Collectibles
PRICE GUIDE 2006

Collectibles
PRICE GUIDE 2006

Judith Miller
and Mark Hill

LONDON, NEW YORK,
MELBOURNE, MUNICH AND DELHI

A joint production from DORLING KINDERSLEY
and THE PRICE GUIDE COMPANY

THE PRICE GUIDE COMPANY LIMITED

Publisher Judith Miller

Collectibles Specialist Mark Hill

Publishing Manager Julie Brooke

European Consultants Martina Franke,
Nicolas Tricaud de Montonnière

Senior Managing Editor Carolyn Madden

Assistant Editor Sara Sturgess

Digital Image Co-ordinator Ellen Sinclair

Editorial Assistants Jessica Bishop,
Dan Dunlavey, Sandra Lange, Alexandra Barr

Design and DTP Tim & Ali Scrivens,
TJ Graphics

Photographers Graham Rae, Bruce Boyajian,
John McKenzie, Byron Slater, Steve Tanner,
Heike Löwenstein, Andy Johnson, Adam Gault

Indexer Hilary Bird

Workflow Consultant Bob Bousfield

Business Advisor Nick Croydon

DORLING KINDERSLEY LIMITED

Publishing Director Jackie Douglas

Managing Art Editor Heather McCarry

Managing Editor Julie Oughton

DTP Designer Adam Walker

Production Elizabeth Warman

Production Manager Sarah Coltman

While every care has been taken in the compilation of this guide, neither the authors
nor the publishers accept any liability for any financial or other loss incurred by
reliance placed on the information contained in *Collectibles Price Guide 2006*

First American Edition, 2005
00 01 02 03 04 05 10 9 8 7 6 5 4 3 2 1

Published in the United States by
DK Publishing Inc.
375 Hudson Street
New York, New York 10014

The Price Guide Company Ltd
info@thepriceguidecompany.com

A CIP catalog record for this book is available from the Library of Congress.

ISBN 0-7566-1339-6

Printed and bound in Germany by GGP Media GmbH

Discover more at
www.dk.com

CONTENTS

6 CONTENTS

INTRODUCTION

Welcome to the fourth edition of my Collectibles Price Guide, published in association with Dorling Kindersley. As I compile these books each year, I am constantly amazed at the breadth of completely new information that becomes available. Collectors, researchers and my team track down company brochures, price lists, key reference works and, where possible, the actual makers or artists themselves – all in the pursuit of precious pearls of collecting wisdom.

All this new information allows a greater and more accurate understanding of an area, as well as adding great vibrancy to the collectibles market. This year we have reflected this by adding even more information than ever before, in the form of extra footnotes and more of our familiar 'Closer Look' features. Over 30 years, I have learnt that knowledge counts for so much when collecting, affecting desirability and prices considerably. With this in mind, we believe that this year's guide will help you stay very much 'top of the tree' in this respect! We've also taken a generous slice through the world of collecting, covering well over 150 different areas from Beswick to books and from pot lids to Pez. With this much diversity and extra information, I believe this once again makes our price guide the essential collecting companion this year!

Judith Miller.

LIST OF CONSULTANTS

Advertising
Rick & Sharon Corley
Toy Road Antiques, OH

Art Deco
Vanessa Strougo
Deco Etc, NY

Ceramics
Judith Keefer
Flow Blue Shoppe, MI

Nick Ainge
Decoseek.decoware.co.uk, UK

Chocolate Molds
Butch Hanes
Dadsfollies.com

Costume
Stacey LoAlbo
Neet-O-Rama, NJ

Dolls
Susan Brewer
Britishdollshowcase.co.uk, UK

Glass
Mark Block
Blockglass.com

Gary Lickver

Inuit Art
Duncan McLean
Waddington's, Canada

Marbles
Robert Block
Auctionblocks.com, CT

Posters
Robert Chisholm & Lars Larsson
Chisholm Larsson Gallery, NY

Sporting
John Kanuit
Vintage Sports Collector, CA

Stamps
Rowan S. Baker
usa-stamps.com

Tools
Tony Murland
Toolshop Auctions,
Needham Market, UK

Toys
Richard & Jeanne Bertoia
Bertoia Auctions, NJ

Watches
Mark Laino
South Street Antiques Center, PA

We are also very grateful to our friends and experts who gave us so much help: Sasha Keen of Neetorama, New Jersey; Barbara Mitchell of Barbara Mitchell Fine Art, Toronto; June O'Neil of R.A. O'Neil, Toronto; Nicholas Lowry of Swann Galleries, New York; Sharon & Joe Happle of Sign of the Tymes, New Jersey.

INTRODUCTION

HOW TO USE THIS BOOK

Category Heading
Indicates the general
category as listed in
the table of contents
on pp.5-6.

Subcategory Heading
Indicates the subcategory of
the main category heading
and describes the general
contents of the page.

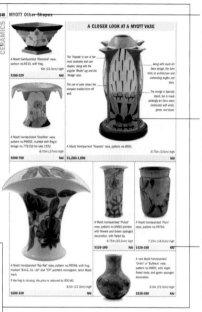

A Closer Look at...
Here, we highlight particularly
interesting items or show
identifying features, pointing
out rare or desirable qualities.

The Source Code
The image is credited to its
source with a code. See the
"Key to Illustrations" on
pp.576-580 for a full listing of
dealers and auction houses.

The Caption
Describes the item and can
include the maker, model,
year of manufacture, size
and condition.

The Price Guide
All prices are shown in ranges and
give you a 'ball park' figure close to
what you should expect to pay for
a similar item. The great joy of
collectibles is that there is not a
recommended retail price. The
price given is not necessarily that
which a dealer will pay you. As a
general rule, expect to receive
approximately 30 per cent less.
When selling, pay attention to the
dealer or auction house specialist
to understand why this may be, and
consider that they have to run
a business as well as make a
living. When buying, listen again.
Condition, market forces and
location of the place of sale will all
affect a price. Prices are expressed
in US$ (even for Canadian
antiques shown). Canadian
readers should refer to the latest
currency conversion rates at
http://finance.yahoo.com/. If no
price is available, the letters NPA
will be used.

Collectors' Notes
Provides background
information on the
designer, factory or
make of the piece or
style in question.

The Object
All collectibles are
shown in full color,
which is a vital aid to
identification and
valuation.

Find out more...
To help you seek further
information, these boxes
list websites, books, and
museums where you
can find out more.

COLLECTORS' NOTES

■ Coca-Cola was invented by Dr. John Pemberton of Atlanta, Georgia in 1886 and was initially marketed as a medicinal pick-me-up called 'Pemberton's French Wine Coca'. The name Coca-Cola was taken from the fact it contained cocaine made from coca leaves and was flavored with kola nuts.

■ The company was sold to Asa Griggs Candler in 1887 who began an aggressive marketing campaign, which accounts for much of the company's success today.

■ Magazine advertisements appeared from 1902 and were soon followed by a huge range merchandizing including ephemera, trays, signs and clocks, produced for a wide range of countries. Due to the vast selection on the market, collectors tend to specialize in one area such as bottles, signs or tip trays.

■ Items from the turn of the 20thC are scarce and tend to be most valuable, though condition is an important factor. Example featuring artwork by popular artists such as Haddon Sundblom, Norman Rockwell or Hamilton King are also sought-after. Becoming familiar with the changing styles of the logo and bottles will help date pieces as well as recognize fakes and reproductions.

A Coca-Cola tip tray, light surface wear to outer edge in a few spots.

1906   *4in (10cm) diam*

$1,000-1,500   **JDJ**

A Coca-Cola 'Exhibition Girl' tip tray, a few minuscule chips to outer rim.

1909   *6in (15cm) wide*

$500-700   **JDJ**

A Coca-Cola tip tray, titled "Drink Delicious Coca-Cola", designed by Hamilton King.

1910   *6.25in (16cm) high*

$500-800   **DC**

A Coca-Cola tip tray, light surface crazing to varnish, designed by Hamilton King.

1913   *6in (15cm) wide*

$600-900   **JDJ**

A Coca-Cola tip tray, with slight dimple to lower left and edge wear.

1914   *6in (15cm) wide*

$180-220   **JDJ**

A Coca-Cola tip tray, with small amount of pitting and a few small chips to perimeter.

1916 6in (15cm) wide

$220-280   **JDJ**

A Coca-Cola serving tray, featuring a reclining lady.

Rectangular trays replaced round or oval ones in 1910 and continued for 50 years.

1936

   13.5in (34cm) high

$500-700   **DC**

A Coca-Cola Selecto-clock, by Selected Devises Company, Chicago, the painted metal dial in oak case.

16in (40.5cm) wide

$280-320 JDJ

A CLOSER LOOK AT A COCA-COLA CLOCK

These early Baird clocks come in two styles, this figure of eight shape and a simpler round one, known as a 'Gallery' clock.

Edward Baird started producing clock cases in Canada in 1888 and moved to Plattsburg, New York in 1890 when he began making these papier-mâché cases for Coca-Cola.

The 'Ideal Brain Tonic' slogan is early. It was replaced with "Drink Coca-Cola. Delicious. Refreshing.", which is preferred less by collectors.

These clocks typically come with mechanisms made by Seth Thomas.

A Coca-Cola advertising clock, by Baird, captioned 'Relieves Exhaustion-Delicious Refreshing', retaining original interior paper label, both papier-mâché bezels restored, clock face shows some discoloration typical of these clocks, includes pendulum and key.

1893-96 *30.5in (77.5cm) high*

$2,200-2,800 JDJ

A Coca-Cola tin advertising sign, featuring an early cardboard six-pack holder and captioned 'Take Home a Carton', dated, light surface scuffs and scrapes.

1939 *27.5in (70cm) high*

$800-1,200 JDJ

An early Coca-Cola menu, featuring Hilda Clark.

Actress and singer Hilda Clark first appeared on Coca-Cola advertising in 1899.

1903

$800-1,200 DC

A 1920s Coca-Cola lithographed metal sign, depicting a six-pack with bottles, Coke-color contents, some fading to carrier.

The six-bottle pack was introduced in the 1920s, enabling customers to take the refreshing drink home.

13in (33cm) wide

$70-100 TA

A scarce Coca-Cola 'Verbena' die-cut cardboard festoon, complete with original satin ribbon garlands, with one leaf tip broken off and some tears and creases.

1932 *33in (84cm) wide*

$1,200-1,800 JDJ

A large printed Coca-Cola advertisement, from part of a shop festoon.

c1958 *18.5in (47cm) high*

$50-70 DC

FIND OUT MORE...

Petretti's Coca-Cola Collectibles Price Guide, by Allan Petretti, published by Krause Publications, 11th edition, July 2001.

www.cocacola.com, official company website.

COLLECTORS' NOTES

■ Vintage advertising provides a fascinating document of social trends and aspirations throughout the years. Collectors might be interested in one area, such as tobacco advertising; a certain brand, such as Coca-Cola; or even a particular character, for example Planter's Mr. Peanut.

■ Countless products have used colorful characters and witty devices in their advertising campaigns since the early 20thC. The highest prices are usually paid for advertising relating to established and popular brands. Breweriana, or beer-related memorabilia and tobacco advertising, are two of the hottest areas in this sector.

■ Prices range from a few dollars for more recent campaigns to upwards of $1,000 for rarer and larger items dating from the 1920s or before. Anything that has crossover appeal, for example to a collector of railway memorabilia or a fan of a particular cartoon character, will usually attract a premium.

■ Never designed to stand the test of time, many advertising figures and products have degraded with age. Flimsy materials such as card, foam, and vinyl are susceptible to wear and can lose value quickly if not properly cared for. Evidence of restoration will generally depress the value of any given object.

A 1950s Miss Dairylea painted ceramic advertising figurine.

6in (15cm) high

$80-120   **PA**

An Legee Co. 'Ma Brown' vinyl advertising doll, for Ma Brown Pickles.

c1960   15in (38cm) high

$25-35   **PA**

A set of 1960s Snap, Crackle & Pop vinyl advertising figures for Kellogg's Rice Krispies, each with molded Kellogg Co. copyright wording.

8.5in (21.5cm) high

$70-90   **HH**

A 1960s Pillsbury 'Poppin' Fresh Doughboy' jack-in-the-box type advertising figurine, with hollow vinyl figurine and tube with paper label.

An 'Archie' painted hard foam advertising figurine, for Archway Cookies.

Archie the baker is standing on one of Archway's famous cookies!

6.75in (17cm) high

$150-200   **PA**

A 'Chucky Cheese' hard plastic mouse advertising money box, made in China by Dennis Foland Inc. for Showbiz Pizza Time Inc.

1993   5.75in (14.5cm) high

$10-15   **PA**

Push the Doughboy into the tube and close the lid. Striking the tube down makes him pop characteristically out of the tube! The Pillsbury Doughboy was developed at ad agency Leo Burnett in 1965 and the original poseable clay figure used in TV advertisements cost a staggering $16,000 at the time! When Pillsbury released a Doughboy toy in 1972, he was named the most popular toy of the year.

5in (13cm) high

$120-180   **PA**

A 'Winni The First' vinyl advertising money bank figurine, for Winn-Dixie grocery stores.

8.5in (21.5cm) high

$70-100   **PA**

A 1960s-70s 'Mr Pig' advertising plastic money box, for Piggly Wiggly stores.

Founder Clarence Saunders of Piggly Wiggly, the first true self service grocery store in the US, never explained the origin of the very unusual name.

$55-65   **PA**

A Spanish 'Fanta' colored molded soft foam jester.

Like many soft foam toys, his surface is in poor condition. Nevertheless, this is a rare advertising figure.

5.25in (13.5cm) high

$65-75　　　　　　**PA**

A CLOSER LOOK AT AN ADVERTISING FIGURINE

Dating from 1947, he is an early figure for this very popular soft drink, which is still available today.

In 1946 owners Herbert Bishop and Ed Mehren began promoting Squirt nationwide - this counter top figurine also comes from an important period in the company's history.

He is in excellent condition, with no damage to the body or any wear or repainting to the original paint finish.

He retains his original bottle, which is an actual empty bottle of Squirt.

A Squirt boy painted plaster advertising figurine, with 'Just Call Me Squirt' to front and copyright wording to reverse of the base.

Loveable character 'Little Squirt' was born in 1941, the brainchild of co-owner Ed Mehren who understood the need for excellent promotion and advertising to make a brand successful.

1947　　　　　　　　　12.25in (31cm) high

$550-650　　　　　　**PA**

A 1950s Stoney's Beer plastic painted advertising figurine, for the Jones Brewing Company.

Beer advertising, often known as 'Breweriana', is one of the most popular collecting areas all over the world.

9.5in (24cm) high

$220-280　　　　　　**PA**

A 1930s/40s Bulmer's Cider latex advertising figurine.

The material shows this to be an early example, later examples are made in plastic.

8.25in (21cm) high

$60-80　　　　　　**PA**

A 1960s/70s 'Chilly Willee' hard vinyl plastic advertising figurine, for Chilly Willee flavored ice drinks.

Chilly Willee is now fronted by a blue sea lion, rather than this All-American boy.

10.5in (27cm) high

$65-75　　　　　　**PA**

A 'Little Hans The Chocolate Maker' soft vinyl advertising doll, for Nestlé, with leatherette lederhosen, impressed on back of head "1969 The Nestlé Co".

Hans was the first character to advertise Nestlé's 'Nesquik' milk drink. During the 1970s he was replaced by the now famous bunny.

1969　　　　12.25in (31cm) high

$80-120　　　　　　**PA**

An 'Elsie the Cow' glazed ceramic lampbase, showing Elsie with a baby cow.

Elsie had four babies, which may help to date her. Beulah the cow was born in 1940, followed by Beauregard the bull in 1947 and finally cows Larabee and Lobelia in 1957.

c1950　　　　9.5in (24cm) high

$100-150　　　　　　**PA**

A 'Big Bob Kinderlotion' hard plastic advertising figurine.

7in (18cm) high

$70-90 PA

A Parke-Davis talcum powder advertising counter top display stand, in the form of a baby with a nappy, with Art Deco design talc bottle.

c1935 14in (35.5cm) high

$250-350 DETC

An early 1960s Escondido Datsun 'Dat-Man' painted Melamine money bank, made for a Datsun dealer in Escondido CA, by Rubens Originals in British Hong Kong.

The Nissan Motor Corp. was established in California in 1960 using the name Datsun, although the Escondido dealership cannot yet be traced. Little was known of Japanese cars when they arrived in the US. They very clearly played on the popular 1960s TV series 'Batman' for recognition.

8.25in (21cm) high

$80-120 PA

A 1940s Red Goose Shoes counter display, a couple of small specks of paint loss.

Red Goose Shoes, founded in 1896, was originally known as 'Gieseke-D'Oench-Hayes' after its founders. Upon deciding to rename, 'Gieseke' is German slang for 'Goose'.

12in (30.5cm) high

$120-180 JDJ

A 'Barnaby' bee ceramic advertising savings money bank.

6.75in (17cm) high

$35-45 PA

A Lamtex Rugs painted hard plastic advertising lamb.

9.5in (24cm) high

$70-100 PA

An 'Energizer Bunny' soft vinyl toy, for the Eveready Battery Company Inc, mint in bubble pack.

Designed by Chiat/Day/Mojo, the Energizer Bunny first appeared in 1989. This model lights up when his stomach is squeezed.

1991

$10-15 PA

A 1970s/80s Best Western hotels advertising ceramic money box, with paper hat band reading "Before you buy, call B-W supply 1-800-528-3601/".

6.25in (16cm) high

$80-120 PA

A 1960s rare Semco Ltd 'STUIF' vinyl/soft plastic advertising figurine for Hoover vacuum cleaners, possibly Dutch.

This was one of the 'nasty' types of grime collected from homes by Hoovers, the others being 'Fluff', 'Dirt', and Grit'.

5.25in (13.5cm) high

$650-750 PA

COLLECTORS' NOTES

■ Advertising beer trays have been produced since the end of the 19th century when most beer was consumed in bars or taverns rather than at home. The trays were initially made with an enamel or porcelain coating onto which the decoration was applied. This was replaced with lithographed tinplate. Shapes are typically round, oval or rectangular with tip trays usually being smaller versions of serving trays.

■ They can generally be divided into pre-Prohibition (pre-1920) and post-Prohibition (post 1933) with early trays being much more desirable. Well-known breweries such as Budweiser, Beck's, and Miller's are always popular, but so are smaller, and now obsolete companies. Many smaller breweries did not survive the effects of Prohibition and the only record of their existence is advertising such as trays.

■ Plastic replaced metals in the late 1960s and these later versions are much less sought after. As many of these trays were well used commercially, condition has a huge effect on value.

An Angeles Brewing & Malting Co. tip tray, featuring a bottle against an arctic background, with a few small rubs to field color.

4.25in (11cm) diam

$100-200   **JDJ**

A 15th Anniversary of the Brewers Local Union No.5 tip tray, dated Nov. 4th 1907.

1907

$400-500   **DC**

A Drink Lehnert's Beer, Catasaqua, Pennsylvania tip tray.

$400-500   **DC**

A Liberty Beer American Brew. Co., Rochester, New York tip tray.

$300-400   **DC**

A Millers Brewing Company, Milwaukee Wisconsin lithographed tin tip tray, marked "Thos. A Shutz Co. Chicago".

6.5in (16.5cm) wide

$15-20   **BH**

An Adam Scheidt Brewing Co. 20th Century Ale tip tray.

$400-500   **DC**

A Stegmaier Brewing Co. of Wilkes-Barre, PA advertising tip tray, with embossed center for cigarettes.

4.25in (10.5cm) diam

$220-280   **TRA**

A La Toco Havana Cigars printed tin tip tray.

4.25in (11cm) diam

$400-500   **DC**

A Baker's Cocoa tip tray, with 'Le Chocolatier' illustration for the Walter Baker Co., Dorchester, Massachusetts, with slight surface wear.

6in (15cm) diam

$100-150   **JDJ**

A Moxie tip tray, featuring a Victorian lady saluting with a glass of Moxie stating "I just love Moxie, don't you?", with few paint chips to bottom perimeter edge.

6in (15cm) diam

$300-400   **JDJ**

A Kenny's Teas & Coffees advertising tip tray, with "Hear No Evil, See No Evil, Speak No Evil" motto.

$400-500   **DC**

A White Rock advertising tip tray.

6.25in (16cm) high

$300-400   **DC**

A John W. Merriam & Co. Havana Segars tip tray, with bulldog.

c1900   *7in (18cm) high*

$300-400   **DC**

A Red Raven Splits advertising tip tray, marked "World's Fair 1904".

1904

$400-500   **DC**

A San Felice Cigars "For Gentlemen of Good Taste" tip tray.

$200-300   **DC**

A Puritan Hams advertising trip tray.

$300-400   **DC**

A Zipp's Flavoring Extracts advertising tip tray.

$150-250   **DC**

A Best Automatic Electric Iron color lithographed advertising tip tray, by Dover Manufacturing Co, Canal Dover, Ohio.

4.25in (10.5cm) high

$250-350 | **TRA**

A Fairy Soap advertising tip tray.

$70-100 | **DC**

A G.S. & A. Shoe Co. Fine Shoes color lithographed advertising tip tray.

4.25in (10.5cm) diam

$180-220 | **TRA**

A Grand Old Party tip tray, with Howard Taft and other GOP presidents from 1856-1908, light surface crazing to varnish.

1908   4in (10cm) diam

$180-220 | **JDJ**

A Gypsy Hosiery tip tray, featuring a bejeweled gypsy and a campfire, with light surface wear.

6in (15cm) diam

$200-300 | **JDJ**

A Resinol Soap and Ointment color lithographed advertising tip tray.

4.25in (10.5cm) diam

$120-180 | **TRA**

A 'Your Credit is Good – The Household, New Bedford, Mass." advertising tip tray.

The figure echoes James Montgomery Flagg's famous poster of Uncle Sam recruiting soldiers for WWI, later reissued for WWII and much parodied.

$400-500 | **DC**

A Wise Furnace Company advertising tip tray.

$200-300 | **DC**

An American Lion Coffee pin, the back with "It's Perfectly Pure Lion Coffee" printed paper.

0.75in (2cm) diam

$25-35 TRA

An American Lion Coffee advertising pin, with paper insert to back advertising the product.

0.75in (2cm) diam

$25-35 TRA

An American Black Cross Coffee advertising pin, by the Whitehead Hoag of Newark, New Jersey.

0.75in (2cm) diam

$15-20 TRA

An American 'Liquozone Gives Life Destroys Diseases Germs' advertising pin.

1.25in (3cm) diam

$50-70 TRA

An American 'Golden Crisp Potato Chips' advertising pin.

0.75in (2cm) diam

$25-35 TRA

An American 'Paradise Crackers Double Your Money' advertising pin.

0.75in (2cm) diam

$28-32 TRA

An American 'Honey and Sonny Bread' pinback, celluloid cracked.

1in (2.5cm) diam

$28-32 TRA

An American 'Pikle-Rite Mr Pikle' advertising pin.

1in (2.5cm) diam

$28-32 TRA

An American 'Alderney Butter' advertising button.

1.25in (3cm) diam

$50-60 TRA

An American 'Its Very Difficult, To "Buster Brown" Hose Supporter' advertising pin.

0.75in (2cm) diam

$45-55   **TRA**

An American 'You Can't "Buster Brown" Hose Supporter' advertising pin.

0.75in (2cm) diam

$45-55   **TRA**

An American 'I Wear Poll Parrot Shoes' advertising pin, the back printed with "Poll Parrot All Leather Shoes Good for Growing Feet".

0.75in (2cm) diam

$28-32   **TRA**

A Hamilton Brown Shoe Co. 'Twinkies' Happy Club' advertising pin.

0.75in (2cm) diam

$35-45   **TRA**

A 'Randolph Cuties' advertising pin, for children's hosiery.

0.75in (2cm) diam

$55-65   **TRA**

A 'Bear Brand Hosiery Wears' advertising pin.

1in (2.5cm) diam

$60-70   **TRA**

A Wool Soap advertising pin, by the Whitehead Hoag Co. of Newark, New Jersey.

0.75in (2cm) diam

$45-55   **TRA**

A National Lead Co. 'Pure White Lead Old Dutch Process' advertising pin.

0.75in (2cm) diam

$50-70   **TRA**

A rare Infallible Smokeless Shotgun advertising pin, with printed card insert for "Dupont Powders The Result of 107 years' experience".

1in (2.5cm) diam

$80-120   **TRA**

A Schaeffer Pianos cut celluloid piano-shaped swing pin, by Whitehead Hoag.

0.75in (2cm) diam

$30-40   **TRA**

A Pied Piper Shoes advertising sign, wear and flaking to painted outside border and minor wear and scratches.

57.75in (146.50cm) wide

$180-220 JDJ

A Schuliens 'We Sell Good Luck Shoes' embossed tin sign.

20in (51cm) wide

$80-120 TRA

A CLOSER LOOK AT A SIGN

This extremely rare sign is one of only two known examples.

Dating from the late 1800s, it is an early example. Tobacco advertising is also currently one of the hottest and most sought after areas of the advertising market.

It is visually stunning with a complex design. It is considered the finest graphic American advertising sign, particularly with the repeated stars and stripes motifs.

The endorsement has a double meaning – both the cigars and the beautiful girl are meant to have no equal.

A 'Yankee Girl Cigar' tin advertising sign, lithographed by the Standard Adv. Co., Coshocton, Ohio.

c1880s *27.50in (70cm) high*

$18,000-22,000 JDJ

A 'Pabst Original Blue Ribbon Beer' lithographed tin advertising sign, nail holes in the sides and color faded.

59.5in (151cm) high

$50-80 JDJ

An 'Ale-8-One – It Glorifies' printed tin advertising sign.

13.75in (35cm) wide

$280-320 TRA

A 'Star Tobacco' porcelain advertising sign, slightly bent.

24in (61cm) wide

$400-500 JDJ

A 1940s British Bear Brand 'Crapo Barbed Wire' tin sign.

19.25in (49cm) high

$450-550 TRA

A 'Crush International Ltd' blue enamel tin advertising thermometer.

A 'Brown's Jumbo Bread' elephant-shaped die-cut tinplate sign.

Shaped signs are particularly sought after.

15.25in (39cm) wide

A 'Bell Systems' double-sided enameled telephone sign, for New England Telephone and Telegraph/ATT.

16in (40.5cm) high

16in (40.5cm) wide

$500-600   **TRA** | **$220-280**   **TRA** | **$120-180**   **EG**

An Art Deco 'Four Roses Whiskey' reverse-painted glass counter-top advertising sign, made by Crystal Mfg Co. of Chicago, with inset clock.

c1935   18in (45.5cm) wide

$850-950   **DETC**

A 'Hires Root Beer' easel back die-cut card standee, "The Symbol of Delicious Taste", edge loss, bottom corners and top of hat, missing rear easel.

c1925   32in (81.5cm) wide

$400-500   **JDJ**

A rare Wrigley's Chewing Gum large die-cut stand-up card standee, split and repaired at the mother's neck, the surface with some wear and staining.

William Wrigley backed his gum with strong advertising so that by 1911, Wrigley's was the best selling brand in the US. The large size, shape, and fine advertising add to an early date to make this highly sought after. Wrigley began his business in 1891 in Chicago.

c1915   36in (91.5cm) high

$1,200-1,800   **JDJ**

A 1950s Wrigley's Juicy Fruit Chewing Gum advertising card standee.

'Juicy Fruit' was developed by William Wrigley in 1893 and is the oldest Wrigley brand.

14.25in (36cm) high

A 1930s Canadian Wrigley's Spearmint Chewing Gum advertising card standee.

'Spearmint' followed 'Juicy Fruit' after a few months, also being introduced in 1893. If the stains were not present, the value would rise to $400.

14.25in (36cm) high

A 1930s Wrigley's Chewing Gum shop advertising leaflet, with different flavors of gum.

'Doublemint' was introduced in 1914, the name referring to the double distillation process used by Wrigley to make this flavor.

1935 6in (15cm) high

$300-400   **DCOL** | **$150-200**   **DCOL** | **$70-100**   **TRA**

A Monarch Pumpkin Pie Spice tin.

3.25in (8cm) high

$30-40　　　　　　　　**TRA**

A Wigwam Mustard tin, with paper label.

2.5in (6cm) high

$100-170　　　　　　　　**TRA**

A Three Crow Ginger tin, with paper label.

3in (7.5cm) high

$100-150　　　　　　　　**TRA**

A Puck Pure Ground Allspice tin, with paper label.

4.25in (10.5cm) high

$180-220　　　　　　　　**TRA**

A very rare Monarch Cocoa square tin, with round top.

The shape of this tin is very rare for Monarch. The other Monarch tin on this page is much more common. The pattern is also detailed and well printed.

4.5in (11.5cm) high

$120-180　　　　　　　　**TRA**

A Buckingham Smoking Tobacco lithographed tin, by John J. Bagley & Co.

5in (12.5cm) high

$70-90　　　　　　　　**BH**

A Big Buster Yellow Pop Corn lithographed tin, by Dickinson's, retains contents.

4.75in (12cm) high

$100-140　　　　　　　　**BH**

A Williams Talc Powder tin, from Williams Co., Glastonbury, Connecticut.

6in (15cm) high

$100-150　　　　　　　　**TRA**

A Rawleigh's Antiseptic Salve printed tinplate tin, some wear to transfer on base.

c1910　　　　3.5in (9cm) diam

$18-22　　　　　　　　**PKA**

An Art Deco style box of 500 Sunshine Straws, by The Hertz Straw Co. Inc, dated.

1928   *8.75in (22cm) high*

$40-50   **TRA**

A Sweetheart Mother Goose Drinking Straws box, by Maryland Paper Products of Baltimore, Maryland.

19in (48cm) high

$40-50   **TRA**

A box of Mother Goose straws, by Maryland Paper Products of Baltimore, Maryland, showing Humpty Dumpty.

8.75in (22cm) high

$60-80   **TRA**

A Two Orphans wooden cigar box, with color printed label, dated "Registered in Patent Office 1875".

1875   *5.25in (13.5cm) high*

$60-80   **TRA**

A Chubbies small cigar box, marked "copyright by Donaldson Bros 1893, litho'd by Witsch & Schmidt of NY".

7in (18cm) long

$70-100   **TRA**

An American card Sunbeam Wafers box.

6.75in (17cm) high

$100-150   **TRA**

A Kellogg's Pep Wheat Flakes lithographed card cereal packet.

Cereal packets have become immensely collectible, particularly if they show celebrity endorsement or film or favorite characters within promotions.

c1963   *4in (10cm) high*

$20-30   **BH**

A late 1920s Canadian Woods Hatchway No Button Underwear card box, for Wood Underwear Company of Toronto.

14.5in (37cm) high

$70-100   **TYA**

A Whale Smoking Tobacco canvas bag, unopened with label and unbroken paper label.

7.5in (19cm) high

$200-300   **TRA**

A rare large Hold Tight Hair Nets shop display and storage counter top box, printed tin on wooden frame, by Adolph Klar, complete.

Fewer counter top display boxes were made compared to other advertising items such as signs or card standees, making this rare. The condition is also superb, with the tin lithographed to imitate wood grain and bearing all it's original lettering and detailed pictorial decals.

1921   16.25in (41.5cm) wide

$800-1,200   **TRA**

A CLOSER LOOK AT A DISPLAY BUST

Large sized wax busts are extremely rare, particularly of this fine quality and life-like modeling.

The hair and eyelashes are synthetic, but threaded into the wax head, and the eyes are made of glass adding to the realistic appearance.

It was used to display jewelry in shop windows. Wear was common as wax is easily damaged.

It is signed by the artist on the side and would have been designed and then carefully hand carved by him.

A 1950s Canadian Eaton's felted card hat shop gift certificate holder, in a miniature Eaton's hatbox.

The hat would have held a gift certificate to spend on a hat in Eaton's. Made from the 1930s/50s, these were popular gifts.

Hat 2.75in (7cm) high

$70-100   **TYA**

A rare 1920s French wax jewelry display bust, hand signed 'Maurice Lue' (or similar) on the side.

22.75in (58cm) high

$2,500-3,500   **TRA**

A Kellogg's plastic pencil box, with branded ballpoint pens and an eraser.

c1979

$15-20   **BH**

A set of Budweiser advertising salt and pepper shakers, the glass bottles in original printed box.

Box 4.5in (11.5cm) wide

$10-15   **BH**

A 1960s Pepsi Cola glass bottle, with printed label.

8in (20.5cm) high

$7-10   **BH**

COLLECTORS' NOTES

■ The first manned balloon flight took place in 1783. The balloon was built by the Montgolfier brothers. The 18th and 19th centuries saw a craze for wealthy men to take balloon flights, these always drew a crowd and memorabilia was produced to record the flights.

■ Ferdinand Graf von Zeppelin developed a commercial airship with a rigid hydrogen gas-filled balloon that was capable of transatlantic flights and which saw action in WWI. Following the destruction of the LZ129 Hindenberg in 1937 and the onset of WWII, interest in lighter-than-air flight waned until the late 20thC.

■ Early memorabilia is very scarce and examples that record specific flights are particularly sought after. Examples from the late 19th and 20th centuries are more affordable.

A Creil & Montereau 'Aircraft' plate, with an illustration of an airship.

c1900   8.25in (21cm) diam

$120-180   **ATK**

'Grand Prix De L'Aero Club De L'Atlantique', designed by Wyacauier, printed by Moderne-Beuchet & Vanden Brugge, Nantes.

1925   47in (117.5cm) high

$1,800-2,200   **SWA**

Hans Hildebrant, "Zeppelin-Denkmal für das Deutsche Volk", published by Germania-Verlag, Stuttgart, a history of Count Ferdinand von Zeppelin.

Published on the 25th anniversary of the first successful flight of a Zeppelin.

1925

$280-320   **ATK**

A 'Graf Zeppelin's Weltreise' (The Zeppelin's World Travel) board game, by Klee.

c1928   12in (30.5cm) wide

$280-320   **DH**

An aluminum fruit dish, with a wavy edge, peak in the middle and a silhouette of the Zeppelin and the trademark name "Zeppelin" stamped into the reverse.

11.5in (29cm) diam

$280-320   **AGI**

A flown Stratosphere Mail Explorer II cover, with "July 12, 1935 Rapid City, S. D. cds." and a "White Lake Nov. 11, 4PM" hand cancel on the face indicating where the balloon landed.

1935

$300-500   **AGI**

A limited edition Da Vinci Balloon Flight cover, from an edition of 1,000, with a green printed cachet, canceled with a Las Cruces, NM machine cancel, no marking to indicate that this cover was flown.

1974

$120-180   **AGI**

A Breitling Orbiter 2 flown cover, signed in the center by pilots Bertrand Piccard and Wim Verstraeten and engineer Andy Elson, the cover canceled by a Swiss stamp tied by a fancy ballooning cancel.

1998

$80-120   **AGI**

A 'Bisto' ceramic child's bowl, with scene of Louis Blériot.

This bowl depicts the scene of Louis Blériot taking the first recorded flight over a large body of water, when he flew across the English Channel on July 25, 1909.

c1909   9.25in (23.5cm) diam

$300-500   **AL**

An 'Aero Plate' decorative plate, by Higgins & Seiten, New York, commemorating the Hudson-Fulton Centennial Exhibition, glaze flaw at the lower right.

1909   10.5in (26.5cm) diam

$30-40   **AGI**

A 1920s-30s German Aviator Duck bobble headed candy container, made from painted plaster.

6in (15.5cm) high

$50-80   **HH**

A KLM 'De Groote Sprong' lithographed tin.

This tin commemorates the first crossing of the Atlantic by a KLM plane.

c1934   7in (18cm) high

$50-80   **DH**

A 1960s BOAC cup and saucer, by Copeland Spode.

$20-30   **COB**

A 1960s BOAC plate, by Copeland Spode.

8in (20cm) diam

$12-18   **COB**

A CLOSER LOOK AT A PEENEMÜNDE WORKER'S BADGE

The Heeresversuchsstelle (Army Experimental Station) at Peenemünde was the secret German rocket base where the V-1 and V-2 rockets were developed during WWII.

This identification badge would have been worn by a Peenemünder and would have allowed access to the base.

Original badges are rare but reproductions are known. They are shinier and lighter in weight as they are made from different materials. The numbers are also weaker and usually repeat.

Peenemünde is a village on the German island of Usedom on the Peene River, on the easternmost part of the German Baltic coast.

A Peenemünde worker's 'Access' enameled aluminum badge no. 361, with button back, with a German eagle and swastika in the bottom half below the number.

1937-45

$2,800-3,200   **AGI**

COLLECTORS' NOTES

■ Basketry was originally used to make vessels for both domestic and ceremonial use. Different tribes developed their own styles and methods of production, although as trade increased, tribes began to copy the most popular designs from each other.

■ After the arrival of European settlers and the integration of their utensils, domestic basketry wares became more or less obsolete. When the settlers began to collect the baskets themselves, the basket makers looked to make their wares more attractive and added styles, colors and embellishments, including those from Europe, into their designs.

■ Examples from before the 1880s are extremely rare, so pieces made up to the 1930s are the most commonly collected. Baskets are still made today, often for the tourist trade, and later examples are less desirable.

A CLOSER LOOK AT A SALISH BASKET

The basket retains its original handles, which are intact, increasing its value.

The wide flat coils are typical of Salish work.

Black and red imbricated designs are commonly found in Salish basketry.

The Salish people inhabited an area centered around southwestern British Columbia in Canada and western Washington in the US.

An early 1900s Salish all-woven carrying basket, with overlapping black and red designs, original handles intact.

16in (40.5cm) high

$350-450   **ALL**

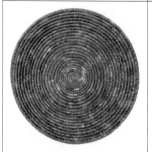

A rare Apache Jicarilla-type black woven basketry bowl, with false weave rim, by "Mae Tilousi, 1960".

c1960   12in (30.5cm) diam

$350-450   **ALL**

An Apache light ground woven basketry tray, with high contrast modified squash blossom design.

c1970   13in (33cm) diam

$150-250   **ALL**

A Navajo woven wedding basket, with black and brown-on-red central design showing spirit release.

c1960   12in (30.5cm) diam

$120-180   **ALL**

A mid-1900s Quinault lidded carry basket, with handles and colorful banded designs.

9in (23cm) high

$180-220   **ALL**

An early 1900s traditional Salish woven basketry carry basket, with red, black, and yellow imbricated designs and intact openwork handles.

15in (38cm) high

$120-180   **ALL**

AMERICANA

COLLECTORS' NOTES

- The Navajo learnt material weaving from the Spanish-influenced Pueblo people in c1650 and used it to make wearable blankets, clothing and accessories. By the 1700s they had developed their own techniques with more complex designs. The quality of their weaving was such that wares were traded with other tribes.

- The establishment by European settlers of commercial weaving mills that mass-produced wearing blankets meant that the Navajo no longer needed to make their own. The craft would have died out were it not for settlers buying the weavings to use as decoration, so the production changed from blankets to rugs.

- Four main trading centers were established, which encouraged production. New styles, specific to each center, were created. Some of these designs are still made today.

A Navajo multi-colored tapestry, from the Four Corners area.

c1980   30in (76cm) long

$300-400   **ALL**

A 1990s Navajo Ganado weaving, by Dwayne G. Holiday.

44in (112cm) long

$200-300   **ALL**

A 1980s Navajo 'Eye Dazzler' weaving, by Lillie Nez, Red Rock, Arizona.

Eye Dazzler blankets were developed in the 1880s when chemical dyes were introduced from Germantown and the Navajo weavers could indulge their love of color and complex patterns.

51in (139.5cm) long

$220-280   **ALL**

A 1980s Navajo multi-colored Teec Nos Pos weaving.

The Teec Nos Pos trading post was established in 1905 and became known for its tight and intricate weavings that utilised small amounts of bright colors.

47in (119.5cm) long

$400-500   **ALL**

A 1980s Navajo Two Gray Hills weaving, by Ramona Tewa, of hand-spun wool.

These weavings were originally made to wear, but Europeans began to collect them as wall hangings and rugs. Early examples intended for wear will not have a border, which was a later addition to the standard design.

41in (104cm) long

$120-180   **ALL**

A Navajo Two Gray Hills weaving, by Annie Lewis.

The Two Gray Hills trading post was established in 1911. The weavers of this area prefer to use natural wool from their own sheep, which is finely spun, allowing for tightly woven and intricate designs. They also avoid chemical dyes and rely on the wool's natural color. This has become a trade mark of the area.

c1990   46in (117cm) long

$450-550   **ALL**

A 1990s Navajo fine weave rug, by Eugenia Begay.

40in (101.5cm) long

$120-180   **ALL**

A Navajo single figure Yei weaving, by Lorraine Mark, in oak frame.

c1980   7in (18cm) long

$40-60   **ALL**

AMERICANA

A Nez Perce hat, from Kooskia, Idaho, made from woven cornhusk and trade yarn.

c1920   8in (20cm) wide

$800-900   **ALL**

An early 1900s beadwork collection, with a pair of Plateau gauntlets and a fringed Plateau drawstring bag, in large Western-framed shadowbox.

34in (86.5cm) high

$700-800   **ALL**

A rare commercial Eskimo fur parka, with sealskin cut-outs.

c1950   50in (127cm) long

$150-200   **ALL**

A pair of early 20thC Woodlands darkened hide moccasins, with puckered toes, ankle flaps, and unique beaded flower trim.

10.5in (26.5cm) long

$220-280   **ALL**

A pair of early 20thC Cree moosehide high-top moccasins, with intricate silk thread embroidered flowers.

10.5in (26.5cm) long

$250-350   **ALL**

A pair of 1960s Cree hand-sewn heavy moosehide moccasins, with high-top wraps and unique black beaded flowers.

10.5in (26.5cm) long

$50-80   **ALL**

A pair of 1960s Crow ladies high-top buffalo hide moccasins, with blue stylized floral designs.

9.5in (24cm) long

$150-200   **ALL**

A pair of early 20thC Sioux fully beaded hard-soled moccasins, with bright blue ground and geometric designs, done in lazy stitch and sinew sewn.

10.5in (26.5cm) long

$450-550   **ALL**

An early 1910s Tlingit bag, of tanned sealskin and sable fur, trimmed with fringed buckskin and with an open beaded top panel done on red tradecloth.

11in (28cm) high

$300-400   **ALL**

A mid-1900s Chippewa dark hide drawstring bag, with well-beaded floral designs on front.

12in (30.5cm) high

$50-60   **ALL**

A rare early 20thC horse feed bag, of very heavy canvas cloth, shaped leather bottom, and leather straps and trim.

12in (30.5cm) high

$30-40   **ALL**

A 1970s Plateau full-front contour beaded bag, with mother and child and floral designs on brain-tanned white buckskin.

15.25in (38.5cm) high

$600-700   **ALL**

A late 1900s Plateau old-style lazy-stitch beaded knife sheath, on white buckskin with geometric designs.

7.25in (18.5cm) high

$150-200   **ALL**

A Plateau full-beaded hide belt, with unusual geometric design.

c1940   *50in (127cm) long*

$100-150   **ALL**

A 1920s Hopi sash belt of Germantown yarn, with an unusual picture of the Virgin Mary, and in pristine condition.

90in (228.5cm) long

$180-220   **ALL**

A Navajo hand-stamped Concho belt, with eight convex segments, plus matching buckle, all of heavy gauge brass.

c1950   *53in (134.5cm) long*

$120-180   **ALL**

AMERICANA

COLLECTORS' NOTES

■ Heishi meaning 'shell' was the first material used by the Native Americans to create jewelry, though the term has come to mean beads produced from any natural materials. European settlers first introduced beads made from glass and ceramics. Good quality hand-made heishi should have an even and uniform appearance.

■ Metal jewelry was only introduced when Atsidi Saani learnt metalworking from the Spanish colonizers in the 1850s. Widespread production developed in the 1870s, particularly among the prolific Navajo, who are noted for their use of silver and turquoise.

■ Late 19th century examples tend to be crudely made due to a lack of tools but they are prized by collectors and difficult to find today. The popularity of this jewelry in the early 20th century saw pre-finished settings and stones being supplied for assembly. Together with modern examples, these are still popular and more affordable.

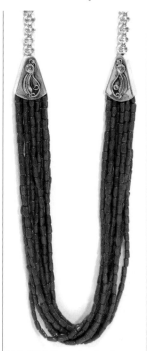

A late 20thC 10-strand coral necklace, of highly polished and shaped blood red corals, with silver tips, beads, and clasp.

26in (66cm) long

$500-600 | **ALL**

A 1980s unique hand-carved turquoise bead and fetish necklace, made from African, Chinese, and King's Manassa turquoise, fetishes by Jackerson Howe.

28in (71cm) long

$280-320 | **ALL**

A late 20thC Pueblo treasure necklace, with stamped sterling crosses, carved bird fetishes, and trade beads all on six strands of Cornaline d'Aleppo beads.

30in (76cm) long

$150-250 | **ALL**

A Pueblo three-strand turquoise and heishi necklace, adorned with agate, shell, hematite, bone, milifiore and gemstone beads with a carved bear fetish pendant.

c1990   *28in (71cm) long*

$150-250 | **ALL**

A 1980s Pueblo five-strand brown shell heishi necklace, with hand-made square-cut shell disc beads.

32in (81.5cm) long

$70-100 | **ALL**

A late 20thC heishi 15-strand necklace, of solid honed turquoise heishi, with string-wrapped top.

28in (71cm) long

$220-280 | **ALL**

A 1970s Navajo hand-honed turquoise bead necklace, made from three sets of jaclas.

Jaclas are short strands of turquoise beads that are hung like a pendant from a necklace. Traditionally they would have been worn as earrings.

18in (45.5cm) long

$200-300 | **ALL**

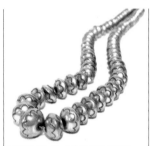

A ladies' Plateau necklace, with bone hairpipes, leather spacers, red 'whiteheart' tradebeads, and cowry shell suspensions.
c1970　　　*55in (139.5cm) long*

$70-100　　　　　　　　　**ALL**

A 1990s seven-strand heishi fetish necklace, with over 100 hand-carved stone, shell, and turquoise animal fetishes with bird spacers and an eagle pendant.
36in (91.5cm) long

$180-220　　　　　　　**ALL**

A 1980s Navajo necklace strand, by F. Laner, of 66 hand-made graduated silver beads, each with stamped designs.
24in (61cm) long

$220-280　　　　　　　**ALL**

A contemporary Son of Bear sterling necklace, made of five segments, four with a Liberty quarter and bear claw, the pendant with two of each.
26in (66cm) long

$280-320　　　　　　　**ALL**

A 1970s Zuni sterling bolo tie, with multi-stone inlay section and single turquoise stone set on stamped and leaf-decorated back.
2.5in (6.5cm) long

$120-180　　　　　　　**ALL**

A late 1900s Zuni sterling man's ring, with twin hand-carved turquoise turtles on top.
Size 11 1/2

$120-180　　　　　　　**ALL**

A 1980s gold bolo tie, with a large single turquoise stone and several inlaid coral stones set in solid 10kt gold, with matching custom tips.
2.75in (7cm) long

$450-550　　　　　　　**ALL**

A 1970s Navajo sterling silver and turquoise 'cluster' style ladies' watch bracelet, signed "HY" in Gothic letters.
5.75in (14.5cm) wide

$150-250　　　　　　　**ALL**

A Navajo coral and sterling watch bracelet, by Lorend Robertson, with 29 natural contour stones set on a heavy band, complete with watch.
c1990　　　*6.75in (17cm) wide*

$250-350　　　　　　　**ALL**

COLLECTORS' NOTES

■ To southwestern tribes, and in particular the Hopi, the Kachina are a group of spirits that represent concepts such as good health, long life and the elements. These spirits are represented by tribesmen dressed in costumes and wearing Kachina masks during ceremonies. Kachina dolls wearing these outfits would be given to women and children.

■ The bodies are traditionally hand-carved from cottonwood root, which was then colored with natural dyes and stains. Look for finely hand-carved and decorated examples and those by noted artists. Modern examples made for the tourist trade will often use other manmade materials.

A 1970s/80s hand-carved and painted Kachina doll, marked "Squash Kachina (Patun)".

10in (25.5cm) high

$120-180　　　　　　　**ALL**

A 1970s/80s hand-carved and painted Kachina doll, marked "Wolf Kachina".

13in (33cm) high

$120-180　　　　　　　**ALL**

A traditional hand-carved and painted Kachina doll, of cottonwood, labeled "Humpbacked Kokopolo Kachina".

c1940　　*7.5in (19cm) high*

$200-300　　　　　　　**ALL**

A traditional hand-carved and painted Kachina doll, of cottonwood, labeled "Mastof Kachina".

c1940　　*8.5in (21cm) high*

$400-500　　　　　　　**ALL**

A late 20thC hand-carved cottonwood root 'Revival' Kachina doll, decorated with pigment paints.

13.5in (34.5cm) high

$800-1,000　　　　　　　**ALL**

A mid-20thC hand-carved and painted Kachina doll, marked "Nihiyo".

10.5in (26.5cm) high

$300-400　　　　　　　**ALL**

A large 1970s Hopi 'Sun' Kachina doll, with feathered 'sun face', signed "Chester".

17in (43cm) high

$350-450　　　　　　　**ALL**

A Navajo large-sized cloth Kachina doll, with traditional red velvet dress, necklace, belt, and yarn hair.

c1970　　　　　23in (58.5cm) high

$100-150　　　　　　　　　**ALL**

A late 20thC Osage hand-made buckskin Kachina doll, with beaded moccasins and dress trim, quilled breastplate, and horsehair.

10in (25.5cm) long

$400-500　　　　　　　　　**ALL**

A 1970s/80s hand-carved and painted cottonwood root kachina doll, marked "Mormon Tea, Myron Gasedma".

14.75in (37.5cm) high

$80-120　　　　　　　　　**ALL**

A late 1900s Cochiti hand-painted pottery 'Storyteller' Kachina doll, with 14 baby/child figures, signed "Hu-u-ca".

9in (23cm) high

$280-320　　　　　　**ALL**

A Navajo folk art wood figure, signed "Delbert Buck".

Self-taught artist Delbert Buck (b.1976) began carving at an early age and had his first show at 13. His love of rodeo can be seen in his common depiction of horses and bulls. His pieces often display a sense of humor.

A Navajo folk art wood figure, signed Delbert Buck.

c1990　　　　12in (30cm) high

$120-180　　　　　　**ALL**

c1990　　　　　　14in (35.5cm) high

$450-550　　　　　　　　　**ALL**

A Navajo folk art 'Koshare and Hair Hungry' wood figure, signed.

c1990　　　　8in (20cm) high

$100-150　　　　　　**ALL**

A Navajo folk art wood figure, by Delbert Buck.

c1990　　　14in (35.5cm)

$120-180　　　　　　**ALL**

A Navajo folk art wood figure, by award-winning Lulu Herbert.

Herbert comes from a family of talented Navajo carvers, famous for their depictions of animals. She is particularly well known for her chickens and ravens.

c1990　　　　35in (89cm) high

$150-250　　　　　　**ALL**

A North West Coast deep relief carved totem, with shaman and other figures.

A mid-20thC North West Coast carved and painted two-figure totem pole, with eagle and bear figures, signed "Chief John Son of Ketchikan, made by David Williams".

c1970   *13in (33cm) high*

$40-50   **ALL**

A late 20thC Kwakiutl hand-carved dance rattle.

16in (40.5cm) high

$150-200   **ALL**

19in (48.5cm) high

$550-650   **ALL**

A late 20thC stretched rawhide and wooden drum, with wolf and spirit painted on front.

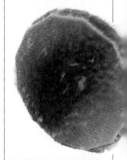

A mid-1900s Zuni (or other Pueblo) upright bear fetish, of carved bone, with incised and inlaid squash blossom.

A rare Plains ceremonial drum, made of stretched beaver hide over a wooden hoop.

6.75in (17cm) high   *6.5in (16.5cm) high*   *c1950*   *17in (43cm) diam*

$40-50   **ALL**   **$200-300**   **ALL**   **$100-150**   **ALL**

A mid-1900s Plains extra long deer and porcupine hair roach headdress.

17.5in (44.5cm) long

A 1970s Apache doll cradle, with old calico padding and rickrack designs.

17in (43cm) high

$180-220   **ALL**   **$70-100**   **ALL**

COLLECTORS' NOTES

■ Black collectibles, as opposed to black historical memorabilia, were primarily made from the 1920s to the 1950s in the US, Japan, and Europe. They feature black people in stereotypical or derogatory situations such as performing household tasks or eating watermelon.

■ In the main, production stopped after the Civil Rights movement of the 1950s and 60s and many examples were thrown away as they were considered insulting. Collections starting to form in the 1970s and interest continued to grow, with a number of high profile collectors like Oprah Winfrey and Spike Lee causing visibility and prices to rise.

■ There is an increased the number of reproductions on the market, so examine materials and stitching, and ensure you are buying from a reputable source.

A folk art handmade fabric black doll, the body made of a fabric covered bottle.

12.5in (32cm) high

$50-80   **PWE**

A folk art handmade fabric doll of a black lady, in a pink floral dress, the body made of a fabric covered bottle.

12in (30.5cm) high

$100-150   **PWE**

A folk art handmade fabric doll of a black lady, washing clothes.

7.5in (19cm) high

$100-150   **PWE**

A folk art handmade fabric black doll of a lady, carrying a basket on her head.

14.75in (37.5cm) high

$100-150   **PWE**

A large felt black memorabilia doll, with weighted feet to make her stand and a felt pocket in the back of her dress.

19.75in (50cm) high

$15-25   **PWE**

A small painted lead figure of a black cook.

$70-90   **SOTT**

A painted bisque souvenir figure of a boy eating watermelon, unmarked.

4.5in (11.5cm) high

$50-70   **SOTT**

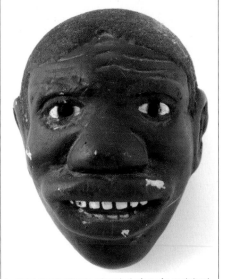

A painted ceramic cigarette ashtray, in the form of a man's head, the smoke coming out of his eyes.

3.25in (8.5cm) long

$150-250   **SOTT**

A handpainted cast iron 'mammy' paper weight, by Hubley.

5.25in (13.5cm) high

$80-120 SOTT

A large pair of 1940s 'Aunt Jemima and Uncle Moses' salt and pepper shakers, by Fiedler & Fiedler Mold & Die Works.

5in (12.5cm) high

$70-90 SOTT

A 1940s handpainted wooden grocery list holder, made in Italy.

9.5in (24cm) high

$30-50 SOTT

A printed wooden shopping list peg board, advertising Torrington Sanitary Baking Co.

10.5in (26.5cm) high

$70-100 SOTT

A wooden plyboard black memorabilia shopping list, with peg holes.

11in (28cm) high

$70-100 PWE

A CLOSER LOOK AT A SUGAR BOWL & CREAMER

The name 'Aunt Jemima' was first used as a trademark to sell a pancake mix in 1889, after becoming a popular Vaudeville song.

Fiedler & Fiedler made a range of kitchen and home ware, featuring Aunt Jemima and Uncle Moses, as promotional giveaways for Quaker Oats. These included cookie jars, salt and pepper shakers and dolls.

Early depictions show her with a headscarf and a broad smile, performing menial tasks while in later examples she appears with her head uncovered.

The company was bought by Quaker Oats in 1926 who continue to use the image of a black 'mammy' up to the present day.

A 1930s Aunt Jemima and Uncle Moses sugar bowl and creamer, by Fiedler & Fiedler Mold & Die Works.

Look for the Fiedler and Fiedler company mark "F&F".

2.25in (5.5cm) high

$180-220 SOTT

THE MANY PURPOSE CLEANER

A Fairbank's Gold Dust
Washing Powder large
lithographed card box,
picturing two black boys, by
Lever Bros.

*Gold Dust soap boxes are
particularly popular with
collectors and as a result are
widely faked. Make sure to
purchase from a reputable
dealer or auction house.*

9in (23cm) high

$70-90   SOTT

A tin of Fairbank's Gold Dust Scouring
Cleanser, by by Lever Bros., with lithographed
paper label picturing two black boys.

4.75in (12cm) high

$30-50   SOTT

A 'Bojangle
Dances Again'
wooden figure, by
the Clown Toy Mfg
Co., Brooklyn, on a
printed tinplate
base marked "Can
be made to dance
to radio or
Phonographic
Music.", with box.

Toy 9in (23cm) high

$100-150   PWE

A 1930s 'Dancing
Sam' painted wood
puppet, with original
packaging and
instructions.

*It is very rare to find
the original packaging
for this toy.*

Toy 9.5in (24cm) high

$120-180   SOTT

A rare 1930s Little Joe craps game figure set, some damage,
repairs.

6in (15cm) long

$500-700   MA

A 1930s kit-made hand-stitched
table cloth, showing a household
chore for each day of the week.

38in (96.5cm) wide

$70-90   SOTT

A woven straw black
memorabilia small child's
handbag.

5in (13cm) high

$15-25   PWE

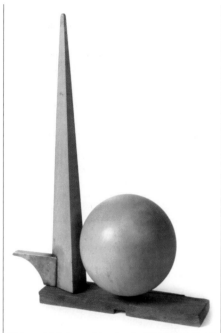

A 1939 New York World's Fair Bakelite desk thermometer.

$40-50   BH

A 1964 New York World's Fair plastic money bank, of an elephant and the Unisphere.

9.75in (25cm) high

$80-120   PA

A Trylon and Perisphere sculpture from the 1939 New York World's Fair, in amber Bakelite mounted on wood base, unmarked.

Of very large size, this was probably made as a display piece around the time of the fair, judging by the 'rough' original base that would have been covered over. It is very unusual to find early plastic items this large and it would have been expensive to produce in its day.

c1939   17.25in (44cm) high

$1,500-2,000   SDR

A 1939 New York World's Fair felt advertising pennant.

8.75in (22cm) high

$70-90   PA

A 1939 New York World's Fair cobalt blue souvenir teapot, by Hall China and sold exclusively at the 1939 New York World's Fair.

6.25in (16cm) high

$700-900   PWE

An American Independence Bi-Centenary commemorative pottery dish, by Mary Wondrausch, slip-decorated with an equestrian portrait within an incised border.

Mary Wondrausch (b.1923) lives in Surrey, England and creates slipwares to commission, in a style similar to late 20thC Pennsylvanian redware. Some of her work is in the collection of the Victoria & Albert Museum, London.

1976   9.5in (23.5cm) diam

$80-120   SAS

An American pearlware feather-edged plate, decorated in brown with a stylized eagle.

8in (20cm) diam

$220-280   SAS

A Ronald Reagan white pottery jug, after Luck & Flaw (Fluck & Law).

$120-180   SAS

An amusing pin tray, by Conte and Boehme, depicting figures representing the US and Cuba tugging at a cigar.

8in (20.5cm) long

$300-500   SAS

COLLECTORS' NOTES

■ Cutting away the fussiness and ornament of the prevailing Art Nouveau style with its clean lines and extreme modernity, Art Deco revolutionized and dominated Western style from the mid-1920s until WWII.

■ Truly a style that could be enjoyed by all, it was one of the first styles that permeated and affected nearly all levels of society in a wider number of countries than before. Modest suburban houses adopted the look as much as grand and glamorous ballrooms and hotels. This leaves a wide array of items for today's collector, from simple but striking wooden mantel clocks to extravagantly designed suites of furniture.

■ The modern appearance of Art Deco means that it fits well into today's homes. Look for clean lines and minimal surface decoration. Where decoration does appear, it is often geometric or stylized, breaking away from the traditional representations of patterns found in the 19th and early 20thC.

■ Colors vary from dramatic monochrome black, white, and silvers to bright and bold reds, oranges, and greens. Consider material as well as form and color. As technologies developed, new materials such as plastics were used. Aluminum, chrome, and enamel are also typical.

■ Themes range from architecture, inspired by the new skyscrapers, to speeding cars and trains and desired luxury, after the deprivations of WWI. Popular areas include lamps, figurines, and small personal objects. As well as considering any marks, decoration or materials, always look for correct signs of construction, age or wear, as the look is so popular that reproductions are very common.

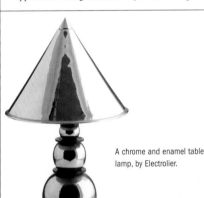

A chrome and enamel table lamp, by Electrolier.

15.5in (39.5cm) high

$700-1,000   DETC

A late 1930s Art Deco 'Machine Age' brushed nickel lamp, the shade clips directly on to the bulb.

11in (28cm) high

$600-800   DETC

A period copy of a chrome desk lamp, designed by Donald Deskey.

Donald Deskey (1894-1989) created a style within the Art Deco movement known as 'Streamlined Modern'. He favored aluminum, chrome, and Bakelite used in a rigidly minimalist, geometric style.

c1935   12in (30.5cm) high

$600-800   DETC

A figural alabaster lamp, depicting a naked female figure holding a drape.

17in (43cm) high

$350-450   DETC

A wood and Lucite banded conical lampstand.

Transparent plastic Lucite was frequently used from the 1930s-50s, and could be carved and painted. Lucite pursees and bangles from the same period are popular with collectors today.

22in (56cm) high

$350-450   DETC

A French Art Deco spelter table lamp, by Fayral, on a two-tier marble base, impressed signature and "Paris France" to reverse.

20.5in (52cm) high

$600-900   ROS

A small chrome figural table lamp, in the form of a stylized donkey, with a beaded cord extending from the tail that operates as a switch.

8.5in (21.5cm) long

$600-800   DETC

An Art Deco style figure of a prancing nude lady, mounted on a plinth.

13.5in (34.5cm) high

$220-280 GAZE

An Art Deco silvered metal and cold painted figure of a female ice skater, on a black marble plinth.

10.25in (26cm) high

$280-320 ROS

An Art Deco ivory figure of a young lady, on a round onyx base, chip to base.

7.75in (20cm) high

$600-800 DN

An Art Deco style 'Hoop Girl' figure, marked "PK".

This figure is a near copy of Ferdinand Preiss' 'Hoop Girl' designed c1930. An original could be worth over $5,000.

8in (20cm) high

$180-220 GAZE

A Goldscheider Art Deco gilt bronze figure of a nude dancer, by P. Philippe, on a hexagonal gray marble base, brass tablet mark to base and signature.

Austrian maker Goldscheider is best known for its Art Deco ceramics, comprising elegant figurines and wall-mounted face masks.

16in (41cm) high

$1,800-2,200 DN

A 1930s black finished ceramic figurine of an African lady, the base with impressed marks for "ANZENGRUBER HAND MADE IN AUSTRIA".

Do not confuse these earlier and very popular figurines with the later examples from the 1950s, which tend to be less valuable. Look for better quality materials, more attention to detail and finer, less 1950s stylized modeling.

5.25in (13.5cm) high

$180-220 PSI

A 1930s black finished ceramic figurine of a small African boy, with ladybird creeping on his leg.

3.25in (8.5cm) high

$100-150 PSI

A 1930s small black ceramic African drummer boy figurine, stamped on the base "ANZENGRUBER", with white glazed drum skin.

4.75in (12cm) high

$100-150 PSI

A pair of Art Deco metal and brass stylized sporting figures, in the style of Hagenauer, both upon black vitrolite bases.

Tallest 7in (18cm) high

$280-320 ROS

A German ceramic vase, with impressed design of figures in a wheat field, with interior glaze.

1934   *8.5in (21.5cm) high*

$300-500   **DETC**

An Art Deco Weatherby of Hanley jug, cream glazed exterior and pink glazed interior, shape no. 82.

7.25in (18.5cm) high

$30-50   **GAZE**

An Art Deco patinated copper vase, unmarked.

8.25in (21cm) high

$70-100   **WW**

A pair of Art Deco-style handpainted vases, Czechoslovakian for the French market, the base with printed "Modele Déposé FAÏENCE TCHÉCHOSLOVAQUIE" marks.

8in (20.5cm) high

$30-50   **PSI**

An Art Deco Karlsruhe lidded bowl, lid with handle, marked.

6.75in (17cm) high

$60-90   **WDL**

A pair of Art Deco Czech ceramic deer bookends, some crazing.

6in (15cm) high

$500-800   **DETC**

A pair of French Art Deco ceramic bookends, modeled in the Cubist manner, signed "E. Hadji" and "Made in France".

9.25in (23.5cm) high

$150-200   **DN**

An ABCO lamp, mounted behind an American bisque bust of an Art Deco woman, on a wooden base, dated.

1934   *9in (23cm) high*

$700-1,000   **DETC**

A 1930s American Seth Thomas mantel clock, with brass accents.

Established in 1813, Seth Thomas is a notable US maker.

11in (28cm) high

$700-1,000   DETC

An Art Deco glass tray with a chrome frame.

Looking at this tray 90 degrees clockwise, you'll note the abstract geometric pattern forms the front or back bumper and wheel of a speeding car.

18in (45.5cm) wide

$350-450   DETC

A Waltham Watch Co. clock mechanism mounted in a crystal-bent green and clear glass case, marked "Process Pat. No. 2,024,775".

Waltham is a well-known US maker of watches, pocket watches and clock mechanisms.

15.5in (39.5cm) wide

$700-1,000   DETC

An Art Deco wall plaque, with a scene of deer jumping in a landscape, etched and silvered on black glass.

c1935   24in (61cm) wide

$350-450   DETC

An Art Deco hand-cut celluloid laminated vanity set, in light green over dark green.

15in (38cm) wide

$500-700   DETC

A 1930s German Art Deco tin-lined leather hip flask, with two integrated cups.

$300-500   CVS

An 1930s American Art Deco Chase 'Pretzelman', whimsical serving piece in polished chrome.

9in (23cm) high

$100-150   DD

A musical cigarette dispenser, in the form of a Turk wearing a fez, dispenses cigarettes from the mouth at the push of a button.

Smoking, gambling and drinking paraphernalia underwent a 'make-over' in the 1920s/30s, becoming more witty, amusing, and frivolous.

8in (20.5cm) high

$500-700   DETC

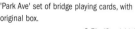

A 1930s American Art Deco geometric 'Park Ave' set of bridge playing cards, with original box.

3.5in (9cm) high

$80-120   DD

FIND OUT MORE...

DK Collectors' Guide: Art Deco, by Judith Miller, published by Dorling Kindersley, 2005.

COLLECTORS' NOTES

- Automobilia covers everything from car parts to items relating to automobile associations, repair and garaging and the wide range of ephemera produced in support of car sales. Most collectors focus on one type, such as car mascots, or on one marque such as Ford. More decorative and easy to display items tend to fetch the highest prices, as do items related to luxury makes such as Hispano Suiza and Rolls-Royce.

- Car mascots are perhaps at the apex of collecting, particularly in terms of desirability and price. The mascot's 'golden period' was from the 1910s to the 1930s. Types include accessory mascots such as animals, characters and figures, manufacturer mascots such as Rolls Royce's legendary 'Spirit of Ecstasy' and advertising mascots such as Michelin's 'Mr Bibendum'.

- Look for figural mascots, which are often designed around themes of speed, strength, satirical humor or good luck. Lively, characterful or dramatic poses are particularly sought-after. Early mascots are usually made from brass or bronze, with alloys coming later. Notable makers include Lalique, Red Ashay, Souest, Bazin and A. & E. Lejeune. Look out for marks as a notable maker can increase value.

- A good level of detail and original plating with good patination increase desirability. Reproductions exist, and watch out for re-plated examples and those that have been over polished. As with much automobilia, mascots from the 1900s-40s are the most desirable, and often valuable, but collectors are turning their attentions towards pieces from the 1950s onwards. As a general rule, look for automobilia by famous marques that represents the glamor and excitement of 20th century motoring, as well as items that are well designed, visually appealing and nostalgic.

A rare 'Aviators' commemorative bronze mascot, depicting the heads of Captain John Alcock and Lieutenant Arthur Whitten Brown, with a deep brown patina.

c1920

$400-500 TCA

A CLOSER LOOK AT A CAR MASCOT

Introduced in 1919 by the Farman car company, this mascot was designed by French sculptor George Colin (1876-1917).

The mascot was intended as a tribute to Brazilian aviator Alberto Santos-Dumont, hence its name and the theme of Icarus. It is based on a commemorative statue.

It was produced in two sizes – a large 6.5in (16.5cm) size was introduced in 1921.

It is stamped 'Finnigans London' - Finnigans were a central London retailer of luxury goods, including luggage and fine car picnic sets.

An early French Farman 'Conquète de l'Air' small nickel-plated mascot, manufactured by Contenot-Lelièvre, with manufacturer's socle, stamped "Finnigans London – Made in France" and "Colin George".

c1920   6in (15cm) high

$650-750 TCA

A 1930s French E. Grégoire horse and jockey chromium-plated mascot, display-mounted on a plinth.

5.5in (14cm) high

$350-450 TCA

A 1930s Augustine & Emile Lejeune cobra snake mascot, for Desmo of Birmingham, with nickel-plated finish and "Desmo Copyright" stamped in the side of the dais.

7.5in (19cm) high

$600-900 TCA

A 1930s chrome-plated car mascot, modeled as kneeling flapper girl with her arms outstretched, with the screw removed and with stamped "12" to base.

6.25in (16cm) high

$500-700 PSI

An American chrome-plated molded angel car mascot, with red Lucite wings, from a Buick 48.

c1955   8in (20cm) long

$600-900 CVS

An American Billiken character mascot, probably designed by L.V. Aronson, with indistinct maker's marks.

The Billiken is a good luck symbol popularized by illustrator Florence Pretz of Kansas City, MO.

c1909-10

5in (12cm) high

$250-350 TCA

COLLECTORS' NOTES

■ Moto Meters were screwed on to a car's front-mounted radiator and measured the temperature of the water coolant to ensure the proper functioning of early engines, which could easily overheat. The most important and prolific maker was the Moto Meter Co. Inc who acquired the Boyce patents in 1912.

■ Car manufacturers such as Packard, Mercer, and Chevrolet soon adopted them and they grew rapidly in popularity during the 1920s. By 1927, company brochures claimed over 10,000,000 Boyce Moto Meters were in use. Other companies such as Jarvis and GideLite sprang up but were not as successful.

■ During the 1930s, more reliable and convenient dashboard-mounted electric sensors replaced Moto Meters. They also became outdated as buyers and manufacturers placed mascots or logos on bonnets, and as car shapes changed.

■ Check that the glass bulb that measured the temperature gauge is intact and look for examples made for popular marques. More prestigious names such as Hispano Suiza, Rolls-Royce, and Duesenberg will fetch a premium, as fewer will have been made. Those that have extra detailing such as illumination, wings or decorative arms are more desirable and valuable, particularly if figurative. Truck examples are also rare. Gauges were also customized for clubs and car dealerships and these can have cross-market appeal.

A Boyce Moto Meter for Paige 'Universal' type temperature gauge, with an intact glass tube, Paige insignia on the black scale plate and chamfered glass.

5.5in (14cm) high

$200-300   **TCA**

A Boyce Moto Meter for Buick 'Universal' type temperature gauge, with an intact glass tube, Buick insignia on the black scale plate and chamfered glass.

5in (12.5cm) high

$220-280   **TCA**

A Boyce Moto Meter for Hudson Super Six 'Universal' type temperature gauge, with an intact glass tube, Super Six insignia on the black scale plate and chamfered glass.

5.5in (14cm) high

$120-180   **TCA**

A Boyce Moto Meter for Cadillac 'Universal' type temperature gauge, with an intact glass tube, Cadillac insignia on the black scale plate and chamfered glass.

5.5in (14cm) high

$200-300   **TCA**

A rare Boyce Moto Meter 'Universal' type temperature gauge, with an intact glass tube and gold-scripted black scale plate, and chamfered glass.

10.5in (26.5cm) wide

$250-350   **TCA**

A Boyce Moto Meter for Chevrolet temperature gauge, with an intact glass tube, a gold script on a black scale plate and chamfered glass.

6in (15cm) wide

$200-300   **TCA**

A Boyce Moto Meter for Buick 'Universal' type temperature gauge, with an intact glass tube, Buick insignia on the black scale plate and chamfered glass.

7.5in (19cm) wide

$250-30   **TCA**

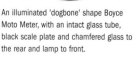

An illuminated 'dogbone' shape Boyce Moto Meter, with an intact glass tube, black scale plate and chamfered glass to the rear and lamp to front.

7in (18cm) wide

$200-300   **TCA**

A Buick logo advertising sign.

48in (122cm) wide

$100-150 AGI

A 'Buick 8' advertising sign.

48in (122cm) wide

$100-150 AGI

A Hillcrest Motor Co. Cadillac dealership sign, part of front missing in one 'ear' of the sign.

48in (122cm) wide

$550-650 AGI

An Esso Gas two-sided porcelain advertising sign, various chips to edges with only a couple small chips to field.

30in (76cm) wide

$700-800 JDJ

A Richfield Gasoline shield sign, reading "Richfield, Gasoline of Power" bearing the Richfield eagle.

48in (122cm) wide

$1,500-2,000 AGI

A Union Gasoline 7600 metal advertising sign.

11.5in (229cm) diam

$40-60 AGI

A Dunlop Tires metal advertising sign, some oxidization on the border and other minor faults.

60in (152.5cm) high

$180-220 AGI

A 'Slow Mud' reflective street sign.

33in (84cm) wide

$20-30 AGI

An 'It's a Duesy! Duesenberg' advertising banner, for the Petersen Automotive Museum Duesenberg exhibition.

48in (122cm) high

$180-220 AGI

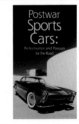

A 'Postwar Sports Cars: Performance and Passion for the Road' sign.

60in (152.5cm) high

$35-45 AGI

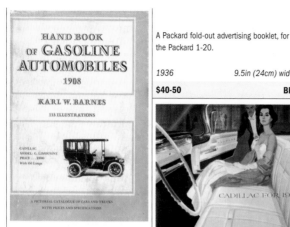

Karl W. Barnes, "Handbook of Gasoline Automobiles", issued annually by the Association of Licensed Automobile Manufacturers, hard cover with dust jacket showing edgewear and stains.

1908

$50-70 AGI

A Packard fold-out advertising booklet, for the Packard 1-20.

1936 9.5in (24cm) wide

$40-50 BH

An American 'Cadillac for 1960' brochure.

1960 10in (25.5cm) wide

$10-20 BH

A Buick 'A Look At The Stars of 1967' advertising brochure.

1967 12.5in (31.5cm) wide

$15-20 BH

Karl Ludvigsen, "Corvette-America's Star-Spangled Sports Car Book", published by Automobile Quarterly, second edition, fourth printing, hard cover with transparent dust jacket.

1977

$100-150 AGI

A Quick Fill racing-style radiator cap, numbered "M95", with modest faults.

7.5in (19cm) wide

$120-180 AGI

A 'Pontiac Indian' radiator cap, by William Schnell, executed in nickel copper on zinc.

5in (12.5cm) high

$400-500 AGI

A 1920s Wolf Whistle car horn, manufactured in Los Angeles by the Yoder Manufacturing company, with original label, minor scratches in the paint and label.

$120-180 AGI

A Ford Motor Co. Mustang lithographed tin advertising tray.

c1979 13.25in (33.5cm) wide

$20-30 BH

COLLECTORS' NOTES

■ Notaphily, the collecting of bank notes, first became popular in the 1960s and grew in the 1970s when it became a separate collecting area from coins.

■ Paper notes, however, have been produced in China since the 7thC by merchants who preferred to transport lightweight paper rather than bulkier coins. The first European country to follow China was Sweden in the 1660s.

■ Notes are often decorated with vignettes and detailed scenes that are not only decorative but are designed to foil counterfeiters. These vignettes often form the basis of a collection with themes including famous people, wildlife, battles or other historical events. Other collecting themes include special or significant serial numbers, wartime currency or notes from a specific country or time period.

■ As most notes were circulated and are therefore worn and soiled, condition has a huge affect on value and uncirculated and therefore mint notes are highly sought-after.

An 1840s Bank of Scotland £50 "Promise to Pay", unissued, some light staining.

$50-70   **BLO**

A Bank of Ireland one pound note, printed in red and black with statues of Hibernia at left and right, heavy circulation, edge splits and few small holes, three heavy hotel stamps at back.
1913

$300-400   **BLO**

A 1970s Bank of England five pound error note, with J.B. Page governor signature and mirror image of Queen on back.

$80-120   **BLO**

An enameled and silvered bronze cigarette case, with engraved design of a Bank of England one pound note, some wear to plating on corners.
c1932

$280-320   **BLO**

A rare Hong Kong & Shanghai Banking Corp $50 note, hand-signed, heavy creases with pinhole in center, some initials on back.
1927

$800-1,200   **BLO**

A scarce Bank of Japan 200 Yen note, Provisional issue, black on pale blue with portrait of Takeuchi Sukune at right, two creases.
1945

$1,200-1,800   **BLO**

A Bank of Japan 200 Yen note, with portrait of Fujiwara Kamatari at right, two creases and minor stain at top.
1945

$600-900   **BLO**

A CLOSER LOOK AT AN AMERICAN DOLLAR NOTE

These are fairly hard to come by, especially in such a good state, as most were used and became tatty, dirty, and worn out.

This example is extremely crisp. Good condition is critical.

The certificate could be exchanged for silver until as recently as the 1950s. The government put a stop to this when they realized the value of the silver was significantly higher than the note.

The two Dollar silver certificate was available with three different seals – red, black, and green. This is a red version.

An American two dollars silver certificate, part of Educational series with group of women and two children, minor ink splashes on bottom corners.

1896

$800-1,200   **BLO**

A scarce Seychelles one rupee note, with no major creases but oil stain at left top, small tear at top right.

1928

$400-600   **BLO**

A Sudanese Seige of Khartoum 100 piastres note, hand-signed by General Gordon.

1884

$700-1,000   **BLO**

A Sudanese Seige of Khartoum 2,500 piastres note, with hectograph signature of General Gordon, stamped on back for M.Tito Figari, advocat in Cairo.

$800-1,200   **BLO**

An American one dollar silver certificate, part of Educational series with reclining woman and boy at left.

1896

$600-900   **BLO**

A scarce American two dollars silver certificate, with red seal.

1917

$280-320   **BLO**

FIND OUT MORE...

International Bank Note Society (IBNS) *General Secretary P.O. BOX 1642, Racine, WI, 53404 USA.*

COLLECTORS' NOTES

■ Barbola was made and sold by Winsor & Newton, a British manufacturer of artists' materials such as oil paints. It was aimed at the home hobbyist or crafts-person of the 1930s and was sold in tins. A thick paste, it could be applied to various objects such as mirrors or boxes, then carved and worked into forms and allowed to dry naturally, without the need for a kiln.

■ Due to its thickness and resilience, it allowed higher relief designs than the 'gesso' also marketed at the time. Once dry, it would be painted in pastel colors and then varnished. Floral patterns typical of chintzware of the period by ceramic makers, such as Royal Winton, were the most popular style.

■ Look for complex, intricate patterns that are well modeled and naturalistically painted all over. Dressing table mirrors were one of the most popular objects to decorate. As protrusions were easily damaged, examine surfaces carefully for signs of damage or restoration, looking for cracks or areas of repainting, often showing as slightly differently colored lines.

A 1930s Barbola ware standing mirror, decorated with green ribbon and flowers.

13.75in (35cm) high

$300-500   **FJA**

A 1930s English Barbola ware plaster mirror.

11.5in (29.5cm) high

$280-320   **FJA**

A 1930s English Barbola ware plaster standing mirror.

8.25in (21cm) high

$220-280   **FJA**

A 1930s Barbola ware toilet mirror, with molded and painted floral border.

10in (25.5cm) diam

$70-100   **B&H**

A 1930s Barbola ware standing mirror, with ball feet.

17in (43cm) high

$300-500   **FJA**

A 1930s English Barbola ware dressing table mirror on stand.

This example is more valuable due to the revolving frame holding the mirror and the decorated base. The design is also more complex and thicker than others and the mirror is beveled, the latter being an attractive feature.

A 1930s Barbola ware mirror, the gilt frame with applied flowers.

10.75in (27cm) high

$180-220   **FJA**

13in (33cm) high

$500-700   **FJA**

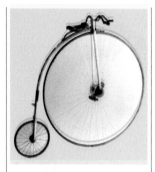

A penny farthing bicycle, sprung leather saddle, finished in white and yellow livery.

$2,800-3,200 LC

A Feho man's bicycle, by Fendt & Hofgärtner, Germany, with pressure pouring wheels, rear wheel-suspension, three course hub circuit and driven by a Cardan shaft.

It is thought that as few as 400 examples of this bicycle were made.

1981

$500-700 ATK

A CLOSER LOOK AT A BICYCLE

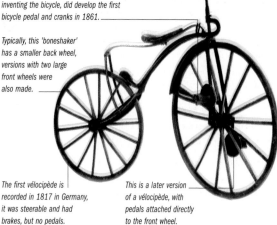

Michaux, once erroneously credited with inventing the bicycle, did develop the first bicycle pedal and cranks in 1861.

Typically, this 'boneshaker' has a smaller back wheel, versions with two large front wheels were also made.

The first vélocipède is recorded in 1817 in Germany, it was steerable and had brakes, but no pedals.

This is a later version of a vélocipède, with pedals attached directly to the front wheel.

An early unmarked 'vélocipède' or 'boneshaker', in the manner of Ernest Michaux, wrought iron frame, wooden spoke wheels with solid iron rims, original leather saddle suspended on large leaf spring, iron pad brake activated by twisting handlebar grip, three-sided pedals, mudguard, with original paint.

c1868 *60in (152cm) high*

$3,000-4,000 ATK

A 19thC 'The Last Lap' woven silk stevengraph, framed and glazed with original mount.

Frame 8.75in (22cm) wide

$700-1,000 MSA

A bicycling tintype, in a daguerreotype/ambrotype like case.

Frame 3.25in (8.5cm) high

$80-120 PWE

A Doulton Lambeth stoneware ewer, with applied molded cycling motifs.

8.25in (15cm) high

$800-1,200 MSA

A Fire Chief lithographed tin bicycle siren, by Ranger Steel Products Corp., in original box.

2.75in (7cm) diam

$30-50 BH

FIND OUT MORE...

The British Cycling Museum, *The Old Station, Camelford, Cornwall.*

The National Cycle Collection, *The Automobile Palace, Temple Street, Llandrindod Wells. www.cyclemuseum.org.uk*

COLLECTORS' NOTES

- Shares as we understand them today were first issued in the Italian port of Amalfi cAD1000. The first shares that came with certificates were produced in the late 17thC in England and the rest of Europe.

- Collectible bonds and shares are those made from the turn of the 18thC up to the mid-20thC with older examples usually being the more sought-after.

- Certificates are often decorated with appealing and detailed printed scenes, usually connected to the product or property they represent. The more decorative the share, generally the more desirable.

- The denomination of the certificate is also an important factor. Higher denominations will be harder to find as fewer were printed and so tend to be more valuable than the same certificate at a lower value.

- Unlike bank notes, it is relatively easy to find certificates in excellent condition as they were often carefully stored in safes and banks.

An English Clarence Railway Co. certificate for one share, black with impressive blue seal.

1828

$700-1,000   **BLO**

A scarce English Forest of Dean Railway Co. certificate for one share, black, very clear embossed seal depicting horse drawing coal wagons.

1826

$1,800-2,200   **BLO**

An English Hammersmith Bridge Co. certificate for one share, printed on vellum, black, pink seal, very clean condition.

1924

$500-700   **BLO**

An English Hope Insurance Co. certificate for one £50 share, imprinted revenue stamp.

1807

$280-320   **BLO**

An English Kent Fire Insurance Office certificate for one £50 share, vignette of prancing horse with fire fighting scenes, on vellum.

1802

$700-1,000   **BLO**

A scarce English Royal Terrace Pier loan certificate for £100 with 5% interest, green seals.

1845

$500-700   **BLO**

An English Stanley Gibbons Ltd. debenture for £500, signed by E.S. Gibbons and C.J. Phillips as directors, four page debenture, further signature of Gibbons, UK revenue stamp.

This is one of only 50 certificates issued.

1890

$280-320   **BLO**

An English West Middlesex Water Works certificate for one share, printed on vellum, black, attached seal.

Only 300 of these early certificates were issued.

1806

$300-400   **BLO**

An American Alaska-Kotsina Copper Co. certificate for 50,000 shares capital stock, made out to and signed by Oliver P. Hubbard.
1906

$70-100   **BLO**

An American Express Co. share certificate, capital 18,000 shares, signed by Henry Wells, William Fargo and Alexander Holland, adhesive revenue stamp, small cancelation stamp, slight discoloration at bottom left.
1866

$300-400   **BLO**

A CLOSER LOOK AT A CHINESE BOND

This bond is for an unusually high denomination, making it desirable. £1,000 in 1912 is the equivalent to over £60,000 ($100,000) today. £500 Chinese bonds are more common.

Chinese bonds are particularly appealing because they are often ornately decorated. Especially attractive ornamentation will increase the bond's value.

Chinese bonds are fairly rare because the Chinese government agreed to convert them back into money during the 1960s. Many individuals chose to cash them in at this time.

The coupons are intact. This is unusual because coupons were used to recoup dividends by the bond owner.

A Chinese Government Gold Loan bond for £1,000, with coupons, central fold, small ink mark at top edge.
1912

$800-1,200   **BLO**

A Kingdom of Bulgaria, 7% Settlement Loan bond for £100, printed by Bradbury Wilkinson & Co., with full coupons.
This appears to be a specimen bond as the serial is No.0000.
1926

$25-35   **BLO**

A Chinese Imperial Government Gold Loan unissued bond for £25, Deutsch-Asiatische Bank issue, with full coupons.
1898

$700-1,000   **BLO**

A French Orleans Railway Co. specimen bond for £1,000, (Comp. du Chemin de Fer de Paris à Orleans) dated, vignette of river scene, printed by Bradbury Wilkinson & Co., with coupons.
1935

$120-180   **BLO**

A Portuguese Loan bond for £100, coat-of-arms at top, ornate border, text in English and Portuguese, with coupons.

1823

$400-600   **BLO**

A scarce Canadian Stewiacke Valley and Lansdowne Railway, incorporated Novia Scotia, uncanceled £100 first mortgage bond, UK revenue stamp.
1889

$120-180   **BLO**

FIND OUT MORE...

Scripophily: Collecting Bonds and Share Certificates, *by Keith Hollender, published by Book Sales, 1985.*
www.scripophily.org, the International Bond and Share Society.

COLLECTORS' NOTES

■ First editions represent the most original version of a book and the one closest to the author's intent. True first editions are from the first printing, or impression, of the first edition. To identify one, look for the number '1' in the series of numbers on the copyright page.

■ Alternatively, some publishers state clearly it is a first edition, or use letters. Always double-check by looking at the publishing date and comparing it to the year that title was first published.

■ Scarcity and condition are major indicators of value – true 'first' numbers are limited – values usually rise as desirability increases. Dust jackets are very important, particularly with modern titles, values can fall by fifty percent or more without them.

■ Authors' signatures are a bonus. Dedications less so, unless that person is famous or important. Signed copies of newly published books are now more commonly available.

■ A good tip is to buy (preferably) signed copies of authors nominated for major prizes, like the Booker, before the winner is announced. A notable example illustrated here is Rushdie's "Midnight's Children".

Nelson Algren, "A Walk on the Wild Side", first edition, published by Farrar, Straus & Cudahy, New York.

1956

$150-250   **BRB**

Maxwell Anderson, "Bad Seed", first edition, published by Dodd, Mead & Company, New York.

This is the dramatization of William March's novel "The Bad Seed".

1955

$150-250   **BRB**

James Graham Ballard, "Empire of the Sun", first trade edition, published by Victor Gollancz, Ltd., London, signed by the author.

A signed limited edition of 100 copies was also issued in 1984 and is worth about ten times as much.

1984

$250-350   **BRB**

Donald Barthelme, "Come Back, Dr. Caligari", first edition, published by Little, Brown & Company, Boston.

1964

$250-350   **BRB**

William S. Burroughs, "Naked Lunch", first American edition, published by Grove Press, New York.

1959

$100-150   **BLO**

Edgar Rice Burroughs, "Tarzan of the Apes", published by A.L. Burt, New York.

1914

$120-180   **BLO**

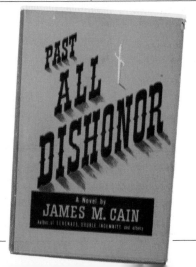

James M. Cain, "Past All Dishonor", first edition, published by Alfred A. Knopf, New York, inscribed by the author.

1946

$850-950   **BRB**

Stephen King, "Carrie", first edition, published by Garden City.

This is King's first novel.

1974

$1,200-1,800   **BLO**

Harry Crews, "The Gospel Singer", first edition, published by William Morrow, New York.

1969

$700-1,100   **BRB**

Don DeLillo, "Players", first edition, published by Alfred A. Knopf, New York, signed by the author.

1977

$700-900   **BRB**

Nicholas Evans, "The Horse Whisperer", first American edition, published by Delacorte Press, New York, signed by the author.

1995

$250-350   **BRB**

William Faulkner, "Pylon", first trade edition, published by Harrison Smith & Robert Haas, Inc., New York.

1935

$800-1,200   **BRB**

John Gardner, "Grendel", first edition, published by Alfred A. Knopf, New York, inscribed by the author.

1971

$700-1,000   **BRB**

A CLOSER LOOK AT A FIRST EDITION NOVEL

Only approximately 2,500 copies of this edition were published, which preceded the English edition by a few weeks.

The American version has a different ending to the English – the Königin Luise is not sunk by the African Queen's torpedo and Allnutt disappears beneath the waves.

Books that have been made into films are often sought after, if the film version has been well received.

Also famous for his Hornblower series of books, this is Forester's most collectible title.

C.S. Forester, "The African Queen", first American edition, published by Little, Brown, & Co., Boston.

1935

$1,500-2,000   **BLO**

Langston Hughes, "The Sweet Flypaper of Life", first edition, New York.

1955

$180-220   **BLO**

John Irving, "The Water-Method Man", first edition, published by Random House, New York.

1972

$600-700   **BRB**

A CLOSER LOOK AT A MODERN FIRST EDITION BOOK

Highsmith (1921-95) is a noted crime writer who developed the genre considerably.

This example is rare and valuable as it is both signed by Highsmith and retains its original dust jacket.

The story was made into a famous film by Alfred Hitchcock in 1951, adding to its popularity.

Highsmith is also famed for creating devious anti-hero Mr Ripley in 1955, played in films by Alain Delon in 1960 and Matt Damon in 1999.

William Irish, "Somebody on the Phone", first edition, published by Lippincott, New York, a scarce title.

William Irish, along with George Hopley were pseudonyms of crime writer Cornell George Hopley-Woolrich.

1940

$350-450   **PB**

Patricia Highsmith, "Strangers on a Train", first edition, New York, signed by the author.

1950

$850-950   **BLO**

Thomas Keneally, "Schindler's Ark", first edition, published by Hodder & Stoughton, London, inscribed with a drawing by the author.

This book was published as Schindler's List in the US.

1982

$800-1,200   **BRB**

Stephen King, "The Shining", first edition, published by Garden City.

1977

$250-350   **BLO**

John Le Carré, "A Small Town in Germany", first edition, published by Heinemann, London, inscribed by the author.

1968

$450-550   **BRB**

Gabriel Garcia Marquez, "One Hundred Years of Solitude", first English-language edition, published by Harper & Row, New York, with first-issue dust jacket.

1970

$2,800-3,200   **BRB**

Gabriel Garcia Marquez, "The General in His Labyrinth", first edition, published by Alfred A. Knopf, New York, from a signed limited edition of 350.

1990

$1,000-1,500 BRB

Richard Matheson, "I am Legend", first hardback edition, published by Walker & Co., New York.

1970

$850-950 BRB

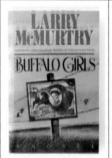

Peter Matthiessen, "At Play in the Fields of the Lord", first edition, published by Random House, New York.

1965

$450-550 BRB

Cormac McCarthy, "All the Pretty Horses", first edition, published by Alfred Knopf, New York.

1992

$450-550 BRB

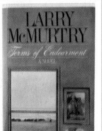

Larry McMurtry, "Terms of Endearment", first edition, published by Simon & Schuster, New York, signed by the author.

1975

$600-800 BRB

Larry McMurtry, "Buffalo Girls", first edition, published by Simon & Schuster, New York, signed by the author.

1990

$200-300 BRB

James A. Michener, "Caravans", first edition, published by Random House, New York, signed by the author.

1963

$350-450 BRB

Arthur Miller, "The Creation of the World and Other Business", first edition, published by The Viking Press, New York, signed by the author.

1973

$300-400 BRB

Bill Naughton, "Alfie", first edition, published by MacGibbon & Kee, London, signed and inscribed by the author.

Signed presentation copies of this title are scarce. The legendary 1966 film with Michael Caine makes this book even more collectible and appealing to fans.

1966

$1,200-1,800 BRB

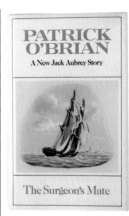

Patrick O'Brian, "The Surgeon's Mate", first edition, published by Collins, London.

Patrick O'Brian, "Master & Commander", first English edition, published by Collins, London.

This is the first UK edition of O'Brian's Aubrey & Maturin series of books and is one of the rarest of that series. It is preferable to the earlier US edition.

Patrick O'Brian, "The Nutmeg of Consolation", first edition, published by Harper Collins, London.

1980

$2,000-3,000   **BRB**

1970

$1,500-2,500   **BRB**

1991

$600-700   **BRB**

Bernard Pomerance, "The Elephant Man", first American edition, published by Grove Press, New York.

Mario Puzo, "The Godfather", first edition, published by G.P. Putnam's Sons, New York.

Salman Rushdie, "Midnight's Children", first American edition, published by Knopf, New York, signed by the author.

Isaac Bashevis Singer, "The Family Moskat", first edition, published by Alfred A. Knopf, New York.

This was the first book by this Nobel Prize-winning author to be translated into English.

1979

$100-200   **BRB**

1969

$1,500-2,000   **BRB**

1981

$1,000-2,000   **BRB**

1950

$750-950   **BRB**

Kurt Vonnegut, Jr., "Mother Night", first hardback edition, published by Harper & Row, New York, with added introduction by the author, signed and dated by the author in 2000.

The hardback version is preceded by the 1962 paperback edition.

Tom Wolfe, "The Bonfire of the Vanities", first trade edition, published by Farrar, Straus and Giroux, New York.

Tom Wolfe, "The Electric Kool-Aid Acid Test", first edition, published by Farrar, Straus and Giroux, New York.

1966

$1,000-2,000   **BRB**

1987

$350-450   **BRB**

1968

$600-800   **BRB**

COLLECTORS' NOTES

- Also known as 'pulp fiction' from the pulped paper they were printed on, paperbacks derived from the mass-produced, inexpensive periodicals or magazines that boomed in popularity during the 1920s and 1930s.

- The golden years are between the late 1940s and 1960s, when they were sold inexpensively to a mass, populist market of both men and women. Many now collect by genre such as gangster/crime, science fiction and Westerns. Look out for key authors, such as Hank Janson, Ben Sarto, A.A. Fair, William Irish, Jim Mayo, Jim Thompson and Bill Lee.

- Today, the stories do not matter to collectors as much as the covers, which became more visual in the late 1940s. During the 1950s, some titles were declared obscene and destroyed for their display of loose morals. Look out for 'dame' covers by Reginald Heade or F.W. Perl, or lively, dramatic or kitsch designs that typify a chosen genre.

- Condition is vital, especially the cover. Creases that damage the image, tears, stains, graffiti and fading all reduce value dramatically. Truly mint or excellent condition examples will often command a financial premium. Some titles and editions are rarer than others; the earliest examples are usually more collectible.

Edgar Rice Burroughs, "Thuvia, Maid of Mars", A Pinnacle Book, published by Mark Goulden Ltd.

Burroughs is a collectible name for his Mars stories as well as Tarzan.

$15-25   **ZDB**

Edgar Rice Burroughs, "Land of Terror", published by Ace Books, New York.

The cover artwork is by popular artist Frank Frazetta.

1944   6.25in (16cm) high

$10-15   **MBO**

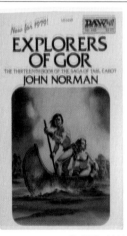

John Norman, "Explorers of Gor", published by Daw Books Inc., New York.

This cover is by Gino D'Achille, look out for Boris Vallejo covers. Gor is a popular series.

1979   7in (17.5cm) high

$15-25   **MBO**

Vargo Statten, "The Avenging Martian", published by Scion Ltd.

Scion was one of the fore-runners of sci-fi pulp fiction and also one of the best. Later novels are less popular than those by Statten or Volsted Gridban.

1951

$22-28   **ZDB**

Murray Leinster, "Operation Outer Space", The New American Library, A Signet Book, New York.

1957   7in (18cm) high

$10-15   **MBO**

J. Hunter Holly, "Encounter", published by Monarch Books.

1962   7in (18cm) high

$12-14   **MBO**

Rafe Bernard, "The Invaders: The Halo Highway", published by Souvenir Press/Corgi Books.

1967

$10-15   **ZDB**

Hank Janson, "Nyloned Avenger", with cover artwork designed by Reginald Heade.

$60-70   **PCC**

Ben Sarto, "Miss Otis Goes Up", published by Modern Fiction Ltd.

Sarto was the pen-name of Frank Dubrez Fawcett (among others who also used this pseudonym) who continued the Miss Otis tales for seven years after introducing her in 1946. Writing over 100 novels between 1946 and 1958, at one point he claimed to be writing a book every fortnight!

1947

$60-70   **PCC**

Anthony Sterling, "King of The Harem Heaven", Monarch Books, New York.

1960   7in (18cm) high

$30-50   **MBO**

A CLOSER LOOK AT A PAPERBACK

Reginald Heade designed the cover and his work is now highly collectible.

The cover is typical of the genre with a lewd lady exposing herself as she drapes provocatively across the cover.

It is more shocking as the lady is being injected, perhaps with drugs, by a man and the title involves vice.

The pseudonym Roland Vane was re-used on postwar books to cash in on the name's excellent pre-war reputation for similar novels – the author's real name was Ernest McKeag.

Roland Vane, "Vice Rackets of Soho", published by Archer Press Ltd.
1951

$70-100   **PCC**

Glenn Canary, "The Damned And The Innocent", published by Monarch Books, Derby, Connecticut.

1961   7in (18cm) high

$12-14   **MBO**

Jim Thompson, "Wild Town", The New American Library published by Signet Books, first printing.

1957   7in (18cm) high

$80-120   **MBO**

William Irish, "Six Nights of Mystery", published by Popular Library, New York.

William Irish was a pseudonym of sought after author Cornell Woolrich, 'father' of noir fiction. The cover artwork is also superb.

1950

    6.25in (16cm) high

$70-100   **MBO**

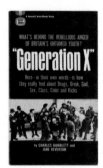

Charles Hamblett & Jane Deverson, "Generation X", A Fawcett Gold Medal Book, first paperback edition.

1964   7in (18cm) high

$15-20   **MBO**

Ralph J. Gleason, "Jefferson Airplane And The San Francisco Sound", published by Ballantine Books, New York.

Rock and pop is a new up-and-coming collecting area.

1969   7in (18cm)

$20-30   **MBO**

Alice Denham, "Coming Together", published by Lancer Books, New York.

Books covering the liberation of women in the 1960s are a popular collecting theme.

1967   7in (17.5cm) high

$15-25   **MBO**

Jack Kerouac, "Maggie Cassidy", published by Panther Books, second issue.

Kerouac is a popular name. Beat genre novels, particularly involving jazz are, sought-after.

1960   6.75in (17cm) high

$40-60   **MBO**

Jim Thompson, "The Alcoholics", published by Lion Books, first paperback edition.

Alcohol and substance abuse and delinquency are currently popular themes, particularly if the artwork bears the theme out in a typical manner.

1953   6.25in (16cm) high

$80-120   **MBO**

Alfred Coppel, "Hero Driver", published by Pocket Books Inc, New York.

1954   6.5in (16.5cm) high

$12-14   **MBO**

Various, "For Bond Lovers Only", published by Dell, New York.

1965   7in (18cm) high

$25-35   **MBO**

William Inge, "Bus Stop", published by Bantam Books, New York, first paperback edition, with Marilyn Monroe cover.

1956   7in (18cm) high

$20-30   **MBO**

H.P. Lovecraft, "The Lurking Fear", published by Avon Book Company, New York.

Horror is a popular genre and Lovecraft is a sought after writer. The artwork is also great!

1947   6.25in (16cm) high

$30-50   **MBO**

FIND OUT MORE...

The Mushroom Jungle – A History of Postwar Paperback Publishing, by Steve Holland, published by Zeon Books, 1997.

Huxford's Paperback Value Guide, by Sharon & Bob Huxford, published by Collector Books, 2003.

COLLECTORS' NOTES

■ As with other books, collectors prefer to buy first editions. Look at the numbers on the inside cover – a '1' in a series of numbers usually means a first edition. Compare the date in the book to the original publishing date to make sure.

■ Authors' signatures add value, as do drawings. Dedications, usually made out if the book is a gift, can reduce the value unless the person is famous – although the personal aspect can be charming.

■ Condition is also important. Doodles and drawings reduce the value dramatically as does a missing dust cover and any damage or wear. Books in fine, excellent or mint condition are more likely to hold their values or rise in the future.

■ Look for classic stories that have entertained many generations of children, or look as if they will continue to entertain in the future as these will be more popular, hence will be in greater demand. Stories made into films also continue to be popular as they revive or further promote interest among a wide audience.

Chris van Allsburg, "Jumanji", first edition, published by Houghton Mifflin Company, New York.

This hit the silver screen in 1995, with Robin Williams as Alan Parrish.

1981

$500-700   **BRB**

Chris van Allsburg, "The Polar Express", first edition, published by Houghton Mifflin Company, Boston, winner of the 1986 Caldecott Medal.
1985

$550-650   **BRB**

Ariane, "The Lively Little Rabbit", first edition, published by Simon & Schuster, New York, with illustrations by Gustaf Tenggren.
1943

$800-1,200   **BRB**

Richard & Florence Atwater, "Mr Popper's Penguins", first edition with illustrations by Robert Lawson, published by Little, Brown and Company, Boston.
1938

$750-850   **BRB**

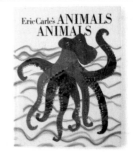

Enid Bagnold, "National Velvet", first edition, published by William Heinemann, London.
1935

$500-700   **BRB**

L. Frank Baum, "Dot and Tot of Merryland", Indianapolis, second edition, with illustrations by W.W. Denslow.
1901

$180-220   **FRE**

Eric Carle, "Animals Animals", first edition, published by Philomel Books, New York, signed by the author.
1989

$150-250   **BRB**

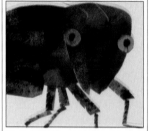

Eric Carle, "The Very Quiet Cricket", first edition, published by Philomel Books, New York, signed by the author.
1990

$200-300   **BRB**

A CLOSER LOOK AT DAHL'S "THE GREMLINS"

This was Dahl's first children's book – it was never reprinted and is very rare.

These Gremlins were personifications of inexplicable problems experienced with WWII planes – Dahl was an ex-RAF pilot.

It was produced for Disney, and contains illustrations by Walt Disney Productions, making it desirable across another collecting market.

A film to be made by Disney was planned, but it was cancelled.

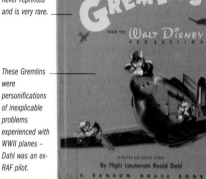

Roald Dahl, "The Gremlins", first edition, published by Random House, New York.
1943

$3,000-4,000   **BRB**

Roald Dahl, "James and the Giant Peach", first edition, first printing, published by Knopf, New York.
1961

$2,000-3,000   **BRB**

Roald Dahl, "Charlie and the Chocolate Factory", first edition, first issue, published by Knopf, New York.
1964

$3,500-4,500   **BRB**

Madeleine L'Engle, "The Twenty-four Days before Christmas", first edition, published by Ariel Books, New York.
1959

$180-220   **BRB**

James Gurney, "Dinotopia", first trade edition, published by Turner Publishing Inc., Atlanta, signed by the author.

1992

$280-320   **BRB**

Albert Neely Hall, "The Wonder Hill, or the Marvelous Rescue of Prince Iota", Chicago, Rand McNally, first edition, illustrated by Norman Hall.
1914

$120-180   **FRE**

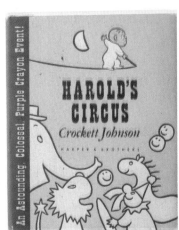

Crockett Johnson, "Harold's Circus", first edition, published by Harper & Brothers, New York.

Robert A. Heinlein, "The Star Beast", first edition, published by Charles Scribner's Sons, New York.

1954

$500-800   BRB

1959

$1,800-2,200   BRB

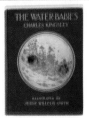

Charles Kingsley, "The Water-Babies", first edition, published by Dodd, Mead & Company, New York, with illustrations by Jessie Willcox Smith.

David Kirk, "Miss Spider's Wedding", first edition, published by Scholastic, New York, signed by the author.

Astrid Lindgren, "Pippi Longstocking", first edition, published by The Viking Press, New York.

1916

$500-800   BRB

1995

$300-400   BRB

1950

$500-700   BRB

Arnold Lobel, "Frog and Toad Together", first edition, published by Harper & Row, New York, signed by the author.

Hugh Lofting, "The Story of Doctor Dolittle", first edition, published by Frederick A. Stokes, New York.

Peter Newell, "The Slant Book", first edition, published by Harper & Brothers., New York.

Wally Piper, "The Gingerbread Boy", first edition, published by Platt & Munk.

1972

$180-220   BRB

1920

$1,000-1,500   BRB

1910

$300-500   BRB

1927

$120-180   BRB

Beatrix Potter, "The Tale of Little Pig Robinson", first American edition, published by David McKay Company, Philadelphia, containing 25 black and white illustrations in addition to those in the UK edition.
1930

$1,000-1,500   **BRB**

Philip Pullman, "Northern Lights", first edition.
1995

$1,800-2,200   **BLO**

Dr. Seuss, "Cat in the Hat", first American edition, published by Random House, New York.
1957

$7,500-8,500   **BRB**

A CLOSER LOOK AT A HARRY POTTER BOOK

Only 500 of this true first hardback edition of Rowling's first book were printed, at a time when Rowling was unknown.

This is in unread condition with no fading or damage, making it rarer still. This first print run was issued without a dust jacket.

Many were sent to libraries, or abroad, meaning that they were stamped or worn through use.

Scholastic published the first US edition as "Harry Potter and The Sorcerer's Stone". The first print run is identified by its purple covers and $16.95 retail price. It can now fetch up to $2,800.

J.K. Rowling, "Harry Potter and the Philosopher's Stone", first edition, original pictorial boards.
1997

$20,000-30,000   **BLO**

J.K. Rowling, "Harry Potter and the Prisoner of Azkaban", first edition, first issue.

This is the first issue with the copyright reading 'Joanne Rowling' (rather than J.K. Rowling) and dropped text on page 7.
1999

$800-1,200   **BLO**

Dr. Seuss, "One Fish Two Fish Red Fish Blue Fish", first edition, published by Random House, New York, in first-issue dust jacket listing no other books.
1960

$800-1,200   **BRB**

Dr. Seuss, "Hop on Pop", first edition, published by Random House, New York.
1963

$600-900   **BRB**

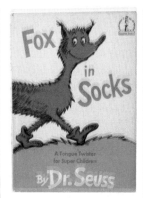

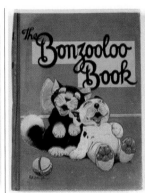

Dr. Seuss, "Fox in Socks", first American edition, published by Beginner's Books, New York.

1965

$1,000-1,500 BRB

Margery Sharp, "The Rescuers", first edition, published by Collins, London.

1959

$300-500 BRB

G.E. Studdy, "The Bonzooloo Book", London, color pictorial bands, 12 color plates, other illustrations.

c1928

$300-400 FRE

G.P. Taylor, "Shadowmancer", first edition, Finland, from an edition of 2,500 privately printed for the author, signed by the author and with a wizard's hat motif, unread with typographical error "right s" on title.

2002

$1,000-1,500 BLO

Kay Thompson, "Eloise", first edition, published by Simon & Schuster, New York, with illustrations by Hilary Knight.

1955

$2,000-3,000 BRB

Kay Thompson, "Eloise", complete set of five first editions, published by Simon and Schuster, New York, each signed by illustrator Hilary Knight.

1955-2002

$5,000-7,000 BRB

Mark Twain, "Adventures of Huckleberry Finn", first edition, published by Charles L. Webster & Company, with rare blue cloth.

The first edition of Huckleberry Finn was issued as standard with a dark green binding. However, purchasers were able to specially request a blue cloth copy to match the previously published "Tom Sawyer" of which this is a sequel. Blue examples are much rarer than green.

1885

$5,000-7,000 BRB

E.B. White, "Stuart Little", first edition, published by Harper & Brothers, New York and London.

1945

$800-1,200 BRB

E.B. White, "Charlotte's Web", first edition, published by Harper & Brothers, New York.

1952

$2,000-3,000 BRB

COLLECTORS' NOTES

■ Photography became more popular during the 1840s. Cameras of the time usually had wooden bodies with brass or other metal fittings. Early 'wet plate' cameras from the 1840s–1880s are often highly desirable, particularly if rigid, sliding boxes. Bellows were developed c1851. Brass lenses are common, and most have a glass back plate to compose the picture and wooden holders for the photographic plates.

■ Most wooden cameras found on the market today will be 'dry plate' folding cameras dating from the 1880s–1920s. Look for a good quality construction and manufacturers' names, such as Watson, Lancaster, and Sanderson. An original case and accessories adds value, as does use of other materials, such as teak.

■ Leica cameras, by Leitz of Wetzlar, Germany, are the most collectible 35mm cameras. The first was developed in 1913 and they are still made today. Screw lens mounts were used 1930–54, with bayonet lens mounts used thereafter, on the 'M' series. Condition is absolutely paramount to collectors, with wear, scratches, scuffs, dents, and broken mechanisms reducing value considerably, depending on the degree of damage.

■ All Leica cameras are numbered, and this gives the model and year of manufacture. Look for unusual engravings, such as 'Luftwaffe Eigentum' (Property of the Luftwaffe), but be aware that fakes are numerous as originals usually fetch high values. Variations in color, form or original use add value and accessories such as lenses can have high individual values.

■ Subminiature, 'detective' and unusually shaped cameras are highly collectible, and can offer a more affordable and 'fun' entry into the market. Condition again is key, particularly for plastic examples and more modern cameras. Other names such as Canon, Zeiss Ikon and Voigtländer are also collectible, with rare models or lenses fetching higher prices. Kodak's 'Box Brownies' were made in vast numbers and are generally of low value.

A Lancaster & Son of Birmingham '1898 Instantograph' camera, with Lancaster brass lens f=10 and two wooden backs.
c1900

$300-500   ATK

A Thornton Pickard Imperial Triple Extension camera, with mahogany frame, Thornton-Pickard roller-blind shutter, with four wooden double backs.
1904-26

$220-380   ATK

A Sanderson half-plate field camera, with brass and mahogany body, Ross No. 2 Wide Angle Symmetric 4in lens and Thornton Pickard roller blind shutter.
c1898

$300-400   ATK

An unmarked mahogany plate camera, with petrol-colored bellows and a Zeiss Tessar 1:4.5, f=21cm lens.
11.25in (28cm) long

$120-180   WDL

A Watson Alpha quarter-plate camera, with mahogany body, black bellows, Beck Isostigmar f=6.3 8.25in lens, set in a Bausch & Lomb shutter and with maker's label "W. Watson & Sons, London Made for H. Carette, Paris", focusing back replaced.

$180-220   EG

A 'Mars' wooden magazine box camera , by Emile Wünsche of Dresden, brass lens with rotating diaphragm.
1895

$700-1,000   ATK

A German Ernemann Ermanox camera, with Ernostar f=1.8 8.5cm lens, Vertex f=4.5 6cm lens and accessories, instructions and maker's fitted leather case.
c1925

$800-1,200   EG

A CLOSER LOOK AT A LEICA CAMERA

Only 984 Leica 'Reporter' cameras were ever made – it has a film capacity of 250 exposures.

Look out for the version with an electric motor drive – only 29 examples were made and it can fetch $50,000 or more.

This is from the first series of only 246 cameras, modeled after the Leica III.

This is in black (top plate and bottom plate) – look out for the extremely rare model with chrome top and base plates.

A Leica 'Reporter' 250 FF camera, serial no. 135642, with Elmar 3.5/5 cm lens.

1934

$10,000-15,000   **ATK**

A Leica chrome IIIa camera, synchronized, with Summar f=2/5cm lens and lens cap.

1935

$280-320   **ATK**

A Leica IIIb camera, with Leitz Summar f=2 5cm lens, in brown leather case.

1938   *5.5in (14cm) w*

$300-400   **GORL**

A rare Leica IIIa 'Monté en Sarre' camera, fitted with an Elmar 3.5/5cm lens, original invoice and with maker's case.

Part of Leica's production was moved to Sarre in 1949-51 to avoid high French tax duties. Around 500 IIIa models were produced, engraved 'Monté en Sarre' and retailed for the French market.

1950

$2,800-3,200   **ATK**

A Leica IIIf 35mm camera with 'Red-Dial', with Summaron f=3.5 3.5 cm lens.

The IIIf was the first Leica to have flash synchronization. Look out for the Canadian model, which can be worth up to five times more.

1952-53

$220-280   **EG**

A Leica IG camera, long shutter speed, with Elmar 3.5/5cm lens and 5cm finder, knob damaged, dent behind rewind knob.

1958

$400-600   **ATK**

A Leica M3 camera, with Summicron 2/50 lens, and lens cap.

1960

$1,800-2,200   **ATK**

A Canon Pellix camera, with Canon FL 1.2/58 lens, Canon lens cap, incorrect diaphragm.

$100-150   **ATK**

A 1950s Kiku 16 miniature camera, complete with box, case and extra yellow filter.

Camera 2.25in (6cm) wide

$120-180   **EPO**

A Nikon FM2 N camera, with instructions, papers and box.

1990

$280-320   **ATK**

A rare transparent demonstration model Polaroid Autofocus 660.

$280-320   **ATK**

A Voigtländer Bessamatic CS camera, with Color-Skopar 2.8/50 lens, exposure meter working.

1966

$220-280   **ATK**

A Zeiss Ikon Kolibri camera, with Novar 4.5/5cm lens and Telma shutter, lacks foot.

1928

$280-320   **ATK**

A Zeiss Ikon Contax I camera, version four with Tessar 2.8/5cm lens, marked "A" for conversion or modification by Zeiss Ikon.

1933

$300-500   **ATK**

An early Zeiss Contarex I camera, with Planar 2/50 lens and exposure meter filter secured.

1962

$600-900   **ATK**

A Zeiss Ikon Contarex I camera, with Biogon 4.5/21 lens and viewfinder 435 for 21mm.

1964

$800-1,200   **ATK**

A Japanese Rokuoh-Sha machine-gun camera, by Konishiroku Kogaku, taking single 35mm pictures, with Hexar 4.5/75 lens, working spring motor drive, shutter releases, with accessories and spare parts, in original wooden box.

These cumbersome cameras are scarce, especially in complete condition with their boxes. They were use to train machine gunners and the idea is said to have been copied from the 1915 British 'Hythe' machine gun camera used in WWI.

1943

$1,800-2,200   ATK

A E.R.A.C. Mercury I brown Bakelite pistol camera, by the E.R.A.C. Selling Co. Ltd., London, invented by H. Covill & H Steward.

c1931

$700-1,000   ATK

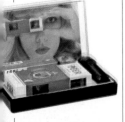

An extremely rare Holly red Bakelite box camera, by Allgäuer Kamerawerkstätte Gomag, Pfronten, with Gomar 4.5/85 lens.

1950

$600-900   ATK

A Coronet Midget olive green plastic subminiature camera.

The red, green, and blue colors are more desirable than brown or black.

1935   0.75in (2cm) high

$220-280   ATK

A Swiss Concava AG Tessina Automatic 35mm wrist-mounted camera, with Tessinon 2.8/25 lens, in original box with wrist strap.

1960   0.75in (2cm) wide

$400-600   ATK

A Kodak Peer 100 pocket camera, in shape of a cigarette box, lacks release, with original box.

1976

$280-320   ATK

A Fotodisc chrome-plated,full-metal subminiature camera, by the American Safety Razor Corp. of New York.

As this lacks both its serial number and photodisc, it is possibly a prototype.

c1960   1in (24cm) high

$800-1,200   ATK

An American Magic Introduction Co. Photoret 'pocket watch' subminiature camera, engraved "A Magazine Snap-Shot Camera".

1894   0.5in (1.5cm) h

$700-1,000   ATK

A Mickey Mouse camera, the lens marked "Copyright Walt Disney Prod.", with f=25 1:9 lens.

1956

$70-100   ATK

A 19thC Canadian redware pitcher, probably from Western Ontario, with incised bands.

8in (20.5cm) high

$60-80   ING

A 19thC Canadian redware crock pot, found in New Hamburg, Waterloo County.

The rare gray-green glaze is unusual but very similar to Joseph Buehler's pottery, also from New Hamburg. The shape helps identify this as coming from Waterloo County.

6.75in (17cm) high

$70-90   ING

A Canadian Sovereign Potters lidded earthenware sugarbowl, with maple leaf mark.

c1945   9in (23cm) diam

$15-25   TCF

A Canadian Sovereign Potters lidded earthenware sugarbowl, with maple leaf mark.

c1945   9in (23cm) diam

$15-25   TCF

A small Deichmann dish, with a running 'goofus', inscribed "Deichmann DK NB" on the reverse.

4in (10cm) long

$100-150   TCF

Blue Mountain is a hot new collecting area. Founded in the mid-1940s, it closed in early 2005. These bookends are an unusual shape. Bowls or vases are much more common.

A pair of 1980s Blue Mountain bookends, with original swing tag to back.

8.25in (21cm) high

$25-35   TJL

A CLOSER LOOK AT A DEICHMANN FIGURINE

These animal figurines are known as 'goofus' and are the pottery's most popular and desirable shape or motif.

Kjell was usually responsible for the modeling, while Erica was responsible for the glazes, developing some 5,000 different types.

Values have risen dramatically for the most characteristic and large pieces over the last decade and look set to continue doing so.

Pieces are always signed, usually with a stylized "D". This one is also signed by Erica who may have made this piece.

A Deichmann 'goofus' figurine, each foot inscribed "Erica", "Canada", "AB" and "D".

Danish immigrants Kjell and Erica Deichmann were among Canada's first studio potters, operating in Moss Glen, New Brunswick from 1935-63. They saw great success in the 1940s and 50s. Kjell died in 1963 and Erica closed the pottery.

c1950   6.75in (17cm) long

$700-900   TCF

A Wedgwood Dominion of Canada commemorative plate, with transfer-printed and handpainted details.

c1920 10in (25.5cm) diam

$70-100 TPF

A Wedgwood commemorative plate for Montreal, with printed and handpainted details.

10in (25.5cm) diam

$100-150 TCF

A Wedgwood Dominion of Canada commemorative plate, with handpainted and transfer details.

c1924 10.5in (26.5cm) diam

$80-120 TPF

An Adams commemorative plate for Prince Edward Island, with armorial.

c1910 9.75in (25cm) diam

$70-100 TPF

A Canadian commemorative plate for the Duke & Duchess of Cornwall's visit to Canada.

1901 8.5in (21.5cm) diam

$70-90 TYA

A limited edition Moorcroft spherical vase, from an edition of 250, with polar bears to represent Canada, the base with painted marks, "J. Moorcroft', 59/250 WM 31.1.88 Moorcroft Made In England".

1988 6.5in (16.5cm) high

$2,500-3,000 TCF

A Torquay ware 'motto ware' souvenir cup and saucer, British for the Canadian market and manufactured for Banff Canada.

5in (13cm) diam saucer

$50-70 TFR

A Royal Doulton figurine of Sir John MacDonald, HN2860, designed by W.K. Harper.

Sir John Alexander MacDonald (1815-91) was the first prime minister of Canada from 1867-73 and from 1878-1891.

1987 9in (23cm) high

$200-300 TCF

A Canadian Sterling souvenir spoon for City Hall, Winnipeg, with enameled Royal crest.

1901   4.25in (10.5cm) long

$15-20   **TFR**

A Canadian Sterling souvenir spoon, with enameled bowl for Owen Sound Ontario, back stamped "E" for Ellis, a Canadian company.

Souvenir spoons are popular with today's collectors and were produced from around 1900. Values depend on the material, the quality and level of decoration, and the theme. Decorated spoon bowls are sought-after, particularly if it shows a famous building. Sporting themes are also popular. Most people collect examples related to areas they have visited or have a personal connection to.

5.75in (14.5cm) long

$18-22   **TFR**

A Canadian Sterling enameled souvenir spoon for Berlin, Ontario.

Berlin was renamed Kitchener in 1916 to commemorate the famous Earl Kitchener who died in that year.

1902   5.25in (13.5cm) high

$15-20   **TFR**

A Canadian Sterling Belleville souvenir spoon, with maple leaf and tennis racquet.

4.25in (11cm) long

$18-22   **TFR**

A Canadian silver-plated EPNS commemorative spoon, with shield and scenes of mining, lumbering, and farming, with engraved bowl "Godrich".

c1900.   6in (15cm) long

$50-70   **TCF**

A Canadian silver-plated Parliament Buildings, Victoria B.C. souvenir spoon, with enameled shield.

4.5in (11.5cm) long

$15-20   **TFR**

A Canadian .925 Sterling souvenir sugar spoon, with enameled maple leaf, and scrolling floral spoon.

4.5in (11.5cm) long

$40-50   **TFR**

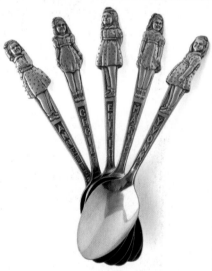

A set of five Carlton Dionne quintuplets silver-plated souvenir spoons, each with the name of one of the sisters.

The Dionne quintuplets were born in Ontario on May 28th, 1934. Their birth captured popular media attention and over 3 million people visited their home to see them, partly due to the Canadian government's intervention.

c1947   6in (15cm) high

$100-150   **TFR**

A Canadian pair of Sterling souvenir sugar tongs, with enameled maple leaf, engraved "Gravenhurst" on the bridge.

2.75in (7cm) long

$22-28   **TFR**

A Clarice Cliff handpainted plate of 'The Mountie', British for the Canadian market, from the Confederation Series.

c1950   *10.5in (27cm) diam*

$350-450   **TCF**

A 1950s Mountie printed metal cocktail tray.

11in (28cm) diam

$15-20   **TPF**

A carved wooden figure of a Mountie.

7.75in (19.5cm) high

$180-220   **TCF**

A limited edition 'Spirit of the Empire Canada' metal figure of a Royal Canadian Mounted Police officer, with French horn, boxed.

1995   *Box 3.5in (9cm) high*

$20-30   **TAM**

A 1960s View-Master picture disc of 'Royal Canadian Mounted Police', by Sawyer's Inc.

4.5in (11.5cm) wide

$7-10   **BH**

A Wedgwood commemorative tankard, British for the Canadian market, for the centenary of the Mounties.

1973   *4.5in (11.5cm) high*

$80-120   **TCF**

A black and white postcard of a North West Mounted Police officer.

c1915   *5.5in (14cm) wide*

$12-18   **TAM**

A medal awarded for long service and good conduct aboard HMS Vernon, struck with a bust of George V.

c1915   *3.75in (9.5cm) long*

$150-250   **TAM**

A set of three early Royal Canadian Mounted Police badges, one for the helmet and one for each shoulder.

Largest 2in (5cm) high

$220-280   **TAM**

A carved pine scoop, from Ontario.

c1880   15.75in (40cm) long

$40-60   **RAON**

A Canadian carved pine cylindrical box, carved from one piece of wood, with two protruding handles.

c1900   4.25in (11cm) high

$45-55   **RAON**

A Canadian folk art carved and painted spoon rack, from Ontario.

c1970   19.25in (49cm) high

$180-220   **RAON**

A Canadian carved and painted wooden garden ornament of a swan, from Ontario.

c1950   19.25in (49cm) high

$70-90   **RAON**

A carved and fretted heart-shaped folk art frame, painted in colors, from Quebec.

c1950   15.5in (39.5cm) high

$40-60   **RAON**

A painted 20thC Canadian folk art windmill model, from Nova Scotia.

                 24.75in (63cm) high

$100-150   **RAON**

A CLOSER LOOK AT A MAUD LEWIS PAINTING

Since the mid-1960s Lewis has become an icon of Canadian folk art - being tagged Canada's own 'Grandma Moses' - values have risen accordingly.

Bright colors are typical of her work as are 'naïve', simple designs of landscapes or harbors. Both reflect the simple life in Nova Scotia as she grew up and her stoically cheerful outlook on life seen through her paintings.

Her materials are typically inexpensive and were often found or scrounged - they include fiberboard, cardboard, and wallpaper, often painted with house or boat paints or sometimes oils or acrylics.

Lewis was effectively self-taught, with her mother providing the earliest instruction when they used to paint Christmas cards together to sell during the 1920s.

A Maud Lewis paint-on-board painting of three cats, signed in capitals in the image.

Maud Lewis, (1903-70) was born with a number of painful physical deformities and lived in a one room wooden house in rural Nova Scotia. Although it had no heating or running water, she decorated it herself with patterns in her typically bright colors. Lewis created many joyful paintings, selling them for only a few dollars each, but sadly contracted pneumonia and died aged 67.

                 13.75in (35cm) long

$3,500-4,500   **BMM**

COLLECTORS' NOTES

■ In 1940 pottery classes were held under Swiss ceramicist Wellie Chochard at the Beauceville High School, Quebec, Canada, leading to the 'Syndicate of the Rural Ceramists of the Beauce' being founded. Their aim was to provide farmers with work they could make and sell during the winter months.

■ In 1943, the potters moved to a vacant factory in St Joseph de Beauce, where production began in earnest and rapidly grew to industrial levels. Raymond Lewis, who had joined as a teacher in 1942, acted as head designer until 1964. Until c1948, red clay was used, but when this could not meet growing needs, it was replaced by a finer white clay from Georgia, which also allowed for more technical possibilities.

■ From 1946-64 the trade name Beauceware was used and is usually found on the base. A 'cb' monogram designed by Andre Roy was used from 1965 until 1989. Numbers relate to the mold or shape number. Although numbers moved upwards consecutively through the years, it is not possible to date a piece by the mold number as a shape could have been made for many years.

■ Glazes can help to date a piece to a period. Early pieces tend to have shaded, sponged or dripped colored glazes, with blue being popular. Surfaces tend to have molded motifs or patterns. During the 1950s,

single solid or toned colors such as green or burgundy were popular. Forms tended to be inspired by leaves, shells or flowers. Many shapes were inspired by those of American pottery companies like McCoy, Hull & Royal Haeger.

■ The 1950s and 1960s saw great expansion in the number of shapes being made. Vases, planters, dishes, lamps, and ashtrays generally dominated production. The 1960s saw more experimentation as colored glazes became dramatic, being dripped, swirled or trailed onto strongly contrasting grounds. This period also saw a focus on tableware, solidifying Beauce's proliferation in North American homes.

■ Key designers included Jacques Garnier, who began in 1963 and introduced a Scandinavian influence, and Jean Cartier, who began in 1970, developing a characteristic style of his own. In 1974 the factory was destroyed by fire. It reopened a year later with a more efficient production process. Despite this, competition from foreign markets forced the factory to close in 1989.

■ Beauceware has become increasingly collectible since the mid-1990s and prices look set to rise. Over 7,000 different designs were produced. Early pieces usually fetch the largest sums. Look out for dramatic glaze colors, unusual shapes and lamps with their original shades.

A Canadian Beauceware light green round dish, shape no.295, with inverted rim.

8in (20.5cm) diam

$12-18　　　　　　　　　　　　　　　**ING**

A 1950s Canadian Beauceware green glazed ashtray, shape no.447.

8.75in (22cm) long

$25-35　　　　　　　　　　　　　　　**RAON**

A Canadian Beauceware light green curving oval dish, shape no.294, with frilled curving edge.

12in (30.5cm) long

$25-35　　　　　**ING**

A Canadian Beauceware molded bulbous green glazed planter, shape no.492.

7.5in (19cm) wide

$20-30　　　　　**ING**

A Canadian Beauceware light green glazed dish, molded as a morning glory flower, unmarked.

8in (20cm) wide

$15-20　　　　　**ING**

A Canadian Beauceware long curving light green dish, shape no.743.

12.25in (31cm) long

$30-40　　　　　**ING**

A Canadian Beauceware dark green glazed asymmetric dish, shape no.934.

9in (22.5cm) long

$10-15   **ING**

A 1950s Beauceware green glazed Cornucopia planter, shape no.394C.

Designed c1945, this was inspired by Royal Haeger's model R-709.

c1955   *15in (38cm) long*

$40-50   **ING**

A 1950s Beauceware large planter, shape no.197, in the form of a shell with a molded coil of beads.

This shape was inspired by a vase made by US maker Royal Haeger.

18.5in (47cm) long

$50-70   **ING**

A Canadian Beauceware gray-green glazed planter, shape no.303, with scalloped corners.

11in (28cm) wide

$22-28   **ING**

A Canadian Beauceware green glazed lidded dish, shape no.637.

7in (17.5cm) high

$40-50   **ING**

A Canadian Beauceware cylindrical dark green glazed vase, with flared rim and light green interior, shape no.270.

c1965   *6.75in (17cm) high*

$20-30   **ING**

A Canadian Beauceware dark green glazed advertising ashtray, shape no.1130, with molded "TU" motif possibly for Trans Union of Canada.

This is the most common form of Beauceware ashtrays found. Advertising examples have become highly collectible.

c1970   *7.75in (19.5cm) diam*

$22-28   **ING**

A Canadian Beauceware green glazed advertising ashtray, shape no.1130, with advertising for Grenier Spring Inc.

7.25in (18.5cm) diam

$22-28   **ING**

A Canadian Beauceware scallop edged dish, shape no.203.

10.75in (27.5cm) long

$30-40 ING

A large Canadian Beauceware red glazed shell or curling leaf-shaped dish, shape no.380, designed c1945.

c1955   13.5in (34cm) long

$50-70 ING

A Canadian Beauceware molded 'Cabbage' bowl, shape no.419.

c1955   6in (15cm) diam

$12-18 ING

A Canadian Beauceware burgundy glazed rectangular dish, shape no.496.

7in (18cm) long

$12-18 ING

A Canadian Beauceware molded fan shaped vase, shape no.286.

12.5in (32cm) long

$25-35 ING

A 1950s Beauceware burgundy glazed ceramic nautilus shell vase, shape no.488.

5.25in (13.5cm) high

$15-20 ING

A Canadian Beauceware molded curling leaf bud vase, shape no.484.

Designed c1949, this was inspired by an example produced by the van Briggle pottery.

c1955   9in (23cm) high

$15-20 ING

A 1950s Beauceware burgundy glazed small flower planter and tray, shape no.J-6.

4.25in (10.5cm) high

$10-15 ING

A 1950s Canadian Beauceware burgundy glazed ball pitcher, shape no.107.

This modern form was inspired by an example produced by the American Hull Pottery and was designed around 1943.

8in (20cm) high

$50-60 ING

A Canadian Beauceware brown Cornucopia
vase, shape no.483.

c1960   *7.5in (19cm) long*

$15-20   **ING**

A Canadian Beauceware black nautilus
vase, shape no.320.

c1960   *6.75in (17cm) high*

$40-50   **ING**

A CLOSER LOOK AT A BEAUCEWARE TANKARD

*This shape was Beauce's main promotional mug
from around 1960 onward. It was
produced in a myriad
of patterns from
advertising to
commemorative
themes making
it a popular
shape to
collect today.*

*Sporting themes are
popular with sporting
collectors, adding
cross-market interest.
Winter sports,
especially curling,
motifs are also
comparatively scarce
and desirable.*

*It was designed around
1942 using an English
tankard produced by Royal
Cauldon as the base example.*

*The maple leaf and
beaver are symbols
of the Canadian
nation and their
appearance adds
appeal.*

A rare Beauceware brown glazed tankard, shape no.105-G, with molded "St-Joseph
BEAUCE" mark and curling and beaver moldings.

5in (12.5cm) high

$60-80   **ING**

A Canadian Beauceware gray-green glazed
dish, shape no.294, with frilled curving edge.

12in (30.5cm) long

$25-35   **ING**

A Canadian Beauceware brown glazed
dish, shape no.450A, with curving rim.

10.5in (26.5cm) long

$30-40   **ING**

A Canadian Beauceware brown glazed advertising ashtray, shape
no.619, for Brocklesby Transport Montreal, impressed "Ceramique
de BEAUCE CANADA - 619".

c1960   *9.5in (24cm) diam*

$60-80   **ING**

An American Royal Haeger
dark green glazed shell
shaped vase, shape
no.R299.

*A number of Royal Haeger designs influenced Beauce – note the
similarities in shape, glaze, and general appearance.*

7in (18cm) high

$50-70   **ING**

FIND OUT MORE...

**Beauce Pottery: The Story of Beauceware and Céramique de
Beauce**, by Daniel Cogné, Richard Dubé and Paul Trépanier,
published by Les Editions CID, Canada, 2004.

COLLECTORS' NOTES

■ Edna Best (1900-74) began her film career in 1921 and grew to be one of the most popular actresses in the 1920s and '30s. She is best remembered for her role as the mother in Alfred Hitchcock's first version of 'The Man Who Knew Too Much', filmed in 1934. From the early 1930s to 1940 she worked in Hollywood, after moving there with her husband.

■ Although she did not design the bright Art Deco ceramics by the Pearl Pottery of Hanley, Staffordshire, England, she did lend her name to them, thereby creating an early instance of 'celebrity endorsement' in homewares.

■ Following the fashion of the day, they are handpainted in bright colors with geometric, stylized patterns somewhat similar to Clarice Cliff's work. Look for those that also follow Art Deco forms as these are often more desirable. Most of the pieces produced were teawares, other items such as vases are scarcer.

An Edna Best Art Pottery round teapot.

c1930   7.75in (19.5cm) high

$280-320   **NAI**

A 1930s Edna Best Art Pottery milk jug.

3.25in (8.5cm) high

$70-100   **NAI**

A 1930s Edna Best Art Pottery teapot.

6.5in (16.5cm) high

$280-320   **NAI**

An Edna Best Art Pottery low teapot.

c1930   *4.25in (10.5cm) high*

$280-320   **NAI**

An Edna Best Art Pottery for Lawley's vase, with two-ring handles.

c1930   *9in (23cm) high*

$300-400   **NAI**

A 1930s Edna Best Art Pottery coffee can and saucer.

4.25in (10.5cm) diam

$70-100   **NAI**

CERAMICS

COLLECTORS' NOTES

■ The Beswick pottery was founded at Loughton, Staffordshire, England, in 1894. Although animal figures were produced in the 1900s, they only formed a larger part of production from the 1930s.

■ In 1939, animal modeler Arthur Gredington joined Beswick, and went on to design most of Beswick's vast range of animals, many produced well into the 1990s. Other modelers of note include Colin Melbourne, known for his CM range and his wildfowl, Graham Tongue, Albert Hallam, and Alan Maslankowski, who also designed Royal Doulton figurines.

■ Collectors tend to focus on one type of animal, with cattle being one of the most popular, particularly among farmers, butchers, and countryside lovers. Prices, particularly for rare variations or models, have rocketed recently, especially for those produced for short periods of time, or that went out of production

after 1969, when the range was rationalized.

■ Also consider the animal itself, as large, visually impressive bulls tend to be slightly more desirable than cows, but both are usually more desirable than smaller calves. Modern limited editions, even from the late 1990s can be valuable too, particularly if the edition was produced in small numbers.

■ Most figures are found in a gloss finish, the matte finish usually having been produced for shorter periods of time as it was less popular. This means some matte pieces can be more valuable today.

■ Colorways that depart from the normal add value too. Roan and Rockinghorse gray are usually more valuable than brown. Always examine protruding parts such as ears and legs for damage as this, or restoration, lowers appeal and thus value considerably.

A Beswick 'Limousin Cow', 3075B, from a limited edition of 656 for the Beswick Collectors' Club.

1998   *5in (13cm) long*

$300-500   **GORW**

A Beswick 'Limousin Bull', 2463B, from a limited edition of 653 for the Beswick Collectors' Club, designed by Alan Maslankowski.

1998   *5in (13cm) long*

$500-700   **GORW**

A Beswick 'Highland Bull' gloss figure, 2008, designed by Arthur Gredington.

1985-89   *5in (13cm) long*

$300-400   **GORW**

A Beswick 'Dairy Shorthorn Ch. Eaton Wild Eyes, 91st', 1510, designed by Arthur Gredington.

1957-73   *4.75in (12cm) long*

$1,800-2,200   **GORW**

A Beswick 'Dairy Shorthorn Ch. Gwersylt, Lord, Oxford, 74th', 1504, designed by Arthur Gredington.

1957-73   *5in (13cm) long*

$1,200-1,800   **GORW**

A Beswick 'Polled Hereford Bull', 2549A, designed in 1975 by Graham Tongue.

1977-97   *5in (13cm) high*

$280-320   **GORW**

A Beswick 'Hereford Bull' gloss figure, 1363A, designed by Arthur Gredington.

This gloss version with his horns protruding from behind his ears is worth up to three times more than the later version with horns set flush to his ears.

Until 1997   *8.5in (11cm) high*

$280-320   **GORW**

A Beswick 'Guernsey Ch. Sabrina's Sir Richmond 14th' gloss figure, 1451, designed by Colin Melbourne, with restored ear.

1956-89   *4.75in (12cm) high*

$280-320   **GORW**

A CLOSER LOOK AT A BESWICK COW

Look out for model number 899 with the horns pointing upward, it was the first version and was produced in 1941 only.

Examine the horns closely for signs of damage or repair.

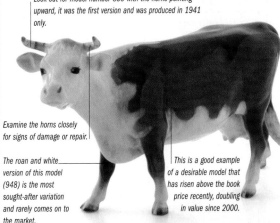

The roan and white version of this model (948) is the most sought-after variation and rarely comes on to the market.

This is a good example of a desirable model that has risen above the book price recently, doubling in value since 2000.

A Beswick 'Hereford Cow', 948, designed by Arthur Gredington.

1941-c1957   *5in (13cm) high*

$800-1,200   **GORW**

A Beswick 'Ayrshire Ch. Ickham Bessie', 1350, designed by Arthur Gredington.

1954-90   *5in (13cm) long*

$300-400   **GORW**

A Beswick 'Jersey Ch. Dunsley Coy Boy' gloss figure, 1422, designed by Arthur Gredington.

1956-97   *4.75in (12cm) high*

$180-220   **GORW**

A Beswick 'Charolais Cow' gloss figure, 3075A.

Look out for the rare matte finish, produced for the first two years of production only, which can be worth around 25 percent more.

1988-97   *5in (13cm) long*

$280-320   **GORW**

A Beswick 'Charolais Bull' gloss figure, 2463A, designed in 1973 by Alan Maslankowski.

1979-97   *5in (13cm) long*

$280-320   **GORW**

A Beswick 'Aberdeen Angus Cow' gloss figure, 1563, designed by Arthur Gredington, with unusual gray hooves.

The matte version can be worth around 25 percent more than the gloss version.

1959-89   *4.25in (11cm) high*

$280-320   **GORW**

A Beswick 'Aberdeen Angus Cow' gloss figure, 1563, designed by Arthur Gredington, with a restored foot.

1959-89   *4.25in (11cm) high*

$280-320   **GORW**

A Beswick 'Aberdeen Angus Bull', 1562, designed by Arthur Gredington.

This model was approved by the panel of judges for the Breed Society.

1958-89   4.75in (12cm) high

$280-320   **GORW**

A Beswick 'Black Galloway Cow', 4113B.

$280-320   **GORW**

A Beswick 'Friesian Ch. Coddington Hilt Bar' gloss figure, 1439A, designed by Arthur Gredington.

1956-97   4.75in (12cm) high

$220-280   **GORW**

A Beswick 'Friesian Bull Ch. Coddington Hilt Bar' matte figure, 1439A, designed by Arthur Gredington.

This is the scarcer matte version of the gloss model also shown on this page. It was produced for a shorter period of 1985-89, and can be worth up to 40 percent more.

4.75in (12cm) high

$300-500   **GORW**

A Beswick 'Belted Galloway Cow', 4113A.

$120-180   **GORW**

A Beswick 'Hereford Cow and Calf' on plinth, 1360 and 1827C, from the 'Plinthed Animals' series.

1993-96   7in (18cm) high

$280-320   **GORW**

A Beswick 'Charolais Cow and Calf' on plinth, 3075 and 1827B, the calf modeled by Arthur Gredington.

1993-96

6in (15cm) high

$280-320   **GORW**

A Beswick 'Jersey 'Ch. Newton Tinkle' and 'Jersey Calf', 1345 and 1249D, both designed by Arthur Gredington.

These models were also released on a wooden plinth as part of the 'Plinthed Animals' series between 1993 and 1997. They would have fetched more on the plinth.

1954-97

$120-180   **GORW**

A Beswick 'Hereford Calf', 1406B, designed by Arthur Gredington.

1956-75   *3in (7.5cm) high*

$280-320   **GORW**

A Beswick 'Hereford Calf', 901B, designed by Arthur Gredington, with restored back leg.

Look for the more valuable roan and white colorway and the early, open-mouthed version.

A Beswick 'Dairy Shorthorn Calf', 1406B, designed by Arthur Gredington.

1956-75   *3in (7.5cm) high*

$600-900   **GORW**

Until 1957   *4in (10cm) high*

$120-180   **GORW**

A Beswick 'Ayrshire Calf' gloss figure, 1249B, designed in 1952 by Arthur Gredington.

The gloss re-issue from 1985-90 is worth around 15 percent less.

1956-75

$220-280   **GORW**

A Beswick 'Guernsey Calf' gloss figure, 1249A, designed by Arthur Gredington, with restored ears.

1985-89   *2.75in (7cm) high*

$80-120   **GORW**

A Beswick 'Limousin Calf', 1827E, designed by Arthur Gredington and from a limited edition of 711 for the Beswick Collectors' Club.

1998   *3in (7.5cm) long*

$300-500   **GORW**

A Beswick 'Charolais Calf' gloss figure, 1827B, designed by Arthur Gredington.

1985-97   *3in (7.5cm) long*

$180-220   **GORW**

A Beswick 'Aberdeen Angus Calf', 1827A, designed by Arthur Gredington.

1985-89   *3in (7.5cm) long*

$400-600   **GORW**

A Beswick 'Aberdeen Angus Calf', 1406A, designed by Arthur Gredington.

1956-75   *3in (7.5cm) high*

$400-600   **GORW**

CERAMICS

A large Beswick 'Mallard Duck', 1518, from the 'Peter Scott Wildfowl' series, designed by Arthur Gredington.

Although this the largest size is the most valuable, look out for the first version of the smallest size, at 4.5in (11.5cm) long, as this is worth around 20-30 percent less than this one, but more than other sizes.

1958-71   6.5in (16.5cm) long

$280-320   **GORW**

A Beswick 'Goosander', 1525, from the 'Peter Scott Wildfowl' series, designed by Colin Melbourne.

1958-71   4.75in (12cm) long

$280-320   **GORW**

A Beswick 'Shelduck', 1527, from the 'Peter Scott Wildfowl' series, designed by Colin Melbourne.

1958-71   4in (10cm) long

$180-220   **GORW**

A Beswick 'Smew Duck', 1522, from the 'Peter Scott Wildfowl' series, designed by Colin Melbourne.

1958-71   3in (7.5cm) long

$180-220   **GORW**

A Beswick 'Teal Duck', 1529, from the 'Peter Scott Wildfowl' collection, designed by Colin Melbourne.

1958-71   2.75in (7cm) long

$180-220   **GORW**

A Beswick 'Mandarin Duck', 1519, from the 'Peter Scott Wildfowl' series, designed by Arthur Gredington.

1958-71

$220-280   **GORW**

A Beswick 'Song Thrush' gloss figure, 2308, designed by Albert Hallam.

The matte finish is worth around 50 percent less.

$180-220   **GORW**

A Beswick 'Gamecock', 2059, designed by Arthur Gredington.

Examine the tailfeathers and beak of this upright and proud bird, as they are prone to breakage.

1966-75   9.5in (24cm) high

$800-1,200   **CHEF**

A Beswick 'Small Owl', 1420, designed by Colin Melbourne, with sgraffito-type detailing, artist's initials and factory paper label to underside.

The stylization of the form and features is typical of the look of the 1950s, when this 'contemporary' range of animals was released. Many are rare and desirable today, but are disliked as much as loved for their modern appearance.

1956-65   5in (13cm) high

$280-320   **ROS**

A Beswick 'Mounted Indian' gloss figure, 1391, designed by Mr. Orwell.

1955-90   8.5in (21.5cm) high

$700-1,000   **PSA**

A CLOSER LOOK AT A BESWICK HORSE FIGURE

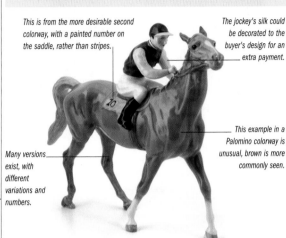

This is from the more desirable second colorway, with a painted number on the saddle, rather than stripes.

The jockey's silk could be decorated to the buyer's design for an extra payment.

Many versions exist, with different variations and numbers.

This example in a Palomino colorway is unusual, brown is more commonly seen.

A rare Beswick 'Racehorse And Jockey' figure, 1037, designed by Arthur Gredington, colorway two with Palomino horse.

$4,000-6,000   **PSA**

A Beswick 'Canadian Mounted Cowboy', 1377, designed by Mr. Orwell.

This large and impressive figurine has cross-market appeal, making it more desirable and hence valuable.

1955-73   8.75in (22cm) high

$2,800-3,200   **PSA**

A Beswick 'Huntsman Standing', 1501, in brown, with six foxhounds and a fox.

Earlier, more valuable, gloss hounds date from 1941-69 and have thicker tails and legs. Look out for this Huntsman in Rockinghorse gray as it can fetch up to six times more than this colorway.

1957-95

Huntsman 8.25in (21cm) high

$800-1,200   **BRI**

A Beswick 'Fox Standing' gloss figure, MN1440, with four gloss foxhounds, 2264, 2262, and 941.

1956-97

Fox 2.5in (6.5cm) high

$300-500   **PSA**

A Beswick 'Zebra' gloss figure, 845B, designed by Arthur Gredington.

The earlier version with black stripes on a tan body is rarer and more desirable, worth up to three times more than this version.

Until 1969

7.25in (18.5cm) high

$220-280   **PSA**

A Beswick 'Small Giraffe' gloss figure, 853, in a realistic colorway, designed by Arthur Gredington.

1940-75   7in (18cm) high

$120-180   **PSA**

A Beswick 'Donkey' matte figure, 1364B, designed by Mr. Orwell.

Look out for the rare earlier version, produced in 1955 with its tail hanging free from the hind leg. This was presumably discontinued as the tail was prone to damage. It was also easier to manufacture with the tail attached to the leg.

1987-89   4.75in (12cm) h

$30-50   **PSA**

A Beswick vase, shape 1649, designed by Albert Hallam.

c1960-65   8in (20.5cm) high

$80-120   **NPC**

A Beswick vase, shape 1653, designed by Albert Hallam.

c1959-66   10.5in (27cm) high

$120-180   **NPC**

A Beswick vase, shape 1402, designed by Colin Melbourne.

c1956   7.25in (18.5cm) high

$50-80   **NPC**

A Beswick vase, shape 1357, designed by Albert Hallam in 1954.

c1957-62   8in (20.5cm) high

$120-180   **NPC**

A Beswick vase, model 128M, molded with rose flowers and a bird, molded and printed marks.

11.5in (29cm) high

$180-220   **WW**

A 1930s Beswick vase, with blue, orange, and yellow glazes.

7.5in (19cm) high

$70-100   **GAZE**

A 1930s Beswick green and mottled glazed jug, no.177/2.

8in (20cm) high

$40-60   **GAZE**

A 1930s Beswick yellow and mottled glazed jug, no.177/2.

8.75in (22cm) high

$40-60   **GAZE**

FIND OUT MORE...

The Charlton Standard Catalogue Of Beswick Animals, *published by The Charlton Press, 2004.*

CERAMICS

COLLECTORS' NOTES

■ Bing & Grøndahl was formed in Copenhagen, Denmark in 1853 by artist Frederick Grøndahl and brothers Jacob and Meyer Bing. Initially, they produced fine quality porcelain tableware. Figures were introduced in c1895.

■ Pieces are typically decorated in soft, pale colors such as gray, blue, brown, and white and are glossily overglazed. The factory's mark is based on Copenhagen's coat of arms and features three towers over the company's initials. If the mark is scratched through, this indicates a second.

■ Figures have always been collectible, although ranges produced for long periods of time tend to be less popular with collectors. Early examples, those produced for a short period of time and large or complex models are sought-after, as are those with unusual variations.

A CLOSER LOOK AT A BING & GRØNDAHL FIGURINE

Henning Seidelin (1904-87) was a Danish industrial designer who worked in a number of media including metalware and ceramics.

This figure is still in production but is large and complex, as well as being very charming and an appealing Danish subject.

Fellow Dane, Hans Christian Anderson is a popular subject with collectors, as are figures inspired by his fairy tales.

2005 is the 200th anniversary of Anderson's birth and this is likely to increase interest in him.

A Bing & Grøndahl 'Hans Christian Anderson' porcelain model, no. 2037, designed by Henning Seidelin.

9in (23cm) high

$300-500 **LOB**

A Bing & Grøndahl 'Who is Calling?' porcelain figurine, no. 2251, designed by Michaela Ahlman.

6in (15cm) high

$120-180 **LOB**

A Bing & Grøndahl porcelain figurine of a boy with a crab at his toes, no. 1870, designed by Ingeborg Plockross Irminger.

c1980   8in (20cm) high

$120-180 **LOB**

A Bing & Grøndahl 'Girl Sitting' porcelain figurine, no. 1879, designed by Ingeborg Plockross Irminger.

7in (18cm) high

$220-280 **LOB**

A Bing & Grøndahl porcelain model of a couple dancing, no. 2385, designed by Claire Weiss.

8in (20cm) high

$120-180 **LOB**

A Bing & Grøndahl porcelain figurine of a terrier, no. 1998, designed by Dahl-Jensen.

6.75in (17cm) long

$220-280 **LOB**

COLLECTORS' NOTES

■ The Brush Pottery was founded by George Brush in Zanesville, Ohio in 1906. When the pottery burnt down 1909, Brush went to work at the J.W. McCoy Pottery as general manager and became a shareholder.

■ The company name became Brush McCoy in 1911 when the two companies merged and Brush took the controlling interest. The name changed again in 1925 to the Brush Pottery Company, a few years after J.W. McCoy died and the family sold its remaining interest.

■ The majority of pieces made under the Brush-McCoy name are unmarked except for the occasional mold number.

■ Brush pieces are typically made of a heavy pottery and unsurprisingly bear many similarities to McCoy examples. Animal-based planters and figures are common and often utilize natural colors such as green, brown or cream.

A Brush frog ornament, unmarked.

7in (18cm) high

$220-280   **BEL**

A Brush frog garden ornament, unmarked.

7.75in (19.5cm) long

$80-120   **BEL**

A Brush frog-shaped flower frog, unmarked.

4.25in (11cm) long

$70-100   **BEL**

A Brush reclining frog ornament, unmarked, hind foot broken off and restored.

10in (25.5cm) long

$40-60   **BEL**

A Brush frog planter, with open top, unmarked.

5.75in (14.5cm) long

$40-60   **BEL**

A scarce Brush ashtray, with two open-mouthed frogs, one on either side, marked "042" on the base.

7in (18cm) long

$150-200   **BEL**

A Brush turtle planter, with open top, marked "B493 USA" on the base.

7.25in (18.5cm) long

$40-60   **BEL**

A Brush turtle ornament, unmarked.

5in (12.5cm) long

$50-80   **BEL**

FIND OUT MORE...

Sanfords Guide to Brush-McCoy Pottery, by Martha & Steve Sanford, published by Adelmore Press, 1992.

The Collector's Encyclopedia of Brush-McCoy Pottery, by Sharon & Bob Huxford, published by Collector Books, 1996.

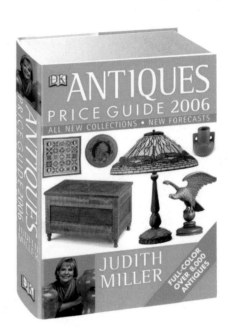

COLLECTORS' NOTES

- Wiltshaw and Robinson established the Carlton Works in Stoke on Trent, England in 1890 and used the trade name Carlton Ware from 1894. The company name became Carlton Ware in 1958.

- Inspired by Wedgwood's successful 'Fairyland' luster range, the company began producing its own richly decorated luster range, with a variety of patterns on different colored grounds, in 1925. The patterns were often influenced by oriental Chinoiserie or ancient Egypt, birds were also a popular theme.

- The 1930s saw the introduction of a molded range of practical tableware decorated with a wide range of flowers, fruit, and vegetables usually in greens, yellows, and pinks. This range was produced in large amounts until the late 1950s and is still affordable today, although rare variations of color and decoration are sought-after.

- The 1960s saw simpler shapes and decoration, often two-tone exemplified by the 'Orbit' range, influenced by the Space Race. Facing financial difficulties due to the recession, the company introduced the Walking Ware range designed by husband and wife team Roger Mitchell and Danka Napiorkoska. The range's popularity helped secure the company and lead to number of variations such as 'Running' and 'Jumping'.

- The company changed hands a number of times in the 1980s before being bought by Francis Joseph in 1997.

A Carlton Ware 'Devil's Copse' pattern vase and flower frog, no.3817, printed and painted marks.

7.75in (20cm) diam

$400-600   **WW**

A Carlton Ware 'Sketching Bird' pattern conical bowl, with printed mark.

9.25in (23.5cm) diam

$800-1,200   **WW**

A Carlton Ware 'Barge' pattern bowl, no.2519, in blue luster glaze.

The 'Barge' pattern is harder to find than some of the other Chinoiserie patterns.

9in (23cm) diam

$180-220   **CA**

A Carlton Ware 'Paradise Bird and Tree' bowl, no. 151, in yellow glaze.

9in (23cm) diam

$280-320   **CA**

A Carlton Ware 'Chinese Dragon' pattern vase, no.3656, printed and painted marks.

6.75in (17cm) high

$300-400   **WW**

A Carlton Ware 'Paradise Bird and Tree With Cloud' pattern vase, no.3144, printed and painted marks.

6in (15.5cm) high

$700-1,000   **WW**

An early Carlton Ware vase, impressed "294".

11.75in (30cm) high

$500-700   **BEV**

A pair of Carlton Ware Rouge Royal candlesticks.

$70-100   **GAZE**

A Carlton Ware green-glazed salad bowl and pair of servers, marked "Registered Australian Design".

$50-80 GAZE

A Carlton Ware cabbage leaf and lobster salad bowl and servers.

The British Public Health service banned the red paint used to decorate these lobsters in 1976 due to its high lead content.

8.75in (22cm) wide

$180-220 BAD

An Art Deco Carlton Ware pear sugar castor.

c1930 *5.5in (14cm) high*

$80-120 BAD

A Carlton Ware 'Fruits' condiment set.

9in (23cm) wide

$40-60 GAZE

A 1930s Carlton Ware 'Cottage' pattern jam pot.

This jam pot will appeal to collectors of cottage ware as well as Carlton ware.

5in (12.5cm) high

$180-220 BEV

A Carlton Ware pen holder, with molded bird decoration.

Carlton Ware produced pen holders for a number of pen companies but are perhaps best known for those made for Parker Pens. Items such as this appeal to both Carlton Ware and pen collectors.

7in (17.5cm) wide

$180-220 BAD

A Carlton Ware toast rack, printed marks including "Registered Australian Design".

6.5in (16.5cm) wide

$30-35 GAZE

A Carlton Ware triple candleholder.

7.5in (19cm) wide

$60-90 NPC

A 1960s Carlton Ware 'Orbit' pattern dish, with two compartments.

$40-60 NPC

CERAMICS

A 1950s Carlton Ware square plate, with abstract turquoise and black decoration.

7in (18cm) wide

$25-35 NPC

A 1960s Carlton Ware 'Flatback' series pig money box.

6in (15cm) long

$70-100 FD

A Carlton Ware 'Bug-Eye' series snail money box.

c1965 *5in (12.5cm) long*

$80-120 FD

A 1960s Carlton Ware 'Flatback' series Noah's Ark money box.

7in (18cm) wide

$70-100 FD

A Carlton Ware 'Walking Ware' teacup, with feet in blue shoes, walking.

4.25in (11cm) high

$40-60 CHS

A Carlton Ware 'Walking Ware' sugar bowl, with feet in yellow shoes, standing, printed marks.

5.5in (14cm) high

$70-100 CHS

A limited edition Carlton Ware 'The Pigeon Fancier' character jug, from an edition of 500.

$50-70 GAZE

A late 1970s Carlton Ware 'Denim' range teapot.

This range was a commercial disaster for Carlton Ware – especially in America where it was thought to have homosexual connotations. It contributed to the closure of the company.

A late 1970s Carlton Ware 'Denim' range salt and pepper shaker.

$50-70 NPC

9in (23cm) high

$80-120 NPC

A J. Meir & Son chintz jug, with registered design mark.

Typical of early chintz patterns, this jug has panels of decoration with space between the flowers and more muted colors. Later examples have brightly colored patterns with tightly packed flowers.

c1866   8.5in (22cm) high

$180-220   **BAD**

A Royal Winton 'Royalty' pattern cup and saucer.

c1930   Saucer 5.75in (14.5cm) diam

$70-100   **BAD**

A 1930s Royal Winton 'Hazel' pattern milk jug.

8.5in (11cm) high

$120-180   **BAD**

A 1950s Royal Winton 'Marion' pattern candy box.

5in (13cm) long

$280-320   **BAD**

A Royal Winton 'Mecca' foot warmer, pattern no.1094, with marks.

When Queen Mary visited the Winton factory in 1913 she was presented with one of these foot warmers.

10in (26cm) high

$280-320   **SWO**

An early 1950s Royal Winton 'Julia' pattern butter dish.

6in (16cm) wide

$280-320   **BAD**

A Royal Winton 'Richmond' pattern trefoil dish.

8in (20cm) wide

$180-220   **BAD**

A 1940s/50s Royal Winton 'Somerset' pattern basket.

This basket is desirable as the pattern covers the majority of the basket with the exception of the inside of the handle.

12.25in (31cm) wide

$280-320   **BAD**

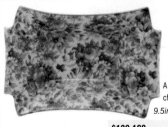

A Royal Winton chintz dish.

9.5in (15cm) wide

$120-180   **BAD**

COLLECTORS' NOTES

■ Clarice Cliff was born in Tunstall, Staffordshire, England, in 1899 and, in a region dominated by the potteries, joined a local company in 1912. In 1916 she moved to A.J Wilkinson's where she was soon promoted to a more influential and artistic position. In 1925, managing director Colley Shorter gave Cliff her own studio at the newly purchased Newport Pottery.

■ This pottery had a large stock of defective blank wares, many in old-fashioned shapes. Cliff covered them in brightly colored and thickly applied patterns, to hide the faults. The new range was given the name 'Bizarre' and was launched in 1928 to great success. The 'Crocus' pattern was particularly popular.

■ The 'Fantasque' line, consisting of similar wares to the 'Bizarre' range, was launched in 1928. As both lines developed, the patterns moved away from the typically Art Deco, simple geometric designs to become more elaborate, abstract and bold, particularly in the 'Fantasque' range.

■ As public tastes changed, the Fantasque name was phased out in 1934, with Bizarre following a year later, although pieces with those backstamps continued to leave the factory. When production restarted after WWII, Cliff, by now art director, continued to design, but not with the success of previous years. When Shorter, by now Cliff's husband, died in 1963 she sold the pottery to rival Midwinter.

■ Items that display a pattern well, such as large plates, jugs and vases are popular. Look for thickly painted wares with visible brushstrokes and black outlines, as these typify early Cliff and are very desirable. Distinctly Art Deco patterns and forms are also favored by collectors, whilst designs in muted colors, or those that are not typical of Cliff, receive less attention.

■ Many patterns were produced in a range of colorways so look out for rare variations: orange is a common color whilst blue and purple are often rarer and more valuable.

A Clarice Cliff Fantasque Bizarre toast rack.

1929-34   6.5in (16.5cm) diam

$500-700   **BEV**

A CLOSER LOOK AT A CLARICE CLIFF PRESERVE POT

Due to its early date, this pot will probably have been handpainted by either Cliff herself or Gladys Scarlett who was the first decorator to work with Cliff.

This early mark with a handpainted "Bizarre" was only used in 1928 before being replaced with a stamped mark.

Typical of the earliest ware, this pot has a relatively simple geometric pattern. It also has visibly handpainted decoration.

The Newport Pottery mark denotes a blank taken from the pottery's unused old stock.

An early Clarice Cliff Bizarre preserve pot, with chromed lid, Newport Pottery mark and handpainted "Bizarre".

c1928   3.25in (8cm) high

$400-600   **NAI**

A rare Clarice Cliff 'Bobbins' pattern Bizarre biscuit barrel, molded with lug handles, slight flaking to orange enamel, printed marks.

c1931-33   6.75in (17cm) wide

$700-1,000   **B**

A Clarice Cliff Fantasque Bizarre 'Canterbury Bells' pattern pot.

1932-33   3in (7.5cm) diam

$500-700   **BEV**

A Clarice Cliff 'Blue Chintz' pattern bowl.

c1932   7.5in (19cm) diam

$400-600   **GORL**

A Clarice Cliff Bizarre 'Crocus' pattern 14-piece part Tankard coffee set.

The most popular design produced by Clarice Cliff, the Crocus pattern was introduced in 1928 and, with the exception of the war years, was made until 1963. It was produced in a number of colorways.

Pot 7in (18cm) high

$2,200-2,800 GORL

A Clarice Cliff Bizarre 'Crocus' pattern Bon Jour preserve pot and cover.

1928-63 4.25in (10.5cm) high

$500-700 BEV

A Clarice Cliff Fantasque 'Melon' pattern beehive honey pot.

c1930-32 3.75in (9.5cm) high

$320-380 GORW

A Clarice Cliff Bizarre 'My Garden Flame' pattern pedestal bowl, "AF" printed marks to underside.

c1934-41 8in (20cm) high

$180-220 ROS

An A.J. Wilkinson 'Orange' pattern Daffodil shape grapefruit dish, designed by Dolly Cliff, marked "Wilkinson, England Honeyglaze Handpainted".

Clarice Cliff's sister Dolly worked as a designer at A.J. Wilkinson at the same time as her.

7in (17.5cm) wide

$50-70 NAI

A Clarice Cliff Fantasque Bizarre 'Pastel Autumn' pattern fern pot, printed marks, introduced in 1934.

3in (7.5cm) high

$300-500 WW

A Clarice Cliff Bizarre 'Pastel Autumn' pattern Conical coffee set.

1932 Pot 7in (18cm) high

$4,000-6,000 GORL

A Clarice Cliff Bizarre 'Pink Pearls' pattern sugar sifter, printed mark.

This is a variation of Rhodanthe with an alternative colorway.

1934-37 5.5in (14cm) high

$300-500 WW

A 1930s Clarice Cliff Fantasque 'Red Trees & House' Conical jug.

6.25in (16cm) high

$1,500-2,000 BEV

A Clarice Cliff 'Tree and Gate' pattern preserve pot, cover glued.

4.25in (11cm) wide

$1,200-1,800   **GORL**

A Clarice Cliff honeyglaze and blue oval meat plate, with matching tureen and cover, gilded with sailing boats.

$40-60   **GORW**

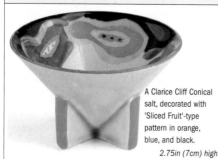

A Clarice Cliff Conical salt, decorated with 'Sliced Fruit'-type pattern in orange, blue, and black.

2.75in (7cm) high

$280-320   **GORL**

A Clarice Cliff Bizarre 'Secrets' pattern charger.

1933-37

10.75in (27cm) diam

$1,200-1,800   **BEV**

A Clarice Cliff Bizarre 'Sliced Fruit' pattern preserve pot and cover, printed mark.

c1930   *3.5in (9cm) high*

$280-320   **WW**

A Clarice Cliff Bizarre 'Viscaria' pattern Liner vase, shape no.469, with printed mark, introduced in 1934

8.25in (21cm) high

$700-1,000   **WW**

A 1930s Clarice Cliff 'Water Lily' planter, shape no.973.

This was the best selling shape in this range.

8.75in (22cm) wide

$80-120   **GAZE**

A Clarice Cliff circular Bon Jour cream jug, painted with a concentric design in brown, yellow, and gray, and a similar sugar bowl.

2.5in (6.5cm) diam

$150-200   **GORL**

A Clarice Cliff Biarritz plate, with abstract design of orange flowers and lines, impressed date.

1935   *9in (23cm) wide*

$180-220   **GORL**

A Gray's Pottery lampbase, probably designed by Susie Cooper, pattern no.9677, printed clipper mark.

8in (20cm) high

$300-400 WW

A Gray's Pottery platter, designed by Susie Cooper, pattern no.2866, painted with flowers, liner mark.

14.5in (37cm) wide

$20-30 WW

A Gray's Pottery coffee can and saucer, designed by Susie Cooper, pattern no.8330, printed liner mark.

2.75in (7cm) high

$300-400 WW

Two of a set of six Susie Cooper Productions dinner plates, retailed by Ingwald Nielsen, Oslo, pattern no.E316, printed and painted marks, minor paint wear.

10in (25.5cm) diam

$1,200-1,400 set WW

A Susie Cooper Productions 'Black Pom and Tango Terrier' lemonade jug, printed in colors, printed mark, hairlines to rim, crazing.

9.5in (24cm) high

$150-200 WW

A Susie Cooper studio ware 'Acorn' pattern jug, in the Kestral shape, signed and dated.

1932 *6.25in (16cm) high*

$150-200 SWO

A Susie Cooper Pottery 'Seagull' pattern side plate, with printed marks.

c1935 *7in (17.5cm) diam*

$450-600 WW

A 1950s Susie Cooper bone china cup and saucer, with spiral decoration.

5in (13cm) diam

$50-70 BAD

CERAMICS

An Adderley bone china coffee cup and saucer, with gilt rim.

Saucer 5in (12.5cm) diam

$25-35 JL

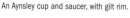

An Aynsley cup and saucer, with gilt rim.

c1920 *Saucer 4.5in (11cm) diam*

$50-70 JL

A Bing & Grøndahl cup and saucer, with a shaped seagull handle and gilt highlights, marked "108b".

Saucer 4.75in (12cm) diam

$80-120 JL

A Bromfield cup and saucer, the cup with painted marks, the deep saucer with impressed marks, dated.

1879 *Saucer 5.25in (13cm) diam*

$70-100 JL

A Carltonware molded trio set, with handpainted decoration and decorative flower handle to tea cup.

A Carltonware Moderne shape cup and saucer, with solid wavy rectangular handle in gilt.

Saucer 5in (13cm) diam

$70-100 BEV

Plate 5.5in (14cm) diam

$100-150 JL

A New Chelsea 'May Time' pattern cup and saucer, with hand-colored printed decoration and gilt trim.

c1935 *Saucer 5.5in (14cm) diam*

$60-90 JL

A Co-Operative Wholesale Society Limited 'Balmoral' china cup and saucer, with floral decoration and gilt trim.

c1960s *Saucer 5.5in (14cm) diam*

$30-40 JL

A Royal Doulton octagonal coffee cup and saucer, with mottled malachite green decoration.

c1935 *Saucer 4.5in (11cm) diam*

$25-35 JL

A Royal Doulton cup and saucer, in blue and white with gilt decoration.

1914　　　*Saucer 7.5in (19cm) diam*

$120-180　　　　　　　　**BAD**

A Royal Doulton 'Felicity' pattern D450 trio set, with an unusual cup, dated.

1934　　　*Plate 7.5in (19cm) diam*

$80-120　　　　　　　　**BAD**

A 1930s Royal Doulton De Lux cup and saucer, with a bold mint green and black design on a white ground.

Saucer 5.5in (14cm) diam

$120-180　　　　　　　　**BAD**

A 1980s Habitat 'Othello' pattern cup and saucer, with printed marks.

Saucer 6in (15cm) diam

$20-30　　　　　　　　**CHS**

A Royal Doulton 'Roses' coffee cup and saucer, with ornate gilt decoration.

c1910-20　　　*Saucer 4.25in (11cm) diam*

$120-180　　　　　　　　**BAD**

A German Hutschenreuther cup and saucer, with painted floral and molded decoration.

Saucer 4.75in (12cm) diam

$40-60　　　　　　　　**JL**

A Jadson & Gosling trio set, hand decorated with blue bands and gilt decoration.

c1920　　　*Plate 6in (15cm) diam*

$80-120　　　　　　　　**JL**

A German Krautheim coffee cup and saucer, with floral painted decoration and gilt rim, marked "scene H".

Saucer 4.5in (11cm) diam

$60-90　　　　　　　　**JL**

A Court China trio set, by William Lowe, with handpainted and gilt decoration.

c1930　　　*Plate 6in (15cm) diam*

$50-70　　　　　　　　**JL**

CERAMICS

A Melba bone china trio, with floral decoration.

6in (15cm) diam

$25-35   **BAD**

A Paragon China small cup and saucer, decorated in colors with budgerigars within a turquoise border.

1930

$70-100   **SAS**

A Paragon China trio set, with handpainted decoration and gilt rim.

c1904   *Plate 7in (17.5cm) diam*

$70-100   **JL**

A Royal Paragon floral trio set, with gilt trim.

Plate 6. 75in (17cm) diam

$80-120   **BAD**

A Royal Paragon trio set, with mint green, pale blue and gilt floral decoration.

Plate 6.5in (16.5cm) diam

$70-100   **BAD**

A Paragon Apple Blossom trio set, with a gilt edge and a six-point star mark.

Plate 4.75in (12cm) wide

$120-180   **BAD**

A Royal Paragon cup and saucer, with flower-shaped handle and foxglove and gilt decoration.

Saucer 5.5in (14cm) diam

$80-120   **BAD**

A Royal Paragon trio set, the reverse inscribed "Replica of Service made for HM The Queen".

$80-120   **SAS**

A 1960s Ridgway's Royal Vale cup and saucer with octagonal cup, with heavy gilt decoration.

Saucer 6.5in (16cm) diam

$30-50   **JL**

A CLOSER LOOK AT A SHELLEY TRIO

The 'Mode' shape was designed by Eric Slater in 1930 and was a radical departure from Shelley's previous traditionally 'Victorian' designs.

The Art Deco shape combines perfectly with the stylized Art Deco decoration.

This impractical solid tea cup handle proved unpopular with the public and was replaced with the 'Eve' shape cup with a cut-out handle in 1932.

Despite being produced for only a few years, over 30 patterns were used on this shape – 'Blue Iris' is one of the most commonly found.

A Shelley Mode 'Blue Iris' trio, comprising cup, saucer and side plate, pattern 11850 printed and painted marks.

1930-32

Cup 3in (7.5cm) high

$400-600

WW

A Rosenthal coffee cup and saucer, with colored and gilt decoration, embossed, marked "Vera".

Saucer 4.25in (10.5cm) diam

$40-60

JL

A Sampson Smith yellow trio set, printed floral decoration and gilt rim, marked "Old Royal China".

c1930   Plate 7in (17.5cm) diam

$50-70

JL

A Sampson Smith green and gilt trio set, handpainted over transfers with flowers, marked "Old Royal China est 1846".

c1930   Plate 6in (15cm) diam

$60-90

JL

A Shelley Mode 'Orange Block' trio comprising cup, saucer and side plate, pattern number 11792, with printed and painted marks.

c1932   Cup 3.25in (8cm) high

$300-500

WW

A Spode Copeland cup and saucer, with gild rim, marked "Ryde".

1953   Saucer 4.75in (12cm) diam

$50-70

JL

A Spode Copeland trio set, comprised of a coffee cup, tea cup and saucer, handpainted over transfer and gilt trim, the cups c1851-1885, the saucer c1891.

Saucer 5.5in (14cm) diam

$80-120

JL

CERAMICS

An English handpainted bone china trio set.

Plate 6in (15cm) wide

$50-70 JL

A paisley pattern coffee cup and saucer, with gilt rim, marked "Made in Czechoslovakia".

Saucer 4.5in (11cm) diam

$60-90 JL

A Victorian trio set, handpainted over transfers with pink flowers among leaves.

Plate 6in (15cm) diam

$70-100 JL

A handpainted trio set, with orange floral decoration.

Plate 6in (15cm) wide

$70-100 JL

A late Victorian handpainted teacup and saucer, with orange and gilt decoration and embossed decoration.

Saucer 5.5in (14cm) diam

$40-60 JL

An English bone china trio set, with shaped octagonal plate and printed and hand-colored decoration.

Plate 6.5in (16cm) diam

$40-60 JL

A molded cup and saucer, the cup with a printed scene titled "Past Church Paignton".

Saucer 5.25in (13cm) diam

$30-50 JL

A handpainted coffee cup and saucer, unmarked.

Saucer 4.5in (11cm) diam

$40-60 JL

A 19thC handpainted cup and saucer, with gilt rim.

Saucer 5.5in (14cm) diam

$70-100 JL

COLLECTORS' NOTES

■ Production of pottery began at Denby in 1809, two years after William Bourne saw the opportunities presented by the discovery of a seam of clay nearby. William's son Joseph ran the pottery, now known as the 'Joseph Bourne' pottery, which soon built up a reputation for its salt-glazed stoneware jars and bottles in subdued colors.

■ The range grew by the 1920s to incorporate functional domestic wares such as dishes, jelly molds, and hot water bottles as well as decorative wares such as vases and bowls. All such decorative wares were stamped 'Danesby Ware'. In 1931, Norman Wood joined and revolutionized production methods enabling brighter glazes to be used.

■ The main designer at this time was Albert Colledge. Others included Alice Teichtner, from the Wiener Werkstätte, and Donald Gilbert, who joined in 1934 and increased Denby's decorative output. During the 1950s, production changed to focus on tableware, for which they are still well known today.

■ 1950 also saw the arrival of Albert Colledge's son, Glyn (1922-2000), and the renaming of hand-decorated 'Danesby Ware' to 'Glyn Ware' in honor of his arrival. Look out for his designs including the 'Glynbourne' range and particularly those signed by him. His earliest designs are inscribed with his signature, later examples until the 1970s are signed with a brush.

A Denby pale green 'Gretna' pattern cigar ashtray, designed by Alice Teichtner, with printed marks to base.

8in (20.5cm) diam

$80-120   **PSI**

A Denby large beige bowl, designed by Alice Teichtner, with printed script Denby mark to base, "AT" monogram and "W.T.L & S 1937" mark.

11.5in (29.5cm) diam

$150-200   **PSI**

A Denby pale green 'Gretna' pattern vase, designed by Alice Teichtner, with printed marks to base.

1937-38 8.5in (22cm) high

$220-280   **PSI**

A pair of Denby Danesby Ware book ends, modeled as angel fish, covered in a pastel blue glaze, printed mark.

6.75in (17cm) high

$180-220   **WW**

A 1930s Denby Orient Ware hand-decorated three-handled vase, script printed mark to base.

Orient Ware, with its recognizable matte blue and brown decoration, became a popular range of giftware during the 1930s. The gloss glaze version is known as 'Electric Blue' and was introduced in 1925.

7.25in (18.5cm) high

$70-100   **PSI**

A 1930s Denby stoneware 'Sylvan Pastel Mushroom Group', designed by Donald Gilbert, design no.SP12.

7in (17.5cm) high

$600-900   **WW**

A Denby 'Danesby Ware' large stoneware single-handled vase, printed mark.

12in (30.5cm) high

$120-180   **WW**

CERAMICS

A 1950s Denby Stoneware handpainted 'Hazlewood' pattern snack dish, with curling sides, designed by Glyn Colledge.

12.25in (31cm) long

$50-70 AGR

A mid-1950s Denby burgundy-striped 'Hazlewood' pattern stoneware posy basket, designed by Glyn Colledge.

5.5in (14cm) wide

$50-70 AGR

A Denby 'Burlington' pattern stoneware ovoid vase, with flared neck.

The Burlington range was introduced in the late 1950s and designed by Albert Colledge, in collaboration with his son Glyn, and was unlike his usual style. Contemporary at the time, its clean lines and black and white decoration were typical of the period.

11.5in (29.5cm) high

$60-90 AGR

A Denby 'Burlington' pattern stoneware tapering vase.

8.25in (21cm) high

$50-70 AGR

A Denby 'Cloisonné' pattern handpainted triangular dish, designed by Glyn Colledge.

Other patterns feature wine glasses, hearts, and stripes.

c1957 6.75in (17cm) wide

$100-150 AGR

A Bourne Denby handpainted vase, designed by Glyn Colledge, with printed Bourne Denby and Glyn Colledge marks to base.

8.5in (21.5cm) high

$60-90 GROB

A Denby 'Arabesque' pattern tankard, designed by Gill Pemberton, unmarked.

'Arabesque' revolutionized tableware and became a highly popular pattern, being produced between 1960 and 1984. It was exported to the US, where it is known as 'Samarkand'.

c1965 5.25in (13.5cm) high

$15-20 GROB

FIND OUT MORE...

Denby Pottery 1809-1997, *by Irene & Gordon Hopwood, published by Richard Dennis Publications, 1997.*

COLLECTORS' NOTES

■ The first Doulton figurines as we know them were launched in 1913 by Royal Doulton's Art Director Charles Noke, although Doulton had made figurines during the 19th century.

■ Over 4,000 different models and color variations are known. Each color variation has its own 'HN' number and a figure may have been produced in a number of different colorways, each often worth a different amount.

■ Many choose to collect by type such as 'fair ladies', children or literary and historical characters. Certain modelers are known for certain types of figurine, such as Harradine and his 'fair ladies'.

■ Ranges such as the 'Dickens' series also prove popular, but some figurines will be rarer and more valuable than others. Figurines only produced before WWII are rare and tend to be very valuable, as are those produced for short periods of time.

■ Figurines produced for long periods like 'The Balloon Man', or those that are still in production today tend to be less valuable or desirable. Condition is directly related to value. Chips and cracks reduce value considerably. Examine all examples carefully.

A Royal Doulton 'The Parson's Daughter' figurine, HN564, designed by Harry Tittensor.

1923-49   9.5in (24cm) high

$180-220   **L&T**

A Royal Doulton 'Victorian Lady' figurine, HN728, designed by Leslie Harradine.

There are 15 different colorways of 'Victorian Lady' known.

1925-52   7.75in (20cm) high

$220-280   **L&T**

A Royal Doulton 'Parson's Daughter' figurine, number HN1356, designed by Harry Tittensor.

1929-38   5.75in (14.5cm) high

$500-700   **DN**

A Royal Doulton 'Sweet Anne' figurine, HN1330, designed by Leslie Harradine.

1929-49 7.25in (18.5cm) high

$120-180   **L&T**

A Royal Doulton 'Miss Demure' figurine, HN1402, designed by Leslie Harradine.

1930-75   7.5in (19cm) high

$80-120   **L&T**

A Royal Doulton 'Pantalettes' figurine, HN1412, designed by Leslie Harradine.

1930-49   7.75in (20cm) high

$220-280   **L&T**

A Royal Doulton 'Chloe' figurine, HN1470, designed by Leslie Harradine.

1931-49   5.5in (14cm) high

$180-220   **L&T**

A Royal Doulton 'Janet' figurine, HN1537, designed by Leslie Harradine.

1932-95   6.25in (16cm) high

$50-70   **L&T**

A Royal Doulton 'Daydreams' figurine, HN1732, designed by Leslie Harradine.

1935-49   5.5in (14cm) high

$70-100   **L&T**

A CLOSER LOOK AT A FAIR LADY

Leslie Harradine is well-known for his fair ladies, which are sought-after by many collectors.

'Camille' was produced for a comparatively short period around WWII, making her scarcer than others.

She was produced in three different colorways – look out for the pink and cream variation, which is even more desirable.

She is one of the most valuable colorways, with handpainted flowers on her dress.

A Royal Doulton 'Margery' figurine, HN1413, designed by Leslie Harradine.

1930-49   11in (28cm) high

$280-320   **SWO**

A Royal Doulton 'Top O'The Hill' figurine, HN1833, designed by Leslie Harradine.

1937-71   7in (18cm) high

$80-120   **L&T**

A Royal Doulton 'Camille' figurine, HN1648, designed by Leslie Harradine.

1935-49   6.5in (16.5cm) high

$300-500   **L&T**

A Royal Doulton 'Autumn Breezes' figurine, HN1913, designed by Leslie Harradine.

Earlier versions of this figurine have two feet showing, later examples have only one, as here.

1939-71   7.5in (19cm) high

$80-120   **L&T**

A Royal Doulton 'Lady Charmian' figurine, HN1949, designed by Leslie Harradine.

1940-75   8in (20cm) high

$80-120   **L&T**

A Royal Doulton 'The Ermine Coat' figurine, HN1981, designed by Leslie Harradine.

1945-67   6.75in (17cm) high

$120-180   **L&T**

A Royal Doulton 'Memories' figurine, HN2030, designed by Leslie Harradine.

1949-59
6in (15cm) high

$120-180   **L&T**

A Royal Doulton 'Hostess of Williamsburg' figurine, HN2209, designed by Margaret Davies, from the Figures of Williamsburg series.

A Royal Doulton 'Judith' figurine, HN2089, designed by Leslie Harradine.

1952-59   *7in (18cm) high*

$120-180   **L&T**

1960-83 7.25in (18.5cm) high

$80-120   **L&T**

A Royal Doulton 'Melanie' figurine, HN2271, designed by Margaret Davies.

1965-81   7.75in (20cm) high

$80-120   **L&T**

A Royal Doulton 'Katrina' figurine, HN2327, designed by Margaret Davies.

1965-69   7.5in (19cm) high

$120-180   **L&T**

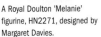

A Royal Doulton 'The Ballerina' figurine, HN2116, designed by Margaret Davies.

1953-73   7.25in (18.5cm) high

$120-180   **L&T**

A Royal Doulton 'Hilary' figurine, HN2335, designed by Margaret Davies.

1967-81 7.25in (18.5cm) high

$50-80   **L&T**

A Royal Doulton 'Loretta' figurine, HN2337, designed by Margaret Davies.

1966-81   7.75in (20cm) high

$50-70   **L&T**

A Royal Doulton 'Masquerade' figurine, HN2251, designed by Margaret Davies.

1960-65   *8.5in (21.5cm) high*

$180-220   **L&T**

A Royal Doulton 'My Love' figurine, HN2339, designed by Margaret Davies.

1969-96   6.25in (16cm) high

$80-120   **L&T**

A Royal Doulton 'Simone' figurine, HN2378, designed by Margaret Davies.

1971-81 7.25in (18.5cm) high

$70-100   **L&T**

A Royal Doulton 'Fiona' figurine, HN2694, designed by Margaret Davies.

1974-81   7.5in (19cm) high

$70-100   **L&T**

A Royal Doulton 'Pensive Moments' figurine, HN2704, designed by Margaret Davies.

1975-81   5in (13cm) high

$80-120   **L&T**

A Royal Doulton red 'Julia' figurine, HN2705, designed by Margaret Davies.

1975-90   7.5in (19cm) high

$70-100   **L&T**

A Royal Doulton 'Veneta' figurine, HN2722, designed by Bill Harper.

1974-81   8in (20cm) high

$70-100   **L&T**

A Royal Doulton red 'Eliza' figurine, HN2543, with painted flowers, designed by Eric Griffiths, from the Haute Ensemble series.

1974-79   11.75in (30cm) high

$180-220   **L&T**

A Royal Doulton 'Clarinda' figurine, HN2724, designed by Bill Harper.

1975-81 8.5in (21.5cm) high

$80-120   **L&T**

A Royal Doulton 'Kate' figurine, HN2789, designed by Margaret Davies.

1978-87   7.5in (19cm) high

$70-100   **L&T**

A Royal Doulton 'Cassim' figurine, HN1231, designed by Leslie Harradine.
1927-38   *3in (7.5cm) high*

$700-1,000   **WW**

A Royal Doulton 'Greta' figurine, HN1485, designed by Leslie Harradine.
1931-53   5.5in (14cm) high

$220-280   **L&T**

A Royal Doulton 'Tootles' figurine, HN1680, designed by Leslie Harradine.
1935-75   4.75in (12cm) high

$25-35   **L&T**

A Royal Doulton 'Little Boy Blue' figurine, HN2062, designed by Leslie Harradine, from the Nursery Rhymes series.
1950-73   5.5in (14cm) high

$80-120   **L&T**

A Royal Doulton 'Baby Bunting' figurine, HN2108, designed by Margaret Davies.
1953-59   5.25in (13cm) high

$180-220   **L&T**

A Royal Doulton 'Pillow Fight' figurine, HN2270, designed by Margaret Davies.
1965-69   5in (13cm) high

$80-120   **L&T**

A Royal Doulton 'Belle' figurine, HN2340, designed by Margaret Davies.
1968-88   4.5in (11.5cm) high

$30-50   **L&T**

A Royal Doulton 'River Boy' figurine, HN2128, designed by Margaret Davies.
1962-75   4in (10cm) high

$80-120   **L&T**

A Royal Doulton 'Alice' figurine, HN2158, designed by Margaret Davies.
1960-81   5in (13cm) high

$50-80   **L&T**

A Royal Doulton 'Georgina' figurine, HN2377, designed by Margaret Davies, from the Kate Greenaway series.

There are 18 characters in the Kate Greenaway series.

1981-86 5.75in (14.5cm) high

$120-180   **L&T**

A Royal Doulton 'Francine' figurine, HN2422, designed by J. Bromley.

Another variation exists with the bird's tail pointing up. It is worth roughly the same as this variation.

1972-onward 5in (13cm) high

$80-120   **L&T**

A Royal Doulton 'Carrie' figurine, HN2800, designed by Margaret Davies, from the Kate Greenaway series.

1976-81 6in (15cm) high

$120-180   **L&T**

A Royal Doulton 'Lucy' figurine, HN2863, designed by Margaret Davies, from the Kate Greenaway series.

1980-84 6in (15cm) high

$120-180   **L&T**

A Royal Doulton 'Hope' figurine, HN3061, designed by S. Mitchell, from the NSPCC Charity series.

Hope was produced, along with Faith and Charity, in a limited edition of 9,500 of each figure for Lawleys By Post.

1984 8.25in (21cm) high

$180-220   **L&T**

A Royal Doulton 'Sleepy Darling' figurine, HN2953, designed by Polly Parsons, from the Royal Doulton International Collectors Club series.

1981 7.25in (18.5cm) high

$80-120   **L&T**

A Royal Doulton 'Tom' figurine, HN2864, designed by Margaret Davies, from the Kate Greenaway series.

1978-81 5.75in (14.5cm) high

$180-220   **L&T**

A Royal Doulton 'Faith' figurine, HN3082, designed by Eric Griffiths, from the NSPCC Charity series.

1986 8.5in (21.5cm) high

$80-120   **L&T**

A Royal Doulton 'Charity' figurine, HN3087, designed by Eric Griffiths, from the NSPCC Charity series.

1987 8.5in (21.5cm) high

$120-180   **L&T**

A Royal Doulton 'The Old Balloon Seller' figurine, HN1315, designed by Leslie Harradine.

7.5in (19cm) high

$120-180   **SWO**

A Royal Doulton 'The Cobbler' figurine, HN1706, designed by Charles Noke.

1935-69   8.25in (21cm) high

$220-280   **L&T**

A Royal Doulton 'Calumet' figurine, HN689, designed by Charles Noke.

1935-49   6.75in (17cm) high

$400-600   **SWO**

A Royal Doulton 'Carpet Seller' figurine, HN1464A, designed by Leslie Harradine.

The earlier version, produced from 1929, has an open outstretched (and easily damaged!) hand. It is harder to find and can be worth up to 20 percent more. The model pictured was withdrawn in 1969.

9in (23cm) high

$220-280   **L&T**

A Royal Doulton 'The Milkmaid' figurine, HN2057A, designed by Leslie Harradine.

The blue, red, and white version of this model is known as 'The Jersey Milkmaid' and can be worth up to 25 percent more, as it was only produced during the 1950s.

1975-81   6.5in (16.5cm) high

$80-120   **L&T**

A Royal Doulton 'The Orange Lady' figurine, HN1759, designed by Leslie Harradine.

1936-75   8.75in (22cm) high

$120-180   **L&T**

A Royal Doulton 'The Balloon Man' figurine, HN1954, designed by Leslie Harradine.

1940-   7.25in (18.5cm) high

$120-180   **L&T**

A Royal Doulton 'Fortune Teller' figurine, HN2159, designed by Leslie Harradine.

1955-67   6.5in (16.5cm) high

$280-320   **L&T**

A Royal Doulton 'Silversmith of Williamsburg' figurine, HN2208, designed by Margaret Davies.

1960-83   6.5in (16cm) high

$120-180   **L&T**

CERAMICS

A Royal Doulton 'Pickwick' figurine, HN556, designed by Leslie Harradine.

1923-39   7in (18cm) high

$280-320   **SWO**

A Royal Doulton 'Micawber' figurine, HN557, designed by Leslie Harradine, from the Dickens series.

There are 24 characters to collect from the Dickens series.

1923-39   7in (18cm) high

$280-320   **SWO**

A Royal Doulton 'Frodo' figurine, HN2912, designed by David Lyttleton, from the Middle Earth series.

Thanks to the popular films, interest in and values of the Middle Earth series have grown.

1980-84   4.5in (11.5cm) high

$180-220   **PSA**

A Royal Doulton 'Sir Walter Raleigh' figurine, HN2015, designed by Leslie Harradine.

1948-55 11.75in (30cm) high

$400-600   **SWO**

A Royal Doulton 'Legolas' figurine, HN2917, designed by David Lyttleton, from the Middle Earth series.

1981-84   6.25in (16cm) high

$180-220   **PSA**

A Royal Doulton 'Florence Nightingale' figurine, HN3144, designed by Polly Parsons.

This was produced in a limited edition of 5,000 for Lawleys By Post in 1988.

1988   8.25in (21cm) high

$280-320   **L&T**

A CLOSER LOOK AT A JESTER

Celebrated modeler Noke was fascinated by the theater and is also noted for his character studies of which this is an excellent example.

It was made before World War II, when comparatively fewer examples were made, some estimates say fewer than 2,000.

All variations of The Jester are scarce and valuable, however those in more muted colorways were less popular at the time and tend to be more valuable.

It was produced between 1918-36, but this example can be dated more precisely as modelers' names were dropped from the bases in c1930.

A rare Royal Doulton 'The Jester' figurine, HN308, in black and lavender suit, designed by Charles Noke and signed "CJ Noke".

1918-c1930   *10.25in (26cm) high*

$5,000-7,000   **PSA**

A Royal Doulton 'Seated Bulldog' figure, DA228, in fawn with white top hat and tails, boxed with certificate.

$120-180　　PSA

A limited edition Royal Doulton 'Bulldog' figure, DA228, in white with a black top hat and tails, boxed with certificate.

$150-200　　PSA

A Royal Doulton 'Character Dog Playing With A Ball' figure, HN1103.

$60-90　　PSA

A Royal Doulton 'Pekinese Puppy Seated' figure, HN832, minor scratches to glaze.

$280-320　　PSA

A Royal Doulton 'Horse Head Tucked Leg Up' brown gloss figure, DA51.

$70-100　　PSA

An early Royal Doulton trial piece matte horse, marked "Property of Royal Doulton Not For Sale" and signed by J.A.J. Brown.

8in (20cm) high

$700-1,000　　PSA

A rare Royal Doulton 'Seated Red Setter' figure, HN976, with collar, in an unlisted flambé glaze.

Doulton's flambé glaze was developed from an appreciation of the Chinese 'sang de bouef' glaze. Working with modeler Charles Noke, chemist Bernard Moore developed a modern version that was used on a number of Noke's figures. It is a popular finish with collectors today. This model was not recorded in a flambé.

$1,000-1,500　　PSA

A Royal Doulton 'Spirit Of The Wild' brown matte figure, DA183, on wooden plinth.

$100-150　　PSA

A Royal Doulton 'Connoisseur Fresian Bull' black and white matte figure, DA23, on wooden plinth.

$280-320　　PSA

CERAMICS

A Royal Doulton 'Bayeux Tapestry' series jug.

4in (10cm) high

$150-200   **GORW**

A rare Royal Doulton 'Aldin's Dogs' series water jug, with a Cecil Aldin character scene, some crazing.

Illustrator Cecil Aldin (1870-1935) was renowned for his illustrations of mischievous dogs, which Doulton used to form a series.

1926-46   *5in (13cm) high*

$500-700   **PSA**

A pair of Royal Doulton Dickens ware candlesticks, featuring 'Alfred Jingle' and 'Barnaby Rudge'.

6.5in (16cm) high

$280-320   **SAS**

A Royal Doulton 'Gibson Girls' series rack plate, light nip to rim.

9.5in (24cm) diam

$150-200   **PSA**

A Royal Doulton 'Golfing' series vase.

2.25in (5.5cm) high

$150-200   **GORW**

A Royal Doulton 'Jackdaw Of Rheims' series oval bowl.

10.5in (27cm) long

$120-180   **PSA**

A Royal Doulton 'Under The Greenwood Tree' series water jug.

5.5in (14cm) high

$180-220   **PSA**

A Royal Doulton David Souter 'Kateroo' mug, restored.

2.75in (7cm) high

$80-120   **PSA**

A Doulton Lambeth stoneware jug, impressed marks to base.

7in (18cm) high

$150-200   **GAZE**

A Doulton Lambeth 'Merry Monks' jar and cover.

$100-150   **GORW**

A Doulton Lambeth tobacco jar and cover, by George Tinworth, decorated with a pipe-smoking mouse.

George Tinworth (1843-1913) studied at the Lambeth School of Art and then the Royal Academy School before being employed by Royal Doulton in 1867 where he spent the rest of his career. He was best known for his terracotta sculptures and produced a terracotta relief for the Doulton building.

6.75in (17cm) high

$1,200-1,800   **GORW**

A pair of Doulton Lambeth faïence vases, of waisted form, initialed "MW" and "EJG".

8.25in (21cm) high

$500-700   **GORL**

A pair of Royal Doulton stoneware vases.

12.5in (32cm) high

$280-320   **GORL**

A Royal Doulton 'Bird of Paradise' handpainted plate, D 4602, printed marks.

$30-40   **GAZE**

A 1930s Royal Doulton white-glazed vase, with heavy base to prevent movement on ship, base with "O.S.N.Co. 165" imprint.

The logo on the vase is for the Orient Shipping Line and was created by designer Edward McKnight Kauffer (1890-1954), famous for his posters for London Transport and Shell Oil as well as theater costume, exhibition designs, murals, book illustrations and textiles.

6.75in (17cm) high

$100-150   **RETC**

A Royal Doulton 'Marriage Day/After Marriage' salt-glazed reversible miniature jug, no. X895.

3.5in (9cm) high

$300-500   **SWO**

A Royal Doulton 'Toby' stoneware figure, impressed marks.

6in (15cm) high

$800-1,200   **WW**

COLLECTORS' NOTES

■ Flow Blue is the term used to describe 19th and early 20th century white or cream earthenwares decorated with underglaze cobalt blue transfer patterns. It takes its name from the fact that the blue transfer pattern has flowed out of its sharp design, creating a blurred effect.

■ At first this may have been a mistake caused by impurities in the clay, but once discovered was continued due to increasing popularity, but also to cover errors in the earthenware blank or the transfer pattern. The addition of lime or chloride of ammonia in kilns created the flowing effect.

■ Flow Blue was primarily made in, and exported to the US from, Staffordshire, England from the 1830s onwards. It was inspired by the designs of popular imported Chinese and French porcelains. It was more affordable as patterns were inexpensively printed rather than handpainted and earthenware was less costly. US makers began to produce wares from the mid-1870s.

■ Patterns can help date Flow Blue. Chinese patterns and landscapes were popular in the 'Early Victorian' period from c1835-60, floral patterns in the 'Mid-Victorian' period from the 1860s/70s and Japanese, Art Nouveau, and other heavy floral patterns with raised designs, gilt details and scalloped edges during the 'late Victorian' period from the 1880s-1900s. Many popular patterns appear throughout the 19th and into the 20thC.

■ Preferably look for a deep cobalt blue coloring against a clean white, avoiding grey tones. An even flow across the piece is also desirable. Certain shapes are rarer or more complex than others, so are usually more expensive. The desirability of the pattern itself will affect value too.

■ Turn a piece over to identify makers and the pattern name as these are often printed on the base. Certain makers are more in demand than others, often due to quality. Damage will reduce value, but if a piece is very rare, it may still be worth buying.

A Davenport 'Macao' pattern Flow Blue platter, with impressed and printed marks.

c1845

15.5in (38.5cm) long

$450-550 **FBS**

A mid-19thC large 'Chusan' pattern Flow Blue platter, possibly by Morley, with gilt highlights.

19.25in (49cm) long

$700-1,000 **FBS**

A Doulton 'Watteau' pattern Flow Blue rectangular charger.

15.25in (39cm) long

$300-400 **FBS**

A Wedgwood & Co. 'Roma' pattern Flow Blue rectangular platter.

c1905 16.25in (41.5cm) diam

$350-450 **FBS**

A late 19thC Ford & Sons of Burslem 'Chatsworth' pattern Flow Blue oval platter, with scalloped edge.

c1893   17in (43cm) long

$350-450 **FBS**

A W.H. Grindley 'Celtic' pattern Flow Blue platter. with registered no.310589 for 1897.

c1898   15.5in (39.5cm) long

$250-350 **FBS**

An unmarked mid 19thC 'Mankin Ware' Flow Blue large oval platter.

17.25in (44cm) long

$600-800 **FBS**

A Johnson Bros. 'Holland' pattern Flow Blue side plate.

c1891   *8in (20.5cm) diam*

$70-100   **FBS**

A Johnson Bros. Royal Semi-Porcelain 'Claremont' pattern Flow Blue side plate, with scalloped edges and white details.

8in (20.5cm) diam

$70-90   **FBS**

An Alfred Meakin Ltd Royal Semi Porcelain 'Belmont' pattern Flow Blue side plate.

c1891   *7in (17.5cm) diam*

$60-80   **FBS**

A Johnson Bros 'Oregon' pattern Flow Blue side plate, with gilt highlights.

c1900   *7in (18cm) diam*

$60-80   **FBS**

A W.H. Grindley 'Melbourne' pattern Flow Blue side plate, with panels of flowers and gilt highlights.

c1900   *8in (20cm) diam*

$85-95   **FBS**

A Prussian 'Spinach' pattern hand-sponged Flow Blue side plate, with three stilt marks on top and bottom of plate.

c1900   *7.5in (19cm) diam*

$70-100   **FBS**

A New Wharf Pottery semi-porcelain 'Waldorf' pattern Flow Blue luncheon plate.

c1892   *8.75in (22cm) diam*

$80-120   **FBS**

A Henry Alcock semi-porcelain 'Touraine' pattern Flow Blue luncheon plate, with registered no.329815 for 1898.

c1900   *29in (22.5cm) diam*

$80-120   **FBS**

A W.H. Grindley 'Alaska' pattern Flow Blue luncheon plate, with gilt highlights and scalloped edge.

c1891   *9in (22.5cm) high*

$80-120   **FBS**

A Johnson Bros. 'Mongolia' pattern Flow
Blue bowl.

c1900-20   6.25in (16cm) diam

$70-100   FBS

A Johnson Bros. 'Mongolia' pattern Flow
Blue large bowl.

c1900-20   9.25in (23.5cm) diam

$180-220   FBS

A Thomas Dimmock Kaolin Ware 'Chinese'
pattern Flow Blue large bowl.

1828-59   10.5in (26.5cm) diam

$150-200   FBS

A Samuel Alcock 'Carlton' pattern Flow Blue soup bowl, with
printed design on the back, marked "SA & Co".

10.5in (26.5cm) diam

$150-250   FBS

A J. Kent 'Brugge'
pattern Flow Blue large
bowl, with scalloped
edge and low relief
white areas.

*This is the same pattern as Wood & Sons' 'Delph' pattern, sold from
around 1907.*

c1910   10.5in (26.5cm) diam

$150-250   FBS

A Johnson Bros. 'Albany'
pattern Flow Blue bowl.

c1900   8.25in (21cm) diam

$100-150   FBS

A New Wharf Pottery 'Conway' pattern Flow
Blue chowder bowl.

c1891   9in (22.5cm) diam

$120-180   FBS

A Ridgways 'Gainsborough' pattern Flow
Blue bowl, with scalloped edge and gilt
highlights.

c1905   8in (20.5cm) diam

$120-180   FBS

An Adams & Co. 'Lily' pattern Flow Blue
bowl.

9in (22.5cm) diam

$70-100   FBS

A Henry Alcock & Co. 'Touraine' pattern Flow Blue coffee cup and saucer, with registered no.329815 for 1898.

Coffee cups are larger and wider than tea cups.

c1900   *cup 4.25in (11cm) diam*

$100-150   **FBS**

A New Wharf Pottery 'Clyde' pattern Flow Blue tea cup and saucer.

The grey-blue tones on this set are not as desirable as deeper blues and whiter whites. If the colours were stronger and cleaner, it would be worth around $30 more.

c1891   *saucer 6in (15cm) diam*

$70-100   **FBS**

A W.H. Grindley 'Lorne' pattern Flow Blue teacup and saucer.

c1900   *saucer 6in (15cm) diam*

$80-120   **FBS**

A New Wharf Pottery semi-porcelain 'Cambridge' pattern Flow Blue gravy boat and saucer.

Saucer 9in (23cm) long

$150-250   **FBS**

A W.H. Grindley 'Syrian' pattern Flow Blue soap dish, with liner and gold-sponged edging, with registered no.303250 for 1897.

c1900   *5.75in (14.5cm) long*

$280-320   **FBS**

A Burleigh Ware 'Briar' pattern Flow Blue bulbous vase, with gilt highlights.

6.25in (16cm) high

$400-500   **FBS**

A tall-necked Flow Blue shaped vase, with iris pattern and gilt bands, the base with 'Trademark' printed coat-of-arms mark.

9.5in (24cm) high

$280-320   **FBS**

A Doulton 'The Hunt' pattern Flow Blue chamber pot.

c1900   *7.5in (19cm) high*

$600-900   **FBS**

FIND OUT MORE...

Gaston's Flow Blue China Comprehensive Guide, by Mary Gaston, published by Collector Books, 2005.

Flow Blue: A Collectors' Guide to Patterns, History and Values, by Jeffrey Snyder, published by Schiffer Books, 2003.

A Fulper tall cylindrical vase, covered in Chinese Blue flambé glaze, with vertical mark.

13in (33cm) high

$600-700 DRA

A Fulper vase, with crystalline blue glaze, marked with vertical ink stamp with Chinese-style letters.

9in (23cm) high

$200-300 BEL

A Fulper tall flambé vase, small bruise with small chip to rim, vertical mark, paper label.

15in (38cm) high

$800-1,200 DRA

A Fulper urn, with two scrolled handles, covered in blue crystalline glaze, vertical mark.

9in (23cm) high

$500-600 DRA

A Fulper double-handled fan vase, with leopard skin glaze, marked with vertical Fulper ink stamp, crack from the rim and a minor flake from the base.

8in (20cm) high

$150-250 BEL

A Fulper tall vase, covered in a good Leopard Skin crystalline glaze, a few grinding chips and restored chip to base, rectangular vertical mark.

Abraham Fulper took over the running of his employer's pottery in Flemington, N.J. in 1847 and changed the name. It became the Fulper Pottery Company in 1899 when Fulper's grandson took over. William Hill Fulper was interested in glazes and introduced art pottery to the catalog in 1909. The company is well known for its glazes, particularly the flambé, mirrored, matte and crystalline, the quality of which has a great effect on value.

12.5in (31cm) high

$800-1,000 DRA

A Fulper vase, with a rolled-in lip finished in a high glaze, marked with vertical Fulper ink stamp.

7.25in (18.5cm) wide

$280-320 BEL

A bisque ring stand, in the form of a hand.

This would have been used as a ring stand, with rings being placed on the fingers and in the 'sleeve' tray.

4in (10cm) high

A L'Amour China handpainted vase, in the form of a pair of cupped hands.

5.25in (13.5cm) high

$30-50 **DAC**

A small purple-tinted vase/bowl, in the form of a pair of cupped hands.

6.25in (16cm) high

$25-35 **DAC**

$20-30 **DAC**

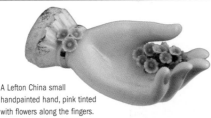

A Lefton China small handpainted hand, pink tinted with flowers along the fingers.

5.5in (14cm) long

$30-40 **DAC**

A ceramic pair of hands, holding a flower-bedecked shoe, unmarked.

Hand-shaped vessels were popular from the 1930s-60s as ladies' dressing table accessories and were used to store and display small items such as earrings, rings or small posies of flowers. Many were made in Japan during the late 1940s and 1950s, usually from the familiar glazed white bisque. Look for large, finely modeled examples and especially those with intricate decoration, such as the flowers on this example. Always examine tips and details carefully as they were prone to breakage and repair.

6.75in (17cm) high

DAC

A gold painted vase, in the form of a pair of hands holding a fan, probably Japanese.

7in (18cm) high

$30-50 **DAC**

A ceramic hand holding a goblet, with applied flowers, base stamped "JAPAN".

5.25in (13.5cm) high

$30-40 **DAC**

A compote, held by a hand, with printed decoration of roses.

dish 7in (18cm) diam

$35-45 **DAC**

A Royal Japan handpainted hand and cornucopia vase.

6in (15cm) high

$30-40 **DAC**

CERAMICS

COLLECTORS' NOTES

- The A.E. Hull Pottery was founded in Crookville, Ohio in 1905. They first produced stoneware and were successful enough to open a second plant two years later.

- The factory expanded its range of art pottery in the 1930s, which was typified by floral decoration executed in pastel colors with a matte finish on vases, planters, ewers and bowls. The success of their Little Red Riding Hood range introduced in 1943 encouraged them to produce novelty items such as the Corky piggy banks into the 1950s.

- A flood destroyed the factory in 1950 and a new factory with modern equipment was built, however the new machinery was not capable of reproducing their signature matte glaze. High gloss artware ranges such as 'Parchment' and 'Ebb Tide' were developed and they continued to produced novelty and figural pieces, as well as dinnerware, into the 1960s.

- The pottery closed in 1985 with production reduced to dinnerware and florist ware in the previous decade.

- Baskets are popular and a premium is paid for undamaged examples as the delicate handles are easily damaged. Look for the 'Bow Knot' range, identified by a bow on the handle, which is particularly sought-after.

A Hull 'Butterfly' pattern basket, marked "Hull USA copyright '56".

10.5in (26.5cm) high

$100-150   **BEL**

A Hull sitting piggy bank, in brown high gloss with blue trim, marked "Hull USA 196", chip partially filled in on the inside of the coin slot.

6.25in (16cm) high

$30-50   **BEL**

A Hull 'Corky' piggy bank, in high gloss brown with pink trim, marked "PAT PEND. Corky Pig HPCo ©1957 USA", with original cork.

7in (18cm) long

$70-100   **BEL**

A 1950s Hull 'Ebb Tide' pattern ewer, finished in a high gloss glaze, the seashell with fish handle and a second fish swimming beneath, marked "A Hull USA E-10".

14in (35.5cm) high

$120-180   **BEL**

A 1950s Hull 'Ebb Tide' pattern large conch basket, with a stylized fish handle, marked "A Hull USA E-11".

16in (40.5cm) long

$100-150   **BEL**

A Hull 'Ebb Tide' pattern tea set, with gold trim, marked "Hull USA E-14", "E-15" and "E-16", tea pot lacks lid, some restoration.

Largest 6.5in (16.5cm) high

$40-60 BEL

A Hull 'Magnolia' pattern pink gloss ewer, with blue floral decoration, marked "USA Hull Art H-3-5 1/2".

5.75in (14.5cm) high

$40-60 BEL

A Hull 'Parchment & Pine' pattern tall ewer, marked "Hull USA S-7", restored chip at base.

14in (35.5cm) high

$40-60 BEL

A Hull 'Wildflower' pattern double-handled vase, in pink and blue, marked "Hull Art USA W-12-9 1/2".

10in (25.5cm) high

$150-200 BEL

A Hull 'Woodland' pattern gloss tea pot, in chartreuse and pink, marked "Hull W26 USA, filled-in chip to lid.

10.75in (27.5cm) long

$30-50 BEL

A pre-1950 Hull 'Woodland' pattern cornucopia, marked "Hull W10-11" USA".

11in (28cm) long

$150-250 BEL

Two Hull 'Woodland' Gloss wall pockets, both marked "Hull USA W13-7 1/2", one with a chip to the top edge and the rear wall bumper.

8in (20cm) high

$60-80 BEL

A Hull pink 'Royal Woodland' pattern ewer, marked "Hull W24-13 1/2" USA".

14.25in (36cm) high

$40-50 BEL

A pair of Hull 'Royal Woodland' blue candleholders, marked "Hull USA W30".

3.25in (8.5cm) high

$30-40 BEL

COLLECTORS' NOTES

- First released in 1935 in Rödental, Germany, Goebel's 'Hummel' figurines were inspired by drawings of children by a nun, Sister Berta Hummel. Since then, over 500 different figurines have been modeled. Examine marks on the base to help you identify the name and the period in which that particular piece was made.

- 'Crown' marks and marks with a large bee motif denote early examples, which are amongst the most valuable. Over time from 1950, the bee becomes smaller in size and moves inside the V shape. After 1964, the bee motif was dropped in favor of text, a large 'G' dominating the mark from 1972.

- As well as early examples from the 1930s-50s, also look for variations in color of certain parts of clothing. These variations can be sought-after and fetch higher prices. Larger examples above the 6in size are also more valuable.

- Dates shown here relate to the time period each piece was produced in, using its mark to help date it. Note that some designs are still in production today.

- Condition is a vital indicator to value. The ceramic chips and cracks easily, so examine figurines carefully for damage or repair, which reduces value. Also take care not to bruise figurines against each other when on display.

A Hummel 'Girl with Nosegay' figure, No. 239A.

This figurine, along with 'Girl With Doll' also on this page and 'Boy With Horse' were released and traditionally sold together from the 1960s as the 'Children Trio' set.

1979-91   3.5in (9cm) high

$30-50   **AAC**

A Hummel 'Girl with Doll' figure, No.239B.

1991-99   3.5in (9cm) high

$18-25   **AAC**

A Hummel 'Birthday Candle' candleholder, No.440, exclusive special edition for the Hummel Collectors' Club.

1983   5.5in (14cm) high

$70-100   **AAC**

A Hummel 'Doll Bath' figure, No. 319, with 1960s smooth finish.

Look out for the ultra-rare early examples with a 'full bee' mark which can fetch up to $2,000 or more.

1964-72   5.25in (13.5cm) high

$120-180   **AAC**

A Hummel 'Little Sweeper' figure, No. 171.

1958-72   4.5in (11.5cm) high

$50-80   **AAC**

A Hummel 'Just Resting' figure, No. 112, with a cracked corner and a three-line mark.

c1964-72 3.75in (9.5cm) high

$50-80   **ERI**

A Hummel 'Smiling Through' figure, No. 408/0, exclusive special edition only for members of the Hummel Collectors' Club.

1983   4.75in (12cm) high

$120-180   **AAC**

A Hummel 'Soldier Boy' figure, No. 332, with red medal, crazing.

The medal on the figure's cap changed from red to blue during the 'Three Line Mark' period. Examples from this period can have either color, but the red is more desirable.

1964-72   6in (15cm) high

$80-120   AAC

A Hummel 'Doctor' figure, No.127.

The more valuable early examples have the figure's feet extending over the edge of the base, a feature changed due to easy breakage.

1958-72   4.75in (12cm) high

$50-80   AAC

A Hummel 'Postman' figure, No. 119, crazing.

1958-72   4.75in (12cm) high

$70-100   AAC

A Hummel 'Boots' figure, No. 143/0.

1972-79   5.5in (14cm) high

$50-80   AAC

A Hummel 'Brother' figure, No. 95, marked "Germany" in black, no decimal.

The earliest, and most valuable, figurines have a blue coat and can fetch up to $300.

1940-59   5.5in (14cm) high

$30-50   AAC

A Hummel 'For Father' figure, No. 87, crazing.

Look at the color of the radishes – if they are green or orange, the value can exceed $800.

1958-72   5.5in (14cm) high

$50-80   AAC

A Hummel 'Boy with Toothache' figure, No. 217, marked with an incised circle and "Germany" in black, damaged.

1958-72   5.5in (14cm) high

$50-80   AAC

A Hummel 'March Winds' figure, No. 43, underbase crazing.

1958-72   5in (12.5cm) high

$50-70   AAC

A Hummel 'I'm Here' figure, No. 478.

1989-91   3in (7.5cm) high

$30-50   AAC

CERAMICS

A Hummel 'Sweet Music' figure, No. 186, with doughnut-shaped base, marked "Germany" in black.

Look out for striped slippers, only found with the early Crown mark, as this rare variation can be worth five times more.

1947-59 5.25in (13.5cm) high

$120-180   **AAC**

A Hummel 'Little Cellist' figure, No. 89/I, crazing.

1958-72 6in (15cm) high

$70-100   **AAC**

A Hummel 'Happy Days' figure, No. 150/2/0.

1972-79 4.25in (11cm) high

$50-80   **AAC**

A CLOSER LOOK AT A HUMMEL FIGURINE

'Little Fiddler' was from the first range of 46 Hummels produced.

Rare, pale-colored 'doll' faces can be worth up to $3,000 or more, and are very early in date.

This example is so valuable as it is large; the standard 6in size is worth around $80-120.

It is undamaged, with no chips or cracks.

A large Hummel 'Little Fiddler' figure, No. 2/II.

1972-79 11in (28cm) high

$280-320   **AAC**

A Hummel 'Happiness' figure, No. 86, incised crown mark and marked "U.S. Zone Germany" in black.

This figurine was modeled in 1938, but the combination of the early Crown mark and the 'US Zone Germany' mark means it can be dated to a four year period of production.

1946-50 4.75in (12cm) high

$120-180   **AAC**

A Hummel 'Serenade' figure, No. 85/0.

1972-79 4.75in (12cm) high

$50-70   **AAC**

A Hummel 'Little Tooter' figure, No. 214H, paint flake.

Although not obvious, this figure comes from Hummel's nativity set.

1964-72 4in (10cm) high

$50-80   **AAC**

A bust of Sister M.I. Hummel, Hu 3, special edition No. 3 for the Goebel Collectors Club, some crazing, with box.

1972-79 5.75in (14.5cm) high

$30-50 AAC

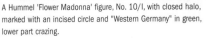

A Hummel 'Flower Madonna' figure, No. 10/I, with closed halo, marked with an incised circle and "Western Germany" in green, lower part crazing.

Examples with 'open' haloes, where the Madonna's hair shows, date from before the mid-1950s and usually fetch more. Also look out for color variations such as royal blue and beiges.

c1955-59 9.25in (23.5cm) high

$180-220 AAC

A Hummel 'Adoration' figure, No. 23/I.

1958-72 6.25in (16cm) high

$120-180 AAC

A Hummel 'Heavenly Protection' figure, No. 88/I.

1972-79 6.25in (17cm) high

$120-180 AAC

A Hummel 'Worship' figure, No. 84/0.

1958-72 5in (12.5cm) high

$70-100 AAC

A Hummel 'Girl with Fir Tree' candleholder, No. 116, crazing.

1958-72 3.5in (9cm) high

$20-30 AAC

A Hummel 'Infant Jesus' figure, No. 214A.

As with all figures numbered 214, they form part of the Hummel nativity set.

1964-72 3.5in (9cm) wide

$20-30 AAC

A Hummel 'Herald Angels' candleholder, No. 37, with high candleholder, incised circle, marked "Western Germany" in black.

A taller candleholder is found on older versions of this piece.

1958-72 4in (10cm) wide

$120-180 AAC

FIND OUT MORE...

Luckey's Hummel Figurines & Plates Price Guide – 12th Edition, by Carl F. Luckey and Dean A. Genth, published by Krause Publications, 2003.

No.1 Price Guide to Hummel Figurines, Plates and More, by Robert L. Miller, published by Portfolio Press, 2003.

CERAMICS

COLLECTORS' NOTES

■ Josef Originals was founded in Arcadia, California by Murial Joseph George in 1945 and went on, like so many US potteries in the postwar period, to become both successful and prolific. The spelling of the name came about when 'Joseph' was misspelt on the first labels, which could not be amended.

■ The 'Birthday Doll' collection was the first range released, with George herself designing this, and the vast majority of the figurines, until her retirement. Ladies, girls, and a few animals dominated production until around 1960 when production moved to Japan. The range was then expanded to include household objects such as sprinklers and planters.

■ Production moved again to Taiwan and then Korea, and in 1982 Murial Joseph George retired. The company was sold to Applause in 1985, which continue to produce the much-loved 'Birthday Doll'

range today. These more modern figurines are of little interest to collectors and usually fetch under $10-20.

■ The lady and girl figurines produced in California before 1960 are the most desirable and valuable and can fetch over $150. These are followed in popularity by figurines produced from the 1960s to c1985, with the later Korean examples being the least valuable. Household wares are popular and also appeal to kitchenalia collectors.

■ Learn how to spot early examples made in California. Labels will often help to date a piece, as they can indicate the country of manufacture. Look out for large figurines with complex molded details such as roses or a butterfly. Damage affects value seriously, so examine protruding parts such as arms, the neck or a birthday number for signs of repair.

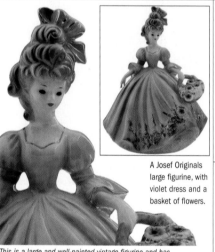

A Josef Originals large figurine, with violet dress and a basket of flowers.

This is a large and well-painted vintage figurine and has comparatively complex features such as the arms, sleeves, hairstyle, basket, and gilt detailing to her dress.

8.75in (22cm) high

$120-180   **DAC**

A 1960s Japanese Josef Originals 'Charmaine' figurine, the base inscribed/stamped "A Josef Original C".

7in (18cm) high

$80-120   **DAC**

A Josef Originals 'Sylvia' figurine, with blue dress highlighted with gold colored glitter.

5.75in (14.5cm) high

$60-90   **DAC**

A Josef Originals 'Russia' figurine.

4.25in (10.5cm) high

$40-60   **DAC**

A Josef Originals figurine, with pink dress, decorated with gold bows and rhinestones.

4.5in (11.5cm) high

$50-70   **DAC**

A Josef Originals 'Spring' figurine, with butterflies, original card swing tag.

6in (15cm) high

$60-90   **DAC**

A CLOSER LOOK AT A JOSEF ORIGINALS FIGURINE

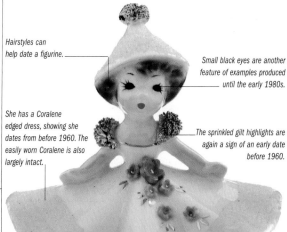

Hairstyles can help date a figurine.

Small black eyes are another feature of examples produced until the early 1980s.

She has a Coralene edged dress, showing she dates from before 1960. The easily worn Coralene is also largely intact.

The sprinkled gilt highlights are again a sign of an early date before 1960.

A Josef Originals yellow girl figurine, for November.

3.75in (9.5cm) high

$30-40　　　　**DAC**

A Josef Originals 8th birthday figurine, the base incised "Josef Originals C".

c1950　　　　5in (12.5cm) high

$25-35　　　　**DAC**

A Josef Originals small figurine of a girl, in a yellow dress and bobble hat, made in California.

c1950　　　　3.5in (9cm) high

$40-60　　　　**DAC**

A Josef Originals 14th birthday figurine.

This series is popular as children were given one every year as a present. Higher numbers towards 20 can tend to be more valuable, probably as many girls had grown out of them by then.

6in (15cm) high

$40-60　　　　**DAC**

A Josef Originals graduation present figurine, of an angel in a pink graduation gown and hat, with gilt detailing.

4.25in (10.5cm) high

$40-60　　　　**DAC**

An unusual Josef Originals bust, with waisted stem.

The rhinestones are an early feature and the faux pearls make her more desirable.

6in (15cm) high

$50-70　　　　**DAC**

FIND OUT MORE...

Josef Originals: Charming Figurines, by Dee Harris, Jim & Kaye Whittaker, published by Schiffer Publishing, 1999.

Josef Originals: A Second Look, by Jim & Kaye Whittaker, published by Schiffer Publishing, 2000.

COLLECTORS' NOTES

- Founded in 1953 in Almacera near Valencia, Spain, by three brothers, Lladró has made over 4,000 designs since its inception. Over 1,200 are still available, with figurines being retired annually. The Nao company was established in 1968 as part of the Lladró group.

- Look on the base for marks, as fakes are known. Pieces from the 1950s are rare and usually have incised marks. Standardized impressed and incised marks were used from c1960. From 1971 the familiar blue stamp was used, but lacked the accent over the 'o' until 1974, when the version still used today was introduced.

- Pastel colors are typical, usually in a high gloss glaze. A matte glaze is scarcer and often fetches higher prices. A third finish, similar to the earthy tones of stoneware, is known as 'Gres', and is often used for large pieces.

- Early preproduction pieces have a plain creamy finish and are sought after and valuable, as are early pieces from the 1950s-70s. Limited editions, popular designs that have been retired, or that were only produced for a short period of time, usually fetch higher values due to their comparative rarity.

- Also look for large or complex moldings but always examine protruding parts carefully for damage or repair, as this reduces value considerably.

- Consider the facial expression, which should be full of character and individuality, something Lladró is known for. Lladró never use black to mark out eyes, brows and lids, a fact that can help identify fakes.

A Lladró 'After School' figure, no.5705, designed by Salvador Debón.

1990-93   10in (25.5cm) high

$120-180   **AAC**

A Lladró 'Dreamer' figure, no.5008, designed by Francisco Catalá.

1978-99   10in (25.5cm) high

$120-180   **AAC**

A Lladró Nao 'Girl with Poodle, Hands Behind Her' figure.

9.25in (23.5cm) high

$70-100   **AAC**

A Lladró 'Girl with Hat in Front' figure.

9in (23cm) high

$50-80   **AAC**

A Lladró Nao 'Girl Running with Puppy' figure, no.1027.

1987-Current   6.25in (16cm) high

$50-80   **AAC**

A Lladró 'Spring is Here' figure, no.5223.

1984-Current   6.75in (17cm) high

$80-120   **AAC**

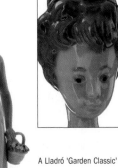

A Lladró 'Garden Classic' figure, no.7617, an 'event' figure, designed by Juan Huerta.

1991   9in (22cm) high

$220-280   **AAC**

A Lladró Nao 'Girl with Violin' figure, no.1034.

1987-Current   7.5in (19cm) high

$80-120   **AAC**

A Lladró Nao 'Girl with Cello' figure, no.1035.

1987-Current   7.5in (19cm) high

$70-100   **AAC**

A Lladró 'Girl with Turkey' figure, no.4569, designed by Fulgencio García.

1969-81   5.5in (14cm) high

$120-180   **AAC**

A Lladró 'Boy with Pails' figure, no.4811, designed by Salvador Furió.

1972-88   8.5in (21cm) high

$120-180   **AAC**

A Lladró 'Winter' boy and dog figure, no.5220, designed by Juan Huerta.

1984-2001 8.5in (21cm) high

$120-180   **AAC**

A Lladró 'Bird Watcher' figure, no.4730, designed by Vicente Martínez.

1970-85   6.5in (16cm) long

$220-280   **AAC**

A Lladró 'Puppy Love' figure, no.1127, designed by Vicente Martínez.

1971-96   10.5in (26cm) high

$280-320   **AAC**

A Lladró 'Good Night' figure, no.5449, designed by Juan Huerta.

1987-91   8.5in (21cm) high

$120-180   **AAC**

A Lladró 'Children at Play' figure, no.5304, designed by Regino Torrijos.

1985-90 11.25in (28.5cm) high

$280-320   **AAC**

A Lladró 'Aranjuez Little Lady' figure, no.4879, designed by Vicente Martínez.

1974-96   12.5in (32cm) high

$220-280   **AAC**

A Lladró 'Evita' figure, no. 5212, designed by José Puche.

1984-98   7.25in (18cm) high

$120-180   **AAC**

A Lladró 'Trying on a Straw-Hat' figure, no.5011, designed by Francisco Catalá.

1978-98   10.5in (26cm) high

$120-180   **AAC**

A Lladró 'Ingenue' figure, no.5487, designed by José Puche.

1988-91   8in (20cm) high

$70-100   **AAC**

A Lladró 'Quixote Standing Up' figure, no.4854, with matte finish, designed by Salvador Furió.

Popular Spanish character, Don Quixote was produced in a number of different poses with different values. This figurine displays the sought-after elongation typical of Lladró designs.

A Lladró 'Buenas Noches' (Good Night) figure, no.5449, designed by Juan Huerta.

1987-91   8.5in (21cm) high

$220-280   **AAC**

1973-91   12in (30cm) high

$120-180   **AAC**

A Lladró 'Shepherdess with Rooster' figure, no.4677, designed by Juan Huerta.

Look for the matte version, also retired in 1991, as it can be worth half as much again.

1969-91 7.75in (19.5cm) high

$50-80   **AAC**

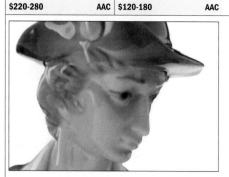

A Lladró 'Countryman' figure, no.4664, designed by Salvador Furió.

1969-79   11.75in (30cm) high

$220-280   **AAC**

A Lladró 'Japanese Girl Decorating' figure, no.4840, designed by Vicente Martínez.

1973-97   7.5in (19cm) high

$80-120   **AAC**

CERAMICS

A Lladró 'Eskimo Playing With Bear' figure, no.1195, with matte finish, designed by Juan Huerta.

1972-91   *4.75in (12cm) high*

$70-100   **AAC**

A Lladró 'Pekinese Sitting' figure, no.4641, designed by Salvador Furió.

1969-85   *6in (15cm) high*

$180-220   **AAC**

A Lladró 'It Wasn't Me!' figure, no.7672G, Collector's Society piece, designed by Antonio Ramos.

1998   *4in (10cm) high*

$220-280   **AAC**

A CLOSER LOOK AT A LLADRÓ FIGURINE

A Lladró 'Kitty Confrontation' figure, no.1442, designed by Juan Huerta.

1983-91   *3.5in (9cm) wide*

$120-180   **AAC**

This figure was designed by Juan Huerta, one of Lladró's most celebrated sculptors.

He is known for his children and animals that incorporate a 'story' into the design.

The series was only produced between 1978 and 1981, making it comparatively scarce today.

This was part of the 'Painful Animals' series of six wounded animal figurines – collectors like to collect an entire series.

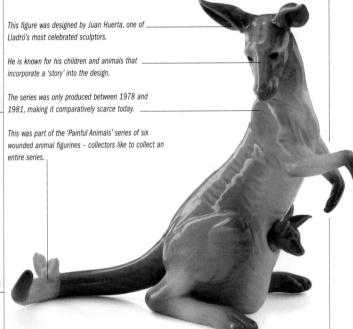

A Lladró 'Koala Love' figure, no.5461G, designed by Antonio Ramos.

1988-93   *8.5in (21cm) high*

$180-220   **AAC**

A Lladró 'Painful Kangaroo' figure, no.5023, designed by Juan Huerta.

1978-81   *7in (18cm) high*

$400-600   **AAC**

A Lladró 'Swan with Wings Spread' figure, no.5231, designed by Francisco Catalá.

1984-91   *7.5in (19cm) high*

$120-180   **AAC**

FIND OUT MORE...

Collecting Lladró: Identification & Price Guide, by Peggy Whiteneck, published by Krause, 2003.

Lladró Authorised Reference Guide, by Lladró, published by Lladró US Inc, 2000.

CERAMICS

COLLECTORS' NOTES

- What is now known as the Lomonosov Porcelain Factory was founded in St Petersburg in 1744, initially to produce porcelain for the Russian royal household. During the reign of Catherine The Great it was known as The Imperial Porcelain Factory, becoming the State Porcelain Works after the Revolution in 1917. Later it was renamed Lomonosov after the founder of the Russian Academy of Science.

- Figurines produced in the late 20thC are becoming more desirable to collectors and prices are rising. A large variety of animals were produced with bears, closely tied in with Russian folklore and legend, being particularly favored. All are handpainted with smooth, glossy glazed finishes. Sizes range from very small to very large examples, often in dramatic poses.

- Often now known as the 'Sèvres of Russia', the factory is still producing today. Look closely at the mark on the base as this can help with dating. Most desirable are earlier figurines. Green, black or blue stamped marks generally date from the 1930s-1960s.

- However, most collectors will find printed marks in red, dating from the late 1960s onward. Examples marked "MADE IN USSR" are sought-after, dating from before the 1980s when Russia went into turmoil as Communism was overthrown. Later examples from after the late 1980s onward are marked "MADE IN RUSSIA". Beware of "Russia" marks that have been altered to look like more valuable, earlier "USSR" marks.

A 1950s Lomonosov she-bear figure, with "Made in the USSR" mark, no longer in production.

6.25in (16cm) high

$120-180   **DSC**

A Lomonosov inkwell, in the form of two bear cubs playing, with "Made in the USSR" stamp, lacks liner under the lid, out of production.

5in (13cm) high

$150-200   **DSC**

A 1950s Lomonosov bear cub figure, with "Made in the USSR" stamp.

Earlier pieces were more 'bumpy' than later smoother examples.

5in (12.5cm) high

$25-35   **DSC**

A 1970s Lomonosov bear cub figure, with "Made in the USSR" stamp.

5.75in (14.5cm) high

$25-35   **DSC**

A 1950s Lomonosov lion and hare figure, with "Made in the USSR" stamp.

The theme of this figurine is taken from a popular Russian folk tale. It is no longer produced.

5in (13cm) high

$150-200   **DSC**

A Lomonosov large 'Misha' mascot figure, with "Made in the USSR" stamp.

Misha was the official mascot of the 1980s Olympic Games, held in Moscow.

4.25in (11cm) high

$70-100   **DSC**

A 1970s Lomonosov seated lion cub figure, with "Made in the USSR" stamp.

4in (10cm) high

$40-60   **DSC**

A 1970s Lomonosov reclining lion cub figure, with "Made in the USSR" stamp.

5in (13cm) wide

$40-60   DSC

A 1960s Lomonosov crouching snow lynx figure, with "Made in the USSR" stamp.

5in (13cm) long

$40-60   DSC

A 1970s Lomonosov seated fox figure, with "Made in the USSR" stamp.

4.25in (11cm) high

$40-60   DSC

A 1960s/70s Lomonosov Afghan hound figure, with "Made in the USSR" stamp.

6in (15.5cm) high

$50-70   DSC

A 1990s Lomonosov seated hedgehog figure, with "Made in Russia" stamp.

3in (7.5cm) high

$15-25   DSC

A late 1960s Lomonosov small wren figure, with "Made in the USSR" stamp.

2.25in (6cm) long

$30-40   DSC

A late 1980s Lomonosov small seated gray rabbit figure, with "Made in the USSR" sticker.

$15-25   DSC

A late 1960s Lomonosov seated rabbit figure, with "Made in USSR" stamp.

2.25in (6cm) long

$25-35   DSC

A late 1960s Lomonosov badge figure, with "Made in the USSR" stamp.

4.75in (12cm) long

$25-35   DSC

FIND OUT MORE...

250 Years of Lomonosov Porcelain Manufacture at St Petersburg 1744-1994, by Galina Agarkova & Nataliya Petrova, published Palgrave Macmillan, 2002.

COLLECTORS' NOTES

- W.R. Midwinter was founded in 1910, moving to Burslem, Staffordshire in 1914. Art Deco style tableware such as tea sets dominated production until WWII saw the closure of much of the factory.

- Midwinter's turning point came in the late 1940s, when the factory began to modernise. By 1950, Roy Midwinter had risen through the company to become Sales and Design Director and he encouraged new, young designer Jessie Tait, who had joined in 1946, to develop her designs.

- Modern patterns began to replace the stylized floral designs dominant at the time, but traditional shapes were still used. Roy Midwinter visited the US in 1952, and saw the innovative modern designs by potters such as Raymond Loewy and Russell Wright and was inspired to move the company along these lines.

- The result was the 'Stylecraft' shape and range, launched in 1953, with a variety of modern patterns designed by Tait. Some were hand-painted. This was followed by the 'Fashion' range in 1955, which saw even more modern and clean-lined shapes being introduced. The ranges were targeted at, and became popular with, young homemakers.

- Look for patterns that sum up the style and feeling of the day as these are usually the most popular. Period textiles were often an inspiration. Abstract patterns and highly stylized floral, fruiting or foliate designs are typical, usually executed in bright colors. More traditional floral designs tend to be less sought-after.

- Characteristic pieces that combine a typically modern shape with a modern pattern are ideal. Tea cups and saucers and plates are common and worth less than items such as vases, teapots and coffee pots, which are harder to find, and complex items such as cake stands. Look out for designs by notable designers Terence Conran and Hugh Casson, as these are also popular.

A 1950s Midwinter Pottery Stylecraft tea set for six, designed by Jessie Tait, decorated with roses.

$100-150   **GORW**

A 1960s Midwinter Pottery Fashion shape 'Homespun' pattern coffee set, designed by Jessie Tait.

7.5in (19cm) high

$400-500   **GGRT**

A Midwinter Pottery Fashion shape 'Cannes' pattern coffee set, designed by Hugh Casson.

1960   *8in (20cm) high*

$500-600   **GGRT**

A Midwinter Pottery Fashion shape 'Whispering Grass' pattern cup and saucer, designed by Jessie Tait.

1960   *saucer 6.25in (16cm) diam*

$80-90   **GGRT**

A Midwinter Pottery Fashion shape 'Zambesi' early morning teapot.

This is both a desirable shape and pattern.

c1956   *5in (13cm) high*

$250-350   **AGR**

A Midwinter Pottery Fashion shape 'Whispering Grass' pattern coffee pot, designed by Jessie Tait.

1960   *7.5in (19cm) high*

$200-300   **GGRT**

A Midwinter Pottery Fashion shape 'Graphic' pattern trio, designed by Jessie Tait.

1964 (17.5cm) diam

$30-50   **GGRT**

A Midwinter Pottery 'Mosaic' pattern celery vase, designed by Jessie Tait.

Unlike many, this pattern is textured, with impressed lines created by the mould. The decoration is sponged on, so can vary in depth of colour and placement.

1960   6.75in (17cm) high

$600-700   **GGRT**

A Midwinter Pottery 'Mosaic' pattern bowl, designed by Jessie Tait.

1960   4in (10cm) high

$200-300   **GGRT**

A Midwinter Pottery 'Mosaic' pattern cake stand, designed by Jessie Tait.

1960   3.75in (24cm) wide

$200-300   **GGRT**

A Midwinter Pottery 'Mosaic' pattern hors d'oeuvres dish, designed by Jessie Tait.

1960   6.75in (17.5cm) wide

$100-150   **GGRT**

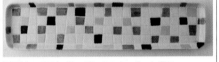

A Midwinter Pottery 'Mosaic' pattern Long Tom buffet tray, designed by Jessie Tait.

1960   22.25in (56.5cm) long

$400-500   **GGRT**

A Midwinter Pottery Fashion shape 'Chequers' plate, designed by Terence Conran.

1957   8.75in (22cm) diam

$100-150   **GGRT**

A Midwinter Pottery 'Flower Mist' pattern plate, designed by Jessie Tait.

This were made for the American market with a speckled background, which was not very popular in England. The pattern reflects contemporary textile designs.

1956   9.75in (25cm) diam

$120-180   **GGRT**

A Midwinter Fashion shape 'Rose' plate.

6in (15.5cm) wide

$10-15   **GROB**

CERAMICS

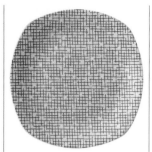

A Midwinter Pottery Stylecraft Modern Shape plate, with printed hatched blue pattern.

7.5in (19cm) wide

$20-30　　　　　　　　　**GROB**

A Midwinter Pottery royal blue Fashion shape sauce boat.

4.5in (11.5cm) high

$25-35　　　　　　　　　**GROB**

A CLOSER LOOK AT A MIDWINTER VASE

Vases are more scarce and sought-after than other shapes such as plates or cups and saucers.

Jessie Tait had learned tube-lining in 1945 when she worked as a decorator under Charlotte Rhead at H.J. Wood in Burslem. Rhead is famous for her tube-lined designs.

The pattern is not printed like 'Zambesi', but is raised to the touch – black slip has been trailed onto the white body in a process known as 'tube-lining'.

As well as the pattern, Tait unusually also designed the shape. In 1956 she designed ten vase and flask shapes, the only ones she designed for Midwinter.

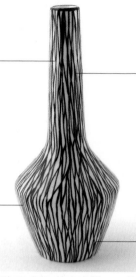

A Midwinter Pottery 'Tonga' vase, designed by Jessie Tait, covered in tube-lined black lines, printed mark.

c1956　　　　　　　　　　　　　　　　　7in (17.5cm) high

$400-500　　　　　　　　　　　　　　　　　　　　**WW**

A late 1950s Midwinter Pottery 'Stubble' pattern vase, designed by Jessie Tait.

9in (23cm) high

$450-650　　　　　　　**PC**

A late 1950s Midwinter Pottery 'Bands and Dots' pattern small vase, designed by Jessie Tait.

6.75in (17.5cm) high

$600-700　　　**GGRT**

A pair of late 1950s Midwinter Pottery 'Bands and Dots' pattern tube-lined studio vases, designed by Jessie Tait.

$700-1,000　　　**PC**

A late 1950s Midwinter Pottery 'Banded' pattern carafe, designed by Jessie Tait.

11.25in (28.5cm) high

$600-900　　　**PC**

A Midwinter figure, 'Madonna', with stamped marks.

10.75in (27cm) high

$120-180　　　**WW**

COLLECTORS' NOTES

■ Myott, Son & Co. Ltd was founded by Ashley Myott in 1898 in Staffordshire, England, expanding in the late 1920s to form the 'Alexander Potteries'. At this time, they also expanded their traditional tableware range to include handpainted decorative wares in the new Art Deco style. It is this range that interests collectors most.

■ Decorators followed a pattern guide but as each is handpainted, differences do occur meaning each piece is effectively unique. Red paint is very rare, with 'autumnal' oranges and browns being more common, along with greens and blues. Decorators did not sign or date their work.

■ A gold stamped mark was used 1930-42, and this Art Deco period is the most desirable one. The printed number is the pattern number. Impressed marks relate to a part of the production process.

■ Some pieces are marked 'B.A.G. Co. Ltd' indicating that they were made for British American Glass for export. 'BAG' pieces are often more finely painted and there may have been exclusive BAG patterns.

■ A fire at the Myott factory in 1949 destroyed all records and pattern books making it hard for collectors to find out more. This may explain why interest in and values for Myott have not risen as much as for its contemporary Clarice Cliff. However, this is changing rapidly.

■ Shape and pattern are the main indicators to value. Beaky jugs (with long beak-like spouts) are sought after, often fetching $3,000-5,000. 'Wedge' and 'Cone' or 'Owl' vases are also prized and can be worth $2,000-2,500 each. Condition is important – brown and orange paints flake easier than other colors and reduces value considerably on common pieces.

A Myott handpainted medium 'Pinchtop' jug, pattern no.8974.

The 'Pinchtop' is also known as 'Persian'. This is an unusual colorway - very light blue is a rare shade.

7.25in (18.5cm) high

$120-180　　　　　　　**NAI**

A Myott handpainted large 'Pinchtop' jug, pattern no.8678.

These jugs were also available in sets of three. It is very rare to find a pattern that combines floral and geometric decoration.

8in (20cm) high

$280-320　　　　　　　**NAI**

A Myott handpainted large 'Pinchtop' jug, pattern no.H8301.

This common pattern was copied by Wade Heath.

8in (20cm) high

$50-80　　　　　　　**NAI**

A Myott handpainted 'Balloon Tree' pattern small 'Pinchtop' jug, pattern no.1143FO.

$120-180　　　　　　　**NAI**

A Myott handpainted small 'Pinchtop' jug, pattern no.H8319.

$70-100　　　　　　　**NAI**

A Myott handpainted large 'Pinchtop' jug, pattern no.H8339.

8in (20cm) high

$120-180　　　　　　　**NAI**

A Myott handpainted large 'Pinchtop' jug, pattern no.2682F.

8in (20cm) high

$120-180　　　　　　　**NAI**

CERAMICS

A Myott handpainted 'Diamond' vase, pattern no.8515, with frog.

6in (15.5cm) high

$180-220   **NAI**

A Myott handpainted 'Overflow' vase, pattern no.P9652, marked with Reg'd design no.779153 for late 1932.

6.75in (17cm) high

$500-700   **NAI**

A CLOSER LOOK AT A MYOTT VASE

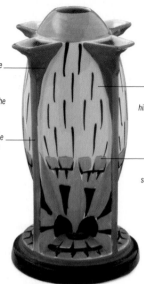

The 'Torpedo' is one of the most desirable and rare shapes, along with the angular 'Beaky' jug and the 'Wedge' vase.

The use of color shows the complex molded form off well.

Along with much Art Deco design, the form hints at architecture and contrasting angles and lines.

The orange is typically Myott, but is made strikingly Art Deco when contrasted with white, green, and black.

A Myott handpainted 'Torpedo' vase, pattern no.8981.

8.75in (22cm) high

     NAI

$1,200-1,800

A Myott handpainted 'Top Hat' vase, pattern no.P9566, with frog, marked "B.A.G. Co. Ltd" and "CP" painters monogram, lacks Myott mark.

If the frog is missing, the price is reduced by $50-80.

8.5in (21.5cm) high

$280-320   **NAI**

A Myott handpainted 'Fluted' vase, pattern no.HW93 painted with flowers and brown sponged decoration, with flared lip.

8.75in (22.5cm) high

$120-180   **NAI**

A Myott handpainted 'Plain' vase, pattern no.P9764.

7.25in (18.5cm) high

$120-180   **NAI**

A rare Myott handpainted 'Onion' or 'Bulbous' vase, pattern no.HW94, with slight flared body, and green sponged decoration.

8.5in (21.5cm) high

$220-280   **NAI**

A Myott handpainted large bowl, pattern no.H2086.

9in (23cm) diam

$80-120 NAI

A Myott handpainted medium bowl, pattern no.P9532.

8in (20.5cm) diam

$70-100 NAI

A Myott handpainted medium bowl, pattern no.8072.

8in (20.5cm) diam

$70-100 NAI

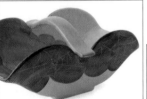

A Myott handpainted small bowl, pattern no.P9531, with rare decoration of oranges.

7in (18cm) diam

$50-80 NAI

A rare Myott chevron dish/fruit bowl, with rounded feet.

12in (30.5cm) high

$120-180 NAI

A Myott handpainted trug, pattern no.P9602.

13.5in (34cm) wide

$400-600 NAI

A Myott handpainted beaker, pattern no.9375.

4.5in (11.5cm) high

$50-80 NAI

A Myott handpainted beaker, pattern no.H8286.

4.5in (10.5cm) high

$50-70 NAI

A Myott handpainted powder box.

5in (13cm) diam

$50-80 NAI

FIND OUT MORE...

The Mystery of Myott by Anne Myott & Philip Pollitt, privately published, 2003.

www.myottcollectorsclub.co.uk

COLLECTORS' NOTES

■ Carter & Co. Pottery of Poole began producing domestic ware in 1921, through their subsidiary company, Carter, Stabler & Adams.

■ Truda Adams was a key designer. Her pieces were typically handpainted with geometric or floral designs on pale backgrounds. Impressed shape numbers and painted letters for the pattern name are often found. Her stylized geometric pieces, large examples and items with animals are desirable.

■ After WWII, Alfred Burgess Read became chief designer. He worked with painter Ruth Pavely and thrower Guy Sydenham to create hand-thrown and decorated pieces, which are effectively unique.

■ The Swedish-inspired 1950s Contemporary range, with bold stripes and wavy lines, is very desirable today.

A Poole Pottery hand-thrown 'LE' pattern vase, decorated by Nicola Massarella, the unusual elaborate design with gray birds.

6.5in (16.5cm) high

$100-150   C

A 1930s Poole Pottery hand-thrown 'AT Abstract Deco' pattern vase.

4in (10cm) high

$250-350   C

A 1930s Poole Pottery hand-thrown 'Leo The Lion' pattern pot, decorated by Myrtle Bond, shape 986.

4in (10cm) high

$100-150   C

A Poole Pottery hand-thrown 'YE Abstract Yellow' pattern vase, shape 443, with a red body.

7in (18cm) high

$300-400   C

A Poole Pottery hand-thrown 'TY' pattern vase, shape 401, with a red body and two handles.

4.5in (11.5cm) high

$300-400   C

A Poole Pottery hand-thrown 'PH' grey and black pattern vase, shape 199.

6in (15cm) high

$350-550   C

A Poole Pottery hand-thrown 'CS' pattern step-handled vase, shape 995, painted by Anne Hatchard from a design by Truda Carter, red earthenware body.

Geometrically stylised Art Deco floral or foliate designs on unusual shapes tend to fetch a premium amongst collectors.

1928-34

9in (23cm) high

$1,500-2,000   C

A Poole Pottery 'Persian Deer' pattern plate, painted by Betty Gooby.

c1950s   10in (25.5cm) diam

$200-300   C

A Poole Pottery 'BN' pattern plate, shape 413, painted by Hilda Trim.

c1930s   8in (20cm) diam

$60-90   C

A Poole Pottery hand-thrown 'AQ Abstract Floral' pattern bowl, painted by Anne Hatchard.

13.5in (34.5cm) diam

$350-450   C

A Poole Pottery hand-thrown 'RH' abstract floral pattern plate, on a red body.

9in (23cm) diam

$150-250   C

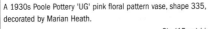

A 1930s Poole Pottery 'UG' pink floral pattern vase, shape 335, decorated by Marian Heath.

6in (15cm) high

$400-600   C

A 1930s Poole Pottery hand-thrown 'AT Abstract Deco' jug.

4in (10cm) high

$200-300   C

A Poole Pottery perfume bottle, with label for W. H. Smith, The Square, Bournemouth.

$40-60   C

A 1930s Poole Pottery small lidded biscuit barrel, shape 926, sprayed in pastel yellow.

$60-90   C

A single 1930s Poole Pottery 'Elephant' bookend, No. 813, designed by Harold Brownsword, finished in a pale gray glaze.

$200-300   C

A Poole Pottery 'PRP' pattern plate, in the 'Bracken' colorway.

c1953-54   13in (33cm) diam

$300-400   **NPC**

A Poole Pottery 'Freeform' low bowl, shape 676, painted by Gwen Haskins, in the 'PRP' pattern.

c1953-54

$150-250   **C**

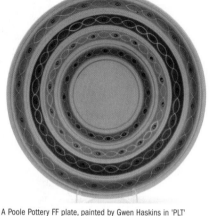

A Poole Pottery FF plate, painted by Gwen Haskins in 'PLT' pattern.

c1959-67   13in (33cm) diam

$300-400   **NPC**

A Poole Pottery cucumber dish, painted in the 'Contemporary' TNC design, designed by Alfred Read.

16in (40.5cm) wide

$200-300   **C**

A Poole Pottery 'PF' pattern dish, shape 338.

The long, slim form with its upwardly curving side was made for display on narrow 1930s window sills.

17.25in (44cm) wide

$120-180   **NPC**

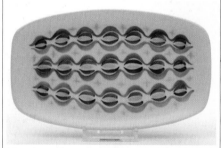

A Poole Pottery 'FT' Onions pattern plate, in shape 361.

c1957   7in (18cm) wide

$50-70   **NPC**

A 1950s Poole Pottery 'Slits' pattern shaped dish.

$50-70   **NPC**

A Poole Pottery 'YHP' design carafe, shape 690.

10in (25.5cm) high

$100-150   **C**

A Poole 'Contemporary' vase, painted by Iris Downtow in the 'PRP' pattern, designed by Alfred Read.

7in (18cm) high

$150-200   **NPC**

A CLOSER LOOK AT A POOLE POTTERY VASE

The modern shape and pattern are typical of Read's innovative 'Contemporary' range launched in 1953 that reflected the spirit of the 1950s.

At over 15in (38cm), this example is extremely large, making it more valuable.

The charcoal gray, Purbeck and lime color combination is harder to find than others.

The carafe's clean-lined shape, numbered 698, had been used before and works well with the linear pattern.

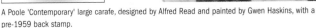

A Poole 'Contemporary' large carafe, designed by Alfred Read and painted by Gwen Haskins, with a pre-1959 back stamp.

c1954-59   15.25in (39cm) high

$600-800   **NPC**

A 1950s Poole Pottery 'Contemporary' flask vase, 'PJB' pattern painted by Gwen Haskins.
1955-59

$250-350   **C**

A Poole 'Contemporary' large vase, designed by Alfred Read, potted by Guy Sydenham, 'PLT' pattern painted by Diane Holloway.

c1953-54   8.75in (22cm) high

$400-600   **NPC**

A Poole Pottery 'Contemporary' large egg-cup shaped pot, shape 721, 'HOL' pattern painted by Gwen Haskins.

9in (23cm) high

$500-800   **C**

A Poole Pottery 'PF Butterfly' pattern vase, in shape 653 designed by Alfred Read, potted by Guy Sydenham and designed by Ruth Pavely in 1957.

c1958

$300-400   **NPC**

A Poole mushroom posy vase, in 'PRP' pattern with Bracken colorway, painted by Diane Holloway.

5in (13cm) diam

$40-60   **NPC**

A Poole 'FF' pattern 'Tea for Two' set.

Teapot 8in (20cm) wide

$150-200   **NPC**

CERAMICS

COLLECTORS' NOTES

■ Robert Jefferson succeeded Alfred Read as chief designer at Poole Pottery in 1958. He developed kitchen wares and set up studios producing artistic pieces, employing painter Tony Morris in 1963.

■ The studio's handmade and decorated pieces formed the new 'Delphis Collection', launched in 1963, using bright natural or abstract designs. From 1966 the Delphis name was applied to mass-produced pieces, with bright glazes. These do not have the word 'Studio' in the backstamp and are less desirable.

■ In 1970, a similar range with a grainier texture, 'Aegean', was introduced. Both ranges were phased out in 1980 and are becoming popular with collectors as prices for 1930s and 1950s Poole soar. Early Studio pieces are still the most desirable.

A Poole Pottery Delphis charger, painted with a scorpion in black and purple, printed and painted marks.

Delphis is the Greek word for 'dolphin', and is the logo of the factory.

13.75in (35cm) diam

$300-400 **WW**

A Poole Pottery Delphis charger, shape number 5, by Cynthia Bennett, printed and painted marks.

13.75in (35cm) diam

$100-150 **WW**

A Poole Pottery Delphis deep dish, painted by Carol Cutler in an abstract red and dark blue design.

c1969-75 *11in (28cm) diam*

$100-150 **C**

A Poole Pottery Delphis plate, painted in an abstract floral design.

8in (20cm) diam

$50-70 **C**

A Poole Pottery Delphis plate, painted by Jean Millership, in an abstract circle and spoke design.

c1966-69 *8in (20cm) diam*

$120-180 **C**

A Poole Pottery Delphis plate, painted by Susan Allen in a starburst red and orange design.

8in (20cm) diam

$120-180 **C**

A Poole Pottery Delphis deep bowl, shape 57, painted in a multitude of colors.

11in (28cm) diam

$250-350 **C**

A Poole Pottery Delphis small pin tray, painted by Jean Millership in the abstract yellow and black design.

$50-70 **C**

A Poole Pottery Delphis vase, shape number 85, by Loretta Leigh, printed and painted marks.

15.75in (40cm) high

$280-320 WW

A Poole Pottery Delphis cushion vase, shape 90, painted by Angela Wyburgh with a brown design on white ground with a magnolia back and a blue stamp.

c1968 *8in (20cm) high*

$280-320 C

A Poole Pottery Delphis cushion vase, shape 90, possibly by Shirley Campbell, painted in the abstract wheel design on a green background.

c1966-69

$220-280 C

A Poole Pottery Delphis bowl, shape 40, decorated by Janet Laird (1969-74) with an abstract petal design against a bold orange ground, with painted artist's monogram.

10.5in (27cm) wide

$280-320 GORL

A Poole Pottery Delphis 'Abstract Floral' pattern hand-thrown vase, shape 85.

16in (40.5cm) high

$300-500 C

A Poole Pottery Aegean wall plate, decorated by Diana Davis, with a full-rigged galleon on a turbulent sea, in russet, brown and yellow tones, impressed marks and painted "D.Davis".

12.5in (32cm) diam

$180-220 DN

A Poole Pottery Aegean wall plate, decorated with black outline of a tree, and splashes of bright orange, against a speckled ground, impressed "Poole England" and stamped "Aegean".

12.5in (32cm) diam

$180-220 DN

A Poole Pottery Aegean wall plate, a collaboration between Leslie Elsden and Jane Brewer, decorated with an owl perched on a tree stump, flanked by foliage and a sun, stamped mark with dolphin, and "Aegean by Leslie Elsden" and "design by J. Brewer".

c1973 *13.75in (35cm) diam*

$280-320 DN

A Poole Pottery Aegean 'Catapult' pattern vase, shape 85, in an unusual pale blue.

16in (40.5cm) high

$280-320 C

CERAMICS

A CLOSER LOOK AT A POOLE DISH

This is a one-off, unique 'Studio' piece. It is thus earlier and rarer than other examples in standard production.

It was decorated by painter Tony Morris, an important name amongst Poole collectors, and bears his monogram on the reverse.

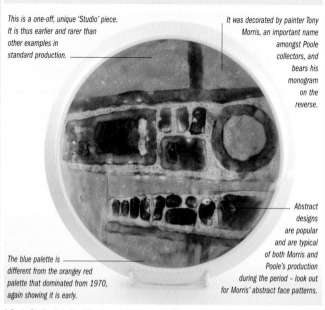

Abstract designs are popular and are typical of both Morris and Poole's production during the period - look out for Morris' abstract face patterns.

The blue palette is different from the orangey red palette that dominated from 1970, again showing it is early.

A Poole Studio dish, No. 47, with a decorated inner of turquoise and blue on a white ground, and with impressed Studio mark and Tony Morris monogram to back.

11in (28cm) diam

$3,000-4,000　　C

A limited edition Poole Pottery Medieval Calendar plate for July, designed by Tony Morris.

c1974　　13in (33cm) diam

$150-200　　C

A Poole Pottery Medieval Calendar plate for March, designed by Tony Morris and painted by S. M. Allen, from a limited edition of 1,000.

c1973　　13in (33cm) diam

$150-200　　C

A Poole Pottery plate, with unusual sgraffito design showing a racing yacht and three sailors on a stormy sea.

8in (20cm) diam

$80-120　　C

A Poole Pottery Atlantis Gourd pot, A52, by Jennie Haigh with deep carving and glazing to exterior.

The Atlantis range was introduced in 1972 and withdrawn in 1977. Guy Sydenham was part of the team that worked on its development.

4in (10cm) high

$300-500　　C

A Poole Pottery Ionian heavy charger, carved, glazed and finished by Jane Brewer, with a signature to reverse and "Cottage in Forest".

The Ionian range, developed by Julia Wills, was only produced during 1974 and 1975.

c1974　　17in (42cm) diam

$500-800　　C

A limited edition Poole Pottery Eclipse plate.

This limited edition was designed by Alan Clarke to commemorate the total eclipse of the sun in 1999 and uses Poole's famed 'Living Glaze' technique.

14in (35.5cm) diam

$150-200　　C

FIND OUT MORE...

Poole Pottery by Leslie Hayward and edited by Paul Atterbury, published by Richard Dennis Publications, 2002.

Collecting Poole Pottery by Robert Prescott Walker, published by Kevin Francis Publishing, 2001.

COLLECTORS' NOTES

- The Ransbottom brothers began as pottery distributors in south eastern Ohio. In order to maintain a consistent supply source, they took over the Oval Ware and Brick Company in 1900 and began to produce their own wares. They initially comprised jardinières, cuspidors, flowerpots, and stoneware jars for which they developed a reputation.

- In 1920, the company merged with the Robinson Clay Products Company in Roseville, Ohio and expanded its range further.

- The pottery continued to produce many of the same lines, employing traditional handcrafted techniques until it closed in May 2005.

A Robinson Ransbottom hand-decorated vase, by Dorothy Archer, marked "RRPCo Roseville O. USA" stamped and signed "D.A. 77" on the side.

1977   *10in (25cm) high*

$70-100   **BEL**

A Robinson Ransbottom hand-decorated vase, by Dorothy Archer, signed "D.A. 78" and stamped "RRPCo".

1978   *6in (16cm) high*

$40-50   **BEL**

A Robinson Ransbottom hand-decorated floor vase, with floral decoration, the whitish stoneware body colored to look like terracotta, marked "RRPCo USA Roseville O".

The factory mark, as above, is often mistaken for the Roseville Pottery stamp.

19.75in (50cm) high

$150-200   **BEL**

A massive Robinson Ransbottom strawberry pot, in yellow high glaze, marked "RRPCo Roseville Ohio No 139".

17.25in (44cm) high

$70-100   **BEL**

A Robinson Ransbottom urn, with green drip glaze, unmarked.

14.25in (36cm) high

$80-120   **BEL**

A pair of Robinson Ransbottom 'Old Colony' slender vases, with double handles and hand-decorated grapes, marked "Old Colony Hand Decorated RRPCo Roseville, O".

8.75in (22cm) high

$70-90   **BEL**

A Robinson Ransbottom 'Tweed' vase, marked "RRPCo Roseville, Ohio, No. 412-10".

10.25in (26cm) high

$35-45   **BEL**

A pair of Robinson Ransbottom 'Old Colony' vases, marked "Old Colony Hand Decorated RRPCo Roseville O", each has a large chip from the underfoot of the base.

8.5in (21.5cm) high

$40-60   **BEL**

A Robinson Ransbottom falcon figure, in high gloss tan and brown, with unmarked open bottom, tip of beak and bottom tip of wings repaired.

10.75in (27.5cm) high

$50-80   **BEL**

A Rookwood Standard Glaze vase, painted by Elizabeth Lincoln, a few scratches, flame mark/734DD/LNL.

Rookwood was established by Maria Nichols in 1880 who left the running to William Watts Tyler, the administrator, after 10 years. Tyler was an innovator and oversaw the introduction of new lines and techniques. Today it is one of the most collectible and sought after American art potteries.

1900   6.75in (17cm) high

$450-550   **DRA**

A Rookwood Standard Glaze vase, painted by Lorinda Epply, seconded for separations in decoration, a few short scratches, flame mark/V/922D/LE/X.

1905   7in (18cm) high

$800-1,000   **DRA**

A Rookwood Standard Glaze vase, painted by A.M. Valentien, overfiring around base caused crazing lines, flame mark/734D/A.M.V.

1898   7in (18cm) high

$1,500-2,000   **DRA**

A rare Rookwood Carved Standard Glaze bottle-shaped vase, unknown artist, flame mark/433B/Artist cipher.

1900   8in (20cm) high

$1,000-1,500   **DRA**

A CLOSER LOOK AT A ROOKWOOD VELLUM VASE

Vellum Glaze pieces are typically decorated in blues and creams. The addition of yellows and greens, such as in this example, increases the value.

The restored hole to the bottom may be the result of the vase being converted to a lamp base and has reduced the value.

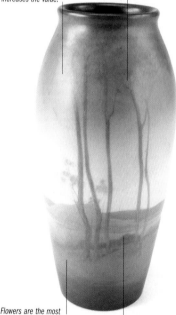

Flowers are the most common decoration, followed by landscapes, any other design would command a premium.

This is a large size for Vellum Glaze, 8in (20cm) high is more typical.

A Rookwood Scenic Vellum Glaze ovoid vase, painted by Lorinda Epply, restored hole to bottom, flame mark/XVI/925C/V/LE.

1916   11in (28.5cm) high

$1,200-1,800   **DRA**

A Rookwood Iris Glaze ovoid vase, painted by Sally Coyne, seconded mark for minor glaze scaling to rim, flame mark/VIII/604D/SEC/W/X.

1908   7in (18cm) high

$1,000-1,500   **DRA**

A Rookwood Iris Glaze bulbous vase, painted by Clara Lindeman, minimal crazing, flame mark/IV/916C/C.C.L./W.

1904   7in (17cm) high

$1,200-1,800   **DRA**

COLLECTORS' NOTES

■ Roseville was founded in 1890 and began by producing utilitarian items such as stoneware and flower-pots. After a move to a new factory their first 'art' pottery range, 'Rozane', was introduced in 1900 and produced until the 1920s.

■ Noted designer and ceramicist Frederick Rhead joined in 1904 and introduced high quality lines such as 'Della Robbia' and 'Aztec', which are scarce and sought after today. In 1919, Frank Ferrell and George Krause designed the molded floral and foliate ranges for which Roseville is best known today.

■ By then, demand for more affordable, commercially produced pottery had grown, and these new ranges became immensely popular. Look for desirable or collectible ranges such as 'Sunflower', 'Futura', 'Blackberry' and 'Pine Cone'.

■ During the 1940s, further ranges were introduced, many of which tend to be less desirable to collectors – although some such as 'Bittersweet' are now increasing in popularity. Despite selling in large quantities, the company was forced to close in 1954.

■ Many collectors focus on one pattern, collecting all the shapes available, or on collecting one shape in all the patterns it was made in. Look for detailed and strong molded patterns, and bright, strongly colored carefully applied glazes.

■ Factory flaws and damage reduce value, but as supplies of first-rate examples dry up, those with slight flaws or professional restoration are becoming more acceptable. Serious glaze crazing also reduces value, but is acceptable again if it is not too pronounced.

A Roseville blue 'Zephyr Lily' pattern cookie jar, with lid, marked "USA 5-8", extensive repairs to the lid and base, flakes.

Introduced in 1946 and produced in blue, green and brown colorways, 'Zephyr Lily' pieces have molded Roseville marks along with a shape number. This piece would have fetched more if it had not been damaged and restored so extensively.

A Roseville blue 'Zephyr Lily' pattern flower pot, with matching saucer, marked "USA 672-5", the saucer marked "USA", saucer repaired.

5.5in (14cm) high

$80-120   **BEL**

10.5in (26.5cm) high

$220-280   **BEL**

A Roseville blue 'Zephyr Lily' pattern basket, marked "USA 393-7", small flat repaired chip to base.

7.5in (19cm) high

$100-200   **BEL**

A Roseville brown 'Zephyr Lily' pattern vase, marked "USA 136-9".

9.5in (24cm) high

$150-250   **BEL**

A Roseville brown 'Zephyr Lily' pattern wall pocket, marked "USA 1297-8".

8.25in (20.5cm) high

$200-300   **BEL**

A Roseville brown 'Zephyr Lily' pattern ashtray, number 29 in the line, unmarked, chips to two leaf points.

6.75in (17cm) wide

$30-40   **BEL**

A Roseville green 'Zephyr Lily' pattern bowl, marked "USA 671-4", flake to one petal.

4.25in (11cm) high

$100-200   **BEL**

A Roseville 'Dahlrose' triple candle holder, with flower moldings.

The inset image shows the foil label sometimes found on these pieces, which are otherwise largely unmarked apart from a shape number handwritten on the base in red. Dahlrose was introduced in 1928.

A Roseville 'Dahlrose' pattern bud vase, with winged handles, unmarked.

8.25in (21cm) high

$350-450   **BEL**

6.25in (16cm) high

$150-250   **PAC**

6.25in (16cm) high

PAC

A Roseville 'Dahlrose' pattern bud vase, with swooping handles, unmarked.

This shape is hard to find without damage to the handles, which can reduce the value by 50% or more.

7.25in (18.5cm) high

$300-400   **BEL**

A Roseville 'Dahlrose' pattern double-bud gate, shape 79-6", marked with black 'Roseville Pottery' paper label and original 'Elder's' retail label with a price of $1.50.

6.25in (16cm) high

$250-350   **BEL**

A Roseville 'Dahlrose' pattern candleholder, marked with black paper label.

3.5in (9cm) high

$100-150   **BEL**

A Roseville 'Dahlrose' pattern 363-6" vase, unmarked.

6.25in (16cm) high

$150-250   **BEL**

A Roseville 'Dahlrose' pattern vase, 364-6", marked with black paper label, filled-in chip on base.

6.25in (16cm) high

$180-220   **BEL**

CERAMICS

A Roseville brown 'Fuchsia' pattern vase, marked "895-7".

7.25in (18.5cm) high

$180-220 BEL

A Roseville brown 'Fuchsia' pattern vase, marked "901-10" and with a silver foil label.

10.25in (26cm) high

$250-350 BEL

A Roseville brown 'Fuchsia' pattern vase, marked "896-8", repaired chip to one leaf.

8.25in (21cm) high

$120-180 BEL

A Roseville brown 'Fuchsia' pattern vase, marked "USA 891-6".

6.25in (16cm) high

$180-220 BEL

A Roseville brown 'Fuchsia' pattern urn vase, marked "646-5".

5.5in (14cm) high

$220-280 BEL

A Roseville brown 'Fuchsia' pattern broad vase, marked "347-6", small glaze skip to the white of one flower.

8.5in (21.5cm) wide

$180-220 BEL

A Roseville green and brown 'Fuchsia' pattern vase, marked "891-6".

6.25in (16cm) high

$180-220 BEL

A Roseville green 'Fuchsia' pattern vase, marked "Roseville 903-12".

Introduced in 1938, Fuchsia can be found in blue, green and brown colorways and usually has an impressed shape number mark on the base.

12.25in (31cm) high

$400-500 BEL

A Roseville blue 'Fuchsia' pattern vase, marked "895-7", filled-in chip at the rim.

7.25in (18.5cm) high

$180-220 BEL

A Roseville brown 'Pine Cone' pattern vase, marked "Roseville 121-7" and with the remnants of a foil label.

Introduced in 1935, 'Pine Cone' went on to become one of Roseville's most successful lines, resulting in a large number of examples being found in over 75 shapes. It continues to be popular with collectors today and can be found in blue, brown and green. The earliest produced pieces have a foil label. From 1936, impressed marks were used and after 1939, marks were molded.

c1936   7.5in (19cm) high

$250-350   **BEL**

A Roseville brown 'Pine Cone' pattern vase, marked "845-8", minor grinding flake from the base.

8in (20cm) high

$220-280   **BEL**

A Roseville brown 'Pine Cone' pattern jardinière, marked "Roseville USA 401-6".

9.25in (23.5cm) wide

$250-350   **BEL**

A Roseville brown 'Pine Cone' pattern curved vase, the base with molded mark "Roseville U.S.A. 490.8".

c1931   8.75in (22cm) high

$150-200   **PAC**

A Roseville green 'Pinecone' pattern vase, with wide conical foot and tiny side handles.

9.25in (23.5cm) high

$180-220   **PAC**

A Roseville green 'Pinecone' pattern trumpet-shaped vase, with wide conical foot, the base stamped "Roseville 743-10".

10.5in (27cm) high

$220-280   **PAC**

A pair of Roseville green 'Pine Cone' pattern triple candleholders, marked "Roseville 1106-5 1/2 Trip".

5.75in (14.5cm) high

$250-350   **BEL**

A Roseville blue 'Pine Cone' pattern bowl, marked "Roseville 276-9".

11.5in (29cm) long

$220-280   **BEL**

A Roseville deep blue 'Pine Cone' pattern vase, marked "745-7", with original foil label, flake from the corner of the base.

7.25in (18.5cm) high

$200-300   **BEL**

A Roseville 'Blackberry' pattern vase, 567-4", unmarked, glaze flake off and an area of branch repaired.

4in (10cm) high

$300-400   **BEL**

A Roseville blue 'Bleeding Heart' pattern jardinière and pedestal set, raised 651-10" mark.

10in (25.5cm) high

$1,200-1,800   **DRA**

A Roseville blue 'Bleeding Heart' pattern handled basket, good mold and color, marked "Roseville USA 359-8".

8in (20cm) high

$250-350   **BEL**

A pair of Roseville 'Bleeding Heart' pattern bookends, marked "Roseville USA 6".

Bookends are a desirable and sought after shape.

5.75in (14.5cm) high

$280-320   **BEL**

A Roseville 'Carnelian I' drip glaze vase, marked with "335-8" and "RV" ink stamp, repairs to lines at rim.

8in (20cm) high

$120-180   **BEL**

A Roseville 'Carnelian II' glaze vase, with very thick and frog skin-like glaze, green, lavender and shades of blue throughout, marked "331" on the base in red crayon.

7.25in (18.5cm) high

$350-450   **BEL**

A Roseville pink 'Cherry Blossom' pattern two-handled vase, with squat base, unmarked.

8.5in (21.5cm) high

$800-1,000   **DRA**

A pair of Roseville 'Cherry Blossom' pattern candle holders, each marked "1080" in red crayon on the base with a foil label.

Introduced in 1933, the pink colorway as shown here is more desirable than the brown.

4.25in (11cm) high

$700-800   **BEL**

A Roseville green 'Dawn' pattern vase, marked "826-6", outside edges of the base over-sprayed.

6.5in (16.5cm) high

$80-120   **BEL**

A Roseville (smooth) 'Dogwood II' pattern large jardinière, 590-10", unmarked, restoration to a small area of the rim.

10.75in (27.5cm) high

$180-220   **BEL**

A CLOSER LOOK AT A ROSEVILLE VASE

'Falline' was introduced in 1933 and is a popular range.

'Falline' tends to be largely unmarked – some have a paper label or a shape number handwritten in red on the base.

The blue colorway seen here is more desirable than the brown, also seen on this page.

The molding is clean, with strong, bright colors that fade to blue at the base giving a visually stunning appearance.

A Roseville blue 'Falline' pattern bulbous vase, with stepped neck and two handles, with foil label.

7.25in (18.5cm) high

$2,500-3,000   **DRA**

A Roseville 'Falline' pattern amphora-shaped vase, with green peapod design, the base marked "91".

7in (18cm) high

$400-500   **PAC**

A Roseville red 'Ferrella' pattern bulbous vase, restoration to small area of base, unmarked.

8.5in (21.5cm) high

$800-1,000   **DRA**

A Roseville green 'Freesia' pattern flower pot, with saucer, pot marked "USA 670-5", the saucer marked "USA", minute flake and wear to the saucer.

5.5in (14cm) high

$150-250   **BEL**

A Roseville blue 'Freesia' pattern basket, marked "USA 391-8".

8.25in (21cm) high

$120-180   **BEL**

A Roseville brown 'Freesia' pattern wall pocket, marked "USA 1296-8", factory kiln kiss at the rim and on the handle.

Wall pockets are a desirable shape – some collectors focus on collecting wall pockets in as many patterns as possible.

8.5in (21.5cm) high

$100-150   **BEL**

A Roseville 'Futura' funnel-shaped bowl, with feet, unmarked, tight line to one leg, very faint line to rim and some flakes.

This shape is known as the 'sand toy'.

4.25in (11cm) high

$200-300   **BEL**

CERAMICS

A Roseville 'Futura' candleholder, with a crystalline effect to the blue areas, faintly marked "1073" in red crayon.

4in (10cm) high

$180-220 BEL

A Roseville 'Imperial II' pattern wall pocket, covered in mottled green-over-lavender glaze, with paper label.

6.5in (16.5cm) high

$800-1,000 DRA

A Roseville brown 'Magnolia' cookie jar, with matching lid, marked "USA 2-8", minute glaze flake to one tree branch.

Although Magnolia (intro.1940) is generally one of the less sought-after ranges, this example, which retains its lid and is an unusual shape is desirable, hence its higher value.

10.25in (26cm) high

$400-500 BEL

A CLOSER LOOK AT A ROSEVILLE VASE

'Futura' was introduced in 1928 and was produced during the height of Art Deco movement.

The clean lines and asymmetric but modern base and sphere are typical of the geometric style of the Art Deco period.

The stylised leaf shapes and Oriental inspiration for the design are typical of the Art Deco movement.

Look out for quirky and unusual shapes that can be rare, such as the 'Tank' vase, which could fetch over $10,000.

A Roseville 'Futura' pattern Bamboo Leaf Ball vase, in shades of blue and green, unmarked.

This vase would have been worth more if it had not been restored. Among collectors Futura is one of the most enduringly popular lines produced by Roseville.

7.25in (18.5cm) high

$400-500 BEL

A Roseville 'Jonquil' pattern vase, with molded daffodil-like flowers.

9.25in (23.5cm) high

$300-400 PAC

A Roseville red 'Laurel' pattern vase, 668-6", marked with foil label on the base.

6.25in (16cm) high

$280-320 BEL

A Roseville blue 'Magnolia' pattern tea pot, marked "USA 4".

7.75in (20cm) high

$180-220 BEL

A Roseville 'Montacello' pattern small vase, with painted arrow-type design, unmarked.

5in (13cm) high

$100-150 PAC

A Roseville brown 'Montacello' pattern vase, with two small handles, marked "558" in red crayon.

5.25in (13.5cm) high

$400-500   BEL

A Roseville brown 'Montacello' pattern basket, unmarked, handle professionally restored.

6.5in (16.5cm) high

$300-400   BEL

A Roseville brown 'Montacello' pattern bowl, unmarked.

13.5in (34.5cm) high

$350-450   BEL

A Roseville 'Rozane' portrait vase, unsigned but attributed to Dunlavy, depicting a middle-aged man, marked "RPCo Rozane 818 78" on the base, one handle and rim restored.

Introduced in 1901, the Rozane range imitated Rookwood's highly successful Standard Glaze range. Designs showing portraits, particularly of Native Americans, are more valuable than flowers.

12in (30.5cm) high

$700-1,000   BEL

A Roseville 'Sunflower' pattern bulbous vessel, unmarked.

Introduced in 1930 and only produced in this colorway, 'Sunflower' is one of the more popular Roseville ranges. Look for crisp moldings and strong colors carefully applied.

7.25in (18.5cm) diam

$1,000-1,500   DRA

A Roseville brown 'Wisteria' pattern gourd-shaped vase, with foil label.

8in (20cm) high

$800-1,000   DRA

A Roseville 'Sunflower' pattern wall pocket, soft mold due to very rich glazing with a deep green center, dark blue at the base and brown at the top, unmarked apart from some illegible crayon marks.

7.25in (18.5cm) high

$1,000-1,500   BEL

A Roseville matte blue 'Topeo' pattern vase, with green and pink highlights, marked "5X" in blue slip.

6.25in (16cm) high

$280-320   BEL

A Roseville 'Vista' pattern handled vase, unmarked, small chip.

'Vista' was introduced in 1920 and is much sought-after.

9.75in (25cm) high

$350-450   BEL

FIND OUT MORE...

Collectors Encyclopedia of Roseville Pottery, by Sharon & Bob Huxford and Mike Nickel, published by Collector Books, 2001.

Warman's Roseville Pottery: Identification & Price Guide, by Mark Moran, published by Krause Publications, 2004.

COLLECTORS' NOTES

■ Royal Copenhagen was founded in 1775 under the patronage of Queen Juliane Marie of Denmark. Frantz Henrich Müller devoted years to unraveling the secret of making hard paste porcelain, which was known to only a very few European factories at the time.

■ 'Blue Fluted' – the first dinner service made by Royal Copenhagen – remains the most popular line today. The company was known primarily for well-decorated blue and white wares for most of its early history.

■ From the 1950s, luminaries such as Henning Koppel helped to secure Royal Copenhagen's reputation for being at the forefront of the Scandinavian design movement, which influenced global ceramic design.

■ The 'Fayence' range of tin-glazed earthenware is popular with collectors today, as are the human and animal figurines designed by Lotte Benter, Knud Kyhn and others.

A large Royal Copenhagen 'Baca' 'Fayence' vase, designed by Nils Thorsson.

7.5in (19cm) high

$70-100   NPC

A Royal Copenhagen 'Baca' 'Fayence' vase, designed by Nils Thorsson.

5in (12.5cm) high

$35-45   NPC

A Royal Copenhagen 'Baca' 'Fayence' square section vase, designed by Johanne Gerber, with stylized bird decoration.

9in (23cm) high

$80-120   GAZE

A Royal Copenhagen 'Fayence' vase.

11in (28cm) high

$70-100   GAZE

A Royal Copenhagen 'Fayence' vase, the hand-decorated design by Nils Thorsson, marked "870/3740".

6.25in (16cm) high

$70-100   GAZE

A Royal Copenhagen 'Fayence' vase, designed by Nils Thorsson, with birds and fishes.

7.25in (18.5cm) wide

$80-120   FD

A CLOSER LOOK AT A ROYAL COPENHAGEN LAMP BASE

A Royal Copenhagen 'Fayence' vase, designed by Johanne Gerber, marked "780" over "3181".

7.5in (19cm) high

$120-180 FD

A Royal Copenhagen 'Fayence' vase, designed by Kari Christensen, with "KC" cipher, marked "427" over "3114".

8.5in (21.5cm) high

$120-180 FD

Nils Thorsson (1898-1975) became interested in ceramics at an early age and was apprenticed to leading artist Christian Joachim in 1912.

'Fayence' (faience) is a type of earthenware which is tin-glazed to make it impervious to water. It was developed in France in the 16thC.

Lamp bases like this piece were made and sold in smaller numbers than vases, making this a relatively scarce example of Thorsson's work today.

The large size and shape of this lamp makes it desirable to collectors.

A large Royal Copenhagen 'Fayence' lamp base, designed by Nils Thorsson.

11.5in (29cm) high

$180-220 FD

A Royal Copenhagen Aluminia 'Fayence' vase, with "CK" backstamp.

11.5in (29cm) high

$120-180 GAZE

A Royal Copenhagen lamp base, designed by Ellen Malmer.

11.5in (29cm) high

$70-100 FD

A Royal Copenhagen 'Fayence' wall hanging salt pot, with wooden lid.

$12-18 GAZE

A Royal Copenhagen 'Girl From Bornholm' porcelain model, no.1323, designed by Lotte Benter.

c1988   8.5in (22cm) high

$280-320   **LOB**

A CLOSER LOOK AT A ROYAL COPENHAGEN FIGURINE

Between 1911 and 1914 Lotte Benter designed a range of figures featuring girls in national or peasant dress, including 'Girl from Bornholm' also on this page.

Part of a series of nine, this porcelain group is very collectible thanks to its charm and patriotic subject matter.

Amager is a Danish island in the Øresund and Copenhagen lies partly on it.

The group displays the typically muted colors of Royal Copenhagen.

A Royal Copenhagen 'Amager Girls' porcelain model, no.1316, designed by Lotte Benter.

6.75in (17cm) high

$400-600   **LOB**

A Royal Copenhagen 'Woman Knitting' porcelain model, no.1323, designed by Lotte Benter.

c1994   7in (18cm) high

$280-320   **LOB**

A Royal Copenhagen porcelain model of a girl with a calf, no.779.

c1975   6.75in (17cm) high

$280-320   **LOB**

A Royal Copenhagen porcelain model of a girl with a doll, no.1938, designed by Ade Bonfils.

5in (13cm) high

$280-320   **LOB**

A Royal Copenhagen porcelain dish with a mermaid, no.3231, designed by Hans H. Hansen.

c1965   6in (15cm) diam

$100-150   **LOB**

A Royal Copenhagen stoneware model of a bear, designed by Knud Kyhn.

3.5in (9cm) long

$50-70   **LOB**

A Royal Copenhagen stoneware model of a bear, designed by Knud Kyhn.

Kyhn (1880-1969) was a Danish sculptor and painter, well known for his interest in nature and animals. He produced a number of animal figures for Royal Copenhagen as well as Bing & Grøndahl.

4in (10cm) long

$50-70   **LOB**

A Royal Copenhagen porcelain model of a kingfisher, no.1769, designed by Peter Herold.

Herold (1879-1920) designed a number of avian figurines for Royal Copenhagen, which were produced from 1910.

8.5in (11cm) high

$180-220   **LOB**

A Royal Copenhagen porcelain model of a sea lion, no.1441, designed by Th. Madsen.

c1980

$80-120   **LOB**

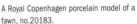

A Royal Copenhagen porcelain model of a polar bear walking, no.320, by Carl J. Bonnesen.

Carl Johan Bonnesen (1868-1933) was well known for his depictions of animals and primitive historical scenes in metal and ceramics. One of his designs stands on top of the Carlsberg brewery in Denmark.

7in (18cm) long

$80-120   **LOB**

A Royal Copenhagen porcelain model of a fawn, no.20183.

c1935   4in (10cm) long

$60-90   **LOB**

A Royal Copenhagen porcelain model of a cock, with its head up, no.1126, designed by Chr. Thomsen.

4.25in (11cm) high

$120-180   **LOB**

A Royal Copenhagen porcelain dish with a crab, no.3131, designed by Jorgen Balslov.

6.25in (16cm) diam

$120-180   **LOB**

A Royal Crown Derby 'Dappled Quail' paperweight, with gold stopper, designed by Louise Adams.

1999

$70-100   PSA

A Royal Crown Derby 'Puffin' paperweight, with gold stopper and box.

1996

$80-120   PSA

A Royal Crown Derby 'Bee Eater Bird' paperweight, with gold stopper and box.

$80-120   PSA

A Royal Crown Derby 'Rough Collie' paperweight, with gold stopper and box.

$120-180   PSA

A Royal Crown Derby 'Fort', from the Treasures of Childhood Series, boxed.

$70-100   PSA

A Royal Crown Derby 'Train', from the Treasures of Childhood Series, boxed.

$80-120   PSA

A Royal Crown Derby porcelain model of an Egyptian cat, boxed.

1986   8.5in (21.5cm) high

$180-220   CA

A Royal Crown Derby porcelain model of a Siamese cat, boxed.

1986   8.5in (21.5cm) high

$220-280   CA

COLLECTORS' NOTES

■ Two of the most important and dominant factories in Scandinavian ceramic design are Sweden's Gustavsberg and Finland's Arabia. Both followed the Scandinavian trend of employing talented designers. Gustavsberg was led by Wilhelm Kage and his successor Stig Lindberg, who introduced modern forms combined with bright, stylized geometric patterns. Arabia's key designer was Kaj Franck.

■ Some of the smaller factories can provide a comparatively inexpensive entry route into the collecting field. Consider Saxbo and Upsala Ekeby, among others. Pieces were designed to be functional – kitchenware from the 1950s and '60s is readily available today, but does not usually fetch as much as more decorative wares such as vases or dishes.

■ Clean-lined, modern forms are typical, and are often asymmetric free form, emphasising a handmade appearance. Decoration varies between muted designs in deep, strong colors and brightly colored, joyful transfer-printed or handpainted patterns. Nature was a key inspiration in terms of form, decoration and often color.

■ The Scandinavian look inspired other potteries such as Rye and Poole in England. It also contributed towards the growth of the global studio pottery movement during the late 20thC.

■ Always look for the hallmarks of Scandinavian design and try to buy pieces by a factory's key designers, as these are most likely to appreciate in value.

A 1950s Rorstrand 'Rubus' range vase, designed by Gunnar Nylund.

Nylund (b.1904) was Art Director at Rorstrand from 1931-58.

9in (22.5cm) high

$50-70　　　**GAZE**

A small 1950s Rorstrand 'Rubus' range vase, designed by Gunnar Nylund.

3.25in (8.5cm) high

$30-50　　　**GAZE**

A 1960s Arabia vase, with striped and square decoration, with printed marks including "5-64".

7in (17.5cm) high

$80-120　　　**GROB**

An Upsala Ekeby vase, with sgraffito decoration.

10.5in (26.5cm) high

$20-30　　　**GAZE**

A 1960s Danish Conny Walther unglazed studio vase, impressed "CW" monogram to base.

6.5in (17cm) high

$250-350　　　**RWA**

A Rorstrand pottery bottle vase, designed by Carl Harry Stahlane, with incised factory marks and initials to the base.

13.5in (34cm) high

$300-400　　　**ROS**

A Gustavsberg yellow glazed asymmetric vase, designed by Stig Lindberg, model number 261, mark and label to base.

c1950　　　7in (18cm) high

$250-350　　　**GAZE**

A 1930s Danish Bode Willumsen studio vase, decorated in relief with a leaping stag and seated horse.

3.5in (9cm) high

$200-250　　　**RWA**

A 1950s/60s Danish Conny Walther squat vase, with matt and high-fired glaze decoration.

3.5in (9cm) high

$180-220　　　　　　　　　**RWA**

A Rorstrand green and black vase, designed by Irma Claesson, with painted marks and initials, crazed.

7in (18cm) high

$100-150　　　　　　　　　**TCM**

A Royal Copenhagen bottle vase, with a peacock design, printed and painted marks.

5.5in (14cm) high

$80-120　　　　　　　　　**TCM**

A 1950s/60s Finnish Kupittaan Savi blue ground studio vase, with green and black stylized vine decoration and brown spots in slip.

Kupittaan Savi was founded in 1712 and was the oldest pottery in Finland. Focusing on bricks and industrial products, production of domestic ware only began in 1915 and had trailed off by the 1930s. It continued, albeit on a smaller but successful scale, until the factory's demise in 1969.

9.25in (23.5cm) wide

$350-450　　　　　　　　　**FD**

A 1960s Danish Palshus vase, by Annelise and Per Linnermann-Schmidt, with incised design.

$150-200　　　　　　　　　**RWA**

A Danish Knabstrup square vase, designed by Erik Reiff, with leaf-pattern design.

c1965-77 9.75in (24.5cm) high

$150-200　　　　　　　　　**RWA**

A 1960s Danish Soholm hand-painted pottery vase, stamped "Handmade in Soholm Denmark".

8.5in (21.5cm) high

$25-35　　　　　　　　　**GAZE**

A 1960s Swedish Niitsjo stoneware cylindrical vase, probably designed by Thomas Stengus, painted "Niitsjo Sweden 7117" and stamped "Thomas Stengus".

$15-20　　　　　　　　　**GAZE**

A Norwegian Figgjo Flint 'Saga' pattern tapered vase, with flared rim and printed marks.

10.25in (26cm) high

$35-45　　　　　　　　　**TCM**

An Uppsala Ekeby Keramic oval dish, with abstract geometric design, designed by Mari Simmulson, with impressed marks.

Estonian designer Simmulson (1911-?) worked for Uppsala Ekeby from 1949-72. The design here is very similar to those by Stig Lindberg for Gustavsberg, where Simmulson had worked from 1945-49.

11.5in (29cm) long

$120-180　　　　　　　　　　　　　　　　　　　**TCM**

A Stig Lindberg studio ceramic bowl, with artist's cipher and marked "Sweden P/46-3".

As well as having an abstract linear design typical of Lindberg's designs, the organically curving linear form, inspired by a leaf, is typical of Scandinavian design at the time. A similar example can be found in the Victoria & Albert Museum collection.

c1950　　　　　　　　　　　　　　9.5in (24cm) wide

A Danish long dish, with an abstract design, printed marks.

12.5in (32cm) long

$80-120　　　　　　**TCM**

$350-450　　　　　　　　　　　　　　　　　　　**FD**

A 1960s Uppsala Ekeby studio ceramic shallow bowl, designed by Sven-Erik Skawonius, stamped "UE Sweden 9037 SES" to reverse.

8.5in (22cm) diam

$15-20　　　　　　　　　　　**GAZE**

A Rorstrand dish, designed by Sylvia Leuchovious, signed "W R WW SWEDEN" and "S-L 8-1" to reverse.

7.5in (19cm) diam

$40-60　　　　　　　　　　　**GAZE**

A Rorstrand handpainted Sgrafo Modern plate, with printed marks.

5.5in (14cm) diam

$50-70　　　　　　　　　　　**TCM**

A 1950s Rorstrand 'Florita' square dish.

8.5in (22cm) wide

$18-22　　　　　　　　　　　**GROB**

A square dish by Stig Lindberg, depicting a maiden in a high tower, painted marks and designer's label.

6.25in (16cm) wide

$80-120　　　　　　　　　　　**TCM**

A Rorstrand Sgrafo Modern footed bowl, with molded foot, wavy rim and impressed marks.

5.5in (14cm) wide

$120-180　　　　　　　　　　　**TCM**

A 1960s Rorstrand wall plaque, designed by Olle Alberius, with incised marks.

Alberius (b.1926), designed for Rorstrand from 1963-71.

12.5in (32cm) wide

$300-400   **TCM**

A Gustavsberg wall plaque of three figures on an elephant, designed by Lisa Larson, stamped "LISA L".

$100-150   **GAZE**

A Nymølle 'Donna Elvira' large oval display plate, designed by Bjørn Wiinblad, printed signature to reverse.

1954

$80-100   **GAZE**

A Bing & Grøndhal snail wall plaque.

5.75in (14.5cm) diam

$40-50   **FD**

A Norwegian Figgjo Flint 'Saga' pattern silk screened plaque, marked "Saga Norske design".

Note the similarity in style to Bjørn Wiinblad's designs. Flint makes more use of color and symmetry.

6.25in (16cm) long

$15-20   **GROB**

A Rorstrand "Bayleaves" storage jar, with wooden lid.

3.5in (9cm) high

$15-20   **GROB**

A 1950s Ganiopta Swedish stylized bird dish, signed to the base and with red foil label.

13in (33cm) long

$60-90   **GAZE**

A Rorstrand lidded ovenware dish, with printed marks.

5.75in (14.5cm) wide

$30-50   **TCM**

An Arabia jug, designed by Kaj Franck, with a green stylized cat design.

4in (10.5cm) high

$40-60   **MHT**

FIND OUT MORE...

Scandinavian Ceramics & Glass in the Twentieth Century, by Jennifer Opie, published by V&A Publications, 2001.

Scandinavian Design, by Charlotte & Peter Fiell, published by Taschen, 2002.

COLLECTORS' NOTES

■ The Shelley Pottery began life as Wileman & Co., when Joseph Ball Shelley went into partnership with Henry Wileman at the Foley China Works of Fenton in Staffordshire, England, in 1827. The Shelley name was in use by 1910, but it was not until 1925 that the factory became known by that name.

■ Their ceramics were executed in bone china or earthenware, with patterns being handpainted or applied by lithographic transfer. Designers included the notable Frederick Rhead, Walter Slater and Eric Slater. Hilda Cowham, who joined in 1925, and Mabel Lucie Attwell, who joined in 1926, are known for their nursery ware.

■ Shelley is very well known for its Art Deco tea wares. Look for an Art Deco shape, such as Vogue, Eve or Mode, combined with a geometric or Art Deco stylized floral or foliate pattern. Cups and saucers are a strong collecting area – over 50 patterns were produced in the Vogue and Mode shapes and over 200 for the Regent shape, so there is plenty to collect.

■ The Shelley factory continued production until 1966 when it was taken over by Allied English Potteries, who themselves became part of the Doulton Group in 1971. Marks can help date pieces, with the word Foley last being used in marks c1916. Most marks are printed in green with the word Shelley inside a shield.

A Shelley Regent shape coffee set for six, including a coffee jug, sugar bowl and milk jug.

Although the shape was introduced in 1932 and continued until the 1960s, this service was manufactured for two years only, starting in 1935, and combines a good Art Deco shape and pattern.

1935-37　　　　　　　　　　pot 7.5in (19cm) high

$450-650　　　　　　　　　　　　　　　　**CA**

A Shelley Regent shape 'Brown Swirls' pattern tea set for six, including two large side plates, a slop bowl and sugar bowl.

c1936
　　　Pot 8in (20cm) high

$450-650　　**CA**

A Shelley Vogue shape part tea service for six, including a cake plate, printed factory mark, painted "11741".

1930-c1933

$2,500-3,500　　**L&T**

A Shelley Princess shape cup and saucer, with stylized flowers in oranges and brown, marked "12227".

c1934

$120-180　　**BAD**

A Shelley Vogue shape trio set, with green rings, marked "11959".

1930-c1933　　*Plate 6.75in (17cm) wide*

$350-550　　**BEV**

A Shelley Mabel Lucie Attwell cup and saucer, with a copyright design.

Beware of the many fakes on the market. Designs that scratch off easily, weaker colors and date marks before 1926, when Attwell joined Shelley, indicate reproductions or fakes.

c1930　　*Saucer 5.5in (14cm) diam*

$40-60　　**BEV**

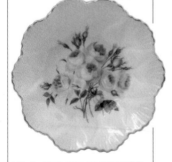

A Shelley Dainty shape nut or sweet dish, decorated with roses and a gilt rim.

4.25in (11cm) wide

$40-60　　**BAD**

CERAMICS

A Shelley Dainty shape rectangular dish, marked "Rd 272101".

5in (13cm) wide

$40-60 **BAD**

An unusual Shelley Ludlow shape handpainted nut dish, with geometric design similar to 'Sunray'.

c1930 *4in (10cm) wide*

$60-80 **BAD**

A CLOSER LOOK AT A SHELLEY FIGURINE

The style of this figure is typical of Attwell, with its rounded face, pudgy body, and bright, appealing colors.

These figures were produced for children as part of Mabel Lucie Attwell's range of nursery ware, which is popular with collectors today.

These figurines are rare – other charming characters can also be found

Like all her nursery ware, this piece is marked with Attwell's name, but beware of modern reproductions by considering marks, colors, and quality.

A Shelley Nursery 'I's Shy' figure, designed by Mabel Lucie Attwell, model no.LA.9, printed mark and facsimile signature.

6in (15.5cm) high

$2,000-3,000 **WW**

A Shelley lustered bowl, designed by Walter Slater.

Walter Slater took over from Frederick Rhead as Art Director in 1905 and remained until 1937, contributing many designs.

c1930 *9.5in (24cm) diam*

$400-500 **BEV**

A Shelley Harmony ware waisted vase, with dripping bands of orange and green.

The Harmony ware range was introduced in 1932. Even though it was molded, it was meant to give the impression of hand-thrown pieces. Drip and banded designs are typical.

c1932 *8.25in (21cm) high*

$200-300 **BEV**

A pair of 1930s Shelley Harmony ware vases, with streaked glaze effects in shades of green, gray, orange, and yellow.

8in (20.5cm) high

$150-200 **GORL**

A pair of 1930s Shelley Harmony ware vases, of waisted form.

4.75in (12cm) high

$100-150 **GORW**

A Shelley 'Groom' figure, designed by Mabel Lucie Attwell.

6in (15.5cm) high

$400-500 **WW**

CERAMICS

A CLOSER LOOK AT A WILLIAM DE MORGAN TILE

William de Morgan (1839-1917) was a prolific, pioneering member of the Arts & Crafts movement.

In 1888, de Morgan established his own pottery at Sands End, Fulham, where some of his finest works were produced.

A rare 1920s Batchelder salesman's tile sample board, with plain and decorated tiles mounted in a metal frame, stenciled "124, BATCHELDER TILES LOS ANGELES".

Successful American ceramicist and Arts & Crafts designer Ernest Batchelder (1875 - 1957) was perhaps best known for his ceramic tiles and coined the phrase "No two tiles are the same".

13.5in (34cm) high

$2,200-2,800   **DRA**

He was particularly well known for his tiles and specialized in their production from 1882.

This example shows de Morgan's typically rich shades of gold, ruby red, and greens.

A pair of William de Morgan tiles, from the early Fulham period and with Sands End Pottery impressed marks.

Each 6in (15cm) wide

$700-1,000   **GAZE**

A T. & R. Boote Art Nouveau-style green tile, with stylized curling leaf and flower decoration.

c1900   *5in (15cm) wide*

$50-70   **AGR**

A California tile table top, the two tiles painted with a scene after Cecil Aldin, mounted on a wrought-iron base, chip to one edge of one and hairline from one to the other.

16.5in (42cm) wide

$280-320   **DRA**

An early 1960s printed tile, designed by Dorin Court, from the 'Rustic Peasants' series, on a Carter blank.

The humor, monochromatic design and style is similar to that of Danish designer Bjørn Wiinblad.

5in (15cm) wide

$20-30   **AGR**

A rare William de Morgan 'Persian' tile, small chip to edge.

6in (16cm) wide

$400-600   **PSA**

A 1950s polychrome stencil printed tile, by Dunsmore, decorated with a lamb, on a Minton blank.

5in (15cm) wide

$30-50   **AGR**

A Minton Hollins handpainted tile, decorated with a design by W.B. Simpson.

c1885   *8in (20cm) wide*

$220-280   **AGR**

A Minton 'Stag & Doe in Pasture' pattern tile, designed by William Wise, from the 'Animals of the Farm' series.

Three Mosaic nursery rhyme-themed tiles, decorated in cuerda seca, mounted in a Arts & Crafts frame, stamped marks.

Roughly translating as 'dry rope', the cuerda seca method outlines the decoration with a mixture of manganese and grease to prevent the different colored glazes mixing.

A 1950s Packard & Ord 'Pilgrim's Progress' handpainted tile.

c1879   5in (15cm) wide

Each 4.5in (11.5cm) wide

4.25in (10.5cm) wide

$100-150   **AGR**

$700-1,000   **DRA**

$25-35   **AGR**

A Packard & Ord 'King Lear' handpainted tile, designed by R. Leeper, from the 'Shakespearean Characters' series, on a Pilkington blank.

The small monogram in the bottom right identifies this as Packard & Ord.

A Poole Pottery Carter tile, depicting rabbits and grass, in a decorative frame.

A set of four Poole Pottery Carter tiles, designed by Cecil Aldin and featuring four different designs of dogs, in original box.

c1953   5in (15cm) wide

c1953

$30-50   **AGR**

$50-80   **C**

$220-280   **C**

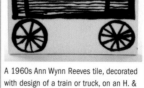

A 1960s Ann Wynn Reeves tile, decorated with a design of chairs, on an H.&R. Johnson blank.

A 1960s Ann Wynn Reeves tile, decorated with design of a train or truck, on an H. & R. Johnson blank.

A 1950s Richards tile, screen-printed with a 'Homemaker' style design.

This pattern was inspired by the success of Ridgway's Homemaker pattern. The design is subtly different and the printing is of poorer quality and is over, rather than under, the glaze as is found on Homemaker.

5in (15cm) wide

5in (15cm) wide

5in (15cm) wide

$35-45   **AGR**

$35-45   **AGR**

$25-35   **AGR**

A CLOSER LOOK AT A SET OF WEDGWOOD TILES

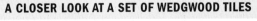

As well as the polychrome versions seen here, this series was also produced in monochrome browns and blues.

The tiles were designed by Thomas Allen, who oversaw Wedgwood's tile production in the late 19thC.

A 1950s polychrome stencil printed tile, designed by E.E. Strickland in the 1920s, with a scene of rabbits from the 'Farmyard' series, on a Carter blank.

5in (15cm) wide

$50-80 **AGR**

A 1950s polychrome stencil tile, designed by Reginald Till, from the 'English Countryside' series, on a Carter blank.

5in (15cm) wide

$70-100 **AGR**

A set of 12 tiles were designed for the series.

This tile was made using the dust-pressed method, patented by William Boulton in 1863. It used dust clay that was pressed into one or more copper plates perforated with the desired pattern.

Four Josiah Wedgwood, Etruria tiles, with scenes from Shakespeare's 'A Midsummer Night's Dream', including Puck, Bottom, Lysander and Hermia, marked "65413" in ink of the reverse.

c1880-90 *Each 6in (15cm) wide*

$800-1,200 **GAZE**

A Villeroy & Bosch 'Acapulco' pattern tile trivet.

8in (20.5cm) wide

$30-40 **GROB**

A Wedgwood 'Old English' tile, designed by Helen J.A. Miles, with underglaze dust pressed technique print of the 'April' scene from the 'Months' series.

c1890 *5in (15cm) wide*

$150-200 **AGR**

A Wedgwood tile, decorated in slip with a patent impressed technique, the floral and foliate pattern on a cream ground numbered "R2738" on the reverse.

c1880 *5in (15cm) wide*

$40-60 **AGR**

A 1960s Italian printed tile, of a stylized teenager's head.

This pattern is usually found on dressing table sets.

6in (15.5cm) wide

$20-25 **GROB**

CERAMICS

COLLECTORS' NOTES

■ Artus Van Briggle (1869-1904) joined Rookwood as decorator in 1887. The company sent him to study in Paris for three years to expand his education.

■ In 1899, tuberculosis forced him and his wife, Anne, to move to Colorado Springs where they established their own pottery.

■ There they produced slip-cast pieces with typically organic shapes, featuring flower petals and leaves. Figural pieces are less common, although his signature piece, 'Lorelei' depicts a woman draped around the neck of a vase.

■ He also worked on perfecting his hallmark matt glazes that had been inspired by the Ming Dynasty pottery he has studied in Paris.

■ Van Briggle died in 1904 and his wife continued running the company until 1912 when it was sold. The company still exists today.

■ The best quality and most desirable pieces were made c1902-04 when Artus was alive and in charge of production. Pieces produced until 1912 under his wife's direction are also sought-after.

A Van Briggle vase, in Ming turquoise glaze, marked "Van Briggle" with logo, "Colo Spgs Co", finisher's initials "GP" and esoteric markings.

10.5in (26.5cm) high

$120-180 **BEL**

A Van Briggle 'Lorelei' vase, in Ming turquoise, marked with logo, "Van Briggle, Colo Spgs Co", finisher's initials "DR" and esoteric markings.

11in (29cm) high

$280-320 **BEL**

A Van Briggle vase, with three Indian faces, marked with logo, "Van Briggle, Colorado Springs Co", finisher's initials "HVM" and esoteric markings.

12in (30.5cm) high

$200-300 **BEL**

A Van Briggle floor vase, with yucca floral decoration in a Persian Rose glaze, marked with logo, "Van Briggle, Colo Spgs Colorado", finisher's initials "BWL" and "VB100".

17.5in (44.5cm) high

$250-300 **BEL**

A Van Briggle massive stoneware lion, probably hand-molded, with a red flambé-like glaze, unmarked.

21in (53.5cm) long

$250-350 **BEL**

A Van Briggle floor vase, with three nudes encircling the body, marked "Van Briggle" with logo, "Colorado Spgs, Colorado", finisher's initials "GP" and esoteric markings.

16.75in (42.5cm) high

$300-400 **BEL**

A pair of Van Briggle bowls, in Persian Rose glaze, marked "Van Briggle" with logo, "Colo. Spgs".

5.75in (14.5cm) long

$40-60 **BEL**

A pair of Van Briggle double-candleholders, in Persian Rose glaze, marked "Van Briggle" with logo, "Colo Spgs".

4.5in (11.5cm) high

$30-50 **BEL**

A J.H. Cope & Co. wall mask, of a lady in a large feathered hat.

c1934   *12in (30.5cm) wide*

$280-320   **BEV**

A rare Royal Doulton 'Jester' wall pocket, D6111, designed by Charles Noke.

c1940-41

$1,000-1,500   **PSA**

A 1950s Austrian 'Keramic' Art Deco mask.

      8.5in (21.5cm) high

$150-200   **GEW**

A CLOSER LOOK AT A WALL POCKET

Royal Doulton wall pockets are generally hard to find, 'Old Charley' is a particularly scarce example.

Wall pockets were only produced for a short amount of time during WWII, which would account for their limited production.

'Old Charley' was designed by Charles Noke, who is well known for his reintroduction of figurines to the Royal Doulton range.

This is the only known colorway for this wall mask.

A rare Royal Doulton 'Old Charley' wall pocket, D6110, designed by Charles Noke.

c1940-41   *7.25in (18.5cm) high*

$1,200-1,800   **PSA**

A small Goebel pottery wall mask of a young woman, with blonde hair, very small chip to base.

      5in (12.5cm) long

$80-120   **CA**

A rare Goldscheider wall mask.

c1925-8   *8.5in (21.5cm) high*

$1,200-1,800   **SCG**

A 1930s Czech Art Deco wall mask, of Marlene Dietrich.

      8in (20.5cm) high

$280-320   **GEW**

A German pottery mask, the stylized face with craquelure glaze, unmarked.

6in (15.5cm) high

$280-320   **WW**

COLLECTORS' NOTES

■ Founded in 1871 in Fultonham, Ohio, Samuel A. Weller began by producing flower pots, jardinières and other everyday earthenwares. Expanding rapidly, he moved to Zanesville in 1888. In 1894, he acquired the Lonhuda art pottery and began producing hand painted art pottery known as 'Louwelsa'.

■ Competing against Rookwood and Roseville, he introduced other art pottery lines, many similar to their production. He aimed to produce fine art pottery on a commercial basis with affordable prices. Like his competitors, Weller employed a number of noted designers such as Frederick Rhead and Frank Ferrell.

■ By 1906, prestigious hand-painted ranges, such as Eocean, Etna and Aurelian, that are popular with collectors today, were being produced. In the early 1920s, a range of production line pottery was introduced alongside the growing number of more prestigious ranges, which now included Hudson and

LaSa. Weller died in 1925, leaving one of the largest pottery factories in the US.

■ The Depression affected the company seriously and by 1935 they had abandoned hand-painted decoration to focus on more inexpensive molded ranges. Many looked like, and were made to compete with, Roseville ranges, but were neither of as fine quality nor as successful. In 1948, after the war, the factory closed.

■ Look out for early hand-decorated ranges produced around the early 1900s such as Dickens, Eocean, Hudson, Aurelian and Sicardo. Artist-signed pieces, large examples and those that are glazed well will fetch higher prices. Damage and crazing affects prices seriously, reducing them by around 50 percent.

■ Damage also affects the later molded wares, often more seriously, as they were produced on an even larger scale. Look for designs that incorporate animals, as these are generally more popular.

A Weller 'Louwelsa' lobed squat jug, with floral decoration, marked with Weller Louwelsa circular stamp and "X519", with darkened crazing.

5.75in (14.5cm) wide

$100-150 BEL

A Weller 'Louwelsa' squat ewer, with clover decoration, marked "Weller Louwelsa X73", some small glaze flakes to the rim of the ewer.

5.5in (14cm) wide

$70-100 BEL

A Weller 'Louwelsa' squat jug, with open rose decoration, marked "Weller Louwelsa 423".

4.5in (11.5cm) wide

$100-150 BEL

A Weller 'Louwelsa' ewer, with floral decoration, marked with Weller Louwelsa circular stamp and "487", glaze flake from the rim.

6.25in (16cm) high

$100-150 BEL

A Weller 'Louwelsa' large vase, with heavy slip decoration, signed "McLaughlin" on the rear, faintly stamped on the base.

'Louwelsa', named after LOUisa (his daughter), WELler (the name of the business) and SA (Weller's initials) was one of his most popular lines and was made in over 500 shapes.

11in (28cm) high

$250-350 BEL

A Standard Glaze cylinder vase, probably Weller 'Louwelsa', with floral decoration, unmarked, restored hairlines to rim and scratches to the glaze.

8.5in (21.5cm) high

$70-100 BEL

A Weller 'Hudson' bulbous vase, by Hester Pillsbury, with flared rim and footed base, marked "Weller" in script and signed "HP" at the base.

10.75in (27.5cm) high

$700-1,000 **BEL**

A CLOSER LOOK AT A WELLER VASE

At over 18in high, this vase is larger than most examples and was made to stand on the floor.

The decoration is hand-painted and is of good quality, but it is not by a noted painter or signed.

The design of birds on a vine is an attractive and more unusual feature.

This vase is from the Hudson range, which is one of the most popular Weller ranges and was developed in the late 1910s to the early 1920s.

A Weller 'Hudson' floor vase, marked "WELLER" in the base, rim restored.

This piece could have been worth about 50 per cent more if the rim had not been restored.

18.5in (47cm) high

$2,200-2,800 **BEL**

A Weller 'Hudson' vase, by Hester Pillsbury, marked "A Weller" in script on the base and signed "HP" near the bottom on the rear of the vase.

10in (25.5cm) high

$1,200-1,800 **BEL**

A Weller 'Hudson' double-handled vase, marked "A Weller Pottery" by hand on the base and signed "Pillsbury", handles professionally restored.

9.75in (25cm) high

$250-350 **BEL**

A Weller 'Hudson' tall vase, marked "WELLER", professionally restored drill hole to the base.

12in (30.5cm) high

$550-650 **BEL**

A Weller 'Hudson' vase, by Claude Leffler, signed "C Leffler" at the base, unmarked, restoration to drill hole in base and fine all-over crazing.

12.25in (31cm) high

$550-650 **BEL**

A Weller 'Hudson' vase, by Dorothy England, marked "A Weller" in block and signed "England" at the base.

8in (20cm) high

$750-850 **BEL**

A Weller 'Hudson' vase, by Sarah Timberlake, marked "Weller Pottery" in script and signed "S.T." at the base, restored chip to rim and some factory glaze flakes at base.

10.75in (27.5cm) high

$300-400 **BEL**

A Weller 'Tutone' vase, marked with Weller Pottery full kiln stamp.

6.75in (17cm) high

$120-180 **BEL**

A Weller 'Tutone' vase, marked with partial Weller Pottery half kiln stamp.

6in (15cm) high

$90-100 **BEL**

A Weller 'Tutone' vase, marked with Weller Pottery half kiln stamp, factory glaze pop at foot of base.

12.75in (32.5cm) high

$200-300 **BEL**

A Weller 'Tutone' triangular vase, unmarked, two corners of base have glaze abrasions.

9in (23cm) high

$120-180 **BEL**

A Weller 'Tutone' vase, marked with a partial Weller Pottery half-kiln stamp.

6in (15cm) high

$70-100 **BEL**

A Weller 'Tutone' vase, marked with Weller Tutone Ware paper label.

7.75in (19.5cm) high

$250-350 **BEL**

A Weller 'Tutone' basket, marked with Weller Pottery half kiln stamp.

5.75in (14.5cm) high

$80-120 **BEL**

A Weller 'Tutone' open-handled basket, unmarked.

7.5in (19cm) high

$150-200 **BEL**

A Weller 'Tutone' rectangular planter, marked with Weller Pottery kiln stamp, some skips to the color along edges.

7in (18cm) wide

$70-100 **BEL**

A Weller green 'Marvo' double-bud gate vase, marked with Weller Ware stamp and Weller Marvo Ware label.

8.25in (21cm) wide

$120-180 BEL

A Weller green 'Marvo' log planter, unmarked.

10in (25.5cm) long

$50-80 BEL

A Weller green 'Marvo' vase, marked with Weller Pottery full kiln stamp.

7in (18cm) high

$120-180 BEL

A Weller 'Marvo' flared trumpet vase, marked with Weller Ware stamp, with some darkened crazing.

11.5in (29cm) high

$150-200 BEL

A Weller 'Marvo' vase, with very heavily embossed leaves in tan and green, unmarked, with factory firing line at the base.

9in (23cm) high

$120-180 BEL

A Weller 'Marvo' jardinière, in tan with green highlights, unmarked, unobtrusive lines at the rim.

8in (20cm) wide

$70-100 BEL

A Weller 'Forest' jardinière, unmarked.

6.5in (16.5cm) wide

$220-280 BEL

A Weller 'Woodcraft' wall pocket, unmarked, outer ear repaired.

'Woodcraft' is one of Weller's most popular molded production ranges.

10in (25.5cm) high

$180-220 BEL

A Weller 'Flemish' tall vase, with apples on a wood-like background, unmarked.

13in (33cm) high

$200-300 BEL

CERAMICS

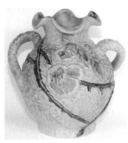

A Weller 'Silvertone' floral vase, with ruffle rim and curving handles, marked with Weller Pottery full kiln stamp, unobtrusive bruise to foot.

8.25in (21cm) high

$180-220 BEL

A Weller 'Silvertone' vase, with grapes on vines with leaves, marked with Weller Pottery half kiln stamp.

6.5in (16.5cm) high

$250-350 BEL

A Weller 'Silvertone' fan vase, with floral decoration, marked with Weller Ware stamp.

8in (20cm) wide

$220-280 BEL

A Weller 'Silvertone' vase, with two squared handles, marked with Weller Ware stamp.

10in (25.5cm) high

$280-320 BEL

A Weller blue 'Delsa' vase, with oak leaves and acorns, marked "Weller Pottery Since 1872".

12in (30.5cm) high

$180-220 BEL

A Weller 'Flemish' hanging basket, marked with Weller Pottery half kiln stamp.

3.5in (9cm) high

$180-220 BEL

FIND OUT MORE...

Collectors Encyclopedia of Weller Pottery, by Sharon & Bob Huxford, published by Collector Books, 1979.

Zane Gray Museum, Zanesville, OH, where Weller's 'largest vase in the world' is on display. A 7ft high 'Aurelian' vase, it was made for the 1904 St Louis Exposition and could fetch well over $250,000 today.

A CLOSER LOOK AT AN EOCEAN VASE

This is unusually large for Weller. Large pieces of Late Line are very rarely found.

It is even rarer to find a large piece of Late Line signed by the artist.

The hand-painted design is typically painted in slip relief.

A Weller Late Line 'Eocean' floor vase, artist signed by Sarah Timberlake, appears unmarked, restoration to drill hole in base may cover up any markings, glaze skip at the base.

The design is signed "S.T" showing it is by Sarah Timberlake, a noted Weller artist.

17.5in (44.5cm) high

$800-1,200 BEL

A Royal Worcester large ovoid vase, with scroll side handles, decorated with flowers on a blush ground, shape '1969'.

c1899   12in (30.5cm) high

$600-900   **WW**

A Royal Worcester globular vase, with a molded mouth, the body decorated with flowers on an ivory ground, puce mark.

c1884   9in (23cm) high

$400-600   **WW**

A CLOSER LOOK AT A ROYAL WORCESTER DINNER SERVICE

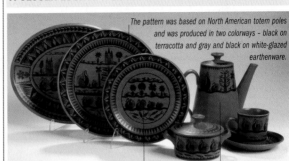

The pattern was based on North American totem poles and was produced in two colorways - black on terracotta and gray and black on white-glazed earthenware.

Royal Worcester commissioned artist Robert 'Scottie' Wilson (1890-1972) to design this dinner service pattern in the early 1960s.

He is well known for his Primitive Style of art featuring stylized floral and fauna and his work was owned by Pablo Picasso. It is also included in the Tate Gallery and the Metropolitan Museum, New York.

Perhaps due to its high cost, the pattern was unsuccessful and was retired in 1965. The design, however, was much admired and it has become a popular with collectors on both sides of the Atlantic.

An early 1960s Royal Worcester 'Cheltenham' pattern part tea, coffee and dinner service, designed by Scottie Wilson, approximately 90 pieces, printed factory marks.

$2,800-3,200   **L&T**

A Grainger & Co. Worcester globular vase, painted with a blue tit on gilded branches.

2.5in (6.5cm) high

$280-320   **SAS**

A Royal Worcester pot pourri centerpiece, of Etruscan shape, on pedestal base, date code.

1895   10in (25.5cm) diam

$350-450   **GORL**

A Royal Worcester centerpiece shell dish, with scalloped rim, on entwined dolphin stem, date code.

1878
                           8.25in (21cm) wide

$280-320   **GORL**

A pair of trumpet vases, after Royal Worcester, each painted with a similar large floral spray, sprigs and an insect against a pale yellow ground.

7.75in (19.5cm) high

$220-380   **GORL**

A CLOSER LOOK AT A ROYAL WORCESTER CANDLE EXTINGUISHER

Royal Worcester have almost continuously produced candle extinguishers since 1850. This particular snuffer was introduced in the 1870s.

With the advent of electricity at the end of the 19thC, snuffers began to become obsolete and later examples were produced for decoration rather than function.

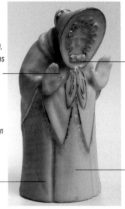

Snuffers were usually available singularly or as a pair, often with a matching stand. They are often decorative and amusing.

Despite heavy use, the vulnerable hands and hat rim have survived in good condition with no damage. This increases the desirability.

A Royal Worcester 'Blue Lagoon' conical candle extinguisher, boxed.

c2001   3.25in (8.5cm) high

$50-70   **GAZE**

A Royal Worcester blush ivory 'Granny Snow' candle extinguisher.

This model was produced in cream-colored Parian as well as this blush and was available in two sizes.

c1903   3in (7.5cm) high

$400-600   **GCL**

A Royal Worcester blush ivory 'The Monk' candle snuffer.

c1899   4in (10cm) high

$300-400   **GCL**

A Royal Worcester 'India' figure, by Freda G. Doughty, no.3071.

Doughty worked as a modeler at Royal Worcester from 1930 to 1963 and is best known for her models of children, often based on those she knew. Although considered old fashioned by some, her designs were extremely popular with the public and were produced for a long period of time.

3.25in (8cm) high

$280-320   **WW**

A Royal Worcester 'Friday's Child' porcelain figurine, modeled by Freda G. Doughty, no.RW3261.

c1950   7in (18cm) high

$280-320   **DN**

A Royal Worcester 'Thursday's Child' porcelain figurine, modeled by Freda G. Doughty, no.RW3260.

6.5in (16.5cm) high

$280-320   **DN**

Two Royal Worcester figures, 'Monday's Child' and 'Saturday's Child', modeled by Freda G. Doughty, hairline crack to first, with printed marks.

$150-200   **WW**

FIND OUT MORE...

Royal Worcester Figurines, *by Anthony Cast, John Edwards, published by Charlton Press, February, 2005.*

An Alpine Pottery hand-decorated vase, by Lori Hammer, marked with "Alpine Pottery Roseville Ohio 2002" ink stamp and signed by the artist.

2002   14.75in (37.5cm) high

$50-80   **BEL**

An American Terra Cotta Co. flower basket doorstop, a few hairlines and small chips, stamped "1925".

1925   6.25in (15.5cm) wide

$280-320   **DRA**

A Burley Winter vase, with blue and purple semi-matte glaze, marked "8" on the base with a small circular guide for un-drilled hole.

12in (30.5cm) high

$200-300   **BEL**

A rare Denver Denaura squat vase, embossed with violets, two small nicks to shoulder, stamped "Denaura" with shield, "184".

5.25in (13.5cm) wide

$1,500-2,000   **DRA**

A Tim Eberhardt vase, marked "Tim Eberhardt St. Louis 4-1-02 #595".

Tim Eberhardt (b.1948) runs a one-man studio pottery working in the spirit of 19thC and 20thC art potters and is based in St Louis. His high-fired porcelain and stoneware vases and bowls are painted with patterns inspired by nature, with Eberhardt seeing himself as much a painter as a potter. He devoted himself to pots in 1993 and his early work can fetch high prices on the secondary market. He often dedicates work to buyers in pen inscriptions on the base.

2002   8.5in (21.5cm) high

$350-450   **BEL**

A Chicago Crucible bud vase, covered in a fine, frothy blue-green and amber glaze, unmarked.

8in (20cm) high

$300-400   **DRA**

A Tim Eberhardt board vase, marked "Tim Eberhardt #644 St. Louis 5-22-02", with a dedication to the buyer.

2002   9.25in (23.5cm) high

$300-400   **BEL**

A Tim Eberhardt vase, depicting four pink peonies, marked "Tim Eberhardt St. Louis 6-5-98".

1998   8.25in (21cm) high

$220-280   **BEL**

A Tim Eberhardt squat vase, covered with hand-carved roses, marked on the base "Tim Eberhardt St. Louis 6-17-99".

1999   6in (15cm) wide

$70-100   **BEL**

CERAMICS

A Tim Eberhardt vase, marked "Tim Eberhardt St. Louis 6-21-'99", with dedication to buyer in pen on the base, uncrazed.

1999   10in (25.5cm) high

$150-200   **BEL**

A limited edition Art Nouveau vase, made by Frankoma to a Gerald Smith design, from an edition of 600, marked "Frankoma GS 50", signed by Gerald Smith in ink.

11.25in (28.5cm) high

$250-300   **BEL**

A Grueby bottle-shaped vase, carved by Gertrude Priest, Grueby Pottery circular stamp and artist cipher.

6.75in (17cm)

$1,200-1,800   **DRA**

A Jugtown squat vessel, covered in Chinese Blue glaze, stamped "Jugtown Ware".

6.5in (16cm) wide

$300-400   **DRA**

A unique Logan Pottery bulldog, incised "D.K.G." and "1940" on the base with "Lena Glass" written in ink.

8.75in (22cm) high

$350-450   **BEL**

A CLOSER LOOK AT A GILHOOLY SCULPTURE

David Gilhooly (b.1943) is an innovative and noted Canadian potter – his works can be found in many museums and public collections around the world.

Some of his first frog pieces explored Pre-Christian, Christian, Greek, Roman, and Egyptian themes – he returned to this Egyptian theme later on.

He began work in earnest on his famous 'FrogWorld' collection in 1969 – this is an early piece from the range, dating from 1970.

It is decorated in modern, bright colors, a typical hallmark of his work which also appeals to children, many of whom have become collectors as adults.

A David Gilhooly glazed ceramic sarcophagus, in two halves, incised "GILHOOLY 70".

1970   28.5in (71cm) long

$2,800-3,200   **FRE**

A Marblehead circular trivet tile, decorated in cuerda seca, small chip, abrasion around rim and flat chip to back.

Marblehead was founded near Boston in 1904 and closed in 1936, remaining a small company for its short lifetime. Ship motifs were commonly used in tiles and trivets during the 1920s/30s, but were primarily embossed in blue and white. The cuerda seca technique, coloring, typical 'misty' effect and shape makes this more valuable.

6in (15cm) diam

$1,500-2,000   **DRA**

A McCoy Loy-Nel-Art vase, marked "02" on the base, some unobtrusive flakes and glaze scratches throughout.

In 1899 James W. McCoy founded the J.W. McCoy Pottery in Roseville, Ohio. The Loy-Nel-Art range is reminiscent of Rookwood's Standard Glaze, Roseville's Rozane range and Weller's Louwelsa line.

$150-250   **BEL**

A McCoy Loy-Nel-Art standard glaze vase, marked "05" on the base, small repair and bruise to rim.

6.25in (16cm) high

$80-120   **BEL**

A McCoy Loy-Nel-Art standard glaze vase, with flowers, unmarked, some unobtrusive scratches to the glaze.

10.5in (26.5cm) high

$180-220   **BEL**

A McCoy stein, the back with "J" and "M" in gold, the base incised "6029 MCP USA" with the McCoy logo, the base signed in gold "Lei' & Nandy Cannon April 24, '71", some wear to gold trim.

This was possibly a wedding present to the Cannons' and could be a unique design.

8.25in (20cm) high

$70-100   **BEL**

A Mosaic Tile Company tray, with a wire hair fox terrier, marked "Mosaic" and "The Mosaic Tile Co. Zanesville Ohio New York NY" on the base, tail repaired and factory firing line to the underside.

5.5in (14cm) high

$100-150   **BEL**

A Merrimac low bowl, a couple minute glaze flakes to inner rim, stamped "Merrimac" with fish mark.

7in (17.5cm) wide

$450-550   **DRA**

A Mosaic Tile Company pin tray, marked on the base "The Mosaic Tile Co. Zanesville O & New York NY" with the "MTC" logo.

8in (20cm) long

$180-220   **BEL**

CERAMICS

A Nicodemus bowl, with stylized pattern of rope around the rim, marked "Nicodemus" on the base.

4.25in (11cm) wide

$100-150   **BEL**

A Niloak Mission Ware vase, stamped "Niloak".

The Niloak Pottery was founded in 1909 in Benton, Arkansas.

$400-500   **DRA**

A North Carolina urn, several nicks and glaze flakes, unmarked.

9in (22.5cm) high

$220-280   **DRA**

A George Ohr log cabin novelty, of unglazed white clay, marked "Geo. E. Ohr Biloxi Miss".

2.25in (6cm) high

$1,000-1,500   **DRA**

A George Ohr small squat vessel, with closed-in rim, script signature.

Known as the 'Mad Potter of Biloxi', George Ohr made his innovative and uniquely shaped pots from 1883 until 1907. A fire destroyed his pottery in 1890, leading to many examples being burnt – he called them his 'burnt babies'. His teapots, two-handled vases and vase forms with areas almost 'folded like fabric' are much sought after by collectors today.

5.75in (14.5cm) wide

$1,500-2,000   **DRA**

A Norweta rare pear-shaped vase, glaze flake to rim, stamped "NORWETA".

8.25in (20.5cm) high

$700-800   **DRA**

An attributed Owens Utopian tall vase, unmarked, tight line at rim and scratches to the glaze, small area of loose crazing on the rear of the vase.

15.25in (38.5cm) high

$250-350   **BEL**

A Owens Utopian tall vase, marked "Owens 012".

The Owens Pottery was founded in 1885, beginning its art pottery lines with the Utopian range in 1886. Art pottery production ceased in 1907 and the factory closed in 1929. The quality of their wares and the fact it won many awards at the time has led many to believe they are currently undervalued, especially when compared to more famous rivals such as Rookwood.

13in (33cm) high

$550-650   **BEL**

A McCoy Loy-Nel-Art standard glaze vase.

McCoy's pieces are often mistaken for Owens as they are so similar.

6.25in (16cm) high

$100-150   **BEL**

An Owens Utopian standard glaze mug, artist signed with a "W" below the decoration and "Owens Utopian 1033".

5in (12.5cm) high

$150-200   **BEL**

An attributed Pauline incised and gilded vase, with three-lobed opening, unmarked.

11.5in (29cm) high

$250-300   **DRA**

A Peters & Reed large standard ware vase, unmarked, unobtrusive scratches to the glaze.

12in (30.5cm) high

$120-180   **BEL**

A Pisgah Forest tall pitcher, grinding chip and small nick to rim, raised mark, dated.

1952   9.5in (24cm) high

$150-200   **DRA**

A Pisgah Forest baluster vase, stamped "Cameo Stephen".

5in (12.5cm) high

$180-220   **DRA**

A Poillon rare flaring vase, with two applied salamanders, two short interior surface Y-lines, stamped "CLP".

5.75in (14cm) wide

$350-450   **DRA**

A large American Albert Radford Pottery standard glaze jardinière, marked "207-12" on base, scratches to the glaze.

16in (40.5cm) wide

$250-350   **BEL**

An unusual Paul Revere baluster vase, dated, "PRP 8/20".

1920   5.75in (14cm) high

$300-400   **DRA**

CERAMICS

A Santa Barbara Ceramic Design lamp, marked "SBCD 4-81" and artist signature "AC" at the base.

10.5in (26.5cm) high

$150-250   **BEL**

A very large and unusual hand-decorated wall plaque, by Rick Wisecarver, signed "Rick Wisecarver 84" near the edge.

Painter and pottery artist Wisecarver is well known for his skilled and evocative portrayals of Native Americans.

1984   *18in (45.5cm) diam*

$500-600   **BEL**

A Rick Wisecarver portrait vase, signed "Rick Wisecarver" next to the portrait and marked "Wihoa's Hand Paint 1996 RS" on the base.

$350-450   **BEL**

A late 1930s Russel Wright 'American Modern' teapot, in the early 'Bean Brown' color.

10in (25.5cm) wide

$300-400   **MI**

A mid-1950s Russel Wright 'American Modern' cantaloupe creamer.

7in (18cm) high

$70-90   **MI**

A late 1930s Russel Wright 'American Modern' coral water pitcher, signed on base "Russel Wright mfg. by Steubenville".

11.25in (28.5cm) high

$80-120   **MI**

A 'Quick Meal' oval stove tile, attributed to Trent, crazing lines, small chips, unmarked.

3.5in (9cm) wide

$380-320   **DRA**

A Zanesville two-handled tall vase, line from rim, unmarked.

15.5in (38.5cm) high

$380-320   **DRA**

A 1950s Gundikins 'Popeye' plush and soft vinyl-headed doll, with card feet and original tag, signs of wear and discoloration.

9in (23cm) high

$30-50   **WAC**

A 1950s Gundikins 'Olive Oyl' plush and soft vinyl doll, with card feet, so she can stand, and original tag.

8.5in (21.5cm) high

$40-60   **WAC**

A CLOSER LOOK AT A POPEYE TOY

This toy was made by Louis Marx Toys, an American tinplate manufacturer and distributor known for their quality and detailing.

It was made between the 1930s and 40s, not long after Popeye's first appearance in the comic strip 'Thimble Theater' in 1929.

This is an early example of a Popeye toy, which is more desirable. It is in relatively good and complete condition.

The Popeye character has since been heavily merchandised, with Marx being responsible for many of the wind-up toys.

A 1930s/40s American Louis Marx 'Popeye' wind-up toy, carrying parrot cages at his side, fading and small abrasions to toy, mechanism working.

8.5in (21.50cm) high

$250-350   **JDJ**

A pair of Japanese Woolikin 'Popeye' and 'Olive' Oyl dolls, by F.W. Woolnough, with vinyl heads.

12.5in (32cm) high

$120-180   **SOTT**

A Gund Mfg. Co. 'Olive Oyl' hand puppet, with original bow.

9.75in (25cm) high

$30-50   **SOTT**

An Aladdin Industries 'Popeye' lunchbox and Thermos flask, with embossed detailing.

1980   *8in (20.5cm) wide*

$70-100   **STC**

A 'Popeye' lithographed tinplate dime register bank.

c1929-30   *2.5in (6.5cm) high*

$70-100   **SOTT**

A 1960s 'Official Batman Batplane' friction-powered plastic toy, marked "©National Periodical Publications Inc. 1976", boxed.

Box 5in (12.5cm) wide

$70-100 GAZE

An Aurora Comic Scenes 'Bat-Man' assembled model kit, marked "©1974 National Publications Inc".

$80-120 NOR

A 'Superman' 204-piece jigsaw puzzle, by APC.

c1974   5.5in (14cm) high

$15-20 BH

A 'Batman and Robin' Society Charter Member's pin, in original packaging.

c1966   3.25in (8.5cm) diam

$35-45 BH

A Toy Biz 'Superman' figurine, with Kryptonite ring that makes the figure fall over.

Superman figures are not common, especially those that are a good likeness.

c1989   10in (25.5cm) high

$70-100 NOR

A printed card packet of Mr. Bubbles 'Super Friends' bubble bath.

c1984   9.75in (25cm) high

$15-20 BH

A 'Super Friends' Thermos bottle, by Aladdin Industries.

6.5in (16.5cm) high

$10-15 BH

A 'Dudley Do-Right' printed glass, from the Pepsi Collector's Series.

5in (12.5cm) high

$7-10 BH

A 'Flub-a-Dub' soft vinyl and cloth hand puppet.

A character on the Howdy Doody show, Flub-a-Dub was an amalgamation of eight different animals. It is one of the hardest characters from the show to find.

9.5in (24cm) high

$50-70 SOTT

CHARACTER COLLECTIBLES

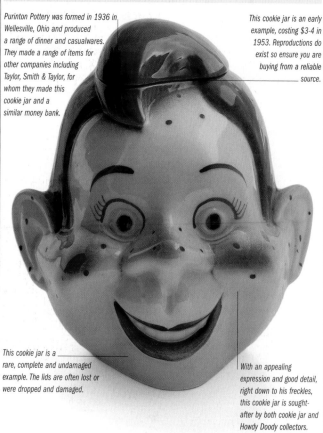

A CLOSER LOOK AT A HOWDY DOODY COOKIE JAR

Purinton Pottery was formed in 1936 in Wellesville, Ohio and produced a range of dinner and casualwares. They made a range of items for other companies including Taylor, Smith & Taylor, for whom they made this cookie jar and a similar money bank.

This cookie jar is an early example, costing $3-4 in 1953. Reproductions do exist so ensure you are buying from a reliable source.

This cookie jar is a rare, complete and undamaged example. The lids are often lost or were dropped and damaged.

With an appealing expression and good detail, right down to his freckles, this cookie jar is sought-after by both cookie jar and Howdy Doody collectors.

A very rare Howdy Doody cookie jar, by Purinton.

c1953   7.75in (19.5cm) high

$500-700   **SOTT**

A 1980s plastic 'Pac-Man' gum ball dispenser, by Superior Toy & Mfg Co.

5.75in (14.5cm) high

$20-30   **WAC**

An American Louis Marx 'Porky the Pig' wind-up tin toy, with vibrating action and spinning umbrella above, marked "USA. © 1939 Leon Schlesinger", soiling and abrasions.

c1939   8in (20cm) high

$180-220   **JDJ**

A Rocky printed glass, from the Pepsi Collector's Series.

5in (12.5cm) high

$7-10   **BH**

An Aladdin Character Kits 'Ronald McDonald – Sheriff of Cactus Canyon' lunchbox, with plastic flask.

c1982   8.25in (21cm) wide

$30-50   **NOR**

A 1970s Woody Woodpecker flashlight, by the Dyno Mdse. Corp.

3.5in (9cm) high

$15-20   **BH**

A Woodstock painted plaster nodder, marked "made in Korea".

c1972   3.75in (9.5cm) high

$30-50   **HH**

COLLECTORS' NOTES

■ Metal molds used to form chocolate into novelty or themed shapes began to be widely used from the late 1800s, growing in popularity and reaching their apex during the 1920s and 1930s. Makers at this time were centered in Germany, but also in France and the US. Use began to tail off during the 1950s.

■ Stamped numbers indicate the catalog number, enabling molds to be ordered from makers' catalogs. Makers included Anton Reiche of Dresden, H.Walter of Berlin, Sommet of Paris and Eppelsheimer of New York. Many molds are unmarked, but their style and manufacture can help to identify makers. Walter, for example, was the only maker that stamped its mold numbers inside the mold.

■ Some makers used a symbol, such as Sommet's stylised fish and Eppelsheimer's spinning top. Marked, and particularly dated, examples are more desirable in general. Materials can also help with dating. Tin-plated copper came first, used until the late 1890s, followed by tin-plated steel (the most commonly found material), and finally nickel-plated steel and nickel silver, both of which have a different feel and shiny silvery appearance.

■ Reiche is considered one of the best and most prolific mold makers. Founded in 1870, over 50,000 designs were produced. The company exported to the US via T.C Weygandt of New York, from 1885 until 1939, when WWII broke out. The factory was destroyed during the war, to re-open in Communist East Germany in 1950 and then to close finally in 1972.

■ Look for good levels of detail and large sizes. Popular themes include transport, characters and Christmas and Easter themes. Unusual details or forms can add value. Clips do not count towards value as they are never the original clips, which were interchanged by the original chocolatiers many times over.

An American Eppelsheimer tin-plated copper chocolate mold, no.8200, in the form of a bunny with a basket on his back.

It is the enormous size of this mold, the notable maker's name, marked date and its extreme rarity that make it this valuable. Used as a shop display piece, the eventual pure chocolate bunny would have weighed in at over 30lbs.

1937   37.5in (95cm) high

$18,000-22,000   **DF**

An early American Eppelsheimer tin-plated copper chocolate mold, no.4743.

Examine the edges for tell-tale copper brown coloring to recognize copper molds.

8.5in (21.5cm) high

$100-150   **DF**

An American Eppelsheimer chocolate mold, no.4723, of a standing bunny with a basket on his back.

8.5in (21.5cm) high

$80-120   **DF**

A German Anton Reiche standing rabbit chocolate mold, no.24458.

6.75in (17cm) high

$80-120   **DF**

A German Anton Reiche small seated rabbit chocolate mold, no.6770, with maker's mark.

3.25in (8.5cm) high

$30-50   **DF**

A German Anton Reiche seated bunny chocolate mold, no.26968.

1930   7in (18cm) high

$80-120   **DF**

A 1930s American Eppelsheimer standing bunny with basket chocolate mold, no.8192.

This mold also bears the stamp "Repaired Eppelsheimer & Co N.Y. Jan 1937". Note the bright tin-plated parts which help the chocolate come out of the mold easier.

6in (15cm) high

$70-100   DF

A rare German Anton Reiche bunny pushing a pram chocolate mold, no.21888S, with indistinct date stamp.

1926/36   5in (13cm) high

$220-280   DF

A rabbit playing a saxophone chocolate mold, no.9.

4.75in (12cm) high

$70-90   DF

A German Walter seated rabbit chocolate mold, no.1521.

Seated bunnies are the most commonly found mold shape.

5.5in (14cm) high

$60-80   DF

A German Walter bunnies around a basket chocolate mold, impressed inside the mold "5306".

6.25in (16cm) high

$280-320   DF

A rare rabbit riding on a dolphin chocolate mold, no.4005.

4.25in (11cm) high

$180-220   DF

A German Anton Reiche 'egg boat' chocolate mold, no.6399, with date mark.

1925   5.25in (13.5cm) long

$100-150   DF

A 1920s American Jaburg Bros. solid nickel silver chocolate mold.

5.25in (13.5cm) long

$60-80   DF

A German Anton Reiche double bunny and basket chocolate mold, no.25523, with date mark and Weygandt importers and date stamp.

This mold appears life-size in a 1930s Anton Reiche catalog.

1935   10.5in (27cm) wide

$350-450   DF

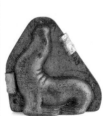

An unmarked cockerel chocolate mold, with chocolate remains.

The oils in the chocolate helped to preserve the mold. Today many collectors use mineral oil.

4.25in (11cm) high

$40-60 DF

A French Letang Fils stork chocolate mold, no.4209.

7.5in (19cm) high

$120-180 DF

A small seated cat chocolate mold, stamped "641" and "48".

3.25in (8cm) high

$60-80 DF

A German Anton Reiche seal chocolate mold, no.26483, with date stamp and additional indistinct French "Georges Diltoer Agent Générale" stamp.

1935   4.5in (11.5cm) high

$180-220 DF

A CLOSER LOOK AT A SOMMET CHOCOLATE MOLD

On Sommet molds, a figure in a diamond is the date mark – here it is "49" for 1949.

Sommet used a stylized fish or dolphin as their maker's mark.

This mold is large and has a 'lid' on the base showing that it could also be used for ice cream - this is borne out by the additional "1L" stamp.

Sommet were the only makers to have overlapping sides.

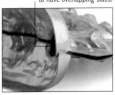

A French Sommet prancing horse chocolate and one litre ice cream mold, no.1436.

1949   9in (23cm) high

$450-550 DF

A French Letang Fils manta ray fish chocolate mold.

These brackets are typical of Letang who were the only maker to use them, even though they do not appear on all of their molds.

5.5in (14cm) long

$80-120 DF

An unusual four part tortoise chocolate mold.

The shell was molded separately from the base, which would then be filled with chocolates and served.

8.5in (21.5cm) long

$300-400 DF

An American Eppelsheimer standing Santa Claus chocolate mold, no.8003.

4.75in (12cm) high

$120-180   **DF**

A modern Chinese reproduction Santa Claus chocolate mold.

Compared to vintage molds, new molds use different materials, have no wear or makers' stamps, are lighter and display less detail.

4.75in (12cm) high

$3-5   **DF**

A standing Santa Claus in a long coat chocolate mold, no.171.

This is a common form for Santa but values can vary depending on the size and number and type of items he is holding.

7.75in (19.5cm) high

$180-220   **DF**

A small German standing Santa Claus in a long coat with clasped hands chocolate mold, unmarked.

4.25in (11cm) high

$100-150   **DF**

A German Anton Reiche standing Santa Claus in a short coat chocolate mold, no.21123S, with date stamp.

This more rounded, more American, form is another commonly found shape for Santa Claus.

1925   5in (12.5cm) high

$100-150   **DF**

A German Hornlein Santa Claus in a Jaguar chocolate mold, no.1013.

This amusing mold shape came in different sizes, like many chocolate molds.

11.75in (30cm) long

$350-450   **DF**

A German Walter 'Bad Boy' Santa Claus chocolate mold, no.131 or 180.

This is the less rare mold of the popular pair.

6.5in (16.5cm) high

$300-400   **DF**

A German Walter 'Good Girl' Santa Claus chocolate mold, stamped "Germany 180A".

This is much rarer than the 'Bad Boy' mold.

7in (17.5cm) high

$700-1,000   **DF**

A German Anton Reiche 'postcard' type chocolate mold, with Santa clutching a Christmas tree and sack, no. 519, with date stamp.

Look for fine details and complex scenes. Reproductions often have badly finished edges and less detail and are also not as inventive in subject matter.

1936   5.75in (14.5cm) high

$500-700   **DF**

An Anton Reiche for the American market 'W.C. Fields' chocolate mold, no. 25628.

5in (13cm) high

$200-300 DF

A Charlie Chaplin chocolate mold, no.17959.

6in (15.5cm) high

$180-220 DF

A German Walter for the American market Popeye mold, no.9034, with US distributor's stamping.

7.25in (18.5cm) high

$350-450 DF

A 1950s Dutch Vormenfabriek 'Puss in Boots' chocolate mold, no.16301, stamped "JKV Tilburg".

5in (13cm) high

$70-100 DF

A German Anton Reiche Felix the Cat chocolate mold, no.13006.

7in (13cm) high

$480-580 DF

A 1950s Dutch Vormenfabriek 'Donald Duck' chocolate mold, no.16358.

5in (13cm) high

$80-120 DF

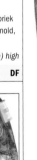

A German Anton Reiche 'Polly on the Potty' chocolate mold, no.16767, with date stamp.

1935

4.75in (12cm) high

$70-100 DF

A 1930s German Anton Reiche 'Mickey Mouse' mold, no.27396, with stamped maker's mark.

As licensing laws did not restrict European makers at this time, they were able to produce molds such as this.

3.25in (8cm) high

$300-500 DF

CHOCOLATE MOLDS

A German Anton Reiche sword in scabbard chocolate mold, no.10013.

14.75in (37.5cm) long

$150-200   **DF**

A large rifle chocolate mold, unmarked.

14.75in (37.5cm) long

$200-250   **DF**

A small key chocolate mold, stamped "5".

6.25in (16cm) long

$70-100   **DF**

A German Anton Reiche radio chocolate mold, no.28448, with date stamp.

1933   *3.5in (9cm) high*

$70-100   **DF**

A German Anton Reiche Halloween pumpkin chocolate mold, no.21836S, with date stamp.

1926   *3.25in (8.5cm) long*

$200-300   **DF**

A French 'Ets Metro Anvers' locomotive chocolate mold.

6.25in (16cm) long

$80-120   **DF**

A postwar Dutch Vormenfabriek fire engine chocolate mold, no.16247.

4in (10cm) long

$50-70   **DF**

A large German Anton Reiche 'Zeppelin' chocolate mold.

The exceptionally large size, rarity and popularity of the subject matter make this a valuable mold.

30.5in (78cm) long

$6,000-7,000   **DF**

FIND OUT MORE...

Chocolate Molds: A History & Encyclopedia, *by Judene Divone, Oakton Hills Publications, 1987.*

The Chocolate Mould, *by Henry & Laure Dorchy, 2000.*

Collectors' Guide to Antique Chocolate Molds, *by Wendy Mullen, published by Hobby House Press, 2002.*

COLLECTORS' NOTES

■ Coin collecting is the oldest of the numismatic fields. The sheer range of types available can seem daunting to a new collector.

■ It is advisable to concentrate on one area such as the ancient world, commemoratives, error coins, or examples from one specific period and place.

■ When buying commemorative issues, take the edition number into account. Those released in large numbers will appreciate less than strictly limited issues.

■ Beware of facsimile collectors coins, which are common. Although not necessarily made to deceive, it can be hard to tell them from the genuine article.

■ As condition is very important, coins should be handled as little as possible. Always hold coins by the edges, and invest in a good quality album and mounts to display and store your collection.

■ Resist the temptation to clean coins – collectors generally prefer coins with an 'original' appearance. Cleaning might reduce values by half or more.

A CLOSER LOOK AT A POST-TREATY NOBLE

The noble was initially introduced during the reign of Edward III. This is an early example from that period.

The coin was worth approximately 6s 8d. It is a high denomination, making it rarer than lower denominations.

The other side depicts Edward the III in a boat, rooting the noble in its historical context and adding appeal.

Although fairly difficult to come by, a hoard of around 130-140 nobles was found in Belgium around five years ago. This increased the number coming to market in the UK.

A post-treaty noble of Calais mint, minted by Edward III, with flag at stern, pellet at center and around fleurs-de-lys, extremely fine. *1327-44*

$2,200-2,800   **BLO**

A long cross Penny, minted by Aethelred II, extra pellet in one quarter and with usual Danegeld chopmarks, very fine condition. *978-1016*

$700-1,000   **BLO**

A quatrefoil-type penny of York, minted by Cnut, in very fine condition. *1016-35*

$300-500   **BLO**

A scarce penny of Winchester, minted by Edward the Confessor, facing right wearing a pelleted helmet, two small annulets in one quarter, in very fine condition. *1042-66*

$500-700   **BLO**

A rare class II groat of London, minted by Richard II, the reverse with bar above second 'N' of London, in very fine condition.

$1,000-1,500   **BLO**

A rosette-mascle issue groat of Calais, minted by Henry VI, the reverse with plain cross, toned and in extremely fine condition. *1422-26*

$400-600   **BLO**

A first bust crown, minted by William III, in very fine condition.

1695

$600-900 BLO

A scarce halfcrown, minted by Anne, with inverted 'A's for 'V's in edge legend, in extremely fine condition.

1713

$500-700 BLO

A half guinea, minted by George I, in extremely fine condition.

1719

$800-1,200 BLO

A 'young head' two guineas, minted by George II, in extremely fine condition.

1738

$1,800-2,200 BLO

A Bank of England dollar, minted by George III, in extremely fine condition.

1804

$220-280 BLO

A crown, minted by George III, attractive rainbow toning, in extremely fine condition.

1819

$300-400 BLO

A scarce 'young head' crown, minted by Victoria, with light hairlines, in extremely fine condition.

1847

$800-1,200 BLO

A scarce Gothic crown, minted by Victoria, inscribed "undecimo", in very fine condition.

1847

$2,200-2,800 BLO

A CLOSER LOOK AT A DUTCH GULDEN

The gulden has been struck by machine.

The coin has a rainbow sheen to the surface. Collectors favor good coloring as it is an indication that the coin has not been cleaned. A cleaned coin can be worth 50 percent less.

This is in remarkable condition for its age. It is one of the finest known examples to come to market.

The reverse depicts the coat of arms of William I of the Netherlands.

A rare Dutch gulden, virtually as struck with super rainbow tones and proof-like fields.

1820

$1,200-1,800   **BLO**

An American trade dollar, some light marks, in extremely fine condition.

1874

$220-280   **BLO**

An Australian shilling, in extremely fine condition.

1911

$120-180   **BLO**

A scarce Austrian thaler, of Vienna mint, as struck with attractive toning.

1829

$280-320   **BLO**

A rare 1800s Belgian gilt bronze franc, date indistinct, superb proof fields, with small toned area on reverse.

$120-180   **BLO**

A German States gulden, Baden, almost as struck, with light gray and rainbow tones.

1838

$120-180   **BLO**

An unusual Irish first Harp issue groat, minted by Henry VIII, with "H.I." for Henry and Jane Seymour, double-striking of obverse legend, in very fine condition.

1509-c1536

$120-180   **BLO**

COLLECTORS' NOTES

- Rarity and condition are crucial to value, the latter particularly so for people who collect for investment rather than for pleasure. The examples in this section are in particularly fine condition, as indicated by their high value.

- Independent third-party companies such as Comics Guaranty LLC will grade the condition of a comic for a fee. The lower the number the poorer the condition.

- The first issue of a title is usually the most desirable, with values dropping considerably even for the second issue. Other sought-after issues feature the first appearance, 'origin' or death of a character.

- Golden Age (1938-c1955) comics continue to be popular and are generally the most valuable, with Superman and Batman the most sought-after.

- Spider-Man is probably the most desirable Silver Age (c1956-c1969) character. Other Marvel titles of that period are currently more popular than titles from the other big publisher DC Comics.

- Comics continue to be a source of material for Hollywood and a number of films released in 2005 including: Batman Begins, Superman; and the Fantastic Four. This should increase interest in the original comics.

"The Amazing Spider-Man", No.5, Oct. 1963, published by Marvel Comics, near mint condition (9.4), off-white to white pages, with cover artwork by Steve Ditko, featuring an appearance by Dr. Doom.

$8,000-12,000   MC

"The Amazing Spider-Man", No.121, Jun. 1973, published by Marvel Comics, near mint condition (9.4), off-white to white pages, featuring the death of Gwen Stacey by the Green Goblin.

$800-1,200   MC

"The Amazing Spider-Man", No.100, near mint condition (9.4), off-white pages.

$600-900   MC

"Action Comics", No.2, Jul. 1938, published by DC Comics, very good to fair condition (5), off-white pages, with cover artwork by Leo E. O'Mealia, featuring the second appearance of Superman.

The number in brackets is the grading given by Comics Guaranty LLC (CGC) for this particular example.

$10,000-15,000   MC

"Adventure Comics", No.48, Mar. 1940, published by DC Comics, very fine condition (8), off-white to white pages, with cover artwork by Bernard Bailey, featuring the first appearance of Hourman.

$12,000-18,000   MC

"The Amazing Spider-Man", No.14, Jul. 1964, published by Marvel Comics, near mint condition (9.4), off-white to white pages, featuring the first appearance of the Green Goblin.

$7,000-10,000   MC

A CLOSER LOOK AT A COMIC

The All Star title was created for the first superhero group, The Justice Society of America.

The title changed to 'All Star Western' from the 58th issue and the Justice Society was retired.

The Green Lantern figure on the cover was cut-and-pasted from the cover of 'All American' comic, issue 16.

The dramatic cover artwork, with its bold use of color, makes this a striking example of a Golden Age comic.

"All Star Comics", No.2, Fall 1940, published by DC Comics, near mint condition (9.2), off-white to white pages.

$20,000-25,000   MC

"The Avengers", No.1, Sep. 1963, published by Marvel Comics, very fine condition (7.5), featuring the origin and first appearance of The Avengers.

$1,200-1,800 MC

"Batman", No.11, Jun/Jul 1942, published by DC Comics, very good to fair condition (5), off-white to white pages, featuring a classic Joker cover by Jerry Robinson.

$1,200-1,800 MC

"Batman", No.1, Spring 1940, published by DC Comics, very good condition (3.5), cream to off-white pages, featuring the origin of Batman and the first appearance of the Joker and Catwoman.

$10,000-15,000 MC

"Batman", No.20, Dec. 1943/Jan. 1944, published by DC Comics, very fine to near mint condition (9), off-white pages, featuring the first appearance of the Batmobile on the cover.

$2,200-2,800 MC

"Batman", No.3, Fall, 1940, published by DC Comics, very fine condition (8), off-white to white pages, featuring the first appearance of Catwoman in costume, with cover artwork by Bob Kane and Sheldon Moldoff.

$5,000-7,000 MC

"Captain America Comics", No.1, Mar. 1941, published by Marvel Comics, fine condition (6), featuring the origin and first appearance of Captain America, with cover artwork featuring Adolf Hitler by Joe Simon.

$7,000-10,000 MC

"Captain Marvel Jr.", No.29, Apr 1945, published by Fawcett Publications, mint condition (9.9), with double cover.

$8,000-12,000 MC

A CLOSER LOOK AT A DETECTIVE COMIC

Issue 27 of Detective Comic saw the first appearance of the ever popular Batman.

Despite the relatively poor condition of this example, its rarity makes it desirable in virtually any state.

'The Batman' was created by artist Bob Kane, who took inspiration from Zorro, Leonardo da Vinci, and the horror film 'The Bat-man', together with writer Bill Finger who is rarely credited.

"Detective Comics", No.27, May 1939, National Periodical Publications, good condition (2.5).

$30,000-40,000 MC

A CLOSER LOOK AT A FANTASTIC FOUR COMIC

The Fantastic Four was Marvel Comics answer to DC Comics popular superhero team, the Justice Society of America.

The team was created by legendary writer Stan Lee and artist Jack Kirby just as Lee was considering leaving the industry.

Unusually for the time, the Fantastic Four had no secret identities and, initially, often appeared without costume. They were also far from infallible and displayed very human traits, common with many of Lee's creations.

The latest film version of the franchise, due for released in 2005, is likely to increase interest in the comics.

"The Fantastic Four", No.1, Nov. 1961, published by Marvel Comics, very fine condition (8.5), off-white pages.

"Doctor Strange", No.169, Jun. 1968, published by Marvel Comics, near mint condition (9.6), white pages.

$700–1,000   MC | **$25,000–35,000**   MC

"The Human Torch", No.3, Winter 1940, published by Timely/Marvel Comics, very fine to near mint condition (9), off-white pages.

$7,000–10,000   MC

"The Fantastic Four", No.112, Jul. 1971, published by Marvel Comics, near mint condition (9.2), white pages, with date stamp to the front cover.

$280–320   MC

"The Fantastic Four", No.12, Mar. 1963, published by Marvel Comics, fine condition (6), off-white pages.

$500–700   MC

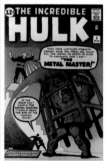

"The Incredible Hulk", No.1, May 1962, published by Marvel Comics, fine to very fine condition (7), off-white to white pages.

In this first issue, the Hulk is gray but due to printing problems, his color was changed to green in issue two, although the gray Hulk briefly appeared again later in the series.

$5,000–7,000   MC

"The Incredible Hulk", No.4, Nov. 1962, published by Marvel Comics, very fine condition (7.5), cream to off-white pages.

$700–1,000   MC

"The Incredible Hulk", No.6, Mar. 1963, published by Marvel Comics, very fine condition (8.5).

$1,800–2,200   MC

A CLOSER LOOK AT A MARVEL COMIC

This was the first and only issue of this title, which became Marvel Mystery Comics from issue two.

Most copies of this issue were over-printed with 'November'; this version retains the original 'October'.

It features the first proper appearance and origin of Namor, the Sub-Mariner and the first appearance of the Human Torch.

This example comes from the collection of Hollywood actor Nicolas Cage, a well-known comic book fan. This adds to the value.

"Marvel Comics", No.1, Oct. 1939, published by Timely Comics, very good to fair condition (5).

$40,000-60,000 MC

"The Silver Surfer", No.2, Oct. 1968, published by Marvel Comics, near mint condition (9.6), off-white to white pages.

$800-1,200 MC

"Superman", No.1, Summer, 1939, published by DC Comics, very fine condition (8), restored.

Superman gained his own title one year after his first appearance and was the first superhero to do so.

$20,000-30,000 MC

"Superman", No. 8, Jan./Feb. 1941, published by Marvel Comics, very fine condition, (7.5), cream pages.

$1,800-2,200 MC

"Tales of Suspense", No. 59, Nov. 1964, published by Marvel Comics, near mint condition (9.4), off-white to white pages, features Silver Age Captain America's first solo story.

$1,200-1,800 MC

"The X-Men", No.2, Nov. 1963, published by Marvel Comics, very fine condition (8.5), off-white pages.

$1,200-1,800 MC

"The X-Men", No.12, Jul. 1965, published by Marvel Comics, very fine condition (8.5), cream-off-white pages, featuring the origin of Professor X.

$280-320 MC

"X-Men Giant Size", No.1, Summer 1975, published by Marvel Comics, near mint condition (9.4), white pages, featuring the first appearance of the new X-Men lineup.

$1,200-1,800 MC

"Adventures Into Terror", No.10, Jun. 1950, published by Atlas Comics, near mint condition (9.2), white pages.

$500-700   MC

"Chamber of Chills", No.15, Jan 1953, published by Harvey Publications, near mint condition (9.4).

$700-1,000   MC

"Chilling Tales", No.13, Dec. 1952, Youthful Publications, very fine to near mint condition (9), with cover art by Matt Fox.

$800-1,200   MC

"The Crypt of Terror", No.18, Jun./Jul. 1950, published by E.C. Comics, very fine to near mint condition (9).

$1,800-2,200   MC

"Dark Mysteries", No.1, Jun./Jul. 1951, published by Master Publications, near mint condition (9.2), off-white pages.

$2,800-3,200   MC

"Dark Mysteries", No.16, Feb. 1954, published by Master/Merit Publications, very fine condition (8), off-white to white pages.

$500-700   MC

"The Haunt of Fear", No.6, Mar./Apr. 1951, published by Fawcett Publications, near mint condition (9.6).

$1,200-1,800   MC

"The Haunt of Fear", No.12, Apr. 1952, published by E.C. Comics, near mint condition (9.2).

$800-1,200   MC

"Fantastic Fears", No.7, May 1953, published by Ajax/Farrell Publications, very fine condition (8.5), off-white to white pages.

$600-900   MC

"Haunted Thrills", No.4, Dec. 1952, published by Ajax/Farrell Publications, very fine to near mint condition (9), white pages.

$700-1,000   **MC**

"Out of the Shadows", No.8, Apr. 1953, published by Standard Comics, very fine condition (8.5).

$800-1,200   **MC**

"Shock SuspenStories", No.8, Apr./May 1953, published by E.C. Comics, near mint condition (9.6).

$1,800-2,200   **MC**

"Strange Suspense Stories", No.1, Jun. 1952, Fawcett Publications, very fine to near mint condition (9).

$1,200-1,800   **MC**

A CLOSER LOOK AT A MARVEL COMIC

Whilst the popularity of superhero comics slumped in the 1950s, horror titles were in great demand.

E.C Comics, run by Will Gaines, produced some of the best horror comics of the period. Companies such as Star Publications, owned by L.B. Cole, also specialized in horror titles.

"Startling Terror Tales", No.11, Jul. 1952, published by Star Publications, near mint condition (9.2).

$5,000-7,000

This example has typically lurid and shocking cover artwork by owner, L.B. Cole, who believed a striking cover was more important than the content.

The horrific nature of these graphically illustrated comics contributed to the creation of the Comic Code Authority in 1954, which changed the industry as a whole.

    MC

"Tales From The Crypt", No.30, Jun./Jul. 1952, published by E.C. Comics, near mint condition (9.4), off-white pages.

$1,200-1,800   **MC**

"The Thing!", No.7, Aug. 1952, very fine condition (8), off-white pages.

$800-1,200   **MC**

"This Magazine is Haunted", No.7, Oct. 1952, published by Fawcett Publications, near mint condition (9.2), graded, white pages.

$1,200-1,800   **MC**

A CLOSER LOOK AT A SCI-FI COMIC

Planet Comics was the first original science fiction comic title released. Previous examples reused material from newspaper strips.

Issue one features the first appearance and origin of Auro, Lord of Jupiter.

"Planet Comics", No.1, Jan. 1940, published by Fiction House Magazines, near mint condition (9.4), off-white pages,

Provenance: From the collection of Nicolas Cage.

$35,000-50,000

The cover art work is by Lou Fine and acclaimed American comic artist Will Eisner.

Its provenance together with its extremely fine condition adds to the value of this rare comic.

MC

"Weird Fantasy", No.15, Sep./Oct. 1953, published by E.C. Comics, near mint condition (9.4).

$2,800-3,200   MC

"Weird Science", No.10, Nov./Dec. 1951, published by E.C. Comics, very fine to near mint condition (9).

$600-900   MC

"Weird Fantasy", No.9, Sep./Oct. 1951, published by E.C. Comics, near mint condition (9.2).

$700-1,000   MC

"Weird Science", No.19, May/Jun. 1953, published by E.C. Comics, near mint condition (9.4).

$1,800-2,200   MC

"Weird Science", No.20, Jul./Aug. 1953, published by E.C. Comics, near mint condition (9.4), white pages.

$1,800-2,200   MC

"Weird Science-Fantasy", No.29, Jun. 1955, published by E.C. Comics, near mint condition (9.4), off-white to white, featuring cover artwork by Frank Frazetta.

$7,000-10,000   MC

"Brenda Starr", Vol.2 No.8, May 1949, published by Superior Comics, near mint condition (9.2), off-white to white pages.

$2,200-2,800   **MC**

"Crimes By Women", No.1, Jun. 1948, published by Fox Features Syndicate, near mint condition (9.2), off-white to white, featuring the true story of Bonnie Parker (Bonnie and Clyde).

Crime comics of the late 1940s and 1950s often featured scenes of torture and violence against women. Many were cited in 'Seduction of the Innocent' by Fredric Wertham in 1953, which asserted that crime comics encouraged children to delinquency. The book contributed to the introduction of the Comic Code Authority in 1954.

$4,000-6,000   **MC**

"Crime Detective Comics", Vol.1 No.1, Mar. 1948, published by Miller Periodicals, near mint condition (9.6), off-white pages, featuring true police cases.

$1,200-1,800   **MC**

"Crime Does Not Pay", No.24, Nov. 1942, published by Comic House, very fine condition (8.5), off-white pages, featuring the first appearance of Mr. Crime.

$4,000-6,000   **MC**

"Detective Picture Stories", No.1, Dec. 1936, published by Comics Magazine Company, fine condition (6.5).

$2,800-3,200   **MC**

"Little Dot", No.1, Sep. 1953, published by Harvey Publications, very fine condition (7.5).

$3,000-4,000   **MC**

"Mad", No.4, Apr./May 1953, published by E.C. Comics, near mint condition (9.4), off-white to white pages.

$1,800-2,200   **MC**

"Mad", No.5, Jun./Jul. 1953, published by E.C. Comics, near mint condition (9.2).

$3,000-4,000   **MC**

"Sgt. Fury and His Howling Commandos", No.1, May 1963, published by Marvel Comics, fine condition (6.5), off-white to white pages.

$400-600   **MC**

FIND OUT MORE...

Official Overstreet Comic Book Price Guide, *by Robert M. Overstreet, published by House of Collectibles, 2004, 34th edition.*

COLLECTORS' NOTES

■ Vintage fashion is popular with both established collectors and casual buyers wanting to create an unusual look. Something can be found for every budget. Clothing made by the top fashion houses tends to attract the highest prices, but interesting and stylish items can be picked up for as little as $10.

■ An appealing area of collecting is 1960s fashion. Clothes often fall into one of two categories – the stark, geometric, space age look of Andre Courreges or the multicolored, ethnic, hippie style.

■ The 1970s saw a diversity of styles including highly patterned clothes inspired by ethnic and peasant dress, brightly colored spandex disco outfits and everyday wear such as tank tops and flares. Clothes by high profile designers, such as Ossie Clark and Yves Saint Laurent, are very desirable, as are unnamed pieces that are typical of the period, or sum up a specific look, such as late 1970s punk.

■ Clothes dating from the 1980s, once considered tasteless and hugely unfashionable, have again found favor with a rapidly increasing number of enthusiasts. Bold glitzy designs, 'power suits' and ra-ra skirts were all popular, as was newly fashionable sportswear by makers such as Nike. Labels were important to the style-conscious 1980s lady and items by well known designers also tend to command a premium today. Look out for Vivienne Westwood, Karl Lagerfeld, Georgio Armani, and Gianni Versace.

An early Ceil Chapman beaded and sequined black dress.

Ceil Chapman was one of a Marilyn Monroe's favorite designers.

$800-1,200   **SM**

A 1980s purple Contempo Casuals cotton and lycra dress, with rigid wired base, pulling in towards the legs.

The Contempo Casuals chain of over 200 stores became part of Wet Seal Inc (founded 1962) in 1995, as the 'forward looking' teen fashion sister brand to Wet Seal. In 2001, the brand disappeared with all stores being renamed Wet Seal. This dress retains its original price tag for $108, so would have been expensive in its day.

31in (79cm) long

$150-200   **NOR**

A CLOSER LOOK AT A GUNNE SAX DRESS

Gunne Sax of San Francisco made dresses to designs by Jessica McClintock, who joined in 1969.

The successful style launched many imitators, which are less desirable, as are Gunne Sax's designs from the 1980s onward.

Gunne Sax produced many successful and popular styles, including 'granny dresses', dresses inspired by Victorian and Edwardian styles, and prairie-style dresses like this one.

Cotton was a typical material, and beige and browns typical colors – both echo the roots of the revivalist style.

An early to mid-1970s Gunne Sax 'prairie' style dress, cotton with cotton lace detailing and string-like soutache detailing.

49.5in (126cm) long

$200-250   **NOR**

An Estelle of Jackson Heights, New York, couture dress, the flesh-colored silk catsuit covered with regular pieces of silver-colored fabric and diamanté set straps and neckline.

c1968   49.5in (126cm) long

$120-180   **NOR**

A 1960s/70s Lanvin polyester shift dress, with belt and geometric abstract print.

40.5in (103cm) long

$80-120   **NOR**

A Lanvin printed polyester chemise, with belt, in green, blue and black.

c1969   42in (107cm) long

$70-100   **NOR**

A CLOSER LOOK AT A JEANNE LANVIN PANTS DRESS

The shimmering exterior is made of silver-colored reflective fabric tape sewn into a woven wool form in horizontal bands.

The form and material exemplifies the 'space-age' look of the late 1960s championed by Andre Courreges, Pierre Cardin and Paco Rabanne, and inspired by man's ventures into outer space.

It has a white label reading 'Lanvin 22 Faubourg St Honore PARIS', meaning it may be an haute couture piece sold in the boutique and made to order.

It was designed by the house of Lanvin's designer at the time, Jules-Francois Crahay, who joined in 1963 and remained there until 1984.

A late 1960s Jeanne Lanvin sleeveless pants dress, with sleeveless coat ensemble, lined with beige wool felt.

51.25in (130cm) long

$500-700   **NOR**

An early 1970s Lanvin block-printed silk chemise, with belt.

Jeanne Lanvin (1867-1946) founded the first haute couture house in France in 1909. Her hallmark designs were the robes de style, with small waists and full skirts, based on 18thC designs. Numerous designers worked for the house, including Giorgio Armani.

42.5in (108cm) long

$100-150   **NOR**

A 1960s 'Waste Basket Boutique' polka dot disposable paper dress, by Mars of Asheville NC.

The Pop Art movement, led by Andy Warhol, led to the use of new materials such as paper. Aimed at being disposable, designs were mass produced and aimed at the mass market.

54in (137cm) long

$70-100   **NOR**

A Lilly Pulitzer 'The Lilly' pink and yellow sleeveless shift dress.

41in (104cm) long

$100-150   **NOR**

COSTUME & ACCESSORIES

A 1970s Lilly Pulitzer 'The Lilly' blue printed floral cotton sleeveless dress, with applied knitted cotton flowers.

39.75in (101cm) long

$50-80   **NOR**

A CLOSER LOOK AT A LILLY PULITZER DRESS

Her name is always incorporated into the design of authentic examples

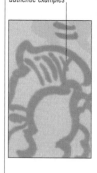

Her hallmark shift dresses are typically sleeveless.

The original was made by Pulitzer's own dress maker and included lining and lace seam beadings around the neck and pocket. Pulitzer continued this attention to detail throughout her career.

As well as being fashionable during the 1960s, the bright floral colors were originally made to conceal orange juice stains as Pulitzer first developed the dress as a uniform for her orange juice stall attendants.

A 1960s Lilly Pulitzer yellow and green sleeveless dress.

When Pulitzer's old school friend Jackie Kennedy began wearing her designs, she shot to fame and her look became popular across the US.

39.5in (100cm) long

$80-120   **NOR**

A Saks Fifth Avenue black and white banded silk sack dress, possibly 1960s, with vertical flat 'ruff' to front.

Starting in 1911, this famous department store carried native and European designs, but closed its couture and custom design department in the 1970s.

91.5in (94cm) long

$30-40   **NOR**

A 1960s 'Malcolm Starr Couture' printed cotton dress, with border of glass jewels.

53.5in (136cm) long

$50-70   **NOR**

A 1980s navy polyester cocktail dress, by Collections, decorated with gold-colored polka dots, size 5-6.

$30-50   **BR**

A 1980s American white knitted cotton dress, by Leslie Fay, with multi-colored geometric design, US size 8.

$15-20   **BR**

A 1960s Mod-style corduroy mini-dress, by Full Circle.

33.5in (85cm) long

$30-50 **NOR**

A 1940s Hawaiian 'Mun' printed silk dress, by Liberty House, Honolulu and Waikiki, size small.

$500-700 **MA**

A 1940s Pake Mud printed Rayon dress, by the Liberty House, Waikiki, size 10.

$800-1,200 **MA**

An American turquoise dress, by International Ladies Garments Workers Union, with ruffled neckline and cuffs.

$20-30 **BR**

An Ondine of California printed pink, green and black tartan sleeveless dress, with black faceted buttons.

38.25in (97cm) long

$50-70 **NOR**

A 1960s polyester bandana print dress, with elasticated cinched waist and flowing sleeves.

51.5in (131cm) long

$40-60 **NOR**

A 1960s printed velvet harlequin-style gown.

70.75in (150cm) long

$50-80 **NOR**

A black polyester dress, with ruffled neck, cuffs, and skirt, decorated with small flower design, size 42.

$15-25 **BR**

A 1930s black gown, with rhinestone and sequin decoration.

$500-700 **MA**

A long red gingham dress, with white collar and cuffs.

$15-20   **BR**

A green evening dress, with matching brocade coat with three-quarter length sleeves.

$15-25   **BR**

A long blue evening dress, with attached overcoat, and beaded detailing.

$25-35   **BR**

A late 1960s metallic thread lace dress.

The overall shape, use of metallic thread and the length of the skirt recall the flapper dresses of the 1920s.

35.5in (90cm) long

$20-40   **NOR**

A printed polyester and silk dress, decorated with Art Nouveau ladies' heads.

The 1960s looked back to the Art Nouveau style for inspiration, but updated it in the bright, psychedelic colors typical of the period. Here the whiplash motif, clouds and flowing tresses of hair, as well as the skirt length are given a truly 1960s makeover. Note the ruff neck, which also copies 19thC style.

$50-80   **NOR**

A 1960s flesh-colored crepé and silk dress, with plastic sequins.

39.75in (101cm) long

$40-60   **NOR**

A late 1960s psychedelic-colored sequin and silk crepé net dress, unlabeled.

35.5in (90cm) long

$50-80   **NOR**

A 1960s border print lurex dress, with button-through top.

39.25in (100cm) long

$40-60   **NOR**

An acetate sack dress, with psychedelic mushroom print.

37.5in (95cm) long

$40-60   **NOR**

A short yellow dress, with zippered back and bold floral design.

$15-20 BR

A 1960s printed cotton dress, decorated with Tudor-type figures, unlabeled.

36.25in (92cm) long

$60-90 NOR

A 1960s handmade blue and green embroidered flower mini dress.

31.5in (80cm) long

$80-120 NOR

A 1960s abstract print cotton sleeveless shift dress.

39in (99cm) long

$20-30 NOR

A Papillon blue and black geometric printed cotton sleeveless dress.

The design of this dress either resembles a Folk Art rug or the geometric prints of Emilio Pucci, who would have been a popular, and expensive, designer name at the time this dress was made.

57in (145cm) long

$40-60 NOR

A pink and black printed white cotton dress, with printed, stylized ruffs and button-down front.

36.25in (92cm) long

$50-70 NOR

A mohair tunic dress, with frayed hem.

$12-18 BR

A 1960s black suede and white leather sleeveless dress, unlabeled.

The style of this dress almost mimics those of Andre Courrèges.

39.75in (101cm) long

$120-180 NOR

A 1960s black silk and rhinestone inlaid Mod dress, with retro 1920s styling.

34.25in (87cm) long

$70-100 NOR

A black and white checkered woven wool coat dress, unlabeled.

40.5in (103cm) long

$100-150 NOR

A 1960s Bergdorf Goodman silk pants suit, with blue and brown 'Maurice' signature floral print.

Pants 41.75in (106cm) long

$70-100   **NOR**

A Bogart of Texas red suede-look velvet hot pants and vest suit, with red polyester polka dot blouse.

Vest 28in (71cm) long

$60-80   **NOR**

A 1980s Contempo Casuals ocher cotton and lycra two-piece suit, with rigid wired base, pulling in towards the legs.

$150-200   **NOR**

A late 1960s Leslie Fay Original gold lamé snakeskin effect two-piece pants suit.

Founded in 1947, Leslie Fay was popular due to its affordable yet appealing designs. Aimed at the middle-aged, it is not known for avant-garde design. Joan Leslie and David Warren are also associated with the brand.

Jacket 29.25in (74cm) long

$50-80   **NOR**

A printed cotton one-piece pants suit, with Aztec designs in bands and card and plastic green belt with card buckle.

52.25in (133cm) long

$30-40   **NOR**

A 1970s/80s Yves Saint Laurent 'Rive Gauche' red woolen jacket, with black and white piping.

Yves Saint Laurent's 'Rive Gauche' ready-to-wear brand was established in 1966. The combination of structured form and strong, powerful colors evoke the 1980s, a decade of power dressing for women.

26.25in (67cm) long

$100-150   **NOR**

A 1960s Shulman Furs of Philadelphia leopard skin fur coat, with black mink fur trim.

30.25in (77cm) long

$2,000-2,500   **PC**

A 1960s Sandy Chrysler faux fur sleeveless coat.

56.75in (144cm) long

$100-150   **NOR**

A 1960s Domani Knits woven wool and cotton sleeveless jacket, with bands of geometric, almost Aztec designs and metallic lion-head buckle fastening.

41.75in (106cm) long

$30-50   **NOR**

A 1960s faux leopard skin sleeveless coat, by Young Generation.

Despite the terrible associations with real fur, fake fur is making a come-back on the catwalks.

43.75in (111cm) long

$80-120   **NOR**

A gold and blue paisley lamé coat, with side fastenings, unlabeled.

56.25in (143cm) long

$70-100   **NOR**

A 1960s suede 'alpine look' cape and matching apron, with applied flowers, unlabeled.

31.5in (80cm) long

$150-250   **NOR**

A 1960s/70s purple and black suede hippie cape.

28.75in (73cm) long

$80-120   **NOR**

A 1960s/70s embroidered green suede poncho, unlabeled.

31.75in (81cm) long

$80-120   **NOR**

A long leather jacket, with popper fastenings, lacks label.

$50-70   **BR**

An early 1960s all hand-embroidered sweater jacket, with triangular designs.

19.75in (50cm) long

$40-60   **NOR**

A Peter Max signature design unisex reversible jumper, the reverse with yellow stripes on red background.

The design, color, form, and material scream the 1980s. Peter Max became famous in the 1960s for his way-out psychedelic designs known as 'Cosmic 60s'. His fondness for bright colors and skill at visually encapsulating the changing styles of an age continued through his career.

c1989   *26in (66cm) long*

$30-50   **NOR**

A ladies' knitted acrylic and nylon sweater, by Destiny.

$15-25 BR

A ladies' knitted sweater, by Jessica at Sears.

$15-20 BR

A ladies' printed sweatshirt, by Les Modes, Minique, Canada.

$20-30 BR

A ladies' knitted sweater, by Mirere, metallic thread geometric decoration, size medium.

$10-15 BR

A ladies' knitted sweater, by Crochetta, Malta, with applied fabric and shell decoration.

$20-30 BR

A ladies' knitted sweater, by Nonpareil, with sequinned decoration, size medium.

$15-20 BR

A ladies' knitted sweater, by Normandy, USA, size large.

$25-35 BR

A ladies' polyester sweatshirt, by Northern Spirit, size small.

$20-30 BR

A ladies' knitted sweater, lacks label.

$10-15 BR

A ladies' paisley pattern tunic, with zippered back.

$6-8 BR

A 1960s Mascot by Trude of California mohair silk and cotton sleeveless top, with Mondrianesque design.

22.5in (57cm) long

$50-70 NOR

A Western-style ladies' shirt, by Karman, size 12.

$15-20 BR

A ladies' floral polyester top, by Mayeelok.

$8-12 BR

A polyester shirt, by Pant Man.

$7-10 BR

A Perfection by Roxanne printed polyester blouse.

$20-30 NOR

A ladies' brown shirt, decorated with orange flowers, lacks label.

$8-12 BR

A ladies' shirt, with floral decoration, lacks label.

$12-18 BR

A ladies' polyester top, with metallic thread decoration, size large.

$15-25 BR

A 1960s brown suede and woven wool hippie top and matching cape, with woven wool tie and bobbles.

28.75in (73cm) long

$150-200 NOR

A ladies' Western-style shirt, by Zazie, London, with red gingham check panel and cuffs.

$7-10 BR

COSTUME & ACCESSORIES

A 1960s Italian 'Mod' woven knit Maxi skirt.

43.75in (111cm) long

$35-45   **NOR**

A 1960s Prestige of Boston 'flower power' printed velvet skirt.

$30-50   **NOR**

A 1960s long skirt, with floral decoration on a black ground.

$12-18   **BR**

A long striped skirt, with pink decoration and long side split.

$8-12   **BR**

A long blue skirt, with floral decoration and elasticated waistband.

$8-12   **BR**

A 1950s long black skirt, with applied patchwork decoration of a basket of balls of wool.

$5-8   **BR**

A 1950s Mexican handpainted cotton full skirt, with design of a Mexican native, highlighted with applied sequins.

$220-280   **MA**

A 1950s Mexican handpainted full skirt, with design of a chief among cacti, with natives and pyramids in the background.

$220-280   **MA**

A 1950s black felt gilt skirt, with applied design of leopard fur and glitter decoration, gold-colored chain belt.

$300-500   **MA**

A 1950s turquoise-blue full circle skirt, with applied glitter and felt decoration of a car at traffic lights.

The condition of the glitter and the appliqué felt decoration is excellent. This, twinned with the stylish motifs, typical of the period, add value.

$280-320   **MA**

A 1980s black and pink net lace layered skirt, by Honey, waist 25in.

$15-20   **BR**

A denim skirt, with indistinct label, size 11.

$10-15   **BR**

A 1970s 'Lick Me' blue printed cotton wraparound skirt.

This print incorporates a slightly naughty version of the now famous Smiley face developed by American artist Harvey Ball in 1963 and popularized during the 1970s.

26in (66cm) long

$35-45   **NOR**

A printed skirt, lacks label, size 44.

$7-10   **BR**

An A-line skirt, with chevron design, lacks label, size 32.

$15-20   **GR**

A pair of multicolored floral culottes.

$8-12   **BR**

A pair of 1960s psychedelic printed cotton hip-hugger jeans, unlabeled.

39in (99cm) long

$50-70   **NOR**

A pair of 1960s psychedelic flower printed pants.

37in (94cm) long

$35-45   **NOR**

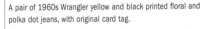

A pair of 1960s Wrangler yellow and black printed floral and polka dot jeans, with original card tag.

It is rare to find jeans like these in such immaculate condition and with their original tag.

$50-70   **NOR**

A 1960s Emilio Pucci for Formfit Rogers polyester slip, with EPFR monogram.

EPFR designs were by Emilio Pucci, but all FormFit Rogers pieces were intended as underwear and were mass-produced.

20.75in (53cm) long

$80-120   **NOR**

A 1970s Emilio Pucci for Formfit Rogers chemise, with EPFR monogram, pink white and black design with border print.

34.25in (87cm) long

$120-180   **NOR**

A 1970s Emilio Pucci for Formfit Rogers four-piece lingerie set, made from nylon, Lycra and Spandex, comprising two sets of knickers, a bra and a sleeveless 'baby doll' tunic, all with EPFR monogram within the printed design.

$200-250   **NOR**

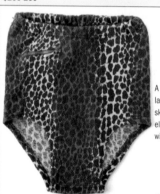

A 1950s leopard skin print bra, unmarked.

$50-80   **SM**

A pair of 1950s lady's leopard skin print elasticated pants, with zip fastener.

11in (28cm) long

$120-180   **SM**

A 1950s Vanity Fair leopard print girdle, with attached suspenders, size 6.

14.5in (37cm) long

$100-150   **SM**

A Rosy white lace waist girdle, with original tags, size 42.

14in (35.5cm) long

$150-200   **SM**

A pair of 1950s 'Good Fairy' nylon pants, with applied fabric and nylon fairy and rhinestones.

11.75in (30cm) wide

$80-120   **SM**

A 1970s denim two-piece suit.

Jacket 23.5in (60cm) long

$80-120   **NOR**

A CLOSER LOOK AT A GOTLOP SUIT

M.S. Gotlop Ltd were a fine quality central London civil, naval and military tailors who first appeared in London listings in 1896.

Based at 49 Whitehall, London, the company changed their name to Lidgett & Sons in 1955 with official records existing until 1969. It is likely that this suit was made around the early 1960s when the Lidgetts may have still liked to use the heritage 'Gotlop' name in their labels.

The long length, fitted, high buttoning, double-breasted design was typical of the 'Mod' look of the 1960s, influenced by Victorian and even Georgian styles.

The pinstripe suit is made from heavy, worsted wool, a quality cloth.

The pants are cut at a very unusual angle, to point towards the toe-cap of a shoe with the creases falling above the laces and giving the impression of matching spats.

A blue worsted wool pinstripe suit by 'Gotlop'. 1960-65

35.5in (90.5cm) long

$180-220   **NOR**

A pair of early 1970s printed cotton 'stars and stripes' hip hugger low-cut jeans, with period stars waistcoat.

This highly patriotic and celebratory clothing was produced in the same decade as the US Bicentenary.

Pants 35in (89cm) long

$120-180   **NOR**

A pair of 1970s 'VOTE' printed cotton pants, in red, white, and blue.

40.25in (102cm) long

$100-150   **NOR**

A late 1970s 'Superfly' style black wool and leather men's coat.

The fit and style of this coat is similar those worn by hip, funky anti-hero 'Priest', played by Ron O'Neal in the 1972 film 'Superfly'.

$70-100   **NOR**

A 1970s Ponzi of Phillipsburg, NJ tuxedo, with velvet collar, satin trim, with shirt, dress pants with satin band, and velvet bow tie.

30.75in (78cm) long

$120-180   **NOR**

A 1960s cobalt blue crushed velvet smoking/dinner jacket, with silk lapels and trim and single button fastening.

34.75in (88cm) long

$120-180   **NOR**

COSTUME & ACCESSORIES

A CLOSER LOOK AT A JOE NAMATH SHIRT

Charismatic baseball player Joe Namath (b.1943) was renowned for his off-pitch social excesses, earning him the nickname 'Broadway Joe'.

Made during the Disco era, this shirt, with its pointed wing collars and all-over print, would have been very fashionable.

His endorsements continued to give him a source of income after his playing years – as well as the Arrow brand shirts, he was spokesman for Dingo boots.

The design shows Arrow advertisements designed by J.C. Leyendecker from the 1920s and '30s, harking back to the historic heritage of the company, which was founded in 1851.

A 1970s Arrow 'Joe Namath' printed polyester shirt.

Namath's road room-mate once observed that being around a 25-year-old Namath was 'like traveling with a Beatle'.

32in (81cm) long

$50-70 | **NOR**

A 1960s batik-style printed cotton jacket, made in Hong Kong, with small lapels.

$50-80 | **NOR**

A 1970s batik-style handprinted cotton men's jacket, made in Great Britain for a retailer in Bermuda.

34in (81cm) long

$80-120 | **NOR**

A 1960s/70s Mexican burnt leather and suede poncho.

The horse head design is burnt into the leather with a thin hot rod.

41in (104cm) long

$120-180 | **NOR**

A 1970s Malber International, Hong Kong multicolored suede men's jacket.

$50-70 | **BR**

A men's short suede jacket, by Lee, lacks label.

$50-70 | **BR**

A 1970s Canadian Jeno de Paris men's cropped leather jacket.

$30-50 | **BR**

COLLECTORS' NOTES

■ Also known as 'Aloha' shirts, colorful Hawaiian shirts have become immensely collectible over the past 20 years, the best fetching hundreds of dollars or more. The mid-1930s to the mid-1950s is considered the 'golden age' of production and examples from this period are the most sought-after due to the quality of their color and design. During this period most were made in rayon, which despite being hot to wear, retains the vibrancy of its colors very well, unlike cotton which fades. The very best rayon shirts have a silky feel, which earned them the nickname, 'silkies' and is different from much modern rayon.

■ Certain brand names, designers and designs are more popular than others. Look out for Kamehama (founded 1936) and Cisco Champion Kahanamoku.

■ Reproductions exist in their millions, so examine labels and cloth for signs of age and wear. Famous wearers of Hawaiian shirts dating from the golden age when they were first popular include Dwight D. Eisenhower, Harry Truman on the front of 'Time' magazine in 1951, and Elvis Presley in 1961's 'Blue Hawaii'. Tom Selleck's TV character, private detective 'Magnum' was also known for his fondness for such garments in the 1980s.

A 1950s printed Hawaiian shirt, by Champion, Kahanamoku, made by Cisco.

$500-700   **MA**

A Champion Kahanamoku Hawaiian shirt, with leaf print.

A shirt of the same design was worn by movie idol Montgomery Clift in the film 'From Here to Eternity' in 1953.

c1940

$500-800   **CVS**

A 1950s Kilohana printed Hawaiian shirt, size medium.

$280-320   **CVS**

A late 1930s Hawaiian shirt, by G. H. Gurupo, Tokyo, with Mount Fuji Japanese print, size XLarge.

This shirt is very rare because of the extra large size.

$400-600   **CVS**

A 1980s Michael Jackson printed cotton short-sleeved shirt.

28.75 (73cm) long

$80-120   **NOR**

A 1940s N. Turk wool and cotton western-style shirt, size medium.

$400-600   **CVS**

A 1960s American printed polyester Dashiki.

Early Afro-American Dashikis, printed on natural fabrics using traditional batik methods, are more desirable than later polyester versions.

28.75in (73cm) long

$25-35   **NOR**

FIND OUT MORE...

The Hawaiian Shirt: Its Art & History, *by Thomas Steele, published by Abbeville Press, 1984.*

A men's cotton work shirt, by Red Kap, USA, with applied patches.

$8-12 BR

A cotton and polyester men's work shirt, by Buckeye.

$12-18 BR

A men's cotton work shirt, by Red Kap, with applied patches.

$12-18 BR

An olive military shirt, label marked "96-100" and "1972".

$25-35 BR

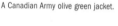

A Canadian Army olive green jacket.

$25-35 BR

A men's printed cotton Army jacket.

The fashion for army-style combat clothing, particularly in camouflage colors, has led to army surplus shops becoming popular shopping destinations – particularly for less formal, non-combat bomber jackets such as these.

$50-80 BR

A men's wool checked jacket, with "Canadian Camper Coat by the Bell Shirt Co.", with mohair and nylon.

$30-50 BR

A men's checked wool shirt, by Pioneer, with knitted cotton waistband.

$30-50 BR

A men's checked cotton shirt, by Romano, Canada, size 16-16 1/2 large.

$18-22 BR

A men's checked shirt, by Bridgeport, Canada.

$12-18 BR

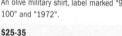

A CLOSER LOOK AT A COWICHAN SWEATER

These sweaters are highly collected. The design should always be considered – shooting motifs are fairly common, a skull-and-crossbones design can be worth over $200, and a shark around $350!

Authentic Cowichan sweaters are hand-knitted by women in the Cowichan Valley, Vancouver Island, Canada, so each one is unique.

The zipper has a 'flash' meaning this example can be dated to the 1950s or '60s.

Colors should be natural, such as brown or white, black is rare.

A men's knitted Cowichan-style sweater, with eagle decoration, lacks label.

$80-120 **BR**

A knitted men's college sweater, by Clover, with applied "OL" patch and "Clover 100% Pure Virgin Wool" label, size small.

$25-35 **BR**

A knitted men's college cardigan, with applied "St Francis Xavier CYO Circuit Champions 1965" patch, lacks label.

$50-70 **BR**

A men's knitted Cowichan-style sweater, by Kingsway Simpson-Sears, with stitched decoration of a hunter and a bird, size medium.

$50-70 **BR**

A men's knitted Cowichan-style sweater, with geometric decoration, lacks label.

$50-70 **BR**

A men's knitted Cowichan-style sweater, with geometric decoration, lacks label.

$50-70 **BR**

A 1960s fraternity jumper, knitted wool with applied leather and felt patches, large size.

$120-180 **MA**

A Levi's denim blouse jacket, with 'Big E' red tab.

The woven red and white Levi's trademark tab was introduced in 1936. Until 1971, all the letters in LEVI'S were in capitals, afterwards, the E became a lower case 'e'. Any labels with a 'Big E' will date from before 1971.

$80-120   **BR**

A Lee denim blouse jacket, size large.

$120-180   **BR**

A pair of Levi's 501 denim jeans, size W30, L36, post 1971.

$80-120   **BR**

A Wrangler denim jacket, with Stars & Stripes patch and metal studs, size small.

$70-100   **BR**

A pair of Levi's denim jeans, size 32.

1971-83

$80-120   **BR**

A pair of Levi's 501 'red line' jeans, size W32 L33.

Levi's denims are considered 'vintage' and collectible if they date from before 1983. Apart from the 'E' in the label, another good way to help identify vintage Levi products is to turn them inside out. Jeans produced before 1983 can be identified by a thin 'red line' sewn into the selvage (the edge of the material) at the seam.

$80-120   **BR**

A pair of late 1960s Lee Riders jeans, size 32.

$120-180   **BR**

A pair of Lee Rider denim jeans, with 'Union Made' label.

Levi's are not the only collectible name in vintage jeans – vintage Lee and Wrangler are also sought-after, although less so. Look out in particular for their 'Cowboy' brand – a 1940s jacket can fetch up to $7,000 or more! Lee Rider jeans were introduced in 1924 in a 13 ounce denim, at the time Levi's were produced in a 10 ounce fabric, making these Riders 'more durable'.

$280-320   **BR**

A Nike nylon jacket, size large.

$20-25 BR

An Adidas blue sweatshirt, marked "Made in Canada", size large.

$18-22 BR

A Nike black sweatshirt, size large.

$12-18 BR

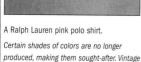

A Ralph Lauren pink polo shirt.

Certain shades of colors are no longer produced, making them sought-after. Vintage examples are also often made of better quality cottons.

$7-10 BR

A Nike red t-shirt.

$5-8 BR

A Menasha Re. Dept. baseball t-shirt, with "Sport-T by Stedman" label.

$8-12 BR

A Nike blue t-shirt, with applied stripes at shoulders, size XL.

$8-12 BR

A black mesh American Football shirt.

$12-18 BR

A 'Five Star' v-neck t-shirt, by Trumark, size M.

$8-12 BR

A Nike navy vest, with white transfer decoration.

$12-18 BR

A large embroidered purse, with a beige ground, decorated with roses and fringes, silver-plated clasp.

c1915   11.5in (29cm) long

$180-220   **WDL**

A 1950s gold-painted straw and wicker purse, with black velvet panel, woven wool poodle, glued sequins, yellow gold silk lining and label for "Midas of Miami".

8.25in (21cm) wide

$300-400   **SM**

A 1950s wicker shopping bag, with applied red felt with hand sewn woolen poodles with inset rhinestone eyes.

12.5in (32cm) wide

$120-180   **MA**

A 1950s fish-shaped plastic-covered wire purse, with fabric-lined interior.

15.25in (38.5cm) long

$400-600   **SM**

An Enid Collins 'By The Roadside' printed and plastic jeweled purse, interior marked with Collins logo and "Copyright The Original Collins of Texas".

Enid Collins opened her purse shop in Medina, Texas in 1959 and produced bags in two main styles – a wooden box bag and a canvas bucket bag. They were decorated by hand with kitsch, glitzy motifs with paint, sequins, and rhinestones. Do-it-yourself kits were also sold. Many designs had titles, which were printed on the bags, together with the Enid Collins' signature. The company was bought out by the Tandy Leather Corporation in 1970.

10.75in (27.5cm) wide

$80-120   **NOR**

A 1960s clear vinyl purse, with internal design of silk flowers and perspex handle.

13in (33cm) wide

$30-50   **MA**

A 1960s wooden box bag, with handpainted 'dining doggies' scene, the interior with mirror and reading "Collectors Item by Gary Jolie Dalas Decorated for you Made in Hong Kong".

6.25in (16cm) wide

$35-45   **NOR**

A 1960s red plush handpainted bag, with 'doggie' scene.

7.75in (19.5cm) high

$50-70   **NOR**

A 1960s Enid Collins 'Do-Drop In' plastic jeweled and printed purse.

10.5in (27cm) wide

$50-70   **NOR**

A 1960s vinyl bag, with colored matchbook design and vinyl interior.

$40-60 NOR

A 1960s Mod box bag, with wooden body, white vinyl and gold bosses, label to red fabric interior "Handmade in British Hong Kong".

7in (18cm) wide

$50-70 NOR

A 1960s/70s box 'Wonder Bag', decorated with applied painted canvas daisies.

10in (25.5cm) wide

$50-70 NOR

The original Jerry Terrence 'Waste Basket' 'For Your Personal Trash' purse, with faux fur panel.

13.75in (35cm) high

$100-120 SM

A green leather satchel, with applied car design.

$12-18 BR

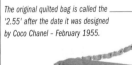

A patchwork bag, decorated with a scene of a musician.

$30-40 BR

A CLOSER LOOK AT A CHANEL QUILTED PURSE

Together with the Hermès Kelly bag, this is one of the most iconic bags ever made. It was Karl Lagerfeld who increased the size of the Chanel Logo and the thickness of the chain.

Although popular when first released, it did not reach iconic status until the 1980s when it was adopted by the label-hungry buyer obsessed with ostentation.

The original quilted bag is called the '2.55' after the date it was designed by Coco Chanel - February 1955.

Coco Chanel preferred understated black, but the quilted bag has since been produced in a huge range of colors, fabrics, and patterns and in 2005, the 20th anniversary year, even as a men's bag.

A Chanel quilted leather purse, in pebble textured leather, with single signature chain strap, open back pocket, interior zip pocket, gold embossed "CHANEL" logo inside with signature zipper pull and all hardware marked "Chanel".

As this bag is widely faked, check the bag is correctly marked and that the construction and material is of suitably high quality.

8.5in (21.5cm) wide

$700-1,000 FRE

A Fun Ship Holidays travel bag.

$12-18 BR

A Canadian Fun Finders Tours travel bag.

$20-25 BR

A Canadian Leo's Travel Ltd, Edmonton travel bag.

$22-28 BR

A Vacances Esprit travel bag.

$15-20 BR

A Trafalgar's Europe and Britain travel bag.

$15-20 BR

A pair of 1960s Taj of India shocking pink silk shoes, with clear soles.

10.25in (26cm) long

$180-220 SM

A pair of flower power printed silk shoes, by 'Schiaparelli Paris & New York'.

9.5in (24cm) long

$30-50 NOR

A pair of Da Venci black satin and fur/plush high heeled shoes, with their original hatbox-shaped box.

$120-180 SM

A pair of 1950s black suedette high heeled shoes, with black bakelite heels and bow, with applied metal 'coins'.

$280-320 SM

A pair of 1970s large orange fading through to clear plastic frames, the arm marked "Frame Hong Kong", with shaped arms and face.

6.25in (16cm) wide

$30-50 BB

A pair of large, mock tortoiseshell gentlemen's frames, the arms stamped "Zyloware U.S.A. 5 1/2" and set into the fronts.

6in (15cm) wide

$30-50 BB

A pair of 1960s clear plastic and fabric laminated sunglasses.

5.75in (14.5cm) wide

$220-280 VE

A pair of 1950s French hand-carved mock tortoiseshell plastic 'mask' sunglasses.

6.25in (16cm) wide

$600-800 VE

A pair of brown striated pearlized 'wood effect' frames, by Fathaway, with chromed metal inserts, the arms marked "Fathaway 5 1/2".

5.25in (13.5cm) wide

$25-35 BB

A pair of 1950s black and white laminated plastic frames.

$30-50 BB

A pair of gray pearlized ladies' frames, with heart-shaped metal inserts, with shaped tips of the arms.

$25-35 BB

A pair of metal bronze colored frames, the arms marked "HUD US 5 1/2".

5in (13cm) wide

$25-35 BB

COSTUME & ACCESSORIES

A gentleman's tie, made to a 1950s design from unused 1950s 'Showgirl' tie silk.

5.25in (13.25cm) long

$220-280 CVS

A 1960s psychedelic purple and orange silk tie.

$10-15 BR

An American handpainted silk tie, by Towncraft Deluxe Cravats, decorated with two swordfish.

$12-18 BR

A handpainted 'Bold Look' silk tie, by Currie.

$12-18 BR

A polyester tie, by Cartier, with geometric design.

$3-5 BR

A Canadian handpainted silk tie, by Rembrandt, with a decoration of a peacock.

$15-25 BR

A silk tie, by Bluestone, with floral decorative panel.

$12-18 BR

A blue polyester tie, decorated with Classical lamp, unmarked.

$6-9 BR

A psychedelic floral cotton tie, made in England.

$7-10 BR

A pair of 1940s apple juice cast phenolic and white dice cufflinks.

Face 0.75in (2cm) wide

$30-50 PC

A pair of 1930s/40s Bakelite dice cufflinks, unmarked.

0.5in (1cm) wide

$100-150 CVS

A pair of late 1960s/early 1970s faceted plastic and gold-colored cufflinks.

0.75in (2cm) diam

$15-20 DTC

A pair of mid-20thC Kreisler Craft gold-filled cufflinks, with reversible pearlized brown and green roller rolling cylindrical 'bars'.

0.75in (2.25cm) wide

$15-25 BB

A pair of 1920s/30s 14ct rose gold Egyptian motif cufflinks, with green painted paste scarab and sarcophagus and ankh-shaped links, unmarked.

Scarab 1.25in (3cm) long

$120-180 BB

A pair of 1950s Mexican silver cufflinks, set with turquoise, with abstract metal pattern.

1in (2.5cm) wide

$120-180 CVS

A pair of 1950s white metal cufflinks, with pink plastic cabochon stones.

1.5in (4cm) wide

$40-60 CVS

A 1970s Swank chrome tie clip bar and cufflinks set, in mint plush box.

$10-15 BB

A pair of 1960s metal cufflinks, in original box.

1in (2.5cm) diam

$20-30 DTC

COLLECTORS' NOTES

■ Named pieces continue to rise in popularity and value, particularly those by Trifari, Coro, Haskell, Joseff, and others. Many people buy to wear, so even unsigned pieces can fetch high prices if the look is fashionable.

■ Well-made pieces from the 1930s-1940s using better quality materials are also increasing in value, particularly if named. Names are often found stamped on the back. Learning how to recognize makers' styles and marks can help with dating.

■ Trifari is one of the most collectible names. It was founded in New York in 1918 by Gustavo Trifari and Leo F. Krussman, with Carl Fishel joining in 1929. This led to the 'TKF' stamped mark.

■ Jaunty, novelty shapes abound, as do floral or foliate designs – particularly pins. Large, brightly colored, complex examples with glittering rhinestones are the most desirable. Look out for designs worn by Hollywood stars from the 1930s-1960s.

A 1950s Trifari pin, in the form of a parrot on a branch, with red rhinestone inset eyes.

1.25in (3cm) high

$70-100   **CRIS**

A 1950s Trifari owl pin.

1.25in (3cm) high

$70-100   **CRIS**

A 1950s Trifari dog pin, with green enamel body and inset rhinestone ears.

1.25in (3cm) high

$80-100   **CRIS**

A 1950s Trifari flapping duckling pin.

1.25in (3cm) high

$70-100   **CRIS**

A 1950s Trifari penguin pin.

Penguins are a comparatively rare animal for Trifari pins.

1.25in (3cm) high

$80-100   **CRIS**

A 1950s Trifari teddy bear pin, with 'faux fur' texture, red enamel and rhinestone inset paws.

The teddy bear pin is relatively scarce. It also appeals to teddy bear collectors, often meaning values are higher.

1.25in (3cm) high

$80-120   **CRIS**

Three 1950s Trifari butterfly pins, with 'plique à jour' colored glass set in gilt frames.

2in (5cm) wide

$70-100 each   **CRIS**

A CLOSER LOOK AT A TRIFARI PIN

This pin was designed by Frenchman Alfred Philippe, Trifari's chief designer from 1930-68, whose designs helped to make Trifari successful.

The design was inspired by the explosion of romantic and historical movies during the 1930s-50s.

It is made from vermeil – gold-plated sterling silver – showing it was made during the 1940s and is thus highly collectible.

Large cabochons are typical of these designs – later reissues from the 1980s are of lesser quality and are less collectible.

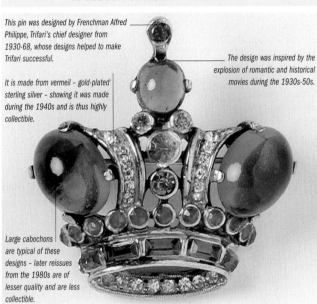

A pair of 1960s Trifari gold-plated and pierced 'sponge' earrings, with their original Trifari tag.

0.75in (2.25cm) diam

$25-35 TR

A 1940s Trifari vermeil crown pin, designed by Alfred Phillippe, with prong-set green glass cabochons, blue baguettes and blue, ruby red, and clear rhinestones, slight wear to gold-plating.

1.25in (3cm) high

$220-280 PC

A pair of mid-1950s Trifari pierced gold-plated pendant fruit earrings.

1.5in (4cm) long

$50-80 CRIS

Four late 1950s Trifari small fruit pins, comprising an apple, a pineapple, a bunch of grapes, and a pear, in matte finish silver and gold alloy.

Largest 1in (2.5cm) long

$25-35 each CRIS

A 1950s Trifari 'retro' flower pin, of pierced silver alloy with pear, navette and round clear rhinestones.

1.5in (4cm) diam

$50-80 ABAA

A 1950s Trifari leaves and berries pin, of matte finish gold alloy, with elongated faux pearls.

4in (10cm) long

$80-120 CRIS

A 1950s Trifari gilt and simulated pearl and rhinestone pin.

4in (10.5cm) long

$80-120 CRIS

An early 1970s Trifari faux fabric black bow-tie pin, designed by Diane Love.

3in (7cm) wide

$70-100 TR

A late 1950s Coro 'space age' pin, of polished and textured white metal, with a round metal cabochon center.

2.25in (5.75cm) diam

$30-50   **MILLB**

A late 1950s Coro 'space age' pin, of gold-tone metal, with clear and ruby red crystal rhinestones.

2.25in (5.75cm) diam

$20-30   **MILLB**

A late 1940s/early 1950s Coro vermeil flower-head pin, with clear crystal rhinestones.

2in (5cm) diam

$50-80   **MILLB**

A pair of 1950s Coro floral motif earrings, of antiqued goldwash metal, with faux baroque pearls and red crystal rhinestones.

1.25in (3.25cm) long

$50-80   **MILLB**

A pair of Coro floral motif earrings, in gold-tone metal with pink, aquamarine, and citrine crystal navettes.

1945-50   *1in (2.5cm) long*

$25-35   **MILLB**

A pair of Coro floral earrings, with pale pink plastic petals and aurora borealis crystal rhinestone centers.

c1955   *2.5in (6.25cm) long*

$25-30   **MILLB**

A mid-1950s Coro floral bracelet and earrings, with white plastic petals and gold-tone metal centers with pale green and blue and clear crystal rhinestones.

Coro was founded in New York in 1919 and continues to produce affordable costume jewelry today on a massive scale. This provides collectors with enormous scope and variety. Look out for their higher end 'Corocraft' name and their 'Duette' pins, made from three detachable pieces.

Bracelet 6in (15.25cm) long

$50-70   **MILLB**

A 1950s Coro Victorian-style love token pin, of gold-tone cast metal in the form of a hand proffering a rose.

2.5in (6.25cm) long

$50-80   **JJ**

A 1960s/70s Coro belt, with silver-tone metal chain and antiqued, mottled silver-tone inverted shield pendant.

Designs derived from African or ethnic forms were very popular in the 1960s and '70s.

Chain 30in (76cm) long

$30-50   **MILLB**

A CLOSER LOOK AT A CHOKER

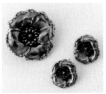

A 1960s ART gilt and silver flower pin and earring set.

Pin 2in (5cm) diam

$50-70 JJ

A 1960s/70s Les Bernard clown with umbrella pin, of gold-tone cast metal with red, black, and white enameling.

2in (5cm) long

$30-50 JJ

Cristobal Balenciaga (1895-1972) was an influential Spanish couturier working in Paris – he launched his couture range in 1919.

This is an haute couture piece, made only to order, so very few examples would have been made.

The very simple lines and colors are aimed to complement the classical elegance of his clothing designs.

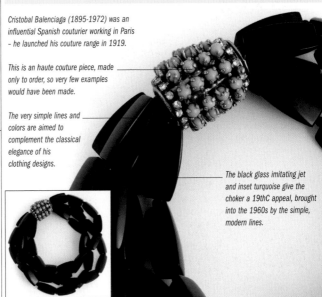

The black glass imitating jet and inset turquoise give the choker a 19thC appeal, brought into the 1960s by the simple, modern lines.

A Balenciaga couture choker, with four interwoven strands of faceted black glass beads and gilt metal clasp with turquoise glass cabochons and clear rhinestones.
c1960 *16.25in (41.5cm) long*

$2,200-2,800 SUM

A 1970s Marcel Boucher turtle pin, of textured gold-tone metal casting with clear crystal rhinestone highlights.

1.5in (3.75cm) long

$30-50 JJ

A 1960s Alice Caviness raspberry and leaf pin, of textured gold-tone metal with pavé-set faux ruby cabochons.

2.75in (7cm) long

$70-100 ABIJ

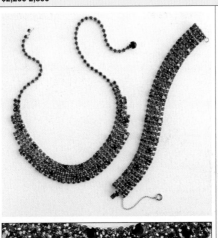

A 1960s Alice Caviness necklace and matching bracelet, of rhodium-plated metal, set with graduated rows of lavender, pink and black rhinestones.

Necklace 16.5in (42cm) long

$350-400 ABIJ

A 1960s Alice Caviness necklace and matching bracelet, of japanned metal with olivine and ruby glass cabochons and prong-set aurora borealis, blue and green rhinestones.

Necklace 16in (40.5cm) long

$300-350 ABIJ

A pair of 1980s Karl Lagerfeld earrings, in the form of 'Louis-style' bérgère armchairs, in gold-washed metal with clear crystal beads to the sides.

1.25in (3cm) long

$70-100 JJ

A 1960s Marvella leaf and buds pin, of gold- and silver-tone metal, with faux pearls and pavé-set clear crystal rhinestones.

1.75in (4.5cm) long

$50-60 ABIJ

A CLOSER LOOK AT A PAIR OF MIRIAM HASKELL EARRINGS

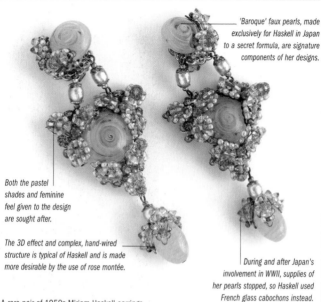

'Baroque' faux pearls, made exclusively for Haskell in Japan to a secret formula, are signature components of her designs.

Both the pastel shades and feminine feel given to the design are sought after.

The 3D effect and complex, hand-wired structure is typical of Haskell and is made more desirable by the use of rose montée.

During and after Japan's involvement in WWII, supplies of her pearls stopped, so Haskell used French glass cabochons instead.

A rare pair of 1950s Miriam Haskell earrings.

If the extremely rare matching necklace could be found, the set could be worth over $3,000!

4in (10cm) long

$700-1,000 BY

A Kramer bracelet and earrings set, with gilt metal clasps and links and clear and textured white glass beads.

1958-62 *Bracelet 7in (17.75cm) long*

$50-70 MILLB

A 1960s/70s Judy Lee floral burst pin and matching earrings, of gold-tone filigree, with navette-cut clear and topaz and round-cut ruby and gray-green rhinestones.

Pin 2.75in (7cm) diam

$50-80 ABIJ

A 1960s Lisner necklace, with gold-tone metal chain and castings, set with Rivoli cabochons and clear crystal rhinestones.

16in (40.5cm) long

$180-220 JJ

A Monet flower pin, with stalk, center and petal borders of gold-plated metal, the petal surface strands of base metal with white enameling.

c1965-75   2in (5cm) long

$25-35   **MILLB**

A 1960s Robert butterfly pin, of gilt metal with black poured glass body and blue and green enamel wings.

1.75in (4.5cm) wide

$50-70   **JJ**

A 1950s Robert bird-on-umbrella pin, of gilt metal casting with red, brown, pink, and green enameling.

2.5in (6.25cm) high

$50-70   **JJ**

A pre-1960s Volupté open bangle, of gold-tone metal, the inner band of wire mesh, the outer band pierced and chased with arabesque patterns.

3in (7.5cm) wide

$70-100   **JJ**

A pair of 1940s Weiss strawberry earrings, with ruby crystal beads and emerald crystal rhinestones in japanned metal settings.

1in (2.5cm) long

$70-100   **JJ**

A pair of 1950s Weiss fleur-de-lys earrings, of antique gold-tone cast metal, with pale green round and dark green navette crystal rhinestones.

1in (2.5cm) long

$25-35   **MILLB**

A pair of 1960s Whiting & Davis pendant snake's head earrings, in punched and engraved silver plate.

1.75in (4.5cm) long

$25-35   **ABIJ**

A 1940s Weiss 'jack-in-the-box' pin, of gilt metal with red and black enameling and clear and emerald rhinestones.

2in (5cm) high

$80-120   **JJ**

A 1960s Whiting & Davis silver-plated coiled snake bangle, with expandable mesh wrist band and solid punched and engraved head.

12in (30.5cm) long

$50-70   **JJ**

An early 1950s Whiting & Davis bracelet, with gold-plated links and safety chain and ruby red glass cabochons.

7.5in (19cm) long

$50-70   **ABIJ**

A 1950s unsigned toucan pin, of gilt cast metal with blue, green, and red enameling and ruby glass cabochon eyes.

2.25in (5.75cm) long

$15-25   CRIS

A 1950s unsigned crested bird-on-a-branch pin, of gold-tone metal with black enameling and clear crystal rhinestones.

3in (7.5cm) long

$15-25   CRIS

A 1960s unsigned stylized humming bird pin, of gold-plated cats metal with turquoise Lucite rings and aquamarine crystal rhinestone eyes.

3.25in (8.25cm) long

$50-70   CRIS

A 1950s unsigned humming bird pin, of gilt cast metal set with clear and ruby rhinestones and pavé-set turquoise crystal cabochons.

2.5in (6.25cm) long

$25-35   CRIS

A 1950s unsigned peacock pin, of gilt cast metal with black enameling and polychrome and clear crystal rhinestones.

2.5in (6.5cm) long

$30-50   CRIS

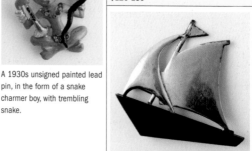

A 1940s unsigned pair of sterling enamel and inset diamanté 'Patriotic' pins, in the form of sailor bunnies.

During WWII, much jewelry was produced in the red, white, and blue colors of the American flag, as well as in patriotic forms such as the US flag or sailors.

1.75in (4.5cm) high

$120-180   BY

A 1960s unsigned caliph pin, of gold-tone cast metal with black enameling, aquamarine and turquoise glass cabochons, round and baguette clear rhinestones and a faux pearl.

2.75in (7cm) long

$70-100   CRIS

A 1930s unsigned painted lead pin, in the form of a snake charmer boy, with trembling snake.

2.25in (5.5cm) high

$50-80   BY

A 1930s dark blue schooner pin, with chrome-plated base metal sails and mast.

2in (5cm) long

$50-70   ABAA

A 1960s-70s unsigned pair of handbag earrings, with gold-tone metal castings and white enameling with 'Organic Modernism' amoeboid pattern.

1.5in (3.75cm) long

$120-180   **LB**

A pair of 1950s German fruit earrings, with red glass and red bead strawberries, green glass leaves, japanned metal stalks and yellow crystal rhinestones.

1.25in (3.25cm) long

$70-100   **BY**

A 1950s fruit pin, with two glass apples with applied tiny glass beads in red and green, with three green glass leaves and single yellow diamanté, stamped on the reverse "MADE IN WEST GERMANY".

2in (5cm) wide

$50-70   **BY**

An early 1920s French 'fruit salad' vase-of-flowers pin, with polychrome French carved glass and clear crystal rhinestones on a sterling silver casting.

2in (5cm) high

$180-220   **CRIS**

A late 1920s/early 1930s brown pin, of scrolling geometric form encrusted with clear rhinestones.

2.5in (6cm) wide

$30-50   **ABAA**

A 1920s dark brown stylized shoe-shape pin, encrusted with clear rhinestones.

2.5in (6cm) long

$30-50   **ABAA**

A 1920s black stylized scrolling leaf pin, with a row of clear rhinestones.

1.5in (4cm) long

$30-50   **ABAA**

A 1930s jade green and black stylized feather pin, with gold edging, incised linear decoration and clear rhinestones.

2.75in (7cm) long

$80-120   **ABAA**

An early 1930s Egyptian-revival motif pin, iridescent pink, red and taupe with a small, central mauve cabochon.

3in (8cm) long

$80-120   **ABAA**

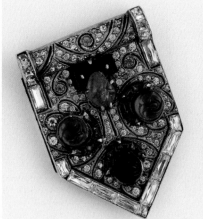

A 1940s unsigned pin, of vermeil sterling silver, with a large aquamarine paste stone and emerald, sapphire, ruby, and aquamarine crystal rhinestones.

4in (10cm) long

$120-180   **CRIS**

A 1920s unsigned shield pin, of sterling silver with faceted and baguette clear crystal rhinestones, and ruby, sapphire, and emerald glass stones.

2in (5cm) long

$220-280   **BY**

A 1960s unsigned, Byzantine-style floral pin, of gilt cast metal set with clear crystal rhinestones and faux pearls.

4in (10cm) long

$70-100   **CRIS**

A 1960s unsigned Maltese Cross pin, with scrolling forms of filigree gold wire set with faux baroque pearls and clear rhinestones.

2.5in (6.5cm) wide

$50-70   **CRIS**

A 1950s unsigned pin, with faux pearl berries, emerald green glass leaves and a mottled jade green glass fruit drop.

2in (5cm) long

$50-80   **ECLEC**

An unsigned entwined snakes pin, in brass with a large jade green plastic stone and four jade green drops.

c1915-20   *2.5in (6.25cm) long*

$220-280   **CGPC**

A 1960s unsigned pair of French earrings, in gold-tone metal, with green and white enameling, clear crystal rhinestones and French jet cabochons.

1.25in (3.25cm) long

$30-50   **CRIS**

A 1950s unsigned pair of star motif earrings, in silver set with bands of round-cut aquamarine crystal rhinestones.

1.25in (3.25cm) diam

$50-70   **CRIS**

A 1960s unsigned pair of oval earrings, with filigree gilt metal castings and matrix faux turquoise centers.

1in (2.5cm) long

$25-35   **CRIS**

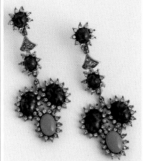

A late 1920s/early 1930s pair of black pendant-hoop clip earrings, encrusted with clear rhinestones and tiny faux pearls.

2.75in (7cm) long

$30-50   **ABAA**

A 1960s unsigned pair of 'Jewels of India' earrings, with starburst drops, of silver-tone metal set with faux lapis and faux coral cabochons and clear crystal rhinestones.

3in (7.5cm) long

$70-100   **CRIS**

A pair of unsigned leaf motif earrings, in hand-beaten white metal with wire wraps.

c1960s   2.5in (6.5cm) long

$80-120   **PC**

A 1930s unsigned necklace and pair of pendant earrings, with faceted rock crystal beads and drops and rock crystal spacers.

Necklace 16in (41cm) long

$120-180   **BY**

A 1920s/30s necklace, with silver links set with clear crystal rhinestones and faceted ruby glass shield motifs.

14in (36cm) long

$120-180   **ECLEC**

A 1920s unsigned necklace, with bunches of grapes of ruby red glass beads alternated with hoops of clear glass.

16.25in (42cm) long

$120-180   **ECLEC**

An unsigned fruit garland necklace, with poured glass leaves and orange and lemon glass bead fruits.

c1930s   16.25in (42cm) long

$120-180   **ECLEC**

An unsigned glass necklace, with pale green, blue, red, black, lilac, and coffee glass beads.

c1930s   15.25in (39cm) long

$70-100   **ECLEC**

A 1920s unsigned faux coral woven bead necklace, with two small rings inset with diamanté near the pendant.

16.5in (42cm) long closed

$220-280   **BY**

A 1920s/30s Czechoslovakian quadruple-pendant necklace, of gilt metal with round-, oval-, and square-cut red glass beads and stones.

Pendant 8.5in (22cm) long

$220-280   **ECLEC**

A 1960s/70s unsigned pendant necklace and earrings, of gold-plated metal with mottled green glass cabochons.

Necklace 14.75in (38cm) long

$70-100   **ECLEC**

A 1920s French floral motif bar pin, with carved blue glass and clear crystal rhinestones on a silver casting.

2.5in (6.5cm) long

$120-180   **CRIS**

A 1960s/70s unsigned Scandinavian pendant necklace, with red plastic neckband and graduated and articulated discs of polished steel.

Pendant 6.25in (16cm) long

$1,800-2,200   **LB**

An 1930s French Art Deco necklace, of matte finish gold-plated metal, with triangular sections of black enameling, unsigned.

17in (43cm) long

$400-600   **CRIS**

An early 1970s unsigned Pop Art open bangle, of gold-tone metal with a shield ornament, stylistically a pastiche of Classical Greco-Roman forms.

3.5in (9cm) wide

$30-50   **MILLB**

COLLECTORS' NOTES

- Color, form, and date are the main indicators of value for the Bakelite and plastic jewelry, which saw its heyday during the 1920s and 30s. Becoming popular by adding a much needed and affordable shot of glamor during the Great Depression, it was produced in a riot of bright and bold colors. The brighter or more numerous the colors, the more desirable a piece is likely to be.

- Consider the form, as this can help you date and value a piece. Forms tended to be plainer and more geometric in the late 1920s, with figurative and animal pins, and more outrageous, novelty designs appearing in the 1930s. Dangling components and an inherent humor and wit also add value, as do sporting themes, including golf and riding.

- Also examine decoration – the plastics used were ideally suited to carving. Hand carved items are the most desirable and the heavier and the more intricate the design, the better. Similarly, pieces that are decorated all over, rather than in panels, are more sought-after. The material also counts. Transparent 'apple juice' Bakelite, a form of Lucite is one of the most sought-after and can be carved and painted, adding yet more value.

- In its day, Bakelite jewelry was stocked by many leading fashionable department stores such as Harrods and Macy's, but after WWII, less expensive plastics were introduced and quality and desirability began to decline. However, the 'Pop' period of the 1960s is fast becoming a popular area, when even leading couturiers re-examined plastic. Look for styling typical of the day and bright colors – pieces can still be found for under $70.

- Reproductions of classic pieces do exist, but materials and therefore colors tend to be different. Reproductions often feel lighter in weight. Gently feel around pieces with your finger nail and examine them closely as scratches and cracks, particularly if deep, can be hard to repair and devalue a piece considerably.

A 1940s orange basketweave carved Bakelite bangle.

6in (8.5cm) diam

$200-250 **BB**

A red 'over-dye' 'creamed corn' Bakelite bangle, engraved with flowers.

3in (7.5cm) diam

$100-150 **EVL**

A carnelian red Bakelite bangle, the outside edges heavily carved with a swirling, stylized, foliate design.

3.5in (9cm) diam

$300-400 **EVL**

A brown Bakelite imitation wood bangle, carved all over with a leaf design and unusually pierced.

3.25in (8cm) diam

$100-150 **EVL**

A 1940s jade green Bakelite bangle, carved with flowers.

This piece is worth less than others as the design is very simple, appears on two panels only and may have been carved on a machine. It is also thinner and is less visually appealing than other examples.

3in (7.5cm) diam

$60-90 **EVL**

A hand carved jade green Bakelite bangle, with inset daisy on a panel of leaves and a carved twist design.

3.25in (8cm) diam

$150-250 **EVL**

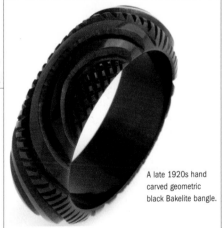

A late 1920s hand carved geometric black Bakelite bangle.

3.5in (9cm) diam

$500-700 **EVL**

A well carved yellow Bakelite bangle, with alternating 'twisting' panels of plain, floral and foliate decoration.

3in (7.5cm) diam

$150-250 EVL

An Art Deco style 'apple juice' Bakelite bangle, reverse carved with grass-like decoration, with black painted inner rim surfaces.

3.25in (8.5cm) diam

$650-750 EVL

A CLOSER LOOK AT A BAKELITE BANGLE

This type of bracelet is known as a 'bowtie' due to the bowtie shapes, made here with the yellowy-orange plastic.

They are comparatively rare and hard to find, as well as being very popular with collectors, making them valuable.

Look out for multi-colored examples using more than two colors – the more colors the more valuable the bangle will be.

Individual sections of Bakelite are assembled to form the bangle – examine the entire bangle as cracks will devalue a piece considerably.

An orange and 'creamed corn' 'bow tie' bangle.

3.5in (9cm) diam

$1,500-2,000 EVL

A laminated colored Bakelite and wood striped bangle.

3in (7.5cm) diam

$150-200 EVL

A 1930s green and yellow mottled cast phenolic hinged bracelet, with two applied carved Scottie dogs.

3in (7.5cm) wide

$250-350 BY

A 1950s pearlized fleck and black fleck curling reeded plastic bangle, with sprung hinge.

3.25in (8cm) diam

$35-45 BB

A contemporary Corian 'granite effect' bangle, by Barry Spector.

Corian is a blend of natural products and pure acrylic polymer and is made by DuPont in a wide range of mottled, stone-like colors.

c2000

3.75in (9.5cm) diam

$80-120 BB

A 'Bambi' fawn 'creamed corn' and painted Bakelite pin.

This characterful pin was probably released around the same time as the Disney film.

c1942   3.25in (8.5cm) high

$150-200   **EVL**

A CLOSER LOOK AT A BAKELITE PIN

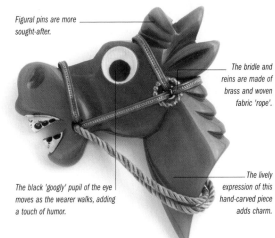

Figural pins are more sought-after.

The bridle and reins are made of brass and woven fabric 'rope'.

The black 'googly' pupil of the eye moves as the wearer walks, adding a touch of humor.

The lively expression of this hand-carved piece adds charm.

A burgundy red cast phenolic horse brooch, with fabric rope and metal harness and bridle.

2.75in (7cm) high

$550-750   **EVL**

A carved wood and green Bakelite leaping gazelle pin.

It is uncommon to find Bakelite jewelry where the wood part is mounted onto the Bakelite part – the other way around is much more common.

2.25in (6cm) high

$250-350   **EVL**

A carved yellow marbled Bakelite pin, in the shape of a chess 'knight'.

2.75 (7cm) high

$80-120   **EVL**

A 1930s green Bakelite figural pin, showing a Chinese man pulling a rickshaw.

2.75in (7cm) wide

$150-200   **EVL**

A 1930s carved jet black Bakelite swordfish pin.

This is both an unusual color and subject matter, almost resembling hardstone jet popular in the Victorian era. Fish and other animals are sought-after subjects.

4in (10cm) wide

$320-380   **EVL**

A carved and painted yellow Bakelite dagger-shaped pin, the painted black grip decorated with wire and pressed brass.

3.25in (8cm) diam

$150-200   **EVL**

An 'apple juice' Bakelite fruit dangling bar pin.

3.25in (8cm) high

$220-280   **EVL**

A rare orangy-red 'over-dye' hunting theme dangling pin, with hunting horn, boot, cap and rhinestone inlaid horseshoe.

Dangling pins are much sought-after, especially when themed. Check the condition carefully as repairs or replaced parts reduce the value.

A dangling bunch of cherries pin, with plastic leaves and plastic-covered string, in excellent condition.

3.5in (9cm) high

3.25in (8cm) high

$300-400   **EVL**   **$350-450**   **EVL**

A well carved 'apple juice' Bakelite Swan pin.

This comparatively complex pin is carved from both the front and the back and is pierced. Furthermore, white paint applied to the back gives the watery swirls their 'depth' and the swan its 'body'.

A 1930s/40s celluloid 'school' themed pin, with dangling slate, painted Bakelite pencil and book.

An 'apple juice' Bakelite bar pin, with reverse-carved and painted Bakelite flowers, with laminated shaped yellow Bakelite ends.

2in (5cm) wide

2.75in (7cm) long

2.75in (7cm) wide

$80-120   **BB**   **$320-380**   **EVL**   **$300-400**   **EVL**

A very rare brown Bakelite-on-silver metal golf clubs and bag shaped pin.

A heavily carved large yellow Bakelite flower pin.

It's the large size – almost the same diameter as a bangle – and the excellent level of hand carving that makes this pin desirable and valuable.

A reverse-carved amber Lucite starfish-shaped pin, carved with a frondy leaf to imitate real amber jewelry.

A red carved wreath pin, carved all over with a stylized foliate pattern.

This is an extremely rare pin – it is unusual for ladies' jewelry to have a golf theme, although more ladies were playing golf in the 1920s and 1930s.

3.25in (8cm) diam

3.25in (8.5cm) diam

2in (5cm) diam

3in (7.5cm) high

$280-320   **EVL**   **$120-180**   **EVL**   **$70-100**   **EVL**   **$320-380**   **EVL**

A contemporary Lea Stein plastic pin, in the form of a dappled cat with reflective eyes and ears.

4in (10cm) long

$70-100 **AGO**

A 1970s vintage Lea Stein brooch, in the form of an elephant with black tusk and ear.

Lea Stein (b.1931) began making rhodoid jewelry in the late 1960s. Her 'vintage' period dated from then until 1981 when her company closed. In 1988 she began making jewelry again and continues to do so today.

2.75in (7cm) long

$70-100 **AGO**

A contemporary Lea Stein plastic brooch, in the form of a red turtle, with glittering patterned shell.

3in (7.5cm) length

$70-100 **AGO**

A contemporary Lea Stein plastic brooch, in the form of a purple poodle.

2.5in (5cm) long

$70-100 **AGO**

A late 1990s Lea Stein 'Panther' pin, made of mottled brown and orange laminated rhodoid.

4in (10cm) wide.

$80-120 **CRIS**

A vintage Art Deco-style Lea Stein brooch, in the form of a bird.

Here Stein strongly harks back to the Art Deco period – not only in the geometric design and bright colors, but also by visually imitating 'shagreen' a luxury material widely used in the 1920s and 1930s.

4.25in (11cm) long

$70-100 **AGO**

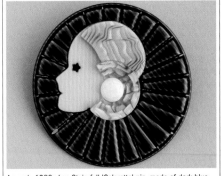

A contemporary Lea Stein plastic pin, in the form of a 1920s flapper, with imitation mother-of-pearl collar.

2.25in (6cm) long

$70-100 **AGO**

An early 1980s Lea Stein full 'Colorette' pin, made of dark blue, ice blue, black and faux pearl laminated rhodoid.

The word 'Colorette' relates to the full, circular fan behind the head.

2in (5.5cm) diam

$80-120 **CRIS**

COSTUME JEWELRY

A pair of 1930s injected cream and brown Bakelite clip loop earrings.

Loop 1.5in (4cm) diam

$180-220 **BB**

A pair of 1960s Pop Art black and green clip earrings, with injection molded green dot.

2.5in (6.5cm) high

$150-200 **BB**

A pair of early 1970s large Pop Art straw boater pendant earrings, unsigned, in candy striped plastic and goldtone base metal.

3.5in (9cm) long

$20-25 **MILLB**

A pair of mid- to late 1960s Pop Art plastic 'flower power' earrings, unsigned, with semi-translucent petals and opaque deep purple centers.

1.5in (4cm) diam

$20-25 **MILLB**

A 1960s Pop Art yellow Bakelite necklace.

This is an unusually late use of Bakelite, as by the 1960s other, less expensive plastics had taken over.

$220-280 **BB**

A 'creamed corn' and black Bakelite articulated necklace.

7in (17.5cm) diam

$80-120 **BB**

A 1960s/70s Lanvin 'Space Age' necklace, with black and red plastic pendant.

Along with other notable designers, Lanvin explored the futuristic space theme that dominated haute couture during the late 1960s.

Pendant 3in (8cm) diam

$220-280 **LB**

An early 1970s unsigned Pop Art belt, with candy colored plastic and goldtone metal links and a long disc pendant.

40in (101.5cm) long

$20-25 **MILLB**

Six 1960s clear and colored laminated Lucite fashion rings.

1.25in (3cm) high

$40-60 each **DTC**

FIND OUT MORE...

DK Collectors' Guide: Costume Jewelry, *by Judith Miller, published by Dorling Kindersley, 2003.*

COLLECTORS' NOTES

■ Type, date, condition, and rarity are the main gauges of value for Disneyana. Many of the items found by collectors are children's toys, which were usually thoroughly play-worn. As a result, mint condition toys, especially if they retain their original box, will fetch a considerable premium over those that have been played with.

■ Memorabilia dating from the 1930s is generally the most sought-after and valuable. When trying to date Disneyana, look first at the shape and design of a character or item as some characters were only made at certain times, and others changed over time – Mickey Mouse is typical of this. Although he is one of the most popular characters, he is not the rarest and rare characters can fetch higher values.

■ Markings are also important. George Borgfeldt's name will generally date an item to the 1930s, as he was the first to receive a license to produce Disney's characters, in 1930. Legendary salesman and marketer Kay Kamen is another early name. He signed a deal with Disney in 1933 that was cut short by Kamen's death in a plane crash in 1949.

■ Before c1939, licenced items were marked 'Walt Disney Enterprises', or 'Walter E. Disney'. Licenced items made in the UK could also be marked 'Walt Disney Mickey Mouse Ltd'. From the 1940s onward, items were marked 'Walt Disney Productions'. Other marks usually indicate unlicensed or later products.

■ From the 1930s to the 1960s, many unlicenced products were made outside the US. Many of these came from Germany, followed by Japan from the late 1940s. Early examples from the 1930s are often desirable and valuable, and those from the 1950s can represent an affordable alternative to collecting period pieces. Many collectors prefer licenced products.

■ As items from the 1930s-1950s become more scarce, collectors are increasingly looking to later decades. Now may be the time to buy, although always aim to go for memorabilia in mint condition. Similarly, paper ephemera from the primary vintage period, such as cards, badges, and paper, is possibly still undervalued.

■ Small limited editions based on characters from recent Disney classics such as The Lion King are currently hot property.

A CLOSER LOOK AT A MICKEY MOUSE FIGURE

An early 1930s German hand-painted ceramic Mickey Mouse figure, marked "820 1/2".

2.25in (5.5cm) high

$30-50 **GAZE**

A Japanese painted ceramic Mickey Mouse figure, stamped "Mickey Mouse" on his front, "MADE IN JAPAN" and "Walt E. Disney" on the back.

4in (10cm) high

$80-120 **PWE**

Mickey has become more 'juvenile' over the years, changing his appearance considerably. This helps to date earlier examples.

His head is smaller, less rounded and more rodent-like than today's Mickey.

This Mickey has a wide smiling mouth with teeth - a scary feature that appears on some very early licenced and unlicenced products including this figurine.

Differences between this Mickey and later incarnations include the tail, longer legs and arms, big hands and striped pants.

A 1930s German large handpainted plaster Mickey Mouse, cracked at the legs and re-glued, molded "1234 GESCH" on back of stand.

7.75in (19.5cm) high

$1,000-1,500 **AMJ**

A 1950s 'Mickey Mouse' collapsible plastic Maxi Puppet, by Kohner, marked "© Walt Disney Productions".

5.5in (14cm) high

$25-35 **SOTT**

A 1970s Mickey Mouse Club 'Minnie Mouse' soft toy, with Mickey Mouse Club badge, faded body, one eye missing.

11in (28cm) high

$25-35 **GAZE**

A 1950s Schuco clockwork Donald Duck tinplate toy, movement in working order, some wear.

Donald Duck first appeared in the Silly Symphony cartoon "The Wise Little Hen" in 1934. Audiences appreciated his characteristic short fuse and during the 1940s he starred in more broadcast cartoons than Disney's 'golden boy' Mickey Mouse.

$300-500 | **LAN**

A 1950s Donald Duck ceramic money bank, with "Japan" foil label.

5.5in (14cm) high

$30-50 | **SOTT**

A late 1930s American Seiberling Latex molded rubber Happy dwarf, marked "© Walt Disney".

5.5in (14cm) high

$80-120 | **PWE**

An American Ideal composition Pinocchio, loosely strung, light soiling to clothing, some crazing to rear of head and split under left ear.

13in (33cm) high

$300-400 | **JDJ**

A late 1930s American Seiberling Latex molded rubber Doc dwarf, by Seiberling Latex and marked "© Walt Disney".

6in (15cm) high

$60-90 | **PWE**

A Japanese Flower ceramic figure, from "Bambi", marked "Disney Japan".

3in (7.5cm) high

$15-20 | **SOTT**

A Britain's Pluto No.18H lead figure.

Pluto's curling tail has been broken, which is a common ailment. A complete set of five Britain's Disney characters, including Mickey, Donald, Goofy, and Pluto, may fetch $3,000.

$70-100 | **GAZE**

A Bambi lithographed die-cut wooden figure, marked "© W.D.P.".

c1942   6in (15cm) high

$30-40 | **SOTT**

A 1940s Mickey Mouse and Donald Duck fire truck rubber toy, by Sun Rubber Co. USA, marked "© Walt Disney Productions".

In 1944, the Sun Rubber Co. also produced a Mickey Mouse gas mask with Walt Disney's full approval, in case of inland attack after the bombing of Pearl Harbor. Few survived and today they are very rare.

6.5in (16.5cm) long

$60-90   **SOTT**

A 1940s Donald Duck and Pluto rubber toy car, by Sun Rubber Co. USA, marked "© Walt Disney Productions".

6.5in (16.5cm) long

$80-120   **SOTT**

A 1960s Walt Disney Club toy car, made in Hong Kong for S.S. Kruesge, marked "© Walt Disney Productions".

5.75in (14.5cm) high

$15-25   **SOTT**

A very rare 1930s 'Funnyflex' painted wood Mickey Mouse on a sledge, with remains of transfer reading "Mickey Mouse Corp by Walt Disney", one ear detached.

6in (15cm) long

$1,500-2,000   **PWE**

A Fisher Price Mickey Mouse 'Puddle Jumper' wooden pull-along toy, with lithographed paper covering.

As you pull the toy along, the back of the car wobbles and makes a noise. It is hard to find the paper on this pull-along toy in such bright, intact and unspoilt condition.

1953-56   *6.5in (16.5cm) long*

$200-300   **SOTT**

A 1950s Fisher Price Donald Duck lithographed paper-on-card and wood pull-along toy drummer.

7.5in (19cm) long

$300-400   **SOTT**

A 1950s/60s Japanese TM Modern Toys battery operated tinplate Mickey Mouse on a buggy, with original box.

8in (20cm) long

$180-220   **W&W**

An American Louis Marx wind-up tinplate and celluloid 'Disney Dipsy Car', with Donald Duck, marked "Walt Disney Prod", mint and boxed.

c1950   *6in (15cm) long*

$600-900   **PWE**

A 1950s Japanese Line Mar Toys wind-up tinplate 'Mechanical Pluto The Drum Major', marked 'Walt Disney Productions', mint and boxed.

6.5in (16.5cm) high

$400-600   **PWE**

A Japanese Pluto bean bag toy, with painted rubber head, marked "© Walt Disney Productions".

7in (18cm) wide

$15-20   **SOTT**

A 1950s Japanese lithographed tin Thumper friction toy, from "Bambi", made by Line Mar Toys, marked "© W.D.P.".

3in (7.5cm) long

$40-60   **SOTT**

A 1950s Japanese lithographed tin Flower friction toy, from "Bambi", made by Line Mar Toys, marked "© W.D.P.".

3in (7.5cm) long

$40-60   **SOTT**

A Mickey Mouse wood and printed paper acrobat toy.

It is hard to find these simply made, delicate toys in this intact and bright condition as they are so easily damaged through play.

A rare 1950s celluloid Mickey and Minnie Mouse see-saw toy, both figures marked, "Japan" at hip, stamped, "Made in Japan" on bottom of tin base.

8in (20cm) high

$70-100   **SOTT**

$700-1,000   **JDJ**

A Donald Duck lithographed tin paint box, by Transorgron Co. Inc., marked "Walt Disney Enterprises".

c1946

$30-50   **SOTT**

A 1960s Mickey Mouse Drawing Tutor, by Welsotoys, no. 9/99, lithographed tinplate, marked "©Walt Disney Productions Ltd".

Box 19.25in (49cm) wide

$40-60   **GAZE**

A 1950s 'Mickey Mouse' lithographed card kaleidoscope, marked "© Walt Disney Production".

7.75in (19.5cm) long

$50-80   **SOTT**

A 1950s American lithographed tin sand pail, by J. Chein, decorated with Mickey Mouse scene, marked "© Walt Disney Productions".

4.25in (11cm) high

$70-90   **SOTT**

A Minnie Mouse vinyl purse, marked "©
Walt Disney Productions".

c1958   *4.25in (11cm) wide*

$30-40   **SOTT**

A 1990s Disney's
'Wonderful World of
Reading' school
book backpack.

*This backpack advertises the popular
children's bookclub run by Disney,
promoting the reading of classic tales for
children.*

$7-10   **BR**

A 1930s Snow
White and the Seven
Dwarfs child's scarf, marked "W.D.E." for
Walt Disney Enterprises.

19in (48.5cm) wide

$40-60   **SOTT**

A 1930s fringed silk scarf, with
printed design of Mickey
catching a football, unmarked.

8.5in (21.5cm) wide

$30-50   **SOTT**

A 1950s pair of Mickey Mouse
socks.

10.5in (26.5cm) long

$10-15   **BH**

A 'Snow White' and 'Dopey' child's
wristwatch, marked "© Walt Disney
Productions".

1in (2.5cm) diam

$100-150   **SOTT**

A 'Mickey Mouse
Globetrotters'
membership badge, by
Kay Kamen Ltd, marked "Eat
Freihofers Perfect Loaf".

*Bread advertising was often tied in to
popular characters. This badge would have
been produced shortly after 1933, the worst
year of the Depression.*

c1934   *1.25in (3cm) diam*

$60-90   **SOTT**

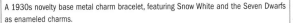

A 1930s novelty base metal charm bracelet, featuring Snow White and the Seven Dwarfs
as enameled charms.

7in (18cm) long

$280-320   **WW**

A Mickey Mouse Bakelite alarm clock, by US Time Ingersoll, marked "© W.D.P."

c1940   4in (10cm) high

$40-60   **JDJ**

A 1950s Minnie Mouse alarm clock, by Bradley, Germany, marked "© Walt Disney Productions".

4.5in (11.5cm) diam

$25-35   **JDJ**

A Walt Disney Pluto plastic clock, by the Allied Manufacturing Company, marked "Walt Disney Productions", mint and boxed.

Box 10.5in (26.5cm) high

$350-450   **PWE**

A German Waechtersbach Donald Duck ceramic clock, marked "© Walt Disney Productions", on a metal base.

9in (23cm) high

$100-150   **PWE**

An early Mickey and Minnie Mouse reverse-painted glass tray, signed on lower right, "A GEORGES GAPIN, VIEN, AMICHLEMENT, E.SEVRE", paint worn in places.

16in (40.50cm) long

$100-150   **JDJ**

A 1950s Donald Duck Chocolate Syrup lithographed tin can, by Atlantic Syrup Refining Corp., marked "©Walt Disney Productions", unused.

4.5in (11.5cm) high

$25-35   **BH**

A Snow White and the Seven Dwarves milk glass child's cereal bowl, by Vitrock, marked "W.D. Ent.".

$70-100   **SOTT**

A pair of Mickey and Minnie Mouse painted cast plastic napkin rings, marked "W.D.P"

3in (7.5cm) high

$30-50   **SOTT**

A 1950s Mickey Mouse painted ceramic ashtray, with Mickey playing the saxophone, marked "Made In Japan".

3in (7.5cm) high

$150-200   **PWE**

A 1950s Three Little Pigs ceramic ashtray, stamped on the bottom "Made in Japan © WALT DISNEY".

3.25in (8.5cm) high

$150-200   **PWE**

A J. Chein Snow White and the Seven Dwarfs electric 78rpm child's record player, marked "PortoFonic", with lithographed tin base.

14in (35.5cm) diam

$200-300   **JDJ**

A 'Mickey Mouse' portable 33 or 45rpm child's turntable, manufactured by General Electric, USA, model RP 3122 B, in a plastic case.

c1970

$150-250   **ATK**

A CLOSER LOOK AT DISNEY STATIONERY

It is very rare to find Horace Horsecollar accompanying Mickey and Minnie as he was a short-lived character. He first appeared in the 1929 film 'The Plow Boy' and he was soon replaced by Goofy.

Horace was not created by Disney himself but, after appearing as a supporting character, appeared in stories of his own.

Disposable and easily used functional items such as children's writing paper can be extremely rare today, despite the large amount originally made – and this is in excellent, bright condition.

Mickey and Minnie both have 'pie-section' eyes indicating a comparatively early date.

Horace Horsecollar can be distinguished from Mickey's other horse Tanglefoot as he walks upright.

An 1930s Walt Disney child's writing paper and envelope, with rare image of Horace Horsecollar.

5.75in (14.5cm) high

$15-25   **SOTT**

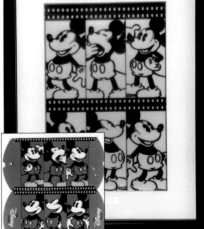

An original Disney Studios Mickey Mouse printing plate, with two original gift box samples, in original frame.

$150-200   **ATK**

A "Walt Disney presents The Jungle Book" 7in mini-LP and 24 page book, LLP319, from Disneyland Records.

1977

$12-18   **GAZE**

A Walt Disney World souvenir book.

1972   *11in (28cm) wide*

$20-30   **BH**

"The Art of Walt Disney: From Mickey Mouse to the Magic Kingdom", 1970s American advertising poster.

40in (101cm) high

$100-150   **CL**

A 1950s Pedigree hard plastic walking doll, marked "Lulu" and "22".

Pedigree was founded by the Lines Brothers in 1919 and began making composition dolls in the 1930s. In the 1950s it turned to hard plastic dolls and it is these that are so sought-after by collectors today.

22in (56cm) high

$180-220   **GAZE**

A 1950s Pedigree clockwork 'Walker' hard plastic doll, with Tri-ang key.

14in (35.5cm) high

$100-150   **DSC**

A 1950s Pedigree 'Knee Joint' hard plastic doll.

She has the same face as the Saucy Walker doll. Her knee joints allow her to sit in a chair and also kneel to pray.

22in (56cm) high

$120-180   **DSC**

A Pedigree hard plastic doll, shoes marked "Cinderella Size 1", in original box.

14.5in (37cm) high

$120-180   **GAZE**

A 1950s Pedigree 'Saucy Walker' hard plastic doll, with 'flirty' eyes and two teeth, with unjointed knees.

This doll has the same face as The Pretty Peepers doll also on this page, and her head turns as she 'walks'. Knee bend examples are more valuable.

21in (53.5cm) high

$100-150   **DSC**

A rare 1950s Pedigree 'Pretty Peepers' hard plastic doll, with jointed knees.

This doll has a plastic plate in her chest which, when pressed, alters the color of her eyes and their position from left to centre to right. They are hard to find in this condition.

22in (56cm) high

$300-400   **DSC**

A 1950s Pedigree 'Little Princess' hard plastic doll.

Based on Princess Anne, this doll was released in the Coronation year, 1953. Her clothes were designed by Norman Hartnell, the Queen's designer but tend to disintegrate, making them rare. An example without clothes would be worth up to $120.

14in (35.5cm) high

$180-220   **DSC**

A 1950s Roddy smiley-faced hard plastic doll.

The company that became known as 'Roddy' in the 1950s was founded in 1948. This example has a slightly less common face. She has plastic eyelashes, which are typical of Roddy. Earlier Roddy dolls had tin eyes.

10in (25.5cm) high

$50-70   **DSC**

A Roddy hard plastic walking doll, boxed.

Box 4.25in (11cm) high

$20-30   **GAZE**

A 1950s Roddy walker pouty-faced hard plastic doll, with turning head mechanism and molded shoes.

The hands with 'thumbs-up' are typical of Roddy. Check the back of the head and lips for paint wear. The molded shoes are also a typical feature of many Roddy dolls.

12in (30.5cm) high

$50-70   **DSC**

A Roddy Maori hard plastic doll and baby, with quill skirt and feather cloak.

14in (35.5cm) high

$50-70   **GAZE**

A 1950s Roddy 'Topsy' hard plastic doll, with molded "Roddy Made in England" mark.

This was also made as a white baby, but as less black dolls were made, they are usually more valuable. The unusual name comes from the hairstyle.

9in (23cm) high

$50-70   **DSC**

A 1950s Tudor Rose straight-legged hard plastic boy doll.

The less valuable white version of this doll is worth approximately $15, but values for Tudor Rose are rising.

8in (20cm) high

$20-25   **DSC**

A 1950s Tudor Rose 'Blondy Blueyes' hard plastic doll, by Rosedale Associated Manufacturing Ltd, with unusual molded clothes and walking action, boxed.

7in (18cm) high

$30-50   **DSC**

A 1950s 'Knee Joint' hard plastic doll, by Rosebud.

17in (43cm) high

$100-150   **DSC**

A late 1950s Rosebud 'Knee Joint' hard plastic doll, with vinyl head.

Late 1950s hard plastic dolls with vinyl heads are known as 'Transitionals' – the vinyl allowed hair to be rooted directly into the scalp rather than being a glued on wig. It was too expensive for all the machinery to be changed as soon as vinyl was introduced, so the new heads were used with old-fashioned style bodies and limbs.

17in (43cm) high

$70-100   **DSC**

DOLLS

A 1980s Peggy Nisbet 'Sarah Ferguson Bride' vinyl doll, with original box.

Peggy Nisbet made her first doll in 1953, to celebrate the coronation of Queen Elizabeth II. Many of her highly detailed dolls are drawn from history, such as Henry VIII and his six wives and the 'Cries of London' series of Victorian dolls. In the 1980s she made a series of Royal dolls, which are popular with collectors. The company became 'House of Nisbet' in the mid-1970s and teddy bears began to take precedence. Although Nisbet herself died in 1985, her dolls were produced until 1999. Mint and complete condition is essential.

16in (10.5cm) high

$100-150   **DSC**

A CLOSER LOOK AT A PEGGY NISBET DOLL

The head and neck are fixed, giving Diana's characteristic look, and her hair is in its original style. ⸻

She is complete with ⸻ *train, veil, necklace and bouquet, which are all in mint condition*

She retains her original box, showing an original price tag of £24.99 at famous London toy store Hamley's.

As they were expensive, most of these dolls were sold to collectors, so it is not hard to find mint and boxed examples.

A 1980s Peggy Nisbet 'My Princess' Diana, Princess of Wales vinyl doll.

16in (40.5cm) high

$100-150   **DSC**

A 1980s Peggy Nisbet 'Prince William Toddler Sailor Suit' vinyl doll, with "PN" monogram on back of neck, mint with original box.

18in (45.5cm) high

$100-150   **DSC**

A mid-to late 1980s Peggy Nisbet 'Prince Harry Baby Sun Suit' vinyl doll, mint with original box.

As this doll has the same face as the Prince William doll, it can often be difficult to tell them apart.

18in (45.5cm) high

$100-150   **DSC**

A 1970s Peggy Nisbet 'Queen Victoria' vinyl doll.

7in (18cm) high

$25-35   **DSC**

A 1970s Peggy Nisbet 'Nefertiti' vinyl doll, with enameled and gilt-decorated metal head dress.

The weighty head dress makes this delicate doll top heavy and unable to stand without support.

8in (20cm) high

$30-50   **DSC**

A 1970s Peggy Nisbet 'Dolls Seller' vinyl doll.

7in (18cm) high

$25-35   **DSC**

A Pedigree Sindy 'Ballerina' doll, mint with original box.

This doll was only made for one year making it scarce. In played-with condition and lacking the box, she would be worth up to $50 if she retained her dress. Sindy was introduced in 1963 and as with Barbie, features help to date her. In 1968 she gained eye lashes, a new side-parted hairstyle and a twist waist, and in 1970 a ball-jointed neck and extra joints at the elbows and knees. By the middle of the decade she had moveable wrists and could point her toes. Despite disappearing in 1997, she reappeared in 1999 under the 'Vivid Imaginations' company.

1985

$120-180   **DSC**

A Pedigree Sindy 'Starlight' doll, mint in box.

This doll has the new Sindy face. The following year, the brand was taken over by Hasbro.

1986

Box 13.5in (34cm) high

$100-150   **DSC**

An early 1980s Pedigree Sindy 'Space Fantasy' doll, with original clothing and shoes.

This was the only Pedigree Sindy made with pink hair.

11in (28cm) high

$100-150   **DSC**

A Pedigree Sindy 'Sweet Dreams' doll, with original nightdress.

This was the only Sindy to be produced with painted sleeping eyes.

1979

$25-35   **DSC**

A 1980s Dutch Fleur doll.

Fleur was the Dutch version of Sindy and had the same body.

11in (28cm) high

$25-35   **DSC**

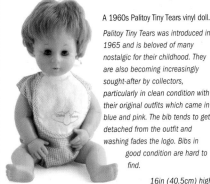

A 1960s Palitoy Tiny Tears vinyl doll.

Palitoy Tiny Tears was introduced in 1965 and is beloved of many nostalgic for their childhood. They are also becoming increasingly sought-after by collectors, particularly in clean condition with their original outfits which came in blue and pink. The bib tends to get detached from the outfit and washing fades the logo. Bibs in good condition are hard to find.

16in (40.5cm) high

$70-100   **DSC**

A 1980s Palitoy 'Tiny Tears' vinyl doll.

16in (40.5cm) high

$70-100   **DSC**

A Pedigree 'First Love' vinyl doll, mint in original box.

She was brought out to rival 'Tiny Tears' and proved successful for 10 years. In played-with but complete condition she can fetch up to $40.

A 1980s Palitoy Teeny Weeny Tiny Tears vinyl doll, in mint condition with original box.

Complete but without the original box, she would be worth up to $50.

8in (20cm) high

$100-150   **DSC**

A 1980s French Miro-Meccano 'Tinnie' vinyl doll, in mint condition with original box.

This is the French version of Tiny Tears.

16in (40.5cm) high

$50-70   **DSC**

c1977   16in (40.5cm) high

$100-150   **DSC**

A Pedigree 'Alice in Wonderland' vinyl doll, in mint condition with original box.

These dolls use a Sindy type body, and are desirable to Sindy collectors. The appealing box makes them highly collectable.

1978   11in (28cm) high

$70-100   **DSC**

A Pedigree 'Snow White' vinyl doll, in mint condition with original box.

1978   11in (28cm) high

$70-100   **DSC**

A 1980s Pedigree 'Matilda' vinyl doll, in mint condition with original box.

7in (18cm) high

$25-35   **DSC**

A 1980s Pedigree Grocer's shop with vinyl doll, in mint condition with original box.

This is part of a series, each in a different shop.

$25-35   **DSC**

A 1980s Hornby Flower Fairies 'Sweet Pea' vinyl doll, in mint condition with original box.

$25-35   **DSC**

A 1980s Hornby Flower Fairies 'Self-Heal Pixie' vinyl doll.

This pixie was usually sold with a fairy, the single boxed versions are much rarer.

Box 9.75in (25cm) high

$25-35   **DSC**

A 1970s Burbank 'Victoria Rose' vinyl doll, with soft body and legs.

Burbank were a short-lived company. As well as the soft body and legs, Victorian styles are typical.

22in (56cm) high

$25-35   **DSC**

A 1960s Amanda Jane Ltd 'Amanda Jane' vinyl doll, with sleepy eyes, in mint condition with original box.

These are commonly copied, but copies are of poorer quality and often have shorter legs. Eyes were painted, not sleepy, from the 1970s onwards.

8in (20cm) high

$25-35   **DSC**

A CLOSER LOOK AT A MORMIT DOLL

These dolls, launched 1945-46, used a heavy, rubbery PVC allowing them to be bathed – an innovation in an age of non-water resistant composition and painted dolls.

The limbs have a push-fit joint, allowing them to be taken apart and drained after bathing.

She is in mint condition with her box and feeding bottle, which are rare.

The coloured dyes used were not 'fast', so can fade or brown in sunlight or due to excessive handling. This one has an excellent complexion with original hair, rouged cheeks and red lips.

A 1950s 'Marie-Mia' hollow, soft plastic feeding and wetting 'Mormit' doll, by Morris Mitchell Ltd.

Founder F.G. Mitchell named the dolls 'Marie' with the second name being those of his five daughters, here 'Mia'.

11in (28cm) high

$80-120   **DSC**

A 1960s Chiltern (H.G. Stone) vinyl girl doll, with tight curl 'Saran' rough textured honey colored hair, in mint condition with original box.

12in (30.5cm) high

$30-50   **DSC**

A 1970s Flair 'Daisy Longlegs' vinyl doll, designed by Mary Quant, with walking/dancing action.

Quant also designed a range of costumes, which help to determine value. Outfits like this example are rare. There was also a smaller version at 11in high.

15in (38cm) high

$25-35   **DSC**

A 1960s Roddy tennis girl vinyl doll, with Saran hair, in mint condition with original box.

15in (38cm) high

$70-100   **DSC**

A 1960s Rosebud 'Bride' vinyl doll, lacks shoes and veil.

Complete she would be worth up to $70.

15in (38cm) high

$25-35   **DSC**

A 1930s hand-painted bisque doll, with googly-eyes and a preying mantis on its head, moveable arms.

6.25in (16cm) high

$40-60　　　　　　**RP**

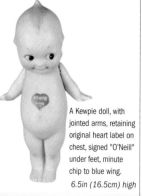

A Kewpie doll, with jointed arms, retaining original heart label on chest, signed "O'Neill" under feet, minute chip to blue wing.

6.5in (16.5cm) high

$80-120　　　　　　**JDJ**

A Kewpie doll, wearing a painted molded Prussian helmet, with outstretched hands.

2.75in (7cm) high

$220-280　　　　　　**JDJ**

A rare German Kewpie soldier doll, with molded clothing, helmet and gun, partial paper label on chest, some damage.

Kewpie was designed by US illustrator Rose O'Neill in 1909. The first dolls were made from around 1912, primarily in Germany but also in the US and Japan, with the craze lasting into the 1920s. Licensed Kewpies are the most desirable, especially if large or in different poses or 'clothes' – look for O'Neill's name on the base of the foot, star-shaped hands or heart-shaped or circular labels.

3.75in (9.5cm) high

$350-450　　　　　　**JDJ**

A Kewpie 'Action' doll.
c1910 　　　*5in (12.5cm) high*

$500-700　　　　　　**BEJ**

A large seated Kewpie doll, playing a mandolin, with original paper label, repair to stem of mandolin.

4in (10cm) high

$120-180　　　　　　**JDJ**

A Kewpie Governor doll, sitting in a wicker chair, with folded arms, marked "C" in a circle on bottom of chair.

$220-280　　　　　　**JDJ**

A large Kewpie Thinker doll, signed on bottom.

4.5in (11.5cm) high

$250-300　　　　　　**JDJ**

A Kewpie Blunderboo doll, minute chip to hair tip.

4.5in (11.5cm) high

$220-280　　　　　　**JDJ**

A Heinrich Handwerck PK doll, with brown sleeping eyes, pierced ears, open mouth with four teeth, the head stamped "109/11 3/4", some wear.

c1900   22in (55cm) high

$700-1,000   LAN

A Hertel, Schwab & Co. PK girl doll, 98/12, with flirty eyes, some damage to eye lids.

20in (50cm) high

$500-700   LAN

A rare Armand Marseille Asian doll, with closed mouth, stamped "353 2 3/4-3 1/2".

A Hertel, Schwab & Co. PK character baby doll, 152/2, with sleeping eyes, open mouth with tongue and two teeth, mohair wig, on a baby body.

c1912   11.25in (28cm) high

$600-900   LAN

Examine the back of bisque dolls' heads to check for marks identifying the maker and the mold number. Look for well painted features and examine the bisque carefully for cracks or damage. Clean bisque is also sought-after, as are large dolls and unusual nationalities, which are generally rarer.

17.25in (43cm) high

$800-1,000   LAN

A Wagner & Zetzsche bisque shoulder head doll, with blue sleep eyes, open mouth, four teeth, jointed body with composition arms.

25in (63.5cm) high

$280-320   W&W

A small French bisque doll, with composition body.

9in (23cm) high   ROS

$150-200   ROS

A German painted bisque boy doll.

c1920   5in (12.5cm) high

$300-500   BEJ

A pair of stone bisque children, with jointed arms and hand-painted details.

c1920   5in (12.5cm) high

$150-200   BEJ

A set of early 1900s bisque 'pudding' dolls.

These miniature hand-painted, simply molded dolls were often put in Christmas puddings as favours.

1.25in (3cm) high

$7-10 each   DSC

A 'Madam Hendron' composition doll, by Universal Talking Toys Co., featuring a spring-driven mechanism concealed in its body, with original dress and two cylinders.

c1922   26in (65cm) high

$500-700   **ATK**

An Italian composition 'Flirty' child doll, dressed in bright clothing with a straw hat.

c1930

$220-280   **BEJ**

A CLOSER LOOK AT A CORONATION DOLL

Her well-painted face is in excellent condition as is her hairstyle, which retains its original, tight curls and hairnet.

She has a disc-playing mechanism in her stomach that makes her sing the English National Anthem and recite a poem about the coronation.

She is in mint condition with all her clothes including her fur-trimmed coronation robe, sash, instructions and the original card box she was mailed in.

She was released at the time of the coronation of Queen Elizabeth II to help girls celebrate.

A 'Queen Elizabeth' speaking/singing composition doll, by Mark Payne Ltd, with original box.

c1953   26in (66cm) high

$700-1,000   **DSC**

A 1940s composition girl doll, probably by Roddy, all original.

18in (45.5cm) high

$50-70   **DSC**

A 1950s Rosebud fairy painted composition doll, with original outfit, wand and box.

7in (18cm) high

$50-70   **DSC**

A 1940s composition boy doll, by Diamond Tile Company, with soft body.

15.5in (39.5cm) high

$50-70   **DSC**

A late 19thC sailor boy doll, with cloth body, hand-painted face and composition head, "VH" mark at the back of the head, a few scratches to the face.

9in (23cm) high

$70-100   **EPO**

A Norah Wellings 'Jolly Toddler' doll, with original clothes and box.

c1930   17in (43cm) high

$600-800   **BEJ**

A 1930s Norah Wellings 'Queen Mary' sailor doll.

This doll is more desirable because it has the name of a well-known ship on the cap.

10in (25.5cm) high

$150-250   **BEJ**

A 1950s Lupino Lane doll, by Dean's Rag Book of London, with dog-tooth check suit and printed facial features.

This doll is modeled after the 1930s music hall star Lupino Lane, who is best known for the song 'The Lambeth Walk' from the musical 'Me and My Girl'.

c1939   11.5in (29cm) high

$350-450   **TCT**

A very rare Steiff British policeman poseable doll, with accurate blue felt uniform, his velvet face with boot button eyes, stitched and printed detail.

It's the early date, condition, subject matter and great rarity that make this doll as valuable as it is.

c1910   18in (46cm) high

$2,200-2,800   **F**

A 1950s Chad Valley 'George' fabric doll, with felt clothes and hat, label to foot.

12in (30.5cm) high

$300-500   **TCT**

A 1930s/40s Chad Valley fabric doll, the painted head with eyes looking to the side, label to foot.

18in (45.5cm) high

$80-120   **GAZE**

A Lenci cloth doll, arms jointed at the shoulders.

24in (61cm) high

$280-320   **GORL**

A 1930s fabric half doll, with painted features and blonde mohair wig, unmarked.

11.25in (28.5cm) high

$40-60   **GAZE**

COLLECTORS' NOTES

■ Technology has developed in leaps and bounds over the past few decades and those with an eye for nostalgia or for collecting important, classic technologies have begun to consider early computers.

■ Many collectors usually use their computers, to play original games that are no longer available, except possibly on emulators. As such, examples must be in working condition and be as complete as possible to fetch the higher values.

■ Look out for models from the 1970s-early 1990s that are considered landmarks of their time. Mass-produced and highly successful models such as Sinclair's Spectrum range or many Commodores are usually of lower value as so many survive today.

■ Certain models are rarer than others. Accessories such as games and power packs are also often sought-after.

■ A single year shown represents the year of introduction, a range gives the years of production.

An Acorn Archimedes A410 home computer.

Despite being at least twice as fast as the – then current – Atari ST and Amiga models, the Archimedes was expensive and saw little success outside of British schools.

1987-89   19in (48.5cm) w

$25-35   **PC**

An Apple IIe (European Model) home computer.

This model was the updated version of the II+, the 'e' standing for 'enhanced'.

1983-93   17in (43cm) wide

$25-35   **PC**

An Apple Mac Classic home computer.

The Classic was the cut-down successor to the Mac SE, with limited features for a budget market, and was thus rather underspecified compared to its siblings.

1990-92

$50-80   **PC**

An Atari 400 home computer, with touch-sensitive keypad and built-in tape drive.

1979-82   13in (33cm) wide

$30-50   **PC**

A Commodore Amiga A1000 home computer and keyboard.

Despite being a high-spec machine, the high price made it unpopular outside of the UK.

1985-87   17.5in (44.5cm) wide

$50-80   **PC**

A Commodore CDTV home computer.

This was designed as a home entertainment system, but was unpopular due to its high cost and lack of software.

1990-93   17in (43cm) wide

$70-100   **PC**

A Commodore Amiga A-500+ home computer.

1986   18in (45.5cm) wide

$8-15   **PC**

A Memotech MTX 512 home computer.

c1983 19in (48cm) wide

$30-50 PC

A Research Machines 380Z professional computer, with 32K RAM, a 5.25in double disc system and keyboard.

These computers were made primarily for use in schools and cost over $3,000 + VAT.

c1982 19.5in (49.5cm) wide

$30-50 PC

A Sinclair ZX Spectrum+ home computer.

c1984 12.5in (31.5cm) wide

$30-50 PC

A New Brain AD home computer, by Grundy Business Systems Ltd, with one line, 16 character screen.

An earlier model 'A' existed, without a screen. Neither were highly successful as, perhaps put off by the poor keyboard, the trade press noted that it was not a good games or business machine.

1982 10.75in (27cm) wide

$120-180 PC

A Sinclair Spectrum ZX 48K home computer, in fitted carrying case with power pack, manual, tape deck and games.

The 16K version is hard to find and can be worth up to twice the value of the 48K version.

1982-84 8.5in (21.5cm) wide

$50-70 PC

A Sinclair ZX Spectrum +3 home computer.

c1987 17in (43cm) wide

$50-80 PC

A TRS-80 color 2 home computer, by Tandy Radio Shack.

c1982 15in (37cm) wide

$30-50 PC

12 issues of 'Popular Electronics' magazine from 1975, including the January edition which showcased the introduction of one of the first mini-computers, the 'Altair 8800' – an event that prompted Bill Gates to found Microsoft five months later.

1975

$400-600 ATK

A CLOSER LOOK AT AN ESQUIRE MAGAZINE PINUP CALENDAR

A 1947 Esquire Girl calendar, unsigned artwork, with original mailing envelope.

In 1946, Vargas and Esquire ended their collaboration and Vargas went on to produce his own pinup calendar in 1948. In the meantime, Esquire released this uncredited calendar using unsigned Vargas artwork.

$80-120   **HH**

Alberto Vargas (1896-1982) started drawing fashion illustrations before being commissioned to paint the Ziegfield Follies in 1919. He worked with them for 12 years.

In 1939 he joined Esquire magazine, producing a center spread. These were collected into the 'Varga Girl' calendars.

The illustrations proved particularly popular with the US armed forces overseas and the designs were copied onto jackets and aircraft nose cones.

Playing to the soldiers over seas, Vargas has illustrated this lady in an army cap from the Signal Corp.

A 1945 Esquire magazine pinup calendar, with artwork by Alberto Vargas and verses by Phil Stack.

12.25in (31cm) high

$80-120   **HH**

A 1948 Varga 'The Varga Girl' calendar, with original mailing envelope, in mint condition, with verses by Earl Wilson.

As Esquire magazine had trademarked the name 'Varga Girls' they were able to continue to publish artwork under that name even though their association with Albert Vargas had ended.

12.25in (31cm) high

$80-120   **HH**

A 'Garden of Eden' poster, artwork by Benito Jacovitti (1923-1997).

Jacovitti is probably the best known Italian satirical cartoonist. His first cartoons appeared in 1939 and his recognizable style is typically absurd, bizarre, and often risqué.

25.25in (65cm) high

$30-50   **CL**

An Italian erotic poster, designed by Benito Jacovitti, copyright Club Anni Trenta, Genova.

1977

$80-120   **CL**

A 1950s 'Bust with Humor' small pamphlet, with drawings of various breast types, shapes and names, such as 'Sunnyside Up', 'Loaded 38s', and the rather unfortunate 'Olives' and 'Sandbags'.

4in (10cm) high

$20-30   **HH**

Gretchen Edgren, "The Playboy Book – 40 Years of Pictorial History", first UK edition, published by Mitchell Beazley.

1994

$80-120   **GAZE**

A late 19thC erotic transformation picture with musical movement and clockwork drive, with two scenes, the Swiss cylinder musical mechanism playing one melody.

$400-600 ATK

A Club Trocadero, Chicago matchbook, the matches with printed images of burlesques, unused.

2in (5cm) high

$30-40 SM

A 'Beautiful Girls' theater lounge matchbook, from the 'Burlesque Lounge' Dallas, the cover and interior printed with naked showgirls, the cover with embossed bosoms.

2in (5cm) high

$25-35 SM

A pair of 1950s terry cotton hand towels, by Cannon, made in the USA, titled 'Boss' and 'Slave', each with a dog, the eyes set with metal studs.

18in (45.5cm) long

$40-60 SM

A 'Glamour Girl' bone china pintray, of a naughty bride, gilt trim on scalloped edge.

4.5in (11.5cm) wide

$40-60 MA

A 1950s Adderley bone china transfer-printed 'Glamour Girl' ashtray.

5in (12.5cm) wide

$30-50 MA

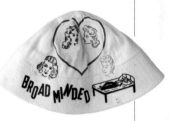

A 1950s cotton 'Broad Minded' hat, with applied cloth patches, made in Japan.

12in (30.5cm) wide

$70-100 SM

COLLECTORS' NOTES

■ Style and design in terms of shape, pattern, and color are of primary importance to most collectors and interior decorators. Pieces by notable designers or factories will fetch more than unnamed items, although a known designer is not always necessary. The 1950s look, even hinted at with a single object, can be acquired without resorting to famous designers or spending large sums of money.

■ Look for rounded, asymmetric and organic forms. Clean-lined kidney and tulip shapes that show patterns off to their best are typical. Angled, spindly legs with ball feet can be found on furniture and other small furnishing items. All are quintessentially modern and represent a stylistic break from the 1940s and traditional designs of previous periods.

■ Patterns are stylized and modern in appearance, ranging from atomic designs to zebra prints, playing cards, polka dots, ballerinas and even pin-up girls.

Parisian and foreign scenes showed a yearning for prosperity, travel, and glamour. Colors tend to be bright and cheerful, appealing to the young, and pastel shades are particularly prevalent. The 1950s saw the birth of the teenager and rock 'n' roll, leading to a fashion for related motifs.

■ Many new materials appeared during this period, such as Formica and different plastics. The early part of the decade saw surplus wartime aluminum being used frequently for domestic products. All these materials allowed for new forms to be made inexpensively.

■ Always consider condition, as many mass-produced pieces were not made to last long. As a result, some can be rare as most examples have long since been broken and discarded. When fashions changed, many 1950s artifacts were stored carelessly, if they were kept at all. In all cases, always aim to collect pieces that fulfil as many of the style criteria as possible.

A 1950s vase, with impressed marks and serial number.

8.25in (21cm) high

$15-25   **TCM**

A 1950s J. & G. Meakin transfer and hand-colored decorated plate.

Meakin ceramics currently have lower values than those by companies such as Midwinter, but this may change as more collectors turn their attention to Meakin's 1950s designs.

10in (25.5cm) diam

$25-35   **PSI**

An H.J. Wood Ltd 'Piazza ware' vase.

As well as the stylized design and colors, the curving asymmetric form and rim is archetypally 1950s.

c1957   9.5in (24cm) high

$50-80   **NPC**

A 1950s Gouda shallow dish, with floral design, printed "Paima Flora Gouda Holland", some crazing.

8in (20.5cm) long

$15-25   **TCM**

A Hornsea Pottery 'Coastline' pattern sugar bowl.

c1955   3.25in (8.5cm) high

$30-40   **AGR**

A Hornsea Pottery 'Elegance' pattern milk jug, sugar bowl and another bowl, designed by John Clappison.

This pattern was also available with a white interior.

c1955-c1959

Jug 4.25in (11cm) high

$100-150   **AGR**

An H.J. Wood Ltd 'Piazza' ware lidded butter dish, marked "845 BM" and "R".

6.5in (16.5cm) wide

$30-50   **FD**

A 1950s French tall hand-painted black asymmetric vase, with impressed and painted marks to base.

16in (40.5cm) high

$70-100   **PSI**

A ceramic 'tiki' mug, in the shape of an Easter Island head, marked "Japan".

Tiki mugs were popular Hawaiian souvenirs during the 1950s and 1960s and were used in 'tiki bars'. Reproductions are sold today, but are usually of poorer quality and not marked "Japan".

6.5in (14cm) high

$40-60   **SM**

A ceramic 'tiki' mug, marked "Orchids of Hawaii" and "Japan".

6in (15cm) high

$40-60   **SM**

A ceramic 'tiki' mug, with a tropical lady, marked "Orchids of Hawaii" and "Japan".

7in (18cm) high

$40-60   **SM**

A 1950s ceramic lady head vase, with umbrella.

6in (15cm) high

$70-100   **DAC**

A 1950s ceramic lady head vase, with green hood, praying hands and ceramic eyelashes.

Always examine the cowl of these vases as they are easily damaged. The more common version, with just one or no hands, is less valuable.

5.75in (14.5cm) high

$100-150   **MA**

A 1950s West German painted ceramic gnome, holding a plastic bird in a cage, the base printed "W.Germany /1".

8.25in (21cm) high

$25-35   **MHC**

A 1950s/60s Italian Raymor ceramic cat, marked "1529 Italy".

The market for Raymor and similar Italian ceramics of the 1950s and 1960s is in its infancy but is growing, with values likely to escalate. Look out for figurative pieces, sculptures or large cylindrical or square rectangular vases. Many share the same colors and impressed 'runic' motifs. Always avoid damaged examples.

15.25in (38.5cm) long

$280-320   **FD**

A 1950s or 1950s-style studio pottery figure of a dachshund, chipped.

Note the similarity of the pattern and colors to some of the 'Contemporary' range patterns produced by Poole Pottery during the 1950s.

6in (15cm) long

$50-70   **BRI**

A 1950s set of conical glasses in a wire frame, with transfer-printed designs of a native islander beating a drum.

Large glasses are more sought-after and valuable than sets of smaller shot glasses.

14.5in (37cm) wide

$80-120   **PWE**

A 1950s 'Stars 'n' Stripes' lemonade set, in bent wire holder.

Glasses screen-printed with colorful designs were produced in vast quantities during the 1950s and 60s. Many were contained in wire stands such as this example. As they were inexpensive at the time and used heavily, many sets are incomplete, which lowers their value considerably. Avoid buying examples that show wear to gilt trim or the transfer. Look out for rock 'n' roll and exotic themes, which fetch more, with scantily clad 'pin-up' girl patterns topping the bill.

17in (43cm) wide

$150-200   **MA**

A 1950s set of six screen-printed tumblers, in wire holder.

6.75in (17cm) high

$70-100   **MA**

A 1950s set of six multicolored screen-printed tumblers, with stylized dancing tribesmen.

5in (12.5cm) high

$70-100   **MA**

A 1950s set of four screen-printed tumblers, with rare top hat and cane design.

5.5in (12.5cm) high

$30-50   **MA**

A pair of tomato juice glasses, with printed decoration.

3.75in (9.5cm) high

$3-5   **BH**

Two 1950s printed 'Ubangi' glasses.

7in (17.5cm) high

$100-150   **CVS**

One of a set of four 1950s printed 'Hi Fi' record album glasses.

5in (12.5cm) high

$100-150 set   **MI**

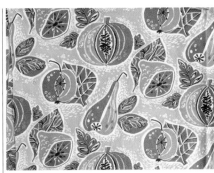

A length of 1950s English bark cloth, printed with a design of stylized fruit.

144in (366cm) long

$30-50 FD

A length of 1950s Swedish fabric, with a stylized foliate design.

144in (366cm) long

$100-150 FD

A length of 1950s cotton fabric, with embroidered silk trees, converted to curtains.

144in (366cm) long

$50-70 FD

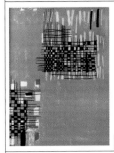

A framed panel of 'Quarto' pattern fabric, by Lucienne Day for Heals.

35.75in (91cm) high

$50-80 GAZE

A pair of 'Plantation' printed curtains, by Lucienne Day.

Lucienne Day (b.1917) is one of Britain's most influential 20thC textile designers. Bringing a new vitality into people's homes, she became known for her abstract designs.

c1958   *84in (213cm) long*

$150-200 GAZE

A small folding table, by Arnold Designs Ltd.

The angled spindle legs, curving form and stylized bull shout the 1950s, when flat-packed occasional furniture such as this became widespread. Arnold Designs of Chalford, near Stroud in Gloucestershire, UK, were known for making giftware, furniture and household goods and employed 25 people by 1972.

20in (51cm) long

$15-25 GAZE

A 1950s/60s kidney or boomerang-shaped laminated wood occasional table.

The kidney-shaped table was a fashionable 1950s favorite, representing a rounded visual departure from the hard angles of utility furniture. It was also practical, as it could fit around the arm of a sofa.

21in (53cm) long

$15-25 GAZE

A 1950s red-painted metal desk light.

$50-70 GAZE

A 1950s plastic-coated wire 78rpm record stand, with treble clef motif.

13.75in (35cm) wide

$100-150 MA

A 1950s pink embossed and printed 'My Favourite Tunes' record holder, by Ponytail.

7.5in (19cm) high

$30-50 MA

A 1950s Max Bill ceramic kitchen wall clock, with timer.

Max Bill (1908-94) studied under Walter Gropius at the Bauhaus from 1927-29 before becoming a prolific architect, artist and designer. He is also known for a small series of simple clocks, of which this is one. The pastel blue color and curving lines are very much of the period.

c1954 *10.5in (27cm) long*

$1,000-1,500 SK

A CLOSER LOOK AT A COFFEE MACHINE

This coffee machine was designed by Giordano Robbiati of Milan in the late 1940s. A patent was granted in the US in 1951.

It is made from aluminum, which was used extensively for domestic objects in the 1940s, partly due to a fondness for new materials and partly to use up surplus wartime stocks.

Its space age design is the epitome of 'modern' and was arguably way ahead of its time.

Made until the early 1980s, vintage models like this one are highly sought-after by collectors of modern design. It also has a legendary ability to make excellent coffee.

A Brevetti Robbiati 'Atomic' aluminum stove-top espresso coffee machine, with original jug.

c1951 *8.25in (21cm) high*

$300-500 SWO

A 1950s 'Mexican playing guitar' novelty bottle opener, with detachable guitar bottle opener, attached to the stand with a magnet.

7in (18cm) high

$15-20 MA

A 1950s American Oster chrome and black Bakelite 'Airjet' tabletop hairdryer, with original box and instructions.

The futuristic Oster Airjet was introduced in 1949.

c1950 *8.5in (22cm) high*

$30-40 NOR

A 1950s ceramic Las Vegas dice-shaped lighter and ashtray set, stamped "Japan".

2.5in (6.5cm) wide

$80-120 SM

COLLECTORS' NOTES

■ As with the 1950s, consider form, pattern and color when looking at 1960s and 1970s memorabilia. Always aim to buy items that fulfil as many of the criteria as possible. Color and pattern are perhaps the most important as they are so characteristic of the age. Bright, acid and often clashing colors dominate, designs explode in psychedelic or 'flower power' patterns. The themes of 'love' and 'peace' recur.

■ The Art Nouveau style of the 1900s also made a comeback, but with a new palette and often with chunkier forms around the sinuous 'whiplash' design. Look out for textiles, which add a notable period touch to any room. Leading names include Heal's of London and Marimekko of Finland.

■ Materials developed too, particularly plastic, which was used heavily for furniture until the petrol crisis of the mid-1970s intervened. Plastic was closely related to an important theme running since the 1950s, that of outer space and the future. As with the 1950s, Sixties style ran through the home, from kitchenware to designer furniture to clothing. As nostalgia is so important to the general market away from notable names, aim to buy brands or designs that inspire fond memories.

A 1960s 'flower power' printed drinking glass, marked "Georges Briard".

Georges Briard was a New York based importer and retailer of decorative and functional glassware.

A 1960s screen printed 'LOVE' drinking glass.

5.75in (14.5cm) high

5.75in (14.5cm) high

$15-20   **NOR**

$15-20   **NOR**

A set of four Ravenhead screen-printed glass tumblers, probably designed by Alexander Hardie Williamson, in original box.

Printed glasses by designers such as the prolific Alexander Hardie-Williamson are becoming more sought-after, particularly in their original box.

c1965   4.75in (12cm) high

$30-50   **DTC**

A 1970s screen printed enameled fondue set, on a stand with a spirit burner.

8in (20cm) high

$30-50   **MTS**

An early 1970s saucepan, with a bright stylized floral design and blue lid.

Kitchenware became more 'fun' and colorful during the 1960s as formal dining declined in popularity, being replaced with dining informally in the kitchen.

7in (18cm) diam

$25-30   **MTS**

A Norwegian enameled kettle, with white stylized leaf pattern.

7.75in (19.5cm) high

$12-18   **GAZE**

A Royal Tudor Ware 'Fiesta' coffee set, by Barker Bros of Staffordshire, comprising a coffee pot, sugar bowl, milk jug and six cups and saucers.

This design was released in the early 1960s and was influenced by Enid Seeney's Homemaker pattern, as can be seen from the design, pattern and color.

Pot 9in (23cm) high

$100-150   **FD**

A Fiesta plastic snack set, made in Spain by Transplastic S.A., in original box.

8.25in (21cm) high

$30-50   **MTS**

A length of 'Fandango' pattern fabric, designed by Maija Isola for Marimekko.

Isola worked for Marimekko from 1951-87 and her designs are among the most familiar Marimekko products, her most notable being 'Unikko' from 1964. The Fandango design is still available today.

1963   *116.75in (210cm) long*

$40-60   **GAZE**

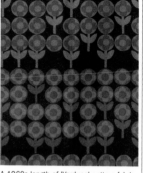

A 1960s length of 'Verdune' pattern fabric, designed by Peter Hall for Heal's.

$50-70   **GAZE**

A length of 1970s 'flower power' material.

$25-35   **GAZE**

A length of heavy cotton fabric, by Heal & Son, in mint condition.

c1964   *144in (366cm) long*

$180-220   **FD**

A pair of 'Watergarden' pattern curtains, designed by David Bartle for Heal's.

$40-60   **GAZE**

A pair of 'Shimma' pattern fabric curtains, by Natalie Gibson for Conran Fabrics.

This was available in different colors and an example is in the collection of the Victoria & Albert Museum, London.

c1967

$20-30   **GAZE**

A pair of 1960s 'Naxos' Op Art-style pattern fabric curtains, designed by Bernard Warde.

100in (254cm) wide

$100-150   **FD**

A 1960s Peter Max designed inflatable plastic cushion, with printed psychedelic design.

Disposable inflatable furniture in new synthetic materials was extremely popular during the 1960s. The most famous example is Zanotta's inflatable PVC 'Blow' armchair. Peter Max (b.1937) is a noted US designer who works in the highly recognizable 'Cosmic 60s' psychedelic style.

11.75in (30cm) wide

$30-50   **NOR**

A 1970s 'LOVE' inflatable plastic coathanger.

15in (38cm) wide

$30-40   **MTS**

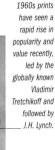

A 1960s 'flower power' printed tin document storage box.

10.25in (26cm) high

$30-50 **NOR**

An Ohio Art 'flower power' printed metal lunchbox.

c1970 *9in (23cm) wide*

$40-60 **NOR**

A CLOSER LOOK AT A MARGARET KEANE PRINT

Big eyed, often weepy waif-like children, such as this girl, are typical of Keane's style – the style was so successful that it was widely copied.

1960s prints have seen a rapid rise in popularity and value recently, led by the globally known Vladimir Tretchikoff and followed by J.H. Lynch.

Initially thought to be by Walter Keane (1915-2000), the original paintings were in fact painted by his wife Margaret and their origins were the subject of a US court case in 1986, which Margaret won.

Color prints are more common, black and white is comparatively rare. They were all sold inexpensively in great quantities, but usually thrown away when the style went out of fashion.

A 1960s Keane 'big-eyed' girl and dog black and white print, designed by Margaret Keane.

Margaret Keane is still a successful artist today and owns a gallery in San Francisco, selling her new works.

frame 25.5in (65cm) high

$100-150 **NOR**

A 1960s teenager's printed plastic singles record holder, with retractable handles.

8.5in (21.5cm) high

$40-60 **MA**

A 1960s vinyl hanging shoe rack, with printed musical decoration.

This example is in mint condition, which is very hard to find as the majority were torn or soiled through use.

31.25in (79.5cm) long

$120-180 **MA**

A 1960s 'Peace' 'flower power' printed tile trivet.

9.5in (24.5cm) long

$15-20 **NOR**

A 1970s cheeseboard and knife, with an inset tile panel.

11.75in (30cm) wide

$15-25 **MTS**

A 1970s Lord Kitchener printed mirror.

13.75in (35cm) high

$25-35 **MTS**

A 1960s German Salvest plastic clock.

4.25in (11cm) diam

$40-60   **MTS**

A Panasonic blue Toot-a-Loop radio.

When closed this radio could be worn around a wrist like a bangle. Produced in a number of colors, lime green, lilac, and mauve are the rarest.

c1972   *6in (15cm) diam*

$80-120   **MTS**

A 1960s/70s stool, with white single-button seat and brushed aluminum base.

17.75in (45cm) high

$50-80   **GAZE**

A 1960s pink and chrome standing 'UFO' circular heater.

$12-18   **GAZE**

A CLOSER LOOK AT A LORD KITCHENER PLATE

'I was Lord Kitchener's Valet' was a famous London shop in the 1960s, selling vintage clothes, regimental uniforms and modern products, usually incorporating similar imagery and the Union Jack.

Images from WWI such as Lord Kitchener were in vogue again during the 1960s, after a period of intense distaste. The Union Jack was a symbol of 'Swinging London', which was given a boost when Britain won the World Cup in 1966.

The shop used the logo seen on this plate, with Kitchener superimposed in a 'pop art' manner over the Union Jack.

Patronized by celebrities like Jimi Hendrix, and representing an 'alternative' street style, the first shop was on Portobello Road and was followed by shops in Chelsea and Soho.

A small 1960s Lord Kitchener plate, marked "I was Lord Kitchener's Valet" to the back.

4.75in (12cm) diam

$70-100   **MTS**

A 1960s RCA clock radio.

9.5in (24cm) wide

$70-100   **MTS**

A Fornasetti cylindrical table lamp base, with leaf design.

Largely ignored in his day, Piero Fornasetti was one of the most prolific designers of the 1950s and '60s. His work is undergoing a revival in popularity today, particularly his ceramics and furniture, the latter in collaboration with Gio Ponti. His style leans heavily on Classical architectural motifs as well as suns, faces, stars and playing cards, usually executed in black and gold.

$100-150   **GAZE**

An Italian yellow and black plastic standard ashtray, the black section pulling off.

21.25in (54cm) high

$25-35   **GAZE**

A Shattaline cast resin paperweight, made in Scotland.

This was retailed along with a series of lamps, which can fetch up to $70-100 with their original shade.

c1968   3in (7.5cm) high

$15-25   **DTC**

A 1970s orange plastic and chrome table lighter.

5.5in (14cm) high

$15-25   **DTC**

A 1970s Circle of Friends telephone and address book.

6.25in (16cm) diam

$15-25   **MTS**

A Mary Quant pastel crayon set.

Fashion designer Mary Quant's name was attached to a variety of objects during the 1960s.

4.25in (11cm) wide

$30-35   **MTS**

A 1960's psychedelic box of Peter John matches.

Note the attention to detail in the differently colored match heads.

$20-30   **GAZE**

A 1960s Russian giraffe figure, marked "Made in the USSR' on the base.

The value of these figures depends of the decoration – circles are more common but flowers or fruit can be worth up to $100-150.

9.5in (24.5cm) high

$50-70   **DSC**

COLLECTORS' NOTES

■ The market in props and costumes from films and TV shows began in earnest during the 1990s. High profile acquisitions by restaurant chains such as Planet Hollywood demonstrated to the studios that these items have value and generate interest even after cinema runs have ended. What was previously discarded or recycled is now traded across the globe.

■ Props are generally designed with a very specific use in mind and, if they are to feature prominently in the foreground, they are likely to be more detailed and better made than items used in the background. Weapons used by lead characters will be more carefully constructed than those carried by extras, and this will be reflected in the price.

■ It is important to be sure of the authenticity of a prop or piece of costume. Look out for the identifying tags that are used by many of the major studios, such as names on a collar. The more characteristic the item is of the film or character, or the more prominent the scene it appeared in affects value.

■ Fluctuations in the market are frequent. There can be a sudden clamor for memorabilia when a production is first shown, so it can be a good idea to wait until the publicity has subsided for an opportunity to buy at more realistic prices.

■ Some of the most dramatic price rises occur when a production is badly received on its initial release only to become a cult phenomenon later on.

A copy of 'The Single Parent's Handbook' from "About A Boy", mounted with stills from the movie showing the book.

2002   *20.5in (52cm) wide*

$500-700   **PSL**

A varsity-style crew jacket and badge from "The Abyss", with patches for 'Benthic Petroleum', the 'U.S.S. Montana' and the 'US Navy SEALs' and an 'I survived the toughest shoot in history' badge, size large.

The badges were made by crew members after shooting to commemorate Cameron's notoriously rigorous style of filmmaking.

1989

$280-320   **PSL**

A prop miniature book from "The Affair of the Necklace", with faux ivory cover and brass clasp, seen carried by a prostitute heading to the Cardinal's quarters.

2001   *4in (10cm) high*

$60-90   **PSL**

An Adrian Brody chair back from "The Affair of the Necklace", some signs of use.

2001   *21in (54cm) wide*

$60-90   **PSL**

A prop Greek sling shot stone from "Alexander", the painted rubber projectile with star symbol to top.

2004   *3in (7cm) high*

$12-18   **PSL**

A prop library scroll from "Alexander", used as set dressing.

2004   *13.5in (34cm) long*

$25-35   **PSL**

A rare prop 'Weyland Yatani' plastic mug from "Alien", with blue corporate logo to one side.

1978   *3.5in (9cm) high*

$700-1,000   **PSL**

A CLOSER LOOK AT A PROP FROM "ALIEN"

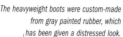

These boots can be seen when Dallas and his crew leave their ship, the Nostromo, to investigate the distress call from the crashed alien ship.

The heavyweight boots were custom-made from gray painted rubber, which has been given a distressed look.

Released over 25 years ago, it is unusual for props from "Alien" to come on the market.

They have the character's name "Dallas" handwritten on the inside of the tongue.

A pair of prop spacesuit boots from "Alien", worn by Dallas (Tom Skerritt).

1978

$1,800-2,200   **PSL**

A prop hand grenade from "Alien Resurrection", used by General Perez (Dan Hedaya), the soft rubber prop painted blue with yellow stripes and two working LEDs, lacks pin section, some paint worn.

1997   *3in (8cm) high*

$280-320   **PSL**

Three souvenir plastic cups from the "Alien War" attraction.

The Alien War attraction was situated in the basement of the Trocadero Center off Piccadilly Circus, London and ran from 1993 to 1996. 'Colonial Marines' would guide people through darkened corridors where 'Aliens' would then appear at opportune moments to terrify the paying guests.

8in (21 cm) high

$25-35 each   **PSL**

A 'Tall Oaks Band Camp' polo shirt from "American Pie 2", made by Jerzees, with camp emblem of an oak leaf on the chest 'Tall Oaks' and 'Band Camp' underneath, child's size large.

2001

$100-150   **PSL**

A 'Guard Dog Security' sew on patch from "Armed and Dangerous".

1986

4in (10cm) diam

$15-20   **PSL**

A mini legal pad from "Austin Powers in Goldmember", by Roaring Spring, used by Mini Me (Verne Troyer), the first eight pages filled with various Austin Powers doodles and scribbles.

2002   *5.25in (13.5cm) high*

$300-500   **PSL**

An alien head appliance from "Babylon 5", worn by Andreas Katsulas as G'kar, the Nam Regime ambassador, made of reinforced foam rubber painted with colored patches and dark colored spots, with evidence of glue inside, small sections of the paint flaked off.

1994-98

$1,000-1,500   **PSL**

A shooting schedule from "Babylon 5", for the season one episode 'Babylon Squared', consisting of 14 A4 pages, signed by Michael O'Hare (Lt Cmdr Jeffrey Sinclair) and dated 1/31/94.

$280-320   **PSL**

A launch bay technicians jumpsuit from the original "Battlestar Galactica" TV series, the cotton jumpsuit with reflective silver taping down both arms and legs and an elasticated waist, embroidered emblem on the left hand side of the chest.

c1980   *size 42*

$600-900   **PSL**

A prop UV bomb from "Blade II", the resin prop painted in black, silver and bronze.

2002   *3in (8cm) high*

$700-1,000   **PSL**

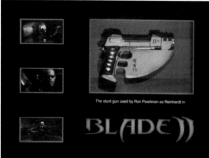

The stunt gun used by Ron Pearlman as Reinhardt in

A stunt gun from "Blade II", used by Reinhardt (Ron Perlman), made from hard rubber, the highly detailed prop with Chinese symbols on the blade and on the barrel, mounted, framed and glazed.

2002   *33.5in (85cm) wide*

$2,200-2,800   **PSL**

A prop 'Sunnydale Rockets' padded cushion from "Buffy the Vampire Slayer", with a letter of authenticity.

The 'Sunnydale Rockets' was the name of the college football team, though there is little mention of them throughout the series. Its lack of air-time has become an in-joke among fans.

1999-2000   *13.5in (34cm) wide*

$500-700   **PSL**

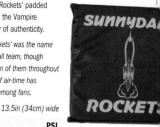

A 'MOO' badge from "Buffy the Vampire Slayer", used in the season three episode 'Gingerbread'.

MOO stands for Mothers Opposing the Occult.

c1998   *2.5in (6.5cm) diam*

$180-220   **PSL**

A prop 'Chicago Evening Star' newspaper display from "Chicago", mounted, framed and glazed.

2002   *33in (83cm) high*

$1,000-1,500   **PSL**

A prop data card from "Cleopatra 2525", used by Drack (Glen Drake) in the season two episode 'Noir or Never', adapted from a Zippo lighter with a lime green Perspex casing.

c2001   *3in (7cm) wide*

$120-180   **PSL**

A CLOSER LOOK AT A "BUFFY THE VAMPIRE SLAYER" PROP

This weapon was used by Buffy (Sarah Michelle Geller) during the show's first season.

The hunga munga is a traditional African throwing knife or iron that often had symbolic or ritualistic uses.

A clip of the character holding the weapon is seen in the opening titles through seasons one and two.

The prop is made of solid metal meaning it would have been made for close-up shots rather than action scenes where a safer, rubber version would have be used.

A prop hunga munga weapon from "Buffy the Vampire Slayer", made from solid metal with distressed effect, mounted framed and glazed.

c1997   *35in (89cm) high*

$3,000-4,000   **PSL**

A pair of Gucci frameless glasses from "Collateral", worn by Max (Jamie Foxx), with fake blood on one lens, the other cracked, together with a black hard case labeled by the prop department and a Dreamworks Studio certificate of authenticity.

There would have been a number of pairs of glasses used throughout the film. This damaged pair was used after the car crash scene.

2004

$500-700   **PSL**

A prop leather wallet from "Collateral", used by Vincent (Tom Cruise), containing a number of fake credit cards and plastic store cards as well as 'Motion Picture Money', some scuff marks.

2004   *4.5in (11cm) wide*

$800-1,200   **PSL**

A digital press pack for "Daredevil", containing a DVD with photographs and production notes, and a small booklet also with production notes.

2003

$40-60   **PSL**

FILM & TV

A stunt throwing star from "Daredevil", used by Bullseye (Colin Farrell), mounted, framed and glazed.

2003   *20.5in (52cm) wide*

$1,200-1,800   **PSL**

A Max Guevara wanted poster from "Dark Angel", used in the season one episode 'Blah Blah Woof Woof', mounted, framed and glazed.

c2000   *27.5in (70cm) wide*

$280-320   **PSL**

A prop 'Hell's Kitchen' cork coaster and a paper napkin from "Dawson's Creek", printed with the restaurant logo in black.

Hell's Kitchen was one of the focal points of the show and a regular meeting point for the main characters.

Coaster 6in (14cm) high

$15-25   **PSL**

A prop bank note from "Dinotopia", printed with "100 Motion Picture Money" and with a dinosaur's head.

2002   *8in (20cm) wide*

$15-20   **PSL**

A Disney Channel promotional jacket.

$120-180   **PSL**

A piece of concept artwork from "Dune", titled "Dune, Guilsman - Front & side elevations" and produced by Don Post Studios, Inc.

The character is incorrectly called a 'Guilsman', rather than 'Guildsman'. This design does not appear to have been recreated on the screen.

c1984   *17in (44cm) high*

$800-1,200   **PSL**

A crew gift organizer from "Elizabeth", the black nylon zip-up case containing an organizer with a color postcard of Elizabeth I on the cover.

1998   *12in (30cm) high*

$25-35   **PSL**

A set of medical scrubs from "ER", worn by Dr. Mark Greene (Anthony Edwards), with 'Costume Collection' tag.

1994-2002

$300-500   **PSL**

Madonna's Brooch worn in

EVITA

A custom-made brooch from "Evita", worn by Eva Peron (Madonna), the flower-shaped brooch set with ruby red and clear stones, mounted, framed and glazed.

1996   *18in (46cm) wide*

$1,500-2,000   **PSL**

A police codpiece from "The Fifth Element", made from vacuum-formed plastic, painted bronze with black distressing.

1997   *9.75in (25cm) long*

$60-90   **PSL**

A tie from "Frasier", worn by Kelsey Grammer in the title role, with maker's label 'Metropolitan View' and handwritten notation by the costume department "F124B, IV".

1993-2004

$100-150   **PSL**

A crew jacket from "The Full Monty", made by Carhartt and customized with the film title over the breast pocket, size 48.

1997

$180-220   **PSL**

A prop appearance generator from "Galaxy Quest", cast from resin with holographic film in the center.

1999   *3in (8cm) diam*

$80-120   **PSL**

A limited edition "Get Carter" script, signed by screenwriter and author Mike Hodges, from an edition of 500, with the original film title "Carter's the Name".

$280-320   **PSL**

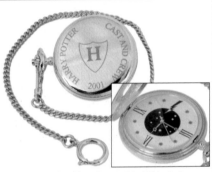

A crew fob watch from "Harry Potter and the Philosopher's Stone", engraved "Harry Potter Cast and Crew 2001", with original presentation box.

c2001

$700-1,000   **PSL**

A London premiere crew zip-up top from "Harry Potter and the Prisoner of Azkaban", size medium.

2004

$150-200   **PSL**

A prop clan MacLeod battle banner from "Highlander", mounted, framed and glazed.

1986   *46in (117cm) wide*

$800-1,000   **PSL**

Two prop Christmas presents from "How The Grinch Stole Christmas".

Largest 12in (30.5cm) wide

$60-90   **PSL**

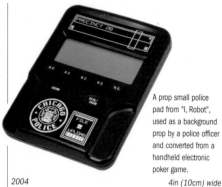

A prop small police pad from "I, Robot", used as a background prop by a police officer and converted from a handheld electronic poker game.

2004   4in (10cm) wide

$40-60   **PSL**

A prop Chicago Police cap badge from "I, Robot", made from resin.

2004
2.5in (6cm) high

$280-320   **PSL**

A European premier party menu for "King Arthur".

2004   8in (21cm) wide

$12-18   **PSL**

A CLOSER LOOK AT AN "I-ROBOT" PROP

These robots are an iconic and integral part of the film and its storyline.

Although many of the robots on the screen were computer generated, a number of real-life models would have been made for close-ups and publicity.

The muscles in the robots arms and legs are based on McKibben's air muscles, used in robots manufacture today.

The custom built stand is a desirable feature, meaning the otherwise unwieldy prop can be more easily displayed.

A full-size NS5 articulated robot from "I, Robot", the resin and fiberglass and metal prop with bright red LED in the chest and white LED in the skull, on custom-made stand.

2004   74.75in (190cm) high

$12,000-18,000   **PSL**

A prop dagger from "King Arthur", used by Galahad (Hugh Dancy), the painted resin giving the effect of a metal blade and leather bound handle with animal head design, with a black leather sheath.

2004   6.5in (42cm) long

$700-1,000   **PSL**

The pistol used by Tom Cruise in

THE LAST SAMURAI

A stunt pistol from "The Last Samurai", used by Nathan Algren (Tom Cruise), made from hard rubber painted to look like metal and wood, mounted, framed and glazed, together with a letter from the film's weapons coordinator.

2003   28in (71cm) wide

$2,800-3,200   **PSL**

A prop 'Daily Planet' newspaper from "Lois & Clark: The New Adventures Of Superman", used in the pilot episode.

1993   *23in (58cm) high*

$300-500   **PSL**

Ian McKellan's ticket to the VIP after premiere party for "The Lord of the Rings: The Return of the King", mounted with a signed photograph of the actor as Gandalf, framed and glazed.

2003   *12in (53cm) wide*

$700-1,000   **PSL**

The gun used by Carrie Anne Moss as Trinity in

A prop Beretta handgun from "The Matrix Reloaded" and "The Matrix Revolutions", used by Trinity (Carrie Anne Moss), the highly detailed rubber weapon with serial number and manufacturer's details clearly visible, mounted, framed and glazed together with a letter of authenticity from the productions weapons coordinator.

2003   *23in (59cm) wide*

$3,000-4,000   **PSL**

A rare Sentinel eye display from "The Matrix Revolutions", made from painted hard black rubber, mounted framed and glazed.

It is very rare to find any original props from the Matrix films.

2003   *22in (56cm) wide*

$500-700   **PSL**

A crew hooded top from "Meet the Parents", size XL.

2000

$60-90   **PSL**

A prop 'Precrime' ID card and strap from "Minority Report", with image of John Anderton (Tom Cruise), produced for the film but not used.

The Precrime ID card was made well into the production process of the film but was never used as 'retinal scans' featured throughout, thus making it redundant.

2002   *3.5in (9cm) wide*

$1,200-1,800   **PSL**

A crew black fleece jacket from "The Mummy", size medium.

c1999

$180-220   **PSL**

A prop Isabel and Jesse wedding photo from "Roswell", seen in the season three episode 'A Tale of Two Parties'.

c2002   *12in (31cm) high*

$100-150   **PSL**

A prison uniform from "The Shawshank Redemption", comprising of striped cotton shirt and blue jeans, the shirt prisoner number across the chest.

1994

$300-500   **PSL**

A pair of prop 'sync device' clone goggles from "The Sixth Day", the painted black metal glasses in original plastic prop storage box.

2000   *7in (18cm) long*

$500-700   **PSL**

A rare prop marine smart grenade from "Space: Above and Beyond", made from plastic and metal, painted dark gray, silver and black.

1995-96   *6in (15.5cm) long*

$280-320   **PSL**

A 'Spice Force 5' sew-on patch from "Spice World".

'Spice Force 5' was a spoof sci-fi adventure that featured in the film.

1997   *3in (8cm) diam*

$12-18   **PSL**

A promotional cap from "Spider-Man".

2002

$15-25   **PSL**

A Mobile Infantry sergeant's cap from "Starship Troopers", worn by Career Sergeant Zim (Clancy Brown), with Infantry insignia on the front and "Zim" written inside.

1997

$500-700   **PSL**

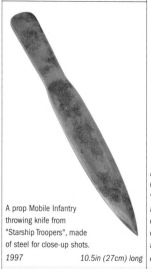

A prop Mobile Infantry throwing knife from "Starship Troopers", made of steel for close-up shots.

1997   *10.5in (27cm) long*

$350-450   **PSL**

A prop alien tool from "Star Trek: The Next Generation", used in the season six episode 'The Quality of Life' as an Exocomp's tool, and reused in the Voyager season four episode 'Random Thoughts', made from part of a Romulan rifle, the main resin body with a metal end and plastic nodules at the top.

c1992   *10in (25.5cm) long*

$1,500-2,000   **PSL**

A spatial trajector device from "Star Trek: The Next Generation", used in the season three episode 'The Dauphin' and reused in the Voyager season one episode 'Prime Factors', made from black painted resin with a transparent orange plastic section, one metal decoration peeling off.

c1989   *8in (20cm) high*

$1,200-1,800   **PSL**

A CLOSER LOOK AT A "STAR TREK" PROP

This style of weapon was used in approximately three episodes of The Next Generation and was a common sight on Deep Space Nine.

It has come from the private collection of the prop maker on the show and is in near mint condition.

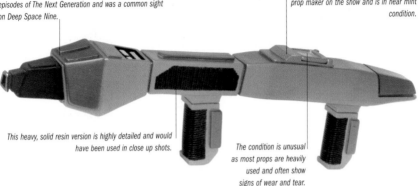

This heavy, solid resin version is highly detailed and would have been used in close up shots.

The condition is unusual as most props are heavily used and often show signs of wear and tear.

A prop type III phaser rifle, from "Star Trek: The Next Generation" and "Star Trek: Deep Space Nine", made from resin sprayed gray and black, with a transparent green insert on top.

25in (64cm) long

$1,800-2,200   **PSL**

A production-used script from "Star Trek: Deep Space Nine", for season four episode 'Our Man Bashir', the blue-colored cover signed by script writer Robert Gillan.

1995

$280-320   **PSL**

A crew fleece top from "Star Wars Episode II: Attack of the Clones", with "Star Wars Episode II" and "Props & Models Australia 2000" embroidered on the chest, size small.

c2000

$280-320   **PSL**

A de-assimilation neural link control box from "Star Trek: The Next Generation", used on Locutus of Borg (Patrick Stewart) by Data (Brent Spiner) in the season four episode 'Best of Both Worlds, part II', the custom made, light-up prop made from resin and plastic with two metal connectors on top where the links were attached.

c1990   *4.5in (11cm) high*

$1,200-1,800   **PSL**

A Cyberdyne tool box from "Terminator 3: The Rise Of The Machines", made from hard rubber painted gray with blue sections and a "Cyber Research Systems" label on one side.

21.5in (54cm) wide

$300-500   **PSL**

A prop small keypad from "Thunderbirds", made from black plastic and silver-painted resin with a plastic screen and numerical keypad.

2004   *7in (12cm) wide*

$40-60   **PSL**

FILM & TV

A prop Thunderbirds 4 access box from "Thunderbirds", made from blue-painted metal labeled "T4, Access 3094-R, For Sequential Routine Checks Refer To Onboard Manual 0923/4 V5".

2004   5.5in (14cm) wide

$60-90   **PSL**

A pair of sunglasses from "2 Fast 2 Furious", worn by Monica Fuentes (Eva Mendes), mounted, framed and glazed.

2003   21in (53cm) wide

$400-600   **PSL**

A cast and crew screening invitation for "Troy", dated May 16th 2004.

8.5in (21cm) high

$12-18   **PSL**

A 'Stop Animal Testing' crew T-shirt from "Twelve Monkeys", size large, in worn condition.

The cast and crew wore animal-themed T-shirts during the production of this film.

1995

$100-150   **PSL**

A prop silver vampire bullet from "Underworld", mounted, framed and glazed.

2003   18in (46cm) wide

$280-320   **PSL**

An ornate vampire-killing stake from "Van Helsing", made from wood-effect resin with silver-colored decoration.

2004   23in (59cm) long

$500-700   **PSL**

A 'Die! Bug Die!' bug spray can from "The X-Files", used in the season three episode 'War of the Coprophages'.

c1995   8in (20cm) high

$150-200   **PSL**

A prop helmet from "Xena: Warrior Princess", worn by Xena (Lucy Lawless) in the season six episode 'Return of the Valkyrie', made of soft silver-painted leather with hard rubber decorations, labeled "Xena".

c2000

$1,500-2,000   **PSL**

An Amazonian necklace from "Xena: Warrior Princess", the leather and suede necklace decorated with colored beads and silver painted stones.

8in (20cm) wide

$70-100   **PSL**

A red crew T-shirt from "The X-Files", printed with the X-Files logo on the front, "Season 9" underneath and "Want it" on the back, size XL.

These were given to crew members by Robert Patrick who played Special Agent John Doggett in season nine.

c2001

$100-150   PSL

A prop vehicle license plate from "The X-Files", used in the season two episode 'Little Green Men' on Dana Scully's jeep.

c1994   *12in (30.5cm) wide*

$280-320   PSL

A sweatshirt and pants from "X-Men", each with the 'X' logo patch with "Xavier's School For Gifted Youngsters", mounted, framed and glazed together with a Fox Studios certificate of authenticity.

2000   *39.5in (100cm) long*

$600-900   PSL

A prop camping blanket and strap from "X-Men 2", with applied logo badge for "Xavier's School For Gifted Youngsters".

2002

$300-500   PSL

A prop missile launching system panel and hard drive from "xXx", with molded resin hard drive and spray painted acrylic, launching system panel, lacking a light-up panel.

2002

12in (30cm) wide

$700-1,000   PSL

FILM & TV

COLLECTORS' NOTES

- The successful return of Doctor Who in 2005 has meant that the profile of cult films and TV series has risen again. Coupled with the nostalgia for all things 1970s and 80s, this has resulted in an increased desire for film and TV toys and memorabilia from that period.

- Early examples are usually the most sought-after and often the hardest to find, particularly in good and complete condition, as few would have been made. The original box and any instructions or certificates will also be desirable.

- While Doctor Who is riding high in the popularity charts, large amounts of toys are being released onto the market. When buying modern examples, look for well-known manufacturers and good quality materials and construction, as these are more likely to hold their value. Limited editions are also a good bet, but only if the number really is limited, ideally to under 1,000.

- As of 2005 there are no new series of Star Trek in production and it will be interesting to see how this affects the market for the toys and memorabilia. The early Mego figures for the original series continue to be sought-after, but later examples, particularly for the last series may suffer.

- As numerous shows and films are being reinvented for the next generation, nostalgia for the originals often increases, bringing with it a demand for vintage memorabilia. Cult film series, such as Star Wars and James Bond, remain extremely popular, with older pieces tending to attract the most interest.

- In the long run, pieces from an unpopular period may prove a good investment as production may be limited and few will have been bought, making them scarce in later years. A new audience may be more appreciative and the toys could become sought-after.

David Banks, "Doctor Who The New Adventures – Iceberg", published by Virgin Publishing.
1993

$10-15　　　　　　　　　　**TP**

Terrance Dicks, "Doctor Who – The Five Doctors", published by Target, 20th Anniversary special edition.
1983　　　　　*7in (18cm) high*

$7-10　　　　　　　　　　**TP**

Paul Cornell, "Doctor Who The Missing Adventures – Goth Opera", published by Virgin Publishing.

This was the first title in Virgin's Missing Adventures series, featuring 'lost' stories of the Doctor's adventures that took place in between episodes of the TV series.
1994

$12-18　　　　　　　　　　**TP**

Howe, Stammers and Walker, "Doctor Who – The Handbook: The Seventh Doctor", published by Virgin Publishing.
1998

$12-18　　　　　　　**TP**

Stephen Marley, "Doctor Who The Missing Adventures – Managra", published by Virgin Publishing.
1995

$10-15　　　　　　　**TP**

Jim Mortimer, "Doctor Who The New Adventures – Parasite", published by Virgin Publishing.
1994

$15-20　　　　　　　**TP**

Jim Mortimer, "Doctor Who The New Adventures – Blood Heat", published by Virgin Publishing.
1993

$10-15　　　　　　　**TP**

Howe and Stammers, "Doctor Who – Companions" book, published by Virgin Publishing.
1995   *12in (30.5cm) high*
$35-33   **TP**

Nigel Robinson, "Doctor Who The New Adventures – Birthright", published by Virgin Publishing.
1993
$10-15   **TP**

Howe, Stammers and Walker, "Doctor Who – The Sixties" annual, published by Virgin Publishing.
1992   *12in (30.5cm) high*
$35-55   **TP**

A Doctor Who "The Pescatons" audio CD, by Silva Screen.
1991   *5.5in (14cm) wide*
$35-45   **TP**

Nigel Robinson, "Doctor Who The New Adventures – Timewyrm: Apocalypse", published by Virgin Publishing. *1991*
$12-18   **TP**

Gary Russell, "Doctor Who The Missing Adventures – Invasion of the Cat-People", published by Virgin Publishing.
1995
$12-18   **TP**

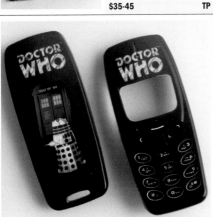

A Doctor Who 'Sonic Screwdriver' ballpoint pen.
c2001   *5in (12.5cm) long*
$18-28   **TP**

A Doctor Who cell phone cover, for a Nokia 3310.
6.75in (17.25cm) high
$18-28   **TP**

A Doctor Who pewter Dalek keyring.
c2001   *1.5in (4cm) high*
$5-9   **TP**

FILM & TV

A Doctor Who pewter TARDIS keyring.

c2001   1.5in (4cm) high

$7-9   **TP**

A Doctor Who Dalek-shaped pewter bottle stopper.

c2002   1.5in (4cm) high

$18-28   **TP**

A Doctor Who 'Cyberman Attacking' figure, by Media Collectables.

c2002   Figure 2in (5cm) high

$10-15   **TP**

A Doctor 'The Mysterious Daleks' black battery-operated figure, by Marx Toys, with eyepiece and weapons, in excellent condition, the box with some graffiti and one indentation.

c1964

$300-400   **GAZE**

A Dr Who 'War of the Daleks' game, by Denys Fisher.

c1975   Box 19.5in (49.5cm) w

$60-80   **GAZE**

A CLOSER LOOK AT A DALEK TOY

As these toys made to be played with and usually were, the delicate eyepiece and weapons are often damaged or missing, and the box also is often missing.

Daleks were one of the first characters from the series to be recreated as toys.

Palitoy and Marx also made Dalek toys, but this is usually considered the most sought-after.

The Daleks were recently voted most evil villains in recent UK survey, and much to fans delight, they have returned in the new series of Doctor Who.

A Codeg (Cowan de Groot) 'Mechanical Dalek' blue plastic figure, 'Strong Clockwork with Realistic Action', with two weapons, lacks eyepiece, toy marked "©BBCTV 1965", box incorrectly marked "Black".

c1965

Box 5.25in (13.5cm) high

$700-900   **GAZE**

An A-Team 'Mr T' action figure, by Galoob, boxed.

Box 15in (38cm) high

$50-80   **GAZE**

A Canadian Battle of the Planets child's record player, by Tele-Tone.

13.5in (34cm) wide

$80-120   **NOR**

A very rare Japanese Official Universal Studios 'Creature From The Black Lagoon' tin and plastic toy, mint & boxed.

c1991   9in (23cm) high

$300-400   **NOR**

A 1960s Bonanza lithographed tin mug, made in Hong Kong.

It is rare to find Bonanza memorabilia that includes an image of Pernell Roberts, who played Adam Cartwight in the series and left in the sixth season.

3.5in (9cm) wide

$12-18   **BH**

A Mego Corp James Bond Moonraker fully poseable figure, in original box.

c1979   Box 13.5in (34.5cm) high

$120-180   **F**

An American 'James Bond 007 Secret Agent' game, by MB Games.

c1964   19in (48cm) wide

$100-150   **NOR**

An early James Bond 007 Thunderball game, by Milton Bradley, made in Australia.

Box 19in (48.5cm) wide

$50-100   **GAZE**

A James Bond "007 Best 4" picture sleeve, OH-27, from United Artists Records.

c1964

$40-50   **GAZE**

A James Bond 'Jaws' action figure, made in Hong Kong, marked "©1979 Eon Productions".

c1979   13in (33cm) high

$10-15   **GAZE**

A Japanese James Bond "From Russian with Love" soundtrack 45rpm, BS-7019, from King Stereo, featuring the 'Kiss-Theme' from Niagara on the B-side.

c1963

$12-18 GAZE

A Timpo 'Captain Scarlet' plastic figure.

2.25in (5.5cm) high

$20-30 GAZE

An IJN E.T. The Extra-Terrestrial poseable toy, mint and boxed.

11in (27.5cm) high

$30-40 NOR

An Aladdin ET lunchbox.
c1982
8.25in (21cm) wide

$100-150 NOR

A Flash Gordon medals and insignia set, by Larami Corp.

c1980 *7in (18cm) high*

$12-18 NOR

A Green Hornet LP record.

12in (32cm) wide

$35-45 NOR

A Record Guild of America 'Flash Gordon' story record.

These story records were cut out from cereal boxes, and it rare to find a two-sided version.

6.75in (17cm) diam

$40-50 NOR

A 'Ming The Merciless' plastic poseable doll, by King Features Syndicate

c1976 *10in (25.5cm) high*

$60-80 NOR

Brandon Keith, "The Green Hornet and the Case of the Disappearing Doctor", illustrated by Larry Pellini, published by the Whitman Publishing Company.

1966 *8in (20cm) high*

$40-50 NOR

A Knight Rider metal lunchbox, by Thermos.

c1982   8.5in (21.5cm) wide

$15-25   **BH**

A Lassie the Wonder Dog 'Timmy' grey cotton outfit, by Wings, size 10.

$80-120   **NOR**

A King Seeley Thermos Mork & Mindy lunchbox.

This appeals to Robby the Robot collectors too, as he also features on the lunchbox.

c1979   9in (23cm) wide

$50-70   **NOR**

A Lost In Space 'Robby the Robot' battery powered robot, manufactured by Remco Industries, marked "©Space Productions".

The character of Robby the Robot first appeared in the film 'Forbidden Planet' in 1956 and was designed by prop maker Robert Kinoshita. The robot suit was altered slightly and was used in the TV series 'Lost in Space' as Robot B-9. Robby went on to appear in a number of other films and shows including 'Mork & Mindy'. This Remco robot was also produced in blue and red colorway.

c1966   11.75in (30cm) high

$350-450   **NOR**

A 'Mork & Mindy ' plastic Mork Eggship, marked "©1979 Paramount Pictures Corp.", with removable Mork figure.

Egg 4.25in (11cm) high

$25-35   **NOR**

A PPC Mork poseable figure in costume.

c1979   9.5in (24.5cm) high

$25-35   **NOR**

An Our Gang 'Darla' carded action figure, by Mego Corp.

c1975   9in (23cm) high

$70-100   **NOR**

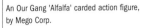

An Our Gang 'Alfalfa' carded action figure, by Mego Corp.

c1975   9in (23cm) high

$60-80   **NOR**

An Our Gang 'Mickey' carded action figure, by Mego Corp.

c1975   9in (23cm) high

$80-120   **NOR**

A Planet of The Apes plush, plastic and furry hand puppet.

9.75in (25cm) high

$70-90   **NOR**

A United Artists Corp Rocky figurine, mint in bubble pack and card.

8.5in (22cm) high

$15-20   **NOR**

An unopened box of Planet of the Apes bubble gum cards.

c1967   7.5in (19cm) high

$180-220   **NOR**

A signed Warrick Davis publicity postcard.

6in (15cm) high

$12-15   **LCA**

A signed Kenny Baker (R2-D2) 'Star Wars' publicity postcard.

6in (15cm) wide

$18-28   **LCA**

A signed Caroline Blakiston (Mon Mothma) 'Return of the Jedi' publicity postcard.

6in (15cm) high

$10-15   **LCA**

A signed Ian McDiarmid (Emperor Palpatine) 'Return of the Jedi' publicity postcard.

6in (15cm) high

$18-28   **LCA**

A signed Jeremy Bulloch (Boba Fett) Return of the Jedi' publicity postcard.

6in (15cm) high

$18-28   **LCA**

A signed Brian Blessed (Boss Nass) 'Star Wars: Episode I – The Phantom Menace' publicity postcard, as Boss Nass.

6in (15cm) high

$12-18   **LCA**

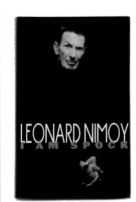

Leonard Nimoy, "I Am Spock", first edition published by Century, London, signed by the author.

1995

$120-180   **PSL**

Three unusual Mego Corp 'Star Trek: The Motion Picture' figures, in original packaging, comprising Spock, Kirk and Willard Decker.

A Star Trek 'Klingon' carded action figure, by Mego Corp, on 'six-face' card.

This was one of the first figures by Mego and is commonly found.

c1974   *Card 9in (23cm) high*

$40-60   **NOR**

Released five years after the original figures, Mego produced a range of smaller figures to complement the first Star Trek movie hoping to emulate the massive success of Kenner and their 3in Star Wars action figures.

c1979   *box 9in (23cm) high*

$120-180   **W&W**

A CLOSER LOOK AT A STAR TREK FIGURE

"TV Century 21 Annual", published by City Magazines Ltd., featuring Stingray, Fireball XL5 and Lady Penelope.

1965   *15.5in (39.5cm) high*

$22-28   **GAZE**

Released one year after the first figures, the Aliens series comprised of four alien characters, Neptunian, Gorn, The Keeper and Cheron.

While none of these new figures were exact replicas of aliens seen on the screen, the Neptunian was entirely created by Mego.

Look for examples that are on a 14-back card, which are much rarer than the 10-back card.

This second series of figures is rarer than the original series, a further four aliens were released, which are considerably harder to find.

A Star Trek Aliens 'Neptunian' carded action figure, by Mego Corp.

c1975

$150-250   **NOR**

FILM & TV

A very rare card, cast iron and tinplate Scarecrow from The Wizard of Oz jigger, the dancing printed card figure moves up and down as a record is played, base molded 'PAT.FEB.11-19'.

c1940   7.5in (19cm) high

$300-500   **PWE**

A limited edition whimsical 'Wizard of Oz' lidded jar, by Rick Wisecarver, from an edition of 30, signed "Rick Wisecarver No-28-95", incised "The Wizard of Oz" on the rear and "Copyrights G931-0999 Roseville Ohio" on the base.

16.5in (42cm) long

$400-500   **BEL**

A mint Aladdin 'Wild Bill Hickock' vacuum bottle, with original box.

c1955   6.5in (16cm) high

$70-100   **NOR**

A mint Aladdin 'Zorro' vacuum bottle, with original box.

c1955   6.5in (16cm) high

$100-150   **NOR**

A Mego Corp Emerald City playset, with Wizard figure, Emerald City, tree, plastic-covered card throne, spinning crystal ball, lacks some parts, but shows very few signs of wear, boxed and complete.

The Wizard of Oz range was particularly successful for Mego, with well-modeled and detailed figures. They were produced in large numbers and are generally easy to find loose but boxed examples are scarce. Three playsets were produced - Munchkinland, Emerald City and Wicked Witch Castle, which is the rarest. Although it is often thought that the Wizard figure was only available with this playset, he could be bought individually. Singularly boxed examples are extremely rare.

Box 14.75in (37.5cm) wide

$300-400   **NOR**

Four Mego Corp Wizard of Oz figures.

These figures came with a range of accessories that are often lost, complete examples are worth over twice as much. The Dorothy figure, which came with a small Toto figure is scarce as are the four diminutive Munchkin figures.

8.25in (21cm) high

$25-35 each   **NOR**

A Venetian glass St Marks lion, awarded at the Venice Film Festival during the 1960s.

18in (45.5cm) wide

$150-200   **GAZE**

COLLECTORS' NOTES

■ Carnival glass is the name given in the 1960s to the colorful, press-molded glass produced in the US and Europe from around 1905-7. It was inspired by Tiffany's iridescent glass, fashionable but expensive at the time. After being inexpensively made in mechanical presses, pieces were sprayed with metallic salts to give them their iridescence.

■ The 'Prime' period of production was from c1910-c1925, with the late 1920s and 1930s being of secondary interest to collectors. Notable factories include Fenton (est.1904), Northwood (1888-1925) who became Dugan & Diamond, and Imperial (est.1903) in the US, Sowerby in the UK, and Brockwitz in Germany. After the 1920s, US production declined in favor of other countries.

■ Prices vary widely from around $15-25 up to a $2,000 or more for the best and rarest pieces. Most pieces can be easily found for $80-200, providing excellent variety. When collecting, consider four main areas – shape, pattern, color, and iridescence. Certain shapes such as plates are scarcer than ruffled bowls, for example, and can fetch a premium.

■ Consider the pattern. Sometimes a combination of pattern and form is rare, some are scarcer than others in general and so command premium. Patterns can also help identify a manufacturer, and although manufacturers produced seemingly identical patterns, there are usually small differences that distinguish them. Pattern variants can make for an interesting collection.

■ To examine the base color, hold it up against strong light to see which color it is. Marigold is one of the most common colors with opalescent colors and red, launched in 1920 by Fenton, being generally scarcer. The base color should be strong. Iridescence should also be strong, with a shimmering quality ranging from deep to light colors across the entire surface. Pieces with excellent levels of iridescence are sought-after.

A Fenton 'Heart & Vine' pattern blue Carnival glass plate.

This large plate is very scarce and is most valuable in this color.

9.5in (24cm) diam

$600-900   **GL**

A Northwood 'Peacocks on a Fence' pattern green Carnival glass plate.

This pattern breaks the usual rule that plates are the rarest shape, as while plates are scarce, the pie-crust and ruffled edge bowls are rarer in this pattern.

9.5in (24cm) diam

$600-900   **GL**

A Fenton 'Sailboats' blue Carnival glass plate.

The plate is very rare in this color, a bowl in this pattern may fetch around $50-70. Look out for the ultra-rare red.

6.25in (16cm) high

$550-650   **GL**

A very rare 'Rose Show' pattern blue Carnival glass plate.

Only found on bowls and a plate, this pattern was only produced in small quantities, making it hard to find today.

9.5in (24.5cm) diam

$1,200-1,800   **GL**

An Imperial 'Open Rose' pattern purple Carnival glass bowl, with paneled pattern on the outside of the bowl and excellent iridescence.

7in (18cm) diam

$100-150   **GL**

GLASS

A Diamond Glass Company 'Brooklyn Bridge' pattern Carnival Glass souvenir ruffled bowl.

This bowl is only known in marigold. Look out for the rare example without the lettering under the Zeppelin. During the 1920s and 30s these German airships ferried passengers and mail between Europe and New York and Brazil until the Hindenburg disaster in 1937 ended their viability as a form of transport.

c1930   9in (23cm) diam

$250-350   **GL**

A CLOSER LOOK AT A CARNIVAL GLASS PLATE

Large plates are rare in the majority of Carnival glass patterns, but there are a few exceptions.

Although the iridescence on this example is good, those with better iridescence can fetch up to $5,000-7,000.

Plates are also desirable as they have great visual impact and show the pattern off to its best. This is also in undamaged condition.

Look out for the rare blue color in this pattern.

A Dugan 'Persian Garden' pattern large amethyst Carnival glass chop plate.

13in (32.5cm) diam

$3,500-4,500   **GL**

An Imperial 'Scroll Embossed' pattern purple Carnival glass bowl.

This is a very common pattern, but this one is made rarer as it has a fluted exterior. Plain examples are more common and worth less.

7.25in (18cm) diam

$100-150   **GL**

A Northwood 'Poppy' pattern ice blue Carnival glass oval pickle dish.

8.5in (21.5cm) diam

$400-600   **GL**

A Fenton 'Kittens' pattern small blue Carnival glass child's cereal bowl.

This pattern was aimed at children and has become very popular with collectors.

c1920   3.75in (9.5cm) diam

$350-450   **GL**

A Fenton 'Open Edge Basketweave' pattern red Carnival glass hat-shaped bowl.

5.75in (14.5cm) wide

$250-350   **GL**

A Northwood 'Wild Rose' pattern marigold Carnival glass footed bowl.

7.75in (19.5cm) diam

$100-150   **GL**

A Dugan or Diamond Glass 'Double Stem Rose' pattern Celeste blue Carnival glass ruffled bowl.

1916-c1926   *4.5in (11.5cm) high*

$500-700   **GL**

A Northwood 'Beaded Cable' pattern aqua opalescent Carnival glass rose bowl.

4.25in (10.5cm) high

$300-400   **GL**

A Northwood 'Peacock at the Fountain' pattern marigold Carnival glass compote, with excellent iridescence and applied clear glass foot.

6in (15.5cm) high

$600-900   **GL**

A Northwood 'Grapes & Cable Banded' pattern green Carnival glass hatpin holder.

The molded 'ring' around the upper part identifies this as a scarce variant of the very common 'Grape & Cable' pattern by Northwood. The shape and color add to this piece's desirability.

7in (17.5cm) high

$350-450   **GL**

An Imperial 'Tiger Lily' pattern purple Carnival glass water beaker.

This pattern is 'intaglio', meaning the pattern is set into the piece rather than protruding from it. It is only found on a water set, the pitcher and the blue color being much sought-after.

4.25in (11cm) high

$80-120   **GL**

An Imperial 'Grapes' pattern purple Carnival glass water bottle.

This is slightly scarcer, but not always more valuable than, the decanter also shown here. It was made from the same mold as the decanter but with the lip flared out.

8.75in (22cm) high

$300-400   **GL**

An Imperial 'Grapes' pattern purple Carnival glass water decanter with stopper.

12in (30.5cm) high

$380-420   **GL**

A rare Fenton 'Kittens' pattern blue Carnival glass child's cup.

2.25in (5.5cm) high

$300-500   **GL**

FIND OUT MORE...

The Standard Encyclopaedia of Carnival Glass, by Bill Edwards & Mike Carwile, published by Collector Books, 2002.

The Pocket Guide to Carnival Glass, by Monica Lynn Clements & Patricia Roser Clements, published by Schiffer Books, 2001.

GLASS

A Canadian Chalet blue and clear glass bowl, with crossing pulled lips and acid-etched mark to base.

Although resembling Murano, particularly with the use of 'sommerso' technique of colored glass cased in clear glass, Chalet pieces are identified by an acid stamp to the base. Decorative Art glass such as this was popular from the 1960s-70s and was sold in department stores. Examples may pulled 'arms' such as here, that have been broken and then smoothed off with rounded ends. Full-length ends will often show marks from the gripping tools used to 'pull' the arm out when molten.

13.5in (34.5cm) wide

$65-75 | ING

A Canadian Chalet red glass dish, with four curling pulled rims parts and acid-etched mark to base.

16.75in (42.5cm) wide

$45-55 | ING

A Canadian Chantili orange glass bowl, with curling pulled ends and acid stamp to base.

13in (33cm) long

$65-75 | ING

A Canadian Chantili yellow glass dish, with pulled tips, and acid-etched stamp to base.

17.75in (45cm) long

$50-60 | ING

A Canadian Chalet swirling orange glass dish, with pulled lip and acid-etched stamp to base.

9.5in (24cm) wide

$50-60 | ING

A Canadian Chalet green, blue, and clear glass triform lobed bowl, with acid stamp to base with Gothic style lettering.

8.75in (22cm) wide

$45-55 | ING

COLLECTORS' NOTES

- Cloud glass is a decorative form of hand or mechanically pressed colored glass, containing coloured, wispy swirls. The swirls are created by adding trails of dark colored glass to a lighter colored glass base. When the mass of glass is pressed into shape in a mold, the characteristic trails are formed. As this trailing is random, the patterns created are unique to each piece.

- The idea was developed by George Davidson & Co, of Gateshead, England, and was introduced from 1923 with production ending by WWII. Some colors were however produced into the 1950s. Other companies also produced cloud glass, such as Sowerby and Jobling of England, Walther and Brockwitz of Germany, and Reich of the Czech Republic, but they were not as prolific.

- Values vary according to a combination of shape, color and patterning. Complex, large shapes, or those made up of different pieces or made for shorter periods of time are more valuable. Look for a good variation of cloud-like wispy trailing, evenly spread across the piece. Colors should be strong. Some colors are rarer and so are more valuable than others. For Davidson, amber is the most common, red the rarest.

- Colors were produced at different times, helping to date pieces to a period. Davidson's colors include purple (1923-34) amber (1928-57), blue (1925-34), green (1934-41), orange (1933-35) and red (1929-32). Shapes were also produced in specific periods and comparing the two can sometimes narrow a period down.

A Davidson purple cloud glass parfait, pattern no.1.

Note the unusual, broad trailing on this example known as 'Ribbon Cloud', which is not as popular with many collectors, but is quite rare.

1923-34 5.25in (13.5cm) high

$50-70   **STE**

A Davidson cloud glass celery vase, pattern no.283.

Although the shape was produced from 1912-42, this pattern was only made in cloud glass in the 1920s.

1923-30   7in (17.5cm) high

$70-100   **STE**

A Davidson purple cloud glass flower bowl set, with stand, pattern no.699C.

The price is comparatively low as this set is not deemed particularly attractive by collectors.

1923-34   10in (25.5cm) diam

$80-120   **STE**

A Davidson matte finish purple cloud glass flower bowl set, with frog and stand, pattern no.1910MD.

This piece is made more unusual as it is matt to both sides, not just the underside.

1923-34   8in (20cm) diam

$80-120   **STE**

A very rare Davidson purple cloud glass number 269 dish.

This is one of Davidson's most long-lived patterns, registered in 1908 and produced into the 1960s. Very few pieces were made in Cloud Glass, making this example rare.

1923-34   5in (13cm) wide

$70-100   **STE**

A rare Davidson purple cloud glass sugar bowl, pattern no.283.

1923-34   7in (18cm) wide

$120-180   **STE**

A Sowerby purple cloud glass bowl, with remains of a label.

1965-70   7in (18cm) wide

$20-30   **STE**

A Davidson amber cloud glass vase, pattern no. 34SVF.

This vase with a flared rim, as here, is rarer than the same shape with a smaller, unflared rim.

1934-42   6in (15cm) high

$50-70   STE

A very rare Davidson amber cloud glass Tutankhamun bulb bowl.

This shape, designed in 1922, had a very limited run and is usually found in black. It was made in amber cloud glass from 1928. Tutankhamun's tomb was discovered in 1922, sparking off 'Egypt-o-mania' in design.

1928-30   6in (15cm) wide

$120-180   STE

A rare J.A. Jobling amber cloud glass flower bowl, with registered no.795794 for 1935.

Jobling is known for making pressed glass and Pyrex and did not produce much cloud glass. Its cloud glass was made by machine whereas Davidson's was hand-pressed. The line was not successful so was quickly abandoned.

1935-38   6in (15.5cm) diam

$100-150   STE

A Davidson amber cloud glass no.1 size cigarette box, for 70 cigarettes.

These were made in three sizes.

1931-42   6.25in (16cm) wide

$50-70   STE

A Davidson amber cloud glass rose bowl, pattern no.10/1910.

The top section was molded in a modified ashtray mold.

1935-c1957   12in (30cm) diam

$50-70   STE

A set of four Davidson amber cloud glass small-size 'Bridge Ashtrays', pattern nos 29, 30, 31, 32.

With their original box, these could be worth up to $300-500.

1933-39   Club 2.25in (6cm) wide

$120-180   STE

A Davidson amber cloud glass vase, with frog, pattern no.278.

1928-37   7in (18cm) high

$70-100   STE

A Davidson amber cloud glass parfait, pattern no.1.

1928-42   5.5in (14cm) high

$30-40   STE

GLASS

A Davidson blue cloud glass faceted 'Column Vase', with flared rim, pattern no.279D.

1928-34   7in (17.5cm) high

$70-100   STE

A pair of Davidson blue cloud glass tall candlesticks, pattern no.283.

1925-34   7.5in (19cm) high

$80-120   STE

A Davidson blue cloud glass no.2 cigarette box, for 50 cigarettes.

1931-34   3.5in (9cm) wide

$60-90   STE

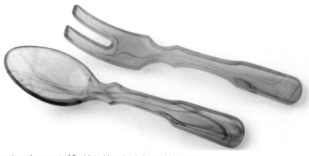

A Davidson blue cloud glass vase, pattern no.277.

Smaller 10in and 16in versions of this vase are available. Very few examples are found in cloud glass, making this rare. It was also made in purple.

1925-34   18in (45.5cm) high

$800-1,200   STE

An extremely rare set of Davidson blue cloud glass salad servers.

Glass salad servers were introduced in 1923, but these are currently the only known cloud glass examples.

1925-34   9in (23cm) long

$350-550   STE

A rare Davidson orange cloud glass cylindrical vase, pattern no.712.

1933-35   8in (20cm) high

$250-350   STE

A very rare Davidson 'modified' orange cloud glass flower dome and bowl, pattern no.1910D.

Only around 50 orange flower domes were ever made in this size.

1933-35   11in (28cm) diam

$450-550   STE

A Davidson 'modified' orange cloud glass flower bowl and frog, pattern no.732.

Davidson produced two types of orange cloud glass, this 'modified' color is the later version.

1933-35   8in (20cm) wide

$120-180   STE

A Davidson unmodified orange cloud glass faceted 'Column Vase', pattern no.279.

This is often thought to be 'yellow' cloud glass but is actually an early attempt at orange.

c1933   10in (25.5cm) high

$450-550   STE

A CLOSER LOOK AT A DAVIDSON CLOUD GLASS TRINKET SET

Davidson's red cloud glass, trade-marked as 'Ora', originally cost around twice as much as ordinary cloud glass.

Their red cloud glass is actually amber or purple cloud glass enameled to one side with red. It had to be fired again after enameling and the enamel rubs off easily.

Red is the rarest color for cloud glass and, despite high hopes, it was unpopular due to its cost and flaking enamel. It was only produced for three years.

This set is missing a pin dish and small pot, a complete set could be worth $2,500-3,500.

A Davidson red cloud glass part trinket set, pattern no.283, with original label to tray.

Fakes are known so look for an original label or traces of a label to identify it.

1929-31   18.25in (35cm) wide

$1,500-2,000   STE

A Davidson red 'Ora' cloud glass flower set, pattern no.700D.

1929-32   11.5in (29cm) wide

$700-900   STE

A Davidson green cloud glass flower bowl, pattern no.204R.

1934-40   12in (30.5cm) diam

$80-120   STE

An unusual Davidson green cloud glass vase, pattern no.34 SVG.

1934-41   7in (18cm) high

$80-120   STE

A Davidson green cloud glass vase, with turned in rim, pattern no.294.

This shape was made 1931-36 and green was made 1934-41, making this piece easy to date.

1934-36   6in (15cm) high

$20-30   STE

A Davidson Topaz-Briar cloud glass fan vase, pattern no.296.

1957-61   5in (13cm) high

$100-150   STE

GLASS

A German Walther violet cloud glass KDG powder bowl.

Walther produced cloud glass from around 1932-39. Violet is popular, sepia is more common. Opposite to Davidson, amber is rare.

1932-39   4in (10cm) diam

$100-150   STE

A German Walther violet cloud glass Zentrum cress strainer and dish.

1935-39   8.5in (22cm) diam

$150-200   STE

A German Walther Prismem violet cloud glass flower bowl.

Walther sold its cloud glass under the trade name Oralit.

1932-39   9.75in (24.5cm) diam

$120-180   STE

A German Walther lilac cloud glass plate.

1932-39   12.25in (31cm) diam

$150-200   STE

A German Walther pink cloud glass bowl.

1935-39   5.25in (13.5cm) wide

$70-50   STE

A German Walther 'malachit' cloud glass 'Lotos' vase.

1935-39   5.75in (14.5cm) high

$180-220   STE

A 1920s/30s Reich gray cloud glass 'Viktoria' vase, pattern no.4857.

Gray cloud glass is hard to come by.

8in (20cm) high

$450-550   STE

A Walther sepia cloud glass 'Lotos' vase, with Oralit label.

Sepia is the most common colour for Walther cloud glass.

1932-1939   7in (18cm) high

$120-180   STE

FIND OUT MORE...

www.cloudglass.com

Davidson Glass – A History, by Chris & Val Stewart, 2005.

COLLECTORS' NOTES

■ Ronald Stennett-Willson founded King's Lynn Glass in King's Lynn, Norfolk in 1967. Before this, Stennett-Willson had worked for J. Wuidart & Co., a UK importer of Scandinavian glass, and been a Reader in Industrial Glass at the Royal College of Art, London.

■ The factory produced high quality tableware and decorative ware in line with the popular Scandinavian style. Forms were clean and modern, relying on the color and clarity of the glass, which ranged from cool icy blues to strong purples.

■ The successful factory was acquired by Wedgwood in 1969. It continued to use Stennett-Willson's designs as well as commissioning new designs until his retirement in 1979. In 1982, Wedgwood acquired a controlling 50

percent stake in Dartington Glass, which was then acquired by Caithness in 1988. The King's Lynn factory was closed in 1992.

■ The many candleholders produced, such as the instantly recognizable 'Sheringham', form the core of many collections. The range, size, and color count towards value. Vases are also popular, as are the numerous animal paperweights, which are at the most affordable and varied end of their production.

■ As simple form and color are so important to the design, always aim to buy pieces in immaculate condition. Chips, especially to the rim, cracks and internal liming reduce the appeal and desirability of a piece, as well as the value.

A 1970s Wedgwood 'Sheringham' topaz candlestick, design RSW13-2, by Ronald Stennett-Willson, with two discs.

5.5in (14cm) high

$40-60 NPC

A 1970s Wedgwood 'Sheringham' amethyst candlestick, design RSW13-2, by Ronald Stennett-Willson, with two discs.

5.5in (14cm) high

$40-60 NPC

A 1970s Wedgwood 'Sheringham' amethyst candlestick, design RSW13-1, by Ronald Stennett-Willson, with single disc and applied boss.

Look out for inset Wedgwood ceramic plaques, celebrating events such as the Queen's silver jubilee in 1977. Amethyst glass was a popular color for commemorating Royal events.

5.5in (14cm) high

$25-35 NPC

A King's Lynn blue glass display vase, designed by Ronald Stennett-Willson, with heavy foot and straight stem and original Lynn paper label.

5in (12.5cm) high

$120-180 GC

A Wedgwood light blue textured tumbler, design RSW128-13, designed by Ronald Stennett-Willson, with molded flame motifs.

These were sold in boxed pairs.

c1969 *5in (13cm) high*

$25-35 GC

A 1970s Wedgwood blue textured candleholder or posy vase, design RSW58, by Ronald Stennett-Willson, with "Wedgwood England" acid stamp to base.

4.25in (11cm) high

$50-70 MHT

A Wedgwood 'Squat Vase', design RSW110, by Ronald Stennett-Willson, with heavy cased clear glass base and pink mottled white internal layer.

c1969 *5in (13cm) high*

$100-150 GC

A very rare Wedgwood heavily cased blue 'ariel' vase, designed by Ronald Stennett-Willson, with internal elliptical bubble patterns.

This is part of a series of unique vases produced under Stennett-Willson's guidance during the late 1970s, shortly before his retirement from Wedgwood. The complex 'ariel' process used was similar to that developed by Orrefors around 1937 where a pattern was sandblasted onto a piece before it was cased, resulting in trapped air bubbles forming the design. Many have natural motifs such as leaves.

c1975-78   *4in (10cm) high*

$500-700   **GC**

A Wedgwood topaz and clear glass decanter, design RSW43, by Ronald Stennett-Willson, with clear stopper with three controlled internal bubbles.

11.75in (30cm) high

$80-120   **GC**

A Wedgwood whiskey decanter, design RSW60, by Ronald Stennett-Willson, with heavy moulded dimpled base.

This was originally designed for King's Lynn Glass in 1967, and was produced until the early 1970s.

c1970   10in (25cm) high

$60-90   **GC**

A 1970s Wedgwood white cased pear paperweight, design RSW231, by Ronald Stennett-Willson, with acid-etched Wedgwood mark to base and paper label.

4.75in (12cm) high

$60-90   **GC**

A Wedgwood 'Galaxy' faceted glass paperweight, design RSW14, by Ronald Stennett-Willson, with two controlled opaque blue internal bubbles.

This was one of the first paperweights designed by Stennett-Willson for Wedgwood in 1970. They were discontinued in 1973, making them hard to find today, particularly in undamaged condition.

1970-73   *4in (10cm) high*

$80-120   **GC**

A 1970s Wedgwood black and white cased panda paperweight, design SG421.

3.5in (9cm) high

$80-120   **GC**

FIND OUT MORE...

Wedgwood Glass, *by Susan Tobin, 2001, ISBN: 0-9580234-0-9.*

COLLECTORS' NOTES

■ Mdina was founded on Malta in 1968 by Michael Harris (1933-94) who had been a tutor in glass at the Royal College of Art, London. Colors are instantly recognizable as the rich blues, greens, sands, and browns of the Mediterranean landscape around the factory. The glass also tends to be thickly rendered.

■ Pieces are typically free blown, with Harris taking the studio glass movement to a new commercial level. Harris left in 1972, and early pieces produced when Harris was at Mdina fetch a considerable premium. Look for his hallmark 'Fish' vases, which are one of his most popular shapes with collectors today. Rounded vase and dish forms are also typical shapes.

■ Souvenir hunting tourists preferred smaller, less expensive examples. Pieces were also exported to Germany, the UK, and the US among other countries. Larger pieces command a premium as fewer were made. Most examples are signed 'Mdina' in script on the base, but look for those signed with Harris' signature as these are extremely rare.

■ Later examples from the 1980s onward are currently less sought-after but, as with all Mdina glass, are growing in desirability and value. Pieces dated or signed by Joseph Said, one of Mdina's blowers and subsequent owner, can also fetch comparatively high prices. Oranges, pinks, and white are all signs of later pieces produced into the 1980s after Harris left.

A Mdina 'Fish' vase, heavily cased in clear glass with internal swirls and cut with two facets on one side, signed "Michael Harris, Mdina Glass, Malta" on the base.

c1970   8.75in (22cm) high

$500-700   **GROB**

A CLOSER LOOK AT A MDINA 'FISH' VASE

The rounded, organic form is typical of Harris' early pieces, if it were signed by Harris with his name, its value would nearly double.

This 'axe-head' shape is known as a 'Fish' vase with the clear parts being like the 'wings' of a manta ray.

These heavy vases were hard to make in the early days of the factory, with Harris being one of a very few who were competent enough.

It is unusual to find an example that has been 'double-cased', with a blue outline under the clear glass.

A rare Mdina 'Fish' vase, designed and made by Michael Harris, cased in clear glass.

Very few of these were made in this large size by Harris at this time.

c1970   11.5in (29cm) high

$500-600   **ART**

A 1980s Mdina blue 'Fish' vase, unsigned.

The green spidery internal patterning combined with the general 'squared off' shape with a thin, elongated neck show this to be a late example. Note that early examples tend to be in the earlier colorways including browns, amethyst, and mottled, rather than striated, greens.

8.25in (21cm) high

$120-180   **NPC**

A Mdina large mold-blown textured vase, of square section with dropped-in circular neck and polished pontil mark.

The texture and polished, lens-like pontil mark means these pieces are often mistaken for Whitefriars. This large size is very rare.

8.75in (22.5cm) high

$120-180   **GC**

A Mdina vase, signed and dated "Mdina Glass 1974".

Dated examples such as this are more desirable among collectors than undated.

6.75in (17cm) high

$80-120 NPC

A Mdina blue and green glass vase, with two pulled handles, signed "Mdina" on the base.

6in (15cm) high

$50-80 NPC

A 1970s Mdina gourd-shaped vase, signed "Mdina" on the base.

8in (20cm) high

$70-100 NPC

A Mdina goblet, with 'craggy' trailed knop and clear stem and foot.

7.5in (19cm) high

$120-180 NPC

A Mdina green and blue swirl pattern vase, signed "Mdina" on the base.

5.5in (14cm) high

$50-80 GAZE

A Mdina glass ball paperweight, signed "Mdina" on the base.

5in (13cm) high

$25-35 GAZE

A Mdina tortoiseshell-colored textured cylindrical vase.

8in (20cm) high

$50-80 NPC

A Mdina orange-amber glass vase, overlaid with randomly applied blue-green straps.

6in (15cm) high

$50-70 GAZE

A 1980s Mdina pink mottled vase, with applied blue trails, with Maltese cross stamped logo.

5in (12.5cm) high

$80-120 JL

COLLECTORS' NOTES

■ After leaving Malta in 1972, Michael Harris founded a second island factory near Ventnor, Isle of Wight. Initial ranges are currently the most desirable and tended to have colored swirling or cloud-like patterns such as 'Pink & Blue Swirls' or 'Blue Aurene'.

■ The factory's major commercial breakthrough came in 1978-79 with the 'Azurene' range, with silver and gold leaf applied to the surface. Developed by Harris and Royal College of Art student William Walker, it was exported all over the world. Black is the most common base glass color, others, such as white, are rarer.

■ Look for a stamped 'flame' mark on the base that indicates production was between c1974 and c1982. A flat, polished base indicates a date after 1982. Labels

can help to date a piece, with a triangular black label being used in the 1980s and a black or gold square sticker from the 1990s.

■ Pieces signed by Harris with his name command a substantial premium, as do large examples. Short-lived 1980s and 1990s ranges tend to be more collectible and valuable today than ranges that were more popular at the time, as fewer examples exist.

■ After Harris' death in 1994, production was continued by his wife and two sons. The factory is still producing today, under the expertise of one of his two sons, Timothy, and his wife. As with Mdina glass, examples are increasing in desirability and value.

An Isle of Wight Studio Glass 'Pink & Blue Swirls' vase, with impressed 'flame' pontil mark.

c1974-c1980   5.75in (14.5cm) high

$80-120   **GC**

A Isle of Wight Studio Glass 'Pink & Blue Swirls' vase, with impressed 'flame' pontil mark.

c1974-78   3.5in (9cm) high

$50-80   **TGM**

An Isle of Wight Studio Glass 'Pink & Blue Swirls' perfume bottle, with impressed 'flame' pontil mark.

Perfume bottles of this period and shape always have clear stoppers.

c1974-c1980   6.25in (16cm) high

$80-120   **PC**

An Isle of Wight Studio Glass brown streaked vase, with an impressed 'coach-bolt' prunt to the base.

A plain applied concave 'prunt' covering the broken pontil mark is a rare feature of early Isle of Wight examples made in 1973 only.

1973   4in (10cm) high

$70-100   **ART**

An Isle of Wight Studio Glass 'Blue Aurene' type cylinder vase.

1973-82   9.5in (24cm) high

$120-180   **GC**

A Isle of Wight Studio Glass 'Blue Aurene' perfume flask, with impressed 'flame' pontil mark.

1973-82
3.75in (9.5cm) high

$80-120   **PC**

An early Isle of Wight Studio Glass 'Black Azurene' cylindrical vase, with polished base and black triangular sticker.

1978-82   7.5in (19cm) high

$70-100   **EAB**

An Isle of Wight Studio Glass 'Pink Azurene' vase, with impressed 'flame' pontil mark.

The Azurene range was made with different base glass colors. Seen without light shining it, the surface effect is similar to the black one also on this page.

c1979-87   7.5in (19cm) high

$70-100   **TGM**

An Isle of Wight Studio Glass 'Poppy' vase, from the 'Meadow Garden' range with polished base.

This shape was issued in 1987 only, although the range was one of their most popular.

1987   9in (23cm) high

$80-120   **TGM**

A 1980s Isle of Wight Studio Glass spherical glass vase, from the 'Meadow Garden' range, with polished base and triangular black label.

This shape was only made in this prolific range in 1986-88 only.

1986-88   6in (15.5cm) h

$80-120   **TGM**

A very rare Isle of Wight Studio Glass 'Allsorts' perfume bottle, from the 'New Bon Bon' range, with deep gold-colored ground and iridescent green and blue spots, signed on the base "Michael Harris Isle of Wight Glass".

This shape was only produced in this colorway in 1989. Its rarity is tripled as it is signed by Michael Harris.

1989   3.75in (9.5cm) high

$220-280   **TGM**

An Isle of Wight Studio Glass small 'Satin & Silk' vase, with polished base and triangular sticker.

1988-91   5in (13cm) high

$30-50   **TGM**

An Isle of Wight Studio Glass pink and white swirled bowl or ashtray, with impressed 'flame' pontil mark.

c1980   4.25in (10.5cm) wide

$35-50   **TGM**

An Isle of Wight Studio Glass for Kerry Glass 'Peat' vase, with reversed, impressed 'flame' pontil mark.

This was part of a range produced by Kerry Glass in Ireland, but designed by Isle of Wight Studio Glass.

1980-82   5.25in (13.5cm) high

$70-100   **TGM**

A scarce Isle of Wight Studio Glass goblet, designed and made by Timothy Harris, with applied abstract rod of colored glass fused into stem.

1992-93   5.5in (14cm) high

$80-120   **MHT**

COLLECTORS' NOTES

■ The Venetian island of Murano has been a center of glass production since the 14thC. The 1950s saw a renaissance of the island's industry via the adoption of modern design principles and a huge range of colors.

■ Figurines of clowns and other novelties are mostly produced on a large scale for the tourist market. These items generally have little value on the secondary market due to the quantity produced.

■ Beware of glass offered as 'Murano style', which will probably have been made in workshops in Asia or South America.

■ Damage will of course devalue a piece of Murano glass. Even minor losses such as 'flea bites' or tiny rim chips will have an adverse affect on most pieces.

■ Collectors pay the highest prices for glass blown by, or at least under the supervision of, well-known glassmasters or designers such as Ercole Barovier, Carlo Scarpa and Fulvio Bianconi. Company names to watch out for include Venini, Fratelli Toso and the innovative Seguso Vetri d'Arte.

■ Murano glassblowers use a wide variety of techniques and forms, including murrines, air bubbles and a method of casing glass known as 'sommerso', which translates as 'submerged'.

■ Value is dependant on many variables including size, color and rarity. Generally, more complex or demanding designs by well-known manufacturers will be more valuable.

A Murano sommerso vase, in four colors.

c1955   6.25in (16cm) high

$100-150   **NPC**

A 1960s Murano large flared rim vase, light amber glass encasing green.

13.75in (35cm) high

$60-80   **GAZE**

A Seguso Vetri d'Arte sommerso vase, pale violet, blue and green cased glass, with vertical ribbing.

c1970   7.5in (18.5cm) high

$400-500   **VZ**

An Anfora sommerso orange and cased clear glass vase, by Andrea Zilio, with trapped air bubbles and gold leaf inclusions and signed to the base "Anfora, Murano '04".

2004   18.5in (47cm) high

$500-700   **VET**

An Arte Nuova Murano clear, blue and light yellow sommerso vase, in the style of Flavio Poli, with maker's label "ARTE NUOVA MURANO GRAND PRIZE ... World Fair Brussels 1958".

c1958   7in (18cm) high

$120-180   **VZ**

A Seguso Vetri d'Arte sommerso vase, designed by Flavio Poli, with burgundy glass cased in yellow and clear glass.

Flavio Poli is one of the earliest and most successful designers working with the sommerso technique. In 1954, he won the prestigious Compasso D'Oro award for his sommerso designs. As here, forms tend to be sculptural and rounded. Look out for larger examples such as his elliptical 'Valva' vases.

c1958   5.75in (14.5cm)

$150-200   **VZ**

A Barovier & Toso vase, designed by Ercole Barovier, clear glass spiralling with overlaid dark-red and cobalt-blue canes, with original paper label to base.

c1966   10.3in (25.8cm) high

$600-800   **VZ**

A Seguso Vetri d'Arte sommerso vase, designed by Flavio Poli, teardrop shape with angled neck.

c1955   9.25in (23.5cm) high

$500-700   **VZ**

A Seguso Vetri d'Arte sommerso vase, designed by Flavio Poli, in gray-green, clear and rosé-flashed glass.

c1958   7.75in (19.5cm) high

$450-650   **VZ**

A Venini vase, the bulbous body with controlled trails of large air bubbles and narrow flared neck, marked on the base "Venini Murano ITALIA".

c1950   10.25in (25.5cm) high

$600-800   **VZ**

A Barovier & Toso 'Efeso' vase, designed by Ercole Barovier, with pale and dark blue powder inclusions and irregular internal glass bubbles.

c1964   6.5in (16.5cm)

$800-1,000   **VZ**

A Venini opaline vase, made to a 1930 design by Napoleone Martinuzzi, with thick horizontal ribbing, signed "Venini 94 Carlo Scarpa" on the base.

1994   11.75in (29.5cm) high

$600-800   **VZ**

A Vistosi Memphis glass vase, designed by Ettore Sottsass, white glass applied with red and green dots.

8.75in (22cm) high

$900-1,200   **WW**

A late 20thC Venini vase, of flattened ovoid form with 'Scotsasi' tartan pattern, with clear plastic label and engraved "Venini Italia".

A 1930s Murano vase, the body of spiralling vertical canes, with zanfirico rods, with applied blue rim, mounted on a hollow base.

7.25in (18.5cm) high

8.75in (22cm) high

$250-450 KAU **$600-800** ROS

A Venini & C. handled vase, designed by Vittorio Zecchin, with ruby-red body, two applied handles, marked "Venini Murano ITALIA" on base.

A Seguso Vetri d'Arte vase, designed by Mario Pinzoni, in chrysoberyl (alexandrite) glass.

c1925   5.5in (14cm) high

c1955   8.5in (21.5cm) high

$250-350 VZ **$350-550** VZ

A Venini clear and red glass stem vase, incised marks to base reading "Venini Italia 14.10.59".

An opaque pink and opaline footed tall vase, possibly Seguso, with tall, elongated neck.

c1959   7in (18cm) high

17in (43cm) high

A Venini & C. vase, with arched rim, cased clear and cyclamen-red glass turning turquoise-blue towards rim.

c1952   10.75in (27.5cm) high

$60-80 GAZE **$100-120** RETC **$450-650** VZ

A CLOSER LOOK AT A MURANO VASE

This vase is by the renowned Fratelli Toso factory, famous for its murrine designs, which use colored 'tiles' of glass.

The murrines are intended to look like the glass shades found on Tiffany lamps.

Rather than using lead, as on a real Tiffany lamp, the iridescent black areas are actually glass and part of the murrine itself.

This style of murrine was designed around the 1960s-70s, when Tiffany lamps became popular collectors pieces, so that the look could be offered to clients who liked the Tiffany design.

The colored strands are formed from diagonal rods laid onto the vase and are known as 'pietini'.

A rare Fratelli Toso 'Tiffany' murrine and opaque white and colored strand pietini vase, designed and made by Vittorio Ferro.

1960-70   5.5in (14cm) high

$2,500-3,500   **PC**

A Venini 'Grenadine' glass vase, designed by Gianni Versace, the clear glass with blue panels with turquoise, yellow and red murrines, engraved "Venini Gianni Versace 1988/57".

1988   9.75in (25cm) high

$700-900   **ROS**

A Venini Murano large glass vase, attributed to Alessandro Mendini, clear cased with applied vertical canes in turquoise, red and blue, with label and engraved "Venini 80" to underside.

1980   15.5in (39.5cm) high

$600-800   **ROS**

A very rare Fratelli Toso 'field flower' and 'grass' murrine vase, designed and made by Vittorio Ferro.

1950-70   6.25in (16cm) high

$2,500-3,500   **PC**

A Murano ruby red lobed bowl, with internal trails of bubbles.

c1965   *5.5in (14cm) diam*

$20-30   **NPC**

A 1950s Seguso glass ashtray, in red, blue and turquoise.

5in (13cm) wide

$80-100   **P&I**

A Venini 'corroso' bowl, designed by Carlo Scarpa, marked on base "Venini Murano".

Corroso glass was developed at Venini in the early 1930s. The 'frosted' or 'veined' effect is gained by applying a wax resist and then acid to the exterior.

c1936   *2.75in (7cm) wide*

$200-300   **VZ**

A Venini bowl, designed by Carlo Scarpa, with trails of internal air bubbles and gold inclusions.

c1940   *2.75in (7cm) wide*

$150-200   **VZ**

A 1950s Murano turquoise trefoil bowl, with silver foil and colored inclusions.

5.25in (13.5cm) diam

$45-65   **AG**

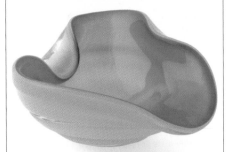

A Murano opaline green cased glass ashtray, with pulled rim.

7in (18cm) high

$70-90   **RETC**

A Seguso Vetri d'Arte ashtray, the opening in the form of a rosette, signed "Seguso V. d'Arte", and with "Seguso Vetri d'Arte Murano Made in Italy" label with handwritten number "13152".

c1970   *8.75in (22cm) diam*

$550-750   **VZ**

A Seguso Vetri d'Arte bowl, with "Seguso Murano Made in Italy" label.

c1960   *3.5in (9cm) wide*

$250-350   **VZ**

A Venini 'corroso' bowl, designed by Carlo Scarpa, in clear and turquoise-blue cased glass, frosted from the base upwards.

c1940   *7.75in (19.5cm) wide*

$250-350   **VZ**

A Seguso Vetri d'Arte bowl, in dark-blue and turquoise cased iridescent glass.

c1965   *2.75in (7cm) high*

$300-400   **VZ**

A Venini & C. small honey-colored glass dish, with trails of regular air bubble inclusions, marked on base "Venini Murano ITALIA".

c1960   *4.5in (11.5cm) diam*

$150-200   **VZ**

A Murano green glass lobed bowl, with four colored openings.

6.25in (16cm) diam

$40-70   **NPC**

A CLOSER LOOK AT A MURANO BOWL

Yoichi Ohira is a respected glass designer who combines Murano glass with Japanese ceramic forms and styles.

The piece uses glass canes typical of Murano and the form resembles a tea bowl.

This is made with the 'incalmo' process, where two separate 'vessels' are made in different types of glass and joined while still hot.

Its simple lines and form are accentuated by the separately applied rim and solid color foot.

A 1980s De Majo bowl, designed by Yoichi Ohira.

5in (12.5cm) high

$350-550   **VET**

A Seguso Vetri d'Arte bowl, with flared rim and applied hollow foot, the black glass cased in opaque white, light green and clear glass, with "Seguso Murano Made in Italy" label and handwritten lot number.

The form of this bowl echoes those produced in Murano in the early 16thC, but with modern colors.

c1960   7.75in (19.5cm) diam

$350-550   **VZ**

A Venini 'fazzoletto' vase, designed by Fulvio Bianconi, clear glass with vertical band inclusions in opaque lobster-red and purplish-black.

The fazzoletto or handkerchief vase was developed by Fulvio Bianconi and Paolo Venini around 1947. Millions of copies have been made by other factories, mainly for the tourist market. Large examples are authentic Venini pieces fetch the most. Look for a delicacy and complexity of form, or an acid etched "Venini Murano Italia" signature, denoting a piece made before 1960.

c1950   4.25in (10.5cm) high

$200-300   **VZ**

A Venini 'fazzoletto' vase, designed by Fulvio Bianconi, marked "Venini murano ITALIA" on base.

c1950   3.75in (9.5cm) high

$250-450   **VZ**

GLASS

A Murano art glass bowl, red and pale blue, encased in clear glass.

18.5in (47cm) wide

$40-50   **GAZE**

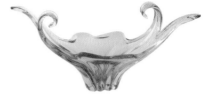

A Murano yellow and green tinted glass 'splash' bowl.

19in (48cm) wide

$50-70   **GAZE**

A 1960s Seguso sommerso orange and green glass vase, with curving leaf-like rim.

14.25in (36cm) wide

$250-350   **RETC**

A Venini bowl, designed by Napoleone Martinuzzi, the deep molded shape with ribbed rosette pattern in the centre and flared rim.

c1930   *19in (47.5cm) diam*

$200-300   **VZ**

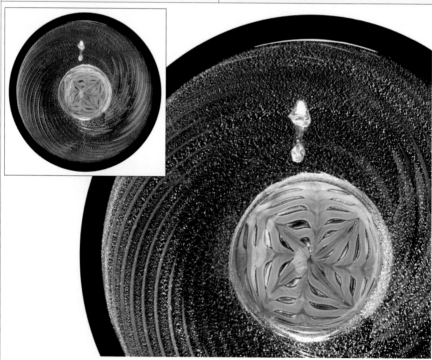

A Barovier & Toso bowl, designed by Angelo Barovier, with gold-foil inclusions in a spiral pulton, clear-glass center with opaque pink and purple lattice work.

c1974   *14.5in (37cm) diam*

$550-750   **VZ**

A Murano glass display piece, of two geese in flight, mounted on an oval sommerso glass base.

c1960   8in (20cm) high

$40-50   **GAZE**

A pair of 1950s Murano sommerso glass swans, in cranberry glass with air bubbles encased in clear glass, standing on bubbly 'rocky' plinths.

6.25in (16cm) high

$150-200   **AG**

A Seguso Vetri D'Arte fish, designed by Mario Pinzoni.

c1965   12.75in (32.5cm) long

$200-300   **VZ**

A Murano glass clown ornament.

Popular tourist pieces, clowns have been produced in great numbers for decades. Larger sizes fetch more, as do those with complex and more finely applied details.

$40-50   **GAZE**

A Venini Murano incalmo glass decanter, designed by Gio Ponti, with stopper, engraved "Venini Italia 83" to underside.

1983   14.25in (36cm) high

$500-600   **ROS**

A Venini 'Acrobat' figure, the design attributed to Fulvio Bianconi, in white and black glass, depicted in a handstand, unsigned.

15in (38cm) high

$700-900   **ROS**

GLASS

A Salviati amber and dark green decorative pear, with "Salviati & C. Made in Italy" label.

A Venini glass pepper, designed by Napoleone Martinuzzi, with applied green stalk, unsigned.

c1930   *4in (10cm) diam*

$600-800   **VZ**

c1965   *7.75in (19.5cm) high*

$250-350   **VZ**

A Seguso Vetri d'Arte sommerso vessel, designed by Flavio Poli.

c1965   *2.5in (15cm) high*

$500-600   **VZ**

A Murano glass tall, yellow, four sided obelisk, unmarked but possibly by Venini, with black, reflective base.

17in (43cm) high

$350-450   **PSI**

A 1950s Murano sommerso glass green and amber cased lamp base.

11in (28cm) high

$70-90   **NPC**

A Fratelli Toso cup, with millefiori-style murrine and applied pulled scroll handle.

c1910   *1.5in (4cm) high*

$120-180   **VZ**

COLLECTORS' NOTES

■ Pressed Glass, also known as 'Pattern' glass, was primarily produced between the 1850s and the 1940s, with the majority being produced around the 1880s. Much was clear and colorless and it was targeted for use in middle class homes, imitating the more expensive cut crystal glass of the time. It was durable and inexpensive, yet fashionable.

■ A number of Canadian factories produced pressed glass including the largest, Dominion Glass, who also bought out a number of other competitors. Other important factories include the Burlington Glass Factory, the Nova Scotia Glass Company, the Jefferson Glass factory in Toronto and Hamilton Glass, which became Diamond Flint and eventually part of

Dominion Glass. American makers also produced glass for the Canadian market.

■ Little was marked and certain patterns were produced by a number of factories, so it can be hard to identify Canadian examples and attribute a factory. Referring to catalogs or identified examples is often the best way to learn which patterns were Canadian. Goblets are a popular collecting area with a great variety to collect. Later reproductions are known, these tend to be lighter in weight and have less pronounced, less sharp details. Although bubbles (if not excessive in number) do not affect value too much, chips or ground down (restored) areas do.

A Canadian 'Dominion' or 'Mascotte' pattern hobnail pressed glass compote, with hand-engraved leaf designs on the plain border.

c1880s-1900s   5.75in (14.5cm) high

$80-120   ING

A Canadian 'King's Crown' pattern pressed glass compote, probably lacks cover.

c1880s-1900s   7in (18cm) high

$45-55   ING

A Canadian 'Pointed Bull's Eye' pattern pressed glass lidded compote.

c1880s-1900s   9.75in (25cm) high

$45-55   ING

A Canadian pressed glass lidded compote, with heraldic motif and palm trees, starburst motifs and zig zag patterns.

c1880s-1900s   11.75in (30cm) high

$60-80   ING

A Canadian 'Frosted Lion' pattern pressed glass lidded compote, with a few chips to base rim.

The lion is also found in clear, unfrosted glass.

c1880s-1900s   7.25in (18.5cm) high

$25-35   ING

A Canadian oval bulls eye and star pattern pressed glass centerpiece dish.

c1880s-1900s   7.25in (18.5cm) diam

$60-80   ING

A Canadian 'Rayed Heart' pattern pressed glass dish, probably by the (Jefferson) Dominion Glass Company, Montreal.

The Rayed Heart pattern is most commonly associated with Canadian pressed glass.

c1900s   8.5in (21.5cm) diam

$120-180   ING

A Canadian amber pressed glass bowl, with crenellated scalloped rim and star and pinwheel design.

c1880s-1900s   8.75in (22.5cm) diam

$40-50   ING

A Canadian hobnail pattern pressed glass vase, with diamond and linear shaped and red painted panels and rim.

4.25in (11cm) high

$15-25   **ING**

A Canadian aquamarine pressed glass toothpick holder, with hobnail four leaf clover type pattern and scalloped rim.
c1880s-1900s   2.75in (7cm) high

$22-28   **ING**

A Canadian amber pressed glass pitcher, with floral and foliate molding, and bands of vertical ribbed and hobnail patterns.
c1880s-1900s   9.25in (23.5cm) high

$30-40   **ING**

A Canadian pressed glass 'Bull's Eye' jug, with gold painted eyes and remainder of gold finish to area around spout.
c1880s   5in (12.5cm) high

$20-30   **ING**

A Canadian pressed glass 'Bull's Eye' and hobnail pattern two-handled goblet, or soup cup, with gold painted areas.
c1880s   4.5in (11.5cm) high

$20-30   **ING**

A Nova Scotia 'Grape & Vine' pattern pressed glass pitcher.

24 patterns are known to have been made by Nova Scotia glass. The slight gray/blue tinge is caused by a type of degradation over the years.

8.75in (22cm) high

$150-200   **TFR**

A Canadian 'Bull's Eye' pattern pressed glass goblet.

6in (15cm) high

$35-45   **ING**

A Canadian amber pressed glass salt and pepper shaker cruet set with hobnail pattern panels and original amber pressed glass base and tin tops.
c1880s-1900s   7in (18cm) high

$70-90   **ING**

A Canadian hobnail and reeded vertical panel pressed glass goblet.

6in (15cm) high

$15-25   **ING**

FIND OUT MORE...

Unitt's Canadian Handbook of Pressed Glass, by Barbara & Peter Sutton-Smith, published by Fitzhenry & Whiteside Ltd, 2003.

COLLECTORS' NOTES

■ Holmegaard was founded in Zealand, Denmark in 1825. From the 1830s, it produced bottles and pressed glass, including tableware. A second glassworks was built at Kastrup in 1847. It was sold in 1873 to allow for expansion of Holmegaard, although the Kastrup factory continued with its own glass production.

■ Holmegaard's first notable modern designer was Jacob Bang (1899-1965) who joined in 1927. He left in 1941 and joined Kastrup in 1957 where he worked until his death. His designs tend to be classical and restrained, with minimal surface decoration.

■ The second notable designer was Per Lütken, who joined in 1942 and is known for his asymmetric, organic and flowing designs that sum up the aesthetic of the 1950s and 1960s. Curving bud-like or teardrop forms are typical, as are 'pulled' rims. Colors tend to be cool,

classical grays or blues and pieces have heavy walls.

■ Apart from the stylistic appearance, Lütken's designs are often recognizable from the inscription on the base which includes his initials and a date. His tend to be among the most consistently popular Holmegaard designs today. In 1965, the Kastrup factory was merged with Holmegaard to enable production to be expanded.

■ Also highly desirable is Lütken's cheerful 'Carnaby' range, which is the polar opposite of his usual aesthetic, being brightly colored and geometric in shape. This mold-blown series is similar to the 'Palet' range produced by Holmegaard & Kastrup and designed by Jacob Bang's son, Michael, between 1968 and 1976. The bright pillar box red is the most typical color and all have a 'plastic'-like appearance.

A Holmegaard smoke gray bubble vase, designed by Per Lütken and signed "HOLMEGAARD PL 1958".

1958   3.5in (9cm) high

$7-10   **NPC**

A Holmegaard heart-shaped aqua blue 'Minuet' vase, designed by Per Lütken, with original label.

c1955   4.25in (11cm) high

$80-120   **NPC**

A Holmegaard capri blue 'Provence' bowl, designed by Per Lütken.

This was made in a similar way to Lütken's earlier small bowls with heavy bodies. Although larger, it used the same amount of glass so was more cost effective, but its thin body made it more vulnerable to damage.

c1962   7in (18cm) diam

$80-120   **NPC**

A rare Holmegaard tall aqua blue glass vase, designed by Per Lütken, with slender neck.

A similar shape was designed by Paul Kedelv for Flygsfors, and used by Whitefriars (with a bubbled base). Flygsfors uses the white, clear, and colored glass typical of that factory. It is sometimes known as the 'dog bone', because of its shape.

c1955   11in (28cm) high

$80-120   **NPC**

A Holmegaard aqua blue glass bowl, designed by Per Lütken and signed on the base.

c1955   6in (15.5cm) diam

$50-70   **GAZE**

A Holmegaard vase, designed by Per Lütken, signed "Holmegaard PL" on the base.

1960   9in (23cm) high

$120-180   **NPC**

A Holmegaard smoke gray glass cylinder vase, designed by Per Lütken, signed on the base.

1969   7in (18cm) high

$70-100   **NPC**

A Holmegaard smoke gray glass dish, designed by Per Lütken, with heavy walls, signed on the base.

1959   8.5in (11cm) diam

$20-30   **NPC**

A CLOSER LOOK AT A HOLMEGAARD VASE

Pulled or everted rims and parts are a typical feature of many of Lütken's designs.

The organic, budlike-form is typical of Lütken's asymmetric designs during the 1950s and of the influence of nature on Scandinavian designers.

The small hole is created by inserting a pin into the bubble of molten glass. As air escapes, the hole opens wider and a randomly sized cavity opens up.

The walls are heavy, with a green glass element being cased in clear glass, and then manipulated with tools while still hot.

A Holmegaard 'Abstraction' vase, designed by Per Lütken, signed "HOLMEGAARD 19 PL 58" to the base.

1958   7in (18cm) high

$120-180   **GAZE**

A 1940s Holmegaard vase, designed by Per Lütken, with early bold signature.

6in (15cm) wide

$80-120   **NPC**

A late 20thC Holmegaard handkerchief-like clear glass vase.

$80-120   **GAZE**

A Holmegaard sapphire blue cylinder vase, designed by Per Lütken, signed.

1965   9in (23cm) high

$70-100   **NPC**

A Holmegaard deep amber glass 'Gulvase', designed by Otto Brauer.

c1960   11.5in (29cm) high

$70-100   **NPC**

A Holmegaard large sapphire blue glass vase.

11.5in (29cm) high

$60-90   **NPC**

An unusually large Holmegaard red glass stepped and tapering vase, with flared rim.

11in (28cm) high

$80-120   **NPC**

A 1960s Holmegaard large tricorn vase, blue encasing green glass, with a flared rim, signed on the base with Holmegaard marks.

The combination of colored glass is highly unusual for Holmegaard and recalls Muranese designs. However, the pulled rim and thick walls echo the designs of Per Lütken.

14.5in (37cm) high

$30-50   **GAZE**

A Holmegaard seven-piece water or lemonade set.

c1957-65

$60-90   **NPC**

A set of six Holmegaard beakers, five with original labels.

$70-100   **NPC**

A 1970s Holmegaard neck glass, designed by Christer Holmgren, with original box.

Christel and Christer Holmgren established their design studio in Denmark in 1971. Designed to hang around the neck, this weighted glass freed the hands of the drinker to 'smoke, eat, shake hands, or even hold another drink'.

3.5in (9cm) high

$50-70   **NPC**

A Holmegaard glass clock, white with green glass applied decoration.

11in (28cm) diam

$30-50   **GAZE**

A group of 1970s Holmegaard red cased 'Gulvase' bottle vases, designed by Otto Brauer.

These were based on a design by Per Lütken from 1958.

c1962   *Left: 17.75in (45cm) high*

$800-1,200

c1962   *Middle: 13.75in (35cm) high*

$700-1,000

c1962   *Right: 19.75in (50cm) high*

$500-800   **EOH**

A Kastrup & Holmegaard red cased 'Carnaby' line vase, designed by Michael Bang in the 1960s.

11.75in (30cm) high

$600-900   **EOH**

A Holmegaard blue bottle vase, with globe stopper.

21.5in (55cm) high inc stopper

$800-1,200   **EOH**

A Kastrup large gray glass floor vase, designed by Jacob Bang, with internal white casing.

17.5in (44.5cm) high

$180-220   **GC**

A Kastrup blue glass vase, designed by Jacob Bang, with paper label.

8.25in (21cm) high

$100-150   **GC**

A Kastrup green glass vase, designed by Jacob Bang.

6in (15cm) high

$80-120   **GC**

A Kastrup smoky gray tapering vase, designed by Jacob Bang.

10.25in (26cm) high

$80-120   **GC**

A smoky gray tapering vase, possibly designed by Jacob E. Bang for Kastrup.

$220-280   **EOH**

COLLECTORS' NOTES

■ Riihimäki (known as Riihimaën Lasi Oy from 1937) was founded in 1910 in Finland and initially produced container, industrial, and domestic glass. The innovative factory held competitions to employ new designers in the 1930s and 1940s.

■ Helena Tynell joined in 1946, Nanny Still in 1949 and Tamara Aladin in 1959. Aimo Okkolin had already joined the factory in 1937, and these names dominated design into the 1960s. A style based around clean-lined geometric form with little surface decoration typifies their production. Colors tend to be jewel-like, bright and rich, and some are more desirable that others.

■ The designs reflecting the 'Pop' style of the age. They employed a manufacturing process, which used molds to ensure consistency of form and color. Aladin is known for her geometric forms, usually incorporating flanges. Pieces showing numerous strong geometrical or curving parts in rich colors tend to be the most desirable and valuable.

■ Initial secondary market interest came from those interested in Scandinavian and interior design, primarily as the designs sit so well within modern interiors. Over the past few years, collecting interest has grown, as has an understanding of Scandinavian glass. Always avoid chipped, cracked or scratched examples as the purity of color and form so typical of Scandinavian glass is disrupted.

A Riihimaën Lasi Oy cased green glass cylindrical vase, designed by Aimo Okkolin.

c1970   7in (18.5cm) high

$30-50   **GC**

A Riihimaën Lasi Oy cased green glass waisted vase, designed by Aimo Okkolin.

c1970   7in (18.5cm) high

$25-35   **NPC**

A Riihimaën Lasi Oy cased green glass vase, designed by Nanny Still.

c1976   9.75in (25cm) high

$40-60   **NPC**

A Riihimaën Lasi Oy green vase, designed by Helena Tynell.

7in (18cm) high

$70-100   **NPC**

A Riihimaën Lasi Oy green geometric 'Disc' vase, designed by Tamara Aladin.

11in (28cm) high

$70-100   **NPC**

A Riihimaën Lasi Oy olive green stepped vase, designed by Tamara Aladin.

11in (28cm) high

$50-80   **NPC**

A Riihimaën Lasi Oy green vase, designed by Tamara Aladin.

c1976   9.75in (25cm) high

$30-50   **NPC**

A CLOSER LOOK AT A RIIHIMÄKI VASE

This is known as the 'Pablo' vase, perhaps due to its 'Cubist' style lines that bring to mind Picasso's paintings.

As with all Riihimäki pieces, it has been made in a mold to ensure consistency of form and color.

A Riihimaën Lasi Oy 'Pompadour' vase, designed by Nanny Still.

c1968   9in (23cm) high

$50-70   NPC

A Riihimaën Lasi Oy blue 'Pompadour'-style vase, designed by Nanny Still.

6.25in (16cm) high

$30-40   NPC

A Riihimaën Lasi Oy blue vase, designed by Helena Tynell.

8.25in (21cm) high

$60-90   NPC

It was designed by Erkkitapio Siiroinen and is very unusual in blue.

Such sharply angled protrusions are comparatively uncommon in Riihimäki's designs.

A rare Riihimaën Lasi Oy vase, designed by Erkkitapio Siiroinen.

c1968   8in (20cm) high

$120-180   NPC

A 1960s Riihimaën Lasi Oy blue 'Tuulikki' vase, designed by Tamara Aladin.

7.5in (19cm) high

$40-60   NPC

A Riihimaën Lasi Oy octagonal bottle vase, designed by Nanny Still, with knobbly decoration and label.

7in (18cm) high

$80-120   NPC

A Riihimaën Lasi Oy blue-gray vase, designed by Helena Tynell.

8.25in (21cm) high

$40-60   NPC

A Riihimaën Lasi Oy smoky blue-gray vase, designed by Nanny Still.

1960-70   25in (63cm) high

$30-50   NPC

GLASS

A Riihimaën Lasi Oy red vase, designed by Nanny Still.

9.75in (25cm) high

$40-60 NPC

A Riihimaën Lasi Oy red glass vase, designed by Tamara Aladin.

c1965 8in (20cm) high

$40-60 NPC

A Riihamaën Lasi Oy red 'Tuulikki' vase, designed by Tamara Aladin.

c1976 8in (20cm) high

$40-60 NPC

A Riihimaën Lasi Oy red waisted 'trumpet' vase, designed by Tamara Aladin, design number 1565, with three thick rings.

c1976 8in (20cm) high

$60-90 NPC

A Riihimaën Lasi Oy tobacco brown vase, designed by Nanny Still.

11in (28cm) high

$40-60 NPC

A Riihimaën Lasi Oy turquoise 'lantern-style' vase, designed by Tamara Aladin.

9.75in (25cm) high

$50-70 NPC

A Riihimaën Lasi Oy blue vase, designed by Tamara Aladin.

25in (63.5cm) high

$40-60 NPC

COLLECTORS' NOTES

■ Iittala was founded in Finland in 1881. As with many other Scandinavian factories, it initially produced domestic glass, such as bottles and traditional tableware. Designs became more modern with a series of competitions in the 1930s that resulted in leading designers, such as Alvar Aalto, joining.

■ Between 1947 and 1954, this escalated further, pushing Iittala to become a cutting edge glass company employing leading designers, such as Gunnel Nyman, Tapio Wirkkala, Timo Sarpaneva and Kaj Franck. Designs were often executed in clear glass and were inspired by the Scandinavian landscape, so incorporated the texture or appearance of bark and ice. These tend to be the most sought-after designs today. Look for good levels of texture and examples free of damage.

An Iittala tripod candle or taper holder, designed by Tapio Wirkkala.

2.75in (7cm) high

$25-35   **NPC**

An Iittala candle holder, possibly designed by Timo Sarpaneva.

3.5in (9cm) diam

$20-25   **NPC**

An Iittala cushion vase, designed by Timo Sarpaneva, with label.

5in (12.5cm) high

$30-50   **NPC**

An Iittala 'Iceberg' vase, designed by Tapio Wirkkala, unusually marked with full signature and serial marks rather than unsigned or initialed "TW".

This design is typical of Wirkkala's interest in the Scandinavian environment and natural textures such as ice or bark.

6.25in (16cm) high

$80-120   **NPC**

A group of three Iittala 'Festivo' candlesticks, designed by Timo Sarpaneva.

Typical of the fashion for textured glass in the 1960s, the popularity of this design endured well into the 1980s. The texture was created by pouring the hot glass into a wooden mold, which burnt each time, altering the texture. This process was initially created for the textured Finlandia range, of which Festivo was a spin-off.

c1968   Largest 7.25in (18.5cm) high

$80-120   **NPC**

An Iittala bamboo beaker.

4.75in (12cm) high

$20-25   **NPC**

An Iittala 'Savoy' clear glass vase, designed by Alvar Aalto.

6in (15cm) high

$80-120   **NPC**

COLLECTORS' NOTES

■ Kosta was founded in 1742 and Boda in 1864, both in Sweden. Like most factories they began to focus on design during the 1920s and 1930s. Always overshadowed by rival Orrefors, their fortunes changed when Vicke Lindstrand joined as Art Director in 1950, from Orrefors.

■ Lindstrand is known for his modern designs, from curving, organic forms to those incorporating internal threading or cut or engraved designs. Goran Warff was employed from 1964-74, and then again from 1985, and often designed sculptural forms.

■ Kosta, Afors and Boda formed an alliance in 1964, becoming Kosta Boda in 1976. Since then, all pieces produced have been under this brand. Bertil Vallien joined Afors in 1964 and transformed the company. He is known for his richly colored designs, often with mottled, matte surfaces, which are popular with collectors today. In 1990, the company merged with Orrefors to become Orrefors Kosta Boda.

A 1950s Kosta organic, near circular dish, designed by Vicke Lindstrand, with small internal bubbles and marked "Kosta".

8in (20cm) wide

$80-120   **NPC**

A Kosta bowl, designed by Ernest Gordon, with sand-blasted panels cut with deep ovals, the base incised "E. Gordon Kosta GS4014".

Ernest Gordon worked briefly at Kosta with eminent designer Vicke Lindstrand between 1953 and 1955. He then joined Afors in Sweden, where he worked as a designer until the early 1960s. He is known for his cut glass designs in the dominant, organic, often asymmetric, styles of the period as shown here.

c1954   *9.5in (24.5cm) wide*

$600-900   **PSI**

A Kosta clear glass knobbly candleholder, designed by Goran Warff.

c1970

$20-30   **NPC**

A Kosta Boda bowl, designed by Kjell Engman, mottled purple decoration with a matte translucent body, signed "KOSTA BODA 58891 K.Engman".

4in (10cm) high

$30-50   **GAZE**

A 1980s Kosta Boda pink vase, designed by Kjell Engman, with leaf motif.

7.5in (19cm) high

$50-70   **NPC**

A Boda handmade vase, designed by Bertil Vallien, the green body with applied decoration signed "BODA B.VALLIEN ATELJE277" on the base.

6.75in (17cm) high

$120-180   **GAZE**

A Kosta Boda 'Points of View' sculpture, by Bertil Vallien, etched for presentation and signed, on a black stand.

1998

$120-180   **NPC**

A pair of Kosta clear cut-glass candlesticks, one with remains of sticker, etched "Kosta 06202".

11in (28cm) high

$50-80   **GAZE**

COLLECTORS' NOTES

- Orrefors was founded in Sweden in 1898 and initially produced bottles and tableware. It became globally renowned in the 1920s and 1930s for its engraved and innovative 'graal' and 'aerial' designs by Knut Bergvist, Simon Gate, and Edward Hald.

- From the 1930s until 1950, Vicke Lindstrand took the company forward with his engraved designs. Other notable designers include Sven Palmqvist, Nils Landberg, and Ingeborg Lundin. Orrefors' reputation for innovative processes was continued with 'Kraka', 'Ravenna', and 'Fuga' ranges. In 1990, it merged with the Kosta Boda and Afors group and still produces today within the 'Royal Scandinavia' group.

An Orrefors 'Polaris' bowl.

6.25in (16cm) wide

$40-60 NPC

An Orrefors light blue dish, with thickly rendered, lobed design.

6.25in (16cm) wide

$40-60 NPC

An Orrefors small red asymmetric footed bowl, the interior with marbled effect, the foot in clear glass, the base incised "Orrefors PU3297/21".

2.75in (7cm) high

$80-120 PSI

An Orrefors 'Selena' bowl, designed by Sven Palmqvist, with engraved decoration inspired by Uppsala Ekeby.

Orrefors are well known for their engraving, particularly that designed by Edward Hald and Simon Gate during the 1930s. Palmqvist worked at Orrefors from 1928-71 and studied under Gate.

c1950 *8in (20cm) diam*

$80-120 NPC

A Orrefors blue 'Fuga' bowl, marked "Fuga ORREFORS".

The Fuga range was manufactured with centrifugal forces, which forced the glass into the mold to form a consistently thick bowl shape. The process was developed by Sven Palmqvist during the 1940s, and introduced in 1954.

c1955 *8in (20cm) diam*

$30-50 GAZE

An Orrefors blue cased glass vase, designed by Sven Palmqvist, inscribed "Orrefors DW 3591/15" on the base.

c1960 *9in (23cm) high*

$70-100 GAZE

A Orrefors clear cylindrical vase, with white stripe decoration and frosted base.

6.75in (17cm) high

$50-70 NPC

An Orrefors blue free-blown decanter, with applied clear glass foot and leaf-shaped pressed stopper, the body with extensive liming from water to the interior.

The liming reduces the value considerably. If it were not limed, it could be worth up to $80-120.

12.5in (32cm) high

$30-50 GC

GLASS

A CLOSER LOOK AT AN EKENAS DISPLAY PIECE

The amber glass block has been hewn or carved and then engraved by hand with a design of three naked ladies on the front and back, creating perspective.

The rough carving has been utilized as part of the design, forming the illusion of the entrance to a cave.

The lady on the front has been engraved with the reflective base of the piece in mind, so that she appears to sit on the floor.

It has been signed by the artist with the designer's name and a serial number probably containing a date.

A unique John Orwar Lake amber glass display piece, signed on the left "J. O. LAKE EKENAS SWEDEN 508.68;710.68".

Ekenas was founded in Sweden in 1917 and closed in 1976. Little is known about the factory, although some smaller factory-made pieces have come to light. John Orwar Lake (b.1921) was their Chief Designer from 1953-76. He was joined by Michael Bang briefly during the 1960s.

1968   9in (23cm) widest

$180-220   **BY**

A Flygsfors 'Coquille' amethyst and clear glass bowl, with pulled rim.

c1963

$30-50   **NPC**

An Alsterfors red vase, designed by Per Ström.

6in (15cm) high

$25-35   **NPC**

A pair of Ekenas blue bubbled glass cylindrical vases, designed by John Orwar Lake, one with original label.

c1960   6in (15cm) high

$70-100   **GAZE**

An Alsterfors molded, textured vase, designed by Per Ström, etched "P Ström 68" on the base.

1968   10in (25cm) high

$40-60   **GC**

A Flygsfors 'Coquille' clear cased amethyst bowl, with undulating rim.

c1963   10.5in (27cm) wide

$25-35   NPC

A CLOSER LOOK AT A FLYGSFORS DISH

The 'Coquille' range was designed by Paul Kedelv, who worked at Flygsfors between 1949 and 1956 after working for Orrefors and, briefly, Nuutajärvi.

It is typified by freeform shapes with pulled rims, loosely inspired by seashells, as the name suggests.

Launched in 1952, it was immensely popular, selling into the 1960s in the US as well as throughout Europe.

Early colors were opaque white glass with either blue, green, red or purple glass, which was then cased in clear glass.

A Flygsfors 'Coquille' amethyst and clear asymmetrical glass bowl.

1952-c1964   6.25in (16cm) wide

$30-50   NPC

A Gullaskruf green vase, designed by Kjell Blomberg, with J. Wuidart & Co. label.

Wuidart was a London-based importer of Scandinavian glass and design. Ronald Stennett-Willson, founder of King's Lynn Glass (later Wedgwood Glass), was sales manager at Wuidart from 1951-64.

c1960   6.25in (16cm) diam

$70-100   GROB

A Gullaskruf tall blue floor bottle, designed by Arthur Percy, with bulbous base and attenuated flaring neck.

Arthur Percy worked as a designer for Gullaskruf between 1951 and 1965.

c1960   19in (48cm) high

$120-180   GC

A clear globular vase, designed by Benny Motzfeldt, with bubbles and metallic oxide inclusions, acid-etched "PLUS BM NORWAY".

Benny Motzfeldt (1909-95) worked at the Norwegian Hadeland factory as part of its design team from 1955-67, as well as Ransfjord later on. After this period he set up his own glass studio to produce primarily one-off pieces. He became one of Norway's most important studio glass artists.

c1970   6in (15cm) diam

$120-180   GROB

A Nuutajävi Nötsjo red and green speckled vase, by Oiva Toikka, on a white ground, with engraved signature to underside.

6.5in (16.5cm) high

$280-320   ROS

FIND OUT MORE...

Collector's Guides: 20th Century Glass, by Judith Miller, published by DK, 2004.

20th Century Factory Glass, by Leslie Jackson, published by Mitchell Beazley, 2000.

Scandinavian Ceramics & Glass in the 20th Century, by Jennifer Opie, Victoria & Albert Museum, 1989.

GLASS

COLLECTORS' NOTES

■ In 1965, the Rudolfova Hut, Hermanova Hut, Libochovice, Rosice and other glassworks were incorporated into Sklo Union, the national glass manufactory. The name 'Royal Bohemia' or 'Bohemia Glass' is often applied as these names are found on labels applied by importers and exporters.

■ All examples here are made from pressed glass. Communist Czechoslovakia developed its own unique design ethic from the 1940s onward. Although made on a factory basis, production standards were very high and were inextricably linked with design, in line with the Industrial design movement.

■ Many highly skilled designers, such as Frantisek Vizner and Adolf Matura are now well known. However others have remained unrecognized outside Czechoslovakia, due to a continuing shortage of information, often leading to erroneous attributions.

■ Many of the modern designs were produced for very long periods, primarily from the 1950s-80s. The dates of introduction of some shapes are known, as indicated. Some shapes were designed before WWII and the molds reused after the war, making it hard to date pieces. It is estimated that in 1965, half the molds being used in Sklo Union factories were of pre-war origin.

■ Charity shops and collectors fairs often have examples and prices are still comparatively affordable. Due to trade sanctions and taxes a great many designs and examples did not make it to the West at all, so were sold within Communist states, where they may be more common.

■ Designers and factories, as well as dates, can only be identified from company brochures and records or trade journals, many in German or Czech. Some information may never be found. As more information is researched and published, already growing interest from collectors in this fascinating, colorful and characterful glass is sure to boom.

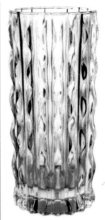

A Sklo Union clear glass cylindrical vase, with vertical wavy textured pattern.

9in (23cm) high

$50-70   **GC**

A Sklo Union clear glass cylindrical vase, designed by Frantisek Vizner, with clear glass molded concave prunts or lenses, retaining original importers silver foil and black "Royal Bohemia" label.

11in (28cm) high

$80-120   **GC**

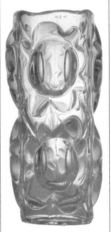

A Sklo Union clear glass cylindrical vase, produced at the Hermanova Glassworks to a design by Frantisek Peceny, with all-round molded design in the form of a Chinese dragon's head, made from 1972.

Peceny (b.1920) began work as a designer at Hermanova in the mid-1940s after studying at the Institute of Applied Arts in Prague. As well as his industrial designs, he is renowned for his improvements to the design and related production of pressed glass.

8in (20.5cm) high

$70-100   **GC**

A Sklo Union small clear glass cylindrical vase, with molded stylized flowers with concave centers.

6in (15.5cm) high

$15-25   **GC**

A Sklo Union clear glass square section vase, produced at the Rosice Glassworks to a design by Vladislav Urban, made from 1967.

This design was also produced in light blue and amber. It is also found in low rectangular bowls, ashtrays and candlesticks.

9.75in (25cm) high

$50-80   **GC**

A Sklo Union clear glass square section candlestick, produced at the Rosice Glassworks to a Vladislav Urban design, with molded geometric design, made from 1967.

3in (7.5cm) high

$15-25   GC

A Sklo Union dark green vase, in an Art Deco style, designed c1925.

This is a typical example of a shape and mold being in use for decades after it was designed.

10in (25.5cm) high

$60-90   GC

A Sklo Union tapering green glass vase, designed by Vaclav Hanus, with alternating stylized leaf like design.

8in (20.5cm) high

$50-80   GC

A Sklo Union green fluted tapering cylinder vase, with flared disc rim, produced at the the Rudolfova Glassworks to a Rudolf Jurnikl design, made from 1964.

This is pattern no.13157 and can also be found in amber. Smaller candleholders can also be found, which are pattern no.13155.

8in (20cm) high

$50-60   GC

A Sklo Union green glass vase, with molded convex teardrop shapes to the bottom half and curving 'cut out' rim.

9.75in (25cm) high

$50-80   GC

A Sklo Union tall green glass vase, made at the Rudolfova Glassworks to a Rudolf Jurnikl design, with two circular areas of molded raised, hobnail-like designs to each side, made from 1964.

This design can be found in a number of different shapes, sizes, and colors, including orange, purple, and light blue. Jurnikl (b.1928) worked in glass design for nearly 30 years and arrived as a designer at Rudolfova in 1960. He became one of the most experienced pressed glass designers, winning many prizes including the gold medal at the International Exhibition of Industrial Design in 1973.

$50-80   GC

A Sklo Union yellow glass tapering cylindrical vase, with molded hobnail-like, pyramidal prunts.

8in (20.5cm) high

$30-50   GC

A Sklo Union amber glass, square section vase, with high relief-molded geometric pattern.

7in (17.5cm) high

$50-80   MHC

GLASS

A Sklo Union graduated red, amber and yellow glass vase, with bulbous body and linear pattern.

6.25in (16cm) high

$60-90   GC

A CLOSER LOOK AT A SKLO UNION VASE

This vase was designed in 1940 by Rudolf Schrötter for the Rudolfova Glassworks based in Teplice, Czechoslovakia.

This design was produced in great numbers from the 1940s into the 1970s, meaning examples can be found comparatively easily today – always look for those in perfect condition.

The machine-cut base with a 'bird bath' like depression is typical of the pressed glass produced by these factories at this time.

It can be found in a variety of jewel-like colors including green and amber. The oval 'lenses' give an interesting optical effect.

A 1940s-70s Sklo Union bullet-shaped glass vase, with molded oval shapes to each of the four sides.

7.75in (19.5cm) high

$25-35   GC

A Sklo Union ashtray, produced at the Rudolfova Glassworks to a Rudolf Jurnikl design, with circular area of molded raised, hobnail-like design on the underside, made from 1964.

6in (15cm) wide

$15-25   GC

A Sklo Union blue glass, tapered vase, with geometric diamond-shaped molded patterns changing to fan shapes near the rim.

This is a pre-WWII shape that remained in production for over 40 years.

16in (5cm) high

$40-60   GC

A Sklo Union light blue glass vase, shape number 13227/13, produced at the Rudolfova Glassworks to a Rudolf Jurnikl design, with a circular area of molded raised, hobnail-like design to each side, made from 1964.

7in (17.5cm) high

$50-70   GC

A Sklo Union lilac glass vase, with stepped, 'festooned' molded pattern.

This is another pre-WWII shape that remained in production for over 40 years.

8in (20cm) high

$40-60   GC

COLLECTORS' NOTES

- The contemporary glass movement for spheres and orbs developed in the late 20thC from the creation of art glass marbles and paperweights by contemporary glass artists, mainly in the US. From functional objects has sprung a new, exciting and dynamic art glass movement. Spheres tend to be larger than marbles, with the tag 'orb' being reserved for the largest examples.

- The designs are not painted on the interior or exterior of the sphere, but are contained within the sphere, being carefully hand-worked in hot, colored glass and most often in more than one layer. The glass designs are then encased in a top layer of clear borosilicate 'crystal' glass.

- Spheres really need to be handled and viewed in person, as this is the best way to appreciate the intricate detail within and myriad reflections and magnifications caused by the curving surface. The skill involved in their creation shows far the studio glass movement has progressed since the late 1960s.

- Names to look out for include Paul Stankard, Jesse Taj, David Salazar, Dinah Hulet, Rolf and Genie Wald, and Josh Simpson. New artists come to the field every year, each bringing their own style and skill, making this a vibrant and ever-changing market. Prices are currently comparatively affordable for such detailed, unique works.

- Watch out for new young makers, examining their work and comparing it to established names. Many artists make their own murrines, which are also known as 'milli', 'millefiori' or 'murrini'. Some artists such as Jesse Taj and David Strobel sell their murrines for others to incorporate into their own designs.

- As well as established marble collectors, a new younger audience has been attracted to the market. Images from cartoons and popular and sub-cultures are often included, making this art form highly relevant to today. Spheres are intricate, easy to display and offer great variety. Values should increase as the market grows.

A Jerry Kelly sphere, with rake-pull patterns around circular set-ups of individual murrines also made by Kelly, signed "JK05".

2005   *1.5in (4cm) diam*

$70-100   **BGL**

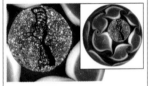

A Jerry Kelly 'Cat In The Hat' sphere, with rake pull forms around a central internal foil decal of Dr Seuss' 'Cat in The Hat', signed "JK2005".

'Rake pull' designs are created by dragging the molten glass into a shaped and swirling pattern with a tool.

2005   *1.5in (4cm) diam*

$100-150   **BGL**

A Rajesh Kommineni 'Reverse Rake' sphere, with layer of rake pulled blue quatrefoils, signed "RK 04".

2004   *2in (5cm) diam*

$80-120   **BGL**

A Raj Kommiene sphere, with internal iridescent swirl core and rake pulled upper layer in a band and floral motifs.

2004   *2in (5cm) diam*

$120-180   **BGL**

A Jerry Kelly 'Bob Marley' sphere, the 'front' with swirls around an internal printed foil decal of Bob Marley, the 'back' with rake pulls surrounding a murrine of a Rastafarian lion with flag.

Kelly has been involved with lamp working since 1993 and is renowned for his attention to detail and is attracted by the variety and challenge offered by marble making.

                    2.5in (6.5cm) diam

$200-250   **BGL**

A prototype David Salazar 'Irises' sphere, signed "DP Salazar".

This unique piece was used to practice the iris pattern before execution on the larger 'Night Sky' piece also shown on this page. Salazar's white ground marbles and spheres are very rare.

2004   1.75in (4.5cm) diam

$350-450   **BGL**

A rare David Salazar experimental 'Irises Over Night Sky', signed "DPSG 6103 1-X".

This combination of a core of blue and yellow swirls and an outer layer of irises was inspired by two of Vincent Van Gogh's most famous paintings. Salazar has been involved in hot glass for over 26 years, and worked as an apprentice at the legendary Lundberg Studios in California in 1972. His love of nature and marine life is apparent in all his works.

3.5in (9cm) diam

$800-1,200   **BGL**

A John Kobuki 'Flower' sphere, signed in kanji.

Kobuki began working in glass in the mid-1990s. His style is typified by floral or seabed designs encased in clear glass that magnifies the internal design in a similar way to a paperweight.

2005   2in (5cm) diam

$60-80   **BGL**

A Christopher Rice 'Butterfly with Flower' sphere, with rake pull back, signed "CYK".

Also known as 'Pan', Rice began working in glass in 1999 and works with pinwheel, vortex and natural motifs.

2005   2.25in (5.5cm) diam

$200-300   **BGL**

A Christopher Rice 'Butterfly' sphere, signed "C Rice 05".

2005   1.5in (4cm) diam

$40-50   **BGL**

A Steve Hitt 'Cedar Trees' sphere, containing butterfly and flower murrines made by Hitt over a layer of cedar trees and a layer of the sky and moon, signed "SH 03".

2003   2in (5cm) diam

$150-200   **BGL**

A large Cathy Richardson Aquarium sphere, signed "Richardson 2002".

Richardson (b.1949) attended Pilchuck Glass School in 1991 and worked at the Corning Glass Studio from 1996-2000.

2002

$400-600   **BGL**

A Christopher Rice 'Frog' sphere, with applied lampwork frog over a sphere with concave swirling interior.

2005

1.5in (4cm) diam

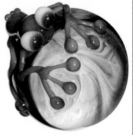

$40-60   **BGL**

A CLOSER LOOK AT A PAUL STANKARD ORB

Stankard is the world's leading paperweight artist - his work is sold by top galleries. It can be found in over 20 public collections including the Metropolitan Museum of Art and The Corning Museum of Glass in New York, the Victoria & Albert Museum, London and the Museum of American Glass, New Jersey.

He is inspired by his love of nature and botany - each individual component is made from glass worked with a hot torch, with the artist concentrating on correct color, form, and detail.

The glass assemblage is then encased in a layer of clear glass, which magnifies certain areas as it is viewed and gives the impression of a moment of living nature trapped in time and glass.

As well as an intricate and accurate visual appearance, Stankard's work considers deeper mystical and poetic themes of the progress of life and nature, involving seeds, flowers, fertility, root systems and decay.

A limited edition Paul Stankard large glass orb, one-of-one from the Whitman Botanical Series, with internal cased lampwork design of a honeycomb, two bees, moss, flowers, and lilies.

Stankard (b.1943) began working with glass around 1961. In 1969 he focused on paperweights, after initially making lampworked animals. During the 1970s, his floral and botanical subject weights, inspired by 19thC French works and friend Francis Whittemore, met with great success. In 1982, he began making a series of botanical obelisks, known as 'Botanicals'. Orbs and spheres are a comparatively new area, only begun in the last few years.

2004   4.25in (11cm) diam

$7,000-9,000   **BGL**

A large Gateson Recko 'Universe' orb, containing a number of planets, a black opal and a nebula, signed "Gateson 2004".

This is the largest 'Universe' orb made to date, taking many days to create. The incredible internal 'space' effect can only be properly appreciated by handling the orb and viewing it from different angles.

2004   3.5in (9cm) diam

$1,000-1,500   **BGL**

A limited edition Josh Simpson 'Planet' sphere, together with a selection of the murrines used, signed "Simpson AP14 2003".

Renowned glass artist Simpson is well known for his fantastical 'Inhabited' and 'Uninhabited' planet orbs and paperweights, as well as other blue glassworks depicting the Mexican night sky.

2003   2.75in (7cm) diam

$280-320   **BGL**

GLASS

A Dustin Morell 'Vortex' sphere, with rake pull reverse design, signed "DKM 2004".

Complex to make, vortex spheres give the impression that the very center of the internal concave vortex is deeper than the corresponding outside surface of the sphere itself.

2004   2.25in (5.5cm) diam

$100-150   **BGL**

A Dustin Morell 'Vortex' sphere, the reverse with randomly shaped colored design, signed "DKM 2004".

2004   2.25in (5.5cm) diam

$80-120   **BGL**

A P. Vogelpohl 'Window Vortex' sphere, with sand-blasted matte areas and clear windows allowing view of the internal vortex, signed "P. Vogelpohl".

2.25in (5.5cm) diam

$120-180   **BGL**

A David Strobel 'Murrini' double-sided sphere, the front with a flat field of orange and yellow stars under a clear dome, the reverse with hemispherical field of many complex murrines, including flying skulls, celtic crosses, jellyfish, Egyptian eyes and a rainbow and clouds over mushrooms, signed "DS04".

Strobel began working in glass in 1991 and has become well known for his complex murrine designs, begun in 1998.

2.25in (6cm) diam

$150-200   **BGL**

A Douglas Sweet 'Fantasy Orb', with sand-blasted areas and clear circular panels showing a set-up of millefiori rods, signed "Sweet".

2005   2in (5cm) diam

$70-100   **BGL**

A Dinah Hulet 'Embellished' lampworked sphere.

Hulet has worked with glass for over 30 years and is one of the best known established studio glass artists working with mosaic glass and spheres.

2005   2in (5cm) diam

$180-220   **BGL**

A limited edition Wendy Bessett 'Stillness of the Night' orb, signed "W Besett C 03 2/4".

2003

2.5in (6.5cm) diam

$280-320   **BGL**

A Mark Matthews 'Windmill Variations' graal sphere, from a series of black and white spheres with various geometric designs, signed to the base "Matthews 2002".

2002   2.75in (7cm) diam

$1,200-1,800   **BGL**

FIND OUT MORE...

Contemporary Marbles & Related Art Glass, *by Mark Block, published by Schiffer Book, 2001.*

The Encyclopedia of Modern Marbles, Spheres, and Orbs, *by Mark Block, published by Schiffer Books, 2005.*

A CLOSER LOOK AT A BLENKO BOWL

It was designed by Blenko's first, and arguably most important, designer Winslow Anderson, around 1950.

Produced in all of Blenko's colors, it is keenly sought after by collectors.

This color, called 'Charcoal', was only produced between 1954 and 1958 although the shape was produced until 1964.

The design won a design award – an example is in the Museum of Modern Art, New York.

A Blenko tall 'Emerald' bottle, designed by Joel Philip Myers, design number 6937.

1969-72	*22in (56cm) high*

$700-1,000   **EOH**

A Blenko gray cornucopia bowl, design 964S.

1954-58	*17.5in (44cm) wide*

$250-350   **EOH**

A Blenko tall 'Charcoal' blue/gray bottle, designed by Wayne Husted, with flat top stopper, design 561.

1956-59	*21.25in (54cm) high*

$600-800   **EOH**

A Blenko 'Wheat' faceted bottle, designed by Joel Philip Myers, with optic rib body and cased stopper, design 6934.

1969-72	*19.25in (49cm) high*

$250-350   **EOH**

A Blenko huge 'Tangerine' bottle, designed by Wayne Husted, with stopper, design 5815L.

Blenko was founded in 1922 and continues today. Loved for their bright, vivid colors, Blenko's most sought after shapes are unusually shaped bottles, preferably in large, floor standing sizes such as this one. Look out for the work of key designers Wayne Husted (designer 1952-1963), and Joel Philip Myers (designer 1963-1972).

1958-70	*30.25in (77cm) high*

$1,200-1,800   **EOH**

A Blenko blue triangular section bottle, with lightly textured sides.

	7.5in (19cm) high

$60-70   **RETC**

A Fenton Blue Overlay double-crimped vase, with clear blue glass over an opaque white glass base.

1943-53	*6.5in (16.5cm) high*

$70-100   **PAC**

GLASS

A Fenton 'Colonial Blue' Hobnail double crimped basket, mold number 3837.

1963-c1973   7in (18cm) high

$30-50   **PAC**

A Fenton Topaz Opalescent Hobnail vase.

Topaz is now becoming second only to Cranberry in desirability levels and also appeals to Vaseline glass collectors. It is also scarcer, having been produced for shorter periods of time.

1940-62   4.5in (11.5cm) high

$80-120   **PAC**

A Fenton Blue Opalescent 'Coin Dot' double-crimped bowl.

Fenton was founded in 1905 and became known for its pressed glass which proved popular from the 1920s-70s, particularly the 'Victorian' style examples with frilled edges. It is still active today.

1947-56   10.75in (27cm) diam

$100-150   **PAC**

A Fenton 'Violets-in-the-snow' pedestal dish with crystal double crimped edge.

c1960s   6in (15cm) high

$40-50   **PAC**

A Hazel Atlas Glass Co. 'Royal Lace' pattern pink depression glass trio set.

1934-41   Saucer 5.5in (14cm) diam

$20-25   **GROB**

A Hazel Atlas Glass Co. 'Moderntone' pattern cobalt blue depression glass cup and saucer, the saucer with gilt trim.

1934-42   Saucer 5.5in (14cm) diam

$25-35   **GROB**

A 1950s American Fire-King Oven range Jadeite cup and saucer.

Saucer 5.75in (14.5cm) wide

$20-25   **GROB**

COLLECTORS' NOTES

■ Holiday memorabilia continues to be popular on both sides of the Atlantic, with Halloween and Christmas examples the most commonly sought-after.

■ German pieces, dating from before WWII, are usually the earliest and most desirable and, as such, command the highest prices.

■ America also started producing its own examples in the 1920s with production carrying through to today. Pieces from the 1950s and later are typically plastic.

■ Many of the early pieces were made of easily damaged materials such as pulped cardboard or lithographed tin, so condition has a great effect on value.

■ Celluloid memorabilia started to appear from Japan in the 1930s and it became an increasingly prolific producer.

■ As earlier pieces become less accessible to new collectors, later, plastic examples from the 1960s onwards are becoming more sought-after and prices are starting to rise.

■ Look for Halloween jack-o-lanterns, particularly double-sided or unusually colored or large versions, as well as black cats and witches.

■ Santa Claus is the most commonly found Christmas character, following by Christmas trees, snowmen and snowbabies.

A 1920s German Halloween 'Betty Boop'-style pumpkin hanging display piece, of molded and painted card.

The Betty Boop style character face is very rare.

9.75in (25cm) high

$70-100   **HH**

A 1920s German Halloween black memorabilia pumpkin, of molded and painted card.

This subject matter is very rare and unusual, and appeals to black memorabilia collectors as well as Halloween collectors.

10.25in (26cm) high

$200-300   **HH**

A 1930s Halloween articulated creeping cat hanging display piece, of printed die-cut card.

13.5in (34cm) long

$35-45   **HH**

A 1920s German painted and molded card Halloween hanging display plaque of a witch on a broomstick.

13in (33cm) wide

$70-90   **HH**

An American Halloween printed and cut card hanging display piece of a witch with devilish pumpkin, by Dennison.

Very few of these were made, making this piece rare.

20.5in (52cm) high

$30-40   **HH**

A German 'Halloween Greetings' color printed card table top decoration of a girl making a potion, some water stains.

4.75in (12cm) high

$30-40   **HH**

A German 'A Happy Halloween' printed card table top decoration of a girl with an owl and a cat.

4.75in (12cm) high

$40-50   **HH**

A 1930s/40s American Halloween printed and die-cut card articulated skeleton, by H.E. Lehr.

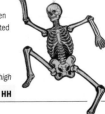

22.75in (58cm) high

$25-35   **HH**

A 1920s/30s Halloween printed tinplate noisemaker, with a devil motif, marked "MADE IN GERMANY".

$40-50   HH

A CLOSER LOOK AT A NOISEMAKER

It is of standard form for a noisemaker.

As well as a witch, it has a devil motif, which is rarer than other decorative forms.

Most tinplate noisemakers are German, not Japanese, making this less common.

It is in very good condition, retaining its paint and with no rust, which is unusual as they were often used roughly over the years.

A 1930s Halloween printed tinplate noisemaker, marked "JAPAN".

6.5in (16.5cm) high

$40-50   HH

A 1950s American Halloween tin noisemaker, with lithographed witches' face.

8.25in (21cm) long

$70-100   SOTT

A 1950s Japanese printed tinplate cylindrical noisemaker, turning the wooden handle activates a spring to beat an internal tin diaphragm made from a beer can, printed "MADE IN JAPAN".

4in (10cm) high

$50-70   HH

An American Halloween tinplate spinning rattle, with a cat motif, marked "TC Made in USA".

4.25in (10.5cm) diam

$20-30   HH

A Halloween printed tinplate tambourine, decorated with a smiley pumpkin.

6.5in (16.5cm) diam

$100-150   HH

A Halloween painted and carved wooden soldier-shaped horn, printed "Czecho-slovakia".

6.25in (16cm) high

$35-55   HH

A 1930s Czechoslovakian Halloween painted wooden horn, with printed decoration of cats.

6in (15cm) high

$35-55   HH

A 1920s German card and crêpe paper candy container, with spherical paper-covered plastic head.

This is unusual as it is female, rather than male.

8in (20cm) high

$250-350   HH

A 1920s German painted composition 'Pumpkin Woman' figurine, with card base and green crêpe paper ruff.

6.25in (16cm) high

$180-270   HH

A scarce 1920s German painted bisque pumpkin head figure.

5.5in (14cm) high

$180-270   HH

A 1970s/80s Halloween plastic push button collapsing pumpkin head doll.

3.5in (9cm) high

$30-45   HH

A CLOSER LOOK AT A HALLOWEEN FIGURINE

It is in very good condition considering its age, with few signs of wear and no damage.

Halloween nodders are scarce. However, there are a number of variations to this color scheme and type.

This one is early, dating from the 1920s - its survival is rare.

It has an oversized head, which is unusual and meant it could have been easily damaged due to its size and weight.

A 1920s American or German pumpkin nodder, unmarked, in painted composition.

6in (15cm) high

$500-700   HH

A German painted ceramic and card candy container, in the form of a cat on a pumpkin, with wire tail.

7in (17.5cm) high

$350-450   HH

A 1930s/40s painted composition trembling skeleton, with wire limbs.

Skeleton models, toys and puppets are also related to the Mexican Day of The Dead.

5.75in (14.5cm) high

$45-65   HH

A 1920s American 'Fibro Toy' pull-along candy holder, by The Dolly Toy Co. of Dayton Ohio, of printed and cut card on wooden wheels.

9.75in (25cm) long

$100-150   HH

HOLIDAY COLLECTIBLES

A 1950s/60s Halloween plastic lamp, of a witch holding a pumpkin.

These lamps have become popular, with demand and thus prices rising over the past two years.

14.5in (37cm) high

$20-30   **HH**

A 1950s/60s Halloween plastic lamp, of a pumpkin emanating from a frying pan.

9in (23cm) high

$20-30   **HH**

A 1920s German Halloween papier-mâché jack-o-lantern.

The airbrushed highlights, color and smiling face are scarce and desirable, hence its higher price. It also retains its original paper insert.

5in (12.50cm) high

$700-1,000   **JDJ**

A 1920s German papier-mâché jack-o-lantern, with original printed paper insert.

This shape with a hat is very rare, as is the larger size.

6in (15cm) high

$200-300   **HH**

An American printed tinplate candy holder, with whistle/noisemaker nose, by the US Metal Toy Co.

3.75in (9.5cm) high

$50-70   **HH**

A 1960s black and orange plastic pumpkin lolly holder.

3in (7.5cm) high

$40-50   **HH**

A 1940s/50s Japanese Halloween finger-operated concertina toy, of wood and printed card, back of card printed "JAPAN".

Card 4.25in (11cm) high

$50-70   **HH**

A complete American printed canvas 'Witch Party' game, by The Saalfield Publishing Co. of Akron, Ohio.

The aim of the game, a variation of 'pin the tail on the donkey', is to pin small cut-out canvas pumpkins on the white space while blindfolded!

c1913   17in (43cm) wide

$80-120   **HH**

A 1950s RCA Victor Walt Disney Production 'Trick or Treat' storybook, and two 78rpm records.

7.5in (19cm) high

$15-30   **HH**

A sitting Santa Claus candy container, with papier-mâché face, red crêpe paper coat, cotton batting beard, hair and other trim, blue crêpe paper hands, and black crêpe paper boots, some dustiness.

18in (45.50cm) high

$1,200-1,400 JDJ

A CLOSER LOOK AT A SANTA

Schoenhut, founded in Philadelphia in 1872 and closed by 1935, is a sought-after American maker.

It is very large in size at 11in (28cm) high and is in excellent condition with only a little in-painting.

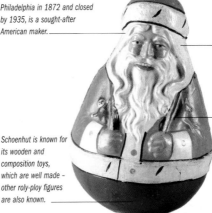

Schoenhut is known for its wooden and composition toys, which are well made – other roly-ploy figures are also known.

This is very early in date for Christmas memorabilia produced in the US, most was produced in Germany at this time.

An early Schoenhut Santa Claus composition roly-poly, retaining partial label on base.

c1920 · 11in (28cm) high

$1,500-1,800 JDJ

A 1920s/30s card, felt and material Santa Claus figure.

9in (23cm) high

$100-150 HH

A German Santa Claus hollow bisque figure, with lantern, marked "Germany".

This shape is extremely rare and is not listed in any of the Santa and Snowbaby reference books.

3in (7.5cm) high

$60-80 HH

An American Santa Claus-on-skis die-cast metal figure, marked "Made in USA".

$40-50 BH

An 1940s/50s American 'King Santa' plastic lamp and money bank, by Harett Gilmar of New York, with coin slot in back of shoulders, in mint condition.

7in (18cm) high

$30-50 HH

A 1940s/50s West German large flock-covered Santa Claus, with bobbing head, faux fur beard and interior printed with a design of flowers and marked "Container made in West Germany".

13.5in (34cm) high

$70-100 HH

A 1950s West German Santa Claus candy holder, the card-bodied figure with bobble head and rare gold glitter decoration.

9in (23cm) high

$60-80 HH

A 1920s German Santa Claus molded, printed and embossed card standee, with silver glitter details.

9.75in (25cm) high

$50-70 HH

A 1920s German papier-mâché snowman decoration.

7in (18cm) high

$40-50 HH

A 1950s snowman white plastic lamp, with green Christmas tree.

The Christmas tree is often missing or broken, and values are greatly reduced, making complete examples rare.

7.5in (19cm) high

$50-70 HH

A 1950s/60s snowman white plastic candy holder, with removable pipe.

Look out for the rare orange Halloween variation, shown on page 357 of the 'DK Collectibles Price Guide 2005' by Judith Miller and Mark Hill, which can fetch up to $90.

2004 5.25in (13.5cm) high

$15-20 HH

A 1950s/60s snowman lolly holder, in blue, red and white plastic, on silver plastic skis.

5.5in (14cm) high

$40-50 HH

A 1960s American friction-driven push-along snowman on a pumpkin, by Fun World Inc.

$30-40 HH

A 'Hi-Ho Santa' pull-along toy-on-wheels, of red, green and tan plastic.

This combination of colors is hard to find.

9.75in (25cm) high

$100-150 HH

A 1950s Santa on cart plastic candy container, with no damage.

9.5in (24cm) long

$60-80 HH

A 1950s Christmas clown and drum, of yellow red and green plastic.

This is a rare shape, with a detailed form and moving wheels. It is rarest in Halloween coloring, with examples in similar condition fetching up to $500.

8in (20cm) high

$200-250 HH

A 1950s small plastic nativity scene.

A 'Christmas Cat' painted bisque cake decoration, the double bass with gold glitter.

1.75in (4.5cm) high

$15-20 LG

A rare pair of 1930s hand-made skiers, with plaster heads, woven wool bodies, metal skis and wooden poles with paper discs.

5.5in (14cm) high

$100-150 HH

These decorations are growing in popularity. This example has palm trees, which is a desirable feature.

7in (18cm) wide

$15-20 HH

A 1950s plastic nativity scene, with silver glitter highlights, in mint condition with original box and price.

5.5in (14cm) high

$12-18 HH

A late 20thC Christmas musical display, of angels in front of an altar, made in Hong Kong.

This example is desirable as it has a musical movement.

4.75in (12cm) wide

$9-12 HH

A 1950s Japanese Christmas bell, with foil and plaster over a card base and molded papier-mâché Santa and embossed card candle and holly decal to reverse, stamped "Made in Japan".

3.75in (9.5cm) high

$45-55 HH

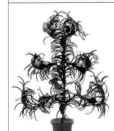

A 1950s/60s Christmas tree, with plastic fronds over paper-covered wire.

This resembles the first artificial Christmas trees, made in Germany in the 1880s, of painted goose feathers on wire branches.

11.75in (30cm) high

$30-40 HH

A 1950s plastic Christmas tree, with faux snow, glass baubles and wooden base.

13.5in (34cm) high

$30-50 HH

A set of four 1950s Japanese Relco Creation Christmas candleholders, with climbing Santas, in original box, each printed "Made in Japan".

Candleholder 3.25in (8cm) high

$20-30 HH

A painted and carved milk glass patriotic candy container, with worn decoration.

The paintwork is often worn through washing.

3.5in (9cm) high

$70-90   SOTT

A 1930s lithographed card patriotic top hat candy container, marked "Germany".

3.5in (9cm) high

$50-70   SOTT

An American lithographed tin patriotic money bank.

3in (7.5cm) diam

$50-70   SOTT

A 1950s lithographed tin patriotic toy drum, made by Noble & Cooley, USA.

9in (23cm) diam

$100-150   SOTT

A late 1940s lithographed tin 'New Deal Bank' money bank, by J. Chein & Co.

In better condition, this bank could fetch up to $85.

3.25in (8.5cm) high

$25-35   SOTT

A 1950s American small lithographed tin sand pail, by T. Conn Co., with patriotic theme.

6.25in (16cm) high

$70-90   SOTT

A 1930s Japanese lithographed card patriotic candy container, marked "Made in Japan".

3in (7.5cm) wide

$70-90   SOTT

A 1930s patriotic Girl Guide chalkware figure, converted to a money bank.

14in (35.5cm) high

$70-100   SOTT

An American Uncle Sam '200 Years' plastic money box, manufactured by 'All States Manuf. Corp. ©1974'.

1974   10.5in (26.5cm) high

$40-50   SOTT

A Japanese Uncle Sam hand-painted ceramic figure, with gilt highlights.

6.5in (16.5cm) high

$70-90 SOTT

An American flag-on-stand patriotic table decoration.

10.75in (27.5cm) high

$10-15 SOTT

An American lithographed tin patriotic radiator hood ornament.

11in (28cm) high

$70-90 SOTT

A patriotic 'Star Spangled Banner' postcard, with postmark for 1909.

5.5in (14cm) high

$12-18 SOTT

A 1950s American card fire cracker candy container.

5.5in (14cm) high

$10-15 SOTT

A 1950s packet of Miss Liberty Sparklers No. 8, manufactured by New Jersey Fireworks Mfg. Co. Inc.

$8-12 SOTT

A 1930s lithographed card and paper patriotic cigar fan.

These patriotic fans were given out on tables at political rallies.

10in (25.5cm) long

$30-40 SOTT

A 1930s length of patriotic crêpe ribbon, made by Dennison, USA.

$8-10 SOTT

An American patriotic lithographed tin horn.

1915-20   12in (31cm) high

$50-70 SOTT

COLLECTORS' NOTES

■ Although enjoying a heritage of many centuries, most of what is known and collected as 'Inuit art' today was made from the mid-20thC onward. In 1949 a young Canadian artist called James Houston visited the Canadian Arctic to find out if the native art was appealing and could be commercial. His initial purchases sold out rapidly and both the government and Hudson Bay Company became involved. During the 1960s, organized trading and collecting began in earnest and popularity swiftly grew.

■ The majority of works are sculptures carved from green or gray hardstone or whalebone. Prints and fabrics are also produced and collected. Subject matter focuses on traditional Inuit life and surroundings including the Inuit themselves, Arctic animals, Inuit myths and more abstracted forms. The artist counts greatly towards value, with works by masters such as Osuitok Ipeelee, John Tiktak, John Pangnark, Jessie Oonark, and Karoo Ashevak being hotly sought-after.

■ Due to the growing popularity of the area and increased trade, there are also a great many mediocre and even poor artworks available. By comparison, these have little chance of becoming desirable or collectible in future, so learn about forms, artists and market trends by reading books and visiting dealers and auctions to view examples. Look for well-executed, stylized and even abstracted designs, often with an inherent wit or humor.

■ Many pieces are signed on the bottom with 'syllabics', the Inuit form of 'verbal' lettering, or with a government controlled 'disc number' beginning with an 'E' or 'W' that also identifies the artist. Numbers in brackets after the caption indicate the disc number if known, and also birth and death dates. The market in Inuit art has seen rapid development over the last 25 years, with interest from across the world, and this looks sets to continue.

An Inuit dark gray soapstone carving of an Inuk hunter with a seal, signed indistinctly to the base.

12in (30cm) high

$550-650   **THG**

An Inuit dark mottled soapstone sculpture of a standing Inuk, by Joe Talirunili (1893-1976), signed in Roman letters.

4in (10cm) high

$850-950   **WAD**

An Inuit carved dark gray soapstone sculpture of an Inuk and polar bear fighting, by Annie Nassak (E8-875, b.1930) of the Kangirsuk community, inscribed on the base with syllabics and disc number.

8in (20cm) cm

$100-150   **MHC**

An Inuit carved dark gray mottled soapstone sculpture of an Inuit mother and child, by S. Weetaluktuk, from the Cape Dorset area.

c1946   *7.25in (18.5cm) high*

$600-700   **THG**

An Inuit mottled dark soapstone carving of a recumbent Inuk, signed indistinctly on the base.

7in (18cm) long

$100-150   **TFR**

A mottled gray soapstone sculpted head of an Inuk, by John Kavik (E2-290) from the Rankin Inlet, signed in syllabics.

John Kavik (1897-1993) is one of the best-known Inuit artists. His work is typified by simple lines but strongly imbued with emotion.

3in (7.5cm) high

$1,500-2,000   **WAD**

A mottled gray soapstone bust of an Inuk, by John Tiktak (E1-266), signed in syllabics.

John Tiktak (1916-81) began carving regularly in the Rankin Inlet after a mining accident in 1959, devoting himself to the art from 1962. He is known for his sculptures of the human face and the mother and child theme, many of which are like the work of Henry Moore. He was the first Inuit artist to be given a retrospective, in 1970, and his work is in many private and public collections.

7.5in (19cm) high

$10,000-15,000   **WAD**

A dark soapstone sculpture of the head of an Inuk, by Francis Kaluraq (E2-179, 1931-90) from Baker Lake.

2in (5cm) high

$1,800-2,200   **WAD**

A mottled soapstone sculpture of a mother and child, by John Pangnark (E1-104, 1920-80) from Arviat, signed in syllabics.

c1965   4in (10cm) high

$2,800-3,200   **WAD**

A CLOSER LOOK AT AN INUIT SCULPTURE

Osuitok Ipeelee (b.1923) is considered the finest Inuit artist and sculptor living today - and perhaps the finest ever - and received a national Aboriginal Achievement Award in 2004.

His work is typified by graceful handling of the subject, with a studied yet often precarious sense of balance as seen here. The abstract, handling of the form is also highly desirable.

He is known for his favorite subjects of birds, caribou, and polar bears, but his shaman sculptures, such as this example, are also celebrated.

Such is the level of interest in his works that pieces are often hotly pursued by avid collectors - this example nearly doubled its original lower auction estimate.

A dark soapstone bust of a hooded Inuk, by Karoo Ashevak (E4-196, 1940-74) from Spence Bay, with inset eyes and mounted on a bone base.

5in (12.5cm) high

$12,000-18,000   **WAD**

A lightly mottled dark green soapstone sculpture of a shaman, by Osuitok Ipeelee (E7-1154, b.1923), from Cape Dorset.

c1966   18.5in (47cm) high

$30,000-40,000   **WAD**

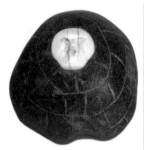

A mottled dark soapstone sculpture of an igloo, by an unknown artist, the inset ivory face of a shaman emerging from the top.

c1950   2.5in (6.5cm) high

$3,500-4,000   **WAD**

A mottled gray Inuit sculpture of an igloo, by an unknown artist, the ivory hands and tattooed face of a spirit emerging from it.

c1950   5in (12.5cm) high

$10,000-15,000   **WAD**

A mottled gray soapstone abstract sculpture of a standing Inuk, by John Kavik (E2-290, 1897-1993), from the Rankin Inlet.

7.5in (19cm) high

$3,500-4,000   **WAD**

A mottled dark soapstone sculpture of an owl, by Davidialuk Alasua Amittu (E9-824, 1910-76) of the Povungnituk community, signed in syllabics and in Roman characters.

7in (19cm) high

$3,200-3,800   **WAD**

A mottled green soapstone abstract sculpture of a spirit bird, by Koomwartok Ashoona (E7-1102, 1930-84), signed in Roman.

c1970   6.3in (16cm)

$2,000-2,500   **WAD**

A mottled green soapstone mythical transformation sculpture of a shaman transforming into a bird, by Latcholassie Akesuk (E7-1055, 1919-2000), from Cape Dorset.

10in (25.5cm) high

$2,200-2,800   **WAD**

A CLOSER LOOK AT AN INUIT SCULPTURE

Stone was not available when Ashevak began carving in 1968, so he used whalebone which was flown in by plane.

Inuit shamans, dreams and mysticism are common themes in Ashevak's highly personal and characteristic work.

Abstraction, humor and a certain animation typify his designs - all can be seen in this exceptional and comparatively very large work.

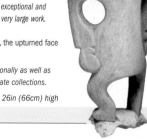

A weathered whalebone sculpture of a standing shaman by Karoo Ashevak (E4-196), the upturned face inset with antler eyes, signed in Roman script.

Seeing success during his short lifetime, Ashevak's works have been shown internationally as well as in New York in 1973 and Ottowa in 1994 and are found in numerous public and private collections.

26in (66cm) high

$60,000-70,000   **WAD**

A mottled gray soapstone sculpture of a polar bear, by Henry Napartuk (E9-1652, 1932-85) from Kuujjuaraapik, with inset eyes, its flanks carved with the face of a shaman, disc number inscribed.

This piece appeared on p151 of "Sculpture of the Eskimo" by early connoisseur and author George Swinton, and published in 1972.

$5,000-6,000 **WAD**

A dark soapstone sculpture of a polar bear/Sedna, by Peter Pitseolak (E7-970, 1902-73) from Cape Dorset, carved with braided hair.

From the Red Petersen collection, sold in 1981. Of this piece Petersen said: "Of all the places in the north, Cape Dorset seems to be the most preoccupied with the spiritual world. This combines the sea-goddess with the polar bear to represent the supreme spirit." Spiritual or mystical themes illustrative of Inuit beliefs are sought-after.

c1960   5.5in (14cm) high

$7,000-8,000 **WAD**

A mottled dark soapstone sculpture of a musk ox, by Judas Ullulaq (E4-342, 1937-98), with antler horns and eyes.

4in (10cm) high

$4,500-5,500 **WAD**

A mottled dark soapstone mystical transformation carving of a shaman/musk ox, by Barnabus Arnasungaaq (b.1924), signed in syllabics.

12.5in (32cm) high

$4,000-5,000 **WAD**

A mottled dark soapstone sculpture of a grazing caribou, by an unknown artist from Povungnituk, with inset antlers.

c1955   4in (10cm) high

$2,000-2,500 **WAD**

A marbled green soapstone sculpture of a rearing caribou, by Osuitok Ipeelee (E7-1154, b.1923), with inset horn antlers.

See the Closer Look on page 365 to see another piece by Ipeelee. Both the subject matter and the use of horn where it would be found naturally are typical features of Ipeelee's work.

c1975   9in (23cm) high

$7,500-8,500 **WAD**

A mottled soapstone sculpture of an owl, by Tudlik (E7-1050, 1890-1966) from Cape Dorset.

Owls are notable artist Tudlik's favorite animal.

3.5in (9cm) high

$3,200-3,800 **WAD**

An Inuit carved mottled green soapstone sculpture of a small owl, the base inscribed "Wolfson Canada".

4.25in (10.5cm) high

$150-250 **THG**

An Inuit carved mottled green/gray soapstone sculpture of a standing seal, by an unknown artist, unmarked.

5.25in (13.5cm) high

$80-120 **TFR**

"The Return of the Sun", by Kenojuak Ashevak, stonecut.

c1961　　　30in (76cm) wide

$4,500-5,500　　　**WAD**

"Animal Kingdom" by Kenojuak Ashevak, felt tip drawing, signed in syllabics.

This drawing is nearly identical to Kenojuak's engraving "Animal Kingdom" of 1967, and to the same image in her 1967 engraving portfolio. It is unknown whether this drawing was for, or from, the engraving, as Kenojuak commonly reworked the same image with slight variations.

　　　26in (66cm) high

$1,200-1,800　　　**WAD**

"Four Women", by Parr (1893-1969), engraving.

c1963　　　12in (30.5cm) high

$1,200-1,800　　　**WAD**

A skin stencil of a Young Curlew, by Kellypalik Mangitak (b.1940).
c1960　　　15.5in (39.5cm) high

$3,200-3,800　　　**WAD**

A CLOSER LOOK AT AN INUIT PRINT

It is by Kenojuak Ashevak (b.1927), who is considered one of Canada's leading artists as well as one of the best Inuit artists.

Animals are a typical motif, particularly birds – she prefers to focus on the overall design and the natural world rather than illustrate Inuit beliefs, myths or legends.

The vibrancy of color is one of her hallmarks and developed from when she began to use colored pencils and felt tips from the 1960s onward.

Forms are clean and hark at her earlier appliqué fabric designs; there is also typically little movement with motifs apparently frozen in a flat plane.

"Night Spirit", by Kenojuak Ashevak, stonecut.

Ashevak's designs gained widespread fame when used on Canadian postage stamps, first in 1970. Since then her work has risen steeply in value, with collectors and collections globally vying to own her latest and most familiar works.

c1960　　　24in (61cm) wide

$6,500-7,500　　　**WAD**

A woman and snow bird, by Pitaloosie Saila (b.1942), stonecut.

Saila uses people, animals and Inuit legends, spirits and events in her work. She began to draw in the early to mid-1960s and is known for her modernism, simplification of form and line and bright color. As well as expressing her own thoughts and concerns, she illustrates important parts of the Inuit way of life and beliefs.

c1973　　　27in (68.5cm) high

$5,500-6,500　　　**WAD**

FIND OUT MORE...

The Inuit Art Center - www.ainc-inac.gc.ca

Inuit Art: An Introduction, by Ingo Hessel, Dieter Hessel & George Swinton, published by *Douglas & McIntyre, 2003.*

Sculpture of the Inuit, by George Swinton, published by *McLelland & Stewart, 1999.*

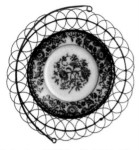

An American 19thC Flow Blue plate, with steel wire basket and handle.

9in (23cm) diam

$120-180 **BCA**

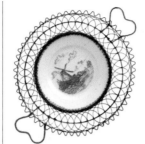

A Delft blue transfer-printed Windmill plate, with wire basket.

11in (27.5cm) diam

$200-300 **BCA**

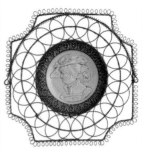

A rare green and brown molded majolica plate, in a squared-off shaped steel wire basket.

c1880 *9.5in (24cm) wide*

$300-400 **BCA**

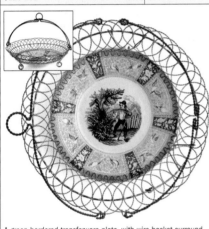

A green-bordered transferware plate, with wire basket surround.

Here, the handle clips together so the basket can be hung from a ceiling to keep the fruit away from mice or rats.

$150-200 **BCA**

A European green majolica plate, molded with grapes and vine leaves, with steel wire basket surround.

Wire fruit baskets can be found with a variety of inserted dishes made from ceramics, glass, and printed card. They were popular from the late 19thC to the early 20thC and made in Europe and the US. Values depend on the complexity, shape, and visual appeal of the pattern of the wire surround, and the value, appeal and desirability of the plate used inside. Notable makers will add value. With many damaged through use, complete examples have recently become highly popular for their vintage, rustic, and Folk Art looks as well as for their variety and complex shapes skillfully created by hand in wire.

12.5in (32cm) diam

$380-420 **BCA**

A handpainted plate, with wire basket edging and handle.

9.75in (25cm) diam

$220-280 **BCA**

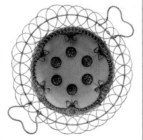

A Villeroy & Boch green stylized topiary box tree plate, with original blue-painted steel wire basket, plate impressed "2044".

9in (23cm) diam

$320-380 **BCA**

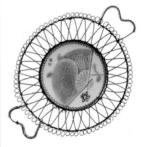

A rare Oriental fan majolica plate, with wire basket.

9in (22.5cm) diam

$350-450 **BCA**

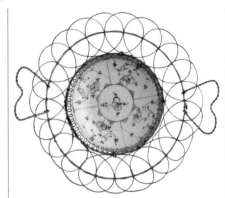

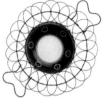

A pair of small blue painted white glazed porcelain serving bowls, with wire baskets.

4in (10cm) diam

$150-200 pair   BCA

A French Opaque de Sarreguemines plate, with blue rims and steel wire basket.

8.5in (22cm) diam

$150-200   BCA

An 'Onion Seed' pattern blue painted white glazed porcelain plate, with steel wire basket.

c1880   *8.75in (22cm) diam*

$200-300   BCA

A Colibri hand-colored transfer-printed plate, with squared-off wire basket and handle.

8.25in (21cm) wide

$150-200   BCA

A handpainted butterfly and sprig of flowers and leaves plate, with wire basket.

9in (23cm) diam

$120-180   BCA

A Villeroy & Boch 'Timor' pattern transfer-printed and handpainted plate, with wire basket.

10.25in (26cm) diam

$150-250   BCA

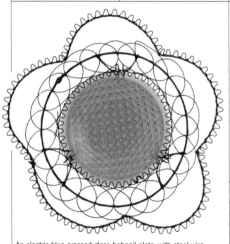

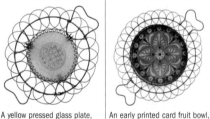

A yellow pressed glass plate, with wire basket surround.

8in (20cm) diam

$80-120   BCA

An early printed card fruit bowl, with wire basket finished in black.

c1880   *9.75in (24.5cm) diam*

$70-100   BCA

An electric blue pressed glass hobnail plate, with steel wire basket.

10.25in (26cm) diam

$100-150   BCA

An early printed card portrait dish, with wire fruit basket surround.

c1900   *8.75in (22cm) diam*

$120-180   BCA

An American 'Heart-Shaped Toaster Universal E 9411', by Landers, Frary & Clark, New Britain, Connecticut.

1929

$400-500 ATK

A Dutch Huza 'turnover' toaster, nickel-plated metal, with white bakelite knobs.

1930

$80-120 ATK

A wooden and brass coffee grinder, the crank lever engraved "Roseta Petrascheck", hinged lid and drawers with brass knob.

c1880   10.5in (26cm) high

$300-400 WDL

A countertop fan-scale, by The Standard Computing Scale Co., Detroit, with sliding weight, hopper, gold finish, lacking back glass.

27in (68.5cm) wide

$80-120 EG

An American Purina Cow Chow milk scale, by Chatillion, with brass front, checkerboard decoration and twin needles.

17in (43cm) high

$100-150 EG

A 1940s Bakelite, wood, chrome and metal desk fan, by Ventaxia, stamped numbers "442469, 429958".

13.5in (34cm) high

$120-180 PSI

An American Art Nouveau-style tabletop fan.

$30-50 GAZE

Two tinned copper cake or jelly molds.

c1860   10in (25cm) diam

$220-280 ATK

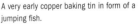

A very early copper baking tin in form of a jumping fish.

c1800   11in (29cm) long

$50-70 ATK

KITCHENALIA & DOMESTIC

A Pyrex Gaiety casserole dish on warmer stand, in unused condition, with original box and packaging.

Corning Glass first released the heat-resistant glass Pyrex in 1924. It became particularly popular when the opaque version was produced in the 1950s with a wide range of patterns and decoration. It was produced in the US and the UK while other companies made their own version of heat resistant oven-to-table glass ware. Vintage pieces are still usable, but don't put them in the dishwasher as this can fade the colors and decoration.

Box 13.75in (35cm) wide

$30-40   **MA**

A Phoenix Glass Grenadier red sprayed Pyrex-type lidded dish, design no. 872873.

9in (23cm) wide

$22-28   **GROB**

A Pyrex saucer boat and underplate, sprayed apple green.

Saucer 8in (20cm) long

$12-18   **GROB**

An American Pyrex tumbler, with yellow holder, and original box, holder marked "Registered 881736", for 1956.

c1960   *5in (12.5cm) high*

$22-28   **MA**

A pair of hobnail glass salt and pepper shakers.

2.5in (6.5cm) high

$10-15   **BH**

A pair of American handpainted ceramic salt and pepper shakers, by Holt-Howard.

c1962   *3.5in (9cm) high*

$7-9   **BH**

A pair of red plastic 'horn of plenty' salt and pepper shakers.

2.5in (6.5cm) high

$3-5   **BH**

A set of 'Model "T"' plastic salt and pepper shakers, the containers formed as the passengers, with original box.

Box 6in (15cm) wide

$20-30   **BH**

A set of four painted tin kitchen canisters, with Bakelite knobs.

Largest 7.5in (19cm) high

$40-50   **BH**

A glass water bottle, with printed decoration and 'E-Z Por' red plastic stopper.

10in (25.5cm) high

$15-25 BH

A glass decanter, with printed striped decoration and an 'E-Z Por' pink plastic pourer.

10.5in (26cm) high

$15-20 BH

A painted and frosted glass syrup pourer, decorated with a rooster.

5.5in (14cm) high

$10-15 BH

A small glass syrup pourer, by the Federal Tool Corp., Chicago, with red plastic top.

4.25in (11cm) high

$8-12 BH

A red plastic watering can, by Celomat New York.

7.5in (19cm) high

$5-7 BH

A 1950s Starnes ceramic telephone cookie jar, with original label.

11in (28cm) high

$50-70 AJK

A Granforest handpainted ceramic cookie jar, with handle.

$15-25 BH

An American yellow ceramic butter dish, made for Westinghouse by Hall China Co., USA.

6.5in (16.5cm) wide

$15-25 BH

A red and white plastic donut maker, by Popeil, with distressed original box.

$18-22 BH

KITCHENALIA & DOMESTIC

A yellow clothes peg-shaped laundry sprinkler.

8.5in (22cm) high

$150-250   **DAC**

A black mammy handpainted laundry sprinkler.

A matching clothes peg holder was also produced and is worth approximately the same amount.

7in (18cm) high

$300-400   **DAC**

A 1930s Myrtle lady sprinkler, by Pfaltzgraff Pottery Co., Pennsylvania, marked "Muggsy" to base.

7in (18cm) high

$280-320   **DAC**

A white poodle sprinkler.

9in (22.5cm) high

$100-150   **DAC**

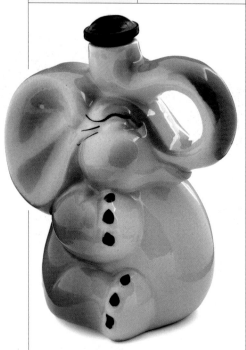

An iron-shaped sprinkler, with scene of girl and boy farmers, with silver "Tilso Japan Handpainted" label to base.

Although the label helps to identify the manufacturer of this example, many were home-made with the value for those examples depending on the quality and decoration of the sprinkler.

7in (18cm) high

$200-300   **DAC**

An American fat elephant bisque laundry sprinkler, by Cardinal China.

As the demand for ceramics and glass sprinklers such as this example rise, together with prices, collectors' interest in plastic sprinklers is beginning to grow.

6.75in (17cm) high

$400-500   **DAC**

FIND OUT MORE...

Collectibles for the Kitchen, Bath & Beyond, by Ellen Bercovici, Bobbie Zucker Bryson and Deborah Gillham, Krause Publications, 2001.

300 Years of Kitchen Collectibles, by Linda Campbell Franklin, Krause Publications, 2003.

COLLECTORS' NOTES

- Marble collectors divide vintage collectible marbles into two distinct types; handmade marbles and machine-made marbles. Handmade marbles were produced primarily in Germany from c1860-1920. Machine-made marbles were primarily produced in the US after M.F. Christensen developed a marble-making machine in 1905. In the 1950s-60s Far Eastern and South American marbles such as 'cats eyes' took over.

- Handmade marbles can be identified by the presence of the remains of a 'pontil' where the marble was broken off from the glass rod and formed into a sphere. These are traditionally the most valuable and sought-after, but have recently fallen slightly behind the best machine-made marbles in popularity.

- Value is primarily indicated by type. Swirls are the most commonly found type, with marbles categorized by the pattern, style and colors. Some are rare. Look for symmetry in design, bright colors and large sizes. More unusual marbles such as the opaque Indians and 'sulphides', with their internal white forms, are also worth looking out for.

- Machine-made marbles have no pontil and grew enormously in popularity during the 1920s eclipsing, and then replacing, German exports. The short-lived Christensen Agate Company produced some of the most colorful and collectible marbles in this sector of the market. Other notable names include the Peltier Glass Company and Akro Agate, who became the largest US producer until their closure in 1951.

- Condition is more important with machine-made marbles than older handmades. Marbles in truly mint condition can sell for up to double the value of marbles with wear such as 'hit' marks, chips and scuffing, especially if they obscure any internal pattern. All marbles shown here are in mint or near-to-mint condition. Restoration can usually be felt as it alters the shape. 'Eye appeal' is also a very important consideration, but factors that appeal to one collector may not appeal to another, making it a matter for personal taste.

A handmade swirl-type 360-degree 'Indian' marble.

Indians have opaque black bases, 'swirl type' examples have strands that run unbroken from pole to pole. Here the bands run all over the marble, which is highly prized, unlike the more common 'paneled' example on the following page. Yellow and white are the most common colors, red being rarer with oxblood being the rarest.

c1860-1920

0.5in (1.5cm) diam

$200-250   **AB**

A handmade End of the Day 'Joseph's Coat' swirl marble.

'End of the Day' refers to the construction of the marble, using stretched flecks of left-over glass instead of rods. 'Joseph's Coat' marbles have closely packed colored strands of bands just beneath the surface with little clear glass showing in between them.

c1860-1920   *0.75in (2cm) diam*

$200-300   **AB**

A handmade 'Solid Core' swirl marble.

c1860-1920

0.75in (2cm) diam

$10-15   **AB**

A handmade 'Mist' marble.

This type has a translucent or transparent base with translucent or transparent colored strands. Blue and green are the most commonly found colors.

c1860-1920   *0.5in (1.5cm) diam*

$40-60   **AB**

A handmade End of the Day 'Joseph's Coat' marble.

Note the very clear, and slightly protruding, pontil mark on the left hand side of this marble. The patterning is unusual and attractive.

c1860-1920   *0.5in (1.5cm) diam*

$80-120   **AB**

A handmade swirl-type 'Banded Opaque' marble.

c1860-1920   *0.75in (2cm) diam*

$150-200   **AB**

A handmade End of the Day 'Onionskin' marble.

Red, blue, and green stripes are more common colors and the more colors present, the rarer and more desirable the marble.

c1860-1920   *1.25in (3cm) diam*

$100-150   **AB**

MARBLES

A handmade 'Latticinio Core' swirl marble.

These are the most common types of handmade marble, but look out for blue core threads, which are rarer than white.

c1860-1920   0.75in (2cm) diam

$10-15   **AB**

A handmade 'Banded' Lutz marble.

A 'Banded' Lutz has two sets of single-colored bands, which are made of finely ground copper.

c1860-1920   0.75in (2cm) diam

$80-120   **AB**

A handmade 'Divided Core' swirl marble, the core with four bands.

The core of this type is formed with three or more separately colored bands, with clear glass between.

c1860-1920   0.75in (2cm) diam

$30-40   **AB**

A 'Solid Core (lobed)' swirl marble.

c1860-1920   0.75in (2cm) diam

$15-25   **AB**

A German handmade 'Sparkler' marble.

c1860-1920
          0.75in (2cm) diam

$20-25   **AB**

A Christensen Agate Company 'Hand-gathered' marble.

A handmade 'Indian' marble.

c1860-1920
          0.75in (2cm) diam

$70-100   **AB**

The Christensen Agate Co. was founded in 1925 and the 'hand-gathered' swirls are their earliest marbles. They can be recognized by their slightly irregular shape and '9' and 'tail' shapes at alternate poles, which are also very rare. There are also a range of four to five different colors, which are unique to this company, again helping with identification.

c1927   *0.5in (1.5cm) diam*

$200-300   **AB**

A handmade 'Confetti' marble.

Confetti marbles are transparent with internal flecks of color. They always have one pontil mark. A colored base glass is very rare.

c1860-1920   0.5in (1.5cm) diam

$80-120   **AB**

An American Transitional 'Leighton Ground Pontil' marble.

These marbles are reputed to have been made by James Leighton & Company in Ohio during the late 1890s. Most contain an 'oxblood' color as here, which triples or quadruples the value. These have a single pontil with the swirling pattern forming a '9' shape at the opposite pole. Some of these marbles have also been found in Lauscha, Germany, opening up discussion as to their precise origins.

c1897   *0.75in (2cm) diam*

$350-450   **AB**

A Christensen Agate Company 'Swirl' marble.

Swirls are the most common marble made by the Christensen Agate Company and can be found in a great many different and typically bright colors.

c1927-29   0.75in (2cm) diam

$20-30   **AB**

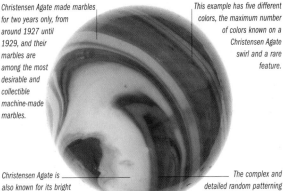

A 1920s/30s American Peltier Glass Company 'National Line Rainbo Tiger' marble.

National Line Rainbo marbles are among the most collectible of Peltier's output. Collectors have given their colorful marbles names based around their colors, as here. They can be differentiated from the similar Miller swirls as they have two seams.

0.75in (2cm) diam

$40-60   **AB**

A Vitro Agate Company 'Sweet Pea Patch' marble.

0.75in (2cm) diam

$15-20   **AB**

An Akro Agate Company 'Swirl Oxblood' marble.

c1930-45   0.5in (1.5cm) diam

$10-15   **AB**

A 1920s/30s Peltier Glass Company 'National Line Rainbo Zebra' marble.

0.75in (2cm) diam

$15-20   **AB**

A Christensen Agate Company 'Moonie' marble.

0.75in (2cm) diam

$100-150   **AB**

A Christensen Agate Company 'Flame Swirl' marble.

Flame Swirls, where the stripes appear in rows (or opposing rows) almost like the flames on a 'hot-rod' car of the 1950s are rare. The colors and pattern affect value, with this example being highly desirable.

c1927-29   0.5in (1.5cm) diam

$200-300   **AB**

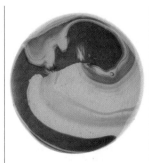

An Akro Agate Company 'Carnelian Oxblood' marble.

Carnelian marbles are very rare. 'Oxblood' refers to the opaque deep rust red-colored glass with black filaments.

0.75in (2cm) diam

$100-150 AB

A CLOSER LOOK AT A MARBLE

The Guinea is one of the most desirable machine-made marbles and also one of the rarest and most sought-after by collectors.

Guineas always have transparent bases – clear is the most commonly found color with amber and blue being much rarer. The rarest are the legendary green and red colored bases.

Guineas have stretched flecks or blotches of colored glass – the name came about as workers were reminded of the colors on guinea cocks running around the factory yard.

The rarest variation is the Guinea Cobra, which has colors inside as well as on the outside like standard Guineas.

A rare Christensen Agate Company 'Guinea Cobra' marble.

Reproductions of Guineas are being made, so if in doubt compare to an original or seek professional advice.

c1927-29   0.75in (2cm) diam

$400-600 AB

A Christensen Agate Company 'Striped Transparent' marble.

This type of marble can be recognized by the stripes predominately confined to or only on one side of the marble – electric colors, as here, are more valuable. The base, transparent on this type, can also be opaque in which case the marble is known as a 'Striped Opaque'.

0.5in (1.5cm) diam

An Akro Agate Company 'Carnelian' marble.

c1930s   0.75in (2cm) diam

$25-35 AB

c1927-1929

$300-500 AB

A Vitro Agate Company '8-Finger Ribbon' marble.

0.75in (2cm) diam

$25-35 AB

A Christensen Agate Company 'Slag' marble.

c1927-29   0.5in (1.5cm) diam

$20-25 AB

An Alley Agate Company 'Flame Swirl' marble.

1929-49   0.75in (2cm) diam

$40-60 AB

FIND OUT MORE...

www.marblecollecting.com

Marbles: Identification & Price Guide, *by Robert Block, published by Schiffer Publishing, 2002.*

COLLECTORS' NOTES

- Forerunners of the moving images we watch today at the movie theater, optical toys developed throughout the 18th and 19thC, catering to a growing public fascination with moving images.

- The first magic lanterns were produced in the 17thC. By the late Victorian period they were a staple of sideshows and fairs everywhere. Showmen would compete to put on the most lavish spectacle.

- Magic lanterns were generally lit by small paraffin lamps and will usually have a funnel or chimney at the top, designed to allow the fumes to escape.

- Many of these pre-cinema toys were discarded or stored carelessly in attics once they were no longer fashionable, falling into disrepair. Examples in good original condition can be hard to find today.

- Stereoscopes reached the peak of their popularity during the later half of the 19thC. They create the illusion of depth by displaying two slightly different views of the same scene, one tailored to each eye.

- The wood used to make stereoscopic viewers was often very thin, and the paper slides were very fragile. Slides are very much in demand today.

A German Ernemann wood-bodied stereoscopic viewer.

Glass or card stereoscopic slides would be inserted into the back plate and viewed through the focusing lenses. Look for decoratively shaped examples in fine woods as these are worth more.

1907   7in (18cm) wide

$350-450   **ATK**

A German Wurzelholz stereoscopic viewer and 116 stereocards, the cards including 21 'tissue' cards of France, 32 cards of views of Switzerland by W. England, and others.

c1905   7in (18cm) wide

$400-600   **ATK**

A French P.H. Suchard Art Nouveau-style printed tinplate stereoscopic viewer, together with ten stereocards.

c1910   Cards 2.75in (7cm) wide

$300-500   **ATK**

A 'La Taxiphote' mahogany tabletop stereoviewer, for stereoscopic slides in magazines, with nickel fittings, and 12 filled magazines containing over 250 slides.

The interior of the box contains a revolving metal rack system to hold the glass slides. Turning the knob on the side revolves the slides, with the upper knobs focusing the eyepiece. A ground glass plate at the back allows light in to illuminate the slides. Further slides are contained in the base. These most commonly contain 'tourist' views of different countries.

c1915   19.5in (49cm) high

$1,000-1,500   **ATK**

A black painted wooden stereographoscope, with a carved floral pattern and six stereocards.

The main lens was used for viewing prints or photographs, the lower dual lenses for stereoscopic cards. Larger and more decorative examples in fine woods command higher prices.

c1880

$200-250   **ATK**

A carte-de-visite graphoscope, of ebonized wood with carved foliate decoration, with some splits to top edge.

c1880   5.5in (14cm) high

$180-220   **EG**

A rare J.T. Chapman of Manchester mahogany and brass magic lantern, with slide carrier and gas light burner.

c1890   21in (53.5cm) high

$1,000-1,500   ATK

An English large professional 'triunnial' magic lantern, the mahogany body with brass lenses and fittings, three original gas burners and accessories, unmarked, chimney replaced.

Triunnial magic lanterns are very rare, this example is of very fine quality, although the chimney has been replaced and is smaller than usual. Using three separate images, the operator could fade between different scenes to tell a story.

c1885   35in (89cm) high

$15,000-20,000   ATK

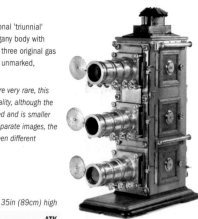

An extremely rare French 'Aubert Brevete' magic lantern, for round picture discs, with one handpainted circular slide, lacks burner.

c1880   14.75in (27cm) high

$800-1,200   ATK

A rare French 'Perfectionnée' Lampascope magic lantern, by Aubert, Paris, with brown body and original chrome burner.

c1870   17.5in (44cm) high

$400-600   ATK

An American 'Sciopticon' magic lantern, by The Pettibone Bros. Mfg. Co. Inc. of Cincinnati, Ohio, with rotating holder for ten slides, box and instruction sheet, electrified, chimney replaced.

c1895   22in (56cm) high

$2,500-3,500   ATK

A German magic lantern, by Georg Carette & Co., with burner, 33 circular glass slides and six mechanical slides.

c1900   10.25in (26cm) high

$220-280   ATK

These sets often contained slides of educational themes or children's tales and were used as toys. The condition of the components and completeness dictates value.

A small magic lantern for 1.7in-slides, with 12 slides and burner, in a wooden box.

c1890   7in (17cm) high

$250-350   ATK

An unusual American 'Comiscope' magic lantern, by Remington-Morse of New York and Chicago, with a cardboard projector in its original box.

This is a very late date for a magic lantern.

1942   9in (23cm) wide

$150-200   ATK

An American mutoscope peep show, by the American Mutoscope & Biograph Co. of New York, with an original Mutoscope reel no. 16T showing a dressed dancer, with repainted exterior and replaced locks.

c1925   56in (144cm) high

$1,500-2,000   ATK

An American floor-standing metal-bodied mutoscope, by the International Mutoscope Corp. of Long Island City, NY, with original Mutoscope reel no.7.365 showing an acrobatic dancer, lacks key for cash box.

Herman Casler patented the 'Mutoscope' in 1897. They soon became popular attractions at seaside resorts or other tourist destinations. The viewer would insert money to watch a titillating, amusing or otherwise entertaining show created by photographic cards flipping at speed to create an illusion of movement.

c1920   75in (191cm) high

$1,500-2,000   ATK

An American coin-operated 'Artist's Models in 3D' floor standing viewer which, for five cents, shows for a full 90 seconds variously posed 'artist's models' in full color, with 18 transparencies.

c1958

$1,000-1,500   ATK

A CLOSER LOOK AT AN OPTICAL TOY

The Filoscope was invented by Henry W. Short and patented on 3rd November 1898.

Short worked as a cameraman for British film pioneers including Robert Paul and Bert Ayres and is known for his work with early cinema.

Handheld and containing a revolving reel of single photographic shots, it was operated by flicking each card past a thumb, creating the sense of movement.

Bridging optical toys with moving images and real cinema further, Short used shots from real films on his Filoscope reels, of which 12 titles are known.

A Japanese 'Cinema Revue' celluloid toy, with key-wound musical movement and moving pictures, and revolving 'merry-go-round' on top.

c1950   9.5in (24cm) high

$200-300   ATK

A British 'Filoscope', manufactured under license from the Mutoscope & Biograph Syndicate, Ltd. for the UK, fitted with 'The Cuddle' flip-film roll.

1898   10in (25.5cm) wide

$500-600   ATK

A French Zoetrope, 'Les Images Vivantes', with a cardboard body and 11 double-sided black-and-white and color paper strips, on a varnished wooden stand.

c1910　　　　　　　10.5in (28cm) high

$700-900　　　　　　　　　　**ATK**

A London Stereoscopic & Photographic Co.'Wheel of Life', with a cast-iron base, tin drum, 12 one-sided color strips and 12 bottom discs with color motifs.

11.75in (37.5cm) high

ATK

An early French 'Ombres Chinoises' shadow theater, by Saussine of Paris, in original box with colored lithograph scene, cut-out stage with red curtain decor and transparent screen, an assortment of cut- and un-cut figures, an original sheet by Pellerin & Cie, Épinal, cover illustrated by B. Condert.

c1860

$2,500-3,000　　　　　　　　　　**ATK**

A French 'Les Anamorphoses' set, comprising 13 hand-colored lithographic anamorphic views about French Royals, with folder.

Anamorphic views look like semi-circles of color until viewed through an upright, cylindrical mirror, which corrects the distortions in the printed image, allowing a face or figure to be viewed. One of the most famous anamorphic views is the skull in Holbein's 1533 painting 'The Ambassadors' in the National Gallery, London.

c1852　　　　　　　7in (19.5cm) high

$800-1,200　　　　　　　　　　**ATK**

A pair of Barr and Stroud military issue binoculars, with leather carrying case, marked "7xCF41".

c1940

$120-180 ROS

An extremely rare 1870s French chromolithograph advertising fan, with magic lantern scenery, showing clowns presenting a magic lantern show and other activities, stamped "Brasserie Vetzel".

15.5in (39cm) high

$1,200-1,800　　　　　　　　　　**ATK**

COLLECTORS' NOTES

■ The first 'golden age' of the paperweight was from 1845-c1855 with production centered in France. Major factories included Clichy, Baccarat, and Saint Louis. Typical designs included lamp worked flowers and often complex 'set-ups' of cut millefiori canes, millefiori being the Italian word for 'a thousand flowers'. The base or 'ground' could be colored or comprise of a number of random canes made from twisted white strands and clear glass known as 'muslin'.

■ Although paperweights continued to be produced, the next major period of production is from the mid-to late 20thC, when Scotland and the US became of greater importance. Names such as Paul Ysart, Caithness, Charles Kaziun, Paul Stankard, and John Deacons led developments, based on 19thC examples, with a more modern slant. Historic French houses such as Baccarat and Saint Louis continue to produce today and their work is much sought-after.

■ Look for complex set-ups and large or very small miniature sizes. The work of notable names is worth looking out for, especially if they have ceased production such as Paul Ysart (now dead) and William Manson, who has changed his career. Many either sign their work on the base or include 'signature canes' showing their initials.

A French Saint Louis limited edition paperweight, from a limited edition of 400, signed and dated "SL 1976".

1976　　　*3.25in (8cm) diam*

$500-700　　　　　**BGD**

A French Saint Louis paperweight, signed and dated "SL 1975".

Saint Louis was founded in Alsace, France in 1767 and its work is typified by a single flower or fruit, often on swirling, white strand grounds. Millefiori is often combined with these two motifs.

1975　　　*3in (8cm) diam*

$600-900　　　　**BGD**

A French Saint Louis paperweight, signed and dated 1970.

1970　　　*3.25in (8cm) diam*

$220-280　　　　**BGD**

A French Saint Louis paperweight, signed and dated "SL 1970".

1970

3.25in (8cm) diam

$600-900　　**BGD**

A French Saint Louis commemorative paperweight, with 'Bicentenaire de la Révolution' inscription to reverse and a small central set-up of millefiori carrying the dates "1789" and "1989".

1989　　*2.75in (7cm) diam*

$220-380　　　　**BGD**

A French Saint Louis scrambled millefiori paperweight, the central cane with a silhouette of a camel.

2in (5cm) diam

$700-1,000　　　　**BGD**

A limited edition Baccarat paperweight, from an edition of 100, signed and dated "B 1994".

1994　　*3.5in (9cm) diam*

$700-1,000　　　　**BGD**

A French Baccarat 'Prince Albert's Bird of Paradise' paperweight, signed and dated "B 1997".

1997   *3.25in (8.5cm) diam*

$800-1,200   **BGD**

A limited edition French Baccarat paperweight, from an edition of 300, signed and dated "B 1977".

1977   *3in (7.5cm) diam*

$700-1,000   **BGD**

A Scottish Perthshire paperweight, with three millefiori and 'silhouette' canes of animals, signed and dated "P 1975".

Silhouette canes show animals in black against a white background, often with extra colored details around them.

1975   *2.75in (7cm) diam*

$300-500   **BGD**

A Scottish Perthshire paperweight, shaped as an ornate star.

2in (5cm) diam

$80-120   **BGD**

A Scottish John Deacons paperweight, signed and dated "JD 2004".

2004   *3.5in (9cm) diam*

$220-280   **BGD**

An Italian Seguso paperweight, signed "Seguso F... 1995".

1995   *3.25in (8cm) diam*

$70-100   **NOR**

A Scottish Paul Ysart paperweight, with a four-leafed clover over a cloudy amber ground.

Paul Ysart's paperweights are highly desirable and he is considered the 'father' of Scottish paperweight making. He worked for Scotland's Moncrieff Glassworks from the 1930s until 1963 when he joined Caithness Glass. From 1970 until 1982 he produced under his own name. Look out for those with animal motifs in particular.

c1975   *5in (7.5cm) diam*

$500-700   **BGD**

A French Val Saint Lambert paperweight, with polychrome marbled decoration pulled into a swirling star shape.

4in (10cm) diam

$120-180   **BGD**

A French commemorative sulphide paperweight, with profile of Benjamin Franklin.

3in (7.5cm) diam

$220-280   **BGD**

COLLECTORS' NOTES

■ Waterman, Parker, Montblanc, and Dunhill Namiki are the most sought after brands, with early, metal-covered pens tending to be the most desirable. The best of Dunhill's 1930s maki-e lacquer models occupy the very high end of the market.

■ In the past, collectors tended to concentrate on pens produced in their own country, probably driven by nostalgia. As the market matures and prices rise, collectors are looking further afield. For example, England's brightly colored and highly useable Conway Stewarts are now proving popular on both sides of the Atlantic.

■ As many collectors use their pens, condition and completeness is very important. Replaceable parts such as nibs and clips should be original and cracked or chipped examples should be avoided.

■ Before the ballpoint became universal, fountain pens were mass-produced, even those with gold nibs. The vast majority are worth under $30, however they can make good writing instruments and are useful for budding repairmen (or women) to practice on.

■ Modern limited editions are often produced in large numbers and, as they are often bought for investment, are kept in pristine condition. This makes used examples undesirable. Values for these are unlikely to rise significantly and collectors should look for early examples, such as Parker's Spanish Treasure and Hall of Independence or those from small editions.

An American Conklin Endura ringtop lever-filler pen, sapphire blue Pyroxlin plastic with Conklin Endura fine nib, in Conklin card box, excellent condition.

c1930-32

$70-100   **BLO**

An American Conklin ringtop lever-filler pen, cream and black celluloid with Conklin Toledo fine nib, in excellent condition, teeth marks on the cap.

c1931

$70-100   **BLO**

A 1930s English Curzons Summit lever-filler pen, blue and bronze marble celluloid with Summit 14ct gold medium nib, a rare color, in very good condition.

$80-120   **BLO**

A limited edition Delta Colosseum lever-filler pen, from an edition of 1,926, marbled yellow celluloid with Delta 18ct gold medium nib, mint condition complete with box and papers.

1997

$280-320   **BLO**

An English Mabie Todd & Co. Blackbird 5277 Self-Filler pen, red celluloid lever-filler with Blackbird nib, in excellent condition.

c1950

$30-50   **BLO**

A rare 1920s English MacNiven & Cameron self-filler pen, checker-design black hard rubber lever-filler with shaped Waverley 14ct nib, in excellent to near mint condition.

$100-150   **BLO**

An extremely rare 1930s Scottish MacNiven & Cameron Waverley pen set, green and black 'tiger-striped' celluloid with Robert Burns clip and shaped Waverley 14ct nib, with matching pencil, and presentation box.

$300-400   **BLO**

A CLOSER LOOK AT A MONTBLANC SAFETY PEN

The Montblanc Pen Company started as The Simplo Filler Pen Company in c1906. This model was made from 1920 to 1928.

Black is the most common color for this model, red and mottled red and black hard rubber versions do exist but are considerably rarer.

Montblanc made this model in a number of sizes from '00' to '12'. The '2' size is the most common, with the smallest and largest being more scarce.

The early models were named 'Diplomat' or 'Rouge et Noir' after the black body and the red 'star' in the cap crown.

A very rare German Montblanc Rouge et Noir 12 M pen, smooth black hard rubber safety filler with Rouge et Noir barrel imprint and Simplo Pen Co. 12 nib, barrel stamp slightly worn, otherwise in very good condition, an unusual nib.

c1920

$5,000-7,000   **BLO**

A rare German Simplo 'Diplomat' 4 safety pen, mottled red and black hard rubber with 'Diplomat' barrel imprint and Warranted 4 14ct nib, and white metal accommodation clip modeled as a monkey, lacks iridium nib tip and cap lip possibly shortened.

1912-28

$500-700   **BLO**

A rare German Simplo safety pen, wave-chased black hard rubber with white cap dome and Gustav Gruber Wien and Sunny Pen barrel imprints and Simplo-style Warranted 2 14ct nib, some polishing.

c1913-15

$120-180   **BLO**

A rare German Montblanc Rouge et Noir 2M safety pen, for the Italian market, smooth black hard rubber, with floral decorated gold-filled bands, 18ct rolled gold Montblanc accommodation clip and 14ct 2 fine-flexible nib, cap possibly replaced or repaired.

1920-23

$300-500   **BLO**

A German Montblanc 1-M safety pen, smooth black hard rubber with Simplo 1 fine nib, in excellent condition.

1920-25

$120-180   **BLO**

A very rare German Montblanc yellow-metal safety pen, with engine-turned and plain panels and Montblanc 2 medium nib, marked "585" on the clip and signed "Mont Blanc", barrel threads replaced with black hard rubber, otherwise in excellent condition.

1925-28

$1,800-2,200   **BLO**

A rare German Montblanc III A-F, Azurite plastic blue push button-filler pen, with later Mont Blanc 14ct 2 nib, tassie and blind cap oxidised, engraved name, in good condition.

The conservative German pen market traditionally favored pens in plain solid colors such as black and red. Examples in other colors, such as this blue marbled Montblanc, will attract a premium.

1932-34

$600-900   **BLO**

A rare German Montblanc 322 EF pen, pearl and black marbled celluloid button-filler with Warranted 'a' nib, barrel slightly amberized, lightly engraved name.

1935-38

$600-900 BLO

A Danish Montblanc 30 Masterpiece pen, black celluloid with 4810 M fine nib, minor brassing otherwise in excellent condition.

Montblanc maintained a factory in Denmark during WWII and due to shortages in parts and materials, produced models such as this example, that were outside the normal catalog.

1935-46

$400-600 BLO

A rare 1930s German Montblanc 72S PIX pencil, chased black hard rubber with alternating columns of engine-turned barley and hatched design, with some brown discoloration otherwise in very good condition.

$180-220 BLO

A rare and unusual Danish Montblanc gold-plated [242] pen, with engine-turned 12-sided faceted overlay signed "Mont-Blanc" around the cap top, and Montblanc 14ct 585 fine nib, light wear to plating, mostly towards the clip.

Produced at the tail-end of WWII when metals would have been in short supply, this gold-plated pen is rare.

1944-54

$300-500 BLO

A Montblanc 144 Meisterstück pen, black celluloid piston filler with two-color 4810 nib, in good condition with loose cap bands.

1949-60

$120-180 BLO

A rare German Montblanc Masterpiece 146 pen, green-striped and visible celluloid with two-color 4810 14ct medium nib, light brassing, clip screw discolored, turning knob replaced.

Despite some discoloration and a replaced part, this pen is made of a variation of the usual celluloid, making it desirable to collectors.

c1949

$500-700 BLO

A German Montblanc 142 F pen, silver pearl striated piston-filler with Montblanc two-color 4810 14ct nib, discolored.

1952-58

$280-320 BLO

A rare 1950s Spanish Montblanc 440 pen, cinnamon pearl-lined piston-filler with yellow ink-window, Montblanc cap band and Montblanc 14ct medium nib, excellent condition.

$400-600 BLO

A very rare English Montblanc 9ct gold Masterpiece 149 pen, fine barley overlay, by S.J. Rose, with 18ct 'tri-color' 4810 fine nib, windmill crest engraved on cap, mechanism stuck, London hallmark for 1972.

Montblanc did not produce their own gold-covered version of the 149 until c1982, so while this customized version by jewelers S.J. Rose is not an 'official' model, it is still sought-after by collectors.

$1,200-1,800 BLO

A German Montblanc M-N 22 pencil, pearl and black marbled celluloid, in excellent condition.

1935-38

$180-220 BLO

A Moore 94A Maniflex pen, silver-brown and black striated celluloid lever-filler with gray cap top, gold-filled trim and Moore Life-Maniflex nib, in excellent condition.

1939-46

$180-220 BLO

An American Parker Maxima Vacumatic pen, silver pearl celluloid with pearl section, metal Speedline-filler, and two-color Arrow fine nib, in excellent condition.

1938

$80-120 BLO

A Canadian Parker Senior Maxima Vacumatic pen, jet celluloid metal Speedline-filler, with medium oblique gold Arrow nib, in good to very good condition.

1940

$220-280 BLO

An American Parker Slender Maxima Blue-Diamond Vacumatic pen, burgundy pearl laminated celluloid, with aluminum Speedline-filler, and two-color Arrow fine-firm nib, in excellent or near mint condition.

The Blue Diamond on the clip denotes Parker's Lifetime guarantee.

1939

$220-280 BLO

An American Parker Senior Maxima Blue-Diamond Vacumatic pen, gold pearl laminated celluloid aluminum Speedline-filler with two-color Parker Arrow fine nib, near mint and exceptionally clean.

1940

$280-320 BLO

A scarce American Parker Duofold pen, silver-blue marble and black-lined celluloid button-filler, with Parker Pen fine nib, in good to very good condition, nib has been restraightened.

1941

$100-150 BLO

An American Parker Duofold Vacumatic pen, silver-red marble and black-lined celluloid aluminum Speedline-filler with Parker Pen medium-fine nib, in excellent condition.

1941

$100-150 BLO

An American Parker Major Blue-Diamond Vacumatic pen, azure blue pearl laminated celluloid with lucite Speedline-filler, gold-filled 'wedding ring' band and gold Arrow nib, in good to very good condition, an unusual variation.

1942

$100-150 BLO

A CLOSER LOOK AT A LIMITED EDITION PARKER

This limited edition was made to commemorate the wedding of Prince Charles and Lady Diana Spencer on July 29th, 1981.

The pen is based on the standard model 105 and can be differentiated by the engraved plaque on the barrel and the top of the cap is engraved with the Prince of Wales' feathers.

It is limited to only 1,000 pieces, a relatively low number for a limited edition. This means pieces are more likely to hold their value.

Collectors look for limited editions that retain all their boxes and paperwork, which will usually include a numbered certificate of authenticity.

A limited edition English Parker 'Royal Wedding' 105 pen, from an edition of 1,000, rolled gold 'royal oak' finish with medium 14ct 585 nib, in original presentation box with card outer, guarantee and certificate of authenticity, in mint condition.

1981

$400-600   BLO

A scarce American Parker Slender Maxima Blue-Diamond Vacumatic pen, jet laminated celluloid with lucite Speedline-filler, gold-filled 'wedding ring' cap band and two-color Arrow medium nib, good condition.

1942

$100-150   BLO

An American Parker Major Blue-Diamond Vacumatic pen, azure blue pearl laminated celluloid, with lucite Speedline-filler, and gold Arrow fine nib, near mint condition.

A late 1950s American Parker 61 Custom pen, black with Insignia design cap and fine nib, in unused condition.

1946

$80-120   BLO | **$50-80**   BLO

A 1960s English Parker 61 Custom Insignia pen, all rolled gold with Insignia design and medium nib, in fair to good condition with light dents and dings from use.

$70-100   BLO

A 1960s English Parker 61 Heirloom pen, rage red with pink and green gold-filled rainbow cap, medium nib and hard box, in excellent to near mint condition.

A 1970s English Parker 61 Custom Insignia pen, all rolled gold with Insignia design and fine nib, in black and white Polka dot Parker 61 box, in mint condition.

$70-100   BLO | **$70-100**   BLO

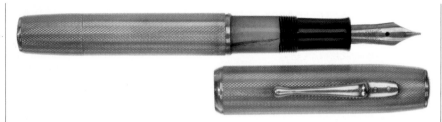

A German Pelikan 100 pen, piston-filler with 14ct solid gold overlay, with Pelikan symbol on cap top, small crack in ink window. *c1935*

$800-1,200   **ATK**

A 1930s Japanese Platinum maki-e lacquer balance piston-filler pen, decorated with gold and silver taka maki-e Japanese coins on a kuro-nuri (black volcanic) lacquer ground.

The tactile textured finish of the background is very unusual.

$1,200-1,800   **BLO**

A 1970s Sheaffer Nostalgia pen, vermeil filigree overlaid cartridge-filler marked ".925", with fine 14K nib, in excellent condition.

This pen is inspired by the attractive filigree overlaid pens of the early 20thC. Vermeil is gold-plated silver.

$400-600   **BLO**

A German Soennecken S13 pen, pearl and black lined marbled celluloid button-filler with chrome trim and medium-oblique Soennecken nib, in excellent condition.

c1947

$180-220   **BLO**

A German Soennecken 304 pen, lapis lazuli blue celluloid button-filler with fine Soennecken nib, in very good condition.

c1933

$220-280   **BLO**

A German Soennecken 222 Extra pen, turquoise green 'lizard' celluloid piston-filler with medium Soennecken nib, in near mint condition.
c1952

$280-320   **BLO**

A German Soennecken 111 Superior pen, silver-gray herringbone celluloid piston-filler with medium-oblique Soennecken nib, in mint condition.
c1954

$300-400   **BLO**

An English Stephens No.106 lever-filler pen, blue and bronze marble with Stephens 106 medium-oblique nib, lacks two fins on feed, otherwise in very good condition.

Writing styles of the time mean that many vintage pens have fine nibs, which are not always suitable for modern writers. Oblique and broad nibs are sought-after, even if fitted in relatively common pens.
c1937

$120-180   **BLO**

An English Summit Savoy button-filler pen, blue and black 'lizardskin' celluloid with Warranted 2 nib, some brassing on clip, blindcap lacks bezel.

c1937

$30-50   **BLO**

A CLOSER LOOK AT A WATERMAN'S LEVER-FILLER

'L.E.C.' stands for Lower End Covered, meaning a fully overlaid barrel; the 'Hand Engraved Vine' is often seen on this version.

Before the introduction of plastics to pen production, the use of precious metals and jewels was the only way to add 'color' to the plain black or red hard rubber bodies.

Waterman's comprehensive numbering code describes the model. '5' in the hundreds column indicates a solid gold model, '5' in the tens column indicates a lever-filler and '2' in the units column is the size of the pen. The '1/2' indicates a slender, but full-length pen.

Engraved initials, names or presentation inscription will generally devalue a pen, though light engravings can be removed.

A rare American Waterman's 552 1/2 L.E.C. 'Hand Engraved Vine' pen, marked "14kt" on the rose-gold cap, barrel, clip and lever, with Waterman's 2 fine nib, in very good condition with lightly engraved name.

1924-27

| **$500-700** | **BLO** |

A late 1930s English Unique lever-filler pen, rose and black 'lizard' celluloid with large Warranted 2 medium nib, in good to very good condition.

| **$70-100** | **BLO** |

A late 1940s Eversharp 'Sixty-Four' duo set, black lever-filler with 14ct gold cap and matching pencil, in fitted gift box.

Based on the 'Fifth Avenue' range, the 'Sixty-Four' was so called because the pen retailed at $64. It also tied into the 'Take it or Leave it' quiz show with the '$64 Question' catch phrase, that Eversharp sponsored.

An American Waterman's 0552 1/2 'Basketweave' pen, gold-filled filigree overlay with Clip-Cap and Waterman's 2 medium-fine nib, in good to very good condition, two initials.

1923-27

| **$120-180** | **ATK** | **$100-150** | **BLO** |

An American Waterman's 55 pen, smooth black hard rubber with Ideal 5 fine nib, light surface scratches otherwise excellent/near mint.

1923-27

| **$180-220** | **BLO** |

A rare American Waterman's 554 'Basketweave' pen, green-gold cap and barrel filigree, clip and lever, marked "14kt", with Waterman's 4 medium nib, in very good condition.

1924-27

| **$700-1,000** | **BLO** |

An American Waterman's 452 'Basketweave' pen, marked "Sterling" on the cap, barrel and Clip-Cap, with Waterman's 2 medium nib, in good to very good condition.

1924-27

| **$280-320** | **BLO** |

A 1920s American Waterman's 'Pansy Panel' gold overlaid pencil, marked "14K", with matching clip, three initials and in near mint condition, nozzle/mechanism needs reconnecting.

$100-150   **BLO**

A 1920s Canadian Waterman's 51V Ripple pen, red and black hard rubber with Waterman's Ideal Canada 1 medium fine nib, lacks clip, otherwise very good condition.

This is an extremely rare short model, with a small no.1 sized nib.

$180-220   **BLO**

An American Waterman's [028]52 pen, smooth black hard rubber with broad gold-filled bands at each end and 18ct gold-filled Clip Cap and Waterman's Reg US 2 fine nib, very good condition.

This rare model was first offered in the 1925 catalog as a 55-size. It is very rare to find in others sizes.

1925-27

$180-220   **BLO**

A 1920s American Waterman's 452 'Basketweave' pen, marked "Sterling" on cap, barrel, Clip-Cap and lever, with Waterman's 2 Canada medium nib, engraved with three fancy initials.

$280-320   **BLO**

An American Waterman's 52 Cardinal pen, red hard rubber with Waterman's Ideal 2 fine nib, in very good to excellent condition.
1928-30

$180-220   **BLO**

A 1920s American Waterman's 0552 1/2 V [L.E.C.] 'Pansy' pen set, gold-filled ringtop lever-filler with Waterman's Reg US 2 nib and matching pencil, engraved Gothic initials on each.

$120-180   **ATK**

A limited edition Waterman Edson Signé Boucheron pen, from an edition of 3,741, with overlaid 18ct gold filigree by Boucheron, with medium nib, boxed, in mint condition.
c1996

$400-600   **BLO**

A 'giant' black hard rubber eyedropper pen, possibly German or English, un-marked smooth hard rubber 8- or 10-size cone-cap with two milled bands on the barrel and one on the cap, lacks nib, cap lip repaired, otherwise excellent or near mint condition.
c1915-20   8.25in (21cm) long

$100-150   **BLO**

FIND OUT MORE...

Fountain Pens of the World, *by Andreas Lambrou, published by Philip Wilson Publishers, 1995.*

The Fountain Pen: A Collector's Companion, *by Alexander Crum Ewing, published by Running Press, 1997.*

The Writing Equipment Society, *www.wesoc.co.uk*

The Pen Collectors of America, *www.pencollectors.com*

COLLECTORS' NOTES

- The mechanical propelling pencil was first patented in 1822 by Sampson Mordan and John Isaac Hawkins and became known as the 'Everpointed' pencil. Hawkins sold his share of the rights to Mordan in 1823, who in turn sold them to a wealthy, successful stationer called Gabriel Riddle. With Riddle's financial support, Mordan was able to build his company into the 19th century success story it became.

- Mordan and Riddle's partnership ended in 1837. Pieces made 1823-37, and particularly before 1825, are scarce and desirable. Many bear an 'SM GR' hallmark and 'S.MORDAN & COs PATENT' wording. Pieces bearing 'S.MORDAN & CO MAKERS & PATENTEES'

date from around 1838 until the 1850s-1860s when 'S.MORDAN & CO MAKERS' was used. From the 1860s onward 'S.MORDAN & CO' was used.

- Mordan worked under Joseph Bramah, who patented a way of cutting quills mechanically in 1809, producing small quill nibs to be fitted into holders with a swiveling clamp. Bramah's patent expired in 1824, and holders were made well into the 1850s, and even beyond on a lesser scale. For both types, look for early examples, ornate decoration and fine materials such as ivory and precious metals. Marked examples are also more desirable. Avoid those with damage or missing parts as these are hard to repair.

A Bramah-type penholder, with agate shaft and gold fittings formed as leaves and set with turquoises.

These precious metal and hardstone holders are scarce. Those with collars covering repairs to the shaft or those that are shorter, due to damage, are worth around 50 percent less.

c1840   6.25in (16cm) long

$1,200-1,800   **PC**

A Georgian silver quill 'presentation' or 'prize' pen, with later Bramah-type holder and London hallmarks for "IR" for 1804.

This would originally have had an integral silver nib but was modified, perhaps due to heavy use, after 1825. Presentation pens were costly and usually given as prizes. They sometimes bear inscriptions relating to the event.

1804   9in (23cm) long

$500-800   **BLO**

A Bramah-type penholder, with a carved ivory shaft, the holder stamped "S.MORDAN'S IMPROV'D".

c1830   6in (15.5cm) long

$120-180   **BLO**

A rare Mordan silver Bramah-type penholder, the grip stamped "S.MORDAN'S IMPROV'D", with ring collar and hobnail terminal.

This is likely to have been made after Bramah's patent expired in 1825 as the only improvement seems to be the way the nib retracts into the holder to protect the nib.

3.25in (8cm) long

$280-320   **BLO**

A very rare Mordan pen and pencil combination, the ivory shaft stamped "S.MORDAN & Co. MAKERS & PATENTEES", the Bramah-type pen holder stamped "BRAMAH PATENT", with sliding ring.

c1820-1830   7in (18cm) long

$700-1,000   **PC**

A Mordan double-ended silver pen and pencil, with reeded body, sliding ring grips and friction fit pen holder, marked "S.MORDAN &Co MAKERS & PATENTEES".

c1840   3.5in (9cm) long

$220-280   **BLO**

A Mordan for Lund silver pen and reeded pencil combination, decorated shaped sliders, stamped "LUND - CORNHILL LONDON", with "SM" hallmarks for London, 1857.

Based in Cornhill, London, Lund was a stationer and retailer of fine, often mechanical objects, such as corkscrews.

1857   3.5in (9cm) long

$180-220   **BLO**

PENS & WRITING

A CLOSER LOOK AT A MORDAN PENCIL

Three colors of cast gold are used, pink, green, and yellow – these were complex and expensive to produce.

Only a handful are known to collectors, making them extremely rare.

It is inset with seed pearls and small ruby cabochons.

The hand engraved gold plated shaft has a split, showing it may have been damaged and shortened slightly.

A small Mordan pencil, with gold shaft engraved with scrolling vines, the screw-off terminal set with seed pearls and rubies in a flowering vine pattern, the slider set with two rubies and pink gold fleur-de-lys, and pink and yellow gold end set with rubies, with fleur-de-lys in pink gold, marked "S.MORDAN & CO."

c1860

2in (5cm) long

$800-1,200

PC

A very rare "S.MORDAN & CO'S PATENT" silver pencil, with "SM*G R" hallmarks for London, 1825, and crown-like terminal.

This is an early example with a Sampson Mordan and Gabriel Riddle hallmark.

1825

4in (10cm) long

$300-500

BLO

An "S.MORDAN & CO MAKERS" silver pencil, with alternating columns of fine barley and line-and-dot, bloodstone-set terminal screwing off to reveal lead storage, "SM" hallmarks for London.

1848

4in (10cm) long closed

$120-180

BLO

A rare "S.MORDAN & CO" silver pencil, with "SM" hallmarks for London 1859, engraved with script presentation engraving "H.T. Lister", and with large screw-off agate set acanthus leaf terminal revealing lead storage.

This pattern is rare. The heavy terminal is similar to the capital of a classical architectural column.

1859

4in (10cm) long

$220-280

BLO

An 1830s "S.MORDAN & Co MAKERS & PATENTEES" silver pencil, with reeded body and citrine-set terminal.

3.5in (9cm) long closed

$120-180

BLO

An "S.MORDAN & CO. MAKERS" 18ct gold pencil, with fine barley shaft and bloodstone-set terminal with two engraved initials, screwing off to reveal lead storage, slider with carved flower and leaf motifs.

As well as the fact it is 18ct gold, it is in mint condition, which is a very rare attribute for such a functional and expensive object.

c1845

3.25in (8.5cm) long

$300-500

BLO

A miniature pencil and penknife, modeled as a musket with mahogany stock.

Novelty shaped pencils were popular during the second half of the 19thC. Look for those made by Mordan, especially in the forms of animals, guns, swords, and other items such as boats.

c1880

3.5in (9cm) long

$80-120

BLO

An ivory Lund pencil, stamped "LUND PATENTEE LONDON", with rotating spiraling silver collar to propel the lead.

c1840

3.75in (9.5cm) long

$80-120

BLO

FIND OUT MORE...

Victorian Pencils: Tools to Jewels, by Deborah Crosby, published by Schiffer Publishing, 1998.

An English Wells & Lambe traveling writing case, the interior stamped "Wells & Lambe Manufacturers to the Queen", covered in green morocco leather.

c1840   9.5in (24cm) wide

$500-700   **BLO**

A rare French traveling writing set, with loops for ruler, seal, paper, pen, pencil, a wafer case, and various accessories, the ends folding-out with a glass inkwell and a pounce pot with brass caps.

c1850   11.5in (29cm) wide

$700-1,000   **BLO**

A globe inkwell, with 12 colored gores on brass sphere, markings in English, hinged cover and inner cover, and glass ink bottle.

1.75in (4.5cm) diam

$120-180   **EG**

A very rare 1950s English Parker Quink black Bakelite ink station, with central covered reservoir for Quink dispenser, some lettering missing paint.

7in (18cm) wide

$120-180   **BLO**

An early English Mabie Todd & Co counter-top display case, with two lift-out trays, repainted MTCo decal and plinth base, lacks inner trays and plaques from tray edges.

c1910   16.25in (41.5cm) high

$700-1,000   **BLO**

A rare 1920s English Mabie Todd & Co. 'Swan Pens' notepad holder, brass with sprung clamp titled in red with a black swan, on four dimpled feet, in excellent condition.

7in (17.5cm) high

$120-180   **BLO**

A German 'Kann Dir die Hand nicht geben' (I can't take your hand) humorous 'inky hand' postcard.

$18-25   **BLO**

A rare and early English Waterman's catalog, with lithographed, embossed and gold-printed covers, 24pp printed in black and white and illustrations.

c1915   8in (20cm) high

$800-1,200   **BLO**

A celluloid alligator paperknife, 'swallowing' a black man-headed pencil.

7in (18cm) long

$50-70   **SOTT**

COLLECTORS' NOTES

■ Pez was invented by Viennese confectioner Eduard Haas III in 1927. Sold in tins, the peppermint flavored sweets were aimed at the adult market in Austria as a breath freshener. In 1948, Oskar Uxa designed a new dispenser shaped like a cigarette lighter. These are known as 'regulars' today.

■ The company expanded into the US in 1952 and, while unsuccessful at first, the addition of character heads to the dispensers and new fruit-flavored sweets aimed at children proved a great marketing ploy.

■ The range initially included Santa Claus, Space Trooper and Popeye and has since expanded to include animals, people (but rarely real-life personalities), cartoon and film characters and holiday-themed dispensers.

■ Companies and organisations have also commissioned promotional dispensers over the years, such as Zielpunkt, eBay, Nivea, and the rare Sparefroh. With such a range, many have crossover appeal.

■ Many characters have been continually produced, with a number of redesigns and variations appearing, and collectors often try to collect the whole set. Earlier examples, lacking the feet which were added in 1987, are generally more desirable and, unusually, the plain 'regulars' from the early 1950s are some of the most sought-after.

■ With such a strong and devoted fan base, Pez now produce a range of dispensers and other merchandise aimed directly at collectors.

An early 1960s Walt Disney's 'Donald Duck' Pez dispenser, with die-cut stem and without feet.

There are five dispensers made with a die-cut stem. The Easter Bunny is the most valuable, worth approximately $450.

4.25in (11cm) high

$120-180   **DMI**

An early 1960s Walt Disney's 'Pluto' Pez dispenser, first version with movable ears and without feet.

4in (10cm) high

$25-35   **DMI**

A mid-1960s Walt Disney's 'Lil' Bad Wolf' Pez dispenser, without feet.

3.75in (9.5cm) high

$35-45   **DMI**

A late 1960s Walt Disney's 'Baloo' Pez dispenser, from "The Jungle Book", with blue-grey head and without feet.

4in (10cm) high

$20-40   **DMI**

A late 1970s Walt Disney's 'Thumper' Pez dispenser, from "Bambi", without feet.

Look for the rare variation that has a copyright symbol together with "WDP" on the head, it could be worth up to $180.

4in (10cm) high

$60-90   **DMI**

A late 1980s Walt Disney's 'Goofy' Pez dispenser, with green hat and with feet.

4.5in (11.5cm) high

$2-4   **DMI**

A 1990s Walt Disney's 'Duck Nephew' Pez character dispenser, with feet.

c1990   4in (10cm) high

$5-10   **DMI**

A 'Popeye' Pez dispenser, with applied hat and plain face and without feet.

4.5in (11.5cm) high

$70-100   **DMI**

A late 1990s 'Asterix the Gaul' Pez character dispenser, from the reissue series.

The original series, made without feet, was released in the mid-1970s, but not in the US, making it very rare here. It can be worth more than $2,000.

5in (12.5cm) high

$4-8   **DMI**

A CLOSER LOOK AT A PEZ DISPENSER

This is one of five dispensers that were produced with a die-cut design cut into the stem. The others were Casper, Donald Duck, Mickey Mouse and the Easter Bunny.

The character of Bozo the Clown was created by Alan W. Livingston in 1946 and the TV show made its debut in 1949. The rights to the character were bought by Larry Harmon in 1956, who then expanded the franchise considerably.

At $350-550, the Easter Bunny version is the most valuable of this range.

Like most of the die-cut dispensers, a solid version of Bozo was also made. Unusually, the solid version is slightly more valuable.

An early 1960s Bozo the Clown Pez dispenser, with die-cut stem.

4.25in (11cm) high

$120-180   **DMI**

A late 1980s 'Papa Smurf' Pez dispenser, from the first Smurfs' series, with thin feet.

4in (10cm) high

$5-10   **DMI**

A 'Batman' Pez dispenser, blue mask version with short ears and with feet.

4.25in (11cm) high

$10-15   **DMI**

An 'R2-D2' Pez dispenser, from the third Star Wars series.

2002   4.5in (11cm) high

$2-4   **DMI**

An 'E.T.' Pez dispenser, manufactured to coincide with the 2002 reissue of the Steven Spielberg film.

2002   4in (10cm) high

$2-4   **DMI**

An 'Easter Bunny' Pez dispenser, with fat ears and without feet.

c1970   *4.25in (11cm) high*

$25-35   **DMI**

A 1990s 'Easter Bunny' Pez dispenser, version 'D' with long ears and plain nose.

4.75in (12cm) high

$2-4   **DMI**

A 'Lamb' Pez dispenser, from the Merry Music Makers series, without feet.

c1985   *4in (10cm) high*

$20-30   **DMI**

A 1980s 'Chick in Egg' Pez dispenser, the thick plastic shell with saw-blade points.

4.75in (12cm) high

$4-8   **DMI**

A 1980s 'Jack-o-Lantern' Pez dispenser, with die-cut face and with feet.

4.25in (11cm) high

$10-15   **DMI**

A Japanese 'Jack-o-Lantern' Pez dispenser, with a blue-tinted crystal head.

4.5in (11.5cm) high

$3-5   **DMI**

An early 1970s 'Angel' Pez dispenser, with yellow hair and feet.

4.75in (12cm) high

$40-60   **DMI**

A 'Santa Claus' Pez dispenser, an unusual colorway with a tan face and white hat.

4.5in (11.5cm) high

$7-10   **DMI**

A 1950s 'Santa Claus' full body Pez dispenser.

Santa Claus dispensers are perennially popular and have been made continually since the 1950s. This is the first version and the most desirable. Examples made from the 1970s are very common.

3.75in (9.5cm) high

$150-200   **DMI**

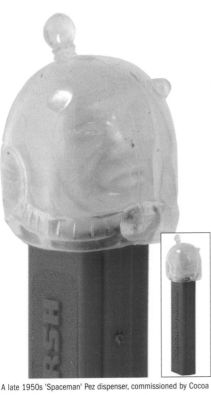

An early 1970s 'Policeman' Pez dispenser, from the Pez Pals series.

4in (10cm) high

$50-70   **DMI**

An African American 'Bride' Pez dispenser, from the Pez Pals series, with feet.

4.25in (11cm) high

$12-18   **DMI**

A late 1950s 'Spaceman' Pez dispenser, commissioned by Cocoa Marsh as a special offer.

The version lacking the 'Cocoa Marsh' on the stem is worth about 15 per cent less.

4.5in (11.5cm) high

$220-280   **DMI**

An African American 'Groom' Pez dispenser, from the Pez Pals series, with feet.

The early version without feet is very rare and can be worth $350-550.

4.5in (11.5cm) high

$10-15   **DMI**

An early 1980s 'Indian' Pez dispenser, from the Merry Music Maker series.

Merry Music Makers feature a whistle on the back of the head of the dispenser and were introduced in the early 1980s. The owl is the rarest version and can be worth up to $2,000.

5in (12.5cm) high

$20-30   **DMI**

A 'Bubbleman' yellow neon Pez dispenser, with feet.

1998   4.25in (11cm) high

$4-8   **DMI**

A mid-1990s 'BP' Pez dispenser, from the Pez Pals series with BP 'Body Parts'.

4.5in (11.5cm) high

$10-15   **DMI**

An early 1980s 'Koala' Pez dispenser, from the Merry Music Maker series, with feet.

4in (10cm) high

$10-15   **DMI**

A mid-1970s 'Rooster' Pez dispenser, with white face and red crop and comb.

White is the most common color for the 'Rooster' dispenser.

4.5in (11.5cm) high

$30-50   **DMI**

A 1990s 'Icee Bear' Pez dispenser.

4.5in (11.5cm) high

$5-7   DMI

A 'Crystal Ball' Pez dispenser on stand, with blue stars.

Produced for a mail-in offer, the first 2,500 were made with silver stars instead of blue stars but there is not a great deal of difference in value at the moment.

2002   5in (12.5cm) high

$20-30   DMI

A limited edition 'Nivea Truck' promotional Pez dispenser, from an edition of 10,000, commissioned by Nivea and made available at the European Nivea Fun Fest.

2003   4in (10cm) long

$12-18   DMI

A 'Smiley' promotional Pez dispenser, commissioned by the Austrian supermarket chain Zielpunkt, depicting their mascot, complete in original packaging.

1999   8.5in (21.5cm) high

$10-15   DMI

A Euro 2004 promotional Pez dispenser, to commemorate Sweden's participation in the European football championships, complete in original packaging.

2004   8.5in (21.5cm) high

$25-35   DMI

An 'LSU Tigers' baseball promotional Pez dispenser.

4in (10cm) high

$20-30   DMI

A 'Silver Glow' Pez regular dispenser, made to commemorate the opening of a new Pez factory in Hungary.

1991   3.5in (9cm) high

$25-35   DMI

A 'Metro Stars' hockey puck Pez dispenser.

4in (10cm) high

$20-30   DMI

An 'eBay' Pez dispenser, commissioned by and sold through eBay.

Pez produced 5,000 dispensers for eBay in yellow, blue, red and green colorways. They were sold online in 2000, and have approximately equal values.

2000   4.5in (11.5cm) high

$15-20   DMI

FIND OUT MORE...

Collector's Guide to Pez, by Shawn Peterson, published by Krause Publications, 2nd edition, 2003.

The Museum of Pez Memorabilia, 214 California Drive, Burlingame, California, 94010, USA.

www.pezcentral.com

www.pezcollectors.com

'Dartmouth Winter Carnival' Canadian tourism poster, designed by Ostberg.

1939   *34in (85cm) high*

$2,200-2,800   **SWA**

'Dartmouth Winter Carnival', Canadian tourism poster, designed by Gish.

1948   *33.25in (83cm) high*

$3,000-4,000   **SWA**

'Nice/Beuil', French tourism poster, designed by Jean Gabriel Domergue.

c1935   *39.5in (99cm) high*

$800-1,200   **SWA**

'Japan XI Olympic Winter Games', Japanese tourism poster, designed by Yosuke Kamekura (1915-97).

1972   *40.75in (102cm) high*

$800-1,200   **SWA**

'Engelberg/Trübsee', Swiss tourism poster, designed by Herbert Matter (1907-84).

1936   *28.75in (72cm) high*

$1,000-1,500   **SWA**

'Sun Valley / "Round House"', American ski poster designed by D.S.

Ski posters have become sought-after due to their bold and visually appealing imagery that combines the romance of foreign destinations with the excitement and fashions of the winter sport. Sun Valley, Idaho was created by Averell Harriman (Chairman of Union Pacific Railroad) as a destination resort to encourage people to ride the railroad out west.

40in (100cm) high

$3,000-3,500   **SWA**

'St. Moritz', Swiss tourism poster, designed by Walter Herdeg (1908-95).

1934   *39.75in (99cm) high*

$800-1,200   **SWA**

'St. Moritz', Swiss tourism poster, designed by Walter Herdeg.

1934   *40in (100cm) high*

$800-1,200   **SWA**

'USA, Psychedelic Travel', 1970s American tourism poster.

39in (100cm) high

$80-120 CL

'State Parks', 1930s American tourist poster, designed by Dorothy Waugh.

41in (104cm) high

$500-800 CL

'See America, Welcome to Montana', 1980s American tourism poster, designed by J.H. Rothstein.

28in (71cm) high

$150-200 CL

'Visit Washington State', 1960s American tourism poster, designed by Harry Bonath.

1964 *29in (73cm) high*

$180-220 CL

'New York Loves You', 1970s American tourism poster showing famous singer Lena Horne wearing an 'I Love NY' badge, photograph by Richard Avedon.

36in (91cm) high

$180-220 CL

'Mexico', 1950s Mexican tourism poster, designed by Espert.

37in (94cm) high

$350-450 CL

'Deutschland', 1920s German tourism poster designed by Friedel Dzubas.

39in (100cm) high

$1,000-1,500 CL

A CLOSER LOOK AT A TRAVEL POSTER

Hohlwein (1879-1934) was one of Germany's most notable poster artists, known for his WWI designs and use of bold colors.

This poster was designed as part of a series of four, advertising Munich Zoo in 1911, the others show a flamingo, eagles and panthers.

Hohlwein was an animal lover and a hunter and often used animals in his designs.

This was the first in the series as the image was also used to advertise the opening of the zoo on August 1st 1911.

'Zoologischer Garten München', designed by Ludwig Hohlwein (1874-1949), printed by G. Schuh, Munich.

1911 *46.75in (117cm) high*

$1,800-2,200 SWA

'Germany, Spring in Wiesbaden', 1930s German tourism poster.

33in (80cm) high

$550-650 CL

'Baden-Baden', 1960s German tourism poster, by an unknown designer.

33in (82.5cm) high

$300-400 SWA

'Saint Aubin', 1930s French tourism poster, designed by A. Galland.

39in (99cm) high

$400-500 CL

'Mont St. Michel', 1950s French tourism poster, designed by E. Thollander.

37in (34cm) high

$120-180 CL

Saison d'Été Menton', 1950s French tourism poster, designed by F. Ferrie.

39in (100cm) high

$500-800 CL

'Egypt', 1950s Egyptian tourism poster, designed by M. Azmy.

39in (99cm) high

$350-450   **CL**

'Egypt', 1950s Egyptian tourism poster, designed by Ihap Hulusi.

Ihap Hulusi studied under German graphic designer Ludwig Hohlwein until 1925. He was one of the earliest, and best known, Turkish graphic designers until the 1960s. He is well known for his travel posters.

39in (99cm) high

$400-600   **CL**

'Finland', 1930s Finnish tourism poster, designed by Bade.

39in (100cm) high

$300-500   **CL**

'Visit India, Kashmir', 1930s Indian tourism poster.

39in (100cm) high

$350-450   **CL**

'Centro Turistico Giovanile', 1950s Italian tourism poster.

39in (100cm) high

$350-450   **CL**

'Poland, Fishing in the Mazurian Lakeland', 1960s Polish tourism poster, designed by Slomczyinski.

39in (100cm) high

$280-320   **CL**

'Ribatejo, Portugal', 1950s Portuguese tourism poster, designed by Gustavo Fontoura.

39in (100cm) high

$150-250   **CL**

'Scotland's Wonderland by MacBraynes Steamers', designed by E.C. Le Cadell, printed by McCorquodale, small losses, tears and pinholes to margin, fold.

40.25in (102cm) high

$500-700   **ON**

COLLECTORS' NOTES

■ Pre-1950s Airline posters evoke an era when air travel was an exciting and glamorous novelty. The designs were often stylish and innovative, reflecting the cutting-edge world of flight and making them particularly popular with today's collectors. 1930s posters featuring Art Deco artwork and notable airlines can command high prices, although examples by unknown designers can be worth less.

■ Air travel had become more common by the 1950s and posters from that period tend to emphasis speed and convenience over glamor. Bold lines, geometric shapes, and flat colors remained predominant.

■ Posters for well-known airline companies, such as Pan Am, British Overseas Airways Corporation (BOAC), and Air France, tend to attract a premium due to the size of their following, as do designs featuring appealing locations.

■ Posters were produced to be used and were often printed on delicate paper, making them susceptible to tears and creases. Condition is important and any damage to the image is likely to seriously affect the value of a poster. Professional restorers can correct many problems and can back them with linen.

■ Beware of reproductions. Learn to recognize the difference in the print qualities of early and contemporary posters by visiting dealers and salesrooms. Later examples tend to be printed on thicker paper with an image made up of pixels.

'AOA USA The Route of the Flagships', poster designed by Lewitt-Him, printed by W.R. Royle.

37.75in (96cm) high

$220-280   **ON**

'American Airlines to New York' poster designed by Edward McKnight Kauffer.

Modernist designer Edward McKnight Kauffer (1890-1954) is perhaps best known for his Art Deco poster designs for Shell. He worked in London from 1914-40, notably for Frank Pick of London Transport, returning to the US in 1940. His work has featured in many exhibitions, including at the Museum of Modern Art, New York, and the Victoria & Albert Museum, London.

c1950   *39.25in (98cm) high*

$700-1,000   **SWA**

'BEA, British European Airways', 1940s English poster, in very good condition.

40in (100cm) high

$500-700   **CL**

'For Better Travel by B.O.A.C.', poster designed by Abram Games (1914-96).

1952   *30in (75cm) high*

$700-1,000   **SWA**

'B. O. A. C. Flies to All 6 Continents', poster designed by Abram Games, printed by Baynard Press.

1952   *40in (100cm) high*

$600-800   **SWA**

'Fly BOAC, It's a Smaller World by Speedbird', 1950s British poster, designed by Beverly Pick.

40in (100cm) high

$250-350   **CL**

'Rome by Clipper, Pan American', 1950s American poster.

39in (100cm) high

$400-600　　　　　CL

A CLOSER LOOK AT AN AIRLINE POSTER

Founded in 1933 by the merger of three companies, Air France is one of the most desirable names in airline posters due to its superb designs.

This is typical of his style for the company, which usually incorporated maps. His posters showing maps of the world are highly sought-after.

This poster was designed by Lucien Boucher (1889-1971), who designed many posters for Air France during the 1940s and 1950s.

Boucher had a Surrealist artistic background – here the wing not only represents flight, but also the shape of South America.

'Air France, South America', 1950s French poster, designed by Lucien Boucher.

39in (100cm) high

$650-750　　　　　CL

'To Paris via Pan American', 1950s French poster, designed by Jean Carlu.

Jean Carlu (1900-97) was the third of France's foremost poster designers during the 1920s and 1930s, after Adolphe Mouron 'Cassandre' and Paul Colin. He is known for his bright colors, strong geometric designs and minimal use of words to create dramatic, eye-catching posters. Cubism and Surrealism were strong influences. This example also shows styling typical of the 1950s. He designed for Perrier and Cinzano, as well as for the US government.

41in (104cm) high

$400-600　　　　　CL

'Round the World, Round the Clock via Pan American', 1950s American poster.

41in (104cm) high

$320-380　　　　　CL

'Seattle United Air Lines', 1960s American poster.

39in (100cm) high

$180-220　　　　　CL

'Fly by West African Airways Corporation', 1950s poster, by an anonymous designer.

30in (76cm) high

$280-320　　　　　ON

A CLOSER LOOK AT A RAILWAY POSTER

Designed by John Hassall in 1908, this poster, incorporating the 'Jolly Fisherman', is perhaps the most famous holiday railway poster ever printed. ——

Produced for the LNER, it —— exists in a number of versions. One features a child pulling the fisherman's scarf and another is in portrait format.

Later Skegness posters, such as BRER's 1958 version, have the addition of Skegness' famous —— pier in the background.

—— The poster was produced to promote Skegness to Londoners. In 1908, the town had 300,000 visitors, making it one of Britain's most popular holiday destinations.

'Skegness Is So Bracing, It's Quicker By Rail', designed by John Hassall, printed for the LNER by Waterlow & Sons Ltd London, mounted on linen.

Hassall (1868-1948) had never visited Skegness when he designed this poster, for which he received 12 guineas! The catchphrase is thought to have been developed by an unknown LNER (London & North Eastern Railway) employee.

50in (127cm) wide

$2,800-3,200 **ON**

'France, Normandy', 1950s English language French poster for French Railways, designed by Raoul Dufy.

Born in Normandy, Raoul Dufy (1877-1953) was a notable French painter and part of the 'Fauve' group. Meaning 'wild beast', they gained their nickname from their wild use of bright color.

39in (99cm) high

$400-600 **CL**

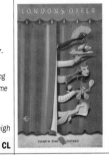

'London's Offer', designed by Jan Lewitt (1907-91) and Jerzy Him (1900-82), printed by Baynard Press, London, for the London Underground.

Each arm holds an item symbolic of the various activities that people can participate in around London.

1938 40in (101.5cm) high

$500-700 **SWA**

'Service To Industry Steel', designed by Norman Wilkinson, published by RELMR, printed by Jordison, mounted on linen.

1949 50in (127cm) wide

$800-1,200 **ON**

'East Coast Frolics Travel Cheaply by L.N.E.R.', designed by Frank Newbould, lithographic print by Chorley & Pickersgill Ltd., published by LNER, unframed.

39.5in (100cm) high

$1,800-2,200 **L&T**

'Demountable Tanks', designed by Kenneth McDonough, published by RELMR, printed by Jordison.

1951 40.25in (102cm) high

$120-180 **ON**

'Bata', 1950s Swiss footwear advertising poster, designed by Birkhauser.

51in (128cm) high

$300-400   **CL**

'Macy's', anonymous American advertising poster.

1938   *33in (82.5cm) high*

$80-120   **SWA**

A CLOSER LOOK AT AN ADVERTISING POSTER

Beginning his poster work in 1899, Cappiello (1875-1942) became one of the most revered and revolutionary 20thC poster designers.

As well as the 'unnecessary' gentlemen's bodies being out of the design, Cappiello's clever design skills show in the reason for gentlemen removing their hats – for a lady, who is also unseen.

This design for a French hat maker honors Surrealist artist René Magritte, who famously painted bowler-hatted men from 1927.

The yellow gloved hand is unusual and hints at the Dandies or show performers of the day, adding a louche but theatrical aspect.

'Mossant', designed by Leonetto Cappiello, printed by Edimo, Paris.

1938   *62.5in (156cm) high*

$2,200-2,800   **SWA**

'Galeries Lafayette', 1980s French poster for the English market, showing an elegant Parisienne, dressed and with a haircut in the style of the day.

66in (167.5cm) high

$280-320   **CL**

'Familistère', designed by Leon Dupin, printed by Joseph-Charles, Paris.

1928   *55in (137.5cm) high*

$700-1,000   **SWA**

'Thonet Seatings Greeting', 1970s American Christmas poster.

Austrian company Thonet (est. 1819) produced fine quality chairs made from bent beech wood from 1859 and, later, chromed metal tubing.

41in (104cm) high

$220-280   **CL**

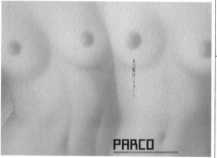

'Parco', by an unknown designer, for a Japanese Department store.

c1975   *40.5in (101cm) high*

$400-600   **SWA**

'Chanel No. 5', American advertising poster, artwork designed by Andy Warhol.

Andy Warhol's (1928-87) 1985 screenprints were produced in four colors, and were used for the perfume's 75th Anniversary in 1996.

1996   *68in (27cm) high*

$220-280   **CL**

'Écoutez La Voix Du Monde', French radio advertising poster designed by René Ravo (1904-98), printed by Réunies, Paris.

c1935   46.25in (115.5cm) high

$1,200-1,800   **SWA**

'Hora Cine Dial', 1930s Spanish advertising poster designed by Kras for Cabouli & Villaro.

39in (100cm) high

$700-1,000   **CL**

A CLOSER LOOK AT AN IPOD POSTER

The use of a strongly colored background is unusual, Apple usually choose white.

The iPod has revolutionized the way we listen to music and has become the 'must-have' for all ages of music lovers.

Rumor has it that Apple demand all advertising is sent back to them for recycling – as the product and campaign is so iconic, examples may become sought-after and collectible.

It is typical of Apple's approach to advertising, showing a young person dancing to music and clearly holding an iPod – encapsulating both brand and lifestyle.

'iPod', American silhouette advertising poster for Apple Computers.

This campaign was produced in myriad colors with people of many races and nationalities. The lack of detail and simple, striking colors work well, leaving the iPod shown in its real-life white. This is one of the more appealing versions.

c2003   36in (91.5cm) high

$80-120   **CL**

'You'll See – Murphy Television', rare and early poster designed by Frederic Henri Kay Henrion (1914-90).

1950   22.5in (56cm) high

$400-600   **SWA**

'Olympia Portable', 1930s French advertising poster.

45in (115cm) high

$300-500   **CL**

'Olivetti Graphika', Italian advertising poster designed by Giovanni Pintori (b.1912), printed by N. Moneta, Milan.

c1958   27.5in (69cm) high

$700-1,000   **SWA**

'Bissell's Cyco-Bearing Carpet Sweeper', American Christmas advertising lithographic poster, by Michigan Litho. Company, Grand Rapids.

50in (127cm) high

$1,800-2,200   **JDJ**

'iPod', American advertising poster for Apple Computers.

c2003   36in (91.5cm) high

$50-70   **CL**

'Papier à Cigarettes Job', 1900s French advertising poster for Job cigarettes designed by Edgard Mascence.

22in (56cm) high

$400-600   **CL**

'Fumar el Papel Job', 1900s Spanish advertising poster for Job cigarettes designed by A. Villa.

22in (56cm) high

$280-320   **CL**

'Marlboro', 1980s American advertising poster.

22in (56cm) high

$25-35   **CL**

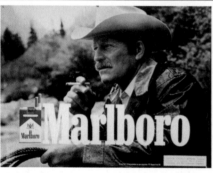

'Marlboro', 1980s American advertising poster.

22in (56cm) wide

$25-35   **CL**

'The New Yorker', 1970s American advertising poster, designed by R.O. Blechman.

40in (101cm) high

$180-220   **CL**

'The New Yorker', 1950s American Christmas advertising poster.

46in (117cm) high

$300-500   **CL**

'It's Spring! And Life is Wonderful!', American LIFE magazine advertising poster, designed by R.M.

c1963   *43.75in (109cm) wide*

$400-600   **SWA**

'Le Parisien', French advertising poster, designed by Phili.

c1946   *63in (160cm) high*

$1,200-1,800   **CL**

'Cacao Lhara', designed by Jules Cheret, printed by Chaix, Paris.

Jules Cheret (1836-1932) is a notable early poster artist, who contributed hugely to the development of the advertising poster. Executed in the Art Nouveau style, his designs also capture the 'laissez-faire' attitude of Belle Epoque Paris.

1893   97in (242.5cm) high

$1,200-1,800   **SWA**

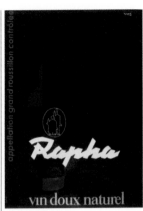

'Rapha', French wine advertising poster, designed by Charles Loupot (1892-1962), printed by I.C.A., Paris.

1958   31in (77.5cm) high

$800-1,200   **SWA**

'Volg Traubensaft', German grape juice advertising poster, designed by Josef Müller-Brockmann (1914-96), printed by A. Trub & Co., one in a series for a brand of grape juice.

c1952   50in (125cm) high

$400-600   **SWA**

'Humber', British bicycle advertising poster designed by French poster designer Clouet.

Humber Bicycles (1898-1976) must have given a truly 'heavenly' ride! It's the superb design and printing quality of this poster, as well as its age and style, that make it so valuable.

c1900   63in (160cm) high

$1,200-1,800   **CL**

'Phillips Bicycles Renowned The World Over', anonymous printed advertising poster.

27.25in (69cm) high

$600-900   **ON**

'Hangi Daitokan', designed by Tadanori Yokoo (b.1936), to advertise a book by Tatsumi Hijikata, reusing an old poster design, central calligraphy by writer Yukio Mishima.

1970   42.75in (107cm) high

$2,800-3,200   **SWA**

'Teinturerie Du Point Noir', designed by Leon Dupin, printed by Joseph-Charles, Paris.

1934   55in (137.5cm) high

$600-900   **SWA**

'For You from Britain', 1960s British advertising poster designed by Eileen Evans.

This poster promoted Britain's innovative modern design during the 1960s, from the 'Mini' to glass, fabric and metalware.

39in (99cm) high

$120-180   **ON**

A CLOSER LOOK AT AN EXHIBITION POSTER

The image shows Hamilton's iconic collage "Just What Is It that Makes Today's Home so Different, so Appealing?" which is considered to be the first true piece of Pop Art.

It shows 'new' domestic appliances of the 1950s such as a vacuum cleaner, tape player, and television, as well as canned foods and other references to the new popular and consumerist culture.

It was initially designed for the poster and catalog of the exhibition 'This Is Tomorrow' at the Whitechapel Gallery, London in 1956.

This poster was produced in the 1970s when Hamilton was internationally famous and enjoying many retrospectives.

'Just What Is It...?', designed by Richard Hamilton (b.1922).

'The London Group – Exhibition of Modern Art', designed by Edward McKnight Kauffer (1890-1954), printed by Dangerfield, London, using two colors.

1919   *29.75in (74cm) high*

$1,200-1,800   **SWA**

1976   *30in (75cm) high*

$800-1,200   **SWA**

'Buy American Art/Art Week', small silk screen poster designed by Joseph Binder (1898-1972), printed by New York City W.P.A. Project.

1940   *12in (30cm) high*

$800-1,200   **SWA**

'Moderne Kunst aus USA', designed by Karl Oscar Blasé (b.1925).

1955   *33in (82.5cm) high*

$220-280   **SWA**

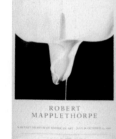

'Bauhaus Exhibition 1968', designed by Herbert Bayer.

1968   *25in (66cm) high*

$120-180   **CL**

'The Guggenheim Museum', designed by Malcolm Grear.

This was produced as a set of four posters.

c1970   *33in (82.5cm) high*

$400-600   **SWA**

'Rokuo Taninchi's Exhibition', by Tadanori Yokoo.

This was produced for the retrospective of painter and illustrator Rokuo Taninchi's work.

1981   *40.5in (101cm) high*

$600-900   **SWA**

'Robert Mapplethorpe', designed by Robert Mapplethorpe.

1988   *33in (91cm) high*

$80-120   **CL**

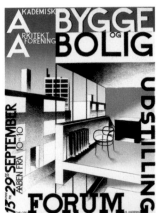

'Bygge og Bolig', Danish exhibition poster, artwork by I.B. Anderson.

Produced for an exhibition of Danish construction and housing, the impactful design is quintessentially of its period. It has strong Art Deco and Bauhaus elements in both the pictorial design and use of font.

1929   33in (80cm) high

$3,200-3,800   **CL**

'International Industries Fair Brussels 1939', anonymous designer, printed by Creations Brussels, tears and folds.

1939   39.75in (101cm) wide

$120-180   **ON**

'International Society for Contemporary Music XVII Festival Krakow Poland 1939', designed by Osiecki and printed for Polish State Railways by W. Glowczewski.

1939   39.75in (101cm) wide

$120-180   **ON**

'Leipzig Fair, 1951', German exhibition poster.

1951   33in (80cm) high

$120-180   **CL**

'Ulster Farm and Factory', Irish exhibition poster, produced to promote regional activities during the Festival of Britain in 1951.

Regional promotions can be rare as fewer examples were produced than for events in London, the center of the exhibition.

1951   29in (73.5cm) high

$100-150   **CL**

'Jens Olsens Verdens ur Københavns Rädhus', Danish poster designed by Aage Rasmussen.

Aage Rasmussen designed this poster to advertise Jens Olsen's (1872-1945) astronomical clock in Copenhagen's town hall. Designed by 1932, and with work beginning in 1943, the clock was completed and opened in December 1955. Rasmussen is a noted Danish poster artist who also worked for Danish railways and produced designs promoting Denmark as a tourist destination.

1957   39in (100cm) high

$80-120   **CL**

'Foire Internationale de Bordeaux', French exposition poster, artwork by Roger Varenne.

1959   39in (100cm) high

$200-250   **CL**

'Carnaval de Nice', 1950s French poster designed by Jean Luc.

    39in (100cm) high

$280-320   **CL**

COLLECTORS' NOTES

■ There are many shapes and sizes of poster available, ranging from small glossy stills to massive 24-sheet bill posters. The most popular, and usually the most valuable, are the US one sheet (27in by 41in) and the British quad (30in by 40in) sizes. The most collectible Polish posters are those in A1 format (23in by 33in).

■ As prices for American and British posters rise exponentially, collectors have developed ever greater interest in movie paper from eastern European countries such as the Czech Republic and Poland.

■ The Golden Age of Polish poster design was from c1955-65, following the alleviation of restrictive government policies regarding art and graphic representation.

■ The state monopoly on film distribution and marketing created a climate in which Polish artists and their personal interpretations of the iconography of film could flourish.

■ Polish posters now enjoy a reputation for innovative, striking and accomplished artwork. Collectors in this area are generally more interested in the artists than the film being depicted, unlike those who collect American or British posters. Masters such as Lucjan Jagodzinski are becoming hot property.

■ Although there is no generally recognized grading system for film posters, any form of folding, tearing or other damage will detract from value. Many valuable posters are backed with linen to better preserve them.

'Czas Apokalipsy' (Apocalypse Now), Polish film poster for the Francis Ford Coppala film, artwork by Waldemar Swierzy.

1981　　　　　39in (100cm) high

$300-400　　　　　**CL**

'Lala' (Big Baby Doll), Polish film poster for the Franco Giraldi Italian film, artwork by Andrzej Krajewski.

1971　　　　　33in (84cm) high

$100-150　　　　　**CL**

'Czarny Narcyz' (Black Narcissus), Polish poster for the Michael Powell film, artwork by Henryk Tomaszewski.

Henryk Tomaszewski was one of the three Polish artists and illustrators first commissioned by Film Polski (the State film distributor) to produce film posters in 1946. This rare, very early poster was re-issued in 1957.

1948　　　　　33in (84cm) high

$500-700　　　　　**CL**

'Kabaret' (Cabaret), Polish film poster for the Bob Fosse film, artwork by Wiktor Gorka.

This is one of the most well-known and desirable of all Polish film posters and is very rare. The frightening image of a 1930s Berlin singer superimposed into a Nazi swastika made up of stocking clad legs is not only highly dramatic but sums up the film perfectly.

1973　　　　　33in (80cm) high

$800-1,200　　　　　**CL**

'Bullitt', Polish film poster for the Peter Yates film, artwork by Marian Stachurski.

1971　　　　　33in (80cm) high

$300-400　　　　　**CL**

'Kabaret' (Cabaret), Polish film poster for the Bob Fosse film, artwork by Andrjez Pagowski.

1988　　　　　39in (100cm) high

$150-250　　　　　**CL**

'Kleopatra' (Cleopatra), Polish film poster for the Joseph L. Mankiewicz film, artwork by Eryk Lipinski.

This is a highly sought-after poster design by a popular artist, as well as being for a popular film.

1968   33in (84cm) high

$400-600   CL

'Zbrodnia w klubie tenisowym' (Crime in the Tennis Club), Polish poster for the Franco Rossetti Italian film, artwork by Andrzej Krajewski.

1973   33in (84cm) high

$180-220   CL

'E.T., the Extra-Terrestrial', 1980s Polish film poster designed by Jakob Erol.

39in (100cm) high

$200-300   CL

'Diabel Wcielony' (Devil in the Flesh), Polish poster for the Claude Autant-Lara French film, designed by Jozef Roszczak.

1956   33in (84cm) high

$350-450   CLG

'Skrzypek na dachu' (Fiddler on the Roof), Polish film poster designed by Wieslaw Walkuski.

39in (100cm) wide

$150-200   CL

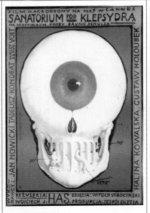

'Upior z Morrisville', (The Ghost from Morrisville), Polish poster for the Borivoj Zeman Czechoslovakian film, art work by Frantiszek Starowieyski.

1967   33in (84cm) high

$320-380   CL

'Sanatorium pod Klepsydra', (The Hour-Glass Sanatorium), Polish poster for the Wojciech J. Has Polish film, artwork by Frantisek Starowieyski.

1973   33in (84cm) high

$280-320   CL

'Ludzie i Wilki' (Humans and Wolves), Polish poster for the Giuseppe De Santis film, artwork by Roman Cieslewicz.

1959   33in (84cm) high

$300-500   CLG

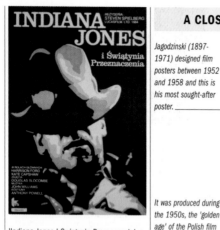

'Indiana Jones I Swiatynia Preznaczenia' (Indiana Jones and the Temple of Doom), Polish film poster for the Steven Spielberg film, artwork by Witold Dybowski.

1985   39in (100cm) high

$280-320   **CL**

A CLOSER LOOK AT A POLISH FILM POSTER

Jagodzinski (1897-1971) designed film posters between 1952 and 1958 and this is his most sought-after poster.

The style of the image and the colors are reminiscent of Toulouse Lautrec's poster designs – Lautrec designed posters when the real Moulin Rouge was at its peak.

It was produced during the 1950s, the 'golden age' of the Polish film poster.

Featuring an absinthe drinking man and a chorus girl, the design ties in with the 'Belle Epoque' Paris theme of the film.

'Moulin Rouge', 1950s Polish poster for the John Huston film, artwork by L. Jagodzinski.

Many experts still cite Jagodzinski's work as being under-valued.

1957   33in (84cm) high

$2,500-3,500   **CL**

'King Kong', Polish poster for the John Guillermin film, artwork by Jakob Erol.

1978   50in (127cm) high

$150-250   **CL**

'Miraz', (Mirage), Polish poster for the Edward Dmytryk film, artwork by Maciej Zbikowski.

1970   33in (84cm) high

$180-220   **CLG**

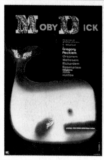

'Moby Dick', Polish poster for the John Huston film, artwork by Wiktor Gorka.

1961   26in (66cm) high

$200-300   **CL**

'Moj Wujaszek', (My Uncle), Polish poster for the Jacques Tati French film, artwork by Pierre Etaix.

1959   33in (84cm) high

$200-300   **CLG**

'SOS Titanic (A Night to Remember)', Polish film poster for the Roy Ward Baker film, artwork by Wojciech Zamecznik.

1961   33in (84cm) high

$350-450   **CL**

'Dawno Temu w Ameryce' (Once Upon a Time in America), Polish film poster for the Sergio Leone film, artwork by Jan Mlodozeniec.

1986   39in (100cm) high

$280-320   **CL**

'Powrot Jedi' (Star Wars Episode VI: Return of the Jedi), Polish film poster, artwork by Witold Dybowski.

1984   *39in (100cm) high*

$220-280   **CL**

'Nieznajomi z Pociagu' (Strangers on a Train), Polish poster for the Alfred Hitchcock film, artwork by Witold Janowski.

1963   *33in (84cm) high*

$280-320   **CL**

'Gwiezdne Wojny' (Star Wars Episode IV: A New Hope), Polish film poster for the George Lucas film, artwork by Jakob Erol.

1980   *39in (100cm) high*

$400-600   **CL**

'Milosc Szesnastolatkow' (Teenage Love), Polish poster for the Herrmann Zschoche film, artwork by Jerzy Czeronawski.

1975   *33in (84cm) high*

$120-180   **CL**

'Wehikul Czasu' (The Time Machine), Polish film poster, artwork by Marian Stachurski.

This is deemed a classic example of the Polish poster.

1965   *33in (84cm) high*

$300-500   **CL**

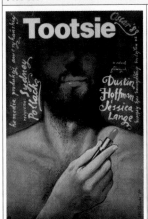

'Tootsie', Polish film poster for the Sydney Pollack film, artwork by Wieslaw Walkuski.

1984   *39in (100cm) high*

$220-280   **CL**

'Wall Street', Polish film poster for the Oliver Stone film, artwork by Andrzej Pagowski.

1988   *39in (100cm) high*

$250-350   **CL**

'Zet i Dwa Zera' (A Zed and Two Noughts), Polish film poster for the Peter Greenaway film, artwork by Wiktor Sadowski.

1994   *39in (100cm) high*

$280-320   **CL**

FIND OUT MORE...

www.cinemaposter.com

'Diamonds Are Forever', American for the foreign market, three-sheet poster, with blue ink Dutch stamp, folded, minor holes, dated.

1971   74.75in (190cm) high

$220-280   SAS

'The Spy Who Loved Me', US one-sheet poster, folded, dated.

1977   41in (104cm) high

$100-150   SAS

'The Man with the Golden Gun', American one-sheet poster for the eastern hemisphere, folded, faded, pinholes.

1974   41in (104cm) high

$180-220   SAS

'Blow-Up', 1960s Italian poster of the Michelangelo Antonioni film.

79in (200.5cm) high

$400-600   CL

'Moonraker', UK three-sheet poster, dated.

1979   75in (190cm) high

$120-180   SAS

'Live And Let Die', US one-sheet poster, for the Eastern hemisphere, dated.

1973   41in (104cm) high

$180-220   SAS

'Café De Paris', French film poster, artwork by René Peron, printed by Baudin, Paris. 1938

62.5in (156cm) high

$1,200-1,800   SWA

'Genesúng', East German film poster, artwork by John Heartfield (1891-1968).

c1956   32.5in (80cm) high

$500-700   SWA

'Tundra', American film poster, artwork by Robert Igot, printed by S.E.G. of Paris.

62.75in (159.5cm) high

$1,000-1,500   SWA

COLLECTORS' NOTES

- Original posters promoting concerts, 'be-ins' and other events from c1965 and into the 1970s are collected for their nostalgia value as well as their highly original and appealing artwork.

- The core value of a poster or flyer is determined by the artist, design, and quality of the paper and the printing process used. Silkscreen printing is more labor intensive than offset, and posters made this way are generally more valuable due to the shorter print runs.

- Posters designed by prolific or cult artists will attract a premium, although any work produced in very large quantities will usually have a lower value. Advertisements for gigs at renowned venues or featuring iconic bands are particularly sought-after.

A Family Dog 'Balloon' poster, FD35, for Daily Flash, Quicksilver Messenger Service and Country Joe & The Fish, at the Avalon Ballroom on November 18 and 19, 1966, artwork by Stanley Mouse and Alton Kelley, marked "San Francisco Poster Co".

21in (53.5cm) high

$220-280   **GAZE**

A Family Dog 'Earthquake' poster, FD21, for Bo Diddley and Big Brother & the Holding Company, on August 12 and 13 1966, by San Francisco Poster Co, artwork by Stanley Mouse.

$120-180   **GAZE**

'Sierra Club Wilderness Conference', psychedelic poster, by the San Francisco Poster Co., designed by Stanley Mouse and Alton Kelley.

1967   *20in (51cm) high*

$70-100   **GAZE**

A 1970s American psychedelic poster for 'Follies', designed by David Byrd.

38in (96.5cm) high

$120-180   **CL**

A 1960s American 'Are You Experienced' psychedelic poster.

This was also the title of Jimi Hendrix' first album, which catapulted him to fame.

35in (89cm) high

$120-180   **CL**

An American psychedelic poster, 'Gloves', designed by Peter Max.
1968   *36in (91cm) high*

$180-220   **CL**

An American psychedelic poster, 'From the Moon – Apollo 11', designed by Peter Max.
1969   *36in (91cm) high*

$120-180   **CL**

An American psychedelic poster, 'Visionaries at the East Hampton Gallery', designed by Peter Max.

This was the first exhibition of psychedelic art, and formed the basis of a book in 1968.

1967   *25in (66cm) high*

$80-120   **CL**

A 1970s Marvel Comics poster, 'Silver Surfer: At Last I'm Free'.

33in (84cm) high

$120-180 CL

A 1970s Marvel Comics poster, 'Thwoom!'.

33in (84cm) high

$120-180 CL

A 1970s Marvel Comics poster, 'Namor the Submariner'.

33in (84cm) high

$120-180 CL

A 1970s Marvel Comics poster, 'So Shall It Be – Odin & Hela'.

31in (78.5cm) high

$80-120 CL

An American neon psychedelic poster, 'Zeus', manufactured and distributed by Third Eye Inc. of New York.

1972 *33.5in (85cm) high*

$30-50 NOR

A 1970s American psychedelic poster, 'Acid Rider'.

$80-120 CL

A 1960s American marijuana related psychedelic poster, 'Crop Rotation Pays'.

This poster is based on Grant Wood's 1930 painting 'American Gothic', one of the most famous images in American art, which depicts the morally virtuous pastoral life in the American Midwest.

35in (89cm) high

$80-120 CL

A CLOSER LOOK AT A PSYCHEDELIC POSTER

This image is a combination of two of Robert Crumb's most famous creations – 'Mr Natural', the dubious guru, and the 'Keep on Truckin'' slogan.

This image lacks the cross-hatching characteristic of Crumb's own work, indicating that it is probably by another hand.

Crumb hit a low ebb in 1976 when a court ruling that 'Keep on Truckin'' was public property coincided with a large bill for unpaid tax on royalties earned.

The laid back ethos encapsulated in Crumb's original 'Keep on Truckin'' panels led to its enthusiastic adoption by the hippie movement.

An American neon poster, depicting 'Mr Natural', with velvet-like black areas, from an original design by Robert Crumb.

Long a counter-cultural hero, Robert Crumb has recently been embraced by the art establishment and his work has been exhibited at high profile galleries. Robert Hughes, art critic for 'Time' magazine, has famously called him the "Brueghel of the last half of the 20th century".

1971   35.5in (90cm) wide

$25-35   **NOR**

A 1970s Canadian psychedelic poster, 'Hair is Beautiful'.

33in (80cm) high

$120-180   **CL**

A 1960s American psychedelic poster, 'New San Francisco, Free City'.

33in (80cm) high

$80-120   **CL**

A 1970s Italian psychedelic poster, 'Cora Americano', designed by M. Lecourt.

33in (84cm) high

$120-180   **CL**

A 1970s American psychedelic poster, 'Psychedelic Cat', artwork by Joe Roberts Jr.

30in (76cm) high

$80-120   **CL**

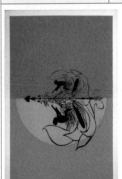

A 1960s American psychedelic poster, 'Psychedelic Surfers'.

40in (101.5cm) high

$180-220   **CL**

A 1960s American poster, 'Love', designed by Robert Indiana.

The use of short words in large colorful letters is typical of Pop artist Indiana's style. This, his most famous image, was created first for a Museum of Modern Art Christmas card in 1964, reused on a USPS stamp in 1973 and also for a sculpture in John F. Kennedy Plaza, Philadelphia.

29in (73.5cm) wide

$180-220   **CL**

John Hassall, 'Bluebeard by Arthur Collins & J. Hickory Wood, Drury Lane Pantomime', printed by Waterlow, small tears.

John Hassall was born in 1868 in Walmer, Kent. After failing to get accepted into the Army on two occasions, he studied art in Antwerp and at Academie Julien, Paris, in 1894, and went on to become a full-time illustrator. As well as producing posters for a number of clients, the most famous perhaps 'The Jolly Fisherman' for the G.N.E.R, he also illustrated children's books. Hassall died in 1948.

30in (76cm) wide

$180-220   **ON**

John Hassall, 'Pontings Xmas Show, Dover to Calais Tube, Change at High Street Kensington'.

30in (76cm) high

$400-500   **ON**

William H. Barribal, 'The Palace, Airs and Graces', printed by David Allen, small tears.

30in (76cm) high

$70-100   **ON**

John Hassall, 'Royal Naval & Military Tournament Olympia May to June', printed by Dobson Molle Ltd, tears and small losses to top margin.

40.25in (102cm) high

$80-120   **ON**

John Hassall, 'Two Little Vagabonds by George Sims & Arthur Shirley from the Royal Princess's Theatre', printed by David Allen.

30in (76cm) high

$100-150   **ON**

John Hassall, 'A Grand Concert will be held at the Albert Hall in aid of the Union Jack Club May 1910', printed by The Avenue Press, tears.

40.25in (102cm) high

$70-100   **ON**

John Hassall, '"Oo-er" Savage Club Ball at the Royal Albert Hall June 1919', printed by Haycock & Cadle Ltd, tears to margin.

30in (76cm) high

$100-150   **ON**

John Hassall, 'The Whole Town's Talking', printed by David Allen.

30in (76cm) high

$120-180   **ON**

'The Man Who Wasted Gas!', designed by H.M. Bateman, issued by the Ministry of Fuel and Power, printed for HMSO by J. Weiner, fold.

15in (38cm) high

$60-90   **ON**

'It does matter: The Country pays for it, Don't waste Here- the fuel you save at Home!', designed by Fougasse, issued by Ministry of Fuel & Power, printed for HMSO by Stafford & Co Ltd, folds.

15in (38cm) high

$50-70   **ON**

'Waste Paper Still Wanted', designed by Eileen Evans, published by Ministry of Supply, printed for HMSO by Hubners Ltd.

28.75in (73cm) high

$30-40   **ON**

'No Llenceu Els Diaris', Spanish Catalan language poster, designed by Miguel, printed by Rieusset, Barcelona.

c1938   *39.25in (98cm) wide*

$600-900   **SWA**

'National Relief Fund two ways of fighting...', designed by John Hassall, printed by David Allen.

30in (76cm) high

$70-100   **ON**

'Buy a Share in America', designed by John Atherton, printed by US Government Printing Office.

Encouraging the public to buy war bonds was a common way of raising money for the war effort on both sides of the Atlantic.

1941   *28in (70cm) high*

$800-1,200   **SWA**

'Post Office Savings Bank', British wartime savings poster designed by Frederic Henri Kay Henrion (1914-90), printed by J. Howitt, Nottingham.

36in (90cm) wide

$1,200-1,800   **SWA**

'Give it your Best!', American poster designed by Charles Coiner, printed by U.S. Government Printing Office.

Charles Coiner (1898-1989) is credited with bringing modern art to US advertising. This simple but striking poster promotes nationalistic support during wartime. In 1933, he also developed the blue eagle motif used by the National Recovery Administration.

1942   *28in (70cm) wide*

$500-700   **SWA**

'Never Was So Much Owed By So Many To So Few', published by HMSO, printed by Lowe & Brydone, folds and small tears.

Winston Churchill spoke this famous line after the decisive airborne Battle of Britain.

1940   *30in (76cm) high*

$400-600   **ON**

'The Freedom of the Seas from the Hun point of view', designed by David Wilson, printed by H. & C. Graham Ltd, folds.

15in (38cm) high

$220-280   **ON**

'VD May Ruin Your Career', 1940s-50s American poster.

22in (56cm) high

$150-250   **CL**

'For Victory, London's Transport No. 1 - 10,000,000 Passengers a Day', GPD 365/13/28.

19.25in (49cm) wide

$70-100   **ON**

'For Victory, The Fleet Air Arm: No. 3 - A "Seafire" fighter takes off'.

19.25in (49cm) wide

$150-200   **ON**

'A Cocoa Estate In Trinidad', RBD3, designed by Frank Newbould, issued by the Empire Marketing Board, printed by Johnson Riddle London, tears into image.

30in (76cm) wide

$80-120   **ON**

'The Market Gardens of the Tropics – Malayan Pineapples', RCB1, designed by Edgar Ainsworth, issued by the Empire Marketing Board, printed by Waterlow, London.

30in (76cm) wide

$180-220   **ON**

'Borneo Sago', RCB2, designed by Edgar Ainsworth, issued by The Empire Market Board, printed by Waterlow, London.

20in (51cm) high

$120-180   **ON**

'Outposts of Britain', designed by Edward McKnight Kauffer.

This series of four posters showed that the General Post Office could reach anywhere in Britain, even a remote Irish crofter's cottage.

1937   *25in (62.5cm) wide*

$700-1,000   **SWA**

'Outposts of Britain', designed by Edward McKnight Kauffer.

The use of broad areas of color and a stylized font is typical of much of Edward McKnight Kauffer's (1890-1954) work.

1937   *25in (62.5cm) wide*

$700-1,000   **SWA**

'United Nations / For All Children a Safe Tomorrow – IF You Do Your Part', American poster.

c1949   *28in (70cm) high*

$400-600   **SWA**

'United Nations / "We the Peoples of the United Nations"' American poster, designed by Ladislav Sutnar.

Sutnar (1897-1976) also designed a wall at N.B.C. in the Rockefeller Center in 1946.

c1949   *28in (70cm) high*

$300-500   **SWA**

'Das letzte Stück Brot', a German political poster, designed by John Heartfield.

Ernst Thälmann (1886-1944) was one of the founders of the German Communist Party, after whom songs were written and streets named in postwar East Germany. This pro-Communist poster, originally printed in 1932, explains that capitalism is stealing the last piece of bread from children.

c1970   *36.25in (90.5cm) high*

$700-1,000   **SWA**

'Tariff Reform Means Happier Dukes', political poster designed by Ernest Noble, published by the Liberal Publication Department.

1903-06   *19.75in (50cm) high*

$30-50   **PC**

'Cigarettes Cause Lung Cancer', designed by Reginald Mount, issued by Central Office of Information, printed by MMP Ltd.

1962-c1963   *30in (76cm) high*

$20-25   **ON**

'Smoking Pollutes...', 1970s American public health poster.

22in (59cm) high

$80-120   **CL**

'Oranges and Their Importance to Health', 1930s American public information poster.

22in (59cm) wide

$120-180   **CL**

'Ignorance = Fear, Silence = Death' 1980s American poster, designed by Keith Haring.

This is from a series of AIDS awareness posters designed by Haring and promoted by the 'ACT UP' group in the late 1980s. The pink triangle was used as a gay 'motif' during the 1970s and 80s – it was previously used by the Nazis to identify gay men, like the Star of David for the Jewish.

43in (109cm) wide

$220-280   **CL**

'Save the Products of the Land, Eat More Fish', 1910s American political poster, artwork by Charles L. Bull.

28in (71cm) high

$600-900   **CL**

'Wait Till It Stops' poster', designed by Zero-Hans Schleger, printed by Loxley.

A pioneer of Modernism, Schleger (1898-1976) uses strong lines and perspective, an eye reflecting a stop sign and different typefaces, (a hallmark of his work) to create a striking image warning of the dangers of getting on or off a tram or bus if still moving.

c1946   *29.75in (74cm) high*

$700-1,000   **SWA**

'Brands Hatch', 1960s English motor racing poster, designed and printed by Briscall Studios, Ashford, Kent, England.

30in (76cm) high

$120-180 CL

'Brands Hatch 1000Kms, September 18', full-color English motor racing poster.

1983 *30in (76cm) high*

$30-50 SAS

'Motor Racing Goodwood', for formula 3 cars, historic and vintage racing by the British Automobile Racing Club.

1966 *30in (76cm) high*

$80-120 SAS

'Nürburgring, 1000-km-Rennen', full-color German motor racing poster, dated 28 May 1967.

1967 *33in (84cm) high*

$80-120 SAS

'The R.A.C. British Grand Prix Silverstone', full-color English motor racing poster, dated 10 July 1965.

When building a collection of motor racing posters, look for popular drivers, marques or teams at well-known tracks. An important or infamous race can also add value. Look for a visual sense of speed or for dramatic images of the cars themselves.

1965 *30in (76cm) high*

$220-280 SAS

'Silverstone, Daily Express 23rd International Trophy Meeting', full-color English motor racing poster.

1971 *30in (76cm) high*

$70-100 SAS

'Monaco 25/26 Mai 1968', French full-color motor racing poster, illustration by Michael Turner, Edition J. Ramel-Nice.

23.5in (60cm) wide

$120-180 SAS

'24 Heures du Mans 13-14 Juin 1981', French motor racing poster, slight water damage.

1981 *21in (53.5cm) wide*

$120-180 AGI

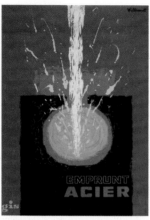

'Emprunt Acier' poster, designed by Bernard Villemot, printed by R.L. Duphy, Paris.

This poster is typical of Villemot's (1911-89) work, being stylized and colorful with a plain background and painterly effect. Villemot also designed posters for high-end shoe shop Bally.

1964   31.5in (79cm) high

$300-500   **SWA**

'(God's Love We Deliver)', 1990s American Pop Art poster designed by Keith Haring.

34in (85cm) high

$80-120   **CL**

'Enjoy Cocaine', 1970s American poster.

This design was developed in late 1970 by Gemini Rising Inc. and is said to have sold over 100,000 copies in two years. Coca-Cola took the company to court around 1972, claiming it damaged their brand. An injunction was granted by the court who found it was likely to tarnish Coca-Cola's 'wholesome' reputation and costly global advertising campaigns. Seen by many as parodying an American national icon, it also plays on the untrue rumor that Coca-Cola contains cocaine, which was said to be the reason why it was marketed as a 'pick-me-up' since its inception in 1886.

33in (80cm) wide

$180-220   **CL**

'"Nonsense! There are no such things as--UHH!"', poster by an unknown designer.

1968   41in (102.5cm) high

$1,000-1,500   **SWA**

'Pays-Bas', Dutch poster designed by Libra Studio, printed by Kühn en Zoon, Rotterdam.

From a group of six posters, each promoting a different aspect of the Dutch economy, the Art Deco photo-montage style is highly desirable. Little is known about the design studio, and the series was aimed at use abroad.

1948   43in (107.5cm) high

$1,000-1,500   **SWA**

COLLECTORS' NOTES

- Pot-lids form one of the earliest types of visually appealing packaging. Products include bear's grease (a hair product), toothpaste, and meat or fish paste. Blue and white printed pot-lids were introduced in the 1820s, with colored examples appearing in the mid-1840s. Makers include F.R. Pratt, T.J. & J. Mayer and Brown-Westhead & Moore.

- It is not possible to date pot-lids precisely as so many were produced over large periods of time, with no records remaining. Events depicted and certain makers' marks can help to date some pot-lids to within a date range, as can the form. Over 350 different images are known, many taken from watercolors by Jesse Austin.

- Earlier lids, from before 1860, are usually flat and light in weight, with fine quality prints and often have a screw thread. Lids from 1860 to 1875 are heavier and have a convex top. Handle as many as possible to gain experience of weights and appearances.

- Look for lids with good, strong colors, as faded, weak examples are worth considerably less. Chips to the flange and rim do not affect value seriously. Chips to the image, or restoration, can lower values by up to 50-75 percent, even if well restored. Complex or colored borders usually add value. Non-circular lids usually date from after the late 1870s.

- Some collectors choose to collect by type. Two of the most popular are lids for bear's grease, or those depicting Pegwell Bay. Beware of reproductions. Run your finger over a lid and if you can feel the transfer, it is likely to be a later reproduction. Numbers given here relate to lid reference numbers in Mortimer's pot-lid reference book, listed at the end of this section.

A 'Bear's Grease Manufacturer' pot-lid, no. 3, no lettering, by the Mayer factory.

Although restored, this is an extremely rare lid, with less than ten thought to exist. Variants with advertising wording can be worth around 20 percent more.

3.25in (8cm) diam

$5,000-7,000   SAS

An 'Alas! Poor Bruin' pot-lid, no. 1, with lantern, double line and dot border.

3.5in (8.5cm) diam

$220-280   SAS

A 'Bear Hunting' pot-lid, no. 4, with advertising for Ross & Sons Bear Grease at 119 & 120 Bishopsgate, blue-checkered border, hairline crack.

3.5in (9cm) diam

$700-1,000   SAS

A 'Shooting Bears' pot-lid, no. 13, no lettering.

3.25in (8cm) diam

$180-220   SAS

A 'The Ins' pot-lid, no. 15, fancy lettering, flange restored.

3.5in (8.5cm) diam

$600-900   SAS

A 'The Outs' pot-lid, no. 16, with fancy border, restored.

The fancy border makes this more valuable. Without the border, the value is around 20 percent less. 'The Ins' is the partner lid and both are early, dating from before the 1860s.

3.5in (9cm) diam

$1,200-1,800   SAS

A 'Polar Bears' pot-lid, no. 18, lacks moon, gold line.

Produced in 1846, this is the earliest known colored pot-lid pattern. The version with a moon in the sky is more valuable.

3.25in (8cm) diam

$500-700   SAS

A CLOSER LOOK AT A POT-LID

The pot-lid shows singer Jenny Lind, the 'Swedish Songbird', who came to England in 1847.

This version with J. Grossmith advertising is extremely rare. Under ten examples are thought to exist.

'Jenny Lind' was produced in two versions, one with just the floral border around the figure, of which around 25 examples are known.

A 'Jenny Lind' pot-lid, no. 180, advertising J. Grossmith & Co. 85 Newgate St. London, stained.

The manufacturer of this lid is not known.

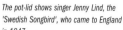

Although stained, the great rarity and bright colors on this lid make it desirable and valuable.

3.5in (9cm) diam

$3,000-4,000   **SAS**

A Pratt 'Queen Victoria and Prince Consort' pot-lid, no. 167, oak leaves and acorn border.

5.5in (14cm) diam

$300-500   **SAS**

A Staffordshire 'Wellington with Cocked Hat' no. 183 pot-lid, with lettering pertaining to his birth and death, restored.

5in (13.5cm) diam

$700-1,000   **SAS**

A large 'Wellington with Clasped Hands' no. 184 pot-lid, with border.

The colors on this large example are particularly rich and the color variation on the border is comparatively unusual.

4.75in (12cm) diam

$1,200-1,800   **SAS**

A Pratt 'The Blue Boy' pot-lid, no. 196.

This is taken from Gainsborough's famous painting. Look for a strong blue, rather than a grayish blue. The version with the 'seaweed' border and flange is the most valuable, and can fetch up to $2,000.

4.75in (12cm) diam

$80-120   **SAS**

A 'Little Red-Riding Hood' pot-lid, no. 200.

3in (7.5cm) diam

$120-180   **SAS**

A 'Windsor Castle or Prince Albert (Hare Coursing)' pot-lid, no. 176, produced by the Mayer factory, minor hairline crack.

4.25in (10.5cm) diam

$220-280 SAS

An 'Albert Memorial' pot-lid, no. 190.

A version with a carriage is also known, but is worth slightly less.

4in (10cm) diam

$120-180 SAS

A 'St. Paul's Cathedral' pot-lid, no. 238, probably by Brown-Westhead, Moore & Co.

4.25in (10.5cm) diam

$220-280 SAS

A 'Belle Vue Tavern' pot-lid, no. 29, flat lid, dark cliffs, no name on the inn.

There are a number of complex variations to this lid, including a domed or flat shape, small or large lettering, a name on the inn, the color of the cliffs, and the presence of a small pile of boulders on the beach.

3.5in (9cm) diam

$1,800-2,200 SAS

A Pratt 'Pegwell Bay, Established 1760' pot-lid, no. 32, with earlier sandy road and pathway design.

4in (10cm) diam

$70-100 SAS

A 'Walmer Castle' pot-lid, no. 45, with two horsemen, probably made by Cauldon.

4.25in (10.5cm)

$70-100 SAS

A 'Royal Harbour, Ramsgate' pot-lid, no. 50, probably by the Cauldon factory.

4in (10cm) diam

$120-180 SAS

A Pratt 'Hauling in the Trawl' pot-lid, no. 60.

Pratt produced this for Cross & Blackwell over many years, making it comparatively common. The pattern was copied from a drawing in the London Illustrated News, 6th March, 1847.

4.25in (11cm) diam

$80-120 SAS

A Pratt 'Letter from The Diggings' pot-lid, no. 131, with fancy border.

Look out for the ultra-rare versions of this lid with 'Valentine's Day' or a retailer's advertising wording.

5in (13cm) diam

$80-120   SAS

A Mayer 'The Boar Hunt' pot-lid, no. 288.

This was reissued up to the 1960s by Kirkhams. Early examples, such as this one, are rarer.

4.25in (10.5cm) diam

$700-1,000   SAS

A 'The Shepherdess' pot-lid, no. 279, produced by Bates, Brown-Westhead & Moore at the Cauldon factory.

4in (10cm) diam

$60-90   SAS

A Pratt 'Master of the Hounds' pot-lid, no. 295.

4.25in (10.5cm) d

$120-180   SAS

A 'Fair Sportswoman' pot-lid, no. 297, produced by Bates, Brown-Westhead & Moore at the Cauldon factory.

4.25in (10.5cm) d

$70-100   SAS

A Mayer or Pratt 'A Fix' pot-lid, no. 302, no border.

4.25in (10.5cm) diam

$280-320   SAS

A Pratt 'The Times' pot-lid, no. 307.

4.25in (10.5cm) diam

$80-120   SAS

A Pratt 'The Queen God Bless Her' pot-lid, no. 319, fancy border.

5in (12.5cm) diam

$70-100   SAS

A CLOSER LOOK AT A PRATT POT-LID

More common versions contain a verse of poetry in the design.

The extra white surround shows a late production. Earlier examples simply have a black line.

A Pratt 'Our Home' pot-lid, no. 329, domed lid, gold-painted border.

A registration mark identifies the earliest date of production as being March, 1852. This lid was produced for Thomas Jackson, a chemist in Manchester.

The reverse is stamped in red for "F.R. Pratt, Potters to HRH Prince Albert". This pot-lid, originally from the Pratt factory archives, is one of only two known examples, the other is not stamped.

This has a gold line and no title, also making it a rare variation.

4.25in (10.5cm) diam

$7,000-10,000   **SAS**

A Pratt 'The Dentist' pot-lid, no. 331.

4.25in (10.5cm) diam

$220-280   **SAS**

A 'Xmas Eve' pot-lid, no. 323, double-lined border in black.

3.75in (9.5cm) diam

$600-900   **SAS**

A 'May Day Dancers and the Swan Inn' pot-lid, no. 324, probably designed by Jesse Austin for Bates, Brown-Westhead & Moore around 1860.

4.25in (10.5cm) diam

$120-180   **SAS**

A 'Children of Flora' pot-lid, no. 326, probably by the Cauldon factory.

4.75in (12cm) diam

$120-180   **SAS**

A Pratt 'The Village Wakes' pot-lid, no. 321, based on a Jesse Austin watercolor, with fancy border and bullnose rim.

Look out for the rare variation without two children, the dog and monkey, as this can fetch over 50 percent more than this version.

4in (10cm) diam

$500-700   **SAS**

A Pratt 'The Poultry Woman' pot-lid, no. 338.

The presence of a wide gold band can fetch up to eight times the value of this example.

4.25in (10.5cm) diam

$220-280   **SAS**

FIND OUT MORE...

'Pot-Lids and Other Coloured Printed Staffordshire Wares', by K.V. Mortimer, published by Antique Collectors' Club, 2003.

COLLECTORS' NOTES

■ Powder compacts first became popular in the 1920s when it became acceptable for women to apply make-up in public. Earlier examples do exist, but they were not intended for use outside of the house.

■ Made to be seen, they are often highly decorative and reflect the fashions of the time. Early examples can be made of early plastics like Bakelite and often feature long tassels. Guilloché enameled pieces with strong geometric Art Deco decoration are sought-after.

■ WWII halted the production of face powders and compacts, although late 1930s examples with a military theme were made for members of the armed forces to send back to their sweethearts. Postwar production saw compacts become larger, with novelties such as musical movements added. Compacts also became thicker as solid face powder replaced the loose variety.

■ In the 1960s powder compacts began to loose their appeal as fashions changed and were more or less obsolete by the 1980s.

■ Some cosmetic companies such as Estee Lauder and Yves St Laurent continue to make compacts as limited editions, often designed to hold solid perfume rather than powder.

■ Elgin in the US and Stratton & Kigu in England were the most prolific producers and collectors often concentrate on their compacts. Ideally, compacts should retain their puffs and sifters, although they are not essential. Examples with cracked mirrors should be avoided, as they are difficult to replace.

■ Any old powder left in the compact should be carefully removed and disposed of as it can cause damage.

A 1920s yellow guilloché enameled silver compact, possibly French, with a silhouette of a lady under a tree, London silver import mark.

1923-24   *1.75in (4.5cm) diam*

$600-800   **MGT**

A rare 1920s/30s Art Deco powder compact, with grinder and powder refill underneath, unmarked.

The grater underneath the compact was used to 'shave' powder from the cake.

2.25in (5.5cm) diam

$220-300   **MGT**

A Shildkraut cloisonné enamel powder compact, with floral top.

c1947   *3in (7cm) diam*

$40-60   **SH**

A late 1950s Stratton 'Swan' Rondette shape powder compact, from the Water Birds series.

3.75in (9.5cm) diam

$35-55   **MGT**

An early Stratton non-spill powder compact, with Art Deco decoration in red enamel and chrome.

c1934   *3.75in (9.5cm) diam*

$100-150   **MGT**

An Elizabeth II coronation souvenir compact, by Le Rage.

1953   *3.5in (9cm) diam*

$80-120   **MGT**

A Kigu 'Celestial' Flying Saucer shape powder compact.

This model was produced with and without a musical movement and also came in green and red.

c1951   *2.5in (6.5cm) diam*

$280-320   **MGT**

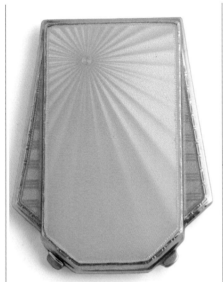

A blue guilloché enameled silver powder compact, with naval emblem, Birmingham hallmarks and makers mark "JWB".

1937 3in (7.5cm) wide

$150-200 **SH**

A 1960s Kigu Cherie shape powder compact, with enameled butterfly top.

3in (7.5cm) long

$60-90 **MGT**

An early 1990s Yves St Laurent heavy gilt heart-shaped compact, embellished with green diamanté stones.

2.5in (6.5cm) wide

$100-150 **MGT**

An Art Deco guilloché enamel and silver compact, London hallmarks.

1936-37 3.5in (9cm) long

$350-450 **MGT**

A 1920s white metal 'tango' powder compact, with guilloché enamel cartouche and blush compartment.

A 'tango' compact comes with a wrist chain attached.

2in (5cm) diam

$100-150 **SH**

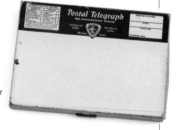

A 1930s American enamel-on-copper butterfly powder compact.

3in (7.5cm) wide

$50-70 **SH**

A 1930/40s DuBarry black enamel powder compact, with applied marcasite basket.

2.5in (6.5cm) wide

$60-80 **SH**

A 1920s Andre Duval 'postal telegraph' enameled powder compact.

The value of this compact would be higher but for a slight chip to the enamel.

3in (7.5cm) wide

$100-150 **SH**

POWDER COMPACTS

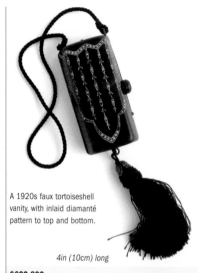

A 1920s faux tortoiseshell vanity, with inlaid diamanté pattern to top and bottom.

4in (10cm) long

$600-800 MGT

An American Platé Trioette Bakelite powder compact, with lipstick in handle.

This was made in seven different colors – ivory, ebony, cornelian, tortoise, briar rose, Nile green, and Rueben blue. The ivory and ebony are the most commonly found and the rose, green and blue are harder to find and more desirable.

c1945

$150-200 SH

A 1920s Houpette Pli swansdown wired puff, with powder in handle, original box and papers.

Box 4in (10cm) high

$80-120 SH

A 1920s/30s Bakelite powder compact, with horse racing scene, unmarked.

3in (7.5cm) diam

$60-90 MGT

A 1940s Coty 'Powder Puffs' plastic powder compact, designed by Lalique.

2.5in (6.5cm) diam

$40-60 MGT

A 1950s Kigu 'Bouquet' shape Lucite powder compact, with movable handle.

2.25in (5.5cm) diam

$100-150 MGT

A promotional Melody record powder compact, marked "Creation JD" on label.

3.5in (9cm) diam

$280-320 MGT

A French Bourjois 'Evening in Paris' blue plastic compact, with embossed Parisian scenes on a chrome lid.

c1938 *2.75in (7cm) wide*

$100-150 MGT

A CLOSER LOOK AT A SCHUCO COMPACT

German toy manufacturer Schuco are well known for their teddy bears and soft toys and in particular for their miniature bears.

This duck compact is a rare variation of the bear compacts and is very desirable.

These teddy bears also concealed perfume bottles, powder compacts and lipsticks or manicure sets. They are all sought-after.

This compact was available in a number of different colorways, which are all of a similar value.

A rare 1920s Schuco duck compact, covered in jade velvet with orange felt feet and beak.

3.5in (9cm) high

$350-550   **MGT**

A 1930s Gwenda painted canvas powder compact, decorated with a kingfisher and with original puff and sifter.

3.25in (8cm) diam

$60-90   **SH**

A 1930s Gwenda tartan fabric-covered hexagonal compact, embroidered souvenir greeting, tartan pad.

2.25in (5.5cm)

$60-90   **MGT**

A 1950s zippered petit point on silk powder compact, probably German.

3in (7.5cm) wide

$40-60   **SH**

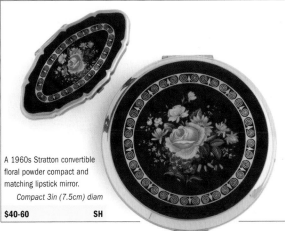

A 1960s Stratton convertible floral powder compact and matching lipstick mirror.

Compact 3in (7.5cm) diam

$40-60   **SH**

A fine petite point compact, depicting a courting couple with musician, black cloth base, no maker's mark.

3.25in (8.5cm) diam

$70-100   **MGT**

A 1940s Coty Air 'Paris' spun face powder box, sealed.

Powder boxes contain the loose powder used to refill a compact and are usually made from lithographed card. They were often made to match the company's own powder compacts such as this example. Examples should ideally be full and unopened.

3.25in (8.5cm) diam

$30-40   **SH**

A 1920s Herbert Roystone 'Poudre L'Ame' powder box, sealed.

This American company offered a $1,000 reward if you could find a better face powder.

2.75in (7cm) diam

$100-150   **SH**

A 1930s Farel Destin USA Strange Music powder box, open.

2.5in (6.5cm) diam

$30-50   **SH**

A 1920s-30s French Houbigant powder box, sealed, with original card outer box.

3in (7.5cm) diam

$40-60   **SH**

A 1930s Luxor sample complexion powder box.

2in (5cm) wide

$20-30   **SH**

A 1930s French Mury, Paris 'Le Narcisse Bleu' powder box.

2.75in (7cm) diam

$50-70   **SH**

A 1930s Princess Pat souvenir trial-size powder tin box.

1.75in (4.5cm) diam

$20-30   **SH**

A 1940s/50s Richard Hudnut 'Three Flowers' face powder, opened, with puff.

3.25in (8.5cm) diam

$40-60   **SH**

A 1920s Pompeian Beauty powder trial tin, with original puff.

1.5in (4cm) diam

$20-30   **SH**

FIND OUT MORE...

Collector's Encyclopedia of Compacts, Carryalls and Face Powder Boxes Vols. I & II, by Laura Mueller, published by Collector Books, 1993 & 1997.

Vintage and Vogue Ladies' Compacts, by Roselyn Gerson, published by Collector Books, 2001.

British Compact Collectors' Club, PO Box 131, Woking, Surrey, GU24 9YR, UK

Compact Collectors, P.O. Box 40, Lynbrook, NY 11563

COLLECTORS' NOTES

■ Look for radios from the 1930s-50s, the golden age of the radio. It is the case that counts the most with shape and color being key factors. Bright colors, produced in cast phenolic plastic known as Catalin, are usually the most desirable. Also look for hallmarks of the Art Deco or 1940s streamlined style. Makers' names also add interest, with FADA, Emerson, Motorola, and EKCO among those being sought-after.

■ Examine all areas of a radio with your hands and eyes for damage such as chips and cracks, warping or burning caused by heat from valves. Original grille cloths and backs add desirability and missing or replaced knobs or grille parts reduce value. Radios can be restored to working order by qualified restorers but never plug a vintage radio into the mains without seeking advice from an electrician first. Also consider more modern transistor radios, as rare models or unusually designed examples can fetch high sums.

An International Radio Corp Kadette Jewel red Catalin radio, with clear Lucite fretwork style grille.

1934   *8in (20cm) wide*

$600-900   **CAT**

A Motorola Model 52 'Aero-Vane' alabaster Catalin radio, with tortoiseshell colored Catalin vertical grille and knobs.

1939   *9.5in (24cm) wide*

$2,800-3,200   **CAT**

A Canadian Addison mottled red Catalin Model 5F radio, with yellow grille and knobs.

1940   *12in (30cm) wide*

$800-1,200   **CAT**

An Emerson Model EP-375 indigo blue Catalin radio, with cream Catalin grille, knobs and handle.

1941   *9.5in (24.5cm) wide*

$2,500-3,500   **CAT**

A FADA 700 'Cloud' alabaster Catalin radio, with mottled red knobs and handle.

The 'Cloud' was available in at least five colors. The 'alabaster' here has discolored to yellow over the years. With much effort, this can be polished away.

1946   *10.5in (27cm) wide*

$800-1,200   **CAT**

A very rare General Television Model 591 turquoise green and cream Catalin radio.

Only General Television and Motorola made radios in this color, which is extremely rare.

1940   *8.75in (22.5cm) wide*

$6,000-9,000   **CAT**

A Philco Model 49-501 brown Bakelite Transitone radio.

Known as the 'Boomerang' this unforgettable radio has become an icon of Pop culture. Its futuristic and modern style typifies postwar spirit.

1949   *11.5in (29cm) wide*

$500-700   **CAT**

A Crosley Model 11-103 U 'Dynamic' bulls-eye style red tabletop radio, with sprayed-on color.

1951   *10.25in (26cm) wide*

$250-350   **CAT**

A Philips 634 A four circuit receiver radio, with five valves.

1933

$500-700 ATK

An Emerson Model 744B black bakelite and white plastic radio.

1954 *11.5in (29.5cm) wide*

$500-700 CAT

A Daniel Weil transistor radio in clear PVC bag, printed "176".

Since designing this 'pop' style radio, Weil has worked for Alessi and Esprit amongst others.

1981 *10.75in (27.5cm) high*

$180-220 WW

A CLOSER LOOK AT A SPARTON RADIO

Sparton made the most famous mirrored radios of the Art Deco period – during this time blue and other mirrored items were the height of fashion.

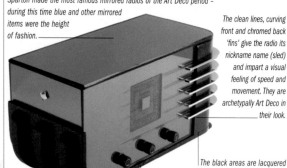

The clean lines, curving front and chromed back 'fins' give the radio its nickname name (sled) and impart a visual feeling of speed and movement. They are archetypally Art Deco in their look.

The black areas are lacquered using a special mixture that gives a distinctive crystalline appearance – look closely as if this is not present, the radio has been refinished.

This was designed, or influenced by, renowned industrial designer Walter Dorwin-Teague who designed the circular blue mirrored 'Bluebird' and ultra-rare 'Nocturne' for Sparton in 1935.

A Sparton Model 557 'Sled' radio, lacking back.

Sparton was the trade name used for the Sparks-Withington Company of Jackson, Michigan.

1936 *17in (43cm) wide*

$1,200-1,800 EG

A Decca model TPW70 radio, the circular burgundy and cream casing with integral speaker and tuning dial.

9.75in (25cm) diam

$120-180 ROS

A scarce Sony ICF-SW1S world-band receiver radio, in complete and working condition.

c1987

$180-220 ATK

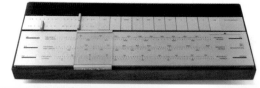

A Bang & Olufsen Beomaster 1900 programing section, with Bevoy S45 speakers and Beomaster 1200 stereo.

The Beomaster 1200 set, introduced in 1969, was designed by Industrial designer Jacob Jensen (b.1926). It set the trend for Bang & Olufsen's designs for years to come.

c1977 *Stereo 20in (51cm) high*

$120-180 GAZE

COLLECTORS' NOTES

- Music fans are always eager to acquire items with a connection to their idols. The Beatles, Elvis Presley, and The Rolling Stones remain the most avidly collected artists in the rock and pop pantheon. It remains to be seen whether more recent acts such as Radiohead and Coldplay will enjoy the same longevity.

- Signatures invariably increase the value of an album or concert ticket, but be aware that facsimile signatures and those done by assistants add little if any additional value.

- Most records fetch low values as so many were made. Rare, often foreign, pressings, early versions and sleeve or label variations can however fetch high sums.

- Items owned, used and, ideally, played by big stars have the most cachet. Instruments, clothing, and original lyric sheets can be worth a great deal of money if properly authenticated and recognizable.

- Some of the highest prices are paid for items relating to icons who died young and at the height of their careers, such as Jimi Hendrix, Janis Joplin, and Jim Morrison. The rock mythology that surrounds these figures acts as a powerful draw for many enthusiasts.

- Condition is very important – toys and games should be complete with original packaging and ephemera should be free from creases and tears as far as possible. Conversely, a guitar famously smashed on stage by The Who's Pete Townshend would be worth far more than an intact one he had used in private.

The Beatles, 'The Beatles featuring Tony Sheridan', stereo 8-track, CN8 2007, released by Contour Records, mounted with a picture of The Beatles including Pete Best.

c1962   14in (35.5cm) high

$30-50   GAZE

The Beatles, 'Please Please Me', mono LP, PMC 1202, released by Parlophone, with black and gold label.

1963

$120-180   GAZE

A CLOSER LOOK AT A SET OF BEATLES' AUTOGRAPHS

'Twist & Shout' was The Beatles' first EP, released in the UK on July 12th, 1963.

Beatles' signatures are among the most faked on the market, so look for a certificate of authenticity or have them approved by a recognized expert.

The historic place of this EP in The Beatles discography further enhances the value of this item.

One item with all four members' signatures is more valuable than four individually signed items.

The Beatles, 'Twist and Shout', mono EP, GEP 8882, released by Parlophone, signed on the reverse by all four members of the band.

1963

$1,200-1,800   GAZE

The Beatles, 'Twist and Shout', German EP, 0 41560, released by Odeon, with green label.

c1963

$12-18   GAZE

The Beatles, 'With the Beatles', LP sleeve, the reverse with four signatures reading the Beatles' names, mounted and framed.

1963   25.25in (64m) high

$220-280   GAZE

The Beatles, 'A Hard Day's Night', stereo LP factory sample, PCS 3058, released by Parlophone, mounted with a ticket from the group's first American concert.

c1964

$80-120   GAZE

The Beatles, 'Please Mister Postman/
Money', Japanese single, EAR 20245,
released by EMI.
1964

$25-35 GAZE

The Beatles, 'The Beatles' Second Album'
American LP, ST 2080, released by Capitol
Records.
1964

$50-80 GAZE

The Beatles, 'Help!', American film
soundtrack LP, SMAS 2386, released by
Capitol Records.
1965

$50-70 GAZE

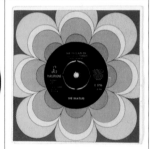

The Beatles, 'The Beatles '65', American LP,
ST-2228, released by Capitol Records.

1964

$25-35 GAZE

The Beatles, 'Yesterday', rare English first
issue picture sleeve mono EP, GEP 8948,
released by Parlophone.
c1966

$50-70 GAZE

The Beatles, 'The Ballad of John and Yoko', stock
record, R5786, on black Parlophone label,
possibly Swedish, with flower design sleeve.
c1969

$30-50 GAZE

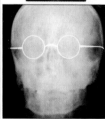

Plastic Ono Band, 'Cold Turkey',
rare picture sleeve issue, Apple
1813, released by Apple
Records.

c1969

$20-25 GAZE

John Lennon & The Plastic Ono Band, 'Unfinished Music No.2:
Life With the Lions', EAS-80701, released by Zapple, with insert.

c1969

$80-120 GAZE

The Beatles, 'The Beatles
Broadcasts', very rare bootleg
picture disc LP, LK4450,
released by Circuit Records,
with die-cut cover.
1982

$70-100 GAZE

The Beatles, 'So Much Younger Then: Beatles BBC Sessions', picture disc, DC 7577-5, released by Democratic Records, from a limited edition set of five picture discs.

1983

$20-30   **GAZE**

A CLOSER LOOK AT A SIGNED JOHN LENNON BOOK

A good condition first edition copy of this book would be worth about 50 percent less if unsigned.

Being a first edition copy also makes this _____ more desirable.

This is one of three books written by Lennon, the other two were 'A Spaniard in the Works' and 'Skywriting by Word of Mouth'.

_____ The provenance from the original owner adds interest.

John Lennon, "In His Own Write", first edition, published by Jonathan Cape, signed by the author. The original owner got this book signed at the Beatles concert, Ipswich Gaumont, 31st October 1964.

1964

$500-700   **GAZE**

An early 1960s Beatles poster, featuring Maureen Cleave interviewing The Beatles for the Evening Standard.

30in (76cm) high

$280-320   **SWO**

A 'The Beatles at Carnegie Hall' booklet, by Ralph Cosham and United Press International, printed by Hamilton Co. Ltd.

1964   *9.75in (25cm) high*

$20-25   **GAZE**

A set of four Beatles color printed publicity photographs, with facsimile signatures.

10.25in (26cm) high

$25-35   **GAZE**

A magazine page with a portrait of John Lennon, with printed signature and mounted with a signed autograph book page, framed and glazed.

c1966

$180-220   **GAZE**

An Apple Corp original production sketch from 'The Yellow Submarine', featuring Fred, mounted with a factory sample film sound track stereo LP and cover.

1968   *42.25in (105.5cm) wide*

$400-600   **GAZE**

A 'The Beatles Magnetic Hair' carded game, by Merit, marked "©1964".

10.5in (26cm) high

$25-35   GAZE

A 1960s Beatles rug, in yellow, oranges, and black, showing the four faces of the group.

34.5in (87.5cm) wide

$300-500   GAZE

A 1960s 'Paul McCartney' rubber doll, by Rosebud of England, with punched nylon hair.

7.25in (18.5cm) high

$50-80   GAZE

A set of four 1960s candy dishes, with gilt scalloped edges, each depicting one of The Beatles.

A framed proof etching by Pietro Psaier, titled 'The Fisherking, Rat Race John Lennon'.

20.5in (52cm) wide

Elvis Presley, 'Rock 'N' Roll No.2', LP, CLP1105, released by HMV.

The poor condition of this album sleeve reduces its value. In excellent condition it could be worth around $800.

1957

$280-320   GAZE $280-320   GAZE $180-220   GAZE

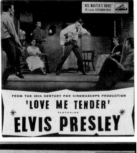

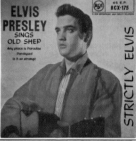

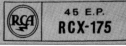

Elvis Presley, 'Love Me Tender', soundtrack EP, HMV 7EG8199, released by HMV.

1957

$180-220   GAZE

Elvis Presley, 'All Shook Up', 45rpm single with purple and silver label and solid centre, HMV POP 359, released by HMV.

Look for the version with the removable center, it can be worth over $200.

$25-35   GAZE

Elvis Presley, 'Strictly Elvis', EP, RCX 175, released by RCA.

1959

$25-35   GAZE

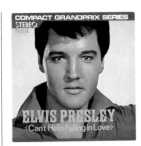

Elvis Presley 'Can't Help Falling In Love', Japanese 45 EP from the Compact Grandprix Series, with gatefold sleeve and orange label, RCA SRA-91, released by RCA.

1961

$40-60   GAZE

Elvis Presley, 'Tickle Me Vol. 2', mono soundtrack EP, RCX 7174, released by RCA.

1965

$25-35   GAZE

Elvis Presley, 'Greatest Hits', seven-disc box set, GELV-6A, released by Reader's Digest.

1978

$8-12   GAZE

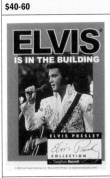

An 'Elvis Is In The Building' framed poster, from Vaughn-Bassett, produced to advertise a range of Elvis-inspired furniture, framed.

2002   *35in (88cm) high*

$50-80   GAZE

The Rolling Stones, 'The Rolling Stones', EP, DFE 8560, released by Decca.

1964

$20-25   GAZE

The Rolling Stones, 'Five by Five' EP, DFE 8590, released by Decca, mounted with a picture of the group, bearing signatures.

c1964   *22in (56cm) high*

$50-80   GAZE

A Rolling Stones US tour picture book program, printed in the US.

1966

$70-100   GAZE

The Rolling Stones, 'Big Hits (High Tide and Green Grass)', LP with gatefold sleeve, TXS 101, released by Decca.

1967

$8-12   GAZE

The Rolling Stones, 'Flowers', rare Belgian LP with unique cover, SSS 120Y, released by Decca.

c1968

$50-80   GAZE

The Rolling Stones, 'Honky Tonk Women', Japanese 45rpm single, TOP 1422, released by the London label.

c1969

$30-50 GAZE

Mick Jagger, 'Just Another Night', 12in single, TA 4722, released by CBS, bears signature, framed with certificate of authenticity.

1985   21.5in (54.5cm) wide

$80-120 GAZE

A 'Life With The Rolling Stones' newspaper, from the Life With The Stars series, printed by East Midlands Printers Ltd for Go Magazine.

1964   16in (40.5cm) high

$20-30 GAZE

David Bowie, 'Man of Words/Man of Music', rare American LP, SR 61246, released by Mercury.

c1969

$80-120 GAZE

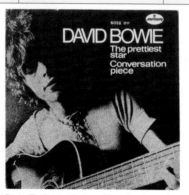

David Bowie, 'The Prettiest Star', rare Norwegian picture sleeve single, MF1153, released by Mercury.

1970

$120-180 GAZE

David Bowie, 'Let's Talk', 1970s Scandinavian 12in interview picture disc, AR 30010, released by NBC.

$8-12 GAZE

Kate Bush, 'The Kick Inside', American LP, SW 17003, released by EMI America, with rare cover.

c1978

$20-30 GAZE

Kate Bush, 'Wuthering Heights', German 7in picture sleeve, LC 0542, released by EMI.

c1978

$8-12 GAZE

Cher, 'All I Really Want To Do', stereo LP, SLBY 3058, released by Liberty.

1965

$12-18 GAZE

The Clash, 'Give 'Em Enough Rope', promotional LP, CBS 82431, released by CBS, lacks poster.

The addition of the original poster could make this album worth around $80.

1978

$30-50   **GAZE**

George Clinton, 'Martial Law', 12in single double pack, PRO-A-5998, released by Paisley Park Records, comprising a red vinyl 'X-Rated Deep Down & Dirty Mixes' disc and a green vinyl 'Clean' disc.

1993

$7-10   **GAZE**

Dave Clark Five, 'Glad All Over/I Know You' 45rpm single, DB 7154, released by Columbia, mounted with a photograph of the group and copy of an autograph book slip bearing signature.

c1963   19.75in (50cm) high

$50-80   **GAZE**

A Duran Duran publicity photograph, with facsimile signatures in silver.

10.75in (27.5cm) wide

$25-35   **GAZE**

Bryan Ferry and Roxy Music, 'Street Life – 20 Greatest Hits', 12in LP, EGCTV1, released by E.G., bears signature.

$20-25   **GAZE**

A reproduction 'Meet The Beat' Billy Fury show poster, for the Britannia Pier, Great Yarmouth, England, framed.

30in (76cm) high

$20-30   **GAZE**

A Genesis handbill, from the Knebworth Festival, other acts including Jefferson Starship and Tom Petty & the Heartbreakers.

1978   11.75in (30cm) high

$50-70   **GAZE**

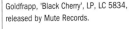

Goldfrapp, 'Black Cherry', LP, LC 5834, released by Mute Records.

2003   12in (30.5cm) wide

$8-12   **GAZE**

A CLOSER LOOK AT A SIGNED GRATEFUL DEAD PICTURE

This is a well-known image and was taken by rock photographer Bill Seidemann for use in the band's eponymous double album released in 1971.

The value would have been greater if the image had not been cut down, losing half of Bill Kreutzman's signature.

The signatures of all the featured band members include Ron McKernan (Pig Pen) who was known for disliking autographs, making this a rare example.

The group disbanded in 1995 following the death of Jerry Garcia, but returned to touring in 2003 as 'The Dead'.

An extremely rare Grateful Dead publicity print, signed by all the members of the Grateful Dead's original five member line-up.

c1971

10.5in (27cm) wide

$4,000-6,000 NOR

Gun, 'Steal Your Fire', limited edition 12in record, AMY-885, released by A&M, with original metal badge and large poster.

c2002

$20-30 GAZE

Rolf Harris, 'Tie Me Kangaroo Down, Sport', 45rpm single, ZSP 59995, released by Epic, mounted with sleeve and slip of paper bearing autographed dedication and image, dated "12/3/63".

27.75in (70.5cm) high

$25-35 GAZE

A Jimi Hendrix Experience 'Axis: Bold as Love' songbook, published by A. Schroeder Music Publishing Co. Ltd.

1968

$40-60 GAZE

Jimi Hendrix, 'Purple Haze', rare Japanese picture sleeve 45rpm single, DP 1559, released by Polydor.

c1968

$50-80 GAZE

Jimi Hendrix, 'Sound Track Recordings From The Film Jimi Hendrix', Japanese two disc stereo LP with gatefold sleeve and obi strip, P 4621 2R, released by WEA, mint condition.

1973

$30-40 GAZE

An Iron Maiden printed glittery glass picture, with wooden frame.

19in (48.5cm) high

$70-100   **NOR**

A novelty postcard of a Life Guard, signed by members of the Jackson Five.

$300-500   **ROS**

A Led Zeppelin at Knebworth official program.

1979   *11.75in (30cm) high*

$20-30   **GAZE**

A 'Led Zeppelin at Earl's Court '75' official concert program.

1975   *11.75in (30cm) high*

$25-35   **GAZE**

Led Zeppelin, 'Led Zeppelin', Italian LP, SM 3721, released by Joker, semi-legitimate recording of a 1971 BBC concert.

1974

$30-50   **GAZE**

Led Zeppelin, 'Trampled Underfoot', special limited edition 45rpm single, DC 1, released by Swan Song.

1975

$30-40   **GAZE**

A limited edition Jerry Lee Lewis poster, reading 'Springhill Salutes The Founders of Rock 'N' Roll', bearing signature, framed.

This poster was also available with an image of Elvis Presley.

22.75in (58cm) high

$70-100   **GAZE**

Little Angels, 'Boneyard', 12in picture disc, LTXP8, released by Polydor, signed by the five band members.

1991

$12-18   **GAZE**

Madonna, 'Crazy For You', picture disc, W008P, released by Sire Records.

1991   *11in (28cm) high*

$30-50   **GAZE**

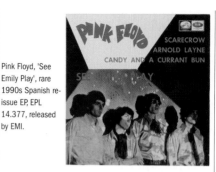

Pink Floyd, 'See Emily Play', rare 1990s Spanish re-issue EP, EPL 14.377, released by EMI.

A photograph of Bob Marley, mounted with signed piece of paper, framed and glazed.

19.5in (49.5cm) high

A Roy Orbison black and white photograph, mounted with a signed autograph book page, framed and glazed.

18.5in (47cm) high

To differentiate between the reissue and the original, look at the upper left hand corner – the original will have the catalog number listed there.

$280-320   **GAZE** | **$120-180**   **GAZE** | **$180-220**   **GAZE**

A run of five tickets for Pink Floyd's 'The Wall' concert, in Dortmund, dated 15th - 19th February.

1981   *6.5in (16.5cm) high*

Cliff Richard, 'Don't Stop Me Now', factory sample LP, S(C)X 6133, released by Columbia, Norrie Paramor signature stamp on sleeve.

Norrie Paramor was the UK recording director of EMI Columbia from 1952 until the late 1960s.

Cliff Richard with The Shadows, 'Wonderful Life', mono soundtrack LP, SX 1628, released by Columbia.

1964

$50-70   **GAZE** | **$50-70**   **GAZE** | **$20-30**   **GAZE**

Cliff Richard, 'Rock 'n' Roll Juvenile', 12in LP, EMC 3307, released by EMI Records, signed on the cover.

1979

Sex Pistols, 'The Great Rock 'n' Roll Swindle', soundtrack LP, VD 2510, released by Virgin.

This is the first version of the LP and contains the track 'Watcha Gonna Do About It'. The second version replaces it with 'I Wanna Be Me' and 'Who Killed Bambi' and is worth less than half of the original version.

1980

Sex Pistols, 'The Great Rock 'n' Roll Swindle', first issue Benelux film soundtrack LP, 70025, released by Virgin Records, with unique cover artwork.

1981

$50-70   **GAZE** | **$40-60**   **GAZE** | **$70-100**   **GAZE**

A Small Faces 'Pop '66' tour program, printed by Hastings Printing Company, together with a ticket for Morecambe April 11th.

1966   *10.5in (26cm) high*

$120-180   **GAZE**

The Spencer Davis Group, 'The Second Album', TL 5295, released by Fontana.

1966

$20-25   **GAZE**

Screaming Lord Sutch, 'Lord Sutch and Heavy Friends' LP, 2400 008, released by Atlantic, with contributions from Jimmy Page, John Bonham and Jeff Beck.

1970

$70-100   **GAZE**

Tyrannosaurus Rex, 'A Beard of Stars', LP, SLRZ 1013, released by Royal Zonophone, with lyric sheet.

1970

$50-80   **GAZE**

Tyrannosaurus Rex, 'By The Light of A Magical Moon', rare 1960s German picture sleeve, released by Polydor.

$80-120   **GAZE**

A very rare Gene Vincent concert flyer, for Shrewsbury, July 1961, printed by Willonns (Printers) Ltd.

1961   *10.25in (26cm) wide*

$120-180   **GAZE**

A limited edition NME front sheet, featuring The Who, live at Leeds, from an edition of 1,300, with facsimile signatures, dated May 23rd, 1970.

30in (76cm) high

$80-120   **GAZE**

The Who, 'Substitute', 45rpm single, 591 001, released by Reaction, mounted with a picture of the band and an autograph book slip bearing signatures.

17.75in (45cm) wide

$70-100   **GAZE**

The Who, 'See Me, Feel Me', 33rpm EP, released by Polydor, with picture sleeve.

1970

$70-100 GAZE

The Who, 'My Generation', LP, LAT 8616, released by Brunswick.

1965

$80-120 GAZE

A John Entwistle's Art The Who – '2000' poster, signed by Entwistle, framed.

26in (66cm) high

$80-120 GAZE

Yes, 'The White Album' LP, OF 722, released by Offshore, Holland.

1972

$40-60 GAZE

A Stranglers 'Strangled – The Peevish Summer of 77' Summer Special booklet, published by Albion Leisure Services.

1977 11.75in (30cm) high

$12-18 GAZE

An Isle of Wight Festival weekend ticket.

1969 6.75in (17cm) high

$50-80 GAZE

A 5th National Jazz & Blues Festival official program, at Richmond, featuring The Who and the Yardbirds.

This rare program was made only for performers.

1965 11.25in (28.5cm) high

$120-180 GAZE

Three Isle of Wight Festival one day tickets, for the reserved enclosure.

1970 4.75in (12cm) long

$70-100 GAZE

Frank Zappa 'Marvellous Stunner' limited edition multi-colored LP, released by Angry Taxman Records, from an edition of 50.

$50-80 GAZE

A Shelley King George VI and Queen Elizabeth Coronation porcelain loving cup, printed with portraits including the Princesses.

c1937   3.5in (9cm) high

$280-320   **SAS**

A pair of Royal Crown Derby King George VI and Queen Elizabeth small square dishes, each printed in sepia with a named and dated portrait, gilt rims.

1937   3in (7.5cm) wide

$220-280   **SAS**

A Royal Crown Derby limited edition footed bowl, commemorating the visit of King George VI and Queen Elizabeth to America, from an edition of 3,000.

1939   5in (12cm) high

$700-1,000   **SAS**

A limited edition Royal Doulton 'The Queen Mother' figure, HN3944, designed by Alan Maslankowski, from an edition of 5,000, no certificate.

1997   10.5in (26.5cm) high

$180-220   **PSA**

A limited edition Royal Doulton 'H.M. Queen Elizabeth The Queen Mother' figure, HN4086, designed by Alan Maslankowski, from an edition of 2,000, commemorating her 100th birthday, with certificate.

2000   9in (23cm) high

$220-280   **PSA**

A Crown Ducal dish, with a sepia portrait of Princess Margaret, named in gilt within a black, red, and gilt dotted border.

c1933   5in (12cm) diam

$180-220   **SAS**

An unusual pair of Crown Ducal Princess Elizabeth and Princess Margaret commemorative dishes, printed with named portraits in sepia.

c1933   6.75in (17cm) high

$280-320   **SAS**

An Aynsley Queen Elizabeth II Coronation plate, the reverse inscribed in gilt.

1953   10.75in (27cm) diam

$280-320   **SAS**

An Aynsley Queen Elizabeth II Coronation plate, the reverse inscribed in gilt.

1953   10.5in (26.5cm) diam

$220-280   **SAS**

A CLOSER LOOK AT A QUEEN ELIZABETH II COMMEMORATIVE CUP

The box and booklet make the piece desirable, but do not have a great effect on the value.

Mugs can be found without the limited edition mark. Unnumbered examples are still valuable, but marked versions command a much higher price.

It is by a fine maker and is of excellent quality, making it highly desirable.

The limited editions of small numbers are more generally more sought-after and tend to keep their value better.

A rare Royal Crown Derby Queen Elizabeth II Coronation loving cup, from a limited edition of 250, with original box and booklet.

c1953

4in (10cm) high

$700-1,000

H&G

A Burleigh Queen Elizabeth II Coronation earthenware loving cup.

c1953   3.25in (8cm) high

$80-120   **H&G**

A Kaiser Queen Elizabeth II Silver Jubilee silhouette vase, the profile of the Queen and the Duke of Edinburgh formed by the shape of the vase.

c1977   8in (20cm) high

$280-320   **H&G**

A limited edition Paragon Queen Elizabeth II Coronation loving cup, from an edition of 1,000, with original certificate.

A similar example was made to celebrate the silver wedding anniversary of Queen Elizabeth and Prince Philip, with silver handles.

c1953   4.75in (12cm) high

$500-700   **H&G**

A limited edition Coalport Queen Elizabeth II Silver Jubilee urn and cover, from an edition of 200, painted with a scene of The Mall, numbered on the base.

1978

11.5in (25cm) high

$280-320   **SAS**

A limited edition Capo di Monte 'H.R.H. The Queen' figure, designed by Bruno Merli, with silver jubilee certificate.

c1973   15.5in (38.5cm) high

$180-220   **SAS**

A limited edition Royal Doulton 'H.M. Queen Elizabeth II' figurine, HN3440, designed by Peter Gee, from an edition of 3,500, with certificate and box.

1992

$220-280   **SAS**

A limited edition Capo di Monte 'H.R.H. Prince Charles' figurine, commemorating his investiture, with certificate.

1969   *15in (37.5cm) high*

$180-220   SAS

A Prince Charles and Lady Diana Spencer Royal Wedding caddy spoon, maker's mark "DSS London", in original fitted box.

c1981   *2.75in (7cm) long*

$120-180   WW

A Derek Fowler Studio Prince Charles and Lady Diana Spencer Royal Wedding ceramic night light.

1981   *8.5in (11.5cm) high*

$60-90   DH

A limited edition Poole Pottery Prince Charles and Lady Diana Spencer Royal Wedding plate, from an edition of 2,000.

1981

$30-50   C

A Caverswall Prince Charles and Lady Diana Spencer Royal Wedding square casket and cover, from a limited edition of 250.

1981   *12.5in (32cm) high*

$300-500   SAS

A Royal Worcester Prince Charles and Lady Diana Spencer Royal Wedding urn and cover, from a limited edition of 750, modeled with Prince of Wales' feathers.

9in (23cm) high

$220-280   SAS

A Spode Prince Charles and Lady Diana Spencer Royal Wedding large chalice and cover, from a limited edition of 500, decorated with enamels and gilt, with certificate.

1981   *12.75in (32.5cm) high*

$180-220   SAS

A Poole Pottery Queen Elizabeth II commemorative tile, in a wooden surround.

$30-50   C

COLLECTORS' NOTES

- Commercial perfumeries boomed in the early years of the 20thC and devised many ingenious marketing and packaging ploys to increase sales of their products.

- Bottles often echo the name of the perfume they contain. Cherigan's 1929 fragrance 'Chance' featured a glass horseshoe on the bottle.

- Collectors will pay more for bottles full of perfume and complete with as much original packaging as possible. Many will even purchase empty packaging in order to reunite it with a stray bottle.

- Bottles with screw tops that have plastic linings can be dated to the 1960s or later. Those with rubber, cork or other linings will probably be older than this.

- One of the most prolific perfumers of the 20thC was Elsa Schiaparelli, an Italian who opened a successful Paris fashion house in 1929. The bottle for 'Shocking', released in 1936, was the first in the form of a female torso – a design since revived by Jean Paul Gaultier.

- A big name will not necessarily fetch a big price. Limited editions and scents that sold badly will be harder to find and therefore are often worth more.

- Scent bottle enthusiasts might organize their collections by designer, company, fragrance or form. Much of the appeal of these bottles lies in the variety of materials used in their design. Glass, silver, fabric, ceramic, wood, and bakelite were all used, often in combination.

A 'Blue Grass' by Elizabeth Arden "Merry Christmas Stocking" holiday gift set, the stocking holding a miniature bottle, with label, in plastic display, introduced in 1934.

'Blue Grass' is Arden's best-selling fragrance.

c1950s   1.75in (4.5cm) high

$280-320   **RDL**

A 1930s 'Carnation' by Elizabeth Arden special miniature scent bottle, the bottle with interior blown flower and hang tag in original window box.

4in (10cm) high

$800-1,200   **RDL**

A 1960s Avon scent bottle, in the shape of a soda siphon, unmarked.

7.5in (19cm) high

$25-35   **LB**

A 1930s 'Evening in Paris' by Bourjois blue bakelite owl-shaped scent bottle and holder.

4in (10cm) high

$120-180   **LC**

A 1930s 'Evening in Paris' by Bourjois scent bottle.

4.5in (11.5cm) high

$80-120   **LB**

A 1930s 'Evening in Paris' by Bourjois scent bottle, in a novelty presentation case shaped as the Eiffel Tower.

2in (5cm) high

$180-220   **LB**

A late 1930s/early 1940s Cardinal 'Tantalux' presentation set, containing 'Bouquet', 'Chypre', and 'Gardenia', in the form of a tantalus with lock.

Also made as a twin set with screw-down top and lock.

4.5in (11.5cm) wide

$120-180   **TDG**

A 'Perfume Hypnotic' by Hattie Carnegie miniature scent bottle, designed by Tommi Parzinger, with paper label, sealed.

c1946 2in (5cm) high

$300-500 RDL

A 'Les Pois de Senteur de Chez Moi' by Caron scent bottle, designed by Baccarat, boxed, introduced in 1947.

4.75in (12cm) high

$300-400 LB

A 'Chance' by Cherigan scent bottle, with applied glass horseshoe and black glass stopper, introduced in 1929.

3.25in (8cm) high

$800-1,000 RDL

A 1940s 'Dashing' by Lilly Dache scent bottle, in faux ivory, with glass interior, on silk base with cover, lacking stopper.

Successful milliner and designer Lilly Dache introduced her two perfumes, 'Dashing' and 'Drifting', in 1941. She was advised by her husband, who had worked for Coty.

7.5in (19cm) high

$800-1,200 RDL

A 1940s 'Pink' by De Raymond holiday presentation bottle, with a glass bottle and fluorescent plastic Christmas tree, with plastic display box.

5in (12.5cm) high

$700-1,000 RDL

A 1950s 'Miss Dior' by Christian Dior scent bottle, with label, introduced in 1947.

5.25in (13.5cm) high

$180-220 LB

A 1910s 'Illusion' by Drallé scent bottle, with box and papers.

Drallé perfumes were packaged in wooden cases.

3.5in (9cm) high

$80-120 LB

A 1920s Fragonard presentation set of perfume solids, containing 'Supreme', '5', and 'Xmas', in wooden containers with labels and box.

Containers 1in (2.5cm) high

$300-500 RDL

A 'Rose' by Gabilla scent bottle, bottle by Baccarat, engraved "ABA" on stopper, introduced in 1912.

2.75in (7cm) high

$280-320 LB

A 'La Vierge Folle' by Gabilla scent bottle, designed by Baccarat, introduced in 1912.

2.75in (7cm) high

$280-320 LB

A 'Cajolerie' by Gilot scent bottle, with original box, introduced in 1930.

Box 3.5in (9cm) high

$70-100 TDG

A 1950s '21' by Goya scent gift set, with two different bottles.

The playful period graphics on this box make it a desirable example.

Larger bottle 2.75in (7cm) high

$120-180 LB

A 1950s 'Gardenia' by Goya small scent bottle.

1.5in (4cm) high

$25-35 LB

A 'Gardenia' by Goya scent bottle, with original box, introduced in 1952.

'Gardenia' bottles were made with varying numbers of rings and collectors often seek to acquire one of each of example.

2.5in (6.5cm) high

$30-50 LB

A 'Contes Choisis' by Marcel Guerlain scent bottle, by Depinoix, with sepia stain and label, introduced in 1926.

3.5in (9cm) high

$1,200-1,800 RDL

A 1900s 'Violettes Prince Albert' by Oriza L. Legrand scent bottle, old factory bottle.

4in (10cm) high

$80-120 LB

A limited edition 'Tropiques' by Lancôme scent bottle, by Jean Sala, with label, in deluxe display box.

1944 *4.75in (11.5cm) high*

$800-1,200 RDL

A 'La Saison des Fleurs' by Lionceau presentation set of perfume solids, in bakelite containers with molded scent names, boxed.

c1936 *Dice 0.75in (2cm) high*

$220-280 RDL

A 'Nuit de Long Champ' by Lubin scent bottle.

A 'Femme Divine' by Loulette scent bottle, made by Depinoix to a Julien Viard design, with pink enamel and gray stain, minor flaw, introduced in 1926.

3.75in (9.5cm) high

$500-700 RDL

A 'Bouquet de Papillons' by Lubin scent bottle, by Depinoix, introduced in 1919.

3in (7.5cm) high | c1935

$500-700 RDL | **$220-280**

6.5in (15cm) high

LB

A 'Prince Douka' by Marquay scent bottle, with jeweled fabric cape and neck label, with box, introduced in 1956.

This bottle was sold with a range of differently colored capes.

4in (10cm) high

$500-700 RDL

A 1950s Mary Chess 'Perfume Gallery' complete presentation of six perfumes, the bottles shaped as chess pieces, with chessboard box.

Box 3.25in (8cm) wide

$800-1,200 RDL

A 1920s 'Princess Maria' by Prince Matchabelli scent bottle, stenciled "France".

2.5in (6.5cm) high

$500-700 RDL

A 1960s 'Chantrelle' by Max Factor scent bottle.

This example was probably a promotional Christmas design. 'Chantrelle' was one of the most popular Max Factor perfumes – it was a well known design and there are many variations on the cat theme. The glass dome echoes Schiaparelli's earlier designs.

6in (15cm) high

$50-70 LB

A 'Habinita' by Molinard scent bottle, with box, introduced in 1925.

3in (7.5cm) high

$220-280 LB

A 'Muguet' by Molinard tester scent bottle, sealed, introduced in 1928.

3.5in (9cm) high

$180-220 RDL

A 1930s 'Oeillet' scent bottle, possibly by Arys, with "Vrai Parfum Oeillet" label.

7in (18cm) high

$120-180   **TDG**

A set of 'Bouquet' by Ota scent bottles, in the form of pearls, each with a stopper to the base, in display box with label, one stained pearl, introduced in 1929.

Box 6in (15cm) high

$800-1,200   **RDL**

A 1900s 'Extrait des Fleurs' scent bottle, retailed by Parfymeri F. Pauli of Stockholm, probably French, with original box.

4in (10cm) high

$50-70   **LB**

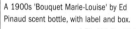

A 1900s 'Bouquet Marie-Louise' by Ed Pinaud scent bottle, with label and box.

4.5in (11.5cm) high

$500-700   **RDL**

A 'Parfum Pompeia' by L.T. Piver scent bottle, with label, seal and box.

c1924   *4.5in (11.5cm) high*

$500-700   **RDL**

A 'Carnet de Bal' by Revillon scent bottle, with gold label attached to neck.

c1937   *3.5in (9cm) high*

$120-180   **LB**

An 'Amour Daria' by Revillon scent bottle, introduced in 1935.

4.25in (11cm) high

$120-180   **LB**

A 'Coeur Joie' by Nina Ricci scent bottle, with box, introduced in 1946.

4in (10cm) high

$280-320   **LB**

An 'Entre Tous' by Robj scent bottle, the bottle with sepia stain and label, with box and cover, paper loss to book interior.

c1925   *3.5in (9cm) high*

$800-1,200   **RDL**

An 'Aladin' by Rosine scent bottle, in cast metal with chain handle and faux ivory stopper, introduced in 1919.

2.5in (6.5cm) high

$300-500 RDL

A 1930s Saturday Night Lotion' bottle, with gold label, embossed "ASJ", probably English.

5in (13cm) high

$30-50 LB

A 'Mischief' by Saville scent bottle, in a bakelite novelty egg-shaped presentation case, introduced in 1935.

2.5in (6.5cm) high

$220-280 LB

A 'Shocking You' by Schiaparelli scent bottle, in novelty cigarette carton style box.

Box 4in (10cm) high

$70-100 TDG

A CLOSER LOOK AT A SCENT BOTTLE

One of Schiaparelli's best known perfumes, introduced in 1936.

This bottle was designed by Eleanore Fini after a bust sent by Mae West for Schiaparelli to fit her clothes to.

Schiaparelli was the first to use the term 'shocking pink' and the color became her trademark .

Her 1949 perfume, Zut, was sold in a bottle shaped as a woman's lower torso, forming a whole with this bottle.

A 1930s 'Shocking' by Schiaparelli scent bottle, in a domed presentation case, with box.

Dome 4in (10cm) high

$300-500 LB

A 'Sleeping' by Schiaparelli scent bottle, introduced in 1938.

6.25in (16cm) high

$300-500 LB

A 'Sleeping' by Schiaparelli miniature scent bottle, with plastic screw cap in the form of a flame and full banner label, introduced in 1938.

3.25in (8cm) high

$80-120 RDL

A 'Success Fou' by Schiaparelli scent bottle, the bottle with enameled and gilt detail and foil label in heart-shaped display box, including advertisement affixed to interior.

1953 *2.5in (6.5cm) high*

$400-600 RDL

A 'Zut' by Schiaparelli scent bottle, the bottle with gold details, in silk-lined box, wear to box exterior, introduced in 1948.

5in (12.5cm) high

$500-700 **RDL**

A 'Zut' by Schiaparelli scent bottle, the bottle with gold details, sealed and labeled, with waist sash and suede drawstring pouch, introduced in 1948.

3.75in (9.5cm) high

$700-1,000 **RDL**

A CLOSER LOOK AT A SCENT BOTTLE

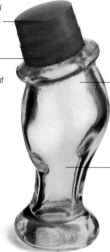

Parisian Suzy was a successful milliner in the 1930s and 40s.

The normal size bottle, designed by Baccarat and produced in crystal, was topped with a stopper shaped as one of Suzy's hats.

The standard bottle was made in three sizes.

'Ecarlate Suzy' was her first scent, followed by 'Golden Laughter', 'Bandbox', and 'Madrigal'.

A rare 'Ecarlate Suzy' by Suzy miniature scent bottle, the glass bottle with plastic screw cap in the form of a hat, introduced in 1939.

1.75in (4.5cm) high

$1,200-1,800 **RDL**

A 'Ze Zan' by Tuvache scent bottle, in gilt glass with wooden screw cap, on wooden stand with gold-glazed ceramic display cover. *1947* *4.25in (10.5cm) high*

$2,200-2,800 **RDL**

A 1930s 'Golliwogg' by Vigny scent bottle, the clear glass bottle forming the head, with plastic screw cap collar and box, tied to hang as a Christmas ornament.

2in (5cm) high

$500-700 **RDL**

A 'Le Chick-Chick' by Vigny scent bottle, with gold-colored detail and yellow metal stopper cover, introduced in 1923.

3.5in (9cm) high

$1,200-1,800 **RDL**

A 'Pourpre d'Automne' by Violet scent bottle, by Lucien Gaillard, with painted detail, some paint loss, introduced in 1922.

3.75in (8.5cm) high

$700-1,000 **RDL**

A 1930s 'Antilope' by Weil scent bottle, with engraved "W" on stopper.

6in (15cm) high

$80-120 **LB**

A late 19thC small brass microscope, probably American, with partial lacquer, pull-tube and stage focusing, on green-painted cast iron base.

8in (20cm) high

$50-80   **EG**

An early 20thC microscope, by Gundlach-Manhattan, Optical Co., Rochester, New York, with pull-tube, rack and micrometer focusing, lacquered-brass bodytube, circular stage with wheel stops, and plano/concave mirror, mounted on twin-pillar support to Y-shaped shoe, in mahogany case.

10.25in (26cm) high

$280-320   **EG**

A mid-19thC German, Oberhauser-type drum microscope, lacquered-brass with pull-tube focusing, detached, bull's-eye condenser, micrometer stage adjustment, wheel stops and reflector in drum, on circular base, with accessories in fitted mahogany case.

8.25in (21cm) high

$220-280   **EG**

A brass drum microscope, by J.H. Steward, London, with three objectives and accessories in a mahogany box.

c1850   *7.25in (18cm) high*

$220-280   **ATK**

A 'Prof. Fuller's Calculating Slide Rule' logarithmic spiral calculator, manufactured and distributed by W.F. Stanley & Co. Ltd., London, with mahogany handle, side ends and original case, brass fittings, no support, original 32-page instruction manual.

c1925   *18in (45.5cm) long*

$300-500   **ATK**

An early logarithmic 'Fuller's Spiral slide rule', with mahogany handle, dated.

1889

$280-320   **ATK**

A German orbit tellurium, by Columbus of Berlin, made for the Scandinavian market, with later electrical fittings.

A tellurium demonstrated the Sun and Earth system.

c1920   *20in (50cm) long*

$700-1,000   **ATK**

A mid-20thC Curta Type I calculator, with original plastic box, shipping carton, and two manuals, mint condition.

This example fetched such a high value as it is unusually totally complete and is in truly mint condition.

$800-1,200   **ATK**

A 19thC English demonstration compass, with printed rose, iron needle and mahogany frame with glazed top.

9in (23cm) diam

$120-180   **EG**

An American brass circumferentor, by William James Young, Philadelphia, magnetic compass surrounded by a divided circle, and equipped with fixed sights, with original wooden case.

c1850   14.25in (35.5cm) long

$500-800   **ATK**

A brass pantograph, by Thomas Rowley, Brighton, with ceramic castors, in shaped mahogany case.

A pantograph (developed by Christoph Scheiner in c1603-c1605) was used for enlarging or reducing the scale of maps when copying them.

c1840   21in (53.5cm) wide

$180-220   **EG**

An early 20thC paper micrometer, by Schopper, Leipzig, with silvered dial, operating lever and foot, agent's label of "Foreign Paper Mills, New York" and cast iron base with gilt decoration.

This is used for measuring the thickness of paper.

11in (28cm) high

$180-220   **EG**

An early American Abbott 'Automatic Check Punch' check protection device, very good condition.

c1890

$400-600   **ATK**

A CLOSER LOOK AT A PERPETUAL FOUNTAIN

This fountain was based on Greek engineer Hero's (10-70 AD) famous mechanical fountain, but used revolving reservoirs to provide perpetual movement.

The water pressure from, and weight of the water in, the revolving reservoirs aimed to cause the fountain to spray and the reservoirs to revolve in perpetuity.

It was patented by Joseph Storer of London in February 1871 and surviving examples are very rare today.

Storer sold the U.S. rights to soda fountain maker John Tufts of Boston, who made them until the early 1900s.

A 'Storer's Patent Perpetual Fountain', manufactured and distributed by J. Defries & Sons, London.

These ornamental table fountains would often contain scented water, so that as the fountain sprinkled, the room's air was delicately fragranced.

1871-1900s   20in (50cm) high

$2,800-3,200   **ATK**

A large Wimshurst's pattern electrostatic generator.

The foil strips and glass rubbed against the wire brushes, generating static electricity.

20in (50cm) high

$1,200-1,800   **ATK**

A telegraph key and sounder, by Manhattan Electrical Supply Co., 20 ohm, with steel lever and twin binding posts on mahogany base.

7in (18cm) wide

$80-120   **EG**

COLLECTORS' NOTES

■ Although sewing is no longer seen as a fashionable pastime, sewing tools are a popular collecting area.

■ A number of patents for sewing machines were granted around the turn of the 19thC. The first useable machine was patented by French tailor Barthelemy Thimonnier in 1830. Elias Howe and later Isaac Merritt Singer added improvements and Singer's name has become synonymous with sewing machines today.

■ The majority of sewing machines can be collected relatively inexpensively, especially Singer machines. Early examples, made for only a short period of time, are more sought-after and valuable.

■ Metal thimbles were made from the mid-18thC and production peaked in the 19thC when sewing was popular. Many were made as souvenir or commemorative pieces. Look for decorative or named examples and those made of precious metal, but be aware that before the 1870s hallmarks were not required on such small items.

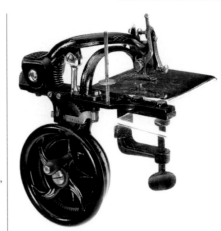

An unusual American Beckwith sewing machine, complete with accessories, manual and original spare needles.
c1875

$2,200-3,200 ATK

A very rare French 'L'Incomparable' sewing machine, retailed by Rumpf of Paris, complete with foot pedal, table clamp and original wooden box.
c1890

$1,200-1,800 ATK

A Wilcox & Gibbs domestic sewing machine, marked "W&G" and with patent date "17 April 1883".
c1884

$250-350 ATK

An English cast-iron domestic sewing machine, by Jones.
c1890

$120-160 ATK

An unmarked cast-iron sewing machine, probably German.

c1895

$300-450 ATK

A 'The Nelson' domestic sewing machine, probably German, retailed in London by the American Sewing Machine Co.
c1900

$120-180 ATK

An English 'Ideal' sewing machine, by Salters.
c1910

$120-160 ATK

A 12 toy sewing machine, by Müller of Berlin, complete and in good condition.
c1935

$600-800 ATK

SEWING

A metal thimble, commemorating Queen Victoria's coronation, reading "Long Live Queen Victoria", lacks glass or stone at top.

c1837

$100-150   **CBE**

A silver-plated thimble, commemorating the Silver Jubilee of King George and Queen Mary of England.

c1935

$60-80   **CBE**

An early 20thC French silver novelty thimble, reading "BONNE ANNEE", with French control marks.

$80-120   **CBE**

A tartanware needle book, printed with the 'Stuart' tartan.

2.25in (5.5cm) high

$80-120   **WW**

An early 20thC German thimble, by Gabler, with enameled band of a landscape scene.

Gabler, which closed in 1963, made many enameled thimbles. It can be recognized by the eight-pointed star motif at the crown of the thimble.

$60-80   **CBE**

A Japanese blue felt plush elephant tape measure.

2.25in (5.5cm) high

$30-40   **SOTT**

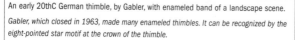

A 19thC rosewood sewing compendium, the turned handle with reel support, a pair of pin cushions flanking a thimble, above a frieze drawer.

5in (12.5cm) high

$300-450   **WW**

A WWI period 'Red Cross' pin cushion, by C.S. Green and Co. of Birmingham.

1914   *3.5in (9cm) diam*

$400-500   **WW**

COLLECTORS' NOTES

■ The excitement, inherent danger, and historical importance of space travel have helped make space memorabilia a rapidly growing area over the past ten years.

■ Flown memorabilia is the most sought-after, with unique items used on lunar missions being the 'holy grail' for many collectors. NASA does not allow items to be taken into space solely to increase their value, meaning numbers are limited.

■ Commemorative pieces are more affordable and varied with autographs and patches being a good start, as so many were produced. Focus on one program, or type such as pre-shuttle missions like Apollo or Gemini, or shuttle missions (STS).

■ Certain objects with astronauts' signatures, such as baseballs, can be rare. Many astronauts still sign today, some for a fee. The autographs of those that no longer sign can rise in value, particularly if the astronaut is especially notable.

■ The condition of flown items, especially equipment, can be poor with signs of wear and use. This is not unexpected and rarity and importance to a mission take precedence over condition.

■ Mass-produced memorabilia should be bought in as close to mint condition as possible. Always try to ensure an autograph comes with a certificate of authenticity, even if obtained personally.

An Apollo 7 Beta cloth crew patch, without cutting lines.

1968   9in (23cm) wide

$120-180   **AGI**

A rare flown Apollo 11 crew-signed Beta emblem, made of teflon-coated fiberglass, signed by Neil Armstrong and Buzz Aldrin and signed and inscribed by Michael Collins with: "Carried to the Moon aboard Apollo XI, July 1969.", together with a letter from Michael Collins.

Apollo 11 crew signed items are very desirable but an item flown to the Moon having their signatures is perhaps the ultimate autograph collectible from this mission. The American Eagle and mission importance make this an iconic emblem.

1969   6in (15cm) wide

$40,000-50,000   **SWA**

A flown to lunar surface Apollo 15 mission patch, carried by Dave Scott, with "XV" stitched in silver, in its flight bag with original tape.

1971

$5,000-7,000   **AGI**

A flown Gemini GT-10 crew patch, together with a handwritten certificate of authenticity.

1966   3in (7.5cm) wide

$2,800-3,200   **AGI**

An extremely rare STS 51L mission patch, together with a crew patch decal.

STS stands for 'Space Transportation System' and refers to the Shuttle. This patch was given to Bob Overmyer by crew member Dick Scobee.

1993

$120-180   **AGI**

A Spacepex Beta cloth patch, distributed at the Manned Spacecraft Center Stamp Club stamp show, "Commemorating Ten Years of U.S. Manned Space Flight, May Fifth, 1961/1971".

1971   8in (20cm) wide

$50-70   **AGI**

A flown Gemini GT-11 Richard Gordon Jr. U.S. Navy patch.

$5,000-7,000   **AGI**

A flown Apollo 11 'United Nations' silk flag, inscribed "Carried to the Moon aboard Apollo XI, Michael Collins" at the bottom, together with a NASA certificate of authenticity signed "Michael Collins".

c1969   12in (30.5cm) high

$5,000-7,000   AGI

A flown Apollo 11 US silk flag, on a presentation certificate inscribed: "This Flag traveled to the Moon with Apollo 11, the first manned lunar landing. July 20, 1969", unsigned.

1969   12in (30.5cm) high

$12,000-18,000   AGI

A flown Apollo 16 United States flag, signed by Charles Duke and inscribed: "This flag—Flown to the Lunar Surface Aboard the Lunar Module "Orion" April 20, 1972. Charles M. Duke, Jr. Apollo 16 LMP", mounted on a NASA certificate.

1972   12in (30.5cm) high

$8,000-12,000   SWA

An extra large flown US silk flag, inscribed and signed by Tom Stafford with: "Flown to the Moon on Apollo X, May 1969, Tom Stafford", with a typed letter signed by Stafford providing additional flight details.

1969 Apollo mission flown flags of this size are extremely rare as they are both heavy and large, taking the space of ten 4in x 6in flags.

1969   18in (47.5cm) wide

$18,000-25,000   SWA

A CLOSER LOOK AT A FLOWN FLAG

This flag was flown on the first manned lunar landing mission, arguably the most important space mission.

It is from Aldrin's personal collection, adding to its desirability.

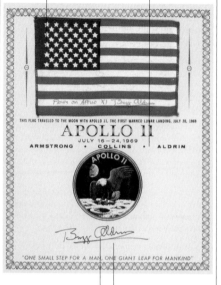

It is signed and inscribed by Buzz Aldrin, one of the first two men to walk on the moon.

It is attractively mounted on a NASA certificate, which is also signed by Aldrin, making it a superb display piece.

A flown United States flag, inscribed and signed by Buzz Aldrin with: "Flown on Apollo XI, Buzz Aldrin", with an NASA certificate reading "This flag traveled to the Moon with Apollo 11, the first manned lunar landing, July 20, 1969" and "Apollo 11, July 16-24, 1969".

1969   12in (30.5cm) high

$25,000-30,000   SWA

A flown United States flag, carried to the Moon on Apollo 14 in the Command Module "Kitty Hawk", inscribed and signed by Mitchell with: "Flown to the Moon--Apollo 14, Edgar Mitchell".

1971

$8,000-12,000   SWA

A flown Texas state flag, carried to the Moon on Apollo 14 in the Command Module "Kitty Hawk", inscribed and signed by Dr. Mitchell with: "Flown to the Moon aboard Kitty Hawk on Apollo 14, Edgar Mitchell, LMP".

1971

$3,000-5,000   SWA

A Russian flight-ready 'Loaf of Bread', consisting of ten thimble-sized mini-loaves, vacuum-wrapped.

3in (7.5cm) wide

$50-70 AGI

A Mercury Program freeze-dried strawberry cereal cube, mounted in a clear Lucite block.

1961-64 Block 2in (5cm) high

$220-280 AGI

A flown Apollo 12 spoon, engraved "Richard F. Gordon Apollo 12 CMP".

c1969

$2,800-3,200 AGI

A CLOSER LOOK AT A TOOTHBRUSH

Toothbrushes are a rare and highly personal item.

This was one of only two toothbrushes taken to the lunar surface by Aldrin and Armstrong.

It was transferred as part of the 'Oral Hygiene' kit from the Command Module to the Landing Module and is complete with its protective case.

It was owned by Buzz Aldrin, the second man to walk on the moon, adding to its value.

A flown Apollo 11 "Tooth Tip" toothbrush and button fastening storage sleeve, model S-19, made by Lactona for NASA/MSC, the sleeve with blue velcro patch and flight designation for the Lunar Module Pilot (LMP), with a typed letter signed by Aldrin.

c1969

8in (20cm) long

$18,000-25,000 SWA

A flown Apollo 12 mechanical pencil, carried by Richard F. Gordon.

c1969

$3,000-5,000 AGI

An unusual Apollo "Lunar Rock Storage Container", the two-part polished stainless steel containment vessel secured by three screws through the bottom, marked "45" on both pieces.

1965-73   2.75in (7cm) long

$700-1,000 AGI

A Mercury orange-flavored drink, in its original intact NASA plastic bottle.

1961-64   3in (7.5cm) high

$300-500 AGI

A Mercury pilot survival kit, made by the ACR Electronics Corp in New York for NASA during the Gemini Program, contents include a signal mirror, fish hook and line, siren whistle, fire starters, flashlight, with label reading "Model 4H-1, Ser No. 5058, Name Combination Survival Light, Cont No. NAS9-5294, Part No. 20538, Date 3.4.66".

1966

$500-700 AGI

A Mercury MR-6 'Friendship 7' black ceramic cookie jar, reading "Friendship 7" on one side and "United States" on the other, a small chip on the bottom.

The proposed Fall 1961 Mercury MR-6 manned flight was canceled in July of that year, and never took place.

c1961   11in (28cm) high

$800-1,200   **AGI**

A Mercury Capsule savings bank, marked "Space Capsule" on one side and "United States" on the other.

4.5in (11.5cm) high

$220-280   **AGI**

An Apollo lunar module model, made for the Grumman Aerospace Corp.

The ascent stage is detachable from the descent stage, as with the actual vessel.

1969   8in (20cm) high

$2,200-2,800   **SWA**

An Apollo 8 painted cast iron money bank, marked "Borman, Lovell, Anders" on one side.

c1968

$80-120   **AGI**

An Apollo 1 gold-plated Robbins medallion, in original Fliteline plastic case.

Gold Robbins Company medallions are ordered by flying astronauts as commemoratives for their wives and families, and are made in strictly limited numbers. The original Apollo 1 mission (previously named AS-204) crew were tragically killed in a training exercise fire.

c1967   1.25in (3cm) diam

$800-1,200   **AGI**

An Apollo 11 souvenir brass bowl, featuring the lunar landing and takeoff, the Apollo 11 emblem, and reading "For your contribution to the first manned lunar landing 1969, NASA MSC".

c1969   4.75in (12cm) diam

$80-120   **AGI**

A sterling silver Robbins STS 107 medallion, in its original case with astronaut's names and dates on the reverse.

Not all Robbins medallions were flown. This example is a restrike, made to commemorate the 2003 Columbia Space Shuttle tragedy. The dates are die-cut, rather than engraved after flying.

$300-500   **AGI**

An Apollo 17 coffee mug, with the official Apollo 17 logo below the inscription "The Beginning!".

c1972

$220-280   **AGI**

An Apollo 15 David Scott signed Rawlings baseball, inscribed "Dave Scott Apollo 15 CDR".

David Scott decided not to autograph baseballs a number of years ago, making this one of the few available. Buzz Aldrin also does not sign baseballs.

$3,000-5,000   **AGI**

An STS 7 Sally Ride signed official NASA photograph.

Ride became the first American woman in space in 1983, on board a space shuttle. The Shuttle was first seen in 1976 and undertook its first mission in space in 1981.

10in (25.5cm) high

$50-70 AGI

A Mercury MR-6 John Glenn signed official NASA lithograph, minor edge bends/faults.

10in (25.5cm) high

$50-70 AGI

An Apollo 7 Walter Cunningham signed NASA color lithograph, inscribed "To Bobby, Study Hard".

10in (25.5cm) high

$50-70 AGI

An Apollo 17 Ron Evans signed photograph of the American flag on the lunar surface, mounted on white matte board.

12in (30.5cm) high

$180-220 AGI

A complete set of Mercury 7 astronaut autographs, comprising Scott Carpenter, Gordon Cooper, John Glenn, Virgil Grissom, Wally Schirra, Alan Shepard, and Deke Slayton, signed on an RCA Photo Lab/Patrick AFB publicity glossy photo.

$5,000-7,000 AGI

STS 107 was the catastrophic final flight for the space shuttle Columbia, which broke up upon re-entry on February 1st, 2003 with the tragic loss of all on board.

2003 *10in (25.5cm) wide*

$18,000-25,000 SWA

An STS 107 signed official NASA lithograph, signed by all crew members, comprising Dave Brown, Rick Husband, Laurel Clark, Kalpana Chawla, Mike Anderson, Willie McCool, and Ilan Ramon, with biographies printed on the reverse side.

A Gemini GT-06 Wally Schirra and Tom Stafford signed NASA reprint photo.

10in (25.5cm) wide

$120-180 AGI

A Mercury MA-8 Wally Schirra signed copy of "The Astronauts, Pioneers in Space", published by Golden Book Press and the Editors of *Life* Magazine.

1961

$50-70 AGI

Three Apollo 11, 12, and 14 Traverses charts, illustrating the lunar EVAs (moon walks) from the first three lunar landings.

1969-71

$5,000-7,000 SWA

COLLECTORS' NOTES

■ Russian space memorabilia is generally less popular than American and as such, usually less valuable. Cosmonauts were allowed to take pieces home after flights, whereas American astronauts were not, or were only allowed a limited numbers of items.

■ Although Americans were the first to land on the Moon, Russian Yuri Gagarin was the first man in space in Vostok I on April 12th 1961, so much memorabilia focuses on this legendary character.

■ Russian space programs are also comparatively less well known and the language barrier makes it hard to understand them, or how a flown piece fits in to a mission.

■ Despite this, posters with their bold and striking artwork and colors, and memorabilia from the earliest years of space travel during the early 1960s are popular.

A Russian 'Glory to the Soviet People, People of Heroes' poster, depicting a revolutionary soldier and a cosmonaut, printed in Leningrad in a quantity of 185,000, some folds and edge faults.
1962 *37in (94cm) wide*

$400-600 **AGI**

A Russian 'Country of October - Country of Cosmonauts'.
1977 *33in (84cm) high*

$700-1,000 **SWA**

A Vostok 1 Yuri Gagarin signed picture postcard.

$220-280 **AGI**

A Russian 'To the Courage, Labor, Mind of the Russian People - Glory!' poster, showing Yuri Gagarin in front of Earth, his flight path marked as a white ring.

1962 *33in (84cm) high*

$700-1,000 **SWA**

Konstantin Eduardovitch Tsiolkovsky, "The Road to the Stars", USSR Academy of Science, 351pp., Russian-language hardback with dust jacket, the science-fiction anthology including "On the Moon", "Dreams about Earth and Sky", "On the Planet Vesta".
1960

$50-70 **AGI**

Evgeny Ryabchikov, "Pilot of the Star Ship", published by The Printing House of Children's Literature of the Department of Education, 48pp., minor faults.

This was the first hardcover book about Gagarin published in the USSR.
1961

$80-120 **AGI**

Yuri Gagarin, "My Blue Planet", 239pp., signed by the author, Russian-language hardback with dust jacket, some wear to dust jacket.

This book is hard to find, particularly with the dust jacket.

$400-600 **AGI**

An 'Order for Conquering Space' enameled award, set with four artificial diamonds.

This is a new decoration from the Russian Republic rather than from the older Soviet times, but it is still awarded with care and respect.

2in (5cm) wide

$70-100 **AGI**

A Russian 'ASTP' enameled press badge.

Distributed to Soviet journalists that attended the Soyuz 19 launch, prior to its docking with Apollo.

1975   3in (7.5cm) high

$120-180   **AGI**

A Mir program Soyuz TM-6 presentation enameled plaque, presented to dignitaries after the flight by the Russians in honor of the first Russian-Afghan space flight.

1988   3.5in (9cm) high

$220-280   **AGI**

A bronze wall hanging, depicting a cosmonaut, a Sputnik and a rocket.

10in (25.5cm) high

$220-280   **AGI**

A Russian lithographed tin container, featuring space dogs "Strelka and Belka" surrounded by stars, minor rubs.

These were the first living creatures to be sent into space and returned safely to Earth. Traveling on Sputnik 5, they spent a day in orbit on August 19th 1960 and were accompanied by 40 mice, two rats, and some plants. One of Strelka's six post-adventure puppies was presented to President Kennedy's daughter as a gift by President Kruschev.

c1960   6in (15cm) diam

$180-220   **AGI**

A Sputnik music box, with engraved inscription "To Lev Stepanovich on his birthday from his co-workers. January 11, 1963".

This was presented to the 37-year-old cosmonaut Stepanovich by his fellow cosmonauts.

c1963   7in (18cm) long

$80-120   **AGI**

A Vostok 1 Yuri Gagarin and Gherman Titov signed photo of them at a parade.

8in (20cm) high

$220-280   **AGI**

A Vostok 1 Yuri Gagarin and Valentina Tereshkova signed Russian 3k postcard, with a red 1964 commemorative cancel.

Valentina Tereshkova became the first woman in space in 1963, orbiting the world 48 times in Vostok 6.

1964

$180-220   **AGI**

A Soyuz TM-11 flown Soviet flag, crew-signed by Viktor Afanasyev, Musa Manarov and Toyohiro Akiyama with black pentagonal and octagonal MIR on-board hand-stamps, with Russian-language certificate of authenticity.

1990   5.5in (14cm) wide

$220-280   **AGI**

COLLECTORS' NOTES

■ Collecting baseball signatures became popular with the arrival of larger-than-life figure 'Babe' Ruth in 1914. While autographs can be collected on any items, baseballs are particularly popular as they are an intrinsic part of the game and are easy to store and display.

■ Signatures should ideally be on official league baseballs, which will carry the printed signature of the league

president of the time. The dates for that president can be checked against the life span of the player for authenticity. The favored place for the signature is the 'sweet spot', a habit popularized by Ruth.

■ Fakes and printed signatures are common, particularly for certain players such as Mickey Mantle and Ted Williams, so ensure you have a certificate of authenticity and buy from a reputable dealer.

A CLOSER LOOK AT A SIGNED BASEBALL

This was signed in Mantle's first year of professional baseball. He stayed with the Yankees for his entire career.

Mantle and DiMaggio only played one season together, as DiMaggio retired at the end of 1951.

The signatures are on an official baseball, which is preferable.

William Harridge was president of the American league from 1931-59 and this helps to confirm the ball's authenticity.

A New York Yankees signed 'Harridge AL' baseball, signatures including Joe DiMaggio on the sweet spot and Mickey Mantle (signed Mick Mantle), with a letter of authenticity from PSA/DNA and letter of provenance.
1951

$15,000-20,000   **HA**

A Connie Mack signed 'Official League' baseball, with a letter of authenticity from PSA/DNA.

$350-450   **HA**

A New York Yankees team signed 'American League' baseball, signed by 29 players including Crosetti, Ruffing, McCarthy, with a letter of authenticity from PSA/DNA.
1945

$400-500   **HA**

A 1946 Kansas City Monarchs signed Goldsmith 'Official 97 League' baseball, signed by 19 members of the team including Satchel Paige, Hilton Smith and Buck O'Neil, with a letter of authenticity from PSA/DNA.

Negro League team signed baseballs are exceedingly rare and seldom offered.

$1,500-2,000   **HA**

A Pittsburgh Pirates team signed 'Giles NL' baseball, signed by 22 players including Clemente, Mazeroski, Friend, and Virdon, with a letter of authenticity from PSA/DNA.

1965

$650-750   HA

A St. Louis Cardinals signed 'Giles NL' baseball, signed by 23 players including Carlton, Brock, Gibson, Cepeda, Schoendienst, and Flood, with a letter of authenticity from PSA/DNA.

1966

$300-400   HA

A Mickey Mantle signed 'B. Brown AL' portrait baseball, signed on the sweet spot in blue ink with handpainted portrait of Mantle on the side panel, with a letter of authenticity from PSA/DNA.

$1,000-1,500   HA

A Mickey Mantle and Roger Maris signed All-Star official baseball, signed by Mantle on the sweet spot and Maris on side panel, with a letter of authenticity from PSA/DNA.

Maris is best remembered for breaking Babe Ruth's single-season home run record in 1961, after a gap of 34 years. Maris' record was broken in 1998. Mantle and Maris were Yankee team mates from 1960 to 1966.

1983

$4,000-4,500   HA

A 500 Home Run Club signed 'Giamatti NL' baseball, signed by 11 members of the 500 Home Run Club including Mantle, Williams, Mays, McCovey, Aaron, Schmidt, and Jackson, with a letter of authenticity from PSA/DNA.

$800-1,000   HA

An Official 2002 World Series ball, signed by 24 members of the World Champion Anaheim Angels team, lacking Troy Glaus and Garret Anderson, with a letter of authenticity from PSA/DNA.

2002

$350-450   HA

A boxed Draper & Maynard Junior League No.150 baseball, in mint condition.

Box 2.75in (7cm) wide

$650-750   VSC

A white Champion baseball, with Goldsmith stamped mark.

$400-500   VSC

COLLECTORS' NOTES

- Gloves form one of the most popular collecting fields in baseball and fall into two main categories – store-bought gloves, sponsored by professional players and often stamped with a facsimile signature, and gloves owned by professional players, which unsurprisingly are considerably more valuable.

- Early store models are harder to find, especially in good condition, than later examples, and are generally more valuable. The endorsing players' names and the manufacturing are also factors.

- The popularity of the player and whether it was game-worn determine the value of professionally owned examples and the provenance should always be carefully checked.

A CLOSER LOOK AT A BASEBALL GLOVE

Reese was a shortstop for the Dodgers team from 1940 to 1958.

Game-worn equipment, particularly from famous games, will always be worth a premium.

Reese had been playing for the Dodgers for 15 years when they won their first and only World Series in 1955.

This glove was given by Reese to a sportswriter who subsequently sold it to a prominent collector.

A significant Pee Wee Reese game-used Rawlings right-hand baseball glove, missing manufacturer's tag on backstrap, checking on interior padding, heavy pocket wear and small tear on the backstrap, number "1" remains on backstrap and signed on the exterior pinky finger, "My 1955 World Series Glove Pee Wee Reese" in black ink, with letter of provenance SCD Authentic and PSA/DNA.
c1955

$30,000-35,000   **HA**

A Joe DiMaggio model baseball glove, by Trio Hollander, signed in black marker on interior pinky finger, manufacturer label missing from backstrap, with a letter of authenticity from PSA/DNA.

$220-280   **HA**

A Don Drysdale model baseball glove, by Spalding.

c1961   10in (25.5cm) high

$100-150   **BH**

A Jerry Koosman model baseball glove, by Spalding, used by Dock Ellis, with "#17" and "Ellis" written in period marker on back of glove, with a letter of authenticity from SCD Authentic.

c1970-75

$180-220   **HA**

A Mickey Mantle Triple Crown model baseball glove, by Rawlings.

10in (25.5cm) high

$200-300   **BH**

A Mickey Mantle baseball MM5 glove, by Rawlings, signed on interior pinky finger, "Mickey Mantle No. 7" in black felt-tip pen, owner's initials on the backstrap, strong Mantle facsimile signature on interior palm, with a letter of authenticity from PSA/DNA.

$550-650   **HA**

A Pee Wee Reese store model right hand baseball glove, by Olympian, signed on interior pinky finger, with a letter of authenticity from PSA/DNA.

$300-400   **HA**

A CLOSER LOOK AT A BASEBALL SHIRT

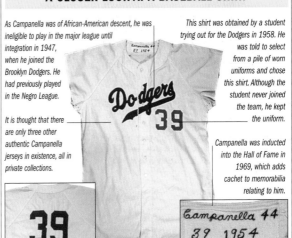

As Campanella was of African-American descent, he was ineligible to play in the major league until integration in 1947, when he joined the Brooklyn Dodgers. He had previously played in the Negro League.

It is thought that there are only three other authentic Campanella jerseys in existence, all in private collections.

This shirt was obtained by a student trying out for the Dodgers in 1958. He was told to select from a pile of worn uniforms and chose this shirt. Although the student never joined the team, he kept the uniform.

Campanella was inducted into the Hall of Fame in 1969, which adds cachet to memorabilia relating to him.

A very rare Roy Campanella Brooklyn Dodgers cream flannel home shirt, strip tag inside the collar with black chain-stitched "Campanella 44 39 1954", original Wilson tag, a few moth holes, with a letter of authenticity from SCD Authentic.

1954

$80,000-100,000   HA

A Harold Baines Chicago White Sox vest-style pinstriped white knit shirt, original Majestic Athletic tag on tail along with "3 48 00" strip tag, very light wear, with a letter of authenticity from SCD Authentic.

2000

$700-800   HA

A John Smoltz Atlanta Braves home professional white knit shirt, Russell Athletic tag on tail front along with "1-00" label, light to moderate wear, with a letter of authenticity from SCD Authentic.

2000

$450-550   HA

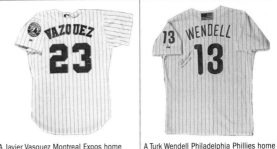

A Javier Vasquez Montreal Expos home professional white knit shirt, Russell Athletic tag remains on tail front along with size/extra length flag tags, wear to lettering and numbers, with a letter of authenticity from SCD Authentic.

c2000

$300-400   HA

A Turk Wendell Philadelphia Phillies home professional white knit shirt, original Sept. 11th US Flag patch on back and Majestic tagging on tail front, signed on back by Wendell, with a letter of authenticity from SCD Authentic.

2001

$150-250   HA

A late 1960s/early 1970s New York Mets heavy royal blue wool warm-up jacket, MacGregor tag inside tail, missing two snap receptacles, vintage piece of tape inside collar with faded #6 in black ink possibly denoting use by Al Weis, with a letter of authenticity from SCD Authentic.

$180-220   HA

A 1970s Philadelphia Phillies ballgirl red knit one-piece uniform, with "P" logo on chest.

$450-550   HA

A Luis Aparicco signed baseball helmet.

9in (23cm) high

$100-150   **BH**

A spider-style catcher's mask, with throat protector, some wear to the headstrap and leather padding.

c1900-10

$500-600   **HA**

A 'Bucky' Walters baseball equipment lidded trunk, used by Walters to hold his baseball equipment for travel, "W.H. Walters" stenciled on end panel, retains original Herkert & Meisel, St. Louis metal manufacturer's tag.

42in (16.5cm) long

$800-1,000   **HA**

A Brooklyn Dodgers heavy blue wool blanket, applied Dodgers felt logo on front, in original handled carrying case.

These were originally given by the Dodgers team as Christmas gifts.

c1950s

$450-550   **HA**

An unusual Mickey Mantle model K55 baseball bat, with applied decal signed in blue felt-tip pen, together with a letter of authenticity from PSA/DNA.

35in (89cm) long

$1,500-2,000   **HA**

A Hillerich & Bradsby Co of Louisville KY Semi-Pro No11B baseball bat, with rare League Regulation transfer decal.

33in (84cm) long

$300-400   **VSC**

An Eddie Collins Stall & Dean baseball bat, with E. Collins signature.

If the bat had been game-used by Eddie Collins, it could fetch around $15,000.

32in (81cm) long

$650-750   **VSC**

A Japanese Boston Red Sox ceramic nodder.

The round white base indicates that this nodder was made between 1961 and 1963. Although it was preceeded by the square colored base, this is usually more popular with collectors.

1961-63   4.5in (11.5cm) high

$200-300   **PWE**

A Japanese Cleveland Indians ceramic mini nodder, with character face.

The character face on this nodder adds value.

1961-63   5in (12.5cm) high

$300-400   **PWE**

A Japanese Detroit Tigers ceramic nodder, with character tiger head.

1961-63   5in (12.5cm) high

$300-500   **PWE**

A Japanese New York Yankees ceramic nodder.

1961-63   5in (12.5cm) high

$250-350   **PWE**

A Japanese Washington Senators ceramic nodder.

1961-63   4.5in (11.5cm) high

$200-300   **PWE**

A Cincinnati Reds World Series press pin, minute hairline in central enamel.

1940

$400-500   **HA**

A Philadelphia Phillies World Series press pin.

1950

$250-350   **HA**

A Pittsburgh Pirates World Series press pin.

1925

$1,500-2,000   **HA**

A Joe Moore New York Giants pin, on card.

1938   Pin 1in (2.5cm) diam

$7-10   **BH**

A rare 1950s Brooklyn Dodgers molded brass bicycle ornament, with enameled decoration, some minor surface wear.

$120-180   **HA**

A CLOSER LOOK AT A BASEBALL PENNANT

Pennants from before 1970 are usually made of felt, making this silk one rare.

The team moved to Los Angeles in 1958, changing their name.

This example celebrates the only time the Dodgers have won the World Series

Pre-1970s pennants are the most popular with collectors.

A rare Brooklyn Dodgers printed silk pennant.

c1955

18in (45.5cm) long

$2,000-3,000

PWE

A rare Brooklyn Dodgers 'team scroll' pennant, players' names in a scroll at left side, with a small edge cutout at top left corner.

1950   *28in (71cm) long*

$400-500   **HA**

A 1940s Philadelphia Stars printed red felt pennant.

The Philadelphia Stars were in the Negro National League, making this desirable.

$220-280   **HA**

A rare 1950s Brooklyn Dodgers Jackie Robinson pennant, with graphic of Robinson at left side along with a facsimile signature, small chip above the "G" in Dodgers.

Jackie Robinson was the first African-American player to join a major league team in nearly 60 years because of an unoffical ban. He joined the Dodgers in 1947 and was initially greeted with abuse, by fans and players from his own and other teams, but went on to win Rookie of the Year. He entered the Hall of Fame in 1962.

$650-750   **HA**

A rare and early St. Louis Browns vs. Boston Red Sox program, some very minor cover toning and a few tiny border tears.

Programs from the early 20thC are some of the most sought-after. Look for unscored examples that are in complete condition.

1904

$1,200-1,800   HA

A scarce Cincinnati Palace of the Fans stadium dedication program, dated May 16th, 1902, light wear, with original string bound spine.

1902

$1,800-2,200   HA

A World Series program and ticket stub, issued for a game played at Philadelphia, some moisture exposure with wrinkling and a few loose pages, ticket stub detached and includes rain check.

1929

$200-300   HA

A Giants vs. Senators World Series program, from October 7th, 1933, in Washington, cover dated in pencil, interior scored.

1933

$400-500   HA

A rare World Series ticket stub, issued for game #1 played at Philadelphia, a few scratches and abrasions.

Ticket have to be from World Series, All-Star or playoff games, or from an otherwise significant game to be of any great value. Whole or unused tickets are also more desirable.

1915

$1,000-1,500   HA

An All-Star game ticket stub, from Brooklyn.

1949

$450-550   HA

An early color lithographed baseball official scorecard.

5.5in (14cm) wide

$100-150   VSC

A 19thC small baseball foldout scorer, with ten interior moveable arrow scorers.

1890

$180-220   HA

A Babe Ruth photograph, picturing Ruth holding bats in front of the dugout, in a vintage matt and frame.

9in (23cm) high

$550-650 HA

A Detroit Tigers team cabinet photograph, including Cobb, Crawford, Jennings, Jones, and Schaefer, Fisher & Kline photographers' stamp to reverse, some typical soiling and a few minor scratches.

1907 *10in (25.5cm) wide*

$5,000-6,000 HA

A rare 1930s/40s Honus Wagner photograph, by George Burke, picturing Wagner in Pirates uniform as a coach, some black paper residue from scrapbook removal, some light soiling to front margins.

14in (35.5cm) high

$1,800-2,000 HA

A Joe DiMaggio photograph, signed in blue felt-tip pen, matted and framed, with a letter of authenticity from PSA/DNA.

20in (51cm) high

$180-220 HA

A Ted Williams and Stan Musial photographic collage display piece, signed by each in blue felt-tip pen, matted and framed, with Mantle Museum hologram sticker and letter of authenticity from PSA/DNA.

20in (51cm) wide

$350-450 HA

A 'Slide, Kelly, Slide' lobby card.

1927 *14in (35.5cm) wide*

$30-40 HA

"Safe at Home!", US one sheet poster, signed "Mickey Mantle No. 7" in blue felt-tip pen at center, a few fold lines and small corner pinholes, matted and framed with a letter of authenticity from PSA/DNA.

1962 *40in (101.5cm) high*

$1,500-2,000 HA

A Mickey Mantle, Willie Mays, and Duke Snider poster, signed by all three players in blue felt-tip pen, with a letter of authenticity from PSA/DNA.

24in (61cm) wide

$350-450 HA

A limited edition Triple Crown award winners poster, issued by Ron Lewis, from an edition of 300, signed by Mickey Mantle, Williams, Yastrzemski, and F. Robinson and signed by artist Robert S. Simon, with a letter of authenticity from PSA/DNA.

24in (61cm) high

$400-500 HA

COLLECTORS' NOTES

■ Baseball cards were introduced by the Goudey Gum Company in 1933, copying the idea from cigarette cards, with the intent of encouraging children to buy more gum. Bowman and Topps starting issuing cards in 1951, and when Topps acquired Bowman in 1956, they became the largest producers in the world.

■ Collecting cards remained a pastime for children until the 1970s when adults began collecting, causing prices to leap in value. Rarity, the even centering of image on the card, condition and errors all affect the value.

A CLOSER LOOK AT A BASEBALL CARD

Topps Chewing Gum Co. of Brooklyn, NY released their first ever cards in 1951, consisting of only two sets of 52 cards, they were not particularly decorative. This 1952 issue was their first true set.

Cards numbered between 311 and 407 were produced in the smallest quantities.

Any card from this set of 407 cards is desirable, but due to its limited production and Mantle's popularity as a player, this is the most valuable.

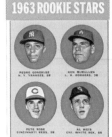

A rare Topps first issue Mickey Mantle #311 card.
This card was issued in Mantle's rookie year with the NY Yankees.
1952
$12,000-18,000   **HA**

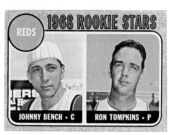

A Topps Johnny Bench #247 card.
1968
$200-300   **HA**

A 'Sporting Life' M116 Ty Cobb card, with rare blue background, light corner crease at top left.
1910-11
$800-1,200   **HA**

A Bowman Bob Feller #30 card.
1951
$800-1,000   **HA**

A Bowman Whitey Ford #1 card.
1951
$2,800-3,200   **HA**

A Topps Mickey Mantle #200 card.
1963
$280-320   **HA**

A Bowman Willie Mays #305 card.
1951
$700-800   **HA**

A rare Topps Pete Rose #537 card.

1963
$1,200-1,800   **HA**

A Crosley Field Burger Beer color lithographed advertising display, with applied advertising logo and depicting game scene at the longtime Reds stadium, framed with some light wear including pinholes.

1960   *38in (96.5cm) long*

$400-500   **HA**

A boxed Babe Ruth All American athletic underwear, the white cotton night gown with stitched Babe Ruth label inside.

13in (33cm) high

$400-600   **VSC**

A Yankee Boy baseball decorated tobacco tin, featuring a boy batting in baseball uniform, some typical surface wear.

c1910

$150-200   **HA**

An RCA Radiotronics printed card advertising standee, promoting baseball scores by radio.

12in (30.5cm) high

$150-250   **VSC**

A rare Brooklyn Dodgers Schaefer Beer advertising stand-up display piece, picturing the World Champion Dodgers.

1955   *5.5in (14cm) wide*

$1,500-2,500   **HA**

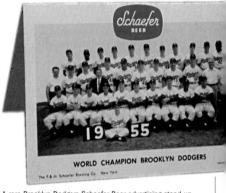

A Blue Ball mahogany cigar box, with impressed sports scene on top and color lithographed interior lid label of identical scene, lid hinge reinforced with period red ribbon, interior remains clean.

c1910   5.5in (13.5cm) long

$80-120   **HA**

A Kibbe's Candies 'You're Sure They're Pure' advertising fan, with a cheering lady at a baseball game and a wooden handle.

13.5in (35cm) high

$100-150   **VSC**

A baseball related advertising fan, with wooden handle, copyrighted by F.A. Schneider, reverse with advertising for Keeley Stove Company ovens.

c1904   13in (33cm) long

$220-280   **VSC**

A rare American Caramel E125 Die Cut Dots Miller card, crease at neck and a few creases.

1910

$800-900   **HA**

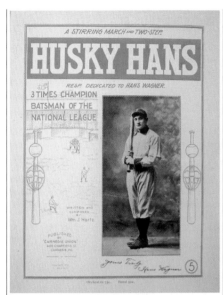

A rare Philadelphia Athletics souvenir book, picturing players photos and biographies inside, some chipping at top left corner.

1910

$250-300   **HA**

A Recess school baseball notebook, with ruled pages and two color printed red and green exterior.

9in (23cm) high

$70-90   **VSC**

A 'Husky Hans – A Stirring March and Two-Step' musical score, composed by William J Hartz, with image of Honus Wagner on the cover.

c1904   *14in (35.5cm) high*

$280-320   **PWE**

"Who's Who In Baseball", dated 1937.

6.5in (16.5cm) high

$100-150   **BH**

"The Sporting News Record Book for 1937", published by Charles C. Spink & Son.

5.5in (14cm) high

$50-70   **BH**

"New Physical Culture", November, 1948, with Babe Ruth cover.

11in (28cm) high

$70-100   **VSC**

"Baseball Digest", dated October 1953.

7.5in (19cm) high

$10-15   **BH**

Dick Schaap, "Mickey Mantle – The Indispensable Yankee", first edition paperback, published by Bartholomew House, Inc.

1961   *7in (18cm) high*

$25-35   **BH**

A Chicago Cubs Official 1962 Roster Book.

7in (18cm) high

$50-60   **BH**

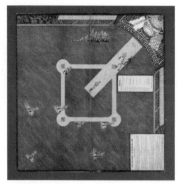

An 'Our National Ball Game' color lithographed baseball board game, matted and framed.

c1886

18in (45.5cm) wide

$300-400 HA

A rare William Hulbert signature, signed "Yours Truly W.A. Hulbert" apparently cut from a document printed with partial name of Harry Wright and "...G. Spalding, Secretary" and "Chicago", with a letter of authenticity from PSA/DNA.

William Ambrose Hulbert (1832-82) helped found baseball's first major league, the National League, of which he later become president. He was also part owner of the Chicago White Stockings club and was elected to the Baseball Hall of Fame in 1995.

4in (10cm) wide

$6,000-7,000 HA

A rare Frank Baker personal check, written and signed "J.Franklin Baker" in black fountain pen, tiny pinhole at center from desk punch, with a letter of authenticity from PSA/DNA.

1922

$1,200-1,800 HA

A Philadelpia 'Big 5' printed plastic megaphone.

8.5in (21.5cm) high

$7-10 BH

A CLOSER LOOK AT A BASEBALL FIGURE

At 17in (43cm) high, this is a particularly large figurine.

The style of this unmarked figure is very similar to that of German porcelain manufacturers Heubach, who are particulary sought-after for their fine quality character dolls.

Despite some restoration to the raised hand, the figurine is in great condition, making it more likely to hold its value.

The complexity of design with the raised arms and the early date all add to the value of this piece.

A rare German handpainted bisque porcelain baseball outfielder figurine, with hand raised to field a ball, stamped on base "Geschützt Gesetzlich DEP", some restoration to raised hand.

c1880s

17in (43cm) high

$5,000-6,000 HA

A 'Bucky' Walters New York Yankees silver-plated presentational plaque, mounted on a mahogany backboard.

13in (33cm) high

$120-180 HA

An 1890s cobalt blue majolica pitcher, with baseball scene on one panel and soccer scene on the other, repaired interior crack and rim chip repair.

8in (20cm) high

$120-180 HA

A plastic baseball-shaped coin bank.

3in (7.5cm) diam

$10-15 BH

A CLOSER LOOK AT A BASKETBALL JACKET

Robertson (b.1938) is regarded as a pioneer 'all-arounder' and was elected to the NBA's 50 Greatest Player list.

In 1971, Robertson helped his team to win their only NBA title.

It has the Bucks logo embroidered on the back. The 'cast iron' provenance, originating from a team source, adds to the value.

It comes with a letter of authenticity from SCD Authentic, which is an important factor to consider when buying memorabilia.

A rare Oscar 'The Big O' Robertson Milwaukee Bucks green knit warm-up jacket, sandknit tag inside collar with green felt tag with chain stitched "1".

c1970-71

$3,500-4,500   **HA**

A green size 40 Harley Davidson basketball shirt, with sewn fabric red "12" on front.

26.75in (68cm) high

$100-150   **VSC**

A Glenn Mosley Philadelphia 76ers blue mesh road jersey, and a pair of 1977 shorts issued to player #11 (Caldwell Jones), with a letter of authenticity from SCD Authentic.

Issued to Mosley as a rookie in 1977 as it was most likely made for Clyde Lee in 1976.

1977

$220-280   **HA**

A 1970s Doug Collins Philadelphia 76ers blue-knit warm-up jacket, with original tag in collar along with player number "20" on strip tag and a letter of authenticity from SCD Authentic.

$200-300   **HA**

A Harlem Magicians basketball cardboard advertising broadside, picturing three players including Marques Haynes, some dings to edges.

26in (66cm) high

$120-180 HA

A Laker Basketball World Champions pictorial album, with pages on key professional players with biographies, awards, and records.

1948 *12.25in (31cm) high*

$70-90 VSC

A Harlem Globetrotters 6th Annual Basketball National Tour Program, for Globetrotters vs All-Stars.

1955 *10in (25.5cm) high*

$70-90 VSC

A scarce 1960s 'Bob Cousy PF Shoes' cardboard easel-back advertising display sign, small pinhole at top and some light wear.

15in (38cm) high

$600-700 HA

A Draper & Maynard basketball blotter, with color lithographed scene of children playing, mounted on a pink card blotter.

6in (15cm) high

$180-220 VSC

An unused 1960s Converse "Chuck Taylor" basketball shoe die-cut cardboard advertising display, for the famous Taylor "All-Stars" sneakers together with an oval Converse sign.

First 23in (58.5cm) high

$300-400 HA

A 1960s Philadelphia 76ers' traveling suitcase, by American Tourister and attributed to Wilt Chamberlain, with vintage Tourister tag with the name of 76ers head coach Roy Rubin addressed to the Spectrum in Philadelphia, with a letter of provenance from the son of Les Yellin.

This suitcase was originally given to longtime collegiate coach Les Yellin by Chuck Daly who was the coach at the University of Pennsylvania at the time.

$1,000-1,500 HA

A 1940s painted metal cased coin-operated basketball game, with lithographic fiberboard background, in working order, backboard stained, some rusting and external glass casing replaced.

22in (56cm) long

$550-650 HA

An American silver-plated basketball bookend, with plaque engraved "OCC 1933 C Kirschner" and with a molded "WB" in a shield mark to reverse, on a black finished metal base.

c1933 *9in (22.5cm) high*

$200-300 VSC

COLLECTORS' NOTES

- American football runs a close second to baseball for collecting memorabilia. First played in the US as a hybrid of rugby and soccer, the first professional game was played in Latrobe, Pennsylvania in 1895.

- The game only became popular with the general public in the 1920s, with the appearance of Harold 'Red' Grange, whose star qualities captured the popular imagination.

- As with other sporting memorabilia, pieces connected to popular players and teams are the most sought after and include uniforms, autographs, photographs, ephemera, and historical items that chart the sport's development.

A YMCA red football jersey, by Draper Maynard, with sewn label.

Draper Maynard is a desirable manufacturer and red is an unusual color for a football jersey.

32.25in (82cm) high

$300-400 **VSC**

A Ray Brown Atlanta Falcons red Durene shirt, Sand Knit and Falcons/Exclusive tagging affixed to tail front, shows some wear, with a letter of authenticity from SCD Authentic.

c1971-77

$120-180 **HA**

A Wilson football helmet, all black leather.

9.75in (25cm) high

$320-380 **VSC**

A rare and early Philadelphia Eagles "Kra-Lite" helmet, by Riddell, with silver Eagle wings on both sides and original chin strap, undrilled for facemask, with a letter of authenticity from SCD Authentic.

c1961-66

$600-700 **HA**

A Morrill football noseguard, with handcarved decor, original canvas strap, player-carved team name "Tigers" (Princeton?), dated.

1903

$550-650 **HA**

An early to mid-1970s New York Jets helmet, by Wilson, with applied logos on both sides, retaining original gladiator chin strap and remains undrilled for facemask attachment, with a letter of authenticity from SCD Authentic.

$120-180 **HA**

A Barry Sanders Detroit Lions professional knit jersey, dazzle cloth and mesh material, Reebok and year tag affixed to tail front, NFL 75th Anniversary patch removed from shoulder, shows some light wear, with a letter of authenticity from SCD Authentic.

1994-95

$1,500-2,000 **HA**

A pair of unused black leather football cleats, with original unused wooden spikes on bottom.

c1910-20

$120-180 **HA**

A used Spalding 'P 3 YALE 0 1922' football, for Princeton & Yale.

1922   *10.75in (27.5cm) high*

$550-650   **VSC**

A Sid Luckman sponsored football, with printed signature.

          12.25in (31cm) wide

$100-150   **VSC**

A Yale football-shaped porcelain stein, with figural player head on thumb press, some restoration to a crack on the body and a chip on lid.

c1905-10   *6in (15cm) high*

$650-750   **HA**

A Princeton University pottery vase, by Doulton, with sterling silver rim, some restoration, marked on base.

c1910-20   *8in (20cm) high*

$40-60   **HA**

A CLOSER LOOK AT A FOOTBALL PITCHER

F. Earl Christy (1882-1961) was a prolific graphic illustrator who is well-known for his portraits and depictions of the female form.

As well as Yale, Christy illustrated for other Ivy League colleges such as Princeton and Harvard, often with sports-related themes.

His images were reproduced on postcards, book and magazine covers, steins and pitchers such as this.

If the handle had been original, the value would be up to double.

A rare Yale football-themed porcelain water pitcher, with Yale player painted on front signed "F. Earl Christy", handle professionally replaced.

c1905-10   *10in high (25.5cm) high*

$800-1,000   **HA**

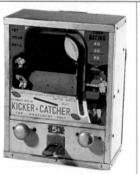

A 1940s 'Kicker & Catcher' coin-operated football game, with moveable player that catches the ball, in working order, replaced backboard.

$180-220   **HA**

A 'Kicker and Catcher' coin-operated football game, by J.F. Frantz Co., probably 1960s/70s, with painted cast iron marquis, in working order with key.

          24in (61cm) high

$250-350   **HA**

A University of Michigan football figural glazed pottery bank, marked "Moyer" on back of base.

8in (20cm) high

$150-250 HA

A 1960s Baltimore Colts figural porcelain decanter, with removable head-shaped stopper, marked "Fred Kail, Jr." on back, some in-painting to shoulder.

10in (25.5cm) high

$180-220 HA

A rare Moyer football player money bank, marked "© Moyer" on side of base, with some wear.

Mr. Moyer reportedly used his own face to model this player, with uniform decorations being added after firing to suit the buyer's preferred team colors.

7.5in (19cm) high

$80-120 BEL

A Heubach-style painted bisque footballer figurine, with impressed sun motif and "ERPHILA GERMANY" printed mark to foot.

6.75in (17cm) high

$550-650 VSC

A 1930s Red Grange children's doll, with composition head and hands, retaining original uniform, marked "Sterling Doll Co., NY", some minor surface scratching under helmet, with a letter of authenticity from PSA/DNA.

$2,200-2,800 HA

A 1920s homemade folk art football player doll, made from fabric, stocking and wool on a poseable wire frame.

12.75in (32.5cm) high

$150-250 VSC

A rare football player still cast iron bank, with original gilt paint.

c1910   6in (15cm) high

$350-450 HA

A figural football player desk clock, retaining most of the original gilt paint, lacks winding key.

4in (10cm) high

$150-250 HA

A pair of 1920/30s figural football painted gesso bookends, with a player tackling a runner.

7in (18cm) high

$650-750 HA

SPORTING MEMORABILIA

A rare Yale vs. Harvard football program, from November 13th, 1897, cover loose from the spine otherwise reasonably clean.

$600-700   HA

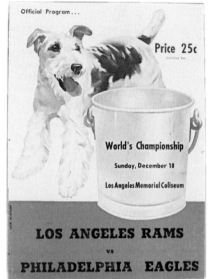

Official Program...

Price 25c

World's Championship

Sunday, December 18

Los Angeles Memorial Coliseum

LOS ANGELES RAMS

vs

PHILADELPHIA EAGLES

A Los Angeles Rams vs. Philadelphia Eagles NFL Championship game program, from December 18th, 1949 at Los Angeles Coliseum, signed on the interior by Steve Van Buren, with letter of authenticity from PSA/DNA.

$650-750   HA

A California Pennsylvania, official souvenir program, from January 1st, 1925.

10.75in (27.5cm) high

$100-150   VSC

An Eagles vs Cardinals NFL Championship program, from December 19th, 1948 at Philadelphia, signed on interior by Steve Van Buren, front cover has an abrasion, with a letter of authenticity from PSA/DNA.

$350-450   HA

A New York Giants vs. Baltimore Colts NFL Championship game program, from December 28th, 1958, at Yankee Stadium, some typical light wear.

$450-550   HA

A World Championship Game Super Bowl I program, from January 15th, 1967, clean example with minimal wear.

$300-400   HA

"Burr McIntosh Monthly", string bound with color lithographic cover featuring Yale football fan holding a ball.

1904

$30-40   HA

A Notre Dame Football Review, with an embossed bust image of Knute Rockne on the front cover, some general wear.

1930

$220-280   HA

"Army Magazine", official program Lon Keller Michie Stadium, October 18th, 1952.

11.5in (29cm) high

$80-100   VSC

A Pennsylvania postcard, with lady's head on the football, with post mark for October 17th 1907.

c1907   *5.75in (14.5cm) wide*

$30-50   **VSC**

A football calendar, by Walter Camp, copyright by Suller & Kleintech.

1916   *10.75in (27cm) wide*

$200-300   **VSC**

A W.V.U. (West Virginia University) card football frame, with inset photographic image of a lady.

10in (25.5cm) wide

$120-180   **VSC**

A rare Harvard fold-out 'pennant' postcard.

c1909   *5.5in (14cm) high*

$70-90   **VSC**

A 1940s Goodrich Shoe Co. die-cut cardboard advertising display set, including Wisconsin football player, very little wear with fresh original colors and clean edges.

Largest 24in (9.5in (high)

$300-400   **HA**

A 1940s Wilson football die-cut cardboard advertising display sign, some light general wear including some corner creasing.

20in (51cm) high

$300-400   **HA**

A 'Big Ten' football game, with original color lithographic envelope.

1926   *20in (51cm) high*

$200-300   **HA**

"Illustrated Football Annual", with superb cover artwork.

1940   *11.5in (29cm) high*

$30-50   **VSC**

A football-related photographic image on paper mounted on canvas, 'Will He Make The College Team? Invest Here for his future education'.

12.25in (31cm) high

$80-120   **VSC**

A 'Johnny Unitas Football Game', featuring image of Unitas on cover.

c1960

$300-400 **HA**

A Touchdown football board game, by Milton Bradley Co., with color lithographed game scene on lid, interior containing board, spinner and wooden ball.

c1915-25

$400-500 **HA**

A rare Harvard vs. Yale football pillowcase top, decorated with a game scene between Harvard and Yale, some toning and a few areas of separations and holes, framed in period oak frame.

c1890-1910 *21in (53.5cm) wide*

$700-800 **HA**

A rare 1940s Red Grange model football photographic box, base missing one side apron.

$300-400 **HA**

An American carved wooden football plaque tie rack.

11in (28cm) widest

$100-150 **VSC**

An Adidas American football-style t-shirt.

$12-18 **BR**

A scarce New York Giants sterling silver football season pass, with raised decoration of a player kicking a ball, inscribed "Harry Colley No. 517" and stamped "Dieges & Clust/sterling".

1926

$1,000-1,500 **HA**

A 1930s/40s Ken Strong die-cut cardboard advertising display sign, with easel back, picturing Strong kicking a ball advertising "Hildick Five" Apple Brandy.

18in (45.5cm) long

$100-150 **HA**

COLLECTORS' NOTES

- Golf is one of the oldest sports still played today, however, most of the memorabilia available today originates in the late 19th century.

- Golf clubs and balls form the basis of many a collection with early, rare or high quality examples forming the upper part of the market. More modern clubs can still be collectible, yet affordable.

- As well as playing equipment, there is a huge range of items carrying a golfing theme, including ceramics, metalware, artwork, and books.

- Ephemera produced for games and tournaments are also popular and come in a wide range of values. Those from very early or landmark games will be the most sought-after.

- Women began playing golf in the early 20th century and the popularity of the game continues to grow. Memorabilia featuring women is harder to find and so can command a premium when it does appear.

A scarce Bramble pattern gutty golf ball, stamped "The Paxton's Brand 1898", wear to paint and some strike marks but retaining good shape.

1.75in (4.5cm) diam

$220-280   **MM**

A scarce 'Scotch Jenny Make' rubber dimple golf ball, made by the St. Andrews Golf Co., some paint wear.

1.75in (4.5cm) diam

$80-120   **MM**

A scarce and unusual 'B. I.' hexagonal mesh pattern rubber core ball, with three strike marks.

c1910   *1.75in (4.5cm) diam*

$70-100   **MM**

A Blue Star paper-wrapped golf ball, complete with original label.

1.75in (4.5cm) diam

$70-100   **MM**

A Dunlop 'Goblin' No.4 paper-wrapped golf ball, complete with original label.

1.75in (4.5cm) diam

$120-180   **MM**

A Dunlop 'Sixty-Five' No.4 paper-wrapped golf ball, complete with original label.

1.75in (4.5cm) diam

$60-90   **MM**

A two-part cast iron cross-hatched golf ball press/mold.

3.75in (9.5cm) wide

$700-1,000   **MSA**

A scarred wooden head putter, by Alexander Patrick, Leven, horn insert to sole, lead counterweight, hickory shaft, wrapped soft leather grip.

Patrick was apprenticed to his cabinetmaker father, who also made clubs, and inherited the family business in 1866. He made clubs at the Royal Wimbledon Golf Club from 1886.

$600-900   **L&T**

A CLOSER LOOK AT A PUTTER

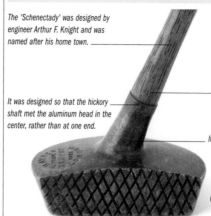

The 'Schenectady' was designed by engineer Arthur F. Knight and was named after his home town.

It was designed so that the hickory shaft met the aluminum head in the center, rather than at one end.

In 1904, the year after it was launched, the 'Schenectady' helped Walter Travis become the first American to win the British Amateur Championship.

It was an extremely popular putter in the US, but was effectively banned by the Royal & Ancient Golf Club (of St. Andrews) Rules of Golf Committee because of its design.

An unusual 'Schenectady' type aluminum putter, stamped on the head "TRUPUT TRADEMARK F H AYRES LONDON", with original hickory shaft and sheepskin grip.
c1910

Head 3.75in (9.5cm) long

$400-600   **MSA**

An Eve smooth-faced putter, the back stamped with trademark, and further marked, "Left 10 degree, weight 8.5oz", hickory shaft, wrapped leather drip.

$120-180   **L&T**

A beech driving putter, by Robert Simpson, the scarred head with horn insert to sole, lead counterweight, hickory shaft, wrapped, white leather grip with silver band mount and cap, engraved initials.

$600-900   **L&T**

An early "Special Patent" wry-neck putter, by Willie Park, smooth face, long crimped hosel, hickory shaft, leather grip.

$280-320   **L&T**

A 'Premier' putter, by Robert Simpson, the iron head with mesh patterned face, the hickory shaft stamped with maker's name, wrapped leather grip.

$700-1,000   **L&T**

An unusual American center-shafted Model AC putter, by Winter Dobson of Dallas, Texas, with Bakelite face and brass sale plate to base of head.
c1945   5in (12.5cm) long

$400-600   **MSA**

A cleek, by Robert Forgan & Son of St. Andrews, showing the Prince of Wales feathers mark and maker's stamp to shaft.

39.5in (100.5cm) high

$80-120   **MM**

A smooth-faced cleek, by Carrick, Musselburgh, stamped "Carrick" and "X", long crimped hosel, hickory shaft, replacement wrapped leather grip.

$220-280   **L&T**

A driving iron, by Tom Morris, of St. Andrews, showing the later Tom Morris head and shoulder stamp mark.

39in (99cm) high

$60-90   **MM**

A Zenith jigger, by Tom Morris of St. Andrews, with unusual Tom Morris color transfer label to shaft inscribed "Open Champion 1861, 62, 64 & 67", together with the maker's autograph shaft stamp.

39in (99cm) high

$180-220   **MM**

A smooth-faced rut niblick, by G. Forrester, Elie & Earlsferry long hosel, hickory shaft, wrapped leather grip.

$500-700   **L&T**

A giant niblick, by James McDowell Turnberry, with a Spalding anvil cleek mark and punch dot facings, fitted with full length original leather grip.

37in (94cm) high

$220-280   **MM**

A persimmon head Sunday club, by J. & H. Scott, Elie, the fancy face head with stamped trademark.

$400-600   **L&T**

A John Letters walking stick golf club, the head bearing transfer trademark.

$300-500   **L&T**

A rare 1920s Prestwick golf scorer, made of nickel-plated brass and ivorine.

4in (10cm) wide

$280-320 MSA

A rare Douglas Golf silver-plated patent 'Sand Tee', unused, in original maker's box priced 3/9d, with instructions and blue paper wrapper.

Box 3.25in (8.5cm) long

$1,200-1,800 MM

A 1920s golf score keeper, the leather wallet with leaves of ivorine set with revolving discs of numbers, the front stamped in gilt with a golf bag.

4.25in (11cm) high

$180-220 MSA

An American clear plastic and paper Strokmaster golf score keeper, made by Healthways of Los Angeles, California, with original box.

4.25in (11cm) high

$120-180 MSA

A rare 1960s Spalding golf clubs store display stand, the wooden easel-back piece having Spalding golf flag style sign at top, and containing a set of four unused Bobby Jones model woods, some light paint flaking.

$300-500 HA

A 1920s Walker & Hall silver-plated nut dish, with squirrel on a twisted horizontal, supported by golf clubs.

8.25in (15cm) wide

$220-280 MSA

A three-piece EPNS condiment set, in the form of Bramble golf balls supported by golf clubs, with stamped registered number 604192 for 1912.

Salt 3.25in (8cm) high

$220-280 MSA

A set of three golf club-shaped pencils, in a papier-mâché golf bag-style case.

c1930s/40s

$80-120 HA

A pair of Hagenauer-style handpainted brass golfing figures.

3in (7.5cm) high

$50-80 MM

A scarce Britains golfer lead figure, with gray jacket, plus-fours and peaked cap, brown socks and shoes, walking with golf club in right hand.

$120-180 W&W

A European handpainted bisque figure of a golf caddy, probably Austrian.

c1910 7in (18cm) high

$400-600 MSA

A pair of green patinated bronze bookends, depicting a golfer and a diminutive caddy with bag of clubs, each on a variegated black/green marble base.

c1930 Largest 9.25 (23.5cm) high

$1,200-1,800 L&T

A pair of Weller Dickens Ware pottery vases, of cylindrical form, each incised and polychrome, decorated with a golfer in a landscape, incised numerals "318/0" to the underside.

7.75in (19.5cm) high

$1,200-1,800 L&T

A Royal Doulton 'The Nineteenth Hole' plate, with printed and handpainted design of two gentlemen enjoying a post game drink.

c1925 10.5in (26.5cm) diam

$500-700 MSA

A Royal Doulton 'Picturesque Scenes' plate, 'Melrose Abbey, Killarney and Stratford', with a transfer scene of a golfer.

10.5in (26.5cm) diam

$400-600 MSA

A Tony Wood Studio ceramic dimple golf ball-shaped teapot, with a club handle and 18th flag mounted to the lid.

7.75in (19.5cm) high

$70-100 MM

SPORTING MEMORABILIA

COLLECTORS' NOTES

- Olympic memorabilia has been collected since the modern games started in 1896, but was mainly collected by people involved in the games, such as the participants and officials.

- The first official piece of memorabilia released was a set of stamps for the 1896 games, issued by the organizing committee to balance the event's budget. Olympic coins followed much later in 1951.

- Lapel badges have been produced since the games restarted. They are an affordable way to start a collection and are usually easy to obtain, with participation medals forming the next step up the ladder. These medals were given to all the participants, officials, and members of the International Olympic Committee, so numbers can be quite large.

- Mascots are a relatively new marketing tool, the first being 'Schuss' – the unofficial mascot of the 1968 games, held in Grenoble. 'Waldi' the dachshund was the first official mascot and presided over the 1972 summer games at Munich.

- Memorabilia from the earliest games tends to be the hardest to find, and so the most valuable, making more recent games a good place to start for collectors on a budget.

- Look for pieces connected to countries that no longer 'exist', such as Eastern Germany or the Soviet Union, as historical interest can add to their value and desirability.

A scarce pewter goblet, relating to the 1912 Olympic games in Stockholm, with a raised acorn leaf design, stamped to base.

1912   *3.5in (9cm) wide*

$70-100   **MM**

A book commemorating the 1912 Olympics, entitled 'Den Femte Olympiaden I Bild och Ord', including a piece on the British gold medal-winning football team.

1912   *12in (30.5cm) wide*

$120-180   **MM**

A 1928 Amsterdam Olympic commemorative plate, decorated in bright colors.

1928   *11.5in (29cm) wide*

$25-35   **SAS**

An official program for the 1936 Winter Olympics, with official Olympic poster design to front cover.

1936   *8.75 (22cm) wide*

$50-80   **MM**

An official 1936 Berlin Olympics brass and white enamel lapel badge, reading "XI Olympiade Berlin", depicting the official games logo.

1936   *1.25in (3cm) wide*

$50-80   **MM**

An official 1936 Berlin Olympics competitor's medal, reading "XI Olympiade Berlin 1936", with the games logo to the reverse.

1936   *2.75in (7cm) wide*

$80-120   **MM**

A gold medal, reading "The 18th Olympic Games Tokyo 1964" to the front, with a Roman chariot scene to the rear, with original box.

2.25in (5.5cm) diam

$700-1,000   **MM**

A 1980 Moscow Olympics walking mug, by Carltonware.

1980   *4.25in (11cm) high*

$30-50   **SAS**

FIND OUT MORE...

www.collectors.olympic.org, *The Olympic Collectors Commission, official collectors association.*

COLLECTORS' NOTES

■ Tennis originated as 'jeu de paume' in France 900 years ago, slowly gaining the use of gloves, then bats, and then rackets in the 16th century, to replace the palm (paume) of the hand. In 1874, Major Walter Clopton Wingfield developed 'Sphairistike', tennis' immediate forerunner.

■ Cans of balls form an interesting collection. Unopened cans are more valuable – check that the colored design goes all the way to the metal band at the top, rather than having a gap showing the opening strip has been torn off. Look at the artwork to discern the period of the can. Card was used during WWII due to a shortage of metal, and plastic was introduced in 1984.

■ Rackets are a popular area. Changing shapes allow them to be dated to a period. Full size rackets were developed by the 1700s and had asymmetrical, lop-sided heads. By the early 1880s, this was replaced

with a 'flat' top and designs gained a concave throat piece (i.e. curved towards the handle).

■ During the 1890s the flat top began to be rounded off, and from 1900-1920s, heads became more oval in shape. Look out for early rackets made before the 1900s with unusual stringing designs and shaped handles and heads, as experimentation was common.

■ The renowned Wimbledon Championships began in 1877, moving to their present site in 1922. They were suspended during WWII. Early programs, especially from the 1930s, are sought after.

■ Novelty memorabilia is also appealing and collectible, with more jewelry and small items found than for other sports, perhaps due to the larger number of female players. Look for quality of design and materials and an early date, from 1880s-1930s.

An early Dunlop 'The Service' blue lawn tennis ball tin, complete with four maker's unused balls including two fully paper-wrapped with original Dunlop labels, all stamped "Service".

1939-45   11in (28cm) high

$280-320   **MM**

A 1940s Dunlop Championship tin tube of tennis balls.

8in (20cm) high

$120-180   **MSA**

A 1950s American Spalding 'Pancho Gonzales' endorsed tin tube of tennis balls.

Pancho Gonzales (1928-95) won the U.S. Championship 1947-48, dominated the professional circuit during the 1950s and played and won the longest ever Wimbledon match, lasting 5 hours and 12 minutes!

8in (20.5cm) high

$80-120   **MSA**

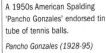

An early Slazenger tin, with two used period balls, removable lid and retaining much original finish.

1900s-1910s   11in (28cm) high

$120-180   **MM**

A Dunlop 'Fort' tennis ball box, complete with six unused balls, dated.

1974   8in (20.5cm) wide

$30-50   **MM**

A 1930s Dunlop Warwick card box of six tennis balls, one with original paper wrapping.

8.25in (15cm) wide

$120-180   **MSA**

A 'Kleenball' patent lawn tennis wooden hand ball cleaner, complete with bristle linings and unusual bowl-shaped body, with turned wooden handles.

4in (10cm) diam

$280-320   **MM**

A rare Hammer Handle flat-top 14oz lawn tennis racket, by F.H. Ayres, handle stamped "Hammer Handle" in script and with reg'd number 37585.

c1880   27.5in (70cm) long

$400-600   **MSA**

A CLOSER LOOK AT A TENNIS RACKET

This racket is named after Ernest & William Renshaw, who were Wimbledon Doubles champions five times from 1884.

It retains its original thick gut stringing, although the strings are distressed with age.

It has a square-shaped head with a flat top and chamfered wedge, indicating an 1880s racket.

Slazenger was founded in 1881, making tennis rackets and balls.

An early Slazenger 'The Renshaw' racket.
c1888   *27.25in (69.5cm) long*

$500-800   **MSA**

A Bussey lawn tennis fishtail 'The Diamond' racket, with unusual grooved handle, with "GEO.G.BUSSEY & CO Ltd" and "THE DIAMOND" stampings.

c1895   27.25in (69cm) long

$400-600   **MSA**

An unmarked fishtail handle racket, stamped "12oz X".

c1905   27.25in (69cm) long

$180-220   **MSA**

A 1920s F.H. Ayres Tournament Model Davis Cup tennis racket, with transfers.

27.25in (69.5cm) long

$180-220   **MSA**

A 1920s American 'Wilding' open throat tennis racket, by Rawlins of St Louis.

27.25in (69cm) high

$120-180   **MSA**

A 1920s good Speedshaft 'Ultra Souple' tennis racket, with transfers, one in a shield reading "Darsonval Brevetee".

27in (68.5cm) high

$120-180   **MSA**

A 19thC mahogany racket press, with brass fitting and painted initials "J.E.B.".

13in (33cm) wide

$280-320   **MSA**

A European handpainted ceramic tennis theme figurine, in the form of a spill vase, of a boy standing next to a tree trunk, unmarked.

5in (12.5cm) high

$120-180   MSA

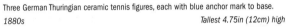

Three German Thuringian ceramic tennis figures, each with blue anchor mark to base.

1880s   Tallest 4.75in (12cm) high

$500-700   MSA

A Spode bone china figure of an Edwardian female tennis player, 'Alexandra', by Paula Shone, wearing a full-length tennis dress and boater, decorated with gold leaf highlights.

c1985   9.5in (24cm) high

$50-80   WW

A Clifton commemorative crested china miniature tennis racket, transfer-decorated.

c1900   4in (10cm) high

$50-80   MSA

A Victorian Denby-style stoneware loving cup with tennis motifs, handles modeled as greyhounds, marked.

8in (20.5cm) wide

$280-320   WW

An Austrian ceramic plate, with molded design of a gentleman tennis player, with painted detailing.

c1880   6in (15cm) diam

$220-280   MSA

A pair of early 20thC printed silk tennis theme lamp shades, with wire bulb grips.

4.25in (11cm) high

$300-500   MSA

A Midwinter tennis theme oval plate, after a design by Shelley, with transfer-printed scene of children playing tennis and a handpainted border, some wear to the transfer.

11.5in (29cm) wide

$180-220   MSA

A Dean leather-bound lawn tennis measure, in exceptional condition with yellow paper label.

A worn example of the this would be worth under half this value.

c1900   5.25in (13.5cm) diam

$280-320   MSA

An American molded composition wall clock, in the form of a tennis racket, fitted with a wind-up movement by the Lux Clock MFG Co Ltd of Waterbury, Conn, USA.

7.5in (19cm) long

$80-120　　　　　　　　　　MSA

A rare S. Mordan & Co. silver slide action pencil, in the form of a Real Tennis racket.

The London firm of Sampson Mordan is well-known for its novelty-shaped pencils, which can be valuable, especially as they appeal also to writing equipment collectors.

c1880

$500-800　　　　　　　　　　GORL

A small wooden tennis racket-shaped '25 Year Silver Anniversary' handheld mirror.

13.5in (34.5cm) high

$220-280　　　　　　　　　　MSA

A Victorian black jet brooch, in the form of a hand holding a racket with tennis ball.

2.25in (5.5cm) high

$80-120　　　　　　　　　　WW

A 1920s 'The Art of Tennis and How To Play It' poster, by an anonymous designer and produced by the Parkstone Film Co. Lytham.

30in (76cm) high

$300-400　　　　　　　　　　CL

A 20thC Wimbledon official member's bow tie.

4.5in (11.5cm) wide

$50-80　　　　　　　　　　WW

A woven fabric and gilt and metal thread 'Tennis Club' blazer pocket badge.

3.5in (9cm) high

$30-50　　　　　　　　　　MSA

A 1980s Snoopy tennis watch, on replaced strap.

$80-120　　　　　　　　　　MSA

An original press photograph of Suzanne Lenglen (1899-1938).

Lenglen won 25 Grand Slam titles between 1919 and 1926.

c1925　　　*9in (23cm) high*

$70-100　　　　　　　　　　WW

Two 19thC feather, blue velvet and pink woven ribbon badminton shuttlecocks.

Largest 5in (12.5cm) high

$300-500   **MSA**

A pair of badminton rackets, stamped "President" and "Army & Navy CTL".

c1900   26.5in (67.5cm) long

$150-180   **MSA**

CHRIS EUBANK

A signed Chris Eubank publicity postcard.

6in (15cm) high

$10-15   **LCA**

A note signed by Gene Tunney, inscribed "P.S. Tell your brother to stop picking on you".

James Joseph "Gene" Tunney was heavyweight boxing champion from 1926 to 1928.

5in (12.5cm) high

$120-180   **MM**

A mechanical boxing toy titled 'Time!', with two lithograph-on-paper board boxing figures operating when tabs are depressed, a few abrasions on the players.

c1911   10in (25.5cm) long

$70-100   **HA**

A bronze group of two men boxing, on a rectangular plinth with outswept marble base, some chips to base.

10.5in (27cm) high

$1,000-1,500   **DN**

A 1950s/60s John L. Sullivan figural advertising display piece, the painted metal statue on original base, marked "James Clark Distilling Co., NY" on back.

11in (28cm) high

$180-220   **HA**

A Joe Louis vs. Joe Walcott Championship program, from June 23, 1948, at Yankee Stadium.

$350-450   **HA**

A pair of Everlast 5403 burgundy leather boxing gloves, printed with Jack Dempsey's signature.

10in (25.5cm) long

$150-200   **VSC**

A five cents red brown stamp, showing Benjamin Franklin, lightly cancelled with postmark.

This was the first American stamp ever issued. The cancellation is light, a positive feature. This example is also well-centered with even margins.

1847   1in (2.5cm) high

$800-1,200   **RSB**

A 1920s American one cent 'Kansas' stamp.

These stamps were overprinted with the name of Nebraska or Kansas states due to organized crime. These are notorious for being off-center, this is a well centered example.

1929   1in (2.5cm) wide

$5-8   **RSB**

A rare block of 12 American three cents rose stamps, with margin and profile of Washington.

It is first of all unusual to find a block of stamps such as this, instead of a single stamp. Furthermore, the block includes the margin with the printed plate number, an interesting feature that is usually removed. An individual stamp in similar condition may fetch around $50.

1861-62   5.5in (14cm) wide

$1,200-1,800   **SST**

An early 1930s Farley unperforated four cents stamp.

US postmaster James A. Farley printed unperforated stamps for selected friends. After continued protests from stamp collectors, the government was forced to reissue the stamps in an unperforated form, which are more appealing to collectors.

1.5in (4cm) wide

$1-2   **RSB**

An American 'Victory' issue stamp.

This example is clean, unhinged and perfectly centered, centering being important to collectors. It was produced in 1919 to commemorate the victory of WWI.

1919   1in (2.5cm) wide

$8-12   **RSB**

Two American 'Family Planning' eight cents stamps, one with perforation shift.

Errors can add value and are always worth looking out for. Note the perforation shift, where the printing has fallen out of kilter. This raises the value of this stamp from up to 40c to around $10.

1972   1.5in (4cm) high

$8-10   **RSB**

A 1985 $10.75 Definitive stamp, showing a Bald Eagle and the Moon.

Most modern stamps generally do not keep their value. This one has two points in favor – birds are a popular collecting theme and it is a high value stamp of which less would have been printed.

1985   2in (5cm) wide

$20-30   **SST**

An American $9.95 Airmail Definitive stamp, showing an American Bald Eagle.

1991   2in (5cm) wide

$20-30   **RSB**

An American $3 Definitive stamp, showing the Space Shuttle Challenger STS-7 in orbit.

Look out for themed stamps. Like birds, space is a popular theme.

1995   1.5in (4cm) wide

$5-8   **RSB**

COLLECTORS' NOTES

- Teddy bears are as valuable and desirable to collectors today as they were to the children that originally owned them. The maker, date and size are the primary indicators to value, followed by color and other features such as facial expression and moving parts. Steiff is the most collectible name, holding the world record with 'Teddy Girl' selling for $200,000 in 1994. Fellow German makers Bing, Schuco and Hermann, English maker Farnell and US maker Ideal follow close behind.

- Look at the shape of a bear as it can help you identify the maker, country of origin and most importantly, the date of manufacture. The face and limbs in particular can help with identifying the maker. Long limbs, a humped back, boot button eyes and a pronounced snout are early features to look for, as are mohair fur and hard, wood wool stuffing. As with any valuable collectible, reproductions do exist so learn how to spot the hallmarks.

- As early bears by major makers become scarcer and more expensive, those from the mid-20thC by lesser known makers are growing in popularity. Much loved names such as Merrythought, Chad Valley and Chiltern are growing in value, particularly if in good condition. As before, consider the shape, material and stuffing, as postwar bears tend to be plumper in form, using synthetic and soft stuffing from the 1960s and 70s.

- Bears that have been well played with and are now lacking their fur, and or have been repaired, are likely to be primarily of sentimental value. Modern limited edition bears, introduced to the collecting market in the 1970s by companies such as Steiff are likely to grow in value, but only if in mint condition with all their paperwork and box, if applicable.

- Despite the dominance of well-known names and condition, 'eye appeal' is another primary consideration. Bears, even home-made ones, with the 'cute' factor will always appeal to collectors, especially if they date from around the mid-20thC.

A large blond mohair teddy bear, stuffed with wood wool stuffing, brown glass eyes, black stitched nose and three stitched claws to each foot.

1920-30   29.5in (74cm) high

$180-220   **WDL**

A beige mohair teddy bear, with hump-backed body, long jointed limbs and neck, black button eyes, pointed snout, suede pads, and oilcloth nose, repair at neck, slight looseness to joints.

The triangular shape of his head and high placed arms suggest an American origin.

c1918   21in (53.50cm) high

$400-600   **JDJ**

An American blond mohair teddy bear, with boot button eyes and stitched black wool nose and mouth.

1906-08   11.5in (29cm) high

$800-1,200   **HGS**

A light-brown teddy bear, with unusual joints, brown wool stitched nose, black card eyes, wood wool stuffing, fur worn away.

c1915   12.5in (31cm) high

$120-180   **WDL**

A gold mohair teddy bear, with glass eyes and brown stitched nose, stuffed with wood wool and with repaired paws, moth damage.

1930-40   28.75in (72cm) high

$150-200   **WDL**

A blond mohair teddy bear, with wood wool stuffed body, with light brown glass eyes and a stitched pointed nose in black, repairs in leather to arms and feet pads.

c1920   13.5in (34cm) high

$220-280   **WDL**

An early English teddy bear, possibly by Farnell, blond plush fur with glass eyes, protruding stitched snout and jointed limbs, formerly with hump, worn.

c1925   23in (58.5cm) high

$800-1,200   **GORL**

A small pink and cream teddy bear, possibly French, with simple visible joints, stuffed with wood wool, growler not working, losses to color.

c1920   *12.5in (31cm) high*

$70-100   **LAN**

A CLOSER LOOK AT A REPRODUCTION TEDDY BEAR

Although he has the form and wear of an old bear, suspicions are raised, starting with the unusual color.

He is still very firmly stuffed, inconsistent with his age and the level of fur wear - it is doubtful he is old and has been re-stuffed.

His pads match his fur color and are suspiciously intact - always smell suspect vintage bears as the odor of years of love and play cannot yet be faked!

The wear to his fur is uneven and inconsistent with play use - he is more 'play worn' around his eyes and snout than on the top of his head or on his arms or chest.

A brown teddy bear, with short mohair fur, small black eyes, black stitched nose, wood wool stuffed body and woven claws.

c1925   *10in (25cm) high*

$70-100   **WDL**

A late 20thC dark cinnamon teddy bear, with all the features of an early 20thC bear including hump, elongated, curved arms and long feet, boot button eyes, stitched nose and mouth.

17in (43cm) high

$30-50   **PC**

An early teddy bear, possibly English, with boot-button eyes, uniform fur loss, heavier on tummy.

c1920   *20in (51cm) high*

$400-600   **JDJ**

A large German or American beige plush teddy bear, with wood-wool filling, glass eyes, upright ears, stitched snout and claws, jointed limbs and felt pads.

c1920   *32in (81.5cm) high*

$280-320   **GORL**

A Steiff miniature blond mohair teddy bear, lacking button and tag, with jointed limbs, revolving head, black eyes and black stitched nose.

c1930   *3.5in (9cm) high*

$80-120   **WDL**

A Steiff blond mohair teddy bear, brown glass eyes, black stitched nose, wood wool stuffed body, with tag, but lacking button and label.

c1950   *5.5in (14cm) high*

$180-220   **WDL**

A German blond plush teddy bear, possibly by Gebrüder Hermann, wood wool stuffed, glass eyes, woven snout and disc joints.

20in (50cm) high

$280-320   **LAN**

A CLOSER LOOK AT A MERRYTHOUGHT BEAR

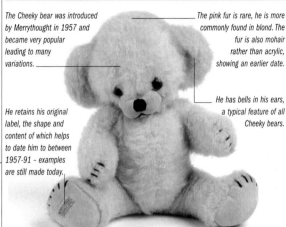

The Cheeky bear was introduced by Merrythought in 1957 and became very popular leading to many variations.

The pink fur is rare, he is more commonly found in blond. The fur is also mohair rather than acrylic, showing an earlier date.

He retains his original label, the shape and content of which helps to date him to between 1957-91 – examples are still made today.

He has bells in his ears, a typical feature of all Cheeky bears.

A rare Merrythought pink mohair Cheeky teddy bear, with velveteen snout.

c1960   *14in (35.5cm) high*

$500-700   **GAZE**

A 1950s Steiff teddy bear, wood wool-stuffed, with glass eyes, lacks button.

This postwar bear shows Steiff's new shape for their Original Teddy, launched in 1951. This form is also typical of other postwar bears. He has a plumper body, a rounder face with ears placed closer together, shorter and straighter arms and a less pronounced muzzle. This is also the most common color found.

18in (45cm) high

$280-320   **LAN**

A 1950s/60s teddy bear, with red tongue, slightly curled synthetic golden plush fur, brown glass eyes, unusual snail-shaped leather nose, long felt tongue, wood wool stuffed body.

15.25in (38cm) high

$40-60   **WDL**

A yellow and black teddy bear, wood wool stuffed, brown glass eyes, yellow and black stitched nose.

20in (50cm) high

$80-120   **WDL**

A black teddy bear, with short synthetic silk plush fur, light nose and ears, brown glass eyes, stuffed with wood wool, pink felt paws.

26in (65cm) high

$50-70   **WDL**

A Merrythought golden mohair Cheeky teddy bear, with velveteen snout, bells in ears and label to foot.

14in (35.5cm) high

$280-320   **GAZE**

A Steiff small mohair teddy bear, with wood wool stuffing, brown stitched nose and light brown felt paws, one eye and button and tag missing.

7.5in (19cm) high

$60-90 **WDL**

A gray brown furry mohair teddy bear, pink paws and three stitched claws to each foot, black stitched nose, brown plastic eyes.

16in (40cm) high

$30-50 **WDL**

A yellow teddy bear, stuffed with wood wool, yellow artificial plush, brown eyes, black stitched nose, some wear.

24in (60cm) high

$15-20 **WDL**

A late 20thC Steiff mohair 'Classic 1920' reproduction teddy bear, with button and tag, disc-joints, glass eyes and growler.

16.5in (41cm) high

$80-120 **LAN**

A late 20thC Steiff Club 'Night' pink and black mohair teddy bear, with growler, button and label.

12in (30.5cm) high

$70-100 **GAZE**

A late 20thC Steiff Club 'Day' cream, pink, and blue mohair teddy bear, with growler, button and label.

12in (30.5cm) high

$60-90 **GAZE**

A Merrythought large gray teddy bear.

c1965 *20in (51cm) high*

$30-50 **GAZE**

A Chiltern Toys plush teddy bear, with glass eyes, white paws and label.

This bear by one of Britain's best loved makers follows the washable synthetic fur bears designed by Wendy Boston and introduced in 1954.

c1960-67 *11in (28cm) high*

$20-30 **GAZE**

A 1980s-90s Steiff soft, unjointed teddy bear, with button and tag in ear.

12.5in (31.5cm) high

$25-35 **GAZE**

FIND OUT MORE...

Bears, by Sue Pearson, published by De Agostini, 1995.

Teddy Bear Encyclopedia, by Pauline Cockrill, published by DK, 2001.

COLLECTORS' NOTES

■ Soft toys pre-date teddy bears, with Margarete Steiff making soft animal-shaped pins as gifts in the 1890s. Steiff soon became the most famous name in teddy bears and also became prolific in making soft toys. Many collectors focus on one maker, or one animal, with cats and dogs being especially popular.

■ The 1920s to the 1950s was the golden age of the soft toy, before Far Eastern imports flooded the market. Pre-1920s soft toys are scarce. Steiff is the most popular and high quality maker, but also look for fellow German maker Schuco (Schreyer & Co), and Dean's, Chad Valley and Merrythought from England, the latter of whom included soft toys in their first catalog from 1930. Such British toys currently offer great value for money by comparison.

■ Consider form, labels, and material as these will help to date a soft toy – many, particularly by Steiff, were produced for long periods of time. Mohair and a hard stuffing will usually indicate an earlier example, but look for signs of age as Steiff still use these high quality materials today.

■ Look for bright, un-faded original colors and avoid buying damaged or dirty soft toys. Animals with concealed features, unusual outlandish creatures and nostalgia-filled characters are popular. As with teddy bears, do not ignore the 'cute' or 'amusement' factors as these often force a collector to add an appealing soft toy to their collections.

A late 20thC Steiff 'Snuffy' plush bunny, in gray and white, blue glass eyes, soft filling, with button, flag and mark.

4.5in (11cm) high

$25-35   **LAN**

A Merrythought novelty soft toy child's purse, modeled as rabbit.

14in (35.5cm) high

$15-20   **F**

A 1950s Steiff 'Tessie' dog, with button, ribbon and original cardboard swing tag, light gray long mohair fur, pivotable head, red collar.

5.25in (13cm) high

$70-100   **WDL**

A Steiff 'Waldi' mohair dachshund, with boot button eyes, stuffed with wood wool and with Steiff ear button, minimal wear, but lacks tag.

10in (25cm) long

$20-30   **LAN**

A hard-filled mohair cow soft toy, possibly by Steiff, with felt udders, lacks one horn and both eyes.

9.75in (25cm) long

$20-30   **GAZE**

A 1960s Steiff 'Zedonk' giraffe soft toy, with button in ear.

15in (38cm) high

$40-60   **GAZE**

A 1960s Steiff koala bear, with pad nose, glass eyes and ear stud with raised "Steiff" logo, in mint condition with original fabric tag.

7in (18cm) high

$300-500   **TCT**

A Steiff life-size peacock soft toy, with molded feet, felt and fur wings, yellow Steiff tag, button and hangtag, slight soiling, some restoration to beak.

31in (79cm) long

$500-800   **JDJ**

A Schuco miniature Yes/No monkey, with orange mohair plush.

The fine condition, the orange color (the brighter, the better) and the Yes/No mechanism, that makes him shake or nod his head, make him this valuable. Look out for other examples that have concealed powder compacts and lipsticks within.

c1920

$500-700 BEJ

A Merrythought large dressed Golly, with internal bell and felt tailcoat.

19in (48cm) high

$150-200 PWE

A Wendy Boston Basil Brush soft toy, with voice box.

14in (35.5cm) high

$15-20 GAZE

A Gabrielle Designs 'Paddington Bear' glove puppet, with felt hat and duffel coat with wooden buttons.

12in (30.5cm) high

$30-50 GAZE

A 1970s Merrythought 'Jerry Mouse' velveteen soft toy, with tag and label.

Jerry was originally designed by deaf and dumb designer Florence Atwood, who used MGM's drawings as inspiration and was chief designer for Merrythought until 1949.

12in (30.5cm) high

$25-35 GAZE

A 1970s Pedigree 'Dougal' soft toy, from 'The Magic Roundabout', with rubber face.

11.5in (29cm) wide

$50-60 GAZE

A Ty 'Clubby III' Beanie, with tag reading "2000 Official Club".

This Beanie bear was only available from September 2000 until January 2001. To be of interest to serious collectors Beanie Babies and Buddies must be in mint condition, retaining their tags and any accessories, also in mint condition.

2000 8.5in (21.5cm) high

$10-15 GAZE

A Ty 'Princess' Beanie Baby, woven rose and tag reading "©1997".

This Beanie Baby was launched on October 29th 1997 and retired on 13th April 1999 with all of Ty's profits from the original sale going to the 'Diana, Princess of Wales Memorial Fund' to carry on the work of the late Princess.

1997 8.5in (21.5cm) high

$7-10 GAZE

COLLECTORS' NOTES

- Until the 1680s, workers would make tools themselves when the need arose. Around 1680-1700, decorative tastes changed and more complex forms and shapes became fashionable. As many new tools were needed, specialist toolmakers sprung up, making a growing range of tools for specific purposes.

- Commercial production began in earnest from c1700 and boomed during the Industrial Revolution. The 'golden age' of the tool lasted until the 1930s-40s and saw a vast number of tools being made. Planes are one of the most popular types to collect – look out for noted names such as Stanley and Norris. Each model is numbered and many collectors aim to collect as many of the models made by a company as possible.

- The Stanley market is dominated by the US and the benchmark currency is in dollars, so currency fluctuations can affect value. The Norris market, dominated by the UK, is similarly affected.

- Collectors also appreciate the design and skill that goes into making a tool. Materials and visual appearance add value, so look for added decorative features such as artistically carved handles and detailed metal plates.

- Specialist tools are another popular area. Tools for coopers (barrel makers), watchmakers, musical instrument makers, and goldsmiths are good examples.

- Tools made for rarely practiced tasks tend to be the most valuable. A large wooden plane used by a great many workers is unlikely to be of value, unless it is old (for example from the 18th century) and thus rarer.

- Tools in unused condition, and even retaining their original packaging, are generally more desirable and valuable. Missing pieces and damage, such as rust and woodworm, reduce value dramatically.

A Stanley 4 1/2 H plane, repainted, in very good condition.

The 'H' series of planes were heavier in weight and were made to satisfy overseas customer demand. As such, they are rarely found in the US and more often in the UK or Europe.

$300-500   **MUR**

A Stanley Victor No.20 black-japanned plane, in fine condition.

$120-180   **MUR**

A Stanley No.85 scraper, in fine condition.

$700-1,000   **MUR**

A Stanley No.113 compass plane, in fine condition.

$120-180   **MUR**

A Stanley 140 skew block plane, in very good condition.

$80-120   **MUR**

A Stanley 140 skew block plane, in fine condition.

$180-220   **MUR**

A rare patent Norris No.13 metal plane, rosewood infill, Ward & Payne parallel iron, in fine condition.

$800-1,200   **MUR**

A CLOSER LOOK AT A PLANE

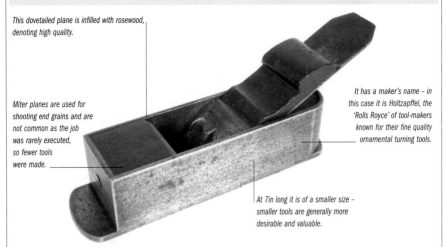

This dovetailed plane is infilled with rosewood, denoting high quality.

Miter planes are used for shooting end grains and are not common as the job was rarely executed, so fewer tools were made.

It has a maker's name – in this case it is Holtzapffel, the 'Rolls Royce' of tool-makers known for their fine quality ornamental turning tools.

At 7in long it is of a smaller size – smaller tools are generally more desirable and valuable.

A very rare Holtzapffel miter plane, dovetailed, with rosewood infill and replaced blade, in very good condition.

7in (18cm) long

$1,800-2,200   **MUR**

A scarce Norris No.20 gunmetal shoulder plane, with original iron, rosewood infill, in very good condition.

1.25in (3cm) wide

$500-700   **MUR**

A postwar Norris A5 smoothing plane.

The 'golden age' of the tool ended during the 1930s-1940s. However, some postwar tools are desirable, especially if by noted names and if few were made, making them rare. The value of this example is increased as it has hardly been used and still retains its box.

$800-1,200   **MUR**

A Record 08 plane, in virtually unused condition.

$220-280   **MUR**

A rare Mathieson smoothing plane, styled on the Stanley 4.5in plane, with rosewood handles, in very good condition.

$80-120   **MUR**

A scarce Preston No.118 block plane, in very good condition.

$120-180   **MUR**

A Scottish gunmetal smoothing plane, with heart and shield lever cap, in fine condition.

$400-600   **MUR**

An Ibbotson brass-plated brace, small chip to head.

$70-100   **MUR**

A CLOSER LOOK AT A BRACE

It is in very good condition, with few signs of wear through use.

It is marked with a maker's name – Pilkington are known for their quality tools but few braces were made, making this comparatively rare.

Pilkington braces were made for, and exported to, the American market.

It has unusual 'artistic' decorative brass plates, which adds interest and value.

A Robert Marples registered octagonal chuck plated brace, in very good condition.

$400-600   **MUR**

A rare Pilkington beech and brass brace, in very good condition.

$1,200-1,800   **MUR**

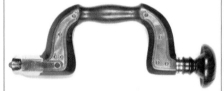

A rare Tillotson brace, with early Ultimatum-style chuck, small chip and crack to head.

$220-280   **MUR**

A Flather plated brace, with 'Eagle' button, for export to the US, in very good condition.

$220-280   **MUR**

An unused Tatham and Darracott brass-framed rosewood brace.

$1,200-1,800   **MUR**

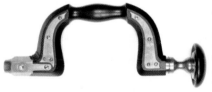

A rare solid macassar ebony plated brace, hairline shrinkage crack to web, in very good to fine condition.

Although this is the basic shape and style for a brace, it is made from ebony rather than the standard beech. This indicates that it may have been a special, 'bespoke' request, or was made for exhibition at a trade fair.

$700-1,000   **MUR**

A very rare Gavin & Cromer's patent brace, with lignum vitae head.

This patent was granted in Eureka, Nevada on July 19, 1887. There are less than five known examples, this is the only one found with a lignum vitae head.

$50-70   **MUR**

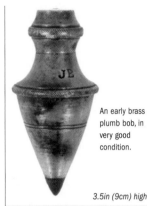

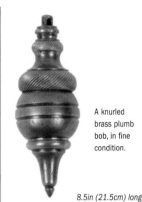

An early brass plumb bob, in very good condition.

A knurled brass plumb bob, in fine condition.

A steel-tipped brass plumb bob, decorated with an engraved brass spool, in very good condition.

3.5in (9cm) high

8.5in (21.5cm) long

3in (7.5cm) long

$120-180   **MUR** | **$300-500**   **MUR** | **$400-600**   **MUR**

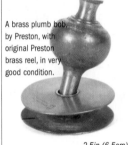

A brass plumb bob, by Preston, with original Preston brass reel, in very good condition.

An early 19thC steel-tipped bronze plumb bob, in very good condition.

An iron plumb bob, knurled brass head, in very good condition.

2.5in (6.5cm) high

8.25in (21cm) high

6in (15cm) high

$180-220   **MUR** | **$220-280**   **MUR** | **$80-120**   **MUR**

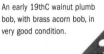

An early 19thC walnut plumb bob, with brass acorn bob, in very good condition.

$120-180   **MUR**

An original 19thC ebony and ivory plumb bob, in very good condition.

A 19thC plumb board, with bronze bob, in very good condition.

The Egyptians were the first civilization recorded using a plumb bob to ensure that walls were vertical. The plumb board also allows good judgment of a horizontal against a vertical. The Industrial Revolution saw the decline of the widespread use of the plumb bob, and it was replaced in many situations by the spirit level.

12.5in (32cm) high

$700-1,000   **MUR** | **$220-280**   **MUR**

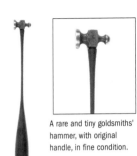

A rare and tiny goldsmiths' hammer, with original handle, in fine condition.

Head 1.25in (3cm) long

$300-500 **MUR**

A watchmakers' hammer, with elaborate knurling to the head, in fine condition.

9in (23cm) long

$280-320 **MUR**

A violin makers' sounding post.

$40-60 **MUR**

An early 19thC jewelry anvil, in a dark oak base, in fine condition.

6in (15cm) long

$280-320 **MUR**

A 19thC brass wheel cutting tool, on a later mahogany stand.

$800-1,200 **GHOU**

An unusual coachmakers' plough, by Tremain, with snicker iron, in very good condition.

$220-280 **MUR**

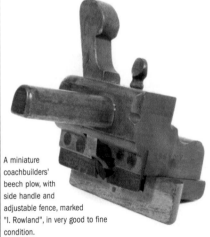

A miniature coachbuilders' beech plow, with side handle and adjustable fence, marked "I. Rowland", in very good to fine condition.

3.5in (9cm) long

$1,200-1,800 **MUR**

A 19thC miniature adze, of unknown purpose, in very good condition.

An adze was used for woodworking (for example on a beam) to chip away slices of wood with an axe-like motion. The blade is thin and the edge is aligned horizontally to the shaft, unlike an axe.

13in (33cm) long

$120-180 **MUR**

A quality rosewood and brass double-bladed cutting gauge, for purling on violins and cellos, in very good condition.

$220-280 **MUR**

A late 18thC veterinary tail docker, iron bound and fruitwood, dated "1787", in fine condition.

This was used for the gruesome task of 'docking', or removing, an animal's tail.

$180-220 **MUR**

A rare brass back tenon saw, by Mathieson, marked on blade and handle escutcheons, in very good condition.

$80-120   **MUR**

An early Groves No.2 handsaw, with ten tines per inch, 1770 escutcheon, in fine condition.

$80-120   **MUR**

A brass and rosewood bevel, in very good condition.

4.5in (11.5cm) long

$280-320   **MUR**

A rare 18thC astragal cove wooden plane, by Richard Burman, in very good condition.

As well as being of an early date and bearing a maker's name, this is indicative of the 'new' tools that needed to be made to create the more complex shapes that became fashionable at this time. An astragal is a narrow, convex shape, often taking the form of beading.

10.5in (26.5cm) wide

$1,200-1,800   **MUR**

An Arts & Crafts architrave molding plane, by Vincent, in very good to fine condition.

2.5in (6.5cm) wide

$120-180   **MUR**

A pair of brass trammels, by Preston, with double pencil holder, in very good condition.

Trammels allow the drawing of ellipses.

6.5in (16.5cm) long

$120-180   **MUR**

A Mathieson No.14C ebony spirit level, in fine condition.

10in (25.5cm) long

MUR

$300-500   **MUR**

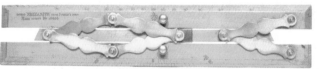

A rare Fields triple-arm rule, boxwood with brass fittings, Hezzanitti patent mark and Hills patent no. 15A55, in fine condition.

$220-280   **MUR**

An original box of Rabone 1167 rules, complete with three unused rules, in fine condition.

$80-120   **MUR**

FIND OUT MORE...

The Ultimate Brace – A Unique Product of Victorian Sheffield, by Reg Eaton, published by Erica Jane Publishing, 1989.

Dictionary of Woodworking Tools, by R.A. Salaman, published by Astragal Press, 1997.

COLLECTORS' NOTES

- Introduced by Mettoy Limited in 1956, Corgi Toys are still in production today.

- They were an innovative company and were the first to add plastic windows and opening doors and boots to their cars, features that helped them compete against rivals Dinky.

- Corgi are also well-known for their film- and TV-related toys, which include various James Bond vehicles, Batman, The Man from U.N.C.L.E., and Chitty Chitty Bang Bang.

- Different variations and versions are sought-after by collectors, and some examples were made for less than one year. Invest in a specialist price guide listing the various examples.

- The original boxes and instructions will add to the value, but like the toys, they must be complete and in good condition to fetch the highest prices.

A scarce Corgi No. 201 Austin Cambridge, silver over metallic green, with two types of white wall over stickers, in original box.
1956-61

$280-320   **W&W**

A Corgi No. 255 Austin Motor School A60, dark blue, spun hubs, export issue, mint condition, in good although grubby carded box.
1964-68

$180-220   **VEC**

A Corgi No.224 Bentley Continental Sports Saloon, cream over green, red interior, spun hubs and another similar but black over silver, in excellent plus to mint condition, in good to very good condition carded boxes.
1961-65

$120-180 each   **VEC**

A Corgi No. 245 Buick Riviera, powder blue, red interior, wire wheels, slightly retouched, and another similar in gold, excellent condition, in good condition carded boxes.
1964-68

$80-120 each   **VEC**

BACK: A Corgi No. 235 Oldsmobile Super 88, metallic blue, red interior, spun hubs, excellent condition, in very good condition carded box.

1962-66

$50-70   **VEC**

FRONT: A Corgi No. 229 Chevrolet Corvair, blue, flat spun hubs, excellent condition, in very good carded box.
1961-66

$50-80   **VEC**

BACK: A Corgi No. 223 Chevrolet 'State Patrol' Police Car, black, lemon interior, flat spun hubs, excellent condition, in good to very good condition box.

1959-61

$120-180   **VEC**

FRONT: A Corgi No. 437 Superior Cadillac Ambulance, red, cream, spun hubs, slight wear to side decals, excellent condition.
1962-65

$120-180   **VEC**

BACK: A Corgi No. 220 Chevrolet Impala, blue, lemon interior, flat spun hubs, in very good to excellent condition, in good although grubby box.
1960-65

$70-100   **VEC**

FRONT: A Corgi No. 248 Chevrolet Impala, brown, cream, cast wheels, very good to excellent condition, in good although grubby carded box.
1965-67

$70-100   **VEC**

A Corgi No. 267 'Batman' Batmobile, gloss black, with sealed secret instructions, one rocket only, near mint condition, in very good condition pictorial card box.
1966-67

$400-600 **GAZE**

A Corgi No. 266 'Chitty Chitty Bang Bang', with four character figures, incorrectly fitted steering wheel, missing front grille, boxed, re-cellophaned.
1968-72

$280-320 **VEC**

A CLOSER LOOK AT A CORGI TOY

These toys appeal to Beatles collectors as well as Corgi collectors.

Film- and TV-related Corgi toys are some of the most sought-after.

This example has two red hatches, and is slightly more desirable than the version with one white and one yellow. The variation with one red and one white hatch can be worth a third as much as this one.

The toy should be complete with the figures John, Paul, George, and Ringo, and in an undamaged picture box.

A Corgi No. 803 'The Beatles' Yellow Submarine, red front and rear hatches, very good condition, although slightly retouched, inner plastic tray is excellent plus, outer box re-cellophaned and slight tears to end flaps.
1970-71

$280-320 **VEC**

A Corgi No. 270 'James Bond' Aston Martin DB5, front and rear number plate decals applied, one side bumper broken.
1968-76

$300-400 **VEC**

A Corgi No. 336 'James Bond' Toyota 2000GI, with red aerial, two figures, secret instruction pack, missing badge, boxed.
1967-69

$400-600 **VEC**

A Corgi No. 261 'James Bond' Aston Martin DB5, bronze, red interior, wire wheels, secret instruction pack containing leaflet, spare bandit figure, lapel badge and a 'Corgi Toys Model Car Makers to James Bond' color leaflet, excellent condition, including inner pictorial, stand outer blue and yellow picture box in very good condition.
1965-69

$500-700 **VEC**

A Corgi No. 277 'Monkees' Monkeemobile, cast wheels, red, white roof, near mint, in excellent although slightly grubby window box, with plastic 'Monkees' Guitar.
1968-72

$300-500 **VEC**

A Corgi No. 258 'The Saint's' Volvo P1800, white, red interior, spun hubs, excellent condition, in excellent condition carded box.
1965-68

$300-500 **VEC**

A CLOSER LOOK AT A CORGI GIFT SET

Corgi Gift Sets are popular with collectors and can fetch more than the individual pieces together.

Look for the variation that contains a green Bentley as it is worth around 20 percent more.

The two cars were only available as a gift set, and were not sold separately.

All the accessories and internal packaging should be present and in good condition to fetch the best price.

A Corgi Gift Set No.4 Bristol Ferranti Bloodhound Guided Missile Set, containing a Bloodhound guided missile with launching ramp, loading trolley and RAF Land Rover, in original box with inner packaging, some age wear to box, paint chips.

1958-60

$400-600   **W&W**

A Corgi Gift Set No.40 'The Avengers', comprising 'John Steed's' Bentley, red and black, with wire wheels and, 'Emma Peel's' Lotus, white and black, with figure and three umbrellas, very good to near mint condition, in good to very good stand and box.

1966-69

$500-800   **VEC**

A Corgi Gift Set No.12 Chipperfields Crane Truck and Cage, with animals, excellent condition, in good condition box.

1961-64

$400-600   **GAZE**

A Corgi Gift Set No.21 ERF Dropside Lorry and Platform Trailer, with milk churns, no decorative accessories, very good condition, in very good condition box.

1962-66

$80-120   **GAZE**

A Corgi Gift Set No.5 Racing Car Set, comprising a No.150 Vanwall, red, flat spun hubs; a No.151 Lotus XI, blue, racing number 3 and a No.152 BRM Grand Prix Car, turquoise, racing number 7, good to excellent condition, in good although grubby inner polystyrene packing and fair condition but complete all-carded box.

1959-60

$280-320   **VEC**

A Corgi No. GS30 Grand Prix Gift Set, including Surtees TS9, Lotus John Player Special, Yardley McLaren, overall conditions are near mint to mint in good box, missing original shrink wrap.

1973

$120-180   **VEC**

A Corgi Gift Set No.2 Land Rover and Pony Trailer, green Land Rover, beige tin canopy, and red trailer with brown horse, excellent condition, with excellent condition inner card and very good condition outer blue and yellow picture box.

1958-68

$300-500   **VEC**

A Corgi Gift Set No.37 Lotus Racing Team, comprising a No. 490 Volkswagen breakdown van and trailer, a No.155 Lotus Climax racing car, a No.318 Lotus Elan coupé, a No.319 Lotus Elan S2, an Elan chassis, boxed, minor wear.

1966-69

$500-700   **W&W**

COLLECTORS' NOTES

- Dinky toys were released as accessories to Hornby's model railways in the UK in 1931, taking on the name 'Dinky' in 1934, just after the first cars were produced. The 1930s grew to be one of Dinky's most important decades, and the same is true for collectors today.

- Supertoys were introduced in 1947, and Speedwheels in 1969, in response to Mattel's 'Hotwheels' brand. The factory closed in 1979. The name was taken over by Matchbox in 1987 but was dropped in 2001.

- Condition and variations are vitally important. To fetch the highest values, toys must be undamaged and in as near to shop-sold condition as possible. If the paintwork is worn, do not repaint it.

- Boxes are very important and can double the value. The box itself should also be in excellent condition. Collectors use terms such as 'good', 'excellent', and 'mint' to describe the condition of the toy and box.

- Variations can be valuable: look closely at color, the transfer, wheels, and other details, such as national variations. All comparative values shown for variations are for items in similar condition to the one pictured.

A Hornby Dinky 22 Series tractor, yellow, blue, red wheels, no hook, good condition.

Although not strictly a car, this is from the earliest series of Dinky Toys, originally produced as Meccano Model Miniatures and as accessories to Hornby train sets.

1933-40

$500-800 VEC

A Dinky No. 38B Sunbeam Talbot, light blue with gray tonneau, in very good condition.

1947-49

$500-800 SAS

A Dinky No. 36C Humber Vogue, with driver and footman, blue, excellent condition, with small glue repair to one mudguard.

The all-over blue color was only produced with figures. Both the excellent condition and fact that this model is complete with both its tin figures account for the high value.

1937-41

$2,200-2,800 SAS

A Dinky No. 110 Aston Martin DB3 sportscar, light green with red hubs, competition number 22, excellent, with small chip to drivers helmet.

This is the most valuable color variation for this car. The gray and a darker green version is worth roughly 50 percent of this variation's value.

c1956

$300-500 SAS

A Dinky No. 167 A.C. Aceca Coupé, gray and red with windows and spun alloy hubs, in good condition box with gray end-spot.

To compete with the newly released Corgi toys with windows, this box advertises the fact that this model too has windows.

1958-60

$500-700 SAS

A rare South African Dinky No. 112 Austin Healy Sprite Mk II, lilac, excellent condition, in very good condition Afrikaans box.

1961-66

$800-1,200 SAS

A Dinky No. 502 Foden Flat Truck, first-type cab, blue cab and chassis, red back and side flash, mid-blue ridged hubs, good condition, some marks to wheel arches, in excellent condition box, some stains caused by rusting to staples.

1948-52

$500-800 VEC

A Dinky No. 903 Foden Flat Truck, with tailboard, second-type cab, mid-blue cab and chassis, fawn back, mid-blue Supertoy hubs, rivetted back, excellent condition, in excellent condition box, a tiny amount of edge ware to box.

1957-60

$120-180 VEC

A French Dinky No. 36A Willeme Log Lorry, orange cab, yellow trailer and hubs, log load, excellent condition, in excellent condition box.

$220-280 VEC

A Dinky No. 935 Leyland Octopus Flat Truck, with chains, mid-green cab and chassis, light gray back and band around cab, red plastic hubs, excellent condition, minor chipping and slight protrusion to flatbed.

If this model retained its box and was in better condition, the value would have been higher. Look out for the valuable variation of the 935 with a blue cab, yellow flash, and gray flatbed.

1964-66

$300-500 VEC

A Dinky No. 513 Guy Flat Truck with tailboard, first type cab, gray, black chassis and mudguards, black ridged wheels, excellent condition, small chip to front right-hand mudguard, in good condition, buff box, split to one end and label attached to one end.

Dark blue rather than black chassis, guards and hubs can more than double the value of this model.

1947-48

$300-400 VEC

A Dinky No. 34B Royal Mail Van, red and black, excellent condition.

1938-47

$400-600 SAS

A Dinky No. 514 Guy Van 'Slumberland', first-type cab, good condition, with box.

The yellow 'Weetabix' Guy Van is the most valuable of this type, and can fetch up to five times more than the 'Slumberland'.

1950-52

$280-320 VEC

A Dinky No. 454 Trojan Van 'Cydrax', mid-green including ridged wheels, roof slightly sunfaded, in good condition box, repair to end flaps and slight graffiti.

1957-59

$180-220 VEC

A scarce Dinky No. 280 South African issue Delivery Van, khaki green including ridged hubs, complete with original trodden tires, good condition.

$500-700 VEC

A Dinky No. 471 Austin Nestlé's van, red body with yellow and beige wheel hubs, Nestlé's decals in gold to the sides, in original box, some wear.

1955-60

$120-180 W&W

A Dinky No. 100 Thunderbirds Lady Penelope's FAB 1, pink including roof slides, missile and harpoons, excellent, slight discoloration to bare metal parts and has been re-touched in places, inner pictorial tray is good, including outer picture box.

1967-75

$220-280 VEC

A Dinky No. 100 Thunderbirds Lady Penelope's FAB1, luminous pink, with Lady Penelope and Parker figures and front rocket, in original box, losses.

The luminous pink variation is more desirable than the standard pink body also shown on this page.

1967-75

$500-700 W&W

A Dinky No. 352 UFO Ed Straker's Car, gold finish, silver engine cover, blue interior, cast wheels mint in good box.

1971-75

$180-220 VEC

A Dinky No. 104 Captain Scarlet Spectrum Pursuit Vehicle, seat and figure attached to door, with leaflet and box.

The earlier variation where the seat and figure is not attached to the door is usually worth slightly more.

1973-75

$120-180 GAZE

A Dinky No. 108 Joe 90 Sam's Car, red, yellow interior, silver rear engine cover, cast wheels, near mint condition, including inner pictorial stand, in excellent condition outer picture box.

Red is one of the most desirable and valuable colors. Surprisingly it is worth slightly more than the silver-gray version that appeared in the TV series.

$300-400 VEC

A Dinky No. 106 The Prisoner Mini Moke, white, brown side steps, excellent condition, in good condition picture box.

1967-70

$280-320 VEC

A Dinky No. 103 Captain Scarlet Spectrum Patrol Car, red, white base and aerial, cast spun hubs, near mint in good box.

1968-75

$280-320 VEC

A Dinky No.354 The Pink Panther's Jet Car, excellent condition, on excellent condition card.

1977-79

$70-100 SAS

A Dinky No.357 Star Trek Klingon Battle Cruiser, excellent condition, box with small fracture to cellophane.

1977-80

$50-80 SAS

A prewar Dinky No. 62m Airspeed Envoy, green, red propellers, G-A ENA, excellent condition.

Dinky began making aircraft just before the start of WWII and today the market is strong and brisk. Postwar, they focused on making models of the new commercial airliners and jet planes. Prewar models are particularly prone to degradation of the metal on parts such as wings, known as 'fatigue', which leads to 'sagging'.

1938-41

$280-320 VEC

A French prewar Dinky No. 60D Breguet Corsair, red, green wing edges, propeller and undercarriage, good condition.

$280-320 VEC

A prewar Dinky No. 60r Empire Flying Boat 'Caledonia', silver, red propellers, red plastic roller, G-A DHM, good condition, no visible signs of fatigue.

1937-40

$220-280 VEC

A Dinky No. 60r Empire Flying Boat 'Cambria', silver, red propellers, red plastic roller, G-A DUV, good condition, slight warpage to wings and minor fatigue, in good condition blue box.

1937-40

$280-320 VEC

A Dinky No. 62w Imperial Airways Liner 'Frobisher', silver, red propellers, gliding pin hole, G-A FDK, excellent condition, in excellent condition box complete with leaflet.

1939-41

$500-800 VEC

A CLOSER LOOK AT A DINKY FLYING BOAT

This was the first 'Supertoys' plane model produced.

It was produced for a short period only, and production began less than two years after the war had ended.

It is in excellent condition and complete with its own labeled box, which is also in good condition.

It shows no sign of metal fatigue, a degradation of the metal associated with prewar Dinky planes.

A Dinky No.701 Shetland Flying Boat, 'G-A GVD' in silver with black propellers and box.

1947-49

$800-1,200 VEC

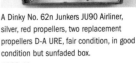

A Dinky No. 62n Junkers JU90 Airliner, silver, red propellers, two replacement propellers D-A URE, fair condition, in good condition but sunfaded box.

1938-41

$300-400 VEC

COLLECTORS' NOTES

- Mattel released its Hot Wheels range in 1968. The intention was to balance out its otherwise girl-orientated catalog and to provide toy 'muscle' cars to boys looking for more exciting models than the relatively sedate British Corgi and Matchbox cars.

- The company developed a special metallic paint called 'Spectraflame', to give the cars a brightly colored 'Californian' look. 14 colors were initially produced and it was expanded to 21, however, not all models were available in all of the colors. Of all the colors produced, pink and purple are the hardest to find, probably as they were considered too feminine by most boys.

- Many collectors concentrate on 'Redline' models, named after the red stripe on the wheels of cars and made between 1968 and 1977.

- As with any other die-cast toy, condition has a great effect on value but unlike manufacturers such as Dinky and Corgi, Mattel packaged their toys in blister packs that were usually destroyed when opened. This means that Hot Wheels are hardly ever found in their original packaging and can command a significant premium when they do come on to the market.

- Mattel still produce Hot Wheels today including a number of limited editions to appeal to adult as well as younger collectors.

A Hot Wheels aqua Heavyweights 'Redline' Cement Mixer, 6450, by Mattel.

1970   3.25in (8cm) long

$50-60   **SOTT**

A Hot Wheels pink 'Redline' Classic '36 Ford Coupe, 6253, by Mattel.

This color was initially referred to as lavender.

1969   2.75in (7cm) long

$220-280   **NOR**

A Hot Wheels purple 'Redline' Classic '32 Ford Vicky, 6250, by Mattel.

1969   2.25in (5.5cm) long

$40-50   **SOTT**

A Hot Wheels silver Corvette Stingray, 1475, by Mattel.

1979   2.75in (7cm) long

$15-20   **SOTT**

A Hot Wheels purple 'Redline' Custom Continental Mark III, 6266, by Mattel.

1969   3.25in (8cm) long

$80-120   **NOR**

A Hot Wheels green 'Redline' Custom Cougar, 6205, by Mattel.

1968   2.75in (7cm) long

$120-180   **SOTT**

A Hot Wheels green 'Redline' Custom Firebird, 6212, by Mattel.

1968   2.75in (7cm) wide

$80-120   **SOTT**

A Hot Wheels purple 'Redline' Custom Fleetside, 6213, by Mattel.

1967 *3in (7.5cm) long*

$40-50 **SOTT**

A Hot Wheels red 'Redline' Custom Volkswagen, 6220, by Mattel.

1968 *2.25in (5.5cm) wide*

$30-40 **SOTT**

A Hot Wheels gold Datsun 200 SX, 3255, by Mattel.

1983 *3in (7.5cm) long*

$18-22 **SOTT**

A Hot Wheels purple 'Redline' Deora, 6210, by Mattel.

1968 *2.75in (7cm) wide*

$80-120 **SOTT**

A Hot Wheels purple 'Redline' Funny Money, 7621, by Mattel, with flower transfer.

1974 *2.75in (7cm) long*

$30-40 **NOR**

A Hot Wheels purple 'Redline' Hot Heap, 6219, by Mattel.

1968 *2in (5cm) wide*

$30-50 **SOTT**

A Hot Wheels black Hotbird, 2014, by Mattel.

1978 *3in (7.5cm) long*

$40-50 **SOTT**

A Hot Wheels metallic gold Jaguar XJS, 2012, by Mattel.

1978 *3.25in (8cm) long*

$15-25 **NOR**

A Hot Wheels green 'Redline' Large Charge, 8272, by Mattel.

1975 *3.25in (8cm) long*

$25-35 **NOR**

A Hot Wheels green 'Redline' Mantis, 6423, by Mattel.

1970　　　　3.25in (8cm) long

$20-30　　　　**NOR**

An Hot Wheels electric blue 'Redline' Mongoose Funny Car, 6410, by Mattel.

1970　　　　3.25in (8cm) long

$70-90　　　　**NOR**

A Hot Wheels red 'Redline' Mercedes Benz C 111, 6196, by Mattel, with plastic baseplate.

1972　　　　3in (7.5cm) long

$80-120　　　　**NOR**

A Hot Wheels blue 'Redline' Neet Streeter, 9244, by Mattel.

1976　　　　2.5in (6.5cm) long

$20-30　　　　**SOTT**

A Hot Wheels 'Redline' Paddy Wagon, 6402, by Mattel.

1970　　　　2.25in (5.5cm) long

$45-55　　　　**SOTT**

A Hot Wheels green Ranger Rig, 7666, by Mattel, replaced wheels.

1975　　　　3in (7.5cm) long

$45-55　　　　**SOTT**

A Hot Wheels yellow 'Redline' Seasider, 6413, by Mattel.

1970　　　　3.25in (8.5cm) long

$60-80　　　　**NOR**

A Hot Wheels yellow 'Redline' Short Order, 6176, by Mattel.

1971　　　　2.5in (6.5cm) long

$30-40　　　　**SOTT**

A Hot Wheels metallic green 'Redline' Silhouette, 6209, by Mattel, with painted base.

1968　　　　3in (7.5cm) long

$15-25　　　　**NOR**

A Hot Wheels orange Spittin' Image, 6261, by Mattel.

1969   *3in (7.5cm) long*

$45-55   **SOTT**

A Hot Wheels turquoise Stripteaser, 6188, with "Firestone" transfer, by Mattel.

c1970   *3in (7.5cm) long*

$80-120   **SOTT**

A CLOSER LOOK AT A HOT WHEELS VAN

The boards are loose and are often missing. The value of the van on its own is about 50 percent less.

This model was introduced in the range's second year and proved very popular.

There is a rare variation, made in Hong Kong which has boards that are mounted through the rear window.

It is thought that as few as 26 of the rare rear-mounted vans exist and they can fetch several thousands of dollars.

A Hot Wheels green 'Redline' Volkswagen Beachbomb, 6274, by Mattel.

1969   *2.5in (6.5cm) long*

$120-180   **SOTT**

A Hot Wheels yellow '57 Thunderbird, 2013, by Mattel.

1978   *2.75in (7cm) long*

$15-25   **SOTT**

A Hot Wheels blue 'Redline' Heavyweights Tow Truck, 6450, by Mattel.

c1969   *2.75in (7cm) long*

$40-50   **SOTT**

A Hot Wheels bronze 'Redline' Twinmill, 6258, by Mattel.

c1968   *3in (7.5cm) long*

$50-70   **SOTT**

A Hot Wheels silver 'Redline' Twinmill, 6258, by Mattel.

1968   *3in (7.5cm) long*

$10-15   **SOTT**

A Mattel Hot Wheels 'Continental Mark III' pin.

The Continental Mark III was released in 1969.

c1969   *1.5in (4cm) diam*

$5-10   **SOTT**

A Mattel Hot Wheels 'Mantis' pin.

The Mantis model was released in 1970.

c1970   *1.5in (4cm) diam*

$5-10   **SOTT**

TOYS & GAMES

COLLECTORS' NOTES

■ Cast iron toys were made from the 1880s until plastic took over from the 1950s. Their heyday was primarily during the 1920s and 1930s. Names to look out for include Arcade, Hubley, Kenton, and Dent. At the time, they were promoted as realistic being full of details, durable, colorful, and even as 'educational'.

■ Values are indicated primarily by type, size, complexity, color, and condition. The maker is also important. Automotive toys are one of the most popular areas, particularly cars of the 1920s and '30s and racing cars. Fire engines are also popular, as are farm vehicles. Do not ignore street furniture such as signs or gas pumps as these can fetch high prices.

■ Larger toys, over the standard 6-8 inches (15-20cm) in length, were more expensive in their day, so less were sold, making them scarcer today. Some makers originally exaggerated sizes in their catalogs as competition was so great. Larger toys also tend to be more complex and realistically modeled. Look for a good level of molded detail such as drivers, headlights, grilles, and badges. Smaller, less detailed and less realistic vehicles will usually be worth less.

■ Bright colors were attractive at the time and still appeal today. Red was one of the most popular. Look for unusual colors or toys decorated for, or bearing wording for, special clients or events. Condition is also of vital importance. The more common a toy is, the better condition it must be in to be of interest and value. A toy in truly mint condition can fetch many times the value of one in poor condition.

■ If a car has damaged paintwork, do not attempt to repaint it, as collectors prefer the original color and finish. Kilgore paintwork often degrades, gaining fragmented 'islands' of color known as 'alligatoring'. Some of the toys shown here are from the Kenton 'Sample Room' and show such high prices due to their scarcity, provenance, and condition.

A Hubley cast iron red 'Kiddie 7' race car.

7in (18cm) long

$60-80 BH

A Hubley cast iron 'No.5 Red Devil Racer', with rubber tires.

This popular car has an aluminum body, an opening hood exposing the engine and an exhaust clicker. A version with electric lights dates from c1934.

$300-400 PWE

A Hubley cast iron yellow grille racer, with separate nickel grille, pistons and driver, rubber tires worn, in very good condition.

4.75in (12cm) long

$200-250 BER

An Arcade cast iron light blue Racer, with two cast figures, "5" embossed behind seat, white rubber tires, in pristine condition.

c1936 *7.75in (19.5cm) long*

$2,500-3,000 BER

An Arcade cast iron No. 8 silver Racer, with white rubber tires, in excellent condition.

c1933 *5.5in (14cm) long*

$150-200 BER

A Hubley cast iron orange 'Golden Arrow Racer', with white rubber wheels.

A larger, and more valuable version can be found at over 10in (25.5cm) in length and with 12 cylinders.

c1931-c1941 *7in (18cm) long*

$120-180 PWE

A rare Hubley cast iron open racer, painted in red overall, features dual seats, opening in boat tail, yellow spoke wheels, in excellent condition.

6.75in (17cm) long

$80-120 BER

A CLOSER LOOK AT A CAST IRON FORD

The car retains its two nickel-plated figures, which are mounted on springs so that they bounce around as the car is moved along.

A variation with an opening trunk was offered in 1926.

It is in overall excellent condition with intact, original paintwork and with only some wear to the wheels.

The Model 'T' Ford was a popular car with children of the period and today's collectors. It was first introduced as a toy in the late 1910s.

A Kilgore cast iron green 'Ford Model 'T' (T-60) Coupé', with nickeled spoke wheels, some wear to wheels, in pristine condition.

c1927 6.25in (16cm) long

$1,000-1,500 **BER**

A Kenton cast iron light blue and black Sedan, with disc wheels, separate driver.

The Sedan was produced from around 1923-29. Examine the black paint used by Kenton as it tends to degrade, this example is in excellent overall condition.

c1925 6.5in (16.5cm) long

$700-900 **BER**

A Hubley cast iron green '665 Coupe' with cast wheels, stamped inside 1499.

Resembling a vintage Dodge, this model was made in five different sizes with the largest being the rarest and most sought after.

c1925-30 8.5in (21.5cm) long

$350-450 **PWE**

A Dent cast iron light blue 'Coupé', with yellow disc wheels, driver's head cast in window, very good condition.

5in (13cm) long

$80-120 **BER**

A Kenton cast iron Pontiac sedan, red body, black frame, Type I nickel grille, white rubber tires.

This toy was from the Kenton 'Sample Room' and is in pristine condition, not having been played with.

4.5in (11.5cm) long

$400-500 **BER**

A rare Arcade Pontiac orange taxi cab, with nickel grille with lights, white rubber tires, stenciled "Yellow Cab Co." on sides, partial label on rear, in good condition.

c1935 6.5in (16.5cm) long

$550-650 **BER**

A 1920s Kenton cast iron red open Roadster, with seated driver and painted disc wheels, wear to wheels, in very good condition.

5.75in (14.5cm) long

$150-250 **BER**

A 1920s Hubley painted cast iron fire truck with cast spoked wheels and two removable firemen and ladder.

15.25in (38.5cm) long

$150-250   **PWE**

A Kenton cast iron red fire pump, with nickel boiler cover, cast driver, rubber tires, in good condition.

5in (13cm) long

$70-100   **BER**

A rare Kenton Pontiac cast iron red and black fire engine, nickel boiler cover, black chassis, cast driver, rubber tires, in good condition.

A rare model with a 'unique' nickel grille cover, the only other example currently known is in the Kenton Museum.

1936   4.75in (12cm) long

$400-500   **BER**

A Kenton cast iron orange and black 1936 Pontiac wrecker, with nickel grille, wire tow hook, in excellent condition.

This toy is rare and from the Kenton factory 'Sample Room', hence its excellent condition. It has a Type II nickel grille.

1936   4.5in (11.5cm) long

$800-1,000   **BER**

A rare Kenton cast iron pickup truck, with red body, black frame, Type I nickel grille, black rubber tires, over spray to grille, in fair condition.

4in (10cm) long

$180-220   **BER**

A Kenton cast iron silver and red Pontiac Wrecker, with tow hook, Type II nickel grille, and white rubber tires.

Also from the Kenton factory 'Sample Room' and in unusual colors.

1936   4in (10cm) long

$1,000-1,500   **BER**

A rare Kenton cast iron green and red pickup truck, with Type II nickel grille, white rubber tires.

Also from the Kenton factory 'Sample Room', and in pristine condition.

4in (10cm) long

$550-650   **BER**

A 1920s A.C. Williams cast iron Fruehauf Trailer Co. gas track, enclosed red cab with green tank body, embossed "Gasoline...Motor Oil...Fruehauf Co.", on sides, nickel spoke wheels together with tin gas sign, in good condition.

7in (18cm) long

$280-320   **BER**

A 1920s Dent cast iron red express truck, with yellow spoke wheels, cast driver, in very good condition.

4.5in (11.5cm) long

$250-350   **BER**

An Arcade cast iron John Deere 'A' tractor, painted in characteristic green with rubber tires, nickel driver, in very good condition with wear to nickel.

c1940   7.5in (19cm) long

$400-500   **BER**

An Arcade cast iron orange 'Allis Chalmers 'WC' Tractor', with nickel driver with drawbar, black rubber tires, decals on body, wear to nickel, in very good condition.

1940-41   7.25in (18.5cm) long

$280-320   **BER**

A 1940s Arcade cast iron red 'Allis Chalmers' tractor, cast driver, rubber tires, in excellent condition with partial label.

6in (15cm) long

$300-400   **BER**

An Arcade cast iron green and red 'Avery Tractor', with spoke wheels, in excellent condition.

This tractor was available in gray or green.

1926-28   4.5in (11.5cm) long

$280-320   **BER**

An Arcade cast iron gray Fordson tractor, with Whitehead and Kales embossed red disc wheels, nickel driver, rubber tires, in good condition.

This toy was a copy of the Whitehead & Kales Industrial Tractor used in factories which would no doubt have 'wowed' small boys who saw it.

1923-30   5.75in (14.5cm) long

$350-450   **BER**

An Arcade cast iron gray and red Fordson tractor, with gold painted highlights, nickel driver, in very good condition with wear to nickel, together with a Fordson tractor manual.

The tread on the back wheels marked wooden floors, so Arcade made a version with smooth wheels. However, fewer were made making it rarer than this model today.

1923-33   5.75in (14.5cm) long

$180-220   **BER**

A 1930s North & Judd cast iron gray and red Fordson tractor, with nickel driver, in very good condition.

This 4in (10cm) toy was the only size made by this Connecticut-based company, who are only known to have made around five models of toy.

4in (10cm) long

$350-450   **BER**

An Arcade cast iron red 'Oliver Plow', with silver blades, one stenciled "Oliver", one with decal, nickel spoke wheels and side gear, in very good condition.

1926-39   6.5in (16.5cm) long

$200-300   **BER**

An Arcade cast iron yellow 'Oliver Superior Spreader', with black trim, three rotating nickel shafts, rubber tires, decals on sides, replaced shafts, in very good condition.

1940-41   10in (25.5cm) long

$400-500   **BER**

TOYS & GAMES

A 1920s Arcade cast iron blue 'Contractor's Dump Wagon', with wording on sides, nickel driver, very good condition.

This is the early version with nickel spoked wheels and is in the desirable blue color. Later versions from c1941 had silver painted wheels with black rubber tires.

A Kenton cast iron blue, yellow, and white horse drawn two-seat Surrey, with cloth canopy, driver and passenger, in pristine condition.

c1918   *12in (30.5cm) long*

$300-400   **BER**

A rare Shimer cast iron red and white Conestoga "Eldorado" ox drawn wagon, with embossed sides and yellow spoke wheels, in very good condition.

                    5.5in (14cm) long

$200-300   **BER**

                    14in (35.5cm) long

$350-450   **BER**

A 1930s Hubley cast iron red, yellow, and blue 'Lindy Glider' pull-along plane.

Planes such as this were made in great variety and quantity to celebrate famed aviator Charles Lindburgh. Beware of examples in suspiciously fine condition and a slightly larger pilot as they were reproduced during the 1980s.

A 1920s Kenton cast iron and green tin yellow kid and goat cart, with red spoke wheels and nickel goat, in very good condition.

                    7.5in (19cm) long

$400-500   **BER**

A Hubley cast iron brown horse and jockey, mounted separate cast jockey wearing white and red colors, in excellent condition.

                    4.75in (12cm) high

$250-350   **BER**

                    6.5in (16.5cm) long

$150-250   **PWE**

An Arcade cast iron double-decker bus, classic design, painted in green overall, nickel grill, upper level contains bench seating and three figures, driver cast in window, rubber tires, in pristine condition.

c1940   *7.75in (19.5cm) long*

$650-750   **BER**

A Hubley cast iron gray 'Lindy Glider' pull-along airplane, with Hubley transfer to tail wing.

This plane was made in many different sizes during its six year run.

1928-33   *9.5in (24cm) long*

$200-300   **PWE**

A small red painted motorbike and black rider, possibly by Hubley, with rubber tires.

                    4.25in (11cm) long

$200-300   **PWE**

A 1930s A.C. Williams cast iron red gas pump, with gold trim, original hose, embossed cast globe.

This is an excellent example in pristine condition with its original hose. There are two versions, with the crank handle placed on the side or on the back, as here.

4.75in (12cm) high

$550-650 BER

An Arcade cast iron red gas pump, with gold trim on embossed "GAS" globe, center dial, base and Arcade decal, in pristine condition.

c1936 6in (15.5cm) high

$800-1,000 BER

A Kilgore cast iron green gas pump, with white highlights, embossed "Gas" on cast globe, gallon meter on front, with retouched paintwork.

This Kilgore pump is one of the rarest toy gas pumps on the market.

c1927 6.5in (16.5cm) high

$350-450 BER

An Arcade cast iron red gas pump still bank, with gold painted cast globe, dial meter on front, slot in back and original hose, in good condition.

1936 5.75in (14.5cm) high

$300-400 BER

An Arcade cast iron yellow and red gas pump, top globe stenciled "Arcade Gas", with Arcade decal, in excellent condition.

1926-31 6.25in (16cm) high

$800-1,000 BER

A Swedish Skolgund & Olson cast iron red gasoline pump, with embossed "MACK" on front and handle to side, in excellent condition.

6.25in (16cm) high

$600-800 BER

An American cast iron red 'GO' sign, embossed wording with gold trimmed letters, in excellent to pristine condition.

This was possibly made by Arcade for a special event.

c1925 5in (13cm) high

$250-350 BER

A scarce 'Warner Bros.' Main Street cast iron green road sign, embossed "Main St" and "Warner Bros' Screen Classic" on two sides of base, in good condition with wear to base paint.

5.5in (14cm) high

$450-550 BER

A 'Barrett Cravens' cast iron red hand truck, with embossed runners, nickel spoke wheels, in excellent condition.

4in (10cm) high

$300-400 BER

A rare Tonka pressed steel private label 'Dobson Movers' Ford semi truck, in very good condition.

Dobson's are based in Bay City, Michigan. Tonka was founded in Mound, Minnesota in 1946 and began producing trucks in 1947. Examples produced until 1964 are the most desirable, with condition and unusual variations or decoration contributing most towards values.

23.5in (59.5cm) long

$800-1,000   **BER**

A 1940s American Grimland Co. lithographed pressed steel Allied Van Lines semi-trailer moving van, with opening top, in excellent condition with original box.

This was given away to children of the company's clients.

7.5in (19cm) long

$180-220   **BER**

A Metalcraft pressed steel Shell Motor Oil truck, with type I grill, in very good condition.

12.5in (32cm) long

$800-1,000   **BER**

A pressed steel 'Coca-Cola' truck, with ten glass bottles.

11in (28cm) long

$600-900   **PWE**

A 1920s/30s Dayton Hillclimber pressed steel fire engine, with driver, missing side ladders.

19.75in (50cm) long

$400-600   **PWE**

A 1930s Kingsbury pressed steel Divco milk truck, Borden's decals on sides, in excellent condition.

Kingsbury stopped making toys in 1942 after contributing to the war effort.

8.75in (22cm) long

$400-500   **BER**

A very rare D.P. Clark wood and pressed steel Hillclimber open touring car, with two correct handpainted tin figures and two cast iron lady passengers.

D.P. Clark were founded in 1898 in Dayton, Ohio and produced toys until 1909, when they were renamed Schieble Toy & Novelty Co. It's the early date, rarity, and excellent, complete condition that make this toy so valuable.

c1905   *10.5in (26.5cm) long*

$1,500-2,000   **BER**

A large Keystone pressed steel ride-on locomotive, with steerable front end, paintwork in fair condition.

25in (63.50cm) long

$120-180   **JDJ**

An Arcade pressed steel flatbed farm wagon, open bench seat with nickel driver, in very good condition.

13in (33cm) long

$300-400   **BER**

COLLECTORS' NOTES

■ Model trains were first produced in the 1850s, but forms tended to be stylized, bulky and rather unrealistic. By the 1890s, German makers such as Märklin (est. 1859) and Gebrüder Bing (1863-1933) had introduced more realistic trains made from tinplate, with clockwork or steam mechanisms. Many of these were exported to the US and other European countries, with the two world wars temporarily stopping exports.

■ The first model trains for adult enthusiasts were developed in the 1900s. These were commonly made from tinplate, propelled by clockwork and handpainted to mimic the liveries of real train operators. Large, well-detailed examples of engines and stock in fine condition are desirable and fetch a premium. Railway accessories from this period, such as stations, are highly prized and certain lamps and other small accessories can be rare and valuable, despite their size.

■ Märklin introduced gauge sizes in 1891. The larger gauges of I, II and III were replaced by 1910 with the smaller gauge 0 as demand for smaller trains grew. The 0 gauge itself was replaced in 1954 with the smaller 00 gauge, and the H0 gauge appeared in 1948.

■ Hornby began making trains in 1920. Its 'Dublo' is highly collectible. Look out for mint, boxed examples as these continue to rise in value. Sets from the 1950s-60s, such as those by Triang, are now worth looking out for if in mint condition with their boxes. These are still reasonably priced, but may rise in value in the future.

■ Condition is of paramount importance, particularly for later trains as they were made to be played with. Collectors therefore seek out examples in the best condition possible as well as rarities and much loved favorites.

A Märklin 0 gauge A-1 steam locomotive with tender, handpainted in green, movement in working order.

$2,800-3,200   LAN

A Märklin 0 gauge B-1 steam locomotive.

The cow catcher on the engine indicates that this train was made for the US market.

12.5in (31cm) long

$4,000-6,000   LAN

A Märklin 1 gauge B-1 steam locomotive with a 2-A tender, movement in working order, handpainted in black, three imitation headlights, hairline cracks to finish.

$1,500-2,000   LAN

A Märklin 2 gauge train set, with B-movement 1022 BN, comprising a 2-A tender, a luggage car and an open goods car with cast iron wheels, two figures, six straight and two half-straight tracks, brake track and buffer, in original box.

It is unusual to find the original box, and the cover picture is rare.

5.75in (14.5cm) wide

$4,000-6,000   LAN

A Märklin 0 gauge clockwork 4-4-2 Great Northern Railway Atlantic locomotive and tender, in green painted finish with white and black lining, for the English Market.

16in (41cm) long

$1,800-2,200   F

Two Märklin H0 gauge electrical locomotives and tenders, both of black cast iron and plastic, one locomotive signed "DB 18 478", together with a four axle tender, the other signed "DC 23015", both marked "Made in Western Germany".

10in (25cm) long

$180-220   WDL

A Märklin 0 gauge 'R 890' locomotive, with tender, of black lacquered sheet metal, on two axles, missing key.

10.5in (26cm) long

$180-220   WDL

A modern Lionel 907 diecast 4-8-2 locomotive, with a 12-wheel Texas & Pacific tender.

$300-500   JDJ

A modern Lionel 2044 4-6-2 locomotive, with a Spokane, Portland & Seattle RY tender.

$150-200   JDJ

A Lionel 763 R locomotive, with 263 W oil tender, in gunmetal gray, slight chipping to frame.

$1,200-1,800   JDJ

A 1970s Lionel No. 3 General engine and tender, with original box.

$50-70   JDJ

A modern Lionel 8960 SP locomotive, an 8961 GP locomotive and four SP freight cars.

$100-150   JDJ

A modern Lionel 490 4-6-4 Chesapeake & Ohio locomotive, with 12-wheel tender.

$500-700   JDJ

A clockwork Hornby No. 1 special tender 0-4-0 locomotive, with a four-wheel tender, in early 1930s LMS maroon livery, RN8712.

$220-280 W&W

A clockwork Hornby Series 1185 4-4-0 locomotive and tender, in LMS livery, fair condition, some wheels replaced.

$280-320 SAS

A electric Hornby O gauge 4-4-2 No. 2 special tank locomotive, in green Southern Railway livery, RN 2091.

$150-200 W&W

A clockwork Hornby O gauge 4-4-2 locomotive in maroon LMS livery, RN 6954, black smoke box and cab roof top.

$280-320 W&W

A Hornby 00-gauge 4-6-0 Black Five locomotive, in LMS livery, with original box.

Box 13in (33cm) long

$70-100 F

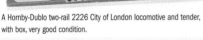

A Hornby-Dublo two-rail 2226 City of London locomotive and tender, with box, very good condition.

$220-280 SAS

A Hornby-Dublo two-rail 2235 Barnstaple locomotive and tender 34005, with box, excellent condition.

$280-320 SAS

A Hornby-Dublo two-rail 2250 SR Electric Motor Coach Brake, lacks two axle guards, with box, very good condition.

$300-500 SAS

TOYS & GAMES

COLLECTORS' NOTES

■ Tinplated steel had overtaken wood as a material for toys by the mid-19thC. Tinplate was less costly to produce and could be fashioned with more intricate details. Germany was the center of production with the US producing toys from the mid-to late 19thC onward. Germany's most notable makers included Märklin (founded 1856), Gebrüder Bing (1863-1933), and Lehmann (founded 1881). US makers included Louis Marx (1896-1982) and Ferdinand Strauss (c1914-42).

■ Tinplate from the 19th and early 20thC was generally handpainted, before the introduction of transfer-printed 'lithography', and is generally very desirable. Handpainted examples can be discerned by a more uneven surface and the presence of brush marks. Lithographed examples have a smooth, often shiny, surface with no brushmarks and usually have finer detailing.

■ After WWII, the Far East took over, with production initially being focused in Japan, followed by China from the late 1960s onward. Toys became brighter in color and more 'novelty' in theme, with 'mystery' actions involving sounds, light and movement. In the West, diecast toys and plastic toys had taken over the market since their introduction in the 1930s and 1950s respectively.

■ Many Japanese examples combine tinplate with plastic. Many are still affordable compared to their earlier cousins, but prices are rising, especially if in mint, working condition with original boxes. Transport toys, including cars, boats and planes are among the most popular toys with collectors, especially if large, early, finely detailed or by major makers. Avoid examples that display rust, splits or missing parts as these are virtually impossible to restore satisfactorily.

A scarce tinplate clockwork tipping lorry, in the Mettoy Wells style, with simple steering system and driver.

9.75in (25cm) wide

$400-600   **W&W**

A German Hausser tinplate pick-up truck, movement in working order, one opening door, steering wheel missing, few marks.

12in (30cm) wide

$1,200-1,800   **LAN**

A rare French C.R. Rossignol lithographed tinplate clockwork Renault petrol tank wagon, with simple steering system, one gear shaft missing.

$150-200   **W&W**

A Distler chromolithographed Dapolin truck 5881, with driver and electrical lighting, movement in good working order.

11.25in (28cm) long

$2,800-3,200   **LAN**

A Schuco 'Constructions' fire engine, no.6080, lacks crew, accessories and hood ornament.

This fire engine was made in three versions between 1956-67. This is the earliest version with Schuco transfers on the doors. Later versions had molded wording and less accessories. The Schuco Constructions range was made from 1949-67.

c1958   *10.75in (27cm) long*

A Minic tinplate clockwork model 'Minic Transport Express' service box van.

5.5in (14cm) long

$70-100   **F**

$2,800-3,200   **LAN**

A rare early 1900s German Ernst Plank town sedan car, with lift-up access interior, two holes to seats for missing figures.

$220-280   W&W

A 1930s American Marx printed tinplate clockwork 'Old Jalopy' limousine.

7.25in (18.5cm) long

$100-150   PWE

An American handpainted tinplate Hill Climber delivery truck, with "J.L. Kessner Co. Sixth Ave 22nd & 23rd Sts" transfer.

c1910   *11in (28cm) wide*

$280-320   PWE

A Mettoy tinplate clockwork model mechanical racing car, in original box.

Box 11in (28cm) wide

$280-320   F

A scarce 1950s Mettoy 'Sparking Racer', 'push 'n' go' mechanism with sparking action, in original box.

$150-200   W&W

A Schuco Studio toy car, with original box and paperwork, including salesman's instructions.

c1935   *Box 5.5in (14cm) long*

$70-100   CA

A 1950s Schuco limousine, No. 1010, movement in working order, with instructions, keys and original box.

$120-180   LAN

A 1960s Japanese Yoneszawa battery-operated tinplate mystery action taxi cab, mint and boxed.

8.75in (22.5cm) long

$40-60   PWE

A Masudaya (TM Modern Toys) battery-operated tinplate Super Patrol Man, boxed with packaging.

9in (23cm) wide

$220-280   W&W

TOYS & GAMES

A Tipp & Co. lithographed tinplate airplane no.60, with retractable undercarriage, movement in working order, electrified.

11.5in (29cm) long

$500-700   **LAN**

A scarce French Joustra Super G Constellation battery-powered tinplate airliner, in Air France blue livery.

19in (48cm) wide

$220-280   **W&W**

A Tipp & Co. painted tinplate propeller biplane, type '1424', removable wings, decorative foil stripes and numbers affixed.

14.75in (37cm) long

$80-120   **WDL**

A Lehmann chromolithographed tinplate airplane He 111 no.831, with accessories and instructions, renewed HK-emblem, original box.

$500-700   **LAN**

A Tri-Ang 'Frog' Mark IV interceptor fighter, in Belgian flying colors, with original orange box.

Box 11in (28cm) long

$100-150   **GORL**

A Günthermann lithographed tinplate water plane 1069, movement in working order, elevator replaced.

12in (30cm) long

$600-900   **LAN**

A 1950s Japanese Bandai 'Space Bus' lithographed tinplate toy, battery-operated via remote control.

$150-200   **W&W**

A CLOSER LOOK AT A MARX ZEPPELIN

The 'MAR' and 'X' in a circle logo identifies it as having been made by notable US maker Louis Marx (1919-79).

For a hollow, tinplate pull-along toy, it is in excellent condition with no dents or scratches and is complete with its wheels and engines.

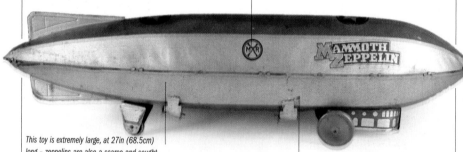

This toy is extremely large, at 27in (68.5cm) long – zeppelins are also a scarce and sought-after tinplate toy, especially in visually impressive sizes.

It dates from the 1930s, before WWII and the tragic Hindenburg disaster in 1937, when the heyday of airships as a mode of transatlantic transport ended.

A large Marx Zepplin tinplate toy, with four facsimile prop motors at side, on three tin wheels with suspended gondola at front, no dents or scratches.

27in (68.5cm) high

$600-900   **JDJ**

A German printed tinplate and metal clockwork boy on a tricycle, with bell.

9in (22.5cm) high

$600-900 **PWE**

A rare large Japanese 'Harley Davidson' police motorbike, chromolithographed tinplate, some wear.

12.25in (31cm) long

$1,500-2,000 **LAN**

A scarce 1950s Japanese Usagiya 'Rabbit' friction-driven lithographed tinplate motorcycle and side car, with original box.

$700-1,000 **W&W**

An American Marx lithographed tinplate coast-to-coast Greyhound bus, with wind-up action, in very good condition.

10in (25.5cm) long

$500-700 **BER**

An Arnold chromolithographed tinplate armored scout car 562, with driver, movement in good order.

10in (25cm) long

$800-1,000 **LAN**

An American Louis Marx tinplate 'Hee Haw' balky mule cart, with wind-up action.

10.5in (27cm) long

$300-400 **PWE**

A scarce early German tinplate penny toy, in the style of an ocean liner.

Penny toys are small tinplate toys that were often sold by street vendors, reaching the height of their popularity around 1900-10. Look for well modeled and detailed examples, as well as popular themes, such as cars. Condition is also paramount for high value.

4.5in (11.5cm) wide

$180-220 **W&W**

A German Lehmann tinplate balky mule cart, for the American market, lacks the back of the cart.

8in (20cm) long

$400-600 **PWE**

An Arnold tinplate boy on a sledge, made in US Zone Germany, with clockwork motor.

c1950

$100-150   **W&W**

An Arnold clockwork tinplate porter, made in US Zone Germany, in original box.

c1950

$150-200   **W&W**

A 1950s Japanese T.P.S. clockwork mechanical 'Suzy Bouncing Ball' toy, lithographed tinplate with plastic head and fabric skirt, in original box.

Box 5.75in (14.5cm) wide

$40-60   **GAZE**

A scarce 1950s Japanese T.P.S. tinplate clockwork 'Mechanical Happy the Violinist', with original clothes and box.

9in (23cm) high

$400-600   **W&W**

A Mattel tinplate mechanical musical Jack-In-The-Box, in original box.

c1968   *6.25in (16cm) wide*

$70-100   **F**

An early 20thC Günthermann clockwork turtle, lacks boy rider to top of shell, some wear to legs.

10.5in (26.5cm) long

$220-280   **W&W**

A rare, early American handpainted tin jockey on an oversized dog pull-along toy, by George W. Brown & Co.

Brown, of Forestville, Connecticut, manufactured toys from 1856-80 and was the first maker to employ clockwork mechanisms. He is known for his boats, vehicles and animals in handpainted tin. In 1868, he merged with J. & E. Stevens.

c1878   *10in (25.5cm) long*

$2,200-2,800   **AMJ**

A 1920s Lehmann tinplate clockwork climbing monkey, gripping a rope that moves him up and down.

$280-320   **TCA**

A Chad Valley lithographed tin drum, with sticks.

c1950   *8.75in (22cm) high*

$15-25   **GAZE**

COLLECTORS' NOTES

■ The majority of space-themed toys traded today were originally made in Japan during the 1950s and 60s. American and Russian models are also available. They reflect the mood of their age, especially the preoccupation with the space race.

■ Yonezawa, Nomura and Masudaya are among the biggest names on the market. Many companies that made these toys have fallen into obscurity, and are now identified only by their stamped initials.

■ The most serious form of damage found on tinplate toys is rust. Even small amounts of rust visible on the surface of a toy can be indicative of an ongoing corrosion problem. Battery leaks will also wreak havoc on metal toys and are extremely hard to rectify.

■ Missing parts can be replaced but are often hard to source. Many collectors are, however, happy to purchase toys that are not in full working order. Repainting invariably detracts from the original aesthetic of a toy and should be avoided.

■ Toys complete with boxes will command a premium, particularly if the box is in good condition. The science fiction inspired designs on these boxes hold great appeal for collectors.

■ More and more toys were made from plastic from the late 1960s onward. This proved a cheaper and more child-friendly alternative to tinplate, eventually replacing it completely. Collectors are increasingly interested in early plastic space toys.

A CLOSER LOOK AT A ROBOT

A Rosko Toy 'Rocket Man' battery operated robot, made in Japan by Alps, remote control, complete with original box with legend.

The box illustration depicts the spaceman with a NASA insignia on his helmet beneath his armor, however on the actual toy this has been obliterated by the addition of a small lamp.

15in (38cm) high

$2,500-3,500   **RSJ**

This is of a large size, which is typical of the 1950s and 1960s as sizes increased.

It is one of the popular 'Gang of Five' skirted toy robots produced by Masudaya, the others include Robot the Robot, Machine Man, Radicon Robot, and Target Robot.

It's nickname 'Train Robot' comes from the train-like sound it makes.

It boasts a mystery 'bump-n'-go' action, with swinging arms and flashing eyes and ears. These actions appeal greatly to collectors. The more the better!

A 1950s Japanese giant Sonic 'Train' battery operated robot, by Masudaya, made by Trademark Toys.

4.5in (37cm) high

$3,500-4,500   **RSJ**

A 1950s Japanese 'Space Man Robot' tinplate astronaut, by Daiya, some wear and faulty switch.

14in (35.5cm) high

$300-500   **W&W**

A 1960s Japanese 'Super Astronaut' tinplate robot, by S.H. Horikawa, boxed, some wear, in working order.

$100-150   **W&W**

A Japanese 'Answer Game' calculating battery operated tinplate robot, by Ichida, with blinking eyes, and a disc revolving in his head.

14in (36.5cm) high

$800-1,200   **ATK**

A Marx Toys plastic and tinplate wind-up walking 'Son of Garloo', made in Hong Kong, with original medallion and box.

6in (15cm) high

$300-400   RSJ

A scarce West German 'Dux Astroman' battery-powered plastic spaceman figure, by Markes & Co, boxed.

c1955

$500-700   W&W

A Japanese Cragstan 'Mr Atomic' battery operated tinplate robot, by Yonezawa, maple leaf insignia.

Although one of the least anthropomorphic of the robots, and certainly not the rarest, Mr Atomic is a particularly popular toy with collectors.

9.5in (24cm) high

$2,800-3,200   RSJ

A Japanese 'Planet' clockwork robot, by Yoshia, with walking mechanism, tin with plastic hands, minor paint wear to back.

1960   8.75in (22cm) high

$280-320   ATK

A Japanese tinplate and plastic battery operated 'Docking Robot', by Daiya, boxed, minor wear, in working order.

16in (40.5cm) high

$80-120   W&W

A Japanese tinplate and plastic 'Apollo 11 Eagle NASA Lunar Module', by DSK Daishin Kogyo Co., battery powered, boxed, in working order.

c1970

$80-120   W&W

A Japanese 'United States Space Capsule', by S.H. Horikawa, Spanish export version, battery powered, boxed, minor wear, in working order.

$80-120   W&W

A Japanese TM Modern Toys battery powered 'Space Ship X5', boxed, some wear, in working order.

$70-100   W&W

A Japanese large lithographed tinplate 'Atom Jet', by Yonezawa, friction-powered, missing windscreen, one new break light.

This is the largest Japanese tin toy car made in the 1950s.

c1950   26.5in (66cm) long

$1,200-1,800   ATK

A Japanese battery operated plastic and tinplate 'Space Rocket Saturn X5', by Alps, boxed, some wear, in good working order.

11.5in (29cm) long

$120-180   W&W

A 1970s Japanese TM Modern Toys battery powered 'Space Ranger No 3', boxed, in working order.

A Japanese battery powered tinplate 'Sky Patrol', by TN.

13in (33cm) long

$80-120   W&W | **$280-320   W&W**

A scarce 1950s Marx 'Tom Corbett Space Cadet 2' space ship, motor in working order.

12.5in (32cm) high

$120-180   W&W

A scarce Tri-Ang Minic 'push and go' tinplate Space Cruiser, in a colorful original box.

10.25in (26cm) long

$220-280   W&W

A Pepys Party Games 'Dan Dare – A Treasure Hunt in Space Ships', boxed.

$50-70   SAS

A 1960s 'Dan Dare Planet Gun' by Merit, with three spinning missiles, boxed.

The box and missiles are hard to find.

Box 10.5in (26.5cm) wide

$80-120   GAZE

A 'Dan Dare, Pilot of the Future' pop up, by Juvenile Productions Ltd.

1953   10.5in (26.5cm) wide

$100-150   GAZE

A 'Dan Dare Planet Gun', by Merit, complete and boxed.

c1953   Box 10.75in (27.5cm) wide

$220-280   GAZE

A Schuco novelty scent bottle, in the form of a plush fabric monkey, with removable head revealing a glass tube insert.

c1920s   4in (10cm) high

$400-600   **RDL**

A Schuco ragged plush monkey, 'Schnico 183', with moving head, movement in working order, some wear.

8.75in (22cm) high

$280-320   **LAN**

A CLOSER LOOK AT A SCHUCO FIGURE

This monkey has a metal body, felt feet and a molded metal face with a painted flock-like textured effect. Any soiling, wear or damage to the felt or fur reduces value considerably.

Look for unusual bright colors, such as the monkey in the purple coat shown on this page. They are scarcer and usually more desirable.

Schuco were well known for their range of innovative figures – they also produced a powder compact, lipstick holder and a lapel badge in the same chimp design.

Look out for the teddy bear version, which is very popular, appealing to arctophiles as much as to collectors of Schuco and perfume bottles.

A 1920s Schuco novelty scent bottle, in the form of a plush fabric monkey, with a glass tube insert, some wear to face.

5in (12.5cm) high

$300-500   **RDL**

A Schuco dancing figure of a piglet, playing the violin in a sailor's outfit, movement in working order, some wear, lacks violin.

$150-200   **LAN**

A Schuco monkey sailor figure.

c1925   4.5in (11.5cm) high

$120-180   **B&H**

A Schuco dancing figure of a Dutch boy with violin, movement in working order.

5.5in (14cm) high

$280-320   **LAN**

A Schuco clown with violin, movement in working order, some wear.

$220-280   **LAN**

COLLECTORS' NOTES

- Star Wars figures have been issued by different companies in many countries worldwide. The most commonly found vintage toys are those made for the US and UK markets by Kenner and Palitoy respectively. More recently, figures have been distributed by Hasbro.

- The first figures could not be manufactured in time for the 1977 holiday season, so Kenner instead issued the 'Early Bird' package with coupons redeemable against the first four figures, including Luke and Leia. These packs can now fetch more than $350.

- Figures and vehicles associated with the first three Star Wars films will generally be more valuable than later issues. Packaging with the original 'Star Wars' logo adds the most value to a toy, especially if combined with a '12-back' reverse design, so called because it depicts the 12 figures that were available at the time.

- The 1985 'Power of the Force' set of 37 figures was issued in limited numbers due to a drop in demand. Today, card-backed examples of these figures are among the most sought-after and the coins included in the original packaging also do a brisk trade.

- The highest prices are reserved for rare variations such as the vinyl-caped Jawa, Boba Fett with rocket-firing backpack, and the original 'Power of the Force' issue of the Anakin Skywalker figure. Even these must be complete with original packaging to realize their full value, and fakes are known to exist.

A CLOSER LOOK AT A STAR WARS ACTION FIGURE

This is an early version of one of the first 12 figures released by Kenner in 1979.

Early examples of this figure were produced with a vinyl cape. Executives felt that, together with the figure's diminutive size, this did not represent good value for money and the cape was therefore changed to cloth.

Beware of fake vinyl capes, which are often cut down from 'Ben Kenobi's' cape. The material should be the same color as the figure's face.

This figure is on a '12-back' card, the first form of packaging that carried illustrations of the first 12 figures on the back. The same figure on a later '20-back' card is worth less than this example.

A Star Wars 'Ben (Obi-Wan) Kenobi' large action figure, by Kenner, mint and boxed.

These large sized (12in) action figures were only issued for two years and are scarce.

c1980   Figure 12in (30.5cm) high

$300-400   **NOR**

A Star Wars 'Jawa' carded action figure, by Kenner, with vinyl cape, on '12-back' card.

If the proof of purchase token at the bottom right hand corner of this card were still intact it could be worth $3,000-5,000.

c1978

$1,000-1,500   **NOR**

A Star Wars – The Empire Strikes Back 'Imperial TIE Fighter Pilot' action figure.

c1982

$100-150   **W&W**

A Star Wars – Return of the Jedi 'AT-AT Commander' action figure, by Kenner, on '65-back' card.

c1982

$40-50   **W&W**

A Star Wars – Return of the Jedi 'Bib Fortuna' action figure, by Kenner.

c1983

$30-40   **W&W**

A Star Wars – Return of the Jedi 'Gamorrean Guard' action figure, by Kenner, on '77-back' card.

c1983

$20-30   **W&W**

A Star Wars – Return of the Jedi tri-logo 'Imperial Stormtrooper -
Hoth Battle Gear' action figure, by Kenner, on '70-back' card.

c1980

$40-60   **W&W**

A Star Wars – Return of the Jedi
'Biker Scout' action figure, by
Kenner.

c1983

$30-50   **W&W**

A Star Wars – Return of the Jedi
'C-3PO' action figure, by Palitoy,
incorrectly sealed on a 'Death
Star Droid' tri-logo card.

*This error variation is
undoubtedly unusual but is of
limited appeal to collectors.*

c1983

$35-45   **W&W**

A Star Wars – Return of the
Jedi 'Emperor's Royal Guard'
action figure, by Kenner, on
'77-back' card.

c1983

$30-50   **W&W**

A Star Wars – Return of the
Jedi 'Klaatu' action figure, by
Kenner.

*Klaatu and his comrades
Barada and Nikto are members
of Jabba's entourage. Their
names are a homage to the film
'The Day the Earth Stood Still'
in which they were used as an
order to stop Gort, a giant
robot, from destroying Earth.*

c1983

$25-35   **W&W**

A Star Wars – Return of the Jedi 'Logray –
Ewok Medicine Man' action figure, by
Kenner, on '77-back' card.

c1983

$30-50   **W&W**

A Star Wars – Return of the Jedi tri-logo
'Squid Head' action figure, by Palitoy,
bubble pack opened.

*Squid Head was renamed 'Tessek' for the
second edition of Power of the Force figures.*

c1983

$20-30   **W&W**

A Star Wars – Return of the Jedi 'Weequay'
action figure, by Palitoy, incorrectly sealed
on a 'Warok' tri-logo card.

c1983

$20-25   **W&W**

A Star Wars - Return of the Jedi 'Ewok' action figure triple pack, by Kenner, containing 'Logray', 'Wicket' and 'Paploo'.

c1984　*Box 5in (12.5cm) high*

$120-180　**KF**

A Star Wars - The Power of the Force second edition 'Chewbacca as Boushh's Bounty' action figure, by Kenner, with Bowcaster, on green 'Freeze Frame' header card.

c1997　*9in (23cm) high*

$8-12　**W&W**

A Star Wars - The Power of the Force second edition 'Luke Skywalker' action figure, by Kenner, with blast shield helmet and lightsaber, on green 'Freeze Frame' header card.

c1997　*9in (23cm) high*

$8-12　**W&W**

A Star Wars Special Edition 300th figure 'Boba Fett' action figure, by Hasbro, with rocket-firing backpack.

This special edition commemorates the first Boba Fett figure that was designed with a rocket-firing backpack. It was considered too dangerous for children and was never properly issued, making it very rare today.

c2000　*8in (20cm) high*

$20-30　**W&W**

A Star Wars - The Power of the Force second edition 'Oola & Salacious Crumb' action figure twin pack, by Kenner.

This pack was an Official Star Wars Fan Club exclusive.

c1998　*5.5in (14cm) high*

$20-30　**W&W**

A Star Wars - The Power of the Force second edition 'Purchase of the Droids' 'Cinema Scenes' triple pack, by Kenner, containing 'Uncle Lars Owen', 'Luke Skywalker' and 'C-3PO', in green box.

All of the 'Cinema Scenes' sets contain at least one exclusive figure, in this case 'Uncle Lars Owen'.

c1998　*10.5in (26.5cm) wide*

$15-25　**W&W**

A Star Wars - The Power of the Force second edition 'Death Star Escape' 'Cinema Scenes' triple pack, by Kenner, containing 'Chewbacca', 'Han Solo' and 'Luke Skywalker' in Stormtrooper outfits.

This set was released exclusively through Toys 'R' Us. The Han Solo figure had previously been available via a Froot Loops mail-in offer.

c1997　*10.5in (26.5cm) wide*

$40-50　**W&W**

A Star Wars - The Power of the Force second edition 'Darth Vader' action figure, by Kenner, with short lightsaber, on multi-language red header card.

Look for the transitional version of this figure which has a short lightsaber and a long slot in the packaging. It can be worth three times more than this version.

c1996　*9in (23cm) high*

$10-15　**W&W**

A Star Wars – Episode 1 'Anakin Skywalker' carded action figure, by Hasbro.

c1998   9in (22.5cm) high

$5-7   KF

A Star Wars – Episode 1 'Destroyer Droid' carded action figure, by Hasbro.

c1998   9in (22.5cm) high

$6-9   KF

A Star Wars – Episode 1 'OOM-9' carded action figure, by Hasbro.

c1998   9in (22.5cm) high

$7-10   KF

A Star Wars – Episode 1 'Obi-Wan Kenobi' carded action figure, by Hasbro.

c1998   9in (22.5cm) high

$5-7   KF

A Star Wars – Episode 1 'Adi Gallia' carded action figure, by Hasbro.

c1998   9in (22.5cm) high

$10-15   KF

A Star Wars – Episode 1 'Qui-Gon Jinn' carded action figure, by Hasbro.

c1998   9in (22.5cm) high

$5-7   KF

A Star Wars – Episode 1 'Ric Olié' carded action figure, by Hasbro.

c1998   9in (22.5cm) high

$7-10   KF

A Star Wars – Episode 1 'Senator Palpatine' carded action figure, by Hasbro.

c1998   9in (22.5cm) high

$7-10   KF

A Star Wars – Attack of the Clones 'Jar Jar Binks (Gungan Senator)' carded action figure, by Hasbro.

c2002   9in (22.5cm) high

$7-10   KF

A Star Wars 'Walrus Man' action figure.

c1979   3.75in (9.5cm) high

$12-15   **KF**

A CLOSER LOOK AT A STAR WARS VEHICLE

This was one of the most expensive vehicles produced by Kenner for the Star Wars line and few were sold at the time.

This toy was initially issued in a Star Wars box, and later re-issued by Kenner Canada in bi-lingual Empire Strikes Back packaging. Boxed examples are extremely hard to find.

Working examples are scarce. The drop-down panel at the side is often broken off and, as in this case, the ladder that attaches to the side of the panel is frequently missing.

While lacking the cachet of the 'Millennium Falcon', this is one of the few remote-controlled vehicles from the original range and is very popular with collectors today.

A rare Star Wars remote-controlled 'Jawa Sandcrawler', the remote control console lacking its battery cover.

A boxed example of this toy could be worth almost $1,000.

c1979   16.5in (42cm) long

$250-350   **KNK**

A Star Wars – Return of the Jedi 'Ree-Yees' action figure.

c1983   3.75in (9.5cm) high

$7-10   **KF**

A Star Wars – Return of the Jedi 'Nien Nunb' action figure.

c1983   3.75in (9.5cm) high

$9-12   **KF**

An unusual set of three Star Wars figures, comprising 'C-3PO', 'B-Wing Pilot' and 'Emperor Palpatine', in generic packaging.

This unusual set does not cite Star Wars on the packaging. These figures may have been bought as surplus stock and repackaged.

9.75in (25cm) wide

$50-70   **W&W**

A Star Wars – The Empire Strikes Back 'CAP-2 Captivator' mini-rig, by Palitoy, boxed.

A slightly more valuable version of this toy has a yellow sticker on the packaging and included a free 'Bossk' action figure.

c1982

$20-30   **W&W**

A Star Wars – Return of the Jedi 'Imperial Shuttle' vehicle, by Palitoy, boxed.

c1983   18in (45.5cm) high

$300-400   **W&W**

A Star Wars die-cast 'Y-Wing Fighter', by Palitoy, boxed, in mint condition.

Die-cast vehicles were issued in boxes and on card blister packs. The boxed versions are much more desirable. Some of the boxed versions of the Y-Wing were issued with special backgrounds and these can be worth nearly three times as much as this example.

1978-80   10.5in (26.5cm) wide

$100-150   **W&W**

A Star Wars Micro Collection 'Death Star Escape' action playset, by Kenner.

c1982   7in (18cm) wide

$50-70   **W&W**

A Star Wars Micro Collection 'Hoth Ion Cannon' action play set, by Kenner, boxed.

c1982   7in (18cm) wide

$30-45   **W&W**

A Star Wars Micro Collection 'Hoth Generator Attack' action play set, by Kenner, boxed.

c1982   7in (18cm) wide

$20-30   **W&W**

A Star Wars Micro Machines 'C-3PO/Cantina' transforming action set, by Kenner, boxed.

c1994   11in (28cm) wide

$12-18   **W&W**

A Star Wars Micro Machines Space 'Rebel Pilot/Hoth' transforming action set, by Kenner, boxed.

c1994   11in (28cm) wide

$15-20   **W&W**

A Star Wars – The Power of the Force second edition Wonder World set, by Kenner, boxed.

c1995   12.25in (31cm) wide

$7-10   **W&W**

A Star Wars – The Power of the Force second edition Micro Machines Space 'Planet Tatooine' playset, by Ideal, boxed.

c1995

$10-15   **W&W**

A Star Wars – Power of the Force second edition 'Speeder Bike', by Kenner, with 'Princess Leia Organa' in Endor gear, with moss air-brushed rocks, boxed.

c1997   9in (23cm) wide

$15-20   **W&W**

A Star Wars Micro Machines Action Fleet 'Ronto' Battle Pack, by Ideal, in sealed, multi-language bubble pack.

c1997   *9.5in (24cm) high*

$7-10   **W&W**

A Star Wars Micro Machines Action Fleet 'Dewback' Battle Pack, by Ideal, in sealed, multi-language bubble pack.

9.5in (24cm) high

$7-10   **W&W**

A Star Wars – The Power of the Force second edition electronic 'Talking C-3PO Carry Case', by Kenner, boxed.

1995-99   *19in (48.5cm) high*

$20-25   **W&W**

A Star Wars 'Darth Vader' Collector's Case, by Kenner, designed to hold 31 figures and containing 26 figures including 'Boba Fett', 'Han Solo', 'R2-D2', 'Ben Kenobi', 'Leia Organa', and others together with an insert depicting 79 characters from the films.

c1980   *14.5in (37cm) high*

$100-150   **W&W**

A Star Wars record tote bag, by Disneyland Vista Records.

c1982   *7.75in (19.5cm) high*

$12-18   **BH**

A Star Wars 'Chewbacca Bandolier Strap', by Kenner, to hold 10 figures, with two containers for accessories.

c1983   *33in (84cm) long*

$7-15   **W&W**

A limited edition Star Wars Coca Cola glass, for Burger King, picturing Darth Vader, Grand Moff Tarkin and a Stormtrooper.

5.5in (14cm) high

$2-4   **BH**

COLLECTORS' NOTES

■ The origins of the game of chess are uncertain, but it is possible that it developed from a 6thC Indian game called 'Chaturanga', although a similar game evolved in China in the 2ndC BC. The game, as it is played today, uses rules set down in the late 15thC in Italy.

■ The style and design of the boards and pieces has changed over the years as well as the rules. The 'Staunton' set, designed by Nathaniel Cook in 1849, was endorsed by famous player Howard Staunton and bears his name. It is one of the most popular designs and is the official set of the World Chess Federation.

■ The majority of chess sets on the market date from the 18thC and later and, although some earlier examples can be found, they tend to be at the high end of the market. As chess is such an international game, sets were manufactured and exported by a number of countries, each with their own style. These include India, China, Germany, and Austria.

■ Sets should be complete and undamaged with the quality, intricacy of carving or manufacture and the materials used also important factors. The inclusion of a chessboard is not important and traditionally they were sold separately to the chess pieces.

■ The market continues to grow with lively internet-based trading. Older, good quality sets are becoming harder to find as demand increases and, as a result, more standard and commonplace sets are rising in value. 'Staunton' sets are doing particularly well at present.

An English 'green-stained' bone barleycorn chess set.

English barleycorn sets are more normally stained red. Green staining is usually associated with chess sets from India.

c1850　　　　　　*King 4.5in (11.5cm) high*

$500-700　　　　　　　　　　　**BLO**

An English ivory chess set.

c1870　　　　　　*King 3.25in (8cm) high*

$220-280　　　　　　　　　　　**BLO**

A mid-19thC English 'Old English' pattern ivory chess set, in a later wooden box with a sliding lid.

c1850　　*King 2.25in (6cm) high*

$1,800-2,200　　　　　**BLO**

A 19thC Jacques Staunton boxwood and ebony weighted chess set, the white king signed "Jacques London", in a mahogany box.

King 3.5in (9cm) high

$1,000-1,500　　　　　　　　　**BLO**

A Silette Catalin Art Deco style chess set, by Grays of Cambridge, in a wooden box with a sliding lid.

c1925　　　　　　*King 2.75in (7cm) high*

$280-320　　　　　　　　　　　**BLO**

An English aluminum 'aircraft' chess set, made of turned aluminum mechanical parts.

Sets such as these were made from the surplus aluminum stocks left over from aircraft manufacture during WWII.

c1948　　　　　　*King 3.25in (8cm) high*

$700-1,000　　　　　　　　　　**BLO**

A US Presidential plastic figural chess set, designed by Alexander Silvery of Graz, Austria.

1972　　　　　　*King 7in (18cm) high*

$80-120　　　　　　　　　　　**BLO**

A 19thC 'Tenniel' pattern bone chess set, the green felt bases probably replaced, in a wooden box with a sliding lid.

The pieces are carved in the style of Sir John Tenniel's (1820-1914) illustrations for Lewis Carroll's 'Alice Through The Looking Glass', which famously included chess pieces among the characters.

King 2.75in (7cm) high

$600-900 **BLO**

A first version Augarten porcelain figural chess set, Vienna, designed by Mathilde Jaksch-Szendro, with "Vienna" mark on the base.

c1929 King 3.25in (8cm) high

$1,200-1,800 **BLO**

Five German 'Reynard the Fox' carved ivory chess pieces, after the illustrations of Wilhelm von Kaulbach, Erbach, all raised on ebony pedestal bases.

3.25in (8.5cm) high

$300-500 **BLO**

A 20thC 'Reynard the Fox' figural chess set, in a fitted presentation case.

King 4.25in (11cm) high

$700-1,000 **BLO**

A mid-20thC European carved ivory 'Egyptology' chess set, in a wooden box.

Despite being relatively modern, this set is well carved in ivory with a popular Egyptian theme.

King 3.25in (8cm) high

$10,000-15,000 **BLO**

A 20thC Bohemian 'Royal Dux' type porcelain figural chess set.

King 4.25in (11cm) high

$400-600 **BLO**

An early to mid-20thC German carved wood and glass-mounted figural chess set, in a walnut board/box with a carved border.

King 4in (10cm) high

$700-1,000 **BLO**

A 20thC German 'Nutcracker' Christmas-themed painted wooden chess set, in a painted wooden box.

King 3.25in (8.5cm) high

$280-320 **BLO**

An early 1970s British politicians resin figural chess set, the red side as Labour, the blue side as Conservatives, the king shown.

King 5in (12cm) high

$600-900 **BLO**

A CLOSER LOOK AT A CHESS SET

The set was officially known as 'The Reds vs The Whites', but became known as 'The Communists vs The Capitalists'.

The use of boats as rooks is a typical feature of Russian chess sets.

This set was in production from 1920 until 1939 and depicts the 'evils' of the Capitalist State.

The Communist pieces are shown as either soldiers of the Red Army or healthy agrarian or industrial workers.

The Capitalist king is portrayed as the grisly figure of Death holding a human thighbone as his scepter, while the pawns are workers bound up in the chains of slavery.

A Soviet Propaganda 'Communists vs Capitalists' porcelain chess set, Lomonosov State Factory, Leningrad, designed by Natalia Danko (1892-1942) and Yelena Danko (1898-1942).

1923-28

King 4.25in (11cm) high

$15,000-20,000　　　　　　　　　　　　　　　　　　　　　　　　　　**BLO**

A 19thC Chinese export Staunton-style ivory chess set, Cantonese.

Although this set is clearly derived from the Staunton style pioneered by Jacques, the style of both the knight and the flat, angular-type carving of the screws reveal that it is, in fact, Cantonese.

King 2.75in (7cm) high

$300-400　　　　　　　　　　　**BLO**

A late 20thC Chinese hardstone figural chess set, Hong Kong.

King 1.5in (4cm) high

$280-320　　　　　　　　　　　**BLO**

A 20thC Indian enamel and silver-colored metal king chess piece, Jaipur, in the form of an elephant with howdah and parasol.

4in (10cm) high

$280-320　　　　　　　　**BLO**

A late 19thC Sumatran carved wooden 'Deity' chess set.

King 4in (10cm) high

$700-1,000　　　　　　　　**BLO**

A 1950s northern Indian Islamic ivory chess set, with a wooden board/box with squares in ebony and ivory.

King 1.75in (4.5cm) high

$800-1,200　　　　**BLO**

FIND OUT MORE...

Master Pieces: The Architecture of Chess,
by Gareth Williams, published by Viking Press and Apple Press, 2000.

Musée International de Jeu d'Eche
(The International Museum of Chess), Chateau de Clairvaux, 86140 Scorbe-Clairvaux, France.

US Chess Hall of Fame & Museum.
US Chess Center, 1501 M Street, NW, Washington DC, 20005, USA.

A Lenormano card game, by Stralsund (North-east Germany), tax stamp "Deutsches Reich No. 4, 30Pf.", in a original cardboard box.

$15-20   **WDL**

A Spears 'Enid Blyton's Noddy Theatre' game, boxed.

Box 15.5in (39.5cm) wide

$180-220   **GAZE**

A German 'Schach – Dame und Mühle' army field games set, including a set of embossed card chess counters and a folding board, boxed.

c1942

$100-150   **BLO**

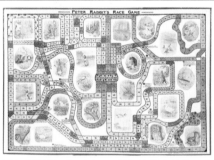

A Peter Rabbit Race board game, published by Frederick Warne & Co, London, complete with board, die, rule sheet and cast metal figural counters, boxed.

This is the favored first edition of the game, which came with metal figures made by the toy soldier manufacturer Johillco. It is in excellent and complete condition, hence its high value.

c1925   *Board 29.5in (75cm) wide*

$700-1,000   **BLO**

A Subbuteo table soccer game, Continental Club edition, with catalog for 1971-72.

Box 18in (45.5cm) wide

$50-70   **GAZE**

A Relum table soccer board game, made in Hungary, boxed.

Box 20.5in (52cm) wide

$20-30   **GAZE**

An Ideal 'Battling Tops' game, complete.

14in (35.5cm) wide

$60-80   **DTC**

An Ideal 'Poppin Hoppies' game.

c1968   *18.5in (47cm) high*

$50-70   **DTC**

A 'Twiggy' game, by MB Games.

The object of the game is to cover Twiggy's face with matching cards.

c1967   *19in (48.5cm) wide*

$100-150   **NOR**

An Atari VCS 2600 games console, with two games and a joystick.

c1977   *10.5in (267cm) wide*

$70-100   **PC**

An Interton Electronic Video 3000 game console, by Grundig, retailed by Dixons.

c1978   *12.5in (31.5cm) wide*

$50-70   **PC**

A Merlin 'Tic-Tac-Toe' game, by Parker Bros., made in Germany.

c1978   *Box 10.25in (26cm) long*

$40-60   **DTC**

A CLOSER LOOK AT A NINTENDO GAME

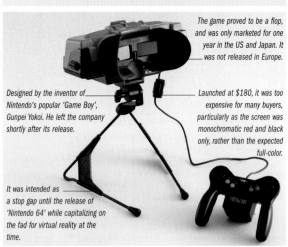

The game proved to be a flop, and was only marketed for one year in the US and Japan. It was not released in Europe.

Designed by the inventor of Nintendo's popular 'Game Boy', Gunpei Yokoi. He left the company shortly after its release.

Launched at $180, it was too expensive for many buyers, particularly as the screen was monochromatic red and black only, rather than the expected full-color.

It was intended as a stop gap until the release of 'Nintendo 64' while capitalizing on the fad for virtual reality at the time.

A Nintendo 'Virtual Boy' 3-D game system.

c1995

$180-220   **HLJ**

A Mattel 'Armor Battle' hand-held game.

c1978   *3.5in (9cm) wide*

$30-50   **HLJ**

A Sega Game Gear set, complete with box and accessories.

c1992   *8in (20cm) wide*

$100-150   **PC**

A Texas Instruments 'Speak & Math'.

One of three popular teaching games released by Texas Instruments that included 'Speak & Spell' and 'Speak & Read'.

c1987   *Box 15.5in (39.5cm) long*

$40-60   **DTC**

A Rolex ladies' silver half-hunter-style wristwatch, with 15-jewel movement.

The 'half-hunter' style reveals the derivation of the earliest wristwatches from pocket watches. 'Half-hunter' pocket watches had an hinged opening metal case over the face with a smaller circular viewing aperture.

1in (3cm) diam

$600-900 **GHOU**

A Rolex WWI military silver wristwatch, with 15-jewel movement.

Rolex was registered in July 1908 by Hans Wilsdorf of Wilsdorf & Davies in London. Founder Wilsdorf started his own wristwatch factory predicting that the wristwatch would overtake the pocket watch for reasons of convenience and fashion. His speculation paid off and by the 1920s the wristwatch had indeed done so. Their more subtle, less 'heavy' watches from the 1950s, particularly in gold, are currently popular with collectors and those choosing to wear them.

1.5in (3.5cm) diam

$700-1,000 **GHOU**

A 1950s Rolex 'Oyster Perpetual' 18ct gold gentleman's wristwatch.

1.5in (3.5cm) diam

$2,800-3,200 **GHOU**

A 1950s Rolex 'Oyster Perpetual Datejust' 18ct gold gentleman's wristwatch, with 25-jewel movement.

Among other developments, Rolex are known for their waterproof 'Oyster' case, developed in 1926 and successfully tested as a publicity stunt by cross-Channel swimmer Mercedes Gleitze in 1927. A clever advertising campaign with shop window displays of a Rolex Oyster in an aquarium created huge brand awareness. The 'Perpetual' automatic movement was developed in 1931 to make the watch yet more hermetic, and the automatic date 'Datejust' in 1945.

1.5in (3.5cm) diam

$2,800-3,200 **GHOU**

A Rolex 'Oysterdate Precision' gentleman's stainless steel wristwatch.

1.5in (3.5cm) diam

$700-1,000 **GHOU**

A Rolex 'Oyster Perpetual' stainless steel gentleman's wristwatch.

1.5in (3.5cm) diam

$700-1,000 **GHOU**

A Rolex 'Oysterdate Precision' gentleman's stainless steel bracelet wristwatch.

1.5in (3.5cm) diam

$800-1,200 **GHOU**

A Rolex 'Oyster Perpetual' ladies' gold and steel bracelet wristwatch.

1in (2.5cm) diam

$800-1,200 **GHOU**

A Rolex 'Oyster Perpetual GMT Master' stainless steel gentleman's bracelet wristwatch.

The GMT Master was released in 1955 and was innovative as it allowed the wearer to read the time in any two time zones.

1.75in (4.5cm) diam

$1,800-2,200 GHOU

An Omega military stainless steel wristwatch.

Military watches typically have black faces, to avoid bright reflections, and a durable, inexpensive stainless steel casing. Many will also bear military markings.

1.5in (3.5cm) diam

$500-800 GHOU

An Omega military stainless steel wristwatch, with 15-jewel movement.

1.5in (3.5cm) diam

$400-600 GHOU

An Omega 'Seamaster' automatic stainless steel gentleman's wristwatch, with 17-jewel movement.

The Seamaster was released in 1948 and is noted for its precision and reliability at sea. In 1993, a model was produced that can function at 1,000 feet (305 meters) beneath sea level. James Bond, played by Pierce Brosnan, in 'Goldeneye' and 'Tomorrow Never Dies' also used a Seamaster Professional Diver's watch, albeit one dramatically modified by Q!

1.25in (3.5cm) diam

$400-600 GHOU

A 1970s Omega 'Chronostop' gentleman's stainless steel wristwatch, with 17-jewel movement.

1.5in (3.5cm) diam

$400-600 GHOU

An Omega Constellation chronometer automatic gold-plated and stainless steel gentleman's wristwatch.

1.5in (3.5cm) diam

$400-600 GHOU

An Omega 'Speedmaster' professional chronograph gentleman's bracelet watch, together with papers and box.

Omega was founded in 1848 in Switzerland by Louis Brandt. It is renowned for its precision and reliability and has been the official timekeeper for 21 Olympic Games. The 'Speedmaster' is one of Omega's key watches and is the only watch to have passed NASA's stringent tests allowing it to be used on space missions, including one to the Moon. Look out for examples with commemorative moon landing engravings, which can fetch $1,000 or more.

1972 *1.75in (4cm) diam*

$800-1,200 GHOU

An Omega 'Seamaster Memomatic' alarm gentleman's stainless steel bracelet wristwatch, with 19-jewel movement.

1.5in (4cm) diam

$500-800 GHOU

A CLOSER LOOK AT A BOREL WRISTWATCH

Ernest Borel, founded in 1859, in Switzerland, is notable for its innovation and avant-garde designs, particularly in the 1950s and 1960s.

The dial moves around as time passes, creating a 'kaleidoscopic' optical effect. Ladies' watches were made in different colors.

The Cocktail watch is one of their most popular, and can be found with five designs including the star (shown here), a flower, a sun, arrows, and a wheel.

It was sold in all parts of the Caribbean but not widely on the US mainland, so you had to travel or be given it as a gift to have one.

A 1950s/60s Ernest Borel men's 'Cocktail' watch, with skeleton display back and 17-jewel movement.

$200-300   **ML**

A 1970s Buler manual wristwatch, deep red plastic bezel, with red dial, clear back, on original red plastic strap.

Face 1.5in (4cm) wide

$50-80   **SEVW**

A Bulova 'flip top' photo wristwatch, with 17-jewel movement and gold-filled case.

The face and bezel of the watch flips up to reveal a space for a small photograph underneath.

c1940

$350-450   **ML**

A Bulova gold-filled doctor's watch, with three registers and 12-jewel movement.

This watch with three dials or 'registers' is rare.

1.75in (4.5cm) high

$1,000-1,500   **ML**

A 1930s Elgin sterling silver wristwatch, with handpainted porcelain dial.

This watch uses a pocket watch movement.

$250-300   **ML**

An early 1920s Elgin two-tone gold-filled wristwatch, with 15-jewel movement and Art Deco enameled details on the case.

$350-450   **ML**

A Gruen 'Precision' 14ct gold rectangular curved wristwatch, with 17-jewel movement, the back dated "8/16/26".

c1926   *1.5in (3.5cm) long*

$400-600   **GHOU**

A Hamilton Flight II asymmetric wristwatch, with 22-jewel movement, gold-filled case and sterling silver dial.

The shape of the case as well as the material it is made from make this watch very desirable. During the 1990s it was re-released due to demand.

1961

$2,800-3,200 ML

A CLOSER LOOK AT AN ELGIN WRISTWATCH

The almost 'digital' readout, known as a jump hour, was called a 'Direct Reader' by Elgin.

The style of the case with its fin-like chevron form not only sums up a style of the age, but also mimics the hands of a watch at ten minutes to two.

This was the style of watch worn by Elvis Presley, although the case on his model was square.

'Lord Elgin' denoted higher-end watches by Elgin, as shown by the 23-jewel movement – high quality movement jump hour watches are scarce.

A Lord Elgin 'Chevron' jump hour or 'Direct Reader' watch, with 23-jewel movement and gold-filled case, together with its original flex gold-filled metal band.

The inclusion of the original metal band makes this more desirable.

c1958

$300-400 ML

A Harwood 'Harwood Automatic' first production automatic wristwatch, with 15-jewel movement and stainless steel case.

Harwood was the first company to produce automatic wristwatches, from around 1926-28. Note the lack of a side winding and setting knob on the bezel. John Harwood had noticed the unreliability of watches in the the trenches of WWI, identifying the hole around the winding stem to be the point of entry for dust and moisture etc. By removing this and placing the setting mechanism inside, he began to develop the idea of a self-winding watch. He had designed the mechanism by 1922 and had registered it a few years later. Watches based on his innovative design are still being made.

c1928

$350-450 ML

An Illinois Watch Co 14ct gold cased gentleman's wristwatch.

1in (2.5cm) long

$400-600 GHOU

A 1930s Illinois Watch Co 'Manhattan' or 'New Yorker' white gold-filled gentleman's wristwatch, with engraved and signed case, two-tone dial with radium numbers.

Founded in 1870 in Springfield, Illinois, and releasing its first watch (The Stuart) in 1872, the company became known as the Illinois Watch Company in 1885. During the late 1920s it was bought out by Hamilton and produced watches for them until 1932 when the last true Illinois watch was produced. After that, all Illinois watches were produced in Hamilton factories.

$350-450 ML

A 1940s/50s Ingersoll Walt Disney Productions Mickey Mouse watch, with chrome-plated case, in very good working condition.

This watch originally sold for $3.95, and the value is largely dependent on whether or not it works, as the movement is hard to fix.

$150-200 ML

An International Watch Co. 18ct gold mid-size wristwatch.

1in (2.5cm) diam

$400-600   **GHOU**

A 1960s Jaeger 'Le Coultre' automatic gentleman's stainless steel wristwatch.

1.5in (3.5cm) diam

$700-1,000   **GHOU**

A Longines 'Flagship' 18ct gold automatic gentleman's wristwatch.

c1970   *1.5in (3.5cm) diam*

$400-600   **GHOU**

A rare 1950s/60s Longines gold-filled gentleman's wristwatch, unusually designed dial with starburst.

$300-500   **ML**

A Movado triple calendar stainless steel gentleman's wristwatch, boxed.

1.5in (3.5cm) diam

$300-500   **GHOU**

A 1940s Girard Perregaux stainless steel gentleman's wristwatch, with 17-jewel movement and rare day, month, and date dial.

$300-400   **ML**

A Piaget 18ct gold gentleman's wristwatch, with 18-jewel movement.

1.25in (3cm) diam

$1,200-1,800   **GHOU**

A 1970s Sicura Chrono 2 wristwatch, steel bezel, black dial, date function, original steel bracelet.

Face 1.75in (4.5cm) wide

$180-220   **SEVW**

A Tag Heuer 'Super Professional' automatic gentleman's steel bracelet wristwatch.

1.75in (4.5cm) diam

$300-500   **GHOU**

A Tissot Bruce McLaren automatic gentleman's stainless steel bracelet wristwatch.

1.75in (4.5cm) diam

$300-400   **GHOU**

A 1970s Tudor 'Oyster Prince Date-Day' stainless steel gentleman's wristwatch, the day and date apertures with Spanish text.

Tudor is a sub-brand of Rolex and hence many Tudor watches bear stylistic resemblances to Rolex watches.

1.5in (3.5cm) diam

$700-1,000   **GHOU**

A CLOSER LOOK AT A MOVADO POCKET WATCH

Known as the 'Ermeto', this style of watch was released by Movado in 1926 and remained popular until the 1940s.

This example is more valuable as the crocodile skin covering is in excellent condition and the face has a moonphase and day, date, and month. Look out for cases with enamel, precious metals or lacquered decoration.

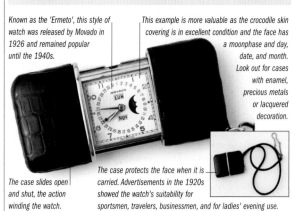

The case slides open and shut, the action winding the watch.

The case protects the face when it is carried. Advertisements in the 1920s showed the watch's suitability for sportsmen, travelers, businessmen, and for ladies' evening use.

A Movado steel-cased traveling watch.

These effectively became the predecessor of the traveling alarm clock, as they had a bracket on the back to allow them to stand up and be viewed from bed.

c1930   *Case 2in (5cm) wide*

$700-1,000   **F**

A 1920s Waltham 18ct gold gentleman's wristwatch, with 15-jewel movement.

1.25in (3.5cm) diam

$300-400   **GHOU**

A Waltham 'jump hour' or 'direct read' gold-filled gentleman's wristwatch, signed "Waltham".

It is very unusual for this watch to be signed.

c1930

$280-320   **ML**

A Waltham 14ct yellow gold gentleman's open-face pocket watch, engraved "JAC" monogram.

1.75in (4.5cm) diam

$80-120   **DAW**

A Canadian gold-filled pocket watch, by James Thomson of Bracebridge, the case marked "A.W.C. Co."

c1915   *1.5in (4cm) wide*

$80-120   **TAB**

A gold mesh-link albert chain, with fancy ball spacers.

One end of an Albert would hold a pocket watch and the other a winding key, pencil or similar useful small object. The watch and item were put in waistcoat pockets, with the chain being pulled through one of the waistcoat buttonholes across the front of the waistcoat. They are seldom used now.

$280-320   **F**

COLLECTORS' NOTES

■ The first range of Swatch watches was released in 1983. These 12 models were plain, quartz wristwatches, almost unrecognizable compared to today's brightly colored, heavily designed models. Since then, the company has released two new collections each year.

■ They were cheaply produced, having only 51 components, and were marketed at an affordable price, although later limited editions were issued at a higher price. They proved extremely popular and by 1984 over one million units had been produced.

■ A number of designers and artists worked with Swatch including Keith Haring, Kiki Picasso, Vivienne Westwood, and Christian Lacroix. Today their models are some of the most sought-after by collectors.

■ Interest in collecting Swatches reached a peak in the early 1990s. While the market is not as strong as it once was, there is a smaller but stable marketplace for discontinued and limited edition models and a number of dedicated websites and internet auctions.

■ Watches in mint, unworn condition, with the original packaging and paperwork are the most desirable and will hold their value better.

■ Check the strap is original and correct for the model, as a replaced strap can reduce the value by half. Straps are also easily marked by the buckle, reducing the value, however, there are methods for removing bends.

A Swatch first series wristwatch, GB 402, with date function.

This was also made with a day and date function, model GB 702, which is worth about the same amount.

1983

$280-320 ML

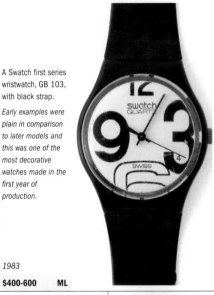

A Swatch first series wristwatch, GB 103, with black strap.

Early examples were plain in comparison to later models and this was one of the most decorative watches made in the first year of production.

1983

$400-600 ML

A Swatch 'Don't Be Too Late' wristwatch, GA 100, from the Memphis series, with original packaging.

1984

$400-600 ML

A Swatch 'Chrono-Tech' wristwatch, GB 403, from the Aspen series.

This was remade in 1985.

1984

$220-280 ML

A Swatch 'Pinstripe' wristwatch, GA 102, from the Carlton series.

1985

$120-180 ML

A Swatch 'Stormy Weather' wristwatch, GV 100, from the Dream Waves series.

Look for the rare version without the Swatch logo at '12', worth about double the normal version.

1989

$120-180 ML

A Swatch 'Nicholette' ladies wristwatch, LB 105, from the Plaza series, with black strap.

This model was relaunched in 1987.

1985

$120-180 ML

A Swatch 'Gamela' ladies wristwatch, LG 102, from the Blue Nile series.

1986

$120-180   **ML**

A CLOSER LOOK AT A 'JELLY FISH' SWATCH

The original version was designed by artist Maryse Schmid and was first issued in 1984. Swatch states that only 200 examples were produced.

The metal dial ring was added to the 1985 version, which is worth double this version.

Thin hands were changed for thick hands in 1986 and the Swatch copyright logo was added to the dial ring that same year.

This version was made in 1986 and is worth about a fifth of the original.

A Swatch 'Jelly Fish' wristwatch, GK 100.

The clear plastic strap and case turn yellow and then brown over time.

1986

$220-280   **ML**

A Swatch 'Nine to Six' wristwatch, GB 117, from the Neo Geo series.

1987

$40-60   **ML**

A Swatch 'Marmorata' wristwatch, GB 119, from the Blake's series.

1987

$40-60   **ML**

A Swatch 'Needles' wristwatch, GB 408, from the Signal Corps series.

1988

$40-60   **ML**

A Swatch 'Sandy Mountains' wristwatch, GG 105, from the Dream Waves series, with replaced textured green strap.

With the correct strap, this watch could be worth up to twice as much.

1989

$50-80   **ML**

A Swatch 'Tango Azul' wristwatch, GX 401, from the Buenos Aires series, with blue leather strap.

1989

$120-180   **ML**

A Swatch 'Sun Lady' ladies wristwatch, LB 125, from the True Stories series.

1989

$60-90   **ML**

A Swatch 'Cosmesis' wristwatch, GM 103, from the Mendini's series.

1990

$30-50   ML

A Swatch 'Hacker's Reward' wristwatch, GK 122, from the Alu Cosmos series.

1990

$25-35   ML

A Swatch 'Patchwork' Pop wristwatch, PWB 150, from the Dancing Art series, with fabric strap.

1990

$120-180   ML

A Swatch 'Reflector' wristwatch, GK 130, from the Bright Flags series, with textured yellow strap.

1991

$70-100   ML

A Swatch 'Stalefish' wristwatch, GG 113, from the Cold Fever series.

1991

$70-100   ML

A Swatch 'Sappho' ladies' wristwatch, LV 101, from the Lovefrieze series, with decorated strap.

1991

$70-100   ML

A Swatch 'C.E.O.' wristwatch, GX 709, from the Grande Capo series, with blue leather strap.

1992

$80-120   ML

A Swatch 'Cappuccino' wristwatch, GG 121, from the Sunday Brunch series.

This was designed by artist Jennifer Morla and was sold with a 'Sunday Brunch' cup. It was also available as a 'Maxi'.

1993

$50-70   ML

A Swatch 'Alabama' chronograph, SCN 105/106.

1993

$80-120   ML

A Swatch 'IOC 100' wristwatch, SCZ 101, from the Olympic series, commemorating 100 years of the International Olympic Committee.

1994

$70-100 ML

A Swatch 'Ramarro' automatic wristwatch, SAK 111, from the Automatic series, with green leather strap.

1994

$70-100 ML

A Swatch 'Cigar' wristwatch, GK 250, from the 1,000 Years series, with 'cigar' strap.

1997

$50-70 ML

A Swatch 'Atlanta Laurels' wristwatch, GZ 145, from the Honor & Glory series commemorating the 1996 Atlanta Olympics, with original packaging.

1995

$80-120 ML

A limited edition Swatch 'Light Tree' Pop wristwatch, GZ 152, from the Christmas series and an edition of 20,000, with LED-tipped fronds, contained in a red Christmas bauble, and original card box.

1996

$180-220 ML

A limited edition Swatch 'Stripp' Scuba 200 wristwatch, SDN 120, designed by Andrea Arrigoni, with extra costumes to dress the spaceman, with original box and packaging.

1996

$50-80 ML

A Swatch 'Centipede' wristwatch, GG 143, from the Comic Hour series.

Designed by the artist Jamie Hewlett, who is better known for his 'Tank Girl' comic series and for his work with the band Gorillaz.

1997

$50-70 ML

Two late 1980s Swatch Guard Too watch guards, mint and boxed.

$7-10 ML

A Swatch clear plastic replacement watch strap.

1995-6 6.75in (17.5cm) high

$25-35 ML

FIND OUT MORE...

www.swatch.com – Official company and collectors' club website.

W.B.S. Collector's Guide for Swatch Watches, by Wolfgang Schneider, published by W B S Marketing, October 1992.

Almost Everything You Need to Know About Dealing & Collecting Swatch Watches, by Roy Ehrhardt, Larry Ehrhardt, published by Heart of America Pr, October 1996.

COLLECTORS' NOTES

■ Wedding collectibles have grown in popularity over the past few years. Most of the items collected comprise the many forms of bride and groom wedding cake toppers. Other themed items bulk out and add variety to a collection. Look for salt and pepper shakers and bride and groom dolls by companies such as Madame Alexander and Peggy Nisbet.

■ Consider the material, plastic is more likely to have been used from the 1940s/50s onward, with bisque being used from the 1920/30s and other ceramics from the 1920s-50s. The complexity, quality and age of the piece will have an effect on value, with better made, earlier pieces from the 1920s fetching higher prices.

■ Examine clothing as styles of wedding dresses can help to date a piece, as can the hairstyles and general appearance of a piece. As a groom's morning dress or tuxedo has remained largely unchanged, this is usually not worth considering. However, look out for grooms wearing other clothes such as army or navy dress uniforms as these are very desirable.

A 1930s German bride and groom painted ceramic salt and pepper set, stamped "GERMANY" on the base.

2.5in (6.5cm) high

$50-70   **DAC**

A 1920s Kewpie-style bisque bride and groom, with crêpe paper clothing, wire-jointed arms and cardboard pads.

These were probably made for the top of a wedding cake. Look out for more accurate Kewpie wedding dolls as these are sought-after, often fetching over $100-120.

3in (7.5cm) high

$50-70   **DAC**

A 1950s small bisque fabric and netting dancing bride and groom.

3.25in (8cm) high

$30-50   **DAC**

A 1930s painted plaster cake topper of an elegant, elongated bride and groom.

6.75in (17cm) high

$50-70   **DAC**

A 1950s painted plaster wedding cake topper with glass dome, the base molded "Our Wedding Day".

3.5in (9cm) high

$30-50   **DAC**

A 1940s cake topper, made from plaster, wire, netting, fabric flowers and ribbon.

8.5in (21.5cm) high

$30-50   **DAC**

A 1940s painted plaster, wire-framed, card, material and ribbon wedding cake topper.

8.5in (22cm) high

$70-100   **DAC**

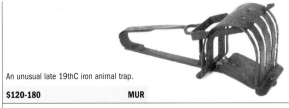

An unusual late 19thC iron animal trap.

$120-180   **MUR**

A 17thC iron dog collar.

Dog collars are often mistaken for early 19thC slave collars, albeit less spikey examples. This early example has spikes to protect the dog's neck from attack by wolves.

An unusual late 19thC iron animal trap.

20in (51cm) long

$70-100   **MUR** | **$120-180**   **ANAA**

An unmarked metal grip, with internal row of spikes and restricted scissor type action.

Some objects were made for a specific use that has since fallen out of favor, or has become obsolete. Despite the opinions of a number of experts, nobody has yet identified this tool. If you know what is, please write in to the address at the front of the book. the first correct answer wins copy of next year's book!

5in (12.5cm) long

A brass and steel hat measure, in very good condition.

NPA   **PC** | **$80-120**   **MUR**

A horn from a German mine, salvaged by Lieutenant W.J. Carver of the Royal Naval Volunteer Reserve in 1918, mounted with descriptive plaque.

The horn was a trigger on German sea mines used extensively during WWI. A mine filled with around 500lbs of explosive would be anchored to the seabed with a wire, and covered with screw-in 'horns'. Any passing ship touching one of these horns would complete a circuit and cause the mine to explode. This example would probably have been unscrewed from a live mine.

c1918

$120-180   **BA**

A rare original US patent mouse trap, by Christopher Lang of Newark, Ohio, together with a copy of the patent of May 23, 1871.

This is one of the rarest mouse traps ever made.

1871

A stilton cheese spoon, with ivory and silver handle, in very good condition.

$400-600   **ATK** | **$100-150**   **MUR**

A collegiate skull porcelain tankard, the metal lid with porcelain inlay and dedication, dated.

The skull is a popular 'memento mori', a reminder of the passing of life and eventual death.

1900   6in (15cm) high

$280-320   **WDL**

A late 19thC French painted canvas and carved wood ventriloquist dummy's head, with glass eyes.

9in (23cm) high

$500-800   **ANAA**

A mid-19thC German commemorative or souvenir bisque model of Chang and Eng, the Siamese twins, impressed on base "Siam Willinc".

A highly realistic fairground horror show painted rubber severed hand.

6.75in (17cm) long

$15-20   **ANAA**

Chang and Eng were born in Siam (now Thailand) in 1811 and were the source of the term 'Siamese Twins'. After being 'discovered' by an English merchant, they traveled in Europe and the USA extensively, taking part in many shows. They eventually settled in North Carolina, assumed the surname 'Bunker', married two sisters and fathered 21 children between them (no pun intended). They died aged 63 in 1874.

3.25in (8.5cm) high

$70-100   **ANAA**

A set of 1930s 'square-dance band' carved and painted wooden figures, base and box stamped "Made in Japan".

Each figure is delicately hand-carved and painted and appears to have no specific use apart from being tiny decorative objects. They are also found in different dance types.

Box 5.5in (14cm) wide

$120-180   **SM**

A wooden auctioneer's gavel, with commemorative stamp for Phillips' the Auctioneers bicentenary celebrations 1796-1996 and original box.

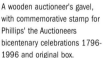

1996   4in (10cm) long

$20-30   **GORL**

A rare set of four brown leather pony or donkey tennis lawn boots, with straps and stamped flower motifs.

These were worn by ponies pulling lawnmowers across lawns and lawn tennis courts to stop their hooves ruining the turf.

Each 4.75in (12cm) high

$280-320   **MSA**

GLOSSARY

A

Acid etching A technique using acid to decorate glass to produce a matt or frosted appearance.

Albumen print Photographic paper is treated with egg white (albumen) to enable it to hold more light-sensitive chemicals. After being exposed to a negative, the resulting image is richer with more tonal variation.

Applied Refers to a separate part that has been attached to an object, such as a handle.

B

Baluster A curved form with a bulbous base and a slender neck.

Base metal A term describing common metals such as copper, tin and lead, or metal alloys, that were usually plated in gold or silver to imitate more expensive and luxurious metals. In the US, the term 'pot metal' is more commonly used.

Bisque A type of unglazed porcelain used for making dolls from c1860 to c1925.

Boards The hard covers of a book.

Brassing On plated items, where the plating has worn off to reveal the underlying base metal.

C

Cabochon A large, protruding, polished, but not faceted, stone.

Cameo Hardstone, coral or shell that has been carved in relief to show a design in a contrasting color.

Cameo glass Decorative glass made from two or more layers of differently colored glass, which are then carved or etched to reveal the color beneath.

Cartouche A framed panel, often in the shape of a shield or paper scroll, which can be inscribed.

Cased Where a piece of glass is covered with a further layer of glass, often of a contrasting color, or else clear and colorless. In some cases the casing will be further worked with cutting or etching to reveal the layer beneath.

Charger A large plate or platter, often for display, but also for serving.

Chromolithography A later development of 'lithography', where a number of printing stones are used in succession, each with a different color, to build up a multi-colored image.

Composition A mixture including wood pulp, plaster and glue used as a cheap alternative to bisque in the production of dolls' heads and bodies.

Compote A dish, usually on a stem or foot, to hold fruit for the dessert course.

Craze/Crazed/Crazing A network of fine cracks in the glaze caused by uneven shrinking during firing. It also describes plastic that is slowly degrading and has the same surface patterning.

Cuenca A technique used for decorating tiles where molded ridges separate the colored glazes, like the 'cloisonné' enameling technique.

Cultured pearl A pearl formed when an irritant is artificially introduced to the mollusc.

D

Damascened Metal ornamented with inlaid gold or silver, often in wavy lines. Commonly found on weapons or armor.

Dichroic Glass treated with chemicals or metals that cause it to appear differently colored depending on how it is viewed in the light.

Diecast Objects made by pouring molten metal into a closed metal die or mold.

Ding A very small dent in metal.

E

Earthenware A type of porous pottery that requires a glaze to make it waterproof.

Ebonized Wood that has been blackened with dye to resemble ebony.

E.P.N.S. Found on metal objects and standing for 'electroplated nickel silver', meaning the object is made from nickel which is then electroplated with silver.

F

Faïence Earthenware that is treated with an impervious tin glaze. Popular in France from the 16th century and reaching its peak during the 18th century.

Faceted A form of decoration where a number of flat surfaces are cut into the surface of an object such as a gem or glass.

Faux A French word for 'false'. The intention is not to deceive fraudulently but to imitate a more costly material.

Finial A decorative knob at the end of a terminal, or on a lid.

Foliate Leaf and vine motifs.

G

Guilloché An engraved pattern of interlaced lines or other decorative motifs, sometimes enameled over with translucent enamels.

H

Hallmark The series of small stamps found on gold or silver that can identify the maker, the standard of the metal and the city and year of manufacture. Hallmarks differ for each country and can consist only of a maker's or a city mark. All English silver made after 1544 was required to be fully marked.

IJKL

Incised Applied to surface decoration or a maker's mark that has been scratched into the surface of an object with a sharp instrument.

Inclusions Used to describe all types of small particles of decorative materials embedded in glass.

Iridescent A lustrous finish that subtly changes color depending on how light hits it. Often used to describe the finish on ceramics and glass.

Lithography A printing technique developed in 1798 and employing the use of a stone upon which a pattern or picture has been drawn with a grease crayon. The ink adheres to the grease and is transfered to the paper when pressed against it.

MNO

Millefiori An Italian term meaning 'thousand flowers' and used to describe cut, multi-colored glass canes which are arranged and cased in clear glass. When arranged with the cut side facing the exterior, each circular disc (or short cane) resembles a small flower.

Mint A term used to describe an object in unused condition with no signs of wear and derived from coinage. Truly 'mint' objects will command a premium.

Mount A metal part applied to an object made of ceramic, glass or another material, with a decorative or functional use.

Nappy A shallow dish or bowl with a handle used for drinking.

Opalescent An opal-like, milky glass with subtle gradations of color between thinner more translucent areas and thicker, more opaque areas.

P

Paisley A stylized design based on pinecones and foliage, often with added intricate decoration. It originated in India and is most often found on fabrics, such as shawls.

Paste (jewelry) A hard, bright glass cut the same way as a diamond and made and set to resemble them.

Patera An oval or circular decorative motif often with a fluted or floral centre. The plural is 'paterae'.

Piqué A decorative technique where small strips or studs of gold are inlaid onto ivory or tortoiseshell on a pattern and secured in place by heating.

Pontil A metal rod to which a glass vessel is attached when it is being worked. When it is removed it leaves a raised disc-shaped 'pontil mark'.

Pot metal Please see 'Base metal'.

Pounce pot A small pot made of wood (treen), silver or ceramic. Found on inkwells or designed to stand alone. It held a gum dust that was sprinkled over parchment to prevent ink from spreading. Used until the late 18th century.

Pressed (Press molded) Ceramics formed by pressing clay into a mold. Pressed glass is made by pouring molten glass into a mold and pressing it with a plunger.

R

Reeded A type of decoration with thin raised, convex vertical lines. Derived from the decoration of classical columns.

Relief A form of molded, pressed or carved decoration that protrudes above the surface of an object. Usually in the form of figures of foliate and foliage designs, it ranges in height from 'low' to 'high'.

Repoussé A French term for the raised, 'embossed' decoration on metals such as silver. The metal is forced into a form from one side causing it to bulge.

S

Sgraffito An Italian word for 'little scratch' and used to describe a decorative technique where the outer surface of an object, usually in glazed or colored ceramic, is scratched away in a pattern to reveal the contrasting colored underlying surface.

Sommerso Technique developed in Murano in the 1930s. Translates as 'submerged' and involves casing one or more layers of transparent colored glass within a layer of thick, clear, colorless glass.

Stoneware A type of ceramic similar to earthenware and made of high-fired clay mixed with stone, such as feldspar, which makes it non-porous.

T

Tazza A shallow cup with a wide bowl, which is raised up on a single pedestal foot.

Tooled Collective description for a number of decorative techniques applied to a surface. Includes engraving, stamping, punching and incising.

V

Vermeil Gold-plated silver.

Vesta case A small case or box, usually made from silver, for carrying matches.

W

White metal Precious metal that is possibly silver, but not officially marked as such.

Y

Yellow metal Precious metal that is possibly gold, but not officially marked as such.

INDEX TO ADVERTISERS

KEY TO ILLUSTRATIONS

Every collectible illustrated in DK Collectibles Price Guide 2005 by Judith Miller has a letter code identifying the dealer or auction house that sold it. The list below is a key to these codes. In the list, auction houses are shown by the letter A and dealers by the letter D. Some items may have come from a private collection, in which case the code is accompanied by the letter P. Inclusion in this book in no way constitutes or implies a contract or a binding offer on the part of any of our contributors to supply or sell the goods illustrated, or similar items, at the prices stated.

AAC (A)
Alderfer Auction Company
501 Fairground Road,
Hatfield, PA 19440
Tel: 215 393 3000
info@alderferauction.com
www.alderferauction.com

AB (A) (D)
Auction Blocks
The Auction Blocks,
P.O. Box 2321, Shelton, CT
06484
Tel: 203 924 2802
auctionblocks@aol.com
www.auctionblocks.com

ABAA (D)
Abacus Antiques
No longer trading

ABIJ (D)
Aurora Bijoux
Tel: 215 872 7808
aurora@aurorabijoux.com
www.aurorabijoux.com

AG (D)
Antique Glass at Frank Dux Antiques
33 Belvedere
Bath BA1 5HR UK
Tel: +44 (0)1225 312 367
m.hopkins@antique-glass.co.uk
www.antique-glass.co.uk

AGI (A)
Aurora Galleries International
30 Hackamore Lane, Suite 2,
Bell Canyon, CA 91307
Tel: 818 884 6468
vcampbell@auroraauctions.com
www.auroragalleriesonline.com

AGO (D)
Anona Gabriel
Otford Antiques Centre, 26-28
High Street, Otford, Sevenoaks,
Kent TN15 9DF UK
Tel: +44 (0)1959 522 025
info@otfordantiques.co.uk

AGR (D)
Adrian Grater
Georgian Village, Camden
Passage, London N1 8DU UK
Tel: +44 (0)208 579 0357
adriangrater@tiscali.co.uk
www.adriangrater.com

AJK (D)
Antiques by Joyce Knutsen
201 Washington Boulavard,
Fayetteville NY 13066
(Summer)
Tel: 315 637 8238 (Summer)
Tel: 352 567 1699 (Winter)
Mob: 315 447 0676
knutsenglass@aol.com

AL (D)
Andrew Lineham Fine Glass
PO Box 465, Chichester, PO18
8WZ UK
Tel: +44 (0)1243 576 241
Mob: +44 (0)7767 702 722
andrew@antiquecolouredglass.com
www.antiquecolouredglass.com

ALL (A)
Allard Auctions
P.O. Box 1030, 419 Flathead
St. 4, St. Ignatius Mt 59865
Tel: 460 745 0500
info@allardauctions.com
www.allardauctions.com

AMJ (D)
American Jazz
Box 302, Ossining, NY 10562
Tel: 914 762 5519
amjazz@optonline.net

ANAA (D)
Anastacia's Antiques
617 Bainbridge Street,
Philadelphia, PA 19147
Tel: 215 928 0256

ART (D)
Artius Glass
Street, Somerset BA16 0AN UK
Tel: +44 (0)1458 443694
Mob: +44 (0)7860 822666
Wheeler.Ron@ic24.net
www.artiusglass.co.uk

ATK (A)
Auction Team Köln
Postfach 50 11 19, Bonner Str.
528-530, D-50971 Cologne,
Germany
Tel: +49 221 38 70 49
auction@breker.com
www.breker.com

B&H (A)
Burstow & Hewett
Lower Lake, Battle, East Sussex,
TN33 0AT UK
Tel: +44 (0)1424 772374
auctions@burstowandhewett.co.uk
www.burstowandhewett.co.uk

B (A)
**Dreweatt Neate, Tunbridge
Wells (formerly Bracketts)**
Auction Hall, The Pantiles,
Tunbridge Wells, Kent TN2 5QL UK
Tel: +44 (0)1892 544 500
tunbridgewells@dnfa.com
www.dnfa.com

BA (D)
Branksome Antiques
370 Poole Road, Branksome,
Poole, Dorset BH12 1AW UK
Tel: +44 (0)1202 763 324

BAD (D)
Beth Adams
Unit GO43/4, Alfies Antique
Market, 13 Church Street,
London NW8 8DT UK
Mob: +44 (0)7776 136 003
www.alfiesantiques.com

BB (D)
Barbara Blau
South Street Antiques Market,
615 South 6th Street,
Philadelphia, PA 19147-2128
Tel: 215 739 4995/ 592 0256
bbjools@msn.com

BBR (A)
BBR Auctions
Elsecar Heritage Centre,
Nr Barnsley,
South Yorkshire, S74 8HJ UK
Tel: +44 (0)1226 745156
www.onlinebbr.com

BCA (D)
**Basketcase Antiques &
Collectibles**
P.O. Box154 S. Dennis NJ
08245
Tel: 609 425 1579
mailgal63@comcast.net

BEJ (D)
Bébés et Jouets
c/o Lochend Post Office, 165
Restalrig Road, Edinburgh EH7
6HW UK
Tel: +44 (0)131 332 5650
bebesjouets@tiscali.co.uk

BEL (A)
Belhorn Auction Services
PO Box 20211, Columbus, OH
43220
Tel: 614 921 9441
auctions@belhorn.com
www.belhorn.com

BER (A)
Bertoia Auctions
2141 Demarco Drive, Vineland
NJ 08360
Tel: 856 692 1881
toys@BertoiaAuctions.com
www.bertoiaauctions.com

BEV (D)
Beverley
30 Church Street, London NW8
8EP UK
Tel: +44 (0)20 7262 1576
www.alfiesantiques.com

BGD (D)
Boisgirard et Associés, SVV
1, rue de la Grange-Batelière,
75009 Paris, France
Tel: +33 1 47 70 81 36
boisgirard@club-internet.fr
www.boisgirard.com

BGL (D)
Block Glass Limited
blockglss@aol.com
www.blockglass.com

BH (D)
**Black Horse Antique
Showcases**
2180 North Reading Road,
Denver PA, 17517
Tel: 717 335 3300
info@antiques-showcase.com
www.antiques-showcase.com

BLO (D)
Bloomsbury Auctions
Bloomsbury House,
24 Maddox Street,
London W1 S1PP UK
Tel: +44 (0)20 7495 9494
info@bloomsburyauctions.com
www.bloomsburyauctions.com

BMM (D)
Barbara M. Mitchell
Ontario, Canada
Tel: 416 699 5582
fineartbarbara@hotmail.com

BR (D)
Beyond Retro
110-112 Cheshire Street,
London E2 6EJ UK
Tel: +44 (0)20 7613 3636
sales@beyondretro.com
www.beyondretro.com

BRB (D)
Bauman Rare Books
535 Madison Avenue, New York,
NY10022
Tel: 212 751 1011
brb@baumanrarebooks.com
www.baumanrarebooks.com

BRI (A)
Brightwells Fine Art
Fine Art Saleroom, Easters
Court, Leominster, Herefordshire
HR6 0DE UK
Tel: +44 (0)1568 611 122
fineart@brightwells.com
www.brightwells.co.uk

BY (D)
Bonny Yankauer
bonnyy@aol.com

C (A)
Cottees
The Market, East Street,
Wareham, Dorset BH20 4NR UK
Tel: +44 (0)1929 552 826
auctions@cottees.fsnet.co.uk
www.auctionsatcottees.co.uk

CA (A)
Chiswick Auctions
1 Colville Road,
London W3 8BL UK
Tel: +44 (0)20 8992 4442
sales@chiswickauctions.co.uk
www.chiswickauctions.co.uk

CAT (D)
CatalinRadio.com
Tel: 419 824 2469
steve@catalinradio.com
www.catalinradio.com

CBE (P)
Christina Bertrand
tineke@rcn.com

CGPC (P)
Cheryl Grandfield Collection

CHEF (A)
Cheffins
Clifton House, 1&2 Clifton
Road, Cambridge CB1 7EA UK
Tel: +44 (0)1223 213 343
fine.art@cheffins.co.uk
www.cheffins.co.uk

CHS (D)
China Search
P.O. Box 1202, Kenilworth,
Warwickshire CV8 2WW UK
Tel: +44 (0)1926 512 402
helen@chinasearch.co.uk
www.chinasearch.co.uk

CL/CLG (D)
Chisholm Larsson Gallery
145 8th Avenue,
New York NY 10011
Tel: 212 741 1703
info@chisholm-poster.com
www.chisholm-poster.com

COB (D)
Cobwebs
78 Old Northam Road,
Southampton SO14 0PB UK
Tel: +44 (0)2380 227 458
www.cobwebs.uk.com

CRIS (D)
Cristobal
26 Church Street,
London NW8 8EP UK
Tel: +44 (0)20 7724 7230
steven@cristobal.co.uk
www.cristobal.co.uk

CVS (D)
Cad Van Swankster at The Girl
Can't Help It
Alfies Antiques Market, Stand
G100 & G90 & G80, 13-25
Church Street, Marylebone,
London NW8 8DT UK
Tel: +44 (0)20 7724 8984
cad@sparklemoore.com

DAC (D)
Dynamite Antiques &
Collectibles
eb625@verizon.net

DAW (A)
Dawson's Auctioneers &
Appraisers now trading as
Dawson & Nye
128 American Road, Morris
Plains, NJ 07950
Tel: 973 984 6900
info@dawsons.org
www.dawsons.org

DC/DCOL (P)
Dust Collectors

DD (D)
Decodame.com
853 Vanderbilt beach Road,
PMB 8, Naples FL34108
Tel: 239 514 6797
info@decodame.com
www.decodame.com

DETC (D)
Deco Etc
122 West 25th Street (between
6th & 7th Aves),
New York, NY 10001
Tel: 212 675 3326
deco_etc@msn.com
www.decoetc.net

DF (D)
Dad's Follies
moreinfo@dadsfollies.com
www.dadsfollies.com

DH (D)
Huxtins
david@huxtins.com
www.huxtins.com

DMI (P)
David Midgley
dgmidgley@yahoo.co.uk

DN (A)
Dreweatt Neate
Donnington Priory Salerooms,
Donnington, Newbury, Berkshire
RG14 2JE UK
Tel: +44 (0)1635 553 553
donnington@dnfa.com
www.dnfa.com/donnington

DRA (A)
David Rago Auctions
333 North Main Street,
Lambertville, NJ 08530
Tel: 609 397 9374
info@ragoarts.com
www.ragoarts.com

DSC (D)
British Doll Showcase
squibbit@ukonline.co.uk
www.britishdollshowcase.co.uk

DTC (D)
Design20c
Tel: +44 (0)794 609 2138
sales@design20c.co.uk
www.design20c.com

EAB (D)
Anne Barrett
Otford Antiques & Collectables
Centre, 28-28 High Street,
Otford, Kent TN15 9DF UK
Tel: +44 (0)1959 522 025
info@otfordantiques.co.uk
www.otfordantiques.co.uk

ECLEC (D)
Eclectica
2 Charlton Place, Islington,
London N1 UK
Tel: +44 (0)20 7226 5625
liz@eclectica.biz
www.eclectica.biz

EG (A)
Edison Gallery
Tel: 617 359 4678
glastris@edisongallery.com
www.edisongallery.com

EOH (D)
The End of History
548 1/2 Hudson Street, New
York, NY 10014
Tel: 212 647 7598

EPO (D)
Elaine Perkins
Otford Antiques & Collectables
Centre, 28-28 High Street,
Otford, Kent TN15 9DF UK
Tel: +44 (0)1959 522 025
info@otfordantiques.co.uk
www.otfordantiques.co.uk

ERI (D)
Eri Jones
Otford Antiques & Collectables
Centre, 28-28 High Street,
Otford, Kent TN15 9DF UK
Tel: +44 (0)1959 522 025
info@otfordantiques.co.uk
www.otfordantiques.co.uk

EVL (D)
Eve Lickver
P.O. Box 1778,
San Marcos CA 92079
Tel: 760 761 0868

F (A)
Fellows & Sons
Augusta House,
19 Augusta Street, Hockley,
Birmingham B18 6JA UK
Tel: +44 (0)121 212 2131
info@fellows.co.uk
www.fellows.co.uk

FBS (D)
Flo Blue Shoppe
Beverly Hills, Michigan
Tel: 248 433 1933
floblueshoppe@hotmail.com

FD (D)
Fragile Design
8 Lakeside, The Custard
Factory, Digbeth, Birmingham
B9 4AA UK
Tel: +44 (0)121 693 1001
info@fragiledesign.com
www.fragiledesign.com

FJA (D)
Feljoy Antiques
Shop 3, Angel Arcade, Camden
Passage, London N1 8EA UK
Tel: +44 (0)20 7354 5336 /
8445 8706
Joy@feljoy-antiques.demon.co.uk
www.chintznet.com/feljoy/

FRE (A)
Freeman's
1808 Chestnut Street,
Philadelphia, PA 19103
Tel: 215 563 9275
info@freemansauction.com
www.freemansauction.com

GAZE (A)
Thos. Wm. Gaze & Son
Diss Auction Rooms. Roydon
Road, Diss, Norfolk IP22 4LN UK
Tel: +44 (0)1379 650 306
sales@dissauctionrooms.co.uk
www.twgaze.com

GC (P)
Graham Cooley Collection
Mob: +44 (0)7968 722 269
graham.cooley@metalysis.com

GCL (D)
Claude Lee
The Ginnel Antiques Centre, off
Parliament Street, Harrogate,
North Yorkshire HG1 2RB UK
Tel: +44 (0)1423 508 857
info@theginnel.com
www.redhouseyork.co.uk

GEW (D)
Eileen Wilson at The Ginnel
The Ginnel Antiques Centre, off
Parliament Street, Harrogate,
North Yorkshire HG1 2RB UK
Tel: +44 (0)1423 508 857
info@theginnel.com
www.redhouseyork.co.uk

GGRT (D)
Gary Grant Choice Pieces
18 Arlington Way,
London EC1R 1UY UK
Tel: +44 (0)20 7713 1122

GHOU (A)
Gardiner Houlgate
Bath Auction Rooms,
9 Leafield Way, Corsham,
Nr Bath SN13 9SW UK
Tel: +44 (0)1225 812 912
auctions@gardiner-
houlgate.co.uk
www.gardinerhoulgate.co.uk

GL (D)
Gary Lickver
P.O. Box 1778,
San Marcos CA 92079
Tel: 760 744 5686

GORL (A)
Gorringes, Lewes
15 North Street, Lewes, East
Sussex, BN7 2PD UK
Tel: +44 (0)1273 472 503
clientservices@gorringes.co.uk
www.gorringes.co.uk

GORW (A)
Gorringes, Worthing
44/46 High Street Worthing
West Sussex BN11 1LL UK
clientservices@gorringes.co.uk
www.gorringes.co.uk

GROB (D)
Geoffrey Robinson
Stand GO77-78 & GO91-92,
Alfies Antiques Market,
13-25 Church Street,
London NW8 8DT UK
Tel: +44 (0)20 7723 0449
www.alfiesantiques.com

H&G (D)
Hope and Glory
131A Kensington Church
Street, London W8 7LP
Tel: +44 (0)20 7727 8424

HA (A)
Hunt Auctions
75 East Ulwchlan Avenue, Suite
130, Exton, PA 19341
Tel: 610 524 0822
info@huntauctions.com
www.huntauctions.com

HGS (D)
Harper General Store
10482 Jonestown Road,
Annville, PA 17003
Tel: 717 865 3456
Lauver5@comcast.com
www.harpergeneralstore.com

HH (P)
Holiday Happenings

HLJ (D)
Hugo Lee-Jones
Tel: +44 (0)1227 375 375
Mob: +44 (0)7941 187 2027
electroniccollectables@hotmail.com

ING (D)
Ingram Antiques
669 Mt. Pleasant Road,
Toronto, Canada M4S 2N2
Tel: 416 484 4601
ingramantiques@bellnet.ca
www.ingramgallery.com/
antiques.htm

JDJ (A)
James D Julia Inc
P.O. Box 830,
Fairfield, Maine 04937
Tel: 207 453 7125
jjulia@juliaauctions.com
www.juliaauctions.com

JJ (D)
Junkyard Jeweler
sales@junkyardjeweler.com
www.junkyardjeweler.com

JL (D)
Eastgate Antiques
Stand S007/009, 13-25 Church
Street,London NW8 8DT UK
Tel: +44 (0)1206 822712
info@alfiesantiques.com
www.alfiesantiques.com

KAU (A)
Auktionhaus Kaupp
Schloss Sulzburg, Hauptstrasse
62, 79295 Sulzburg, Germany
Fax: +49 7634 5038 50
auktionen@kaupp.de
www.kaupp.de

KF (D)
Karl Flaherty Collectables
Tel: +44 (0)2476 445 627
kfckarl@aol.com
www.kfcollectables.co.uk

KNK (D)
Kitsch-N-Kaboodle
South Street Antiques Market,
615 South 6th Street,
Philadelphia, PA 19147-2128
Tel: 215 382 1354
kitschnkaboodle@yahoo.com

L&T (A)
Lyon and Turnbull Ltd.
33 Broughton Place, Edinburgh
EH1 3RR UK
Tel: +44 (0)131 557 8844
info@lyonandturnbull.com
www.lyonandturnbull.com

LAN (A)
Lankes
Triftfeldstrasse 1, 95182,
Döhlau Germany
Tel: +49 (0)928 69 50 50
info@lankes-auktionen.de
www.lankes-auktionen.de

LB (D)
Linda Bee
Stand L18-21, Grays Antique
Market, 58 Davies Street,
London W1Y 2LP UK
Tel: +44 (0)20 7629 5921
lindabee@grays.clara.net
www.graysantiques.com

LC (D)
Lawrence's Fine Art
Auctioneers
The Linen Yard,
South Street, Crewkerne,
Somerset TA18 8AB UK
Tel: +44 (0)1460 73041
enquiries@lawrences.co.uk
www.lawrences.co.uk/

LCA (D)
Lights, Camera, Action
6 Western Gardens, Western
Boulevard, Aspley,
Nottingham, HG8 5GP UK
Tel: +44 (0)115 913 1116
nick.straw@lca-autographs.co.uk
www.lca-autographs.co.uk

LG (D)
Legacy
No longer trading

LOB (D)
Louis O'Brien
Tel: +44 (0)1276 32907

MA (D)
Manic Attic
Stand S48/49, Alfies Antiques
Market, 13 Church Street,
London NW8 8DT UK
Tel: +44 (0)20 7723 6105
manicattic@alfies.clara.net

MBO (D)
Mori Books
Amherst Book Center,
141 Route 101A,
Amherst, NH 03031
Tel: 603 882 2665
richard@moribooks.com
www.moribooks.com

MC (D)
Metropolis Collectibles, Inc.
873 Broadway, Suite 201,
New York, NY 10003
Tel: 212 260 4147
orders@metropoliscomics.com
www.metropoliscomics.com

MGT (D)
Mary & Geoff Turvil
Vintage Compacts, Small
Antiques & Collectables
Tel: +44 (0)1730 260 730
mary.turvil@virgin.net

MHC (P)
Mark Hill Collection
Mob: +44 (0)7798 915 474
stylophile@btopenworld.com

MHT (D)
Mum Had That
info@mumhadthat.com
www.mumhadthat.com

MI (D)
Mood Indigo
181 Prince Street,
New York, NY 10012
Tel: 212 254 1176
info@moodindigonewyork.com
www.moodindigonewyork.com

MILLB (D)
Million Dollar Babies
Tel: 518 885 7397

ML (D)
Mark Laino
South Street Antiques Market,
615 South 6th Street,
Philadelphia, PA 19147-2128
Tel: 215 739 4995

MM (A)
Mullock Madeley
The Old Shippon, Wall-under-
Heywood, Church Stretton,
Shropshire SY6 7DS UK
Tel: +44 (0)169 477 1771
info@mullockmadeley.co.uk
www.mullockmadeley.co.uk

MSA (D)
Manfred Schotten Antiques
109 Burford High Street,
Burford,
Oxfordshire OX18 4RH UK
Tel: +44 (0)1993 822 302
enquiries@schotten.com
www.schotten.com

MTS (D)
The Multicoloured Time Slip
Unit S002, Alfies Antiques
Market, 13-25 Church Street,
London NW8 8DT UK
Mob: +44 (0)7971 410 563
dave_a_cameron@hotmail.com

MUR (A)
Tony Murland Auctions
78 High Street, Needham
Market, Suffolk, IP6 8AW UK
Tel: +44 (0)1449 722 992
tony@antiquetools.co.uk
www.antiquetools.co.uk

NAI (D)
Nick Ainge
Tel: 01832 731063
Mob: 07745 902343
nick@ainge1930.fsnet.co.uk
http://decoseek.decoware.co.uk

NOR (D)
Neet-O-Rama
93 West Main Street,
Somerville, NJ 08876
Tel: 908 722 4600
neetstuff@mindspring.com
www.neetstuff.com

NPC (D)
No Pink Carpet
Tel: +44 (0)1785 249 802
www.nopinkcarpet.com

ON (A)
Onslows
The Coach House, Manor Road,
Stourpaine, Dorset, DT11 8TQ
UK
Tel: +44 (0)1258 488 838
enquiries@onslows.co.uk
www.onslows.co.uk

P&I (D)
Paola & Iaia
Unit S057-58, Alfies Antiques
Market, 13-25 Church Street,
London NW8 8DT UK
Tel: +44 (0)7751 084 135
paolaeiaialondon@hotmail.com

PA (D)
Senator Phil Arthurhultz
P.O. Box 12336,
Lansing, MI 48901
Tel: 517 334 5000
Mob: 517 930 3000

PAC (D)
Port Antiques Center
289 Main Street, Port
Washington, NY 11050
Tel: 516 767 3313
visualedge2@aol.com

PB (D)
Petersham Books
Unit 67, 56 Gloucester Rd,
London SW7 4UB UK
Tel: +44 (0)20 7221 4035
ks@modernfirsts.co.uk
www.modernfirsts.co.uk

PC (P)
Private Collection

PCC (P)
Peter Chapman Collection
pgcbal1@supanet.com

PKA (D)
Phil & Karol Atkinson
May-Oct: 713 Sarsi Tr, Mercer,
PA 16137
Tel: 724 475 2490
Nov-Apr: 7188 Drewry's Bluff
Road, Bradenton, FL 34203
Tel: 941 755 1733

PSA (A)
Potteries Specialist Auctions
271 Waterloo Road, Cobridge,
Stoke-on-Trent ST6 3HR UK
Tel: +44 (0)1782 286 622
enquiries@potteriesauctions.com
www.potteriesauctions.com

PSI (D)
Paul Simons
5 Georgian Village, Islington,
London N1 UK
Mob: +44 (0)7733 326 574
pauliobanton@hotmail.com

PSL (D)
The Propstore of London
Great House Farm, Chenies,
Rickmansworth WD3 6EP UK
Tel: +44 (0)1494 766 485
steve.lane@propstore.co.uk
www.propstore.co.uk

PWE (D)
Philip Weiss Auction Galleries
1 Neil Court,
Oceanside, NY 11572
Tel: 516 594 073
info@philipweissauctions.com
www.philipweissauctions.com

RAON (D)
R.A. O'Neil
Ontario, Canada

RDL (A)
**David Rago/Nicholas Dawes
Lalique Auctions**
333 North Main Street,
Lambertville, NJ 08530
Tel: 609 397 9374
Fax: 609 397 9377
info@ragoarts.com
www.ragoarts.com

RETC (D)
Retro Etc
13-14 Market Walk, Market
Square, Old Amersham,
Bucks HP7 0DF UK
Tel: +44 (0)7810 482900
info@retroetc.com
www.retroetc.com

ROS (A)
Rosebery's
74-76 Knight's Hill, West
Norwood, London SE27 0JD UK
Tel: +44 (0)20 8761 2522
auctions@roseberys.co.uk
www.roseberys.co.uk

RP (D)
Rosie Palmer
Otford Antiques & Collectable
Centre, 26-28 High Street,
Otford, Kent TN15 9DF
Tel: +44 (0)1959 522 025
info@otfordantiques.co.uk
www.otfordantiques.co.uk

RSB (D)
Rowan S. Baker
The Covent Garden Stamp
Shop, 28 Bedfordbury, London,
WC2N 4RB UK
Tel: +44(0) 207 379 1448
rowanbaker@btopenworld.com
www.usa-stamps.com

RSJ (D)
Roger & Susan Johnson
6264 Valley Creek,
Pilot Point, TX 76258
Tel: 940 686 5686
czarmann@aol.com

RWA (D)
Richard Wallis Antiks
Tel: +44(0)20 8529 1749
Mob: +44(0)7721 583 306
info@richardwallisantiks.co.uk
www.richardwallisantiks.com

SAS (A)
Special Auction Services
Kennetholme, Midgham,
Nr. Reading, Berks RG7 5UX UK
Tel: +44 (0)118 971 2949
commemorative@aol.com
www.invaluable.com/sas

SCG (D)
Gallery 1930 Susie Cooper
18 Church Street, Marylebone,
London NW8 8EP UK
Tel: +44 (0)20 7723 1555
gallery1930@aol.com
www.susiecooperceramics.com

SDR (A)
Sollo:Rago Modern Auctions
333 North Main Street,
Lambertville, NJ 08530
Tel: 609 397 9374
info@ragoarts.com
www.ragoarts.com

SEVW (D)
70s Watches
graham@gettya.freeserve.co.uk
www.70s-watches.com

SH (D)
**Sara Hughes Vintage
Compacts, Antiques &
Collectables**
sara@sneak.freeserve.co.uk
http://mysite.wanadoo-
members.co.uk/sara_compacts

SK (A)
Skinner, Inc.
The Heritage on the Garden,
3 Park Plaza, Boston, MA
02116
Tel: 617 350 5400
www.skinnerinc.com

SM (D)
**Sparkle Moore at The Girl
Can't Help It**
Alfies Antiques Market, Stand
G100 & G90 & G80, 13-25
Church Street, Marylebone,
London NW8 8DT UK
Tel: +44 (0)20 7724 8984
sparkle@sparklemoore.com
www.sparklemoore.com

SOTT (D)
Sign of the Tymes
Mill Antiques Center,
12 Morris Farm Road,
Lafayette, NJ 07848
Tel: 973 383 6028
jhap@nac.net
www.millantiques.com

SST (D)
Strand Stamp Centre
The Stamp Centre, 79 Strand,
London, WC2R 0DE UK
Tel: +44 (0)20 7240 3778
enquiries@stamp-centre.co.uk
www.stamp-centre.co.uk

STC (D)
Seaside Toy Center
Joseph Soucy
179 Main St, Westerly, RI
02891
Tel: 401 596 0962

STE (D)
Cloud Glass
info@cloudglass.com
www.cloudglass.com

SUM (D)
**Sue Mautner Costume
Jewellery**
No longer trading.

SWA (A)
Swann Galleries Image Library
104 East 25th Street,
New York, NY 10010
Tel: 212 254 4710
swann@swanngalleries.com
www.swanngalleries.com

SWO (A)
Sworders
14 Cambridge Road, Stansted
Mountfitchet,
Essex CM24 8BZ UK
Tel: +44 (0)1279 817 778
auctions@sworder.co.uk
www.sworder.co.uk

TA (A)
333 Auctions LLC
333 North Main Street,
Lambertville, NJ 08530
Tel: 609 397 9374
info@ragoarts.com
www.ragoarts.com

TAB (D)
Take-A-Boo Emporium
1927 Avenue Road, Toronto,
Ontario Canada M5M 4A2
Tel: 416 785 4555
swinton@takeaboo.com
www.takeaboo.com

TAM (D)
Antiques & Militaria
Toronto Antiques Market, Stand
King Street West, Toronto,
Ontario Canada M5V 1J2
Tel: 416 345 9941
sales@antiquesandmilitaria.com
www.antiquesandmilitaria.com

TCA (D)
Transport Car Auctions
14 The Green, Richmond,
Surrey TW9 1PX UK
Tel: +44 (0)20 8940 2022
oliver@tc-auctions.com
www.tc-auctions.com

TCF (D)
Cynthia Findlay
Toronto Antiques Centre, 276
King Street West, Toronto,
Ontario Canada M5V 1J2
Tel: 416 260 9057
www.cynthiafindlay.com

TCM (D)
Twentieth Century Marks
Whitegates, Rectory Road, Little
Burstead, Nr Billericay,
Essex CM12 9TR UK
Tel: +44 (0)1268 411 000
info@20thcenturymarks.co.uk
www.20thcenturymarks.co.uk

TCT (D)
The Calico Teddy
Tel: 410 433 9202
calicteddy@aol.com
www.calicoteddy.com

TDG (D)
The Design Gallery
5 The Green, Westerham,
Kent TN16 1AS UK
Tel: +44 (0)1959 561 234
sales@designgallery.co.uk
www.designgallery.co.uk

TFR (D)
**Floyd & Rita's Antiques and
Collectables**
Toronto Antiques Centre, 276
King Street West, Toronto,
Ontario Canada M5V 1J2
Tel: 416 260 9066
antiques@floydrita.com
www.floydrita.com

TGM (D)
The Glass Merchant
Tel: +44 (0)7775 683 961
as@titan98.freeserve.co.uk

THG (D)
**Tatiana Kuchinsky at Toronto
Heritage Gallery**
Toronto Antique Centre, 276
King Street West, Toronto
Ontario Canada M5V 1J2
Tel: 416 260 0398

TJL (D)
Josephine Liss
Toronto Antiques Centre, 276
King Street West, Toronto,
Ontario Canada M5V 1J2
Tel: 416 260 9066
www.ohayonantiques.com

TP (D)
Tenth Planet
Unit 37a, Vicarage Field
Shopping Centre, Ripple Road,
Barking, Essex IG11 8DQ UK
Tel: +44 (0)20 8591 5357
sales@tenthplanet.co.uk
www.tenthplanet.co.uk

TPF (D)
Pam Ferrazuti
Toronto Antiques Centre, 276
King Street West, Toronto,
Ontario Canada M5V 1J2
Tel: 416 260 0325
www.pamferrazuttiantiques.com

TR (D)
Terry Rodgers & Melody LLC
30 & 31 Manhattan Art &
Antique Center, 1050 2nd
Avenue, New York, NY 10022
Tel: 212 758 3164
melodyjewelnyc@aol.com

TRA (D)
Toy Road Antiques
200 Highland Street, Canal,
Winchester OH 43110
Tel: 614 834 1786
toyroadantiques@aol.com
www.goantiques.com/members
/toyroadantiques

TYA (D)
Yank Azman
Toronto Antiques Centre, 276
King Street West, Toronto,
Ontario Canada M5V 1J2
Tel: 416 260 5662
yank@yank.ca
www.antiquesformen.com

VE (D)
Vintage Eyeware of New York
Tel: 646 319 9222

VEC (A)
Vectis Auctions Ltd
Fleck Way, Thornaby, Stockton
on Tees TS17 9JZ UK
Tel: +44 (0)1642 750 616
admin@vectis.co.uk
www.vectis.co.uk

VET (D)
Vetro & Arte Gallery
Calle del Cappeller 3212,
Dorsoduro, Venice 30123 Italy
Tel: +39 (0)41 522 8525
contact@venicewebgallery.com
www.venicewebgallery.com

VSC (D)
Vintage Sports Collector
3920 Via Solano, Palos Verdes
Estates, CA 90274
Tel: 310 375 1723

VZ (A)
Von Zezschwitz
Friedrichstrasse 1a, 80801
Munich, Germany
Tel: +49 89 38 98 930
www.von-zezschwitz.de

W&W (A)
Wallis & Wallis
West Street Auction Galleries,
Lewes, East Sussex BN7 2NJ UK
Tel: +44 (0)1273 480 208
auctions@wallisandwallis.co.uk
www.wallisandwallis.co.uk

WAC (D)
What A Character!
hugh@whatacharacter.com
bazuin32@aol.com
www.whatacharacter.com

WAD (A)
Waddington's
Auctioneers & Appraisers
111 Bathurst St., Toronto,
Ontario Canada M5V 2R1
Tel: 416 504 9100
www.waddingtons.ca

WDL (A)
Kunst-Auktionshaus Martin
Wendl
August-Bebel-Straße 4, 07407
Rudolstadt, Germany
Tel: +49 3672 424 350
www.auktionshaus-wendl.de

WW (A)
Woolley & Wallis
51-61 Castle Street, Salisbury,
Wiltshire SP1 3SU UK
Tel: +44 (0)1722 424 500
www.woolleyandwallis.co.uk

ZDB (D)
Zardoz Books
20 Whitecroft,
Dilton Marsh, Westbury,
Somerset BA13 4DJ UK
Tel: +44 (0)1373 865 371
www.zardozbooks.co.uk

DIRECTORY OF SPECIALISTS

If you wish to have any item valued, it is advisable to contact the dealer or specialist in advance to check that they will carry out this service and whether there is a charge. While most dealers will be happy to help you with an enquiry, do remember that they are busy people. Telephone valuations are not possible. Please mention the DK Collectibles Price Guide 2005 by Judith Miller when making an enquiry.

ADVERTISING

Senator Phil Arthurhultz
P.O. Box 12336,
Lansing, MI 48901
Tel: 517 334 5000
Mob: 517 930 3000

Phil & Karol Atkinson
May-Oct:
713 Sarsi Tr, Mercer, PA 16137
Tel: 724 475 2490
Nov-Apr:
7188 Drewry's Bluff Road,
Bradenton, FL 34203
Tel: 941 755 1733

The Nostalgia Factory
Original Movie Posters &
Related Ephemera, Charlestown
Commerce Center, 50 Terminal
St., Bldg. 2, Boston MA 02129
Tel: 617-241-8300 / 800-
479-8754
Fax: 617-241-0710
posters@nostalgia.com
www.nostalgia.com

Toy Road Antiques
200 Highland Street, Canal,
Winchester OH 43110
Tel: 614 834 1786
toyroadantiques@aol.com
www.goantiques.com/members
/toyroadantiques

AMERICANA

Richard Axtell Antiques
1 River St, Deposit, NY 13754
Tel: 607 467 2353
Fax: 607 467 4316
raxtell@msn.com
www.axtellantiques.com

Buck County Antique Center
Route 202, Lahaska, PA 18931
Tel: 215 794 9180

Fields of Glory
55 York St, Gettysburg,
PA 17325
Tel: 717 337 2837
foglory@cvn.net
www.fieldsofglory.com

Larry and Dianna Elman
PO Box 415, Woodland Hills,
CA 91365

Olde Hope Antiques
P.O. Box 718, New Hope,
PA 18938
Tel: 215 297 0200
info@oldehope.com
www.oldehope.com

The Splendid Peasant
Route 23 & Sheffield Rd,
P.O. Box 536,
South Egremont, MA 01258
Tel: 413 528 5755
folkart@splindindpeasant.com
www.splendidpeasant.com

Patricia Stauble Antiques
180 Main Street, P.O. Box 265,
Wiscasset, ME 04578
Tel: 207 882 6341
pstauble@midcoast.com

AUTOGRAPHS

Autographs of America
P.O. Box 461, Provo,
UT 84603-0461
tanders3@autographsofamerica
.com
www.autographsofamerica.com

Platt Autographs
PO Box 135007, Clermont, FL
34711
Tel: 352 241 9164
ctplatt@ctplatt.com
www.ctplatt.com

AUTOMOBILIA

Dunbar's Gallery
54 Haven St. Milford, MA
01757
Tel: 508 634 8697
Fax: 508 634 8697
dunbarsgallery@comcast.net
http://dunbarsgallery.com

BOOKS

Abebooks
www.abebooks.com

Aleph-Bet Books
85 Old Mill River Rd., Pound
Ridge, NY 10576, US Postal
Service
Tel: 914 764-7410
Fax: 914 764-1356
helen@alephbet.com
www.alephbet.com

Bauman Rare Books
535 Madison Ave, between
54th & 55th Streets,
New York, NY 10022
Tel: 212 751 0011
brb@baumanrarebooks.com
www.baumanrarebooks.com

Deer Park Books
Abebooks Inc., #4 - 410
Garbally Road, Victoria, BC V8T
2K1, Canada
Tel/Fax: 860 350 4140
deerparkbk@aol.com
www.deerparkbooks.com

CANADIANA

Yank Azman
Toronto Antiques Centre, 276
King Street West, Toronto,
Ontario, M5V 1J2 Canada
Tel: 416 345 9941
yank@yank.ca
www.antiquesformen.com

The Blue Pump
178 Davenport Road,
Toronto, Canada M5R 1J2
Tel: 416 944 1673
www.thebluepump.com

CERAMICS

The Perrault-Rago Gallery
333 North Main Street,
Lambertville, NJ 08530
Tel: 609 397 1802
www.ragoarts.com

Pair Antiques
12707 Hillcrest Dr, Longmont,
CO 80501-1162
Tel: 303 772 2760

Greg Walsh
P.O. Box 747, Potsdam, NY
13676-0747
Tel: 315 265 9111
gwalsh@northnet.org
www.walshauction.com
(Stoneware)

Happy Pastime
P.O. Box 1225, Ellicott City,
MD 21043-1225
Tel: 410 203 1101
hpastime@bellatlantic.net
www.happypastime.com
(Figurines)

Keller & Ross
47 Prospect Street, Melrose,
MA 02176
Tel: 781 662 7257
kellerross@aol.com
http://members.aol.com/kellerross

Ken Forster
5501 Seminary Road,
Ste 1311, South Falls Church,
VA 22041
Tel: 703 379 1142
(Art Pottery)

Mellin's Antiques
P.O. Box 1115, Redding,
CT 06875
Tel: 203 938 9538
remellin@aol.com

Mark & Marjorie Allen
300 Bedford St. Suite 421,
Manchester, New Hampshire
03101
Tel: 1-603-644-8989
Fax: 1 603 627 1472
mandmallen@adelphia.net
www.antiquedelft.com

Charles & Barbara Adams
By appointment only
289 Old Main St, South
Yarmouth, MA 02664
Tel: 508 760 3290
adams_2430@msn.com

CHARACTER COLLECTIBLES

What A Character!
hugh@whatacharacter.com
bazuin32@aol.com
www.whatacharacter.com

COMICS

Carl Bonasera
A1-American Comic Shops,
3514 W. 95th St,
Evergreen Park, IL 60642
Tel: 708 425 7555

Metropolis Collectibles Inc.
873 Broadway, Suite 201,
New York, NY 10003
Tel: 212 260 4147
Fax: 212 260 4304
orders@metropoliscomics.com
www.metropoliscomics.com

The Comic Gallery
4224 Balboa Ave, San Diego,
CA 92117
Tel: 619 483 4853

COSTUME & ACCESSORIES

Andrea Hall Levy
P.O. Box 1243, Riverdale, NY
10471
Tel: 646 441 1726
barangrill@aol.com

Fayne Landes Antiques
593 Hansell Road,
Wynnewood, PA 19096
Tel: 610 658 0566
fayne@comcast.net

Yesterday's Threads
206 Meadow St, Branford,
CT 06405-3634
Tel: 203 481 6452

Lucy's Hats
1118 Pine Street, Philadelphia,
PA, USA

Vintage Eyeware
Tel: 646 319 9222

COSTUME JEWELRY

Aurora Bijoux
Tel: 215 872 7808
aurora@aurorabijoux.com
www.aurorabijoux.com

Barbara Blau
South Street Antiques Market,
c/o South Street Antiques
Market 615 South 6th Street,
Philadelphia, PA 19147-2128
USA
Tel: 215 739 4995/ 592 0256
bbjools@msn.com

APPENDICES

The Junkyard Jeweler
www.junkyardjeweler.com

Mod-Girl
South Street Antiques Center,
615 South 6th Street,
Philadelphia, PA 19147
Tel: 215 592 0256

Roxanne Stuart
Langhorne PA
Tel: 215 750 8868
gemfairy@aol.com

Terry Rodgers & Melody LLC
30 & 31 Manhattan Art &
Antique Center, 1050 2nd
Avenue, New York, NY 10022
Tel: 212 758 3164
melodyjewelnyc@aol.com

Bonny Yankauer
Tel: 201 825 7697
bonnyy@aol.com

DISNEYANA

MuseumWorks
525 East Cooper Avenue,
Aspen CO 81611
Tel: 970-544-6113
Fax: 970-544-6044
www.mwhgalleries.com

Sign of the Tymes
Mill Antiques Center, 12 Morris
Farm Road, Lafayette, NJ
07848
Tel: 973 383 6028
jhap@nac.net
www.millantiques.com

DOLLS

Memory Lane
45-40 Bell Blvd, Suite 109,
Bayside, NY 11361
Tel: 718 428 8181
memlnny@aol.com
www.tias.com/stores/memlnny

Treasure & Dolls
518 Indian Rocks Rd, N.
Belleair Bluffs, FL 33770
Tel: 727 584 7277
dolls@treasuresanddolls.com
www.treasuresanddolls.com

FIFTIES & SIXTIES

Deco Etc
122 West 25th Street (btw 6th &
7th Aves), New York, NY 10001
Tel: 212 675 3326
deco_etc@msn.com
www.decoetc.net

Kathy's Korner
Tel: 516 624 9494

Lois' Collectibles
Market III, 413 W Main St,
Saint Charles, IL 60174-1815
Tel: 630 377 5599

Nifty Fifties
Tel: 734 782 3974

Neet-O-Rama
93 West Main Street,
Somerville, NJ 08876
Tel: 908 722 4600
neetstuff@mindspring.com
www.neetstuff.com

Steve Colby
Off The Deep End, 712 East St,
Frederick, MD 21701-5239
Tel:800 248 0645
Fax: 301-766-0215
contact@offthedeepend.com
www.offthedeepend.com

FILM MEMORABILIA

STARticles
58 Stewart St, Studio 301,
Toronto, Ontario,
M5V 1H6 Canada
Tel/fax: 416 504 8286
info@starticles.com

Norma's Jeans
3511 Turner Lane, Chevy
Chase, MD 20815-2313
Tel: 301 652 4644
Fax: 301 907 0216

George Baker
CollectorsMart, P.O. Box
580466, Modesto, CA 95358
Tel; 290 537 5221
Fax: 209 531 0233
georgeb1@thevision.net
www.collectorsmart.com

GENERAL

Adamstown Antiques Market
Route 272, Adamstown, PA
19501
Tel: 215-484-4385

Anastacia's Antiques
617 Bainbridge Street,
Philadelphia, PA 19147

Antiques of Cape May
Tel: 800 224 1687

**Black Horse Antique
Showcases**
2180 North Reading Road,
Denver PA, 17517 USA
Tel: 717 335 3300

Bucks County Antique Center
Route 202, Lahaska, PA 18931
Tel: 215 794 9180

Burlwood Antique Center
Route 3, Meredith, NH 03523
Tel: 603 279 6387
www.burlwood-antiques.com

Camelot Antiques
7871 Ocean Gateway,
Easton, MD 21601
Tel: 410 820 4396
camelot@goeaston.net
www.about-
antiques.com/CamelotAntiques

Manhattan Art & Antiques Center
1050 Second Avenue (between
55th & 56th Street) New York,
NY, 10022
Tel: 212-355-4400
Fax: 212-355-4403
info@the-maac.com
www.the-maac.com

The Lafayette Mill Antiques
12 Morris Farm Road (Just off
Rte 15), Lafayette NJ 07848
Tel: 973 383 0065
millpartners@inpro.net
www.millantiques.com

South Street Antiques Market
615 South 6th Street,
Philadelphia, PA 19147
Tel: 215 592 0256.

The Showplace
40 W. 25th St., New York City,
New York, United States
Tel: 212 741 8520

Toronto Antiques Centre
276 King Street West, Toronto,
Ontario M5V 1J2 Canada
Tel: 416 345 9941

GLASS

The End of History
548 1/2 Hudson Street,
New York, NY 10014
Tel: 212 647 7598
Fax: 212 647 7634

Past-Tyme Antiques
Tel: 703 777 8555
pasttymeantiques@aol.com

Jeff F. Purtell
31 Pleasant Point Drive,
Portsmouth, NH 03801
Tel: 800-973-4331
jfpurtell@steubenpurtell.com
www.steubenpurtell.com
(Steuben)

Paul Reichwein
2321 Hershey Ave, East
Petersburg, PA 17520
Tel: 717 569 7637
paulrdg@aol.com

Paul Stamati Gallery
1050 2nd Ave, New York,
NY 10022
Tel: 212 754 4533
Fax: 212 754-4552
www.stamati.com

Suzman's Antiques
P.O. Box 301, Rehoboth, MA
02769
Tel: 508 252 5729

HOLIDAY MEMORABILIA

Chris & Eddie's Collectibles
c/o South Street Antiques
Market, 615 South 6th Street,
Philadelphia, PA 19147
Tel: 215 592 0256

Sign of the Tymes
Mill Antiques Center, 12 Morris
Farm Road, Lafayette, NJ
07848
Tel: 973 383 6028
jhap@nac.net
www.millantiques.com

KITCHENALIA

**Dynamite Antiques &
Collectibles**
eb625@verizon.net

Village Green Antiques
Port Antiques Center, 289 Main
Street, Port Washington, NY
11050
Tel: 516 625 2946
amysdish@optonline.net

LUNCH BOXES

Seaside Toy Center
Joseph Soucy
179 Main St,
Westerly, RI 02891
Tel: 401 596 0962

MARBLES

Auction Blocks
P.O. Box 2321, Shelton, CT
06484
Tel: 203 924 2802
auctionblocks@aol.com
www.auctionblocks.com

MECHANICAL MUSIC

The Music Box Shop
6102 North 16th Street,
Phoenix, AZ 85016
Tel: 602 277-9615
musicboxshop@home.com
www.themusicboxshop.com

Mechantiques
The Crescent Hotel,
75 Prospect St,
Eureka Springs, AR 72632
Tel: 479-253-0405
mroenigk@aol.com
www.mechantiques.com

MILITARIA

Articles of War
358 Boulevard,
Middletown, RI 02842
Tel: 401 846 8503
dutch5@ids.com

PENS & WRITING EQUIPMENT

Fountain Pen Hospital
10 Warren Street,
New York, NY 10007
Tel: 212 964 0580
info@fountainpenhospital.com
www.fountainpenhospital.com

Gary & Myrna Lehrer
16 Mulberry Rd, Woodbridge,
CT 06525-1717
Tel: 203 389 5295
Fax: 203 389 4515
garylehrer@aol.com
www.gopens.com

David Nishimura
Vintage Pens, P.O. Box 41452
Providence, RI 02940-1452
Tel: 401 351 7607
www.vintagepens.com

Sandra & L. 'Buck' van Tine
Lora's Memory Lane, 13133
North Caroline St, Chillicothe, IL
61523-9115
Tel: 309 579 3040
Fax: 309 579 2696
lorasink@aol.com

Pendemonium
619 Avenue G, Fort Madison, IA
52627
Tel: 319 372 0881
Fax: 319 372 0882
www.pendemonium.com

PLASTICS

Dee Battle
9 Orange Blossom Trail,
Yalaha, FL 34797
Tel: 352 324 3023

Malabar Enterprises
172 Bush Lane, Ithaca,
NY 14850
Tel: 607 255 2905
Fax: 607 255 4179
asn6@cornell.edu

POSTERS

Posteritati
239 Center St, New York,
NY 10013
Tel: 212 226 2207
Fax: 212 226 2102
mail@posteritati.com
www.posteritati.com

Chisholm Larsson
145 8th Avenue,
New York, NY 10011
Tel: 212 741 1703
www.chisholm-poster.com

Vintage Poster Works
P.O. Box 88, Pittford, NY 14534
Tel: 585 381 9355
debra@vintageposterworks.com
www.vintageposterworks.com

La Belle Epoque
11661 San Vincente, 3304 Los
Angeles, CA 90049-5110
Tel: 310 442 0054
Fax: 310 826 6934
ktscicon@ix.netcom.com

RADIOS

Catalin Radios
5443 Schultz Drive, Sylvania,
OH 43560
Tel: 419 824 2469
Mob: 419 283 8203
steve@catalinradio.com
www.catalinradio.com

ROCK & POP

Heinz's Rare Collectibles
P.O. Box 179, Little Silver,
NJ 07739-0179
Tel: 732 219 1988
Fax: 732 219 5940
(The Beatles)

Tod Hutchinson
P.O. Box 915, Griffith,
IN 46319-0915
Tel: 219 923 8334
toddtcb@aol.com
(Elvis Presley)

SCENT BOTTLES

Oldies But Goldies
860 NW Sorrento Ln. Port St.
Lucie, FL 34986
Tel. 772 873 0968
email@oldgood.com
www.oldgood.com

Monsen & Baer Inc
P.O. Box 529, Vienna, VA
22183-0529
Tel: 703 938 2129
monsenbaer@erols.com

SCIENTIFIC & TECHNICAL, INCLUDING OFFICE & OPTICAL

George Glazer Gallery
28 East 2nd St,
New York, NY 10021
Tel: 212-535-5706
Fax 212-658-9512
worldglobe@georgeglazer.com
www.georgeglazer.com

Tesseract
coffeen@aol.com
www.etesseract.com

The Olde Office
68-845 Perez Rd, Ste 30,
Cathedral City, CA 92234
Tel: 760 346 8653
Fax: 760 346 6479
info@thisoldeoffice.com
www.thisoldeoffice.com

Jane Hertz
Fax: 941 925-0487
auction01122@aol.com
auction@breker.com
www.breker.com
(Cameras, Office & Technical
Equipment)

SMOKING

Richard Weinstein
International Vintage Lighter
Exchange, 30 W. 57th St,
New York, NY 10019
Tel: 212 586 0947
info@vintagelighters.com
www.vintagelighters.com

Ira Pilossof
Vintage Lighters Inc., P.O. Box
1325, Fairlawn,
NJ 07410-8325
Tel: 201 797 6595
vintageltr@aol.com

Mike Cassidy
1070 Bannock #400,
Denver, CO 80204
Tel: 303 446 2726

Chuck Haley
Sherlock's, 13926 Double Girth
Ct., Matthews, NC 28105-4068
Tel: 704 847 5480

SPORTING MEMORABILIA

Classic Rods & Tackle
P.O. Box 288, Ashley Falls, MA
01222
Tel: 413 229 7988

Larry Fritsch Cards Inc
735 Old Wassau Rd, P.O. Box
863, Stevens Point, WI 54481
Tel: 715 344 8687
Fax: 715 344 1778
larry@fritschcards.com
www.fritschcards.com
(Baseball Cards)

George Lewis
Golfiana, P.O. Box 291,
Mamaroneck, NY 10543
Tel: 914 698 4579
findit@golfiana.com
www.golfiana.com

Golf Collectibles
P.O. Box 165892,
Irving, TX 75016
Tel: 800 882 4825
furjanic@directlink.net
www.golfforallages.com

The Hager Group
P.O. Box 952974, Lake Mary,
FL 32795
Tel: 407 788 3865
(Trading Cards)

Hall's Nostalgia
21-25 Mystic St, P.O. Box 408,
Arlington, MA 02174
Tel: 781 646 7757

Tom & Jill Kaczor
1550 Franklin Rd, Langhorne,
PA 19047
Tel: 215 968 5776
Fax: 215 946 6056

Vintage Sports Collector
3920 Via Solano, Palos Verdes
Estates, CA 90274
Tel: 310 375 1723

TEDDY BEARS & SOFT TOYS

Harper General Store
10482 Jonestown Rd, Annville,
PA 17003
Tel: 717 865 3456
Fax: 717 865 3813
lauver5@comcast.net
www.harpergeneralstore.com

Marion Weis
Division St Antiques, P.O. Box
374, Buffalo, MN 55313-0374
Tel: 612 682 6453

TOYS & GAMES

Atomic Age
318 East Virginia Road,
Fullerton, CA 92831
Tel: 714 446 0736
Fax: 714 446 0436
atomage100@aol.com

Barry Carter
Knightstown Antiques Mall, 136
W. Carey St, Knightstown,
IN 46148-1111
Tel: 765 345 5665
bcarter@spitfire.net

France Antique Toys
Tel: 631 754 1399

Roger & Susan Johnson
6264 Valley Creek, Pilot Point,
TX 76258
Tel: 940 686 5686
czarmann@aol.com

Kitsch-N-Kaboodle
c/o South Street Antiques
Market, 615 South 6th Street,
Philadelphia, PA 19147-2128
USA
Tel: 215 382 1354
kitschnkaboodle@yahoo.com

Litwin Antiques
P.O. Box 5865, Trenton,
NJ 08638-0865
Tel/Fax: 609 275 1427
(Chess)

Harry R. McKeon, Jr.
18 Rose Lane, Flourtown,
PA 19031-1910
Tel: 215 233 4094
toyspost@aol.com
(Tin Toys)

Jessica Pack Antiques
Chapel Hill, NC
Tel: 919 408 0406
jpants1@aol.com

The Old Toy Soldier Home
977 S. Santa Fe, Ste 11
Vista, CA 92083
Tel: 760 758 5481
oldtoysoldierhome@earthlink.net
www.oldtoysoldierhome.com

Trains & Things
210 East Front Street, Traverse
City, Michigan 49684
Tel: 231 947 1353
www.tctrains.com

WATCHES

Mark Laino
c/o South Street Antiques
Center, 615 South 6th Street,
Philadelphia, PA 19147
Tel: 215 592 0256

Texas Time
3076 Waunuta St, Newbury
Park, CA 1320
Tel: 805 498 5644
paul@dock.net

WINE & DRINKING

Derek White
The Corkscrew Pages, 769
Sumter Dr, Morrisville,
PA 19067
Tel: 215 493 4143
Fax: 609 860 5380
dswhite@marketsource.com
www.taponline.com

Donald A. Bull
P.O. Box 596, Wirtz, VA 24184
Tel: 540 721 1128
Fax: 540 721 5468
corkscrew@bullworks.net

Steve Visakay Cocktail Shakers
P.O. Box 1517 West Caldwell,
NJ 07007-1517
svisakay@aol.com

DIRECTORY OF AUCTIONEERS

This is a list of auctioneers that conduct regular sales. Auctioneers who wish to be listed in this directory for our next edition, space permitting, are requested to email info@thepriceguidecompany.com by February 2005.

ALABAMA

Flomaton Antique Auctions
P.O. Box 1017, 320 Palafox Street, Flomaton, AL 36441
Tel: 251 296-3059
Fax: 251 296-1974
www.flomatonantiqueauction.com

ARIZONA

Dan May & Associates
4110 N. Scottsdale Road, Scottsdale, AZ 85251
Tel: 602 941 4200

ARKANSAS

Ponders Auctions
1504 South Leslie, Stuttgart, AR 72160
Tel: 501 673 6551

CALIFORNIA

Aurora Galleries International
30 Hackamore Lane, Ste 2, Bell Canyon, CA 91307
Tel: 818 884 6468
Fax: 818 227 2941
vcampbell@auroraauctions.com
www.auroragalleriesonline.com

Butterfield & Butterfield
7601 Sunset Blvd, Los Angeles, CA 90046
Tel: 323 850 7500
Fax: 323 850 5843
info@butterfields.com
www.butterfields.com

Butterfield & Butterfield
220 San Bruno Ave, San Francisco, CA 94103
Tel: 415 861 7500
Fax: 415 861 8951
info@butterfields.com
www.butterfields.com

Clark Cierlak Fine Arts
14452 Ventura Blvd, Sherman Oaks, CA 91423
Tel: 818 783 3052
Fax: 818 783 3162
gallery@pacbell.net
www.estateauctionservice.com

I.M. Chait Gallery
9330 Civic Center Dr, Beverly Hills, CA 90210
Tel: 310 285 0182
Fax: 310 285 9740
chait@chait.com
www.chait.com

Cuschieri's Auctioneers & Appraisers
863 Main Street, Redwood City, CA 94063
Tel: 650 556 1793
Fax: 650 556 9805
www.cuschieris.com

eBay, Inc
2005 Hamilton Ave, Ste 350, San Jose, CA 95125
Tel: 408 369 4839
www.ebay.com

L.H. Selman
123 Locust St, Santa Cruz, CA 95060
Tel: 800 538 0766
Fax: 408 427 0111
leselman@got.net

Malter Galleries
17003 Ventura Blvd, Encino, CA 91316
Tel: 818 784 7772
Fax: 818 784 4726
www.maltergalleries.com

Poster Connection Inc
43 Regency Dr, Clayton, CA 94517
Tel: 925 673 3343
Fax: 925 673 3355
sales@posterconnection.com
www.posterconnection.com

Profiles in History
110 North Doheny Dr, Beverly Hills, CA 90211
Tel: 310 859 7701
Fax: 310 859 3842
www.profilesinhistory.com

San Rafael Auction Gallery
634 Fifth Avenue, San Rafael, CA 9490
Tel: 415 457 4488
Fax: 415 457 4899
www.sanrafael-auction.com

Slawinski Auction Co.
The Scotts Valley Sports Center, 251 Kings Village Road, Scotts Valley, CA 95066
Tel: 831 335 9000
www.slawinski.com

CONNECTICUT

Alexander Autographs
100 Melrose Ave, Greenwich, CT 06830
Tel: 203 622 8444
Fax: 203 622 8765
info@alexautographs.com
www.alexautographs.com

Norman C. Heckler & Co.
79 Bradford Corner Road, Woodstock Valley, CT 0682
Tel: 860 974 1634
Fax: 860 974 2003
www.hecklerauction.com

Lloyd Ralston Gallery
350 Long Beach Blvd, Stratford, CT 016615
Tel: 203 386 9399
Fax: 203 386 9519
lrgallery@sbcglobal.net
www.lloydralstontoys.com

DELAWARE

Remember When Auctions Inc.
Tel: 302 436 4979
Fax: 302 436 4626
sales@history-attic.com
www.history-attic.com

FLORIDA

Auctions Neapolitan
995 Central Avenue, Naples, FL 34102
Tel: 941 262 7333
kathleen@auctionsneapolitan.com
www.auctionsneapolitan.com

Burchard Galleries
2528 30th Ave N, St Petersburg, FL 33713
Tel: 727 821 1167
www.burchardgalleries.com

Dawson's, now trading as Dawson's & Nye
P.O. Box 646, Palm Beach, FL 33480
Tel: 561 835 6930
Fax: 561 835 8464
info@dawsons.org
www.dawsons.org

Arthur James Galleries
615 E. Atlantic Ave, Delray Beach, FL 33483
Tel: 561 278 2373
Fax: 561 278 7633
www.arthurjames.com

Kincaid Auction Company
3809 East CR 542, Lakeland, FL 33801
Tel: 800 970 1977
www.kincaid.com

Sloan's Auction Galleries
8861 NW 19th Terace, Ste 100, Miami, FL 33172
Tel: 305 751 4770
sloans@sloansauction.com
www.sloansandkenyon.com

GEORGIA

Great Gatsby's
5070 Peachtree Industrial Blvd, Atlanta, GA
Tel: 770 457 1903
Fax: 770-457-7250
www.gatsbys.com

My Hart Auctions Inc
P.O. Box 2511, Cumming, GA 30028
Tel: 770 888 9006
www.myhart.net

IDAHO

The Coeur D'Alene Art Auction
P.O. Box 310, Hayden, ID 83835
Tel: 208 772 9009
Fax: 208 772 8294
cdaartauction@cdaartauction.com
www.cdaartauction.com

ILLINOIS

Leslie Hindman Inc.
122 North Aberdeen Street, Chicago, IL 60607
Tel: 312 280 1212
Fax: 312 280 1211
www.lesliehindman.com

Joy Luke
300 East Grove Street, Bloomington, IL 61701
Tel: 309 828 5533
Fax: 309 829 2266
robert@joyluke.com
www.joyluke.com

Mastronet Inc
10S 660 Kingery Highway, Willobrook, IL 60527
Tel: 630 471 1200
info@mastronet.com
www.mastronet.com

INDIANA

Curran Miller Auction & Realty Inc
4424 Vogel Rd, Ste 400, Evansville, IN 47715
Tel: 812 474 6100
Fax: (812) 474-6110
cmar@curranmiller.com
www.curranmiller.com

Kruse International
5540 County Rd 11A, Auburn, IN 46706
Tel: 800 968 4444
info@kruseinternational.com
www.kruseinternational.com

Lawson Auction Service
P.O. Box 885, North Vernon, IN 47265
Tel: 812 372 2571
www.lawsonauction.com

Stout Auctions
529 State Road 28 East, Willamsport, IN 47993
Tel: 765 764 6901
Fax: 765-764-1516
info@stoutauctions.com
www.stoutauctions.com

IOWA

Jackson's Auctioneers & Appraisers
2229 Lincoln St, Cedar Falls, IA 50613
Tel: 319 277 2256
Fax: 319-2771252
www.jacksonsauction.com

Tom Harris auctions
2035 18th Ave, Marshalltown, IA 50158
Tel: 641 754 4890
Fax: 641 753 0226
tomharris@tomharrisauctions.com
www.tomharrisauctions.com

Tubaugh Auctions
1702 8th Ave, Belle Plaine, IA 52208
Tel: 319 444 2413 / 319.444.0169
www.tubaughauctions.com

KANSAS

Manions International Auction House
P.O. Box 12214, Kansas City, KS, 66112
Tel: 913 299 6692
Fax: 913 299 6792
collecting@manions.com
www.manions.com

CC Auctions
416 Court St, Clay Center, KS 67432
Tel: 785 632 6021
dhamilton@cc-auctions.com
www.cc-auctions.com

Brian Spielman Auctions
PO Box 884, Emporia, KS 66801
Tel: 620-341-0637 or 620-437-2424
spielman@madtel.net
www.kansasauctions.net/spielman

KENTUCKY

Hays & Associates Inc
120 South Spring Street, Louisville, KY 40206
Tel: 502 584 4297
kenhays@haysauction.com
www.haysauction.com

Steffens Historical Militaria
P.O. Box 280, Newport, KY 41072
Tel: 859 431 4499
Fax: 859 431 3113
www.steffensmilitaria.com

LOUISIANA

Morton M. Goldberg Auction Galleries
547 Baronne Street
New Orleans, LA 70113
Tel: 504 592 2300
Fax: 504 592 2311

New Orleans Auction Galleries
801 Magazine Street, New Orleans, LA 70130
Tel: 504 566 1849
Fax: 504 566 1851
info@neworleansauction.com
www.neworleansauction.com

MAINE

James D. Julia Auctioneers Inc.
P.O. Box 830, Fairfield, Maine 04937
Tel: 207 453 7125
jjulia@juliaauctions.com
www.juliaauctions.com

Thomaston Place Auction Galleries
P.O. Box 300, 51 Atlantic Highway, US Rt 1 Thomaston ME 04861
Tel: 207 354 8141
Fax: 207 354 9523
barbara@kajav.com
www.thomastonauction.com

MARYLAND

Guyette & Schmidt
PO Box 1170, St. Michaels, MD 21663.
Tel: 410-745-0485
Fax: 410-745-0457
decoys@guyetteandschmidt.com
www.guyetteandschmidt.com

Hantman's Auctioneers & Appraisers
P.O. Box 59366, Potomac, MD 20859
Tel: 301 770 3720
Fax: 301 770 4135
hantman@hantmans.com
www.hantmans.com

Isennock Auctions & Appraisals
4106B Norrisville Road, White Hall, MD 21161
Tel: 410-557-8052
Fax 410-692-6449
isennock@isennockauction.com
www.isennockauction.com

Sloans & Kenyon
7034 Wisconsin Avenue, Chevy Chase, Maryland 20815
Tel: 301 634-2330
Fax: 301 656-7074
info@sloansandkenyon.com
www.sloansandkenyon.com

MASSACHUSETTS

Eldred's
P.O. Box 796, 1483 Route 6A East Dennis, MA 02641
Tel: 508 385 3116
Fax: 508 385 7201
info@eldreds.com
www.eldreds.com

Grogan & Company
22 Harris St, Dedham, MA 02026
Tel: 800-823 1020
Fax: 781 461 9625
grogans@groganco.com
www.groganco.com

Simon D. Hill & Associates
420 Boston Turnpike, Shrewsbury, MA 01545
Tel: 508 845 2400
Fax: 978 928 4129
www.simondhillauctions.com

Skinner Inc
The Heritage on the Garden, 63 Park Plaza, Boston, MA 02116
Tel: 617-350-5400
Fax: 617-350-5429
info@skinnerinc.com
www.skinnerinc.com

Willis Henry Auctions
22 Main St, Marshfield, MA 02050
Tel: 781 834 7774
Fax: 781 826 3520
wha@willishenry.com
www.willishenry.com

MICHIGAN

DuMouchelles
409 East Jefferson Ave, Detroit, MI 48226
Tel: 313 963 6255
Fax: 313 963 8199
info@dumouchelles.com
www.dumouchelles.com

MINNESOTA

Buffalo Bay Auction Co
825 Fox Run Trail, Edmond, OK 73034
Tel: 405 285 8990
buffalobayauction@hotmail.com
www.buffalobayauction.com

Rose Auction Galleries
3180 Country Drive, Little Canada, MN 55117
Tel: 651 484 1415 / 888-484-1415
Fax: 651 636 3431
auctions@rosegalleries.com
www.rosegalleries.com

MISSOURI

Ivey-Selkirk
7447 Forsyth Blvd, Saint Louis, MO 63105
Tel: 314 726 5515
Fax: 314 726 9908
www.iveyselkirk.com

MONTANA

Allard Auctions Inc
P.O. Box 1030 St Ignatius, MT 59865
Tel: 406 745 0500
Fax: 406 745 0502
www.allardauctions.com

NEW HAMPSHIRE

Northeast Auctions
93 Pleasant St, Portsmouth, NH 03801-4504
Tel: 603 433 8400
Fax: 603 433 0415
contact@northeastauctions.com
www.northeastauctions.com

NEW JERSEY

333 Auctions
333 North Main St, Lambertville, NJ 08530
Tel: 609 397 9374
Fax: 609 397 9377
info@ragoarts.com
www.ragoarts.com

Bertoia Auctions
2141 Demarco Dr, Vineland, NJ 08360
Tel: 856 692 1881
Fax: 856 692 8697
www.bertoiaauctions.com

Craftsman Auctions
333 North Main St, Lambertville, NJ 08530
Tel: 609 397 9374
Fax: 609 397 9377
info@ragoarts.com
www.ragoarts.com

David Rago: Nicholas Dawes Lalique Auctions
333 North Main St, Lambertville, NJ 08530
Tel: 609 397 9374
Fax: 609 397 9377
info@ragoarts.com
www.ragoarts.com

Dawson & Nye
128 American Road, Morris Plains, NJ 07950
Tel: 973 984 6900
Fax: 973 984 6956
info@dawsonandnye.com
www.dawsonandnye.com

Greg Manning Auctions Inc
775 Passaic Ave, West Caldwell, NJ 07006
Tel: 973 883 0004
Fax: 973 882 3499
info@gregmanning.com
www.gregmanning.com

Sollo: Rago Modern Auctions
333 North Main St, Lambertville, NJ 08530
Tel: 609 397 9374
Fax: 609 397 9377
info@ragoarts.com
www.ragoarts.com

NEW MEXICO

Manitou Gallery
123 West Palace Ave., Santa Fe, NM 87501
Tel: 800-986-0440
info@manitougalleries.com
www.manitougalleries.com

Parker-Braden Auctions
P.O. Box 1897, 4303 National Parks Highway, Carlsbad, NM 88220
Tel: 505 885 4874
Fax: 505 885 4622
www.parkerbraden.com

NEW YORK

Christie's
20 Rockefeller Plaza, New York, NY 10020
Tel: 212 636 2000
Fax: 212 636 2399
info@christies.com
www.christies.com

TW Conroy
36 Oswego St, Baldwinsville, NY 13027
Tel: 315 638 6434
Fax: 315 638 7039
info@twconroy.com
www.twconroy.com

Samuel Cottone Auctions
15 Genesee St, Mount Morris, NY 14510
Tel: 585 658 3119
Fax: 585 658 3152
scottone@rochester.rr.com
www.cottoneauctions.com

William Doyle Galleries
175 E. 87th St, New York,
NY 10128
Tel: 212 427 2730
Fax: 212 369 0892
info@doylenewyork.com
www.doylenewyork.com

Guernsey's Auctions
108 East 73rd St, New York,
NY 10021
Tel: 212 794 2280
Fax: 212 744 3638
auctions@guernseys.com
www.guernseys.com

Phillips, De Pury & Luxembourg
450 West 15 Street, New York
NY 10011
Tel: 212 940 1200
Fax: 212 924 3306
info@phillipsdepury.com
www.phillips-dpl.com

Sotheby's
1334 York Ave at 72nd St,
New York, NY 10021
Tel: 212 606 7000
Fax: 212 606 7107
info@sothebys.com
www.sothebys.com

Swann Galleries Inc
104 E. 25th St, New York,
NY 10010
Tel: 212 254 4710
Fax: 212 979 1017
swann@swanngalleries.com
www.swanngalleries.com

NORTH CAROLINA

Robert S. Brunk
P.O. Box 2135, Asheville,
NC 28802
Tel: 828 254 6846
Fax: 828 254 6545
auction@brunkauctions.com
www.brunkauctions.com

Historical Collectible Auctions
24 NW Court, SquareSuite
201, Graham, NC 27253
Tel: 336 570 2803
Fax: 336 570 2748
auctions@hcaauctions.com
www.hcaauctions.com

NORTH DAKOTA

Curt D Johnson Auction Co.
4216 Gateway Dr., Grand
Forks, ND 58203
Tel: 701 746 1378
figleo@hotmail.com
www.curtdjohnson.com

OHIO

Cowans Historic Americana
673 Wilmer Avenue, Cincinnati,
OH 45226
Tel: 513 871 1670
Fax: 513 871 8670
www.historicamericana.com

DeFina Auctions
1591 State Route 45 Sth,
Austinburg, OH 44010
Tel: 440 275 6674
Fax: 440.275.2028
info@definaauctions.com
www.definaauctions.com

Garth's Auctions
2690 Stratford Rd, Box 369,
Delaware, OH 43015
Tel: 740 362 4771
Fax: 740 363 0164
info@garths.com
www.garths.com

Metropolitan Galleries
3910 Lorain Ave, Cleveland, OH
44113
Tel: 216 631 2222
Fax: 216 529 9021
www.metropolitangalleries.com

PENNSYLVANIA

Alderfer Auction Gallery
501 Fairgrounds Rd, Hatfield,
PA 19440
Tel: 215 393 3000
Fax: 215 368-9055
info@alderferauction.com
www.alderferauction.com

Noel Barrett
P.O. Box 300, Carversville,
PA 18913
Tel: 215 297 5109
www.noelbarrett.com

Dargate Auction Galleries
214 North Lexington,
Pittsburgh, PA 15208
Tel: 412 362 3558
info@dargate.com
www.dargate.com

Freeman's
1808 Chestnut Ave,
Philadelphia, PA 19103
Tel: 610 563 9275
info@freemansauction.com
www.freemansauction.com

Hunt Auctions
75 E. Uwchlan Ave, Ste 1, 30
Exton, PA 19341
Tel: 610 524 0822
Fax: 610 524 0826
info@huntauctions.com
www.huntauctions.com

Pook & Pook Inc
463 East Lancaster Ave,
Downington, PA 19335
Tel: 610 269 4040
Fax: 610 269 9274
info@pookandpook.com
www.pookandpook.com

Skinner's Auction Co.
170 Northampton St,
Easton, PA 18042
Tel: 610 330 6933
skinnauct@aol.com
www.skinnersauction.com

Stephenson's Auctions
1005 Industrial Blvd,
Southampton, PA 18966
Tel: 215 322 618
Fax: 215 364 0883
info@stephensonsauction.com
www.stephensonsauction.com

RHODE ISLAND

WebWilson
P.O. Box 506, Portsmouth,
RI 02871
Tel: 800 508 0022
hww@webwilson.com
www.webwilson.com

SOUTH CAROLINA

Charlton Hall Galleries Inc.
912 Gervais St Columbia,
SC 29201
Tel: 803 799 5678
Fax: 803 733 1701
www.charltonhallauctions.com

TENNESSEE

Berenice Denton Estate Sales and Appraisals
2209 Bandywood Drive, Suite C
Nashville, TN 37215
Tel: 615 292 5765
info@berenicedenton.com
www.berenicedenton.com

Kimball M. Sterling Inc
125 W. Market St, Johnson City,
TN 37604
Tel: 423 928 1471
www.sterlingsold.com

TEXAS

Austin Auctions
8414 Anderson Mill Rd,
Austin, TX 78729-4702
Tel: 512 258 5479
Fax: 512 219 7372
www.austinauction.com

Dallas Auction Gallery
1518 Socum St, Dallas,
TX 75207
Tel: 213 653 3900
Fax: 213 653 3912
info@dallasauctiongallery.com
www.dallasauctiongallery.com

Heritage-Slater Americana
3500 Maple Avenue
Dallas, Texas 75219
Tel: 214 528 3500
www.heritagegalleries.com

Heritage Galleries
3500 Maple Avenue
Dallas, Texas 75219
Tel: 214 528 3500
www.heritagegalleries.com

UTAH

America West Archives
P.O. Box 100, Cedar City,
UT 84721
Tel: 435 586 9497
Fax: 435 586 9497
info@americawestarchives.com
www.americawestarchives.com

VERMONT

Eaton Auction Service
Chuck Eaton, 3428
Middlebrook Road, Fairlee, VT
05045
Tel: 802 333 9717
eas@sover.net
www.eatonauctionservice.com

VIRGINIA

Ken Farmer Auctions & Estates
105A Harrison St, Radford,
VA 24141
Tel: 540 639 0939
Fax: 540 639 1759
info@kfauctions.com
www.kfauctions.com

Phoebus Auction Gallery
14-16 E. Mellen St, Hampton,
VA 23663
Tel: 757 722 9210
Fax: 757 723 2280
bwelch@phoebusauction.com
www.phoebusauction.com

Signature House
407 Liberty Ave, Bridgeport,
WV 25330
Tel: 304 842 3386
Fax: 304 842 3001
editor@signaturehouse.net
www.signaturehouse.net

WASHINGTON DC

Weschlers
909 E St, NW Washington,
DC 20004
Tel: 202 628 1281
Fax: 202 628 2366
fineart@weschlers.com
www.weschlers.com

WISCONSIN

Krueger Auctions
P.O. Box 275, Iola,
WI 54945-0275
Tel: 715 445 3845

Schrager Auction Galleries
2915 North Sherman Blvd,
P.O. Box 100043,
Milwaukee, WI 53210
Tel: 414 873 3738
Fax: 414 873 5229
askus@schragerauction.com
www.schragerauction.com

WYOMING

Cody Old West Show & Auction
P.O. Box 2038, 37555 Hum Rd,
Ste 101, Crawfree, AZ 85377
Tel: 307-587-9014
brian@codyoldwest.com
www.codyoldwest.com

CANADA

Pinneys Auctions Les Encans
2435 Duncan Road, Montreal,
Canada H4P 2A2
Tel: 514 345 0571
Fax: 514 731 4081
pinneys@ca.inter.net
www.pinneys.ca

Ritchies
288 King Street East, Toronto,
Ontario Canada M5A 1K4
Tel: 416 364 1864
ritchies.com

Waddington's Auctioneers & Appraisers
111 Bathurst St.,
Ontario Canada M5V 2R1
Tel: 416 504 9100
www.waddingtons.ca

Walkers
81 Auriga Drive, Suite 18,
Ottawa, Ontario
Canada K2E 7Y5
Tel: 613 224 5814
www.walkersauctions.com

CLUBS, SOCIETIES & ORGANISATIONS

ADVERTISING

Antique Advertising Association of America
P.O. Box 1121, Morton Grove, IL 60053
Tel: 708 446 0904
www.pastimes.org

Coca Cola Collectors' Club International
P.O. Box 49166, Atlanta, GA 30359-1166

Tin Container Collectors' Association
P.O. Box 440101 Aurora, CO 80044

AMERICANA

Folk Art Society of America
P.O. Box 17041, Richmond, VA 23226-70

American Political Items Collectors
P.O. Box 340339 San Antonio, TX 8234-0339
www.collectors.org/apic

AUTOGRAPHS

International Autograph Collectors' Club & Dealers' Alliance
4575 Sheridan St, Ste 111, Hollywood, FL 33021-3515
Tel: 561 736 8409
www.iacc-da.com

Universal Autograph Collectors' Club
P.O. Box 6181, Washington, DC 20044
Tel: 202 332-7388
www.uacc.com

AUTOMOBILIA

Automobile Objets d'Art Club
252 N. 7th St. Allentown, PA 18102-4204
Tel: 610 432 3355
oldtoy@aol.com

BOOKS

Antiquarian Bookseller's Association of America
20 West 44th St, 4th Floor, New York, NY 10036
Tel: 212 944 8291

CERAMICS

American Art Pottery Association
P.O. Box 834, Westport, MA 02790-0697
www.amartpot.com

American Ceramics Circle
520 16th St, Brooklyn, NY 11215
Tel: 718 832 5446
nlester@earthlink.net

American Cookie Jar Association
1600 Navajo Rd, Norman, OK 73026
davismj@ionet.net

Style 1900
David Rago, 9 Main St, Lambertville, NJ 08530

U.S. Chintz Collectors' Club
P.O. Box 50888, Pasadena, CA 91115
Tel: 626 441-4708
Fax: 626 441-4122
www.chintznet.com

Goebel Networkers
P.O. Box 396, Lemoyne, PA 17043

Homer Laughlin China Collectors' Association
P.O. Box 1093
Corbin KY 40702-1093
www.hlcca.org
(Fiesta ware)

Hummel Collectors Club
1261 University Dr, Yardley, PA 19067-2857
Tel: 888 548 6635
Fax: 215 321 7367
www.hummels.com

Roseville of The Past Pottery Club
P.O. Box 656 Clarcona, FL 32710-0656
Tel: 407 294 3980
Fax: 407 294 7836
rosepast@bellsouth.net

Royal Doulton International Collectors' Club
700 Cottontail Lane, Somerset, NJ 08873
Tel: 800 682-4462
Fax: 732 764-4974

Stangl & Fulper Club
P.O. Box 538, Flemington, NJ 08822
Tel: 908 995 2696
kenlove508@aol.com

American Stoneware Collectors' Society
P.O. Box 281, Bay Head, NJ 08742
Tel: 732 899 8707

COSTUME JEWELRY

Leaping Frog Antique Jewelry & Collectible Club
4841 Martin Luther King Blvd, Sacramento, CA 95820-4932
Tel: 916 452 6728
pandora@cwia.com

Vintage Fashion & Costume Jewelry Club
P.O. Box 265, Glen Oaks, NY 11004-0265
Tel: 718 939 3095
vfcj@aol.com

DISNEYANA

National Fantasy Club For Disneyana Collectors & Enthusiasts
P.O. Box 106, Irvine, CA 92713-9212
Tel: 714 731 4705
info@nffc.org
www.nffc.org

Walt Disney Collectors' Society
500 South Buena Vista St, Burbank, CA 91521-8028
Tel: 800 932 5749

FIFTIES & SIXTIES

Head Hunters Newsletters
P.O. Box 83H, Scarsdale, NY 10583.
Tel: 914 472 0200

FILM & TV MEMORABILIA

The Animation Art Guild
330 W. 45th St, Ste 9D, New York, NY 10036-3864
Tel: 212 765 3030
theaagltd@aol.com

Lone Ranger Fan Club
19205 Seneca Ridge Court, Gaithersburg, MD 20879-3135

GLASS

American Carnival Glass Association
9621 Springwater Lane, Miamisburg, OH 45342

Land of Sunshine Depression Glass Club
P.O. Box 560275, Orlando, FL 32856-0275
Tel: 407 298 3355

HATPINS

American Hatpin Society
20 Montecillo Dr, Rolling Hills Estates, CA 90274-4249
Tel: 310 326 2196
hatpnginia@aol.com
www.collectorsonline.com/AHS

KITCHENALIA

Kitchen Antiques & Collectibles News
4645 Laurel Ridge Dr, Harrisburg, PA 17119

MARBLES

Marble Collectors Unlimited
P.O. Box 206, Northborough, MA 01532-0206 USA
marblesbev@aol.com

MECHANICAL MUSIC

Musical Box Society International
700 Walnut Hill Rd, Hockessin DE 19707
Tel: 302 239 5658
cotps@aol.com
www.mbsi.org

MILITARIA

Civil War Collectors & The American Militaria Exchange
5970 Toylor Ridge Dr, West Chester, OH 45069
Tel: 513 874 0483
rwmorgan@aol.com
www.civiwar-collectors.com

OPTICAL, MEDICAL, SCIENTIFIC & TECHNICAL

International Association of Calculator Collectors
P.O. Box 345, Tustin, CA 92781-0345
Tel: 714 730 6140
Fax: 714 730 6140
mrcalc@usa.net
www.geocities.com/siliconvalley/park/7227/

PENS & WRITING

The Society of Inkwell Collectors
P.O. Box 324, Mossville, IL 61552
Tel: 309 579 3040
director@soic.com
www.soic.com

Pen Collectors of America
P.O. Box 80, Redding Ridge, CT 06876
www.pencollectors.com

PEZ

Pez Collectors News
P.O. Box 14956, Surfside Beach, SC 29587
info@pezcollectorsnews.com
www.pezcollectorsnews.com

ROCK N ROLL

Elvis Forever TCB Fan Club
P.O. Box 1066, Miami, FL 33780-1066

Working Class Hero Beatles Club
3311 Niagara St, Pittsburgh, PA 1213-4223

SCENT BOTTLES

International Perfume Bottle Association
396 Croton Rd, Wayne, PA 19087
Tel: 610-995-9051
jcabbott@bellatlantic.net
www.perfumebottles.org

SMOKING

Cigarette Lighter Collectors' Club
SPARK International
intSpark@aol.com
http://members.aol.com/intspark

Pocket Lighter Preservation Guild & Historical Society, Inc.
P.O. Box 1054, Addison,
IL 60101-8054
Tel: 708 543 9120

SNOWDOMES

Snowdome Collectors' Club
P.O. Box 53262, Washington,
DC 20009-9262

SPORTING MEMORABILIA

Boxing & Pugilistica Collectors International
P.O. Box 83135, Portland,
OR 97283-0135
Tel: 502 286 3597

Golf Collectors' Society
P.O. Box 24102, Cleveland,
OH 44124
Tel: 216 861 1615
www.golfcollectors.com

National Fishing Lure Collectors' Club
H.C. 33, Box 4012, Reeds
Spring, MO 65737
spurr@kingfisher.com

Society for American Baseball Research
812 Huron Rd, E. 719,
Cleveland, OH 441155
info@sabr.org
www.sabr.org

TEXTILES & COSTUME

The Costume Society of America
55 Edgwater Dr, P.O. Box 73,
Earleville, MD 21919-0073
Tel: 410 275 1619
www.costumesocietyamerica.com

American Fan Collectors' Association
P.O. Box 5473, Sarasota, FL
34277-5473
Tel: 817 267 9851
Fax: 817 267 0387

International Old Lacers
P.O. Box 554, Flanders,
NJ 07836
iolinc@aol.com

TOYS & GAMES

Annalee Doll Society
P.O.Box 1137, Meredith,
NH 03253
Tel: 800 433-6557
Fax: 603 279-6659

The Antique Toy Collectors' of America, Inc
C/o Carter, Ledyard & Milburn,
Two Wall St (13th Floor),
New York, NY 10005

Chess Collectors' International
P.O. Box 166, Commack,
NY 11725-0166
Tel: 516 543 1330
lichness@aol.com

National Model Railroad Association
4121 Cromwell Rd,
Chattanooga, TN 37421
Tel: 423 892 2846
nmra@tttrains.com

Toy Soldier Collectors of America
5340 40th Ave N, Saint
Petersburg, FL 33709
Tel: 727 527 1430

United Federation of Doll Clubs
10920 N. Ambassador Dr,
Kansas City, MO 64153
Tel: 816-891-7040
ufdc@aol.com

WATCHES

Early American Watch Club
P.O. Box 81555, Wellesley Hills,
MA 02481-1333

National Association of Watch & Clock Collectors
514 Poplar St, Columbia,
PA 17512-2130
Tel: 717 684 8261
www.nawacc.org

WINE & DRINKING

International Correspondence of Corkscrew Addicts
670 Meadow Wood Road
Mississauga Ontario,
L5J 2S6 Canada
dugohuzo@aol.com
www.corkscrewnet.com/icca

COLLECTING ON THE INTERNET

- The internet has revolutionised the trading of collectibles. Compared to a piece of furniture, most collectibles are easily defined, described and photographed. Shipping is also comparatively easy, due to average size and weight. Prices are also generally more affordable and accessible than for antiques and the Internet has provided a cost effective way of buying and selling, away from the overheads of shops and auction rooms. Many millions of collectibles are offered for sale and traded daily, with sites varying from global online marketplaces, such as eBay, to specialist dealers' websites.

- When searching online, remember that some people may not know how to accurately describe their item. General category searches, even though more time consuming, and even purposefully misspelling a name, can yield results. Also, if something looks too good to be true, it probably is. Using this book to get to know your market visually, so that you can tell the difference between a real bargain and something that sounds like one, is a good start.

- As you will understand from buying this book, color photography is vital – look for online listings that include as many images as possible and check them carefully. Beware that colors can appear differently, even between computer screens.

- Always ask the vendor questions about the object, particularly regarding condition. If there is no image, or you want to see another aspect of the object – ask. Most sellers (private or trade) will want to realise the best price for their items so will be more than happy to help – if approached politely and sensibly.

- As well as the 'e-hammer' price, you will probably have to pay additional transactional fees such as packing, shipping and possibly regional or national taxes. It is always best to ask for an estimate for these additional costs before leaving a bid. This will also help you tailor your bid as you will have an idea of the maximum price the item will cost if you are successful.

- As well as the well-known online auction sites, such as eBay, there is a host of other online resources for buying and selling, for example fair and auction date listings.

INTERNET RESOURCES

Live Auctioneers
www.liveauctioneers.com
info@liveauctioneers.com
A free service which allows users to search catalogs from selected auction houses in Europe, the USA and the United Kingdom. Through its connection with eBay, users can bid live via the Internet into salerooms as auctions happen. Registered users can also search through an archive of past catalogs and receive a free newsletter by email.

invaluable.com
www.invaluable.com
sales@invaluable.com
A subscription service which allows users to search selected auction house archives from the United Kingdom and Europe. Also offers an extensive archive for appraisal uses.

The Antiques Trade Gazette
www.atg-online.com
The online version of the UK trade newspaper, comprising British auction and fair listings, news and events.

Maine Antiques Digest
www.maineantiquesdigest.com
The online version of America's trade newspaper including news, articles, fair and auction listings and more.

La Gazette du Drouot
www.drouot.com
The online home of the magazine listing all auctions to be held in France at the Hotel de Drouot in Paris and beyond. An online subscription enables you to download the magazine online.

Auctionnet.com
www.auctionnet.com
Simple online resource listing over 500 websites related to auctions online.

AuctionBytes
www.auctionbytes.com
Auction resource with community forum, news, events, tips and a weekly newsletter.

Auctiontalk
www.internetauctionlist.com.com
Auction news, online and offline auction search engines and live chat forums.

Go Antiques/Antiqnet
www.goantiques.com
www.antiqnet.com
An online global aggregator for art, antiques and collectibles dealers who showcase their stock online, allowing users to browse and buy.

eBay
www.ebay.com
Undoubtedly the largest and most diverse of the online auction sites, allowing users to buy and sell in an online marketplace with over 52 million registered users. Collectors should also view eBay Live Auctions (www.ebayliveauctions.com) where traditional auctions are combined with realtime, online bidding allowing users to interact with the saleroom as the auction takes place.

Tias
www.tias.com
An online global aggregator for art, antiques and collectibles dealers who showcase their stock online, allowing users to browse and buy.

Collectors Online
www.collectorsonline.com
An online global aggregator for art, antiques and collectibles dealers who showcase their stock online, allowing users to browse and buy.

INDEX